Microsoft® Excel® 2010

COMPLETE

by Pasewark and Pasewark*, Cable, Romer

COURSE TECHNOLOGY
CENGAGE Learning™

Australia • Brazil • Japan • Korea • Mexico • Singapore • Spain • United Kingdom • United States

Microsoft® Excel® 2010

COMPLETE

by Pasework and Pasework*, Cable, Romer

William R. Pasework, Sr., Ph.D.
Professor Emeritus, Business Education,
Texas Tech University

Scott G. Pasework, B.S.
Occupational Education, Computer Technologist

William R. Pasework, Jr., Ph.D., CPA
Professor, Accounting, Texas Tech University

Carolyn Denny Pasework, M.Ed.
National Computer Consultant, Reading and Math
Certified Elementary Teacher, K-12 Certified Counselor

Jan Pasework Stogner, MBA
Financial Planner

Beth Pasework Wadsworth, B.A.
Graphic Designer

Sandra Cable, Ed. D.
Texas A&M University

Robin M. Romer
Contributing Author

*Pasework and Pasework is a trademark of the Pasework LTD.

COURSE TECHNOLOGY
CENGAGE Learning™

Australia • Brazil • Japan • Korea • Mexico • Singapore • Spain • United Kingdom • United States

COURSE TECHNOLOGY
CENGAGE Learning™

Microsoft® Office Excel® 2010 Complete
Pasewark and Pasewark, Cable, Romer

Author: Sandra Cable

Contributing Author: Robin M. Romer

Executive Editor: Donna Gridley

Product Manager: Allison O'Meara McDonald

Development Editors: Jessica Evans, Ann Fisher

Associate Product Manager: Amanda Lyons

Editorial Assistant: Kim Klasner

Senior Content Project Manager: Catherine DiMassa

Associate Marketing Manager: Julie Schuster

Director of Manufacturing: Denise Powers

Text Designer: Shawn Girsberger

Photo Researcher: Abigail Reip

Manuscript Quality Assurance Lead: Jeff Schwartz

Manuscript Quality Assurance Reviewers:
    Green Pen QA, Susan Pedicini, Marianne Snow

Copy Editor: Michael Beckett

Proofreader: Green Pen Quality Assurance

Indexer: Sharon Hilgenberg

Art Director: Faith Brosnan

Cover Designer: Hannah Wellman

Cover Image: © Neil Brennan / Canopy Illustration / Veer

Compositor: GEX Publishing Services

For product information and technology assistance, contact us at
Cengage Learning Customer & Sales Support, 1-800-354-9706
For permission to use material from this text or product, submit all requests online at **www.cengage.com/permissions**
Further permissions questions can be emailed to
permissionrequest@cengage.com

Library of Congress Control Number: 2010936381

Hardcover:
ISBN-13: 978-1-111-52952-9
ISBN-10: 1-111-52952-3

Course Technology
20 Channel Center Street
Boston, Massachusetts 02210
USA

Cengage Learning is a leading provider of customized learning solutions with office locations around the globe, including Singapore, the United Kingdom, Australia, Mexico, Brazil, and Japan. Locate your local office at:
international.cengage.com/region

Cengage Learning products are represented in Canada by Nelson Education, Ltd.

To learn more about Course Technology, visit **www.cengage.com/coursetechnology**

Visit our company website at **www.cengage.com**

Any fictional data related to persons or companies or URLs used throughout this book is intended for instructional purposes only. At the time this book was printed, any such data was fictional and not belonging to any real persons or companies.

To access additional course materials [including CourseMate], please visit www.cengagebrain.com. At the CengageBrain.com home page, search for the ISBN of your title (from the back cover of your book) using the search box at the top of the page. This will take you to the product page where these resources can be found.

Printed in the United States of America
1 2 3 4 5 6 7 14 13 12 11 10

ABOUT THIS BOOK

Microsoft Excel 2010 Complete is designed for beginning users of Microsoft Excel 2010. Students will learn to use the application through a variety of activities, simulations, and case projects. *Microsoft Excel 2010 Complete* demonstrates the tools and features for this program in an easy-to-follow, hands-on approach.

This self-paced, step-by-step book with corresponding screen shots makes learning easy and enjoyable. End-of-lesson exercises reinforce the content covered in each lesson and provide students with the opportunity to apply the skills that they have learned. It is important to work through each lesson within a unit in the order presented, as each lesson builds on what was learned in previous lessons.

Illustrations provide visual reinforcement of features and concepts, and sidebars provide notes, tips, and concepts related to the lesson topics. Step-by-Step exercises provide guidance for using the features. End-of-lesson projects concentrate on the main concepts covered in the lesson and provide valuable opportunities to apply or extend the skills learned in the lesson. Instructors can assign as many or as few of the projects at the end of the lesson as they like.

In the **Introductory Excel** unit, students learn spreadsheet basics: how to enter and edit data; how to change the appearance of worksheets; how to organize a worksheet; how to prepare a worksheet for printing; how to enter formulas and functions; how to enhance a worksheet with graphics, conditional formatting, and comments; how to work with multiple worksheets and workbooks; and how to create and modify charts.

The lessons in the **Advanced Excel** unit teach students advanced spreadsheet features: how to apply advanced formats to worksheets; how to use advanced chart features; how to improve data accuracy; how to create PivotTables and PivotCharts; how to use advanced functions such as VLOOKUP and HLOOKUP; how to create macros; how to protect, share, and track data; and how to import and export data.

Please note that some concepts introduced in the Introductory unit will be expanded upon in the Advanced unit.

To complete all lessons and end-of-lesson material, this book will require approximately 36 hours.

Start-Up Checklist

Hardware

- Computer and processor: 500-megahertz (MHz) processor or higher
- Memory: 256 megabytes (MB) of RAM or higher
- Hard disk: 3.5 gigabyte (GB) available disk space
- Display 1024 × 768 or higher-resolution monitor

Software:

- Operating system: Windows XP with Service Pack 3, Windows Vista with SP1, or Windows 7

INSIDE THIS BOOK

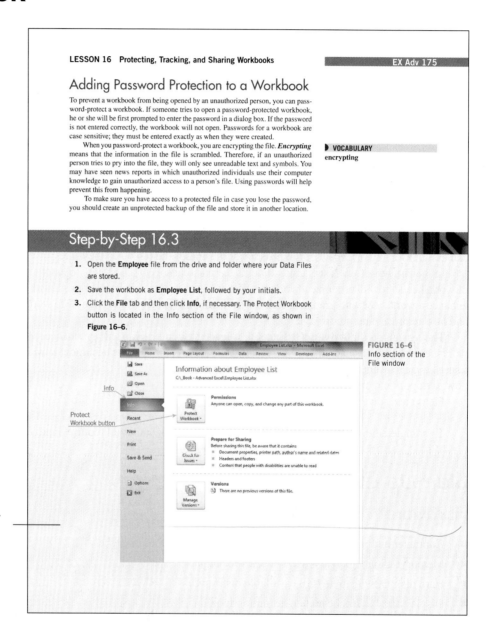

LESSON 16 Protecting, Tracking, and Sharing Workbooks

EX Adv 175

Adding Password Protection to a Workbook

To prevent a workbook from being opened by an unauthorized person, you can password-protect a workbook. If someone tries to open a password-protected workbook, he or she will be first prompted to enter the password in a dialog box. If the password is not entered correctly, the workbook will not open. Passwords for a workbook are case sensitive; they must be entered exactly as when they were created.

When you password-protect a workbook, you are encrypting the file. *Encrypting* means that the information in the file is scrambled. Therefore, if an unauthorized person tries to pry into the file, they will only see unreadable text and symbols. You may have seen news reports in which unauthorized individuals use their computer knowledge to gain unauthorized access to a person's file. Using passwords will help prevent this from happening.

To make sure you have access to a protected file in case you lose the password, you should create an unprotected backup of the file and store it in another location.

▶ VOCABULARY
encrypting

Step-by-Step 16.3

1. Open the **Employee** file from the drive and folder where your Data Files are stored.

2. Save the workbook as **Employee List**, followed by your initials.

3. Click the **File** tab and then click **Info**, if necessary. The Protect Workbook button is located in the Info section of the File window, as shown in **Figure 16–6**.

FIGURE 16–6
Info section of the File window

Information about Employee List

Permissions
Anyone can open, copy, and change any part of this workbook.

Prepare for Sharing
Before sharing this file, be aware that it contains:
- Document properties, printer path, author's name and related dates
- Headers and footers
- Content that people with disabilities are unable to read

Versions
There are no previous versions of this file.

Step-by-Step Exercises offer "hands-on practice" of the material just learned. Each exercise uses a data file or requires you to create a file from scratch.

Lesson opener elements include the **Objectives**, **Suggested Completion Time**, and **Vocabulary Terms**.

End-of-lesson elements include the **Summary**, **Vocabulary Review**, **Review Questions**, **Lesson Projects**, and **Critical Thinking Activities**.

Instructor Resources Disk

ISBN-13: 978-0-538-47523-5
ISBN-10: 0-538-47523-4

The Instructor Resources CD or DVD contains the following teaching resources:

The Data and Solution files for this course.

ExamView® tests for each lesson.

Instructor's Manual that includes lecture notes for each lesson and references to the end-of-lesson activities and Unit Review projects.

Answer Keys that include solutions to the end-of-lesson and Unit Review questions.

Critical thinking solution files that provide possible solutions for critical thinking activities.

Copies of the figures that appear in the student text.

Suggested Syllabus with block, two quarter, and 18-week schedule.

Annotated Solutions and Grading Rubrics.

PowerPoint presentations for each lesson.

Spanish glossary and Spanish test bank.

Appendices that include models for formatted documents, an e-mail writing guide, and a letter writing guide.

Proofreader's Marks.

ExamView®

This textbook is accompanied by ExamView, a powerful testing software package that allows instructors to create and administer printed, computer (LAN-based), and Internet exams. ExamView includes hundreds of questions that correspond to the topics covered in this text, enabling students to generate detailed study guides that include page references for further review. The computer-based and Internet testing components allow students to take exams at their computers, and save the instructor time by grading each exam automatically.

Online Companion

This book uses an Online Companion Web site that contains valuable resources to help enhance your learning.

- Student data files to complete text projects and activities
- Key terms and definitions for each lesson
- PowerPoint presentations for each lesson
- Additional Internet boxes with links to important Web sites
- Link to CourseCasts

CourseCasts

CourseCasts—Learning on the Go. Always Available…Always Relevant.

Want to keep up with the latest technology trends relevant to you? Visit our site to find a library of podcasts, CourseCasts, featuring a "CourseCast of the Week," and download them to your mp3 player at http://coursecasts.course.com.

Our fast-paced world is driven by technology. You know because you're an active participant—always on the go, always keeping up with technological trends, and always learning new ways to embrace technology to power your life.

Ken Baldauf, a faculty member of the Florida State University Computer Science Department, is responsible for teaching technology classes to thousands of FSU students each year. He knows what you want to know; he knows what you want to learn. He's also an expert in the latest technology and will sort through and aggregate the most pertinent news and information so you can spend your time enjoying technology, rather than trying to figure it out.

Visit us at http://coursecasts.course.com to learn on the go!

SAM 2010 *SAM*

SAM 2010 Assessment, Projects, and Training version 1.0 offers a real-world approach to applying Microsoft Office 2010 skills. The Assessment portion of this powerful and easy to use software simulates Office 2010 applications, allowing users to demonstrate their computer knowledge in a hands-on environment. The Projects portion allows students to work live-in-the-application on project-based assignments. The Training portion helps students learn in the way that works best for them by reading, watching, or receiving guided help.

- SAM 2010 captures the key features of the actual Office 2010 software, allowing students to work in high-fidelity, multi-pathway simulation exercises for a real-world experience.
- SAM 2010 includes realistic and explorable simulations of Office 2010, Windows 7 coverage, and a new user interface.
- Easy, web-based deployment means SAM is more accessible than ever to both you and your students.
- Direct correlation to the skills covered on a chapter-by-chapter basis in your Course Technology textbooks allows you to create a detailed lesson plan.
- SAM Projects offers live-in-the-application, project-based assignments. Student work is automatically graded, providing instant feedback. A unique cheating detection feature identifies students who may have shared files.
- Because SAM Training is tied to textbook exams and study guides, instructors can spend more time teaching and let SAM Training help those who need additional time to grasp concepts

Note: This textbook may or may not be available in SAM Projects at this time. Please check with your sales representative for the most recent information on when this title will be live in SAM Projects.

MESSAGE FROM THE AUTHORS

About the Pasewark Author Team

Pasewark LTD is a family-owned business with more than 90 years of combined experience authoring award-winning textbooks. They have written over 100 books about computers, accounting, and office technology. During that time, they developed their mission statement: To help our students live better lives.

Pasewark LTD authors are members of several professional associations that help authors write better books. The authors have been recognized with numerous awards for classroom teaching and believe that effective classroom teaching is a major ingredient for writing effective textbooks.

Sandra Cable, Texas A&M University – Commerce

Sandra Cable received her doctorate in Education from Texas A&M University – Commerce in 2003. In addition to working as an adjunct professor, she teaches computer classes at corporations that want to enhance the computer skills of their employees. Sandra also volunteers at schools and not-for-profit organizations, giving seminars that demonstrate simple approaches to using computer applications.

I would like to thank the great team at Course Technology: Donna Gridley, Executive Editor; Allison O'Meara McDonald, Product Manager; and Cathie DiMassa, Senior Content Project Manager. This team is truly the best group of individuals with whom I have worked! I would also like to give special thanks to Ann Fisher, the Developmental Editor. Thank you so much for all of your great work, coordination efforts, and incredible sense of humor. You are truly wonderful to work with.

To the thousands of students and clients that I have taught over the years, many thanks for your encouragement and for all you have taught me. Finally, I am very grateful to my family, Keith and Meridith Albright, for their enduring support. — **Sandra Cable**

From the Contributing Author

Many thanks to my talented co-authors and the dedicated editorial and production team at Course Technology. Thank you to Donna Gridley for the continued opportunity to be part of your team. Thank you to Allison O'Meara McDonald, Amanda Lyons, and Cathie DiMassa for keeping everything on track. Thank you to Jess Evans for the detailed, thorough edit. Much love to my family for their constant support. A special thank you to Brian and Jake for your patience and endurance. — **Robin M. Romer**

ADDITIONAL MICROSOFT OFFICE 2010 TITLES

Microsoft® Office 2010 Advanced
Casebound
ISBN-13: 978-0-538-48129-8
ISBN-10: 0-538-48129-3
Hard Spiral
ISBN-13: 978-0-538-48142-7
ISBN-10: 0-538-48142-0
Soft Perfect
ISBN-13: 978-0-538-48143-4
ISBN-10: 0-538-48143-9

Microsoft® Access® 2010 Complete
Hardcover
ISBN-13: 978-1-111-52990-1
ISBN-10: 1-111-52990-6

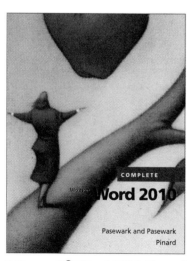

Microsoft® Word 2010 Complete
Hardcover
ISBN-13: 978-1-111-52951-2
ISBN-10: 1-111-52951-5

Microsoft® PowerPoint® 2010 Complete
Hardcover
ISBN-13: 978-1-111-52953-6
ISBN-10: 1-111-52953-1

CONTENTS

INTRODUCTORY UNIT

INTRODUCTORY MICROSOFT EXCEL 2010

ADVANCED MICROSOFT EXCEL

LESSON 14
Creating and Using Macros   EX Adv 125

LESSON 15
Working with Auditing and Analysis Tools   EX Adv 149

LESSON 16
Protecting, Tracking, and Sharing Workbooks   EX Adv 171

LESSON 17
Importing and Exporting Data   EX Adv 191

EXCEL 2010 COMPLETE
DATA FILES GRID

APPLICATION	LESSON	DATA FILE	SOLUTION FILE
INTRODUCTION	1	Class Descriptions.docx	Blackfoot Resort.pptx
		Clients.accdb	Final Spectrum Follow-up.docx
		Historic Preservation.pptx	First Qtr Sales.xlsx
		January Sales.xlsx	Historic Housing.pptx
		JC's Data.mdb	JC's Updated Data.accdb
		Sales Report.xlsx	Revised Sales Report.xlsx
		Spectrum Follow-up.docx	Updated Class Descriptions.docx
			Updated Clients.accdb
INTRODUCTORY EXCEL	1	Frogs.xlsx	Activity 1-1.docx
		Homes.xlsx	Activity 1-2.docx
		Names.xlsx	Frogs Census.xlsx
		Properties.xlsx	Home Ownership.xlsx
			Last Names.xlsx
			Properties Estimates.xlsx

APPLICATION	LESSON	DATA FILE	SOLUTION FILE
INTRODUCTORY EXCEL	2	Birds.xlsx	Activity 2-1.docx
		Cassidy.xlsx	Activity 2-2.docx
		Central.xlsx	Birds Census.xlsx
		Mileage.xlsx	Cassidy Budget.xlsx
		Shop.xlsx	Central Conference.xlsx
		TechSoft.xlsx	Mileage Chart.xlsx
		Wireless.xlsx	Technology Shop.xlsx
			TechSoft Balance Sheet.xlsx
			Wireless Bill.xlsx
INTRODUCTORY EXCEL	3	Assets.xlsx	Activity 3-1.xlsx
		Chemistry.xlsx	Assets Statement.xlsx
		Club.xlsx	Chemistry Grades.xlsx
		Creston.xlsx	Club Equipment.xlsx
		Inventory.xlsx	Creston Pool.xlsx
		Time.xlsx	Inventory Purchase.xlsx
		Trade.xlsx	Time Sheet.xslx
		Utilities.xlsx	Trade Balance.xlsx
			Utilities Expenses.xlsx

APPLICATION	LESSON	DATA FILE	SOLUTION FILE
INTRODUCTORY EXCEL	4	Formula.xlsx	Activity 4-1.xlsx
		Investment.xlsx	Formula Practice.xlsx
		Juice.xlsx	Investment Record.xlsx
		Mackenzie.xlsx	Investment Record Updated.xlsx
		Operation.xlsx	Juice Sales.xlsx
		Zoo.xlsx	Mackenzie Development.xlsx
			Operation Results.xlsx
			Zoo Invoice.xlsx
INTRODUCTORY EXCEL	5	Coyotes.xlsx	Activity 5-1.xlsx
		Exam.xlsx	Activity 5-3.xlsx
		Finances.xlsx	Coyote Stats.xlsx
		Functions.xlsx	Exam Scores.xlsx
		Golf.xlsx	Finances for *Student Name*.xlsx
		National.xlsx	Functions Worksheet.xlsx
		Reynolds.xlsx	Golf Tryouts.xlsx
		Xanthan.xlsx	National Bank.xlsx
			Reynolds Optical.xlsx
			Xanthan Promotion.xlsx

APPLICATION	LESSON	ECO.XLSX	SOLUTION FILE
INTRODUCTORY EXCEL	6	Bamboo.png	Activity 6-1.xlsx
		Beautiful.xlsx	Activity 6-2.xlsx
		Bus.bmp	Beautiful Blooms.xlsx
		City.xlsx	Bus Records.xlsx
		Creative.xlsx	City Facts.xlsx
		Eco.xlsx	Compact Cubicle.xlsx
		Logo.docx	Eco Container.xlsx
		Salary.xlsx	Roberts Statement.xlsx
		Stock.xlsx	Salary List.xlsx
		Tax.xlsx	Stock Quotes.xlsx
		Titus.xlsx	Tax Estimate.xlsx
		Top.xlsx	Time Card.xlsx
		Travel.xlsx	Titus Oil.xlsx
		Tulips.jpg	Top Films.xlsx
		Zoom.xlsx	Travel Expenses.xlsx
			Travel Expenses 2003.xlsx
			Travel Expenses Web.mht
			Zoom Salaries.xlsx

APPLICATION	LESSON	DATA FILE	SOLUTION FILE
INTRODUCTORY EXCEL	7	Alamo.xlsx	Activity 7-1.docx
		Annual.xlsx	Alamo Industries.xlsx
		Crystal.xlsx	Annual Income.xlsx
		Delta.xlsx	Crystal Sales.xlsx
		March.xlsx	Delta Circuitry.xlsx
		Rain.xlsx	March Income.xlsx
		Vote.xlsx	Rain Records.xlsx
			Vote Tally.xlsx
INTRODUCTORY EXCEL	8	Cash.xlsx	Activity 8-1.docx
		Chico.xlsx	Activity 8-2.xlsx
		Concession.xlsx	Cash Surplus.xlsx
		Coronado.xlsx	Chico Temperatures.xlsx
		Education.xlsx	Concession Sales.xlsx
		Great.xlsx	Coronado Foundries.xlsx
		Largest.xlsx	Education Pays.xlsx
		McDonalds.xlsx	Great Plains.xlsx
		Red.xlsx	Largest Cities.xlsx
		Run.xlsx	McDonalds Report.xlsx
		Starburst.xlsx	Red Cross.xlsx
		Study.xlsx	Run Times.xlsx
			Starburst Growth.xlsx
			Study and Grades.xlsx

APPLICATION	LESSON	DATA FILE	SOLUTION FILE
INTRODUCTORY EXCEL	Unit Review	Club.xlsx	Club Members.xlsx
		CompNet.xlsx	Coffee Prices Job 1.xlsx
		Computer.xlsx	Coffee Prices Job 2.xlsx
		Gas.xlsx	CompNet Expenses.xlsx
		Java.docx	Computer Prices Job 1.xlsx
		Organic.xlsx	Computer Prices Job 2.xlsx
			Gas Sales.docx
			Java Menu.docx
			Java Menu Revised.docx
			Organic Financials.xlsx
ADVANCED EXCEL	9	Bakery.xlsx	AppliedThemes2.xlsx
		Budget.xlsx	AppliedThemes.xlsx
		Coach Assignment.xlsx	BakerySales.xlsx
		Customer.xlsx	CoachAssignmentInformation.xlsx
		Employee.xlsx	CustomerList.xlsx
		Home Sales.xlsx	EmployeeList.xlsx
		StoreLeaseDates.xlsx	HomeSales-2014.xlsx
		Team - Revised.xlsx	ProposedBudget.xlsx
		Team.xlsx	StoreLeaseDatesInformation.xlsx
		Themes.xlsx	TeamAssignments.xlsx

APPLICATION	LESSON	DATA FILE	SOLUTION FILE
ADVANCED EXCEL	9	Tool.xlsx	TeamList.xlsx
		Trendy Resort.xlsx	ToolSales.xlsx
			TrendyResortProjectedSales.xlsx
ADVANCED EXCEL	10	Byars Pizza.xlsx	Byars Pizza Sales.xlsx
		College Book.xlsx	College Book Sales.xlsx
		College Clothing.xlsx	College Bookstore.xlsx
		College.xlsx	CollegeClothing Sales.xlsx
		Donation.xlsx	Donation Goal.xlsx
		GMRE Real Estate.xlsx	GMRE Real Estate Listings.xlsx
		Income.xlsx	Income Statement.xlsx
		Pie Sales.xlsx	Pie Sales First Quarter 2013.xlsx
		Projected Earnings.xlsx	Projected Earnings by Department.xlsx
		Rain Totals.xlsx	Rain Totals Change.xlsx
		University Expenses.xlsx	University Expenses Chart.xlsx

DATA FILES

APPLICATION	LESSON	DATA FILE	SOLUTION FILE
ADVANCED EXCEL	11	Arts&Crafts.xlsx	Arts & Crafts Inventory.xlsx
		CollegeBookSales.xlsx	College Book Sales and Expenses.xlsx
		ComputerTrainingStudents.xlsx	Computer Training Students List.xlsx
		Employees.xlsx	Employees List.xls
		FanFair.xlsx	Fan Fair Inventory - 2.xlsx
		LocalDeptSales.xlsx	Fan Fair Inventory.xlsx
		NewLock.xlsx	Household Inventory.xlsx
		PacificSales.xlsx	Local Dept Sales and Expenses.xlsx
		Pharmacy.xlsx	New Lock Sales.xlsx
			Pacific Sales by Employee.xlsx
			Pharmacy Refills.xlsx
			Watch Window.xlsx
ADVANCED EXCEL	12	Discount Internet.xlsx	Discount Internet Sales.xlsx
		Division Sales.xlsx	Division Sales for Hawaii.xlsx
		Electricity.xlsx	Electricity Usage.xlsx
		P K Industries.xlsx	P K Industries Analysis.xlsx
		Spelling Bee.xlsx	Spelling Bee Groups.xlsx
		Student Loans.xlsx	Student Loans - 2014.xlsx
		Virginia Sales.xlsx	Virginia Sales by Region.xlsx

APPLICATION	LESSON	DATA FILE	SOLUTION FILE
ADVANCED EXCEL	13	AntiqueClass.xlsx	Antique Class Enrollment.xlsx
		Bonus.xlsx	Bonus for Sports.xls
		Booth.xlsx	Booth Sales.xlsx
		ChineseClass.xlsx	Chinese Class Enrollment.xlsx
		ClassEnrollment.xlsx	Class Enrollment Totals.xlsx
		LibraryVolunteers.xlsx	Library Volunteers - June 2014.xlsx
		PCISales.xlsx	PCI Sales Bonuses.xlsx
		Sales.xlsx	Sales Commissions.xlsx
		SpanishClass.xlsx	Spanish Class Costs.xlsx
		StudentGymnastics.xlsx	Student Gymnastics - Paid.xlsx
ADVANCED EXCEL	14	Arts and Crafts.xlsx	Arts and Crafts Expenses.xlsm
		College Book.xlsm	College Book Sales.xlsm
		College Budget.xlsx	College Budget - Annual.xlsm
		Month End.xlsm	Month End Budget.xlsm
		Pet Store.xlsm	Pet Store Inventory.xlsm
		Project Sales.xlsx	Project Sales Totals.xlsm
		School Budget.xlsx	School Budget First Year.xlsm
ADVANCED EXCEL	15	Auto Parts.xlsx	Auto Parts Sales.xlsx
		Blooming Yards.xlsx	Blooming Yards Income and Expenses.xlsx
		Book Sales.xlsx	Coastal Sales - First Quarter.xlsx
		Coastal Sales.xlsx	College Fund Goal.xlsx
		Credit Card.xlsx	Credit Card Payoff.xlsx
		Grades.xlsx	Down Payment Goal.xlsx
		International Sales.xlsx	History Grades.xlsx
		Supplies.xlsx	International Sales Financials.xlsx
		Trees and Landscaping.xlsx	Office Supplies.xlsx
			Payoff.xlsx

DATA FILES

APPLICATION	LESSON	DATA FILE	SOLUTION FILE
ADVANCED EXCEL	15		Trees and Landscaping Financials.xlsx
			Yearly Book Sales.xlsx
ADVANCED EXCEL	16	Airline Rates.xlsx	Airline Rates Shared.xlsx
		Best Diamonds.xlsx	Best Diamonds List.xlsx
		Cost and Sales.xlsx	Cost and Sales Prices.xlsx
		Employee.xlsx	Employee List - Revised.xlsx
		Hobby Store.xlsx	Employee List.xlsx
		New York College.xlsx	Hobby Store Inventory.xlsx
		State College.xlsx	New York College Sports.xlsx
		Water Usage.xlsx	State College Inventory.xlsx
			Water Usage by Department.xlsx
ADVANCED EXCEL	17	Angelina Tarrant signature.tif	A&C Imported File.xlsx
		Arts and Crafts.txt	Access Import.xlsx
		Customer.accdb	Computer Students.pdf
		Doctors.accdb	Computer Students.xlsx
		Household.xlsx	Doctors Import.xlsx
		Income.xlsx	Household Addresses.pdf
		Pacific Sales.txt	Income Statement for Verification.xlsx
		Regional Managers.xlsx	Income Statement.xlsx
		Students.xlsx	Regional Managers Weekly Sales.xlsx
			Text Import.xlsx
ADVANCED EXCEL	Unit Review	Corporate.xlsx	Discount Interior Inventory.xlsx
		Corporate Tees.xlsx	Imports Unlimited.xlsx
		DiscountInterior.xlsx	Law School Budget.xlsm
		Imports.xlsx	New Western Sales.xlsx
		LawSchool.xlsx	Trip Planning Estimates.xlsx
		NewWestern.xlsx	
		TripPlanning.xlsx	

ADVANCED

INTRODUCTION

LESSON 1   2 HRS.

Microsoft Office 2010 and the Internet

LESSON 1

Microsoft Office 2010 and the Internet

■ OBJECTIVES

Upon completion of this lesson, you should be able to:

■ Apply basic Microsoft Word, Excel, Access, PowerPoint, and Outlook features.

■ Search for information on the World Wide Web.

■ Evaluate Web sites.

■ Bookmark favorite Web sites.

■ Manage the history of the Web sites visited.

■ VOCABULARY

bookmark

browser

hits

keywords

search engine

wildcard

Microsoft Office 2010 is a complete set of computer applications that equips you with the tools you need to produce a variety of documents and files, and to help streamline your everyday computing activities. This course focuses on the more complex and advanced capabilities of the Word, Excel, Access, PowerPoint, and Outlook applications.

This lesson provides a review of basic application features and will help you refresh your application skills. In this lesson, you will also learn more about how to access resources on the World Wide Web.

Applying Word Features

As you know, Microsoft Word is a powerful, full-featured word processor with comprehensive writing tools. You've already learned many of the basic features that enable you to complete common word-processing documents. The Word lessons in this course will introduce you to features that will enable you to further enhance the appearance of your documents and save time preparing and editing documents. Developing a document often involves multiple team members, and Word offers several tools to help you share documents and effectively collaborate on projects.

However, before you begin to explore these and other advanced features in Word, complete the following Step-by-Step, which provides a review of many basic Word skills.

Step-by-Step 1.1

1. Launch Word and then open the **Class Descriptions.docx** file from the drive and folder where your Data Files are stored. Save the document as **Updated Class Descriptions**, followed by your initials.
2. Edit the document as shown in **Figure 1–1**.

Health and Nutrition Class ~~Descriptions~~ *es*

For many months we have anticipated the opening of the new Family Fitness Facility in Columbus, and we are now counting down the days for our grand opening on October 1.

As we approach our grand opening day, I am finalizing the class schedule. You will recall that when we met last week we discussed several health and nutrition classes. Before I finalize the class schedule, I would like for you to reveiw the updated class descriptions shown below and respond to the questions on the following page.

Weight Management will help individuals identify their recommended weight. The focus will be on sound advise for exercise and diet programs that will help individuals acheive ideal body weight.

Cooking for Good Health will provide information on selecting and preparing food. Participants will learn about the nutritional benefits of a variety of foods from organic products to frozen dinners. The focus will be on making good choices, cooking foods properly, and creating wholesome menus.

Reading Food Labels will be a short class defining the information included in food labels and explaining its relevance to diet.

Value of Vitamins will explore the advantages and disadvantages of supplementing diets with vitamins. The benefits of a variety of vitamins will be described.

Strengthening Your Immune System will explore how regular exercise, a healthy diet, and reduce *ing* emotional stress help strengthen the immune system.

Please email me your responses to these questions by the end of the day tomorrow.

Regarding the proposed health and nutrition lasses:

- Does each class description adequately describe the objectives of the class?

- Are these classes necessary, and will they complement our instruction on physical training?

- Do you think our family members will be interested in these classes?

- Should we offer more than one class on cooking and design the instruction for specific age groups? *target   to*

- Do you have suggestions for any other health and nutrition classes that you think we should offer?

FIGURE 1–1
Edits for document in
Step-by-Step 1.1

3. Center and bold the title, and then change the font to Arial 18 point. Change the title text to all uppercase.

4. Select the paragraphs that describe the five classes and format all the paragraphs with a left indent of 0.5" and a right indent of 5.5" (0.5" from the right margin).

5. Select the list of bulleted questions at the end of the document and apply the number format (1., 2., 3.) to create an enumerated list.

6. Position the insertion point anywhere in the first numbered paragraph and add space after the paragraph. Then use the Format Painter feature to copy the new paragraph format to the other paragraphs in the numbered list.

7. Search for the word *email* and replace it with **e-mail**.

8. Change the document margins to **Office 2003 Default** setting (1" top and bottom and 1.25" left and right).

9. Position the insertion point in front of the paragraph that begins *Regarding the proposed...* and insert a page break.

10. Create a header for only the second page of the document. Use the Blank (Three Columns) format for the header, and then type the title **Health and Nutrition Classes** in the center of the header.

11. Check the document for spelling and grammar and make any necessary corrections. The spelling checker doesn't catch mistypes if they are the same as correctly spelled words.

12. Save the changes. Close the document, and then exit Word.

Applying Excel Features

Excel is the spreadsheet application in the Office suite. As you've discovered, spreadsheets are used for entering, calculating, and analyzing data. You should now be familiar with the basic features for creating, editing, and formatting worksheet information. Excel's advanced features enable you to perform complex calculations and in-depth analysis that you'd normally leave up to an economist or mathematician! With Excel's data analysis tools, you can generate reports, charts, and tables that are every bit as professional looking and accurate as those created by the experts. In this course, you'll also learn how to share workbooks with colleagues.

Before you venture into the advanced features of Excel, complete the following Step-by-Step, which provides a review of the Excel basic skills.

Step-by-Step 1.2

1. Launch Excel and then open the **Sales Report.xlsx** file from the drive and folder where your Data Files are stored. Save the workbook as **Revised Sales Report**, followed by your initials.

2. Go to cell M5 and type the column heading **TOTAL**.

3. Go to cell M6 and enter a formula to calculate the sum of the numbers in cells B6:L6. Fill the formula down through cell M12.

4. Go to cell A14 and type the row heading **TOTAL**.

5. Go to cell B14 and enter a formula to calculate the sum of the numbers in cells B6:B13. Fill the formula across through cell M14.

6. Insert a new column to the left of the *TOTAL* column. In the new column, type the heading **Dec**, and then enter the following data in the new column:

   61258

   50211

   61858

   50212

   61855

   50215

   61852

7. Copy the formula in cell L14 and paste it in cell M14.

8. Merge and center the title *Division Sales Report* over cells A1:N1. Format the title text bold and italic, and change the font size to 14 point.

9. Delete rows 2 and 3.

10. Format the column and row headings bold, and then center the column headings.

11. Apply a currency format to all the numeric data, with no decimal points. If necessary, automatically adjust the column widths.

12. Create a 3-D pie chart on a new sheet, using only the data in the cell ranges A4:A10 and N4:N10. Add the title **Total Sales by Division** to the chart and apply a chart style of your choice.

13. Format the worksheet to fit on one page in landscape orientation.

14. Save the changes. Close the file, and then exit Excel.

Applying Access Features

Access is the database application in the Office suite that is used for storing and organizing information. Databases are made up of objects, including tables, queries, forms, and reports. You now should be familiar with the basic techniques for creating these objects. In the advanced lessons, you will learn about features that give you even more control over how database records are viewed, edited, and professionally analyzed. You'll learn how to streamline data entry and editing and to present the data in an attractive, reader-friendly manner.

Before you begin exploring advanced features in Access, walk through the following Step-by-Step to review the application's basic features.

Step-by-Step 1.3

1. Launch Access and open the **JC's Data.accdb** file from the drive and folder where your Data Files are stored. Save the database as **JC's Updated Data**, followed by your initials.

2. Open the EMPLOYEE table in Design View. Between the *Employee ID* and *Last Name* fields, insert a new field titled **Department**. Define the field data type as **Text**.

3. Save the changes to the table and then switch to Datasheet View.

4. Sort the table alphabetically by last name and then update the records to include the department name in which each employee works:

Dominquez:	**Marketing**
Gonzalez:	**Administrative**
Keplinger:	**Sales**
Mann:	**Accounting**
Pullis:	**Accounting**
Thomsen:	**Sales**
Ti:	**Marketing**
Wong:	**Sales**

5. Sort the table by Employee ID, and then add a new record to the table and enter the following information:

Employee ID:	**9**
Department:	**Sales**
Last Name:	**Barkin**
First Name:	**Dave**
Salary:	**$145,000**
Home Phone:	**608-555-5121**
Date Hired:	**3/24/13**

6. Adjust the column widths to show all the data, and then show the table in Print Preview.

7. Change the page layout to **Landscape** and close Print Preview. Save the changes and close the table.

8. Open the PRODUCTS table and filter the data to show only those products with a price greater than $10. The filter should produce eleven records. Remove the filter and close the table. When prompted, save the changes.

9. Use the Form Wizard to create a form based on the EMPLOYEE table.
   a. Include all the fields in the form.
   b. Select the **Columnar** layout.
   c. Name the form **EMPLOYEE FORM**.

10. Use the Report Wizard to create a report based on the EMPLOYEE table.
   a. Include all the fields except *Salary* and *Date Hired*.
   b. Group the records by **Department**.
   c. Sort the records in ascending order by **Last Name**.
   d. Apply the **Stepped** layout and **Portrait** orientation.
   e. Name the report **EMPLOYEE TELEPHONE REPORT**.

11. Close the report and the form, and then exit Access.

Applying PowerPoint Features

PowerPoint is a presentation graphics program that enables you to create presentation materials for a variety of audiences, including slide shows using a projector and online presentations that everyone on a network can view. In the PowerPoint unit, you will explore some of its more advanced features. To make your presentations more interesting and effective, PowerPoint provides tools to add multimedia effects to your slides. The many customizing features PowerPoint offers enable you to create your own color schemes, backgrounds, and design templates. When preparing for your final presentation, PowerPoint has many options for distributing your slide show, including sharing via e-mail or presenting it remotely over a Web page or network.

Before you explore these advanced PowerPoint features, complete the following Step-by-Step to review your PowerPoint skills.

Step-by-Step 1.4

1. Launch PowerPoint, and then open the **Historic Preservation.pptx** file from the drive and folder where your Data Files are stored. Save the presentation as **Historic Housing**, followed by your initials.

2. On the title slide, replace *Your Name* with your own first and last names.

3. Add a new slide after the title slide, using the **Two Content** layout for the new slide.

4. In the title placeholder, type **Stabilization**. In the text placeholder on the left, type the following two lines of text. The text should automatically be formatted with bullets.

   Reestablish structural stability.

   Maintain essential form.

5. Move slide #5 (with the title *Resources*) so it is the last slide in the presentation.

6. Add graphics to slides 2–9. If possible, search Office.com for the graphics. *Hint*: Try search terms such as *house*, *fix*, *historic*, *tools,* and *blueprints*.

7. Apply a built-in design, and, if desired, change the color theme and/or fonts.

8. Apply a transition to all slides in the presentation. Adjust the timing of the transitions as needed.

9. Apply custom animations to the text and graphics on slides 2–10 to control when and how the objects appear.

10. Run the slide show and observe your transitions and animations, and make any necessary changes.

11. Save your changes. Close the presentation, and then exit PowerPoint.

Applying Outlook Features

Outlook is a desktop information management application. As you already know, using Outlook helps you keep track of e-mail messages, appointments, meetings, contact information, and tasks you need to complete. In this course, you will explore some of Outlook's more advanced features. You will learn about features that make it even easier to manage contact information, manage e-mails, and communicate with others. You will also learn about many features and tools that make it easier for you to schedule events and track progress on tasks.

Before you explore Outlook's advanced features, complete the following Step-by-Step to review the basic skills and features for Outlook.

Step-by-Step 1.5

1. Launch Outlook. Open a new journal entry and enter the information below. Then start the timer and leave the journal entry open.

   Subject: **Step-by-Step 1.5**

   Entry type: **Task**

2. Open the Contacts folder. Create a new contact group and name the group **Fitness Trainers**.

3. Add the following contacts to the new group and save the group.

Name:	**Sharon McKee**
E-mail:	**smckee@familyfit.xyz**
Name:	**Ronald DeVilliers**
E-mail:	**rdevillers@familyfit.xyz**
Name:	**Alisa Mandez**
E-mail:	**amandez@familyfit.xyz**

4. Create a new e-mail message. Send the message to the Fitness Trainers group, and type **Health and Nutrition Classes** in the Subject box. Then type the following in the message area:

   Please review the attached document and give me your feedback by the end of the day tomorrow.

5. Attach your solution file **Updated Class Descriptions.docx** to the e-mail message, and save the e-mail message as a draft. Do not attempt to send the e-mail.

6. Create the following two notes:

   Upload the health and nutrition class descriptions to the Web site.

   Confirm yoga class schedule with Bonnie.

7. Open the Calendar and show the calendar for a week from the current date. Create an appointment with your dentist for 10 a.m. and set a reminder. The appointment should last 45 minutes.

8. Open the Tasks folder and create the following new task. Give the task high priority and specify that it be completed within a week.

   Gather information for dental bills to submit for insurance.

9. Delete the dentist appointment.

10. Delete the contact group and contacts you created, and then delete the e-mail draft.

11. Delete the insurance task.

12. Delete the two notes.

13. Return to the journal entry and pause the timer. Make note of how much time you spent on this activity, and then delete the journal entry.

14. Exit Outlook.

Accessing Internet Resources

Microsoft Office 2010 is designed to give you quick and easy access to the World Wide Web, regardless of which Office application you are currently using. A *browser* is a program that connects you to remote computers and gives you the capability to access, view, and download data from the Web. Microsoft's browser program is Microsoft Internet Explorer.

▶ **VOCABULARY**
browser

Searching for Information and Evaluating Web Sites

Each day, millions of people use the World Wide Web to find information. To get the information they're looking for, they must navigate through an enormous amount of data. As a result, even with high-speed connections and powerful search engines, searching for specific information can be very time consuming.

ADVANCED Introduction Unit

▶ VOCABULARY
search engine

keywords

hits

wildcard

A *search engine*, such as Microsoft's Bing, is a tool designed to find information on the Web. When you enter *keywords*, words that describe the information you are seeking, the search engine generates a list of Web sites that potentially match the search criteria. These search results (the best matching Web sites) are often referred to as *hits*. Searches often produce a long list of hits; if you wish to narrow the search results, you need to be more specific in the keywords that you provide. **Table 1–1** describes several options for refining a search so you can find information quickly and effectively.

TABLE 1–1 Options for refining searches

SEARCH OPTIONS	DESCRIPTION
Capitalization	If you want the results to include occurrences of both upper and lowercase letters, enter the keywords using all lowercase letters. However, if you want to narrow your results to words that begin with capital letters (such as Central Intelligence Agency) or all capital letters (such as CIA), enter the keywords with the same capitalization.
Plurals	Most search engines consider singular keywords as both singular and plural. For example, results for the keyword *agent* will include hits with the word *agents*. If you want the results to include only hits with a plural word, be sure the keyword is plural.
Phrases	Search for a group of words by including quotation marks before and after the sequence of words. With the quotation marks, only hits with all of the words in the exact same sequence will appear in the results. Without the quotation marks, the results will include hits that contain all or most of the words anywhere within a Web site.
Operators	Narrow or broaden the search using operators including *+*, *&*, *and*, *-*, *not*, and *or*. For example, if you are searching for information about international exchange students, use the following keywords in the search engine to exclude hits for currency exchange rates: **+international +exchange +students -currency** or **international and exchange and students not currency**
Related pages	Many search engines provide options to include hits for Web pages with similar information. Look for links such as *Similar pages*, *Also try*, or *Related searches*.
Truncation	Some search engines support the use of a symbol, sometimes referred to as a **wildcard**, that allows for variations in the spelling of words. When an asterisk (*) symbol is used in a word, the search results include hits with alternate spellings for the word at the point that the asterisk appears. For example, *extra** generates hits for Web pages with *extra*, *extras*, *extract*, and *extraordinary*.
Domains	You can limit search results to a specific domain, such as an educational institution or a government Web site. For example, to find information about environmental research at an educational institution, in the search engine, enter the following keywords: **+domain:edu +environmental +research** or **domain:edu and environmental and research**

When the search results appear, read the information carefully before clicking any of the links. You can determine the validity of some of the hits by looking at the URLs. For example, if you're looking for information about deadlines for filing forms for personal income taxes, you want to click a link that includes IRS in the URL. Also, domain name extensions help to identify the type of entity. **Table 1–2** shows common domain extensions and the type of entity related to them.

TABLE 1–2   Common domain extensions

DOMAIN EXTENSIONS	DESCRIPTIONS
.com	Commercial business
.edu	Educational institution
.gov	Governmental institution
.org	Nonprofit organization
.mil	Military site
.net	Network site
.us	Abbreviation that indicates a country; for example: .us (United States), .ja (Japan), .uk (United Kingdom), .ca (Canada), and .hk (Hong Kong)

TIP

Clicking a link on a Web site can distract you and take you off task. Before you click a link, try to determine if the link will take you where you want to go. If you click a link and see that the target is not what you expected, click the Back button to return to the previous Web page and stay on task.

Just about anyone can publish information on the Web—often for free, and usually unmonitored. So how do you know if you can trust the information that you find? When you depend on the Web for sources of information, it is your responsibility to determine the integrity and validity of the information and its source. **Table 1–3** provides questions that will guide you through an evaluation process.

TABLE 1–3   A guide for evaluating information on the Web

QUESTIONS TO ASK	WHAT TO CONSIDER
Is the information relevant to my query?	The information should help you to accomplish your goals and objectives. Make sure you analyze the information and determine if it meets your needs.
Is the information current?	Check for a date on the Web page that indicates when the information was last updated.
Is the Web site published by a company or an entity, or is it a personal Web site?	The URL often includes a company name. If you are familiar with the company or entity, consider whether you trust information from this source. If you are not familiar with the company, or the individual, look for links such as *About Us*, *Background*, or *Biography*.
What is the purpose of the Web site?	Use the domain name to identify the type of Web site. For example: a domain name ending with .com is a business, and the intent of the Web site is to sell or promote a product or service.
Who is the author?	Look for information that explains who the author is and how the author is connected to the subject. Verify that the author is qualified to address the subject. Individuals sometimes falsify their credentials, so research the author's background and confirm that the author is credible. For example, if information at the Web site indicates that the author is a professor at a university, go to the university Web site and check the faculty roster.
Is the author biased in his/her opinion?	When looking for facts, be sure the author provides objective viewpoints and cites information with credible sources.
Is the Web site presented professionally?	Information should be well organized and presented accurately, free from spelling and grammar errors.
Are the links legitimate and credible?	Confirm that links are up to date. Links to a credible Web site, such as a business or an organization, do not mean that the business or organization approves of or supports the content on the linked Web page.

12. Click **Delete Browsing History** to open the dialog box in **Figure 1–8**. If necessary, change the settings so they match those shown in the figure, and then click **Delete**.

FIGURE 1–8
Delete Browsing History
dialog box

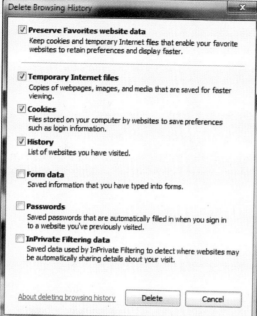

13. Click the **Favorites** button. Click the **Favorites** tab, and in the Favorites list, right-click the **Research** folder, and then click **Delete** in the shortcut menu. Click **Yes** to confirm the deletion.

14. Close Internet Explorer.

SUMMARY

In this lesson, you learned:

Microsoft Word is a powerful, full-featured word processor. Its advanced features enable users to further enhance the appearance of documents and save time preparing and editing documents. Developing a document often involves multiple team members, and Word offers several tools to help you share documents and effectively collaborate on projects.

Excel is the spreadsheet application in the Microsoft Office suite. Spreadsheets are used primarily for calculating and organizing data, and Excel's advanced features enable you to perform complex calculations and in-depth analysis. Excel offers many features that enable you to generate accurate professional-looking reports, charts, and tables.

- Access is the database application in the Office suite. Databases are used for storing and organizing information. The advanced features in Access give you more control over how database records are viewed, edited, and professionally analyzed. Effectively designed forms and reports help to streamline data entry and editing.

- Microsoft PowerPoint is a presentation graphics program that enables you to create materials for presentations of many kinds. Its advanced features include several tools for customizing slide designs and using multimedia effects to enhance your content. Remote publishing features in PowerPoint enable you to share presentations over the Internet or a network.

Step-by-Step 1.6

1. If necessary, log onto the Internet and open your browser.

2. In the address bar, type **www.bing.com** and then press **Enter** to open the Bing search engine.

3. In the Bing search box, type **lake tahoe ski** and then click the **Search** button, or press **Enter**.

4. Note that the number of hits is indicated at the top of the search results. Scroll down and review the first set of results. Each link provides a brief preview of the Web page content, and the keywords are highlighted in the preview. Occurrences of the word *skiing* may also appear highlighted in the previews.

5. Edit the text in the search box to read **+lake +tahoe +ski -water**. Click the **Search** button, or press **Enter**. Scroll down through the first set of results. Note that the number of hits is greatly reduced, and the word *water* is not found in any of the previews.

6. Edit the text in the search box to read **"lake tahoe water ski"** and then click the **Search** button, or press **Enter**. Note that the number of hits is considerably less because adding more keywords often narrows the search.

7. Delete the text in the search box and then type **domain:org and tahoe and ski**. Click the **Search** button, or press **Enter**. Scroll down through the first set of results. Notice every URL has a .org extension.

8. Type **www.nasa.gov** in the address bar and then press **Enter**. The NASA home page opens.

9. Navigate the Web site and find the following information:
   a. the date when the site was last updated
   b. NASA locations
   c. blogs
   d. the names of the authors of the site's articles and blogs
   e. any available information about the authors' backgrounds
   f. information for contacting NASA

10. Return to the home page for the NASA Web site.

11. Leave the NASA Web site open for the next Step-by-Step.

Revisiting Web Sites

As you rely more and more on the Web as a primary source of information on any topic, you'll find that there are sites you visit frequently or that you know you'll want to access again. You can create a bookmark for quick and easy access to a Web page. A ***bookmark*** is a link that navigates you to the Web page, and it is saved in a Favorites folder. You can create additional folders inside the Favorites folder to keep the list of sites organized.

▶ **VOCABULARY**
bookmark

Your browser keeps track of the sites you have visited, so you can also quickly revisit a site by selecting the Web site from the History list. The History list can be organized by date, site, most visited, and the order the sites were visited on the current day. You can easily delete the History list, as well as temporary Internet files, cookies, form data, and passwords.

Step-by-Step 1.7

The following steps describe bookmarking Web pages using Internet Explorer features. If you are not using Internet Explorer as your browser, you can still explore the features for creating the bookmarks, but these steps will not exactly describe your browser features.

1. If necessary, log onto the Internet, open your Internet Explorer browser, and open **www.nasa.gov**. Or navigate to the NASA home page, if necessary.

2. Click the **Favorites** button on the Command bar in the upper-left corner of the screen, as shown in **Figure 1–2**.

FIGURE 1–2
Favorites button on the Internet Explorer browser

Favorites button

3. If necessary, click the **Favorites** tab to show a list of your favorite sites. Your favorites list will be different than the one shown in **Figure 1–3**.

FIGURE 1–3
Folders on the Favorites tab

History tab
Favorites list

4. Click the **Add to Favorites** button to open the Add a Favorite dialog box shown in **Figure 1–4**.

FIGURE 1–4
Add a Favorite dialog box

5. In the Name text box, *NASA - Home* appears. Leave the name as is and click **New Folder** on the dialog box. The Create a Folder dialog box similar to the one shown in **Figure 1–5** opens. In the Folder Name text box, type **Research** and then click **Create**. The Add a Favorite dialog box is still open. Click **Add**.

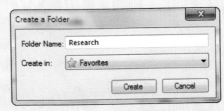

FIGU
Create

6. Click the **Favorites** button to show your list of favorites. Click the new folder **Research** and you will see the *NASA - Home* site. You can move favorites into folders by dragging the site name to the desired folder.

7. Click the **History** tab on the Favorites pane. Click the **View By...** button at the top of the History list, and then click **View By Order Visited Today**. Notice that the NASA Web page is included in the list of documents and Web sites accessed today. Click the **View By...** button at the top of the History list again, then click **View By Most Visited**. The list is rearranged.

8. Right-click one of the Web sites in this list, click **Delete** in the shortcut menu, and then click **Yes** to confirm the deletion.

9. Click the **Favorites** button, and on the History tab, click any one of the site names on the History list. The Web page opens.

10. Click the **list arrow** at the right side of the address bar in the browser, as shown in **Figure 1–6**. A history of accessed Web sites is displayed, as well as a list of favorite sites. Click anywhere outside the History list to close it.

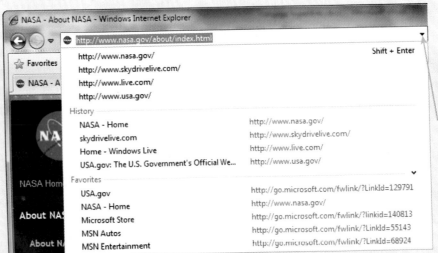

FIGURE 1–6
History and Favorites lists on the address bar

Click to display history of accessed Web sites and favorite sites

11. Click the **Safety** button on the browser toolbar, as shown in **Figure 1–7**.

Safety button

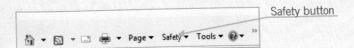

- Microsoft Outlook is a desktop information management program that provides several tools for scheduling appointments and meetings, managing and delegating tasks, and communicating with others. Advanced features help you customize the tools to fit your needs.

- An enormous amount of information is available on the World Wide Web. Effective search strategies not only save you time, but they also lead you to more relevant sources.

- When you depend on the Web for sources of information, it is your responsibility to determine the integrity and validity of the information and its source.

- You can bookmark Web sites that you visit frequently and save the links to the Favorites folder. You can create additional folders to organize your Favorites list.

- You can also quickly revisit a site by selecting the Web site from the History list, which can be organized by date, site, most visited, and the order the sites were visited on the current day.

 # VOCABULARY REVIEW

Define the following terms:

bookmark

browser

hits

keywords

search engine

wildcard

REVIEW QUESTIONS

MATCHING

Match the most appropriate application in Column 2 to the application described in Column 1.

Column 1

_____ 1. A graphics application with multimedia capabilities that can be used to create materials to present and share information with others

_____ 2. An application designed for entering, calculating, and analyzing data

_____ 3. An application used for storing and organizing information

_____ 4. A desktop information management application

_____ 5. An application that provides comprehensive writing tools for sharing information with others

Column 2

A. Microsoft Outlook

B. Microsoft PowerPoint

C. Internet Explorer

D. Microsoft Word

E. Microsoft Excel

F. Microsoft Access

MULTIPLE CHOICE

Select the best response for the following statements.

1. A _____ is a program that gives you the capability to access, view, and download data from the Web.

    A. search engine

    B. Web page

    C. browser

    D. tracking device

2. _____ are used to broaden or narrow an online search.

    A. Keywords

    B. Phrases

    C. Operators

    D. all of the above

3. Non-profit organizations commonly use the _____ extension in the domain name.

    A. .net

    B. .org

    C. country abbreviation

    D. .com

4. _____ are the results generated by a search engine.

    A.   Hits   C.   Wildcards

    B.   Domains   D.   Quick links

5. You can organize your Internet Explorer History list based on _____.

    A.   the date sites were accessed   C.   the order in which sites were visited today

    B.   the names of the sites   D.   all of the above

WRITTEN QUESTIONS

1. Explain how the search results are affected when you include quotation marks before and after a group of words when entering keywords in a search engine.

2. Explain how the domain name can help you identify the purpose of a Web site.

3. Give an example of when you would include operators with the keywords in a search engine.

4. How can you validate that a Web site author has credibility?

5. Name some examples of related pages options provided by some search engines.

■ PROJECTS

If you have a SAM 2010 user profile, your instructor may have assigned an autogradable version of the indicated project. If so, log into the SAM 2010 Web site at *www.cengage.com/sam2010* to download the instruction and start files.

PROJECT 1–1

1. Launch Word, then open the **Spectrum Follow-up.docx** data file from the drive and folder where your Data Files are stored. Save the document as **Final Spectrum Follow-up**, followed by your initials.

2. Make the edits indicated in **Figure 1–9**.

3. Change the left and right margins to 1.25 inches.

4. Justify the alignment of the paragraphs in the body of the letter.

5. Indent the bulleted list .5 inches from the left margin.

6. Adjust the paragraph spacing as needed to fit the entire document on one page.

7. Proofread and check for spelling and grammar errors, and make any necessary corrections.

8. Save the changes and leave the document open for the next project.

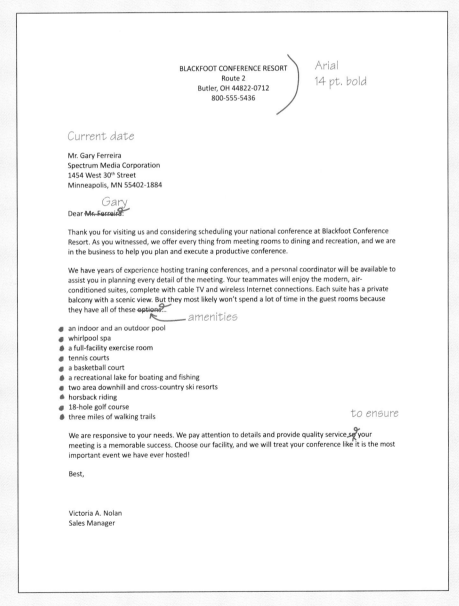

FIGURE 1–9   Edits for the Word document in Project 1–1

SAM PROJECT 1–2

1. Launch PowerPoint and open a new presentation. Save the presentation as **Blackfoot Resort**, followed by your initials.

2. Create a slide show highlighting the guest amenities described in the Blackfoot Conference Resort letter in Project 1-1. This presentation will be distributed on the Internet to promote the resort.

3. Add pictures and graphics to help viewers visualize the amenities.

4. Add a creative title slide at the beginning of the presentation, and add a slide for closure at the end of the presentation.

5. Apply an appropriate design or background colors to the slides.

6. Add transitions to the slides, animations to the text, and objects on the slides to produce special effects and keep the viewer's attention.

7. Save the changes and exit PowerPoint.

PROJECT 1–3

1. If necessary, log onto the Internet and open your browser.

2. In the address bar, type **www.bing.com** and press Enter.

3. Enter the keywords **Conference Resorts Ohio** to search for Ohio-based conference resort sites that offer options for guests that are similar to the options described in the Blackfoot Conference Resort document you edited in Project 1-1.

4. When you find at least two Web sites promoting a conference center similar to the Blackfoot Conference Resort, save the sites to your Favorites list in a Conference Resort folder. *Hint*: Several hits may be sites that showcase multiple resorts, and you will need to navigate to the individual resort pages to get the required information.

5. Evaluate the Web sites and answer the following questions about each Web site.
   a. Were you able to find relevant information to compare resorts?
   b. Is the information at the site current?
   c. When was the site last updated?
   d. Is the site organized well, and is the information presented accurately and professionally?
   e. Does the site provide background information about the resort?
   f. Can you easily access information to contact the resort?
   g. Would you recommend this resort? Explain the reasons for your answer.

6. Close the browser.

PROJECT 1–4

1. Launch Excel and open the **January Sales.xlsx** file from the drive and folder where your Data Files are stored. Save the workbook as **First Qtr Sales**, followed by your initials.

2. In cell C1, type the column heading **February**. In cell D1, type the column heading **March**. In cell E1, type the column heading **Total**. In cell A7, type the row heading **Total**.

3. Enter the following data in the new columns.

	February	March
Byron Store	23112	42109
Fenton Store	38432	41002
Holly Store	31902	48111
Howell Store	27656	39202
Linden Store	29211	43007

4. Proofread the data entries to make sure you entered the numbers correctly.

5. Apply the Accounting number format to all the cells with numbers and remove the decimal places.

6. Enter a formula to calculate the sum of the cell range B2:D2 in cell E2, then fill the formula down through cell E6.

7. Enter a formula to calculate the sum of the cell range B2:B6 in cell B7, then fill the formula across through cell E7.

8. Create a 3-D column chart on the same sheet showing total sales by store. Apply a design of your choice.

9. Add a centered overlay title and type **First Qtr. Sales**. Turn off the legend options.

10. Reposition the chart on the sheet so you can see the sales data in the worksheet.

11. Save the changes and close the document.

PROJECT 1–5

1. Launch Access and open the **Clients.accdb** file from the drive and folder where your Data Files are stored. Save the database as **Updated Clients**, followed by your initials.

2. Open the CLIENTS table in Datasheet View.

3. Delete the record for Daniel Warner.

4. Update the address for Helen Sanderson. Her street address is now **709 Vienna Woods Drive, Cincinnati, OH 45211**.

5. In Design View, add a new field named **Mobile Phone**. Save the changes to the table and then switch back to Datasheet View.

6. Delete the home phone number for Paula Trobaugh and add her mobile phone number, **513-555-4465**.

7. Add two new clients:

   Penelope Rausch

   5074 Signal Hill

   Cincinnati, OH 45244

   Home Phone 513-555-0133

   Mobile Phone 513-555-0899

   Roger Williamson

   722 Red Bud Avenue

   Cincinnati, OH 45229

   Mobile Phone 513-555-1055

8. Save and close the database, then exit Access.

 ## CRITICAL THINKING

ACTIVITY 1–1

Excel and Access have some similarities because both applications are used to organize data. If possible, look at two computer screens, side by side. On one computer, open an Excel worksheet. On the other computer, open an Access database table in Datasheet View. Compare the two screens, and create a list of similarities and differences between the worksheet and the database table. You should point out at least four similarities and four differences.

ACTIVITY 1–2

Open your browser and go to *www.bing.com*. Search for the keywords *Top Ten Search Engines*. Find the most current information available, and confirm that the sources are credible. Then, from the two sources, choose two search engines that you have never used and explore the features in each. Write a brief description of the features you like and why you would use them.

INTRODUCTORY UNIT

MICROSOFT EXCEL 2010

LESSON 1

Microsoft Excel Basics

■ OBJECTIVES

Upon completion of this lesson, you should be able to:

- Define the terms *spreadsheet* and *worksheet*.
- Identify the parts of a worksheet.
- Start Excel, open an existing workbook, and save a workbook.
- Move the active cell in a worksheet.
- Select cells and enter data in a worksheet.
- Edit and replace data in cells.
- Zoom, preview, and print a worksheet.
- Close a workbook and exit Excel.

■ VOCABULARY

active cell

active worksheet

adjacent range

cell

cell reference

column

formula

Formula Bar

landscape orientation

Microsoft Excel 2010 (Excel)

Name Box

nonadjacent range

portrait orientation

range

range reference

row

sheet tab

spreadsheet

workbook

worksheet

Numbers are everywhere. Spreadsheets make it simple to perform calculations with these numbers and resolve problems based on those calculations. People rely on numbers and spreadsheets to do such things as track inventories, set up budgets, determine grades, create invoices, evaluate attendance records, to name just a few examples.

Introduction to Spreadsheets

▶ **VOCABULARY**

Microsoft Excel 2010

Excel

spreadsheet

worksheet

workbook

Microsoft Excel 2010 (or *Excel*) is the spreadsheet program in Microsoft Office 2010. A *spreadsheet* is a grid of rows and columns in which you enter text, numbers, and the results of calculations. The primary purpose of a spreadsheet is to solve problems that involve numbers. Without a computer, you could try to solve these types of problems by creating rows and columns on paper and using a calculator to determine the results (see **Figure 1–1**). Spreadsheets have many uses. For example, you can use a spreadsheet to calculate grades for students in a class, to prepare a budget for the next few months, or to determine payments for repaying a loan.

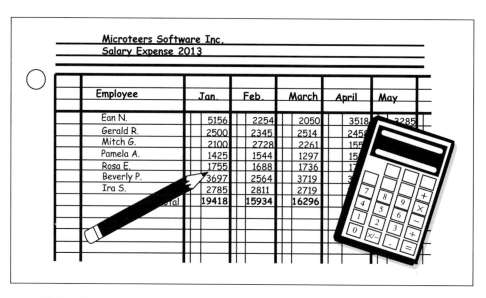

FIGURE 1–1   Spreadsheet prepared on paper

Computer spreadsheets also contain rows and columns with text, numbers, and the results of calculations. But, computer spreadsheets perform calculations faster and more accurately than you can with spreadsheets you create on paper, using a pencil and a calculator. The primary advantage of computer spreadsheets is their ability to complete complex and repetitious calculations quickly and accurately.

Computer spreadsheets are also flexible. Making changes to an existing computer spreadsheet is usually as easy as pointing and clicking with the mouse. Suppose, for example, you use a computer spreadsheet to calculate your budget (your monthly income and expenses) and overestimate the amount of money you need to pay for electricity. You can change a single entry in the computer spreadsheet, and the computer will recalculate the entire spreadsheet to determine the new budgeted amount. Think about the work this change would require if you were calculating the budget by hand on paper with a pencil and calculator.

In Excel, a computerized spreadsheet is called a *worksheet*. The file used to store worksheets is called a *workbook*. Usually, a workbook contains a collection of related worksheets.

Starting Excel

You start Excel from the Start menu in Windows. Click the Start button, click All Programs, click Microsoft Office, and then click Microsoft Excel 2010. When Excel starts, the program window displays a blank workbook titled *Book1*, which includes three blank worksheets titled *Sheet1*, *Sheet2*, and *Sheet3*. The Excel program window has the same basic parts as all Office programs: the title bar, the Quick Access Toolbar, the Ribbon, Backstage view, and the status bar. However, as shown in **Figure 1–2**, Excel also has additional buttons and parts.

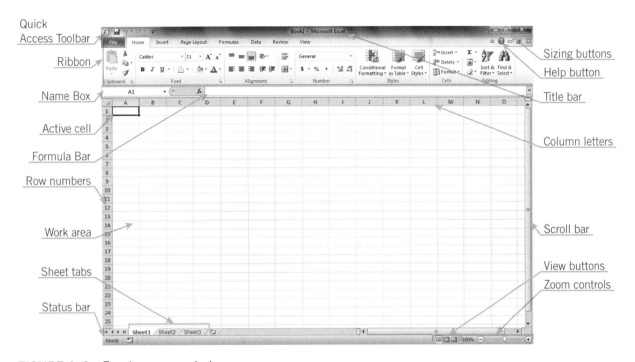

FIGURE 1–2   Excel program window

Step-by-Step 1.1

1. With Windows running, click the **Start** button 🔘 on the taskbar.

2. Click **All Programs**. The Start menu shows all the programs installed on the computer.

3. Click **Microsoft Office** to display a list of programs in the folder, and then click **Microsoft Excel 2010**. Excel starts and opens a blank workbook, titled *Book1*, as shown in Figure 1–2.

4. If the Excel program window does not fill your screen, click the **Maximize** button 🔲 in the title bar.

5. Leave the workbook open for the next Step-by-Step.

▶ **VOCABULARY**

sheet tab

active worksheet

column

row

cell

cell reference

active cell

Name Box

Formula Bar

formula

Exploring the Parts of the Workbook

Each new workbook contains three worksheets by default. The name of each worksheet appears in the *sheet tab* at the bottom of the worksheet window. The worksheet that is displayed in the work area is called the *active worksheet*. *Columns* of the worksheet appear vertically and are identified by letters at the top of the worksheet window. *Rows* appear horizontally and are identified by numbers on the left side of the worksheet window. A *cell* is the intersection of a row and a column. Each cell is identified by a unique *cell reference*, which is formed by combining the cell's column letter and row number. For example, the cell that intersects at column C and row 4 has the cell reference C4.

The pointer changes shape as you move it around the Excel window. The pointer becomes a thick white plus sign ✚ when it is in the worksheet. If you move the pointer to a button on the Ribbon, the pointer changes to a white arrow ⊳.

The cell in the worksheet in which you can type data is called the *active cell*. The active cell is distinguished from the other cells by a dark border. In your worksheet, cell A1 has the dark border, which indicates that cell A1 is the active cell. You can move the active cell from one cell to another. The *Name Box*, or cell reference area located below the Ribbon, displays the cell reference of the active cell.

The *Formula Bar* appears to the right of the Name Box and displays a formula when the cell of a worksheet contains a calculated value (or the results of the formula). A *formula* is an equation that calculates a new value from values currently in a worksheet, such as adding the numbers in cell A1 and cell A2.

Opening an Existing Workbook

Opening a workbook means loading an existing workbook file from a drive into the program window. To open an existing workbook, you click the File tab on the Ribbon to display Backstage view, and then click Open in the navigation bar. The Open dialog box appears. The Open dialog box shows all the workbooks in the displayed folder that you can open with Excel. When you open another workbook, the *Book1* workbook that opened when you started Excel disappears.

TIP

To open a workbook that you recently worked on, click the File tab on the Ribbon, and then click Recent in the navigation bar. The right pane contains the Recent Workbooks list. Click the workbook you want to open to open it in Excel.

Step-by-Step 1.2

1. On the Ribbon, click the **File** tab. Backstage view appears.

2. In the navigation bar, click **Open**. The Open dialog box appears.

3. Navigate to the drive and folder where your Data Files are stored, open the **Excel** folder, and then open the **Excel Lesson 01** folder.

4. Double-click the **Frogs.xlsx** workbook file. Depending on how Windows is set up on your computer, you might not see the file extension after the file name; in that case, double-click the **Frogs** workbook file. The workbook appears in the program window, as shown in **Figure 1–3**.

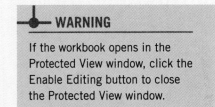

WARNING

If the workbook opens in the Protected View window, click the Enable Editing button to close the Protected View window.

Current workbook name (you might not see the file extension)

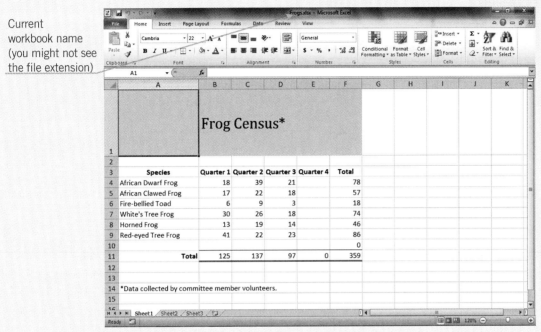

FIGURE 1–3
Frogs workbook open in Excel

5. Leave the workbook open for the next Step-by-Step.

Saving a Workbook

Saving is done two ways. The Save command saves an existing workbook, using its current name and save location. The Save As command lets you save a workbook with a new name or to a new location.

The first time you save a new workbook, the Save As dialog box appears, as shown in **Figure 1–4**, so you can give the workbook a descriptive name and choose a location to save it. After you have saved the workbook, you can use the Save command in Backstage view or the Save button on the Quick Access Toolbar to periodically save the latest version of the workbook with the same name in the same location. To save a copy of the workbook with a new name or to a different location, you need to use the Save As dialog box. You'll use this method to save the Frogs workbook you just opened with a new name, leaving the original workbook intact.

Address bar shows the current drive and folder path

Use the Navigation pane to change the current save location

Workbooks saved in the current folder

Depending on how Windows is set up on your computer, you might not see the .xlsx file extension

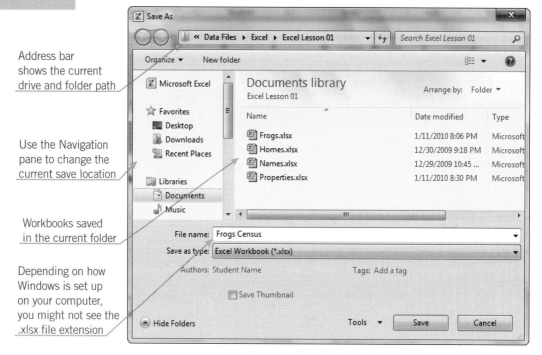

FIGURE 1–4   Save As dialog box

Step-by-Step 1.3

1. On the Ribbon, click the **File** tab. In the navigation bar, click **Save As**. The Save As dialog box appears.

2. Navigate to the drive and folder where you store the Data Files for this lesson, if necessary.

3. In the File name box, type **Frog Census** followed by your initials. Your dialog box should look similar to Figure 1-4.

4. Click **Save**.

5. Leave the workbook open for the next Step-by-Step.

Moving the Active Cell in a Worksheet

The easiest way to change the active cell in a worksheet is to move the pointer to the cell you want to make active and click. The dark border surrounds the cell you clicked, and the Name Box shows its cell reference. When working with a large worksheet, you might not be able to see the entire worksheet in the program window. You can display different parts of the worksheet by using the mouse to drag the scroll box in the scroll bar to another position. You can also move the active cell to different parts of the worksheet using the keyboard or the Go To command.

TIP

The column letter and row number of the active cell are shaded in orange for easy identification.

Using the Keyboard to Move the Active Cell

You can change the active cell by pressing the keys or using the keyboard shortcuts shown in **Table 1–1**. When you press an arrow key, the active cell moves one cell in that direction. When you press and hold down an arrow key, the active cell shifts in that direction repeatedly and quickly.

TABLE 1–1 Keys for moving the active cell in a worksheet

TO MOVE	PRESS
Left one column	Left arrow key
Right one column	Right arrow key
Up one row	Up arrow key
Down one row	Down arrow key
To the first cell of a row	Home key
To cell A1	Ctrl+Home keys
To the last cell of the column and row that contain data	Ctrl+End keys
Up one window	Page Up key
Down one window	Page Down key

Using the Go To Command to Move the Active Cell

You might want to change the active cell to a cell in a part of the worksheet that you cannot see in the work area. The fastest way to move to that cell is with the Go To dialog box. In the Editing group on the Home tab of the Ribbon, click the Find & Select button, and then click Go To. The Go To dialog box appears, as shown in

EXTRA FOR EXPERTS

You can change the active worksheet in a workbook to next worksheet by pressing the Ctrl+Page Down keys or to the previous worksheet by pressing the Ctrl+Page Up keys. You can also use the mouse to click the sheet tab of the worksheet you want to make active.

Figure 1–5. Type the cell reference in the Reference box, and then click OK. The cell you specified becomes the active cell.

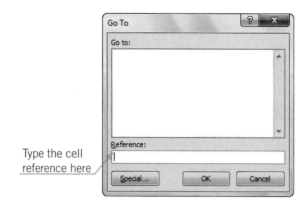

Type the cell reference here

FIGURE 1–5   Go To dialog box

Step-by-Step 1.4

1. Press the **Ctrl+End** keys. The active cell moves to cell F14, which is the cell that intersects the last column and row that contain data in the worksheet.

2. Press **Home**. The active cell moves to the first cell of row 14—cell A14, which contains the text *Data collected by committee member volunteers.*

3. Press the **Up arrow** key six times to move the active cell up six rows. The active cell is cell A8, which contains the words *Horned Frog.*

4. On the Ribbon, click the **Home** tab, if the tab is not already active.

5. In the Editing group, click the **Find & Select** button 🔍 to open a menu of commands, and then click **Go To**. The Go To dialog box appears, as shown in Figure 1–5.

6. In the Reference box, type **B4**.

7. Click **OK**. The active cell moves to cell B4, which contains the number *18*.

8. Leave the workbook open for the next Step-by-Step.

> **TIP**
>
> You can also open the Go To dialog box by pressing the Ctrl+G keys or by pressing the F5 key.

Selecting a Group of Cells

> **VOCABULARY**
> **range**
> **adjacent range**
> **range reference**

Often, you will perform operations on more than one cell at a time. A group of selected cells is called a *range*. In an *adjacent range*, all cells touch each other and form a rectangle. The range is identified by its *range reference*, which lists both the cell in its upper-left corner and the cell in its lower-right corner, separated by a colon (for example, A3:C5). To select an adjacent range, click the cell in one corner of the range, drag the pointer to the cell in the opposite corner of the range, and then release the mouse button. As you drag, the range of selected cells becomes shaded (except for the first cell you selected), and the dark border expands to surround all the selected cells. In addition, the column letters and row numbers of the range you select change to orange. The active cell in a range is white; the other cells are shaded.

You can also select a range that is nonadjacent. A ***nonadjacent range*** includes two or more adjacent ranges and selected cells. The range reference for a nonadjacent range separates each range or cell with a semicolon (for example, A3:C5;E3:G5). To select a nonadjacent range, select the first adjacent range or cell, press the Ctrl key as you select the other cells or ranges you want to include, and then release the Ctrl key and the mouse button.

EXTRA FOR EXPERTS

Have a classmate call out cell references so you can practice moving the active cell in a worksheet using the methods you have learned.

▶ **VOCABULARY**
nonadjacent range

Step-by-Step 1.5

1. Click cell **B3** to make it active.

2. Press and hold the left mouse button as you drag the pointer to the right until cell **F3** is selected.

3. Release the mouse button. The range B3:F3 is selected, as you can see from the shaded cells and the dark border. Also, the column letters B through F and the row number 3 are orange. See **Figure 1–6**.

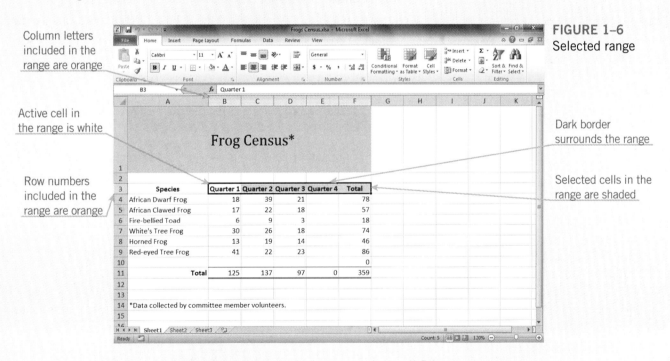

Column letters included in the range are orange

Active cell in the range is white

Row numbers included in the range are orange

Dark border surrounds the range

Selected cells in the range are shaded

FIGURE 1–6
Selected range

4. Click cell **B4**. The range B3:F3 is deselected when you select cell B4.

5. Press and hold the left mouse button as you drag down and to the right until cell **F11** is selected.

6. Release the mouse button. The range B4:F11 is selected.

7. Leave the workbook open for the next Step-by-Step.

TIP

After you type data in a cell, the active cell changes, depending on how you enter the data. If you click the Enter button on the Formula Bar, the cell you typed in remains active. If you press the Enter key, the cell below the cell you typed in becomes active. If you press the Tab key, the cell to the right of the cell you typed in becomes active.

Entering Data in a Cell

Worksheet cells can contain text, numbers, or formulas. Text is any combination of letters and numbers and symbols, such as headings, labels, or explanatory notes. Numbers are values, dates, or times. Formulas are equations that calculate a value.

You enter data in the active cell. First, type the text, numbers, or formula in the active cell. Then, click the Enter button ☑ on the Formula Bar or press the Enter key or the Tab key on the keyboard. The data you typed is entered in the cell. If you decide not to enter the data you typed, you can click the Cancel button ☒ on the Formula Bar or press Esc to delete the data without making any changes to the cell.

If you have already entered the data in the cell, you can undo, or reverse, the entry. On the Quick Access Toolbar, click the Undo button ↺ to reverse your most recent change. To undo multiple actions, click the Undo button arrow ↺▾. A list of your previous actions appears, and you can choose how many actions you want to undo.

Step-by-Step 1.6

1. Click cell **E4** to make it active.

2. Type **17**. As you type, the number appears in the cell and in the Formula Bar.

3. Press the **Enter** key. The number 17 is entered in cell E4, and the active cell moves to cell E5. The totals in cells F4, E11, and F11 change as you enter the data.

4. Type **24**. As you type, the number appears in the cell and in the Formula Bar.

5. On the Formula Bar, click the **Enter** button ☑. The totals in cells F5, E11, and F11 change as you enter the data.

6. On the Quick Access Toolbar, click the **Undo button arrow** ↺▾. A menu appears listing the actions you have just performed, as shown in **Figure 1–7**.

TIP

If a cell is not wide enough to display all the cell's contents, extra text extends into the next cells, if they are blank. If not, only the characters that fit in the cell appear, and the rest are hidden from view, but they are still stored. Numbers that extend beyond a cell's width appear as #### in the cell.

FIGURE 1–7
Undo menu

Click the Undo button arrow to open the menu

Typing '24' in E5
Typing '17' in E4
Cancel

Any entries you select will be reversed when you click

7. Click **Typing '24' in E5**. The data is removed from cell E5, and the data in cells F5, E11, and F11 return to their previous totals.

8. Click cell **A10**, and then enter **Pac Frog**. The Pac Frog species is added to the Frog Census.

9. In the range **E5:E10**, enter the data, as shown in **Figure 1–8**, to include the number of frogs sighted for each species in Quarter 4.

TIP

The instruction to click a cell and then enter data means you should click the specified cell, type the data indicated, and then enter that data in the cell by pressing the Enter key, pressing the Tab key, or clicking the Enter button on the Formula Bar.

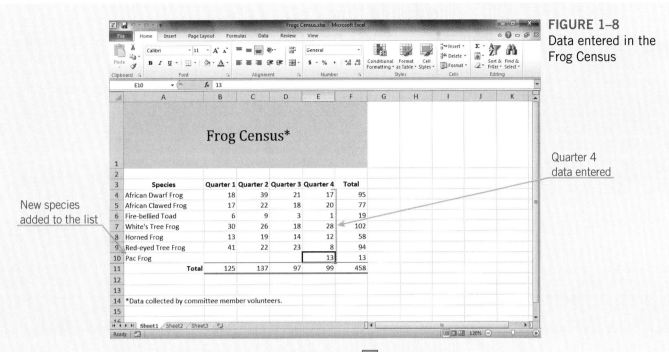

10. On the Quick Access Toolbar, click the **Save** button to save the workbook.

11. Leave the workbook open for the next Step-by-Step.

Changing Data in a Cell

After you enter data in cells in the worksheet, you might change your mind or discover a mistake. If so, you can edit, replace, or clear the data.

Editing Data

When you need to make a change to data in a cell, you can edit it in the Formula Bar or in the cell. The contents of the active cell always appear in the Formula Bar. To edit the data in the Formula Bar, click in the Formula Bar and then drag the pointer to select the text you want to edit. You can also use the arrow keys to position the insertion point. Then, press the Backspace key or the Delete key to remove data, or type the new data. To edit the data directly in a cell, make the cell active and then press the F2 key or double-click the cell to enter editing mode, which places the insertion point within the cell contents. An insertion point appears in the cell, and you can make changes to the data. When you are done, click the Enter button on the Formula Bar or press the Enter key or the Tab key.

TIP

If you need help while working with any of the Excel features, use the Excel Help feature. Click the Microsoft Excel Help button. In the Excel Help window, type a word or phrase about the feature you want help with, and then click the Search button. A list of Help topics related to the word or words you typed appears. Click the appropriate Help topic to learn more about the feature.

Replacing Data

Sometimes you need to replace the entire contents of a cell. To do this, select the cell, type the new data, and then enter the data by clicking the Enter button on the Formula Bar or by pressing the Enter key or the Tab key. This is the same method used to enter data in a blank cell. The only difference is that you overwrite the existing cell contents.

Clearing Data

Clearing a cell removes all the data in the cell. To clear the active cell, you can use the Ribbon, the keyboard, or the mouse. On the Home tab of the Ribbon, in the Editing group, click the Clear button to display a menu with options, and then click Clear Contents. To use the keyboard, press the Delete key or the Backspace key. To use your mouse, right-click the active cell, and then click Clear Contents on the shortcut menu.

> **TIP**
>
> As you type, the AutoComplete function displays the full text entered in other cells that begins with the same letters you have typed. To make a different entry, keep typing the new data. To accept the entry, press the Enter key.

Step-by-Step 1.7

1. Click cell **A10** to make it the active cell.

2. Press the **F2** key. A blinking insertion point appears in cell A10.

3. Press the **left arrow** key five times to move the insertion point after *Pac*.

4. Type **Man**, and then press the **Enter** key. The contents of cell A10 are edited to *PacMan Frog*.

5. Click cell **D9**, and then type **19**.

6. On the Formula Bar, click the **Enter** button ✓. The number 19 is entered in cell D9, replacing the previous contents.

7. Click cell **A3**, and then press the **Delete** key. The contents are cleared from cell A3. Your screen should look similar to **Figure 1–9**.

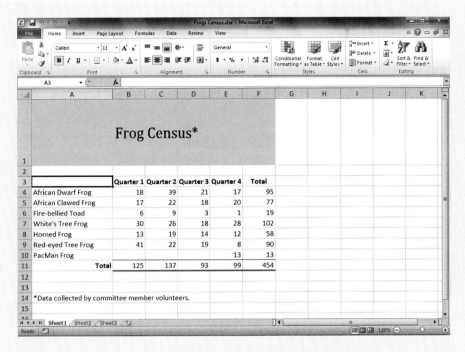

8. Save the workbook, and leave it open for the next Step-by-Step.

Searching for Data

The Find and Replace dialog box enables you to locate specific data in a worksheet. If you like, you can then change data you find.

Finding Data

The Find command locates data in a worksheet, which is particularly helpful when a worksheet contains a large amount of data. You can use the Find command to locate words or parts of words. For example, searching for *emp* finds the words *employee* and *temporary* It also finds Employee and TEMPORARY because the Find command doesn't match the uppercase or lowercase letters you typed unless you specify that it should. Likewise, searching for *85* finds the numbers *85, 850,* and *385*. On the Home tab of the Ribbon, in the Editing group, click the Find & Select button, and then click Find. The Find and Replace dialog box appears, with the Find tab active.

Replacing Data

The Replace command is an extension of the Find command. Replacing data substitutes new data for the data that the Find command locates. As with the Find command, the Replace command doesn't distinguish between uppercase and lowercase letters unless you specify to match the case. On the Home tab of the Ribbon, in the Editing group, click the Find & Select button, and then click Replace. The Find and Replace dialog box appears, with the Replace tab active.

EXTRA FOR EXPERTS

You can use wildcard characters in the Find what box to search for data that matches a particular pattern. Use ? (a question mark) for a single character. Use * (an asterisk) for two or more characters. For example, Br?an finds Brian and Bryan, whereas Sam* finds Samuel, Samantha, Sammy, and Sammi.

You can perform more specific searches by clicking the Options button in the dialog box. **Figure 1–10** shows the Replace tab in the Find and Replace dialog box after clicking the Options button.

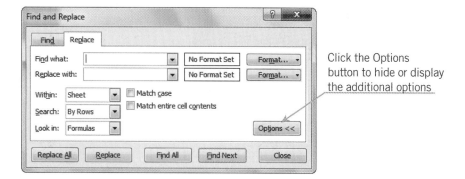

Click the Options button to hide or display the additional options

FIGURE 1–10   Find and Replace dialog box expanded

Table 1–2 lists the options you can specify in the Find and Replace dialog box.

TABLE 1–2   Find and Replace options

SEARCH OPTION	SPECIFIES
Find what	The data to locate
Replace with	The data to insert in place of the located data
Format	The format of the data you want to find or replace
Within	Whether to search the worksheet or the entire workbook
Search	The direction to search: across rows or down columns
Look in	Whether to search cell contents (values) or formulas
Match case	Whether the search must match the capitalization you used for the search data
Match entire cell contents	Whether the search should locate cells whose contents exactly match the search data

Step-by-Step 1.8

1. Click cell **A1**.

2. On the Home tab of the Ribbon, locate the **Editing** group.

3. Click the **Find & Select** button, and then click **Find**.

4. In the Find what box, type **Quarter**.

5. Click **Find Next**. The active cell moves to cell B3, the first cell that contains the search data.

6. In the Find and Replace dialog box, click the **Replace** tab. A Replace with box appears.

7. In the Replace with box, type **Month**.

8. Click **Replace**. The word *Quarter* is replaced by *Month* in cell B3, and the active cell moves to cell C3, which is the next cell that contains the search data.

9. Click **Replace All**. A dialog box appears, indicating that Excel has completed the search and made three additional replacements of the word *Quarter* with the word *Month*.

10. Click **OK**.

11. In the Find and Replace dialog box, click **Close**.

12. Save the workbook, and leave it open for the next Step-by-Step.

Zooming a Worksheet

You can change the magnification of a worksheet using the Zoom controls on the status bar. The default magnification for a workbook is 100%, which you can see on the Zoom level button. For a closer view of a worksheet, click the Zoom In button ⊕, which increases the zoom by 10% each time you click the button, or drag the Zoom slider to the right to increase the zoom percentage. The entire worksheet looks larger, and you see fewer cells in the work area. The Sheet1 worksheet you are working on is zoomed to 120% so you can more easily see the contents in the cells. If you want to see more cells in the work area, click the Zoom Out button ⊖, which decreases the zoom by 10% each time you click the button, or drag the Zoom slider to the left to decrease the zoom percentage. The entire worksheet looks smaller. To select a specific magnification, click the Zoom level button 100% to open the Zoom dialog box, type the zoom percentage you want in the Custom box, and then click OK. The Zoom level button shows the current zoom level percentage. **Figure 1–11** shows the Zoom dialog box and the zoom controls.

TIP

Zoom controls are also available on the Ribbon. Click the View tab, and then in the Zoom group, click the Zoom button to open the Zoom dialog box. Click the 100% option button to zoom the worksheet to 100% magnification. Click the Fit selection option button to zoom the worksheet so the selected range fills the worksheet window.

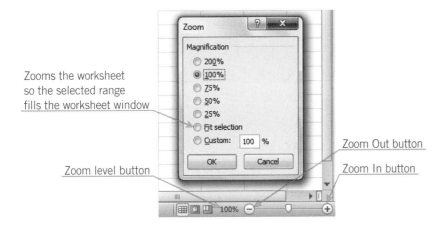

FIGURE 1–11   Zoom dialog box and controls

Step-by-Step 1.9

1. On the status bar, click the **Zoom In** button ⊕ two times. The worksheet zooms to 140%, and you see a closer view of fewer cells.

2. On the status bar, drag the **Zoom slider** ▽ right to approximately 200%. The view of the worksheet is magnified even more.

3. On the status bar, click the **Zoom level** button. The Zoom dialog box appears, as shown in Figure 1–11.

4. Click the **50%** option button, and then click **OK**. The view of the worksheet is reduced to half of its default size, and you see many more cells.

5. On the status bar, click the **Zoom In** button ⊕ seven times. The worksheet returns to zoom level of 120%.

6. Click cell **A16**, and then enter your name.

7. Save the workbook, and leave it open for the next Step-by-Step.

Previewing and Printing a Worksheet

Sometimes you need a printed copy of a worksheet to give to another person or for your own files. You can print a worksheet by clicking the File tab on the Ribbon, and then clicking Print in the navigation bar to display the Print tab (see **Figure 1–12**). The Print tab enables you to select the number of copies to print, a printer, the parts of the worksheet to print, and the way the printed worksheet will look. The print settings include the page orientation (**portrait orientation** for a page turned so that its shorter side is at top and **landscape orientation** for a page turned so that its longer side is at top), the paper size, and the margins. For now, you will print the entire worksheet using the default settings.

▶ **VOCABULARY**
portrait orientation

landscape orientation

Click to print the worksheet

Select the number of copies to print

Click to select the printer to use

Click to select what to print

Click to select the paper orientation

Click to select the margins

Preview of the worksheet as a printed page

Click the Next Page and Previous Page buttons to scroll through the preview

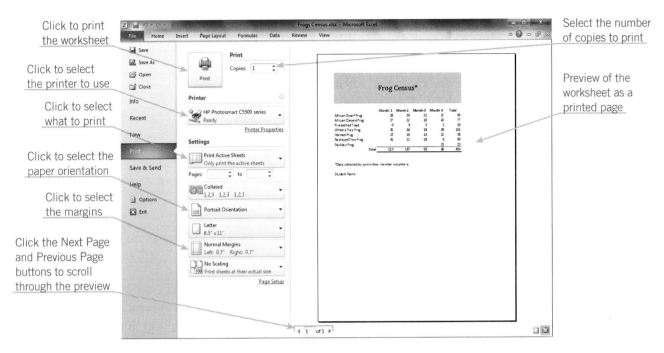

FIGURE 1–12   Print tab

The Print tab also shows you how the printed pages will look before you use the resources to print a worksheet. You can click the Next Page and Previous Page buttons to display other pages of your worksheet. You can click the Zoom to Page button, which shows a closer view of the page (see **Figure 1–13**). When you have finished previewing the printed pages and are satisfied with the print settings, you click the Print button.

Use the scroll bars to shift different parts of the page into view

Click to display other pages of a longer worksheet

Zoom to Page button

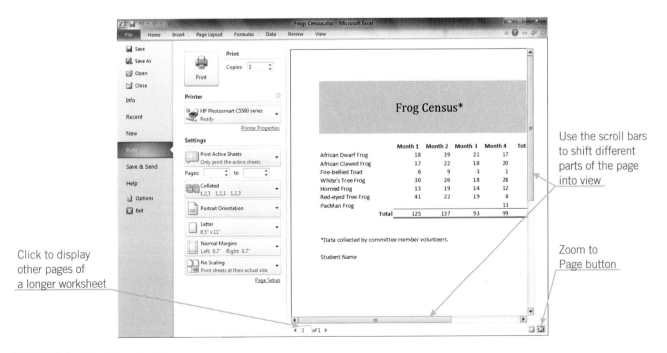

FIGURE 1–13   Zoom to Page

Step-by-Step 1.10

1. On the Ribbon, click the **File** tab. In the navigation bar, click **Print**. The Print tab appears, as shown in Figure 1–12.

2. Review the default settings on the Print tab. If the printer you want to use is not in the Printer button, click the **Printer** button, and then click the appropriate printer name.

3. Click **Zoom to Page** button. The previewed page becomes larger so you can examine it in more detail, as shown in Figure 1–13.

4. Drag the scroll bars to display different parts of the previewed page.

5. Click **Zoom to Page** button. The preview returns to its original size.

6. If your instructor asks you to print the worksheet, click the **Print** button. The active worksheet is printed. If you do not need to print, click the **File** tab on the Ribbon to return to the worksheet.

7. Leave the workbook open for the next Step-by-Step.

Closing a Workbook and Exiting Excel

You can close a workbook by clicking the File tab on the Ribbon, and then clicking Close in the navigation bar. If you use the Close command to close a workbook, Excel remains open and ready for you to open or create another workbook. To exit the workbook, click the Exit command in the navigation bar.

If you try to close a workbook that contains changes you haven't saved, a dialog box opens, asking whether you want to save the file. Click Yes to save and close the workbook. Click No to close the workbook without saving. Click Cancel to return to the Excel program window without saving or closing the workbook.

> **TIP**
>
> You can also close the workbook and leave Excel open by clicking the Close Window button located below the sizing buttons in the title bar. To close the workbook and exit Excel, you can click the Close button in the title bar.

Step-by-Step 1.11

1. On the Ribbon, click the **File** tab, and then in the navigation bar, click **Close**.

2. If you are asked to save changes, click **Save**. The workbook closes.

3. On the File tab, in the navigation bar, click **Exit**. The Excel program window closes.

SUMMARY

In this lesson, you learned:

- The primary purpose of a spreadsheet is to solve problems involving numbers. The advantage of using a computer spreadsheet is that you can complete complex and repetitious calculations quickly and accurately.

- A worksheet consists of columns and rows that intersect to form cells. Each cell is identified by a cell reference, which combines the letter of the column and the number of the row.

- The first time you save a workbook, the Save As dialog box opens so you can enter a descriptive name and select a save location. After that, you can use the Save command in Backstage view or the Save button on the Quick Access Toolbar to save the latest version of the workbook.

- You can change the active cell in the worksheet by clicking the cell with the pointer, pressing keys, or using the scroll bars. The Go To dialog box lets you quickly move the active cell anywhere in the worksheet.

- A group of selected cells is called a range. A range is identified by the cells in the upper-left and lower-right corners of the range, separated by a colon. To select an adjacent range, drag the pointer across the rectangle of cells you want to include. To select a nonadjacent range, select the first adjacent range, hold down the Ctrl key, select each additional cell or range, and then release the Ctrl key.

- Worksheet cells can contain text, numbers, and formulas. After you enter data or a formula in a cell, you can change the cell contents by editing, replacing, or deleting it.

- You can search for specific characters in a worksheet. You can also replace data you have searched for with specific characters.

- The zoom controls on the status bar enable you to enlarge or reduce the magnification of the worksheet in the worksheet window.

- Before you print a worksheet, you should check the page preview to see how the printed pages will look.

- When you finish your work session, you should save your final changes and close the workbook.

■ VOCABULARY REVIEW

Define the following terms:

active cell

active worksheet

adjacent range

cell

cell reference

column

formula

Formula Bar

landscape orientation

Microsoft Excel 2010 (Excel)

Name Box

nonadjacent range

portrait orientation

range

range reference

row

sheet tab

spreadsheet

workbook

worksheet

■ REVIEW QUESTIONS

TRUE / FALSE

Circle T if the statement is true or F if the statement is false.

T   F   **1.**   The primary advantage of the worksheet is the ability to solve numerical problems quickly and accurately.

T   F   **2.**   A cell is the intersection of a row and a column.

T   F   **3.**   You use the Go To command to get a closer view of a worksheet.

T   F   **4.**   You can use the Find command to substitute *Week* for all instances of *Period* in a worksheet.

T   F   **5.**   Each time you save a worksheet, you must open the Save As dialog box.

WRITTEN QUESTIONS

Write a brief answer to the following questions.

1. What term describes a cell that is ready for data entry?

2. How are rows identified in a worksheet?

3. What term describes a group of cells?

4. What key(s) do you press to move the active cell to the first cell in a row?

5. If you decide not to enter data you just typed in the active cell, how do you cancel your entry without making any changes to the cell?

FILL IN THE BLANK

Complete the following sentences by writing the correct word or words in the blanks provided.

1. A(n) _____ is a computerized spreadsheet.

2. Each cell is identified by a unique _____, which is formed by combining the cell's column letter and row number.

3. The contents of the active cell always appear in the _____.

4. _____ a cell removes all the data in a cell.

5. You can increase or decrease the magnification of a worksheet with the _____ controls on the status bar.

PROJECTS

If you have a SAM 2010 user profile, your instructor may have assigned an autogradable version of the indicated project. If so, log into the SAM 2010 Web site at *www.cengage.com/sam2010* to download the instruction and start files.

PROJECT 1–1

In the blank space, write the letter of the key or keys from Column 2 that correspond to the movement of the active cell in Column 1.

Column 1

_____ 1. Left one column

_____ 2. Right one column

_____ 3. Up one row

_____ 4. Down one row

_____ 5. To the first cell in a row

_____ 6. To cell A1

_____ 7. To the last cell containing data

_____ 8. Up one window

_____ 9. Down one window

Column 2

A. Up arrow key

B. Page Up key

C. Left arrow key

D. Home key

E. Down arrow key

F. Right arrow key

G. Ctrl+End keys

H. Ctrl+Home keys

I. Page Down key

SAM PROJECT 1–2

1. Start Excel. Open the **Homes.xlsx** workbook from the drive and folder where your Data Files are stored.

2. Save the workbook as **Home Ownership** followed by your initials.

3. In cell A15, enter **Colorado**.

4. In cell B15, enter **67.30**.

5. In cell C15, enter **62.20**.

6. In cell A16, edit the data to **Connecticut**.

7. In cell B16, edit the data to **66.80**.

8. In cell A5, delete the data.

9. In cell A2, enter your name.

10. Change the page orientation to landscape orientation.

11. Save, preview, and print the workbook. Close the workbook and exit Excel.

PROJECT 1–3

1. Start Excel. Open the **Properties.xlsx** workbook from the drive and folder where your Data Files are stored.

2. Save the workbook as **Properties Estimates** followed by your initials.

3. Enter the square footages in the following cells to estimate the home costs. The estimated home cost in each neighborhood will change as you enter the data.

CELL	ENTER
C5	1300
C6	1550
C7	2200
C8	1500

4. After selling several houses in the Washington Heights neighborhood, Neighborhood Properties has determined that the cost per square foot is $71.25, rather than $78.50. Edit cell B7 to **$71.25**.

5. In cell A3, enter your name.

6. Save, preview, print, and then close the workbook. Exit Excel.

PROJECT 1–4

1. Start Excel. Open the **Names.xlsx** workbook from the drive and folder where your Data Files are stored.

2. Save the workbook as **Last Names** followed by your initials.

3. Use the Find command to locate the name *CRUZ*. The active cell should be cell A123.

4. Click in the worksheet outside the dialog box, and then press the Ctrl+Home keys to return to cell A1.

5. Click in the Find and Replace dialog box, and then locate the name *BOOTH*. The active cell should be cell A595. (*Hint*: The Find and Replace dialog box remains on-screen from Steps 3 and 4. You can simply enter the new search in the Find what box.)

6. Click in the worksheet, and then press the Ctrl+Home keys to return to cell A1.

7. Click in the Find and Replace dialog box, click the Replace tab, and then replace the name *FORBES* with **FABERGE**. The active cell should be cell A988.

8. Undo the last change you made to the workbook.

9. Search for your last name and the last names of three of your friends in the workbook. These names might not appear in the workbook.

10. Save and close the workbook. Exit Excel.

CRITICAL THINKING

ACTIVITY 1–1

The primary purpose of a spreadsheet is to solve problems that involve numbers. Identify two numerical situations in each of the following categories that might be solved by using a spreadsheet.

1. Business

2. Career

3. Personal

4. School

ACTIVITY 1–2

In your worksheet, you have selected a large range of adjacent cells that extends over several screens. You realize that you incorrectly included one additional column of cells in the range.

To reselect the range of cells, you must page up to the active cell (the first cell in the range) and drag through several screens to the last cell in the range. Is there a better way to remove the column from the range, without having to reselect the entire range? Also, is there a faster way to select such a large range—one that doesn't include dragging through several screens?

Start Excel, and use the Help system to learn more about how to select fewer cells without canceling your original selection. Then research how to select a large range without dragging. Use Word to write a brief explanation of the steps you would take to change the selected range and to select a large range without dragging.

LESSON 2

Changing the Appearance of a Worksheet

■ OBJECTIVES

Upon completion of this lesson, you should be able to:

- Change column widths and row heights.
- Position data within a cell by aligning, wrapping, rotating, and indenting.
- Change the appearance of cells using fonts, font sizes, font styles, colors, and borders.
- Designate the number format used for data stored in a cell.
- Use the Format Painter to copy formatting from one cell to another.
- Apply and clear cell styles.
- Find and replace cell formats.

■ VOCABULARY

align

AutoFit

border

cell style

clear

column heading

fill

font

font size

font style

Format Painter

indent

merge

number format

orientation

row heading

style

theme

truncate

wrap text

Worksheet contents should be easy to read and attractive. You can use formatting to provide visual cues to help determine the purpose of different data in the worksheet as well as to make the data visually pleasing. Changing column widths and row heights ensures that all the contents are visible. How data is positioned in cells helps improve readability by lining up items, wrapping long entries onto multiple lines, rotating text for interest, and indenting subentries. You can also change fonts, sizes, colors, and borders to distinguish different parts of the worksheet and highlight key sections. Values are more understandable when the appropriate number format is applied. As you apply formatting to a worksheet, it's often faster to copy formatting with the Format Painter than to reapply several formats. You can also apply a variety of preset formatting using cell styles. If you want to change a specific format, you can quickly find and replace cell formats.

Resizing Columns and Rows

Worksheets are most valuable when the information they present is simple for the user to understand. Data in a worksheet must be accurate, but it is also important that the data be presented in a visually appealing way.

Changing Column Width

Sometimes the data you enter in a cell does not fit in the column. When you enter information that is wider than the column, one of the following situations occurs:

- Text that fits in the cell is displayed in the cell. The rest is stored but hidden when the next cell contains data.

- Text that does not fit in the cell extends into the next cell when that cell is empty.

- Numbers are converted to a different numerical form (for example, numbers with many digits are displayed in exponential form).

- Numbers that do not fit in the cell are displayed as a series of number signs (######).

You can resize a column to fit a certain number of characters. Place the pointer on the right edge of the *column heading* (the column letter) until the pointer changes to a double-headed arrow. Click and drag the column's edge to the right until the column expands to the width you want. Drag the column's edge to the left to reduce the column width. As you drag, a ScreenTip appears near the pointer, displaying the new column width measurement.

If you want to use a precise column width, it's easiest to enter that value in the Column Width dialog box shown in **Figure 2–1**. To access the dialog box, click any cell in the column you want to change. On the Home tab of the Ribbon, in the Cells group, click the Format button, and then click Column Width. In the Column width box, type the width you want, and then click OK. The column resizes to fit the number of characters you specified.

TIP

You can also open the Column Width dialog box by right-clicking the column heading of the column you want to resize, and then clicking Column Width on the shortcut menu.

Type the number of characters to display in the column

FIGURE 2–1　Column Width dialog box

Changing Row Height

The process for changing row height is similar to how you change the column width. Place the pointer below the **row heading** (the row number) until the pointer changes to a double-headed arrow. Click and drag the border of the row heading down until the row has the height you want. You can also use the Row Height dialog box to specify an exact row height. Click a cell in the row you want to resize. On the Home tab of the Ribbon, in the Cells group, click the Format button, and then click Row Height to open the Row Height dialog box. In the Row height box, type the height you want, and then click OK.

Using AutoFit to Change Column Width or Row Height

Columns often contain data of varying widths. To make the worksheet easier to read, a column should be wide enough to display the longest entry, but no wider than necessary. **AutoFit** determines the best width for a column or the best height for a row, based on its contents. Place the pointer on the right edge of the column heading (or below the row heading) until the pointer changes to a double-headed arrow. Then, double-click to resize the column or row to the best fit.

> **VOCABULARY**
> **row heading**
> **AutoFit**

> **EXTRA FOR EXPERTS**
>
> You can resize several columns or rows at once. Select the columns or rows to resize. Then, use the pointer to click and drag the right edge of a selected column heading or the bottom edge of a selected row heading to the desired width or height.

Step-by-Step 2.1

1. Open the **Cassidy.xlsx** workbook from the drive and folder where your Data Files are stored.

2. Save the workbook as **Cassidy Budget** followed by your initials. Notice that the text in some cells extends into the empty cells in the next column; for example, the month name in cell D3 extends into column E. Some text is hidden because the adjacent cell contains data, such as the text in cell A6.

3. Place the pointer on the right edge of the column D column heading. The pointer changes to a double-headed arrow **+**.

4. Click and drag to the right until the ScreenTip reads *Width: 10.00 (75 pixels)*, as shown in **Figure 2–2**. Release the mouse button. The entire word *September* now fits within column D.

As you drag, the ScreenTip shows the new width

Column resize pointer

Text is hidden because the adjacent cell contains data

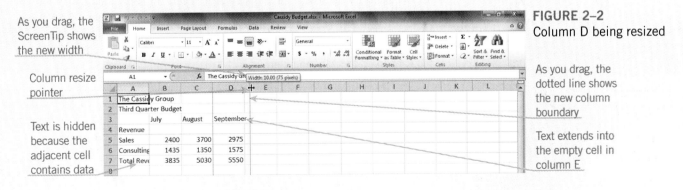

FIGURE 2–2
Column D being resized

As you drag, the dotted line shows the new column boundary

Text extends into the empty cell in column E

5. Point to the **column B** column heading. The pointer changes to the column selection pointer ⬇. Click and drag across the **column B** and **column C** column headings. Both columns B and C are selected. Release the mouse button. You want the two selected columns to be the same width as column D.

6. On the Ribbon, click the **Home** tab, if necessary, and then locate the **Cells** group.

7. Click the **Format** button, and then click **Column Width**. The Column Width dialog box appears, as shown in Figure 2–1.

8. In the Column width box, type **10**. Click **OK**. The widths of the selected columns change to 10 characters.

9. Place the pointer on the bottom edge of the row 18 row heading. The pointer changes to a double-headed arrow ⬍.

10. Click and drag down until the ScreenTip reads *Height: 18.00 (24 pixels)*, and then release the mouse button.

11. Look at the data in column A. Some cells are not wide enough to display all their contents.

12. Click cell **A19**. You see only a portion of the words *Cumulative Profit* in the cell. The Formula Bar shows the complete contents of the cell.

13. Double-click the right edge of the column A column heading. Column A widens to display the longest cell contents in the column, which, in this case is cell A2. You can now see all the contents in column A, and including the contents of cell A19.

14. Save the workbook, and leave it open for the next Step-by-Step.

Positioning Data Within a Cell

Unless you specify otherwise, text you enter in a cell is lined up along the bottom-left side of the cell, and numbers you enter in a cell are lined up along the bottom-right side of the cell. However, you can position data within a cell in a variety of ways, as described in **Table 2–1**. All of these positions are available on the Home tab of the Ribbon, in the Alignment group.

TABLE 2–1   Positioning data within a cell

POSITION	DESCRIPTION	BUTTON	EXAMPLE
Alignment	Specifies where data is lined up within the cell		Align Text Left is the default for text
			Align Text Right is the default for numbers
			Center is often used for title text
Indent	Changes the space between the cell border and its content		Increase Indent adds space; used for subheadings
			Decrease Indent removes space
Orientation	Rotates cell contents to an angle or vertically		Labels in a narrow column
Wrap Text	Moves data to a new line when the cell is not wide enough to display all the contents		Long descriptions
Merge	Combines multiple cells into one cell		Title across the top of a worksheet; Merge & Center centers contents in the merged cell

Aligning Text

You can *align* the contents of a cell horizontally and vertically within the cell. Horizontal alignments are left, centered, or right. Vertical alignments are top, middle, or bottom, as shown in **Figure 2–3**. Excel left-aligns all text and right-aligns all numbers. All data is bottom-aligned. You can select a different horizontal and vertical alignment for any cell.

▶ **VOCABULARY**
align
alignment

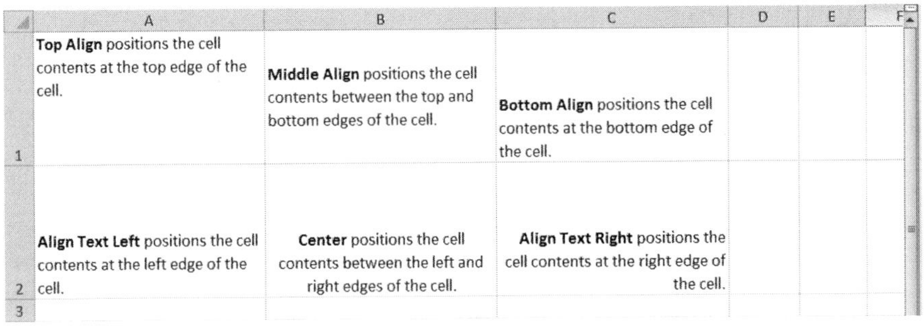

FIGURE 2–3   Horizontal and vertical alignments

     To change the *alignment* of a cell, select the cell and then click an alignment button in the Alignment group on the Home tab of the Ribbon. For other alignment options, click the Format Cells: Alignment Dialog Box Launcher to display the Alignment tab in the Format Cells dialog box. In the Text alignment section, click the alignment you want in the Horizontal or Vertical boxes, and then click OK.

Merging and Centering Data

You can also center cell contents across several columns. Select the cells, and then click the Merge & Center button in the Alignment group on the Home tab of the Ribbon. The selected cells *merge*, or combine into one cell, and the contents from the upper-left cell are centered in the newly merged cell.

Indenting Data

Data can be *indented* (or shifted to the right) within cells to help distinguish categories or set data apart. Instead of trying to indent data by pressing the spacebar, you should use the Increase Indent button in the Alignment group on the Home tab of the Ribbon. This way, all cells' contents are indented evenly. To move the indent in the other direction, click the Decrease Indent button.

▶ **VOCABULARY**

merge

indent

— WARNING

When you merge cells, only the content in the upper-left cell of the range is entered in the merged cell. Any content from the other cells in the range is deleted from the worksheet after merged. When you click the Merge & Center button, a dialog box appears, reminding you of this. Click OK to complete the merge. Click Cancel to return to the worksheet without completing the merge.

Step-by-Step 2.2

1. Select the range **B3:D3**.

2. On the Home tab of the Ribbon, locate the **Alignment** group. All the positioning buttons are located in this group.

3. Click the **Center** button ▤. The headings are centered horizontally in the cell.

4. Click cell **A7**.

5. On the Home tab, in the Alignment group, click the **Align Text Right** button ▤. *Total Revenue* is aligned at the right of the cell.

6. Click cell **A16**, press and hold the **Ctrl** key, click cells **A18** and **A19**, and then release the **Ctrl** key. The nonadjacent range is selected.

7. On the Home tab, in the Alignment group, click the **Align Text Right** button ▤. The contents of the three cells are right-aligned.

8. Select the range **A1:D1**.

9. On the Home tab, in the Alignment group, click the **Merge & Center** button ▦. Cells A1 through D1 are combined into one cell, and the title *The Cassidy Group* is centered in the merged cell.

10. Select the range **A2:D2**. On the Home tab, in the Alignment group, click the **Merge & Center** button ▦. Cells A2 through D2 are merged, and the subtitle *Third Quarter Budget* is centered in the merged cell.

11. Click cell **A5**. On the Home tab, in the Alignment group, click the **Increase Indent** button. The contents of cell A5 shift to the right.

12. Click cell **A6**. On the Home tab, in the Alignment group, click the **Increase Indent** button. The contents of cell A6 shift to the right and line up with the contents of cell A5.

13. Select the range **A10:A15**. On the Home tab, in the Alignment group, click the **Increase Indent** button. The contents of the cells in the range shift to the right.

14. Save the workbook, and leave it open for the next Step-by-Step.

Changing Text Orientation

Sometimes labels that describe the column data, or the data itself, are longer than the column widths. To save space in the worksheet, you can change each cell's text *orientation* to rotate its data to any angle. Changing the text orientation of some cells can also help give your worksheet a more professional look.

To change text orientation, select the cells whose contents you want to rotate. Then, on the Home tab of the Ribbon, in the Alignment group, click the Orientation button. A menu of orientation options appears, with commands for angling the text at 45-degree angles clockwise or counterclockwise, stacking the text vertically, or rotating the text up or down.

If you want to use a different angle, you need to use the Alignment tab in the Format Cells dialog box, as shown in **Figure 2–4**. Click the Format Cells: Alignment Dialog Box Launcher to display the Alignment tab in the Format Cells dialog box. In the Orientation box, click a degree point, drag the angle indicator, or type the angle you want in the Degrees box. Click OK.

> **VOCABULARY**
> orientation

> **TIP**
>
> Rotated text is often used for labels on charts. Angled or vertical text fits more data in a label, while remaining readable.

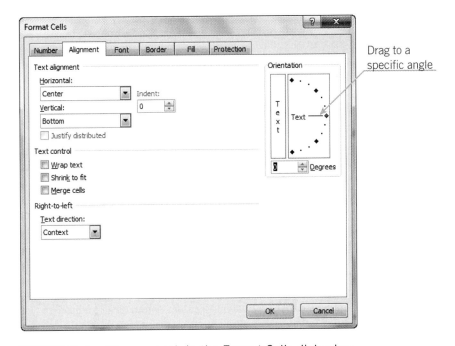

FIGURE 2–4   Alignment tab in the Format Cells dialog box

Step-by-Step 2.3

1. Select the range **B3:D3**.

2. On the Home tab, in the Alignment group, click the **Orientation** button . A menu appears with the most common orientations.

3. Click **Angle Counterclockwise**. The text in cells B3 through D3 shifts to a 45-degree angle, and the height of row 3 increases to accommodate the angled text, as shown in **Figure 2–5**.

FIGURE 2–5
Modified alignments

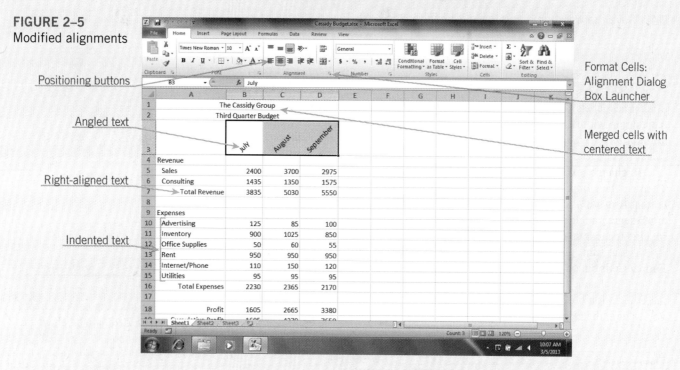

Positioning buttons

Angled text

Right-aligned text

Indented text

Format Cells:
Alignment Dialog
Box Launcher

Merged cells with
centered text

4. Save the workbook, and leave it open for the next Step-by-Step.

▶ **VOCABULARY**

truncate

wrap text

📟 **EXTRA FOR EXPERTS**

You can choose where a new line begins in a cell. Double-click in the cell to position the insertion point in the cell. Use the arrow keys to move the insertion point to where you want the new line to begin. Press the Alt+Enter keys to insert a line break. Press the Enter key to accept the change.

Wrapping Text

Text that is too long to fit within a cell is displayed in the next cell, if it is empty. If the next cell already contains data, any text that does not fit in the cell is *truncated*, or hidden from view. One way to see all the text stored in a cell is to *wrap text*. The row height increases automatically to display additional lines until all the text is visible. When you wrap text, the column width is not changed.

To wrap text, select the cells in which you want to wrap text. Then, on the Home tab of the Ribbon, in the Alignment group, click the Wrap Text button. If the cells already contain text, the row height increases as needed to display all the content. If you enter text after you turn on wrap text, the row height expands to fit the text as you type. To turn off wrap text, click the Wrap Text button again.

If you change the column width for a cell with wrapped text, the contents readjust to fit the new size. Be aware that row height does not automatically adjust, so you might need to AutoFit the row height to eliminate extra blank lines within the cell.

Step-by-Step 2.4

1. Scroll the worksheet down until row 21 is visible.

2. Click cell **A21**. Type **Third Quarter Budget submitted**. Click the **Enter** button ✓ on the Formula Bar.

3. On the Home tab, in the Alignment group, click the **Wrap Text** button 📑. The text wraps in the cell, the row height adjusts to fit both lines of text, and the Wrap Text button remains selected, as shown in **Figure 2–6**.

Wrap Text button

Text wrapped to two lines within the cell

	A	B	C	D	E	F	G	H	I	J	K
15	Utilities	95	95	95							
16	Total Expenses	2230	2365	2170							
17											
18	Profit	1605	2665	3380							
19	Cumulative Profit	1605	4270	7650							
20											
21	Third Quarter Budget submitted										
22											

FIGURE 2–6
Wrapped text

4. Save the workbook, and leave it open for the next Step-by-Step.

Changing the Appearance of Cells

You can change the appearance of cells to make them easier to read, to differentiate sections in a worksheet, or to create a specific look and feel for the worksheet. To do this, you can modify the cell's default font, font size, font style, font color, fill color, and borders.

The fonts and colors used in each workbook are part of a theme. A *theme* is a preset collection of design elements, including fonts, colors, and other effects. By default, the Office theme is applied to each workbook. To change a workbook's appearance, you can select a different theme, or you can format cells with other fonts and colors. If you select another theme font or theme color, it will change when you apply a different theme. Or, you can choose non-theme or standard fonts and colors that stay the same no matter which theme is applied to the workbook.

As you format cells, *Live Preview* shows the results of the different formatting options you can choose. Select the cell or range you want to format, and then point to the formatting option you are considering. The cell or range changes to reflect that option. To accept that format, click the option.

Changing Fonts and Font Sizes

A *font* is the design of text. The default font for cells is Calibri. *Font size* determines the height of characters, as measured in *points*. The default font size for cells is 11 points. You can choose different fonts and font sizes in a worksheet to emphasize part of a worksheet or to distinguish worksheet titles and column headings from other data. The fonts and font sizes you use can significantly affect the readability of

▶ VOCABULARY

theme

Live Preview

font

font size

points

▣ EXTRA FOR EXPERTS

You can select a different theme for your workbook. Click the Page Layout tab on the Ribbon. In the Themes group, click the Themes button to display a gallery of themes. Point to different themes to see how your workbook changes. When you find a theme you like, click that theme to make the change.

TECHNOLOGY CAREERS

Excel workbooks are helpful to people and businesses in sales. Salespeople use worksheets to determine what items are available in inventories, to analyze sales performance, and to track customer orders.

TIP

You can also use the Mini toolbar to change the font, font size, font style, and font color. Double-click the cell, select the text in the cell to format, and then click the appropriate buttons on the Mini toolbar to apply the formatting.

▶ **VOCABULARY**
font style

EXTRA FOR EXPERTS

You can quickly apply a font style to a selected cell or range. Press the Ctrl+B keys to apply bold. Press the Ctrl+I keys to apply italics. Press the Ctrl+U keys to apply underlining. Press the same keys to remove that font style from the selected cell or range.

the worksheet. Office comes with many fonts and sizes for text. However, the available fonts and sizes can change from one computer to another, depending on which fonts are installed on each computer.

To change fonts and sizes, you first select the cells you want to change. Then, on the Home tab of the Ribbon, in the Font group, click the Font arrow to display a gallery of available fonts or click the Font Size arrow, to display a gallery of available font sizes. When you point to a font or a size, Live Preview changes the cell contents to reflect that selection. Click the font or size you want to use.

Applying Font Styles

Bold, *italic*, and <u>underlining</u> can add emphasis to the contents of a cell. These features are referred to as ***font styles***. You can also combine font styles to change the emphasis, such as ***bold italic***. To apply a font style, select the cell or range you want to change. Then, on the Home tab of the Ribbon, click the appropriate button in the Font group. To remove a font style from the cell contents, simply click the button again.

Step-by-Step 2.5

1. Scroll the worksheet up until row 3 is displayed. Select the range **B3:D3**.

2. On the Home tab, in the Font group, click the **Font** arrow. A gallery appears, listing the fonts available on your computer, as shown in **Figure 2–7**.

FIGURE 2–7
Font gallery

Theme fonts

Font names appear
in that font

Non-theme fonts

Scroll to see
more fonts

3. Scroll down the list and click **Times New Roman** (or a similar font). The font of the month names in cells B3, C3, and D3 changes from Calibri to Times New Roman.

4. On the Home tab, in the Font group, click the **Font Size** arrow. A gallery appears, listing the available font sizes. Click **10**. The font size of the month names in cells B3, C3, and D3 is reduced from 11 points to 10 points.

5. Click cell **A1** (the cell you merged from the range A1:D1). On the Home tab, in the Font group, click the **Font** arrow. Scroll down the list and click **Times New Roman**. The font of the company name in cell A1 changes to Times New Roman. Cell A1 remains active.

6. On the Home tab, in the Font group, click the **Font Size** arrow. Click **16**. The font size of the company name in cell A1 increases to 16 points. Cell A1 remains active.

7. On the Home tab, in the Font group, click the **Bold** button **B**. The text in cell A1 changes to bold, and the button remains selected to show it is toggled on.

8. Click cell **A2**. On the Home tab, in the Font group, click the **Bold** button **B**. The text in cell A2 changes to bold.

9. Apply bold to cells A4, A7, A9, A16, A18, and A19.

10. Select the range **A5:A6**. On the Home tab, in the Font group, click the **Italic** button **I**. The revenue items are italicized.

11. Apply italics to the range A10:A15.

12. Select cell **A4**. On the Home tab, in the Font group, click the **Underline** button 🔲. *Revenue* is underlined.

13. On the Home tab, in the Font group, click the **Underline** button 🔲. The underlining is removed from the text.

14. Save the workbook, and leave it open for the next Step-by-Step.

Choosing Font and Fill Colors

You can use color to emphasize cells or distinguish them from one another. The default font color is black, but you can select a different color to emphasize the cell contents. The default *fill* (or background) color of cells is white, but you can change this background color to help draw attention to certain cells, such as descriptive labels or totals.

To change the color of text in a cell, select the cell you want to change. On the Home tab of the Ribbon, in the Font group, click the Font Color button arrow. A gallery appears showing a palette of colors, as shown in **Figure 2–8**. Click the color you want the text in the cell to change to.

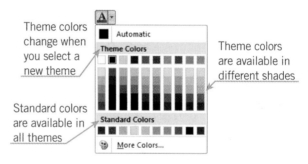

FIGURE 2–8   Font colors

To change the background color of a cell, select the cell you want to change. On the Home tab of the Ribbon, in the Font group, click the Fill Color button arrow. A gallery appears with a palette of colors, as shown in **Figure 2–9**. Click the color you want to fill the cell with.

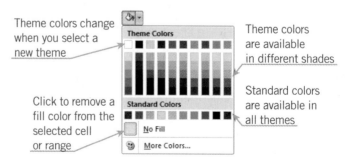

FIGURE 2–9   Fill colors

Step-by-Step 2.6

1. Click cell **A1**.

2. On the Home tab, in the Font group, click the **Font Color** button arrow ⒜▾. A gallery appears with a palette of colors, as shown in Figure 2–8.

3. Point to the **Red** color (the second color in the Standard Colors section). A ScreenTip displays the name of the color, and *The Cassidy Group*, the text in cell A1, changes to red, showing you a Live Preview of that selection.

4. Point to the **Dark Blue, Text 2** color (the fourth color in the first row of the Theme Colors section). A ScreenTip displays the name of the color, and Live Preview shows the company name in dark blue.

5. Click the **Dark Blue, Text 2** color. The gallery closes and the company name remains dark blue. Cell A1 is still the active cell.

6. On the Home tab, in the Font group, click the **Fill Color** button arrow ⒜▾. A gallery appears with a palette of colors, as shown in Figure 2–9.

7. Click the **Dark Blue, Text 2, Lighter 80%** color (the fourth color in the second row of the Theme Colors section). The cell background becomes light blue. Cell A1 is still the active cell.

8. Save the workbook, and leave it open for the next Step-by-Step.

Applying Cell Borders

You can add emphasis to a cell by applying a *border* (or line) around its edges. You can apply the border around the entire cell or only on certain sides of the cell. You can also select different border styles, such as a thick border or a double border.

▶ **VOCABULARY**
border

TIP

The Borders button shows the most recently selected border style. To apply that border style to a selected cell or range, click the Borders button (instead of the arrow).

To apply a border, select a cell or range. Then, on the Home tab of the Ribbon, in the Font group, click the Borders button arrow. A menu appears with border styles, as shown in **Figure 2–10**. Click the border style you want to add. You can remove the borders from a selected cell by clicking No Border in the border style menu.

Preset border styles you can select

FIGURE 2–10   Borders styles

Step-by-Step 2.7

1. Select the range **B7:D7**.

2. On the Home tab, in the Font group, click the **Borders** button arrow . A menu of border styles appears, as shown in Figure 2–10.

3. Click **Top and Double Bottom Border**. Click cell **A8** to deselect the range. A single border appears above the range B7:D7 and a double border appears below the range. The Borders button changes to Top and Double Bottom Border.

4. Select the range **B16:D16**.

5. On the Home tab, in the Font group, click the **Top and Double Bottom Border** button. Click cell **A17** to deselect the range. A single border appears above the range B16:D16 and a double border appears below the range.

6. Save the workbook, and leave it open for the next Step-by-Step.

TIP

Standard accounting format uses a single border below a column of numbers and a double border below the total.

Selecting Number Formats

Number formats change the way data looks in a cell. The actual content you entered is *not* changed. The default number format is General, which displays numbers the way you enter them. However, you can select any of the number formats described in **Table 2–2**. Be aware that changing a number format affects only the appearance of the data in the cell. The actual value is not affected. The Formula Bar shows the actual value of the contents you see in the active cell. For example, the actual value shown in the Formula Bar might be 1000, whereas the number you see in the active cell is $1,000.00 if the cell uses the Currency number format.

▶ **VOCABULARY**
number formats

TABLE 2–2   Number formats

FORMAT	EXAMPLE	DESCRIPTION
General	1000	The default format; displays numbers as entered; if the number doesn't fit in the cell, decimals are rounded, or the number is converted to scientific notation
Number	1000.00	Displays numbers with a fixed number of places to the right of the decimal point; the default is two decimal places
Currency	$1,000.00	Displays numbers with a dollar sign, a thousands separator, and two decimal places
Accounting	$1,000.00 $ 9.00	Displays numbers in the Currency format but lines up the dollar signs and the decimal points vertically within a column
Date	6/8/2013	Displays numbers as dates
Time	7:38 PM	Displays numbers as times
Percentage	35.29%	Displays numbers with two decimal places and a percent sign
Fraction	35 7/8	Displays decimal numbers as fractions
Scientific	1.00E+03	Displays numbers in exponential (or scientific) notation
Text	45-875-33	Displays text and numbers exactly as you type them
Special	79410-1234 (503) 555-4567	Displays numbers with a specific format: zip codes, zip+4 codes, phone numbers, and Social Security numbers
Custom	000.00.0	Displays data in the format you create, such as with commas or leading zeros

To change the number format for a selected cell or range, click the Number Format arrow in the Number group on the Home tab of the Ribbon, and then select the appropriate number format from the menu that opens. You can also change the number format for a selected cell or range by clicking the appropriate button in the Number group. The Accounting Number Format button quickly applies the Accounting number format; click the button arrow to select a different currency symbol, such as Euros. The other buttons let you choose whether the number includes a percent sign, whether it uses a thousands separator (a comma), and how many decimal places to show.

Copying Cell Formatting

The *Format Painter* enables you to copy formatting from one worksheet cell and paste it to other cells without pasting the first cell's contents. This is especially helpful when the cell formatting you want to copy includes several formats. For example, after formatting a cell as a percentage with a white font, a green fill, and a double bottom border, you can use the Format Painter to quickly format other cells the same way.

To copy a cell's formatting, select the cell that has the format you want to copy. On the Home tab of the Ribbon, in the Clipboard group, click the Format Painter button. Then, click another cell or drag to select the range of cells you want to format in the same way.

TIP

You can use the Format Painter to copy the formatting to nonadjacent cells or ranges. Double-click the Format Painter button in the Clipboard group on the Home tab of the Ribbon. Select the cells or ranges to format. Click the Format Painter button again when you are done.

Step-by-Step 2.8

1. Select the range **B5:D5**, press and hold the **Ctrl** key, select the range **B7:D7**, and then release the **Ctrl** key. The nonadjacent range is selected.

2. On the Home tab, in the Number group, click the **Number Format** arrow. A menu of number formats appears.

3. Click **Accounting**. The numbers in the selected ranges include a dollar sign, a thousands separator, and two decimal places, which is the standard Accounting number format.

4. Click cell **B5**. Compare the value in the Formula Bar with the value in the active cell. The Formula Bar shows *2400*, which is the actual value stored in cell B5. Cell B5 shows *$2,400.00*, which is the stored value formatted for display.

5. On the Home tab, in the Clipboard group, click the **Format Painter** button . The pointer changes to a paintbrush next to the white plus pointer 🗗🖌 when placed over worksheet cells. A flashing dashed border surrounds cell B5 to remind you that the formatting from this cell is being copied.

6. Click and drag from cell **B10** to cell **D10**, and then release the mouse button. The format of the range B10:D10 changes to the Accounting number format.

7. Select the range **B11:D15**.

8. On the Home tab, in the Number group, click the **Number Format** arrow, and then click **Number**. The cells in the range are formatted with two decimal places.

9. On the Home tab, in the Number group, click the **Comma Style** button. A thousands separator is added to the number with four digits in cell C11 and the decimal points align with the values you formatted in row 10 with the Accounting number format.

10. On the Home tab, in the Clipboard group, click the **Format Painter** button. The range B11:D15 is surrounded by a flashing dashed border.

11. Click and drag from cell **B6** to cell **D6**, and then release the mouse button. The format of the range B6:D6 is formatted with both the Number and Comma Style number formats that you applied to the range B11:D15.

12. Apply the **Accounting** number format to the ranges B16:D16 and B18:D19.

13. Click cell **A2** to deselect the range. Your screen should look similar to **Figure 2–11**.

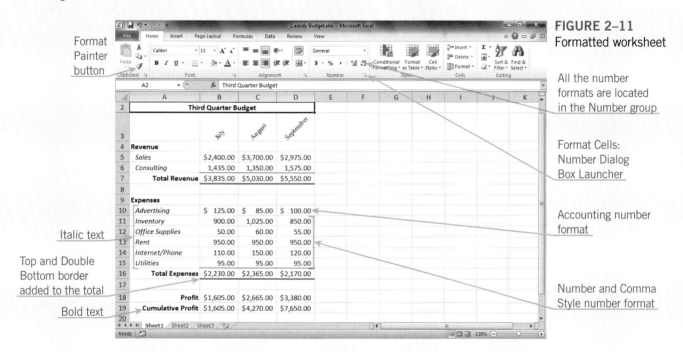

Format Painter button

Italic text

Top and Double Bottom border added to the total

Bold text

FIGURE 2–11
Formatted worksheet

All the number formats are located in the Number group

Format Cells: Number Dialog Box Launcher

Accounting number format

Number and Comma Style number format

14. Save the workbook, and leave it open for the next Step-by-Step.

Using the Format Cells Dialog Box

The Format Cells dialog box provides access to all the formatting options available on the Ribbon, as well as some additional formatting options. To open the Format Cells dialog box, you can click the Dialog Box Launcher in the Font, Alignment, or Number group on the Home tab of the Ribbon, or you can

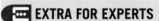 **EXTRA FOR EXPERTS**

The Format Cells dialog box also includes a Protection tab, which has options for locking and hiding cells in a protected workbook. You can protect a workbook to prevent others from making changes to the workbook.

press the Ctrl+1 keys. As shown in **Figure 2–12**, the Format Cells dialog box has Number, Alignment, Font, Border, and Fill tabs. You can use these tabs to change the number format, position of data, font options, borders, and cell background color as you have done so far.

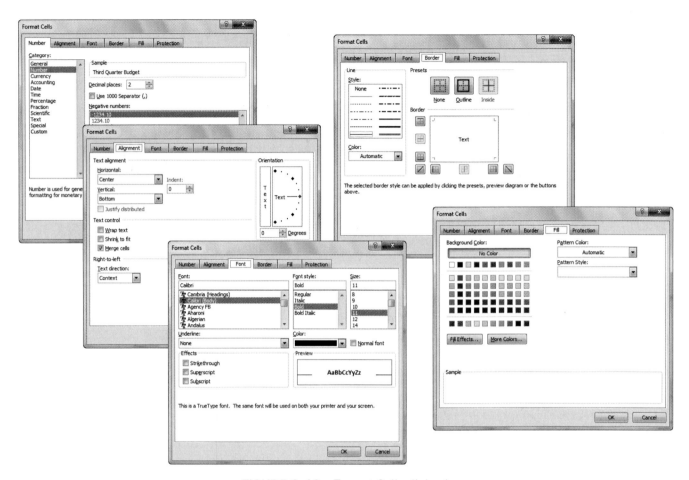

FIGURE 2–12   Format Cells dialog box

Using Styles to Format Cells

▶ **VOCABULARY**
style
cell style

A *style* is a combination of formatting characteristics such as alignment, font, font size, font color, fill color, and borders. When you apply a style to a cell, you apply all the formatting characteristics simultaneously, saving you the time of applying the formats individually. Styles also help you format a worksheet consistently. When you use a style, you know that each cell with that style is formatted the same way.

Applying Cell Styles

A *cell style* is a collection of formatting characteristics you apply to a cell or range of data. To apply a cell style, select the cells you want to format. On the Home tab of the Ribbon, in the Styles group, click the Cell Styles button. The Cell Styles gallery appears, as shown in **Figure 2–13**. Point to a cell style in the gallery to see a Live Preview of that style on the selected cell or range in the worksheet. When you find a style you like, click the style to apply it. To remove a style from the selected cell, simply click Normal in the Good, Bad and Neutral section of the Cell Styles gallery.

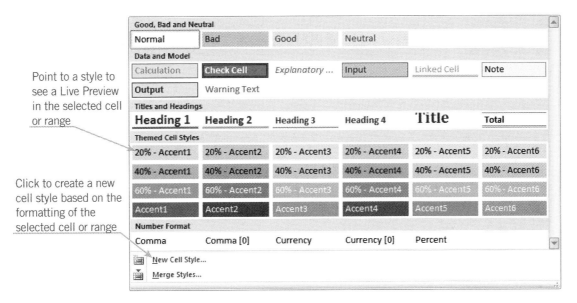

Point to a style to see a Live Preview in the selected cell or range

Click to create a new cell style based on the formatting of the selected cell or range

FIGURE 2–13   Cell Styles gallery

The Cell Styles gallery includes many predefined styles. However, if none of these styles meets your needs, you can define your own styles. First, format a cell with the exact combination of formats you want. Then, select the formatted cell, and click New Cell Style at the bottom of the Cell Styles gallery. In the Style dialog box that opens, shown in **Figure 2–14**, type a descriptive name for the style in the Style name box, verify the formatting in the Style Includes (By Example) section (uncheck any format you don't want to include), and then click OK. When you open the Cell Styles gallery again, the custom style you created appears in the Custom section at the top of the gallery.

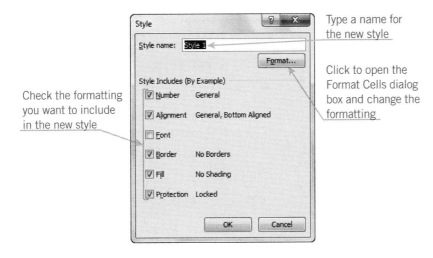

Check the formatting you want to include in the new style

Type a name for the new style

Click to open the Format Cells dialog box and change the formatting

FIGURE 2–14   Style dialog box

Clearing Cell Formats

You have learned how to change the appearance of cells in a worksheet by applying individual formats as well as cell styles. At times, you might need to remove, or *clear*, all the formatting applied to a cell or range of cells. Select the cell or range, click the Clear button in the Editing group on the Home tab of the Ribbon, and then click Clear Formats. Only the cell formatting is removed; the cell content remains the same.

▶ VOCABULARY
clear

Step-by-Step 2.9

1. Select the range **A4:D4**.

2. On the Home tab, in the Styles group, click the **Cell Styles** button ▨. The Cell Styles gallery appears, as shown in Figure 2–13.

3. In the Titles and Headings section, point to **Heading 2**. Live Preview shows the selected range with the font, font size, color, and border in that style.

4. In the Titles and Headings section, point to **Accent1** to see the Live Preview of the style applied to the cells in the selected range. Click **Accent1**. Blue fill and white font colors are applied to the cells in the selected range.

5. Select the range **A9:D9**.

6. On the Home tab, in the Styles group, click the **Cell Styles** button ▨.

7. In the Cell Styles gallery, in the Titles and Headings section, click **Accent1**. Blue fill and white font are applied to the cells in the selected range.

8. Click cell **A1**. On the Home tab, in the Styles group, click the **Cell Styles** button ▨.

9. In the Cell Styles gallery, in the Titles and Headings section, click **Heading 1**. Click cell **E1** to deselect the merged cell A1. The formatting for this style is added to the formatting you already applied to cell A1, as shown in **Figure 2–15**.

FIGURE 2–15
Cell styles applied to cells and ranges

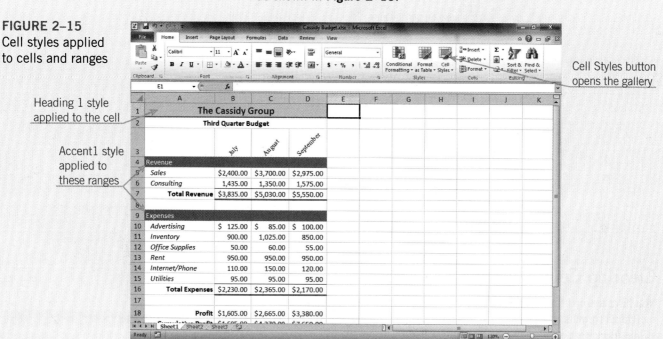

Heading 1 style applied to the cell

Accent1 style applied to these ranges

Cell Styles button opens the gallery

10. Scroll down until you can see row 21, and then click cell **A21**. On the Home tab, in the Styles group, click the **Cell Styles** button 🖼.

11. In the Cell Styles gallery, in the Titles and Headings section, click **Accent3**. The cell is formatted with the selected style.

12. On the Home tab, in the Editing group, click the **Clear** button ⌫. A menu appears with the Clear commands.

13. Click **Clear Formats**. All the formatting applied to cell A21 is removed. The cell returns to the default font color and fill color and text wrap.

14. Click cell **A22**, and then enter your name. Save, print, and close the workbook.

Finding and Replacing Cell Formatting

You have already learned to find and replace data in a workbook. You can also find and replace specific formatting in a workbook. For example, you might want to replace all italicized text with bold text, or you might want to change all cells with a yellow fill color to another color.

Step-by-Step 2.10

1. Open the **Central.xlsx** workbook from the drive and folder where your Data Files are stored.

2. Save the workbook as **Central Conference** followed by your initials.

3. On the Home tab, in the Editing group, click the **Find & Select** button 🔍, and then click **Replace**. The Find and Replace dialog box appears, with the Replace tab displayed.

4. Click the **Options** button to expand the Find and Replace dialog box, if it is not already expanded.

5. If any entries appear in the Find what or Replace with boxes, delete them.

6. Click the top **Format** button. The Find Format dialog box appears. This dialog box has all the same tabs and options as the Format Cells dialog box.

7. Click the **Font** tab if it is not the active tab. In the Font style list, click **Bold Italic**. This is the formatting you want to find.

8. Click **OK**. The Find Format dialog box closes, and the Find and Replace dialog box reappears. The Find what Preview box shows the bold italic formatting you want to find.

9. Click the lower **Format** button. The Replace Format dialog box appears. This dialog box has all the same tabs and options as the Format Cells dialog box.

> **⊢ WARNING**
>
> Clicking the Format button arrow opens a menu instead of the dialog box. If the menu appears, click Format to open the dialog box.

10. On the Font tab, in the Font style list, click **Regular**.

11. Click **OK**. The Replace Format dialog box closes, and the Find and Replace dialog box reappears. The Replace with Preview box shows the regular formatting you want to use instead of the bold italics, as shown in **Figure 2–16**.

FIGURE 2–16
Find and Replace dialog box

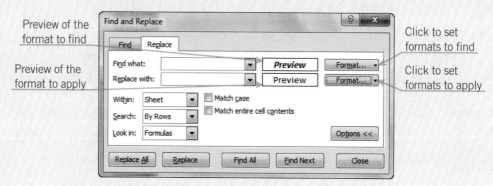

12. Click **Replace All**. A dialog box appears, stating that Excel has completed the search and has made 12 replacements.

13. Click **OK**. The dialog box closes.

14. Click **Close**. The Find and Replace dialog box closes. Your screen should look like **Figure 2–17**.

FIGURE 2–17
Worksheet with formatting replaced

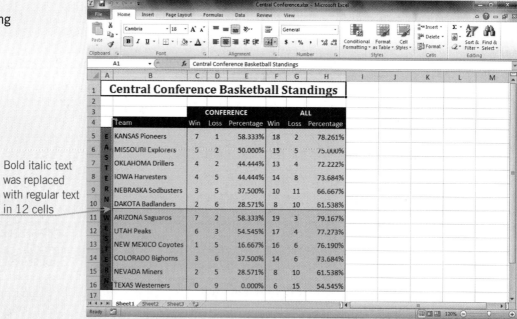

15. Click cell **B2**, and then enter your name.

16. Save, print, and close the workbook.

SUMMARY

In this lesson, you learned:

- If data does not fit in a cell, you can resize the columns and rows to make the data easier to read.

- You can align, indent, rotate, wrap text, and merge cells to reposition data in worksheet cells.

- You can change the appearance of cells to make the worksheet easier to read or to create a specific look and feel. Choose the appropriate fonts, font sizes, font styles, font and fill colors, and borders.

- Using a number format enables you to change how a number is displayed in a cell. No matter which number format you select, the actual value stored in the cell does not change. You can see this by comparing the formatted value in the active cell with the value displayed in the Formula Bar.

- Format Painter copies all the formatting from one cell and pastes it to another cell or range without copying the contents of the cell.

- The Format Cells dialog box provides all the number, alignment, font, border, and fill formatting options available on the Ribbon, as well as some additional options.

- A style is a combination of formatting characteristics, such as alignment, font, font size, font color, fill color, and borders that you can apply simultaneously. The Cell Styles gallery lets you quickly apply a style to selected cells or create a new style.

- You can use the Find and Replace dialog box to find and replace cell formatting.

■ VOCABULARY REVIEW

Define the following terms:

align	font	orientation
AutoFit	font size	row heading
border	font style	style
cell style	Format Painter	theme
clear	indent	truncate
column heading	merge	wrap text
fill	number format	

■ REVIEW QUESTIONS

TRUE / FALSE

Circle T if the statement is true or F if the statement is false.

T F **1.** A series of number signs (######) in a cell indicates that the data entered in the cell is unformatted.

T F **2.** AutoFit determines the best width for a column or the best height for a row based on its contents.

T F **3.** The Merge & Center button combines several selected cells into one cell and places the data in the center of the merged cell.

T F **4.** You can apply a border around the entire cell or on any side of the cell.

T F **5.** The default number format for a cell is General.

WRITTEN QUESTIONS

Write a brief answer to each of the following questions.

1. Which cell formats display numerical data with a dollar sign?

2. What can you do if text is too long to fit within a cell?

3. What is one reason for changing the orientation of text in a cell?

4. What is the difference between fill color and font color?

5. What is an advantage of using cell styles?

FILL IN THE BLANK

Complete the following sentences by writing the correct word or words in the blanks provided.

1. Text that does not fit in a cell is _____ or hidden from view.

2. A(n) _____ is a preset collection of design elements, including fonts, colors, and other effects.

3. Bold, italic, and underlining are examples of font _____.

4. The default _____ (or background) color of cells is white.

5. The _____ copies all the formatting from one cell and pastes it to another cell or range without copying the contents of the cell.

◼ PROJECTS

If you have a SAM 2010 user profile, your instructor may have assigned an autogradable version of the indicated project. If so, log into the SAM 2010 Web site at *www.cengage.com/sam2010* to download the instruction and start files.

PROJECT 2–1

Write the letter of the cell format option in Column 2 that matches the worksheet format described in Column 1.

Column 1

_____ 1. Displays data as entered

_____ 2. Displays numbers with a fixed number of decimal places

_____ 3. Displays numbers with a dollar sign, a thousands separator, and two decimal places; however, dollar signs and decimal points do not necessarily line up vertically within a column

_____ 4. Displays numbers with a dollar sign, a thousands separator, and two decimal places; dollar signs and decimal points line up vertically within a column

_____ 5. Displays numbers as dates

_____ 6. Displays numbers as times

_____ 7. Displays numbers with two decimal places and a percent sign

_____ 8. Displays the value of 0.5 as 1/2

_____ 9. Displays numbers in exponential (or scientific) notation

_____ 10. Displays numbers as zip codes, zip+4 codes, phone numbers, or Social Security numbers

_____ 11. Displays data in a format you design

Column 2

A. Time

B. Date

C. Scientific

D. Fraction

E. Accounting

F. General

G. Special

H. Number

I. Currency

J. Custom

K. Percentage

SAM PROJECT 2–2

1. Open the **Birds.xlsx** workbook from the drive and folder where your Data Files are stored.

2. Save the workbook as **Birds Census** followed by your initials.

3. Change the width of column A to 25.00 characters.

4. Merge and center the range A1:F1 and the range A2:F2.

5. Format cell A1 with the Title cell style and change the fill color to Orange, Accent 6.

6. Change the fill color of cell A2 to Accent6.

7. Bold the range A6:F6.

8. Angle the data in the range B6:F6 counterclockwise.

9. Change the width of columns B through E to 6.00 characters.

10. Bold the range A14:F14.

11. Indent and italicize the range A7:A13.

12. Right-align the text in cell A14.

13. Format the range B14:F14 with a top and double bottom border.

14. Change the font color of the text in the range F6:F14 to Orange, Accent 6, Darker 25%.

15. In cell A4, type **Prepared by:** followed by your name.

16. Save, print, and close the workbook.

PROJECT 2–3

1. Open the **Shop.xlsx** workbook from the drive and folder where your Data Files are stored.

2. Save the workbook as **Technology Shop** followed by your initials.

3. AutoFit column A.

4. Change the width of columns B, C, and D to 12.00 characters.

5. Bold and center the text in the range B5:D6.

6. Bold the text in cell A6.

7. Indent the range A7:A10.

8. Change the text in cell A1 to 16-point Cambria. Merge and center the range A1:D1.

9. Change the fill color of cell A1 to Green (in the Standard Colors section).

10. Change the fill color of the range A2:D2 to Yellow (in the Standard Colors section).

11. Change the fill color of the range A3:D3 to Red (in the Standard Colors section).

12. Format the range C7:D10 and cell D11 with the Currency number format.

13. Format cell D11 with the Total cell style. Change the fill color of cell D11 to Yellow.

14. Add a thick bottom border to the range A6:D6.

15. In cell A3, enter your name.

16. Save, print, and close the workbook.

PROJECT 2–5

1. Open the **TechSoft.xlsx** workbook from the drive and folder where your Data Files are stored.

2. Save the workbook as **TechSoft Balance Sheet** followed by your initials. This workbook contains a *balance sheet*, which is a financial statement that lists a corporation's assets (resources available), liabilities (amounts owed), and equity (ownership in the company).

3. Change the column width of column C to 4.00 characters.

4. Format cell A1 with the Heading 1 cell style.

5. Format the range A2:A3 with the 40% - Accent1 cell style.

6. Merge and center the ranges A1:E1, A2:E2, and A3:E3.

7. Bold cells A5, A6, A20, D5, D6, D17, and D21.

8. Apply a bottom border to cells B8, B13, E11, and E19. Apply a top and double bottom border to cells B20 and E21.

9. Format cells B7, E7, B20, and E21 in the Accounting number format with no decimal places.

10. Format the ranges B8:B19, E8:E15, and E18:E20 in the Number format with a thousands separator and no decimal places.

11. In cell A4, enter your name, and then bold and italicize the text.

12. Save, print, and close the workbook.

PROJECT 2–4

1. Open the **Wireless.xlsx** workbook from the drive and folder where your Data Files are stored.

2. Save the workbook as **Wireless Bill** followed by your initials.

3. In cell A1, type **Wireless Bill Estimate**.

4. Bold the text in cell A1.

5. Change the font size of the text in cell A1 to 18.

6. Merge and center the range A1:D1.

7. Change the fill color of cell A1 to Dark Blue, Text 2.

8. Change the font color of the text in cell A1 to White, Background 1.

9. Underline the contents of cell A1.

10. Center the contents of the range B3:C3. Italicize the range B3:C3.

11. Format the range C4:D8 with the Currency number format.

12. Format cell D8 with a Thick Box Border.

13. Widen column A to 14.00 characters. In cell A4, wrap text.

14. Middle-align the range B4:D4.

15. Apply the 40% - Accent1 cell style to the range D4:D7. Apply the Accent1 cell style to cell D8.

16. In cell A2, enter your name.

17. Save, print, and close the workbook.

PROJECT 2–6

1. Open the **Mileage.xlsx** workbook from the drive and folder where your Data Files are stored.

2. Save the workbook as **Mileage Chart** followed by your initials.

3. Change the font size of the range A1:O15 to 8 points.

4. Format the range B2:O15 in the Number format with a thousands separator and no decimal places.

5. Bold the ranges B1:O1 and A2:A15.

6. Change the width of column A to 10.00 characters.

7. Right-align the content of the range A2:A15.

8. Change the orientation of the range B1:O1 to Angle Clockwise.

9. Change the width of columns B through O to 5.00 characters.

10. In cell A1, enter your name, and then change the font size to 12 points and wrap text.

11. Save, print, and close the workbook.

■ CRITICAL THINKING

ACTIVITY 2–1

To be useful, worksheets must convey information clearly, both on-screen and on the printed page. Identify ways to accomplish the following:

1. Emphasize certain portions of a worksheet.

2. Make data in a worksheet easier to read.

3. Distinguish one part of a worksheet from another.

4. Format similar elements in a worksheet consistently.

ACTIVITY 2–2

You have been spending a lot of time formatting worksheets. A friend tells you that you could save some time by using the Mini toolbar to apply formatting. Use Excel Help to research the following:

1. How do you access the Mini toolbar?

2. What formatting can you apply using the Mini toolbar?

3. How do you use the Mini toolbar to apply formatting to text in a cell?

4. How does the Mini toolbar save you time when formatting a worksheet?

LESSON 3

Organizing the Worksheet

■ OBJECTIVES

Upon completion of this lesson, you should be able to:

- Copy and move data in a worksheet.
- Use the drag-and-drop method and Auto Fill options to add data to cells.
- Insert and delete rows, columns, and cells.
- Freeze panes in a worksheet.
- Split a worksheet window.
- Check spelling in a worksheet.
- Prepare a worksheet for printing.
- Insert headers and footers in a worksheet.

■ VOCABULARY

automatic page break

copy

cut

fill handle

filling

footer

freeze panes

header

manual page break

margin

Normal view

Office Clipboard (Clipboard)

Page Break Preview

Page Layout view

paste

print area

print titles

scale

split

Data in a worksheet should be easy to locate, read, and interpret. You can reorganize data by moving it to another part of the worksheet. You can also reduce the time it takes for data entry time by copying or cutting data and pasting it in another part of the worksheet. If you no longer need certain data, you can delete entire rows or columns. If you want to include additional information within existing data, you can insert another row or column. You can also display different parts of the worksheet at one time. Before sharing a workbook, you should check and correct any spelling errors to present a positive impression. Finally, you can set up a worksheet to print attractively on paper and add headers or footers to provide summary information, such as page numbers or your name, on each worksheet.

Copying and Moving Cells

VOCABULARY

copy

cut

paste

Office Clipboard (Clipboard)

When creating or editing a worksheet, you might want to use the contents of one or more cells in another part of the worksheet. Rather than retyping the same content, you can copy or move the contents and formatting of a cell or range to another area of the worksheet. *Copying* duplicates the cell or range in another location, while also leaving the cell in its original location. *Cutting* removes a cell or range from its original location in the worksheet. *Pasting* places the cell or range in another location.

WARNING

Be sure to check the destination cells for existing data before moving or copying. Pasting replaces any content already in the cell.

Copying and Pasting Cells

When you want to copy a cell or range, you first select the cell or range. Then, you use buttons in the Clipboard group on the Home tab of the Ribbon. To duplicate the cell or range without affecting the original cell or range, you click the Copy button. The selected data is placed as an item on the Office Clipboard. The *Office Clipboard* (or *Clipboard*) is a temporary storage area for up to 24 selections you copy or cut. A flashing border appears around the copied selection, as shown in **Figure 3–1**.

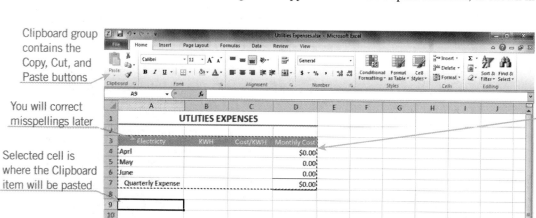

Clipboard group contains the Copy, Cut, and Paste buttons

You will correct misspellings later

Selected cell is where the Clipboard item will be pasted

Flashing border surrounds selected cells copied or cut to the Clipboard

FIGURE 3–1   Range copied to the Clipboard

Next, you select the cell or upper-left cell of the range where you want the copied item to appear in the worksheet. Click the Paste button in the Clipboard group on the Home tab. The Clipboard item is pasted into the selected cell or range. Pasting places the last item from the Clipboard into the selected cell or range in the worksheet. You can continue to paste that item in the worksheet as long as the flashing border appears around the copied cell or range. Just select the new destination cell or range, and then click the Paste button again.

Before pasting, you can click the arrow below the Paste button to open the Paste gallery, which provides additional commands. For example, the Formulas button pastes the actual formulas entered in the cells. The Values button pastes the formula results. The Transpose button pastes a row of cells into a column, or a column of cells into a row. For even more options, you can click the Paste Special command to open the Paste Special dialog box. As you point to a button in the Paste gallery, Live Preview shows the results of clicking that button.

Cutting and Pasting Cells

The process for moving a cell or range is similar to copying a cell or range. First, select the cell or range you want to move. Then, click the Cut button in the Clipboard group on the Home tab of the Ribbon. A flashing border appears around the selection, and the selected cell or range is placed as an item on the Clipboard. Next, select the cell or upper-left cell of the range where you want to move the cut item. Click the Paste button in the Clipboard group on the Home tab. When the cell or range is removed from its original position and placed in the new location, the flashing border disappears from the worksheet. Unlike copying, you can paste a cut cell or range only once.

EXTRA FOR EXPERTS

You can paste any of the last 24 items you cut or copied to the Clipboard. On the Home tab, click the Clipboard Dialog Box Launcher. The Clipboard task pane appears along the left side of the worksheet. In the worksheet, click the cell where you want to paste an item. In the Clipboard task pane, click the item you want to paste. When you are done, click the Close button on the task pane title bar.

TIP

You can use shortcut keys to quickly cut, copy, and paste cells. Click the Ctrl+X keys to cut selected cells. Click the Ctrl+C keys to copy selected cells. Click the Ctrl+V keys to paste the selected cells.

Step-by-Step 3.1

1. Open the **Utilities.xlsx** workbook from the drive and folder where your Data Files are stored.

2. Save the workbook as **Utilities Expenses** followed by your initials. Some words in the workbook are misspelled. Ignore them for now.

3. Select the range **A3:D7**.

4. On the Home tab of the Ribbon, locate the **Clipboard** group. This group includes all the buttons for cutting, copying, and pasting.

5. Click the **Copy** button 📋. A flashing border surrounds the selected range to indicate that it has been placed on the Clipboard.

6. Click cell **A9**. Cell A9 is the upper-left cell of the range in which you want to paste the copied cells, as shown in Figure 3–1.

7. On the Home tab, in the Clipboard group, click the **Paste** button. The range A3:D7 is copied from the Clipboard to the range A9:D13. All the formatting from the range A3:D7 is copied along with the data. The flashing border surrounds the range A3:D7 until you click another button on the Ribbon or type in a cell.

TIP

After pasting, the Paste Options button appears next to the cell or range with the pasted item. Clicking the Paste Options button opens a gallery of options that you can use to choose how to format the pasted item.

8. In cell **A9**, enter **Natural Gas**. The flashing border disappears from the range A3:D7.

9. In cell **B9**, enter **100 cf** to indicate the number of cubic feet in hundreds. In cell **C9**, enter **Cost/100 cf** to indicate the cost per hundred cubic feet.

10. Select the range **A9:D13**.

11. On the Home tab, in the Clipboard group, click the **Cut** button ✂. A flashing border surrounds the range you selected.

12. Click cell **A8**.

13. On the Home tab, in the Clipboard group, click the **Paste** button. The data moves to the range A8:D12.

14. Save the workbook, and leave it open for the next Step-by-Step.

Using the Drag-and-Drop Method

> **TIP**
>
> The drag-and-drop method is the fastest way to copy or move data short distances in a worksheet. When you need to copy or move data to a part of the worksheet you can't see, copy or cut the data, scroll to the new location, and then paste the data.

You can quickly move or copy data using the drag-and-drop method. First, select the cell or range you want to move or copy. Then, position the pointer on the top border of the selected cells. The pointer changes from a white cross to a four-headed arrow. To move the selected cells, drag them to a new location. As you move the selected cells, a dotted border shows where they will be positioned after you release the mouse button, and a ScreenTip lists the destination cell or range address, as shown in **Figure 3–2**. When the destination you want is selected, release the mouse button. To copy the cells, press and hold the Ctrl key to include a plus sign above the pointer as you drag the cells to a new location, release the mouse button, and then release the Ctrl key.

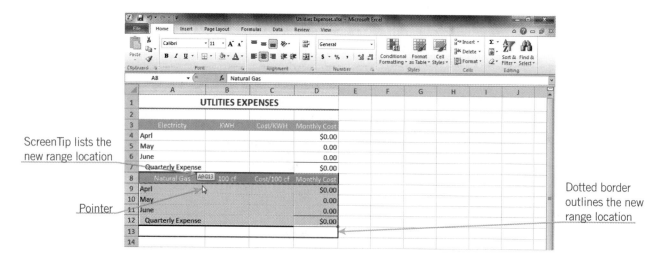

FIGURE 3–2   Range during drag and drop

Step-by-Step 3.2

1. Make sure the range **A8:D12** is selected.

2. Move the pointer to the top edge of cell A8 until it changes to a white arrow with a black four-headed arrow.

3. Click the top border of cell **A8**, press and hold the **left mouse** button, and then drag down to cell **A9** until the ScreenTip reads *A9:D13*, as shown in Figure 3–2.

4. Release the mouse button. The data moves to range A9:D13 and remains selected.

5. Move the pointer to the top edge of cell A9 until it changes to a four-headed arrow.

6. Press and hold the **Ctrl** key. The pointer changes to a white arrow with a plus sign.

7. Click and drag down to cell **A15** until the ScreenTip reads *A15:D19*.

8. Release the mouse button, and then release the **Ctrl** key. The data is copied from range A9:D13 to range A15:D19.

9. In cell A15, enter **Water**.

10. In cell B15, enter **1000 gallons**.

11. In cell C15, enter **Cost/1000 gal** to indicate the cost per 1000 gallons of water.

12. Save the workbook, and leave it open for the next Step-by-Step.

Using the Fill Handle

Filling copies a cell's contents and/or formatting into an adjacent cell or range. Selecting the cell or range that contains the content and formatting you want to copy displays a *fill handle* in the lower-right corner of the selection. When you point to the fill handle, the pointer changes to a black cross. Click and drag the fill handle over the cells you want to fill. Then, release the mouse button. The cell contents and formatting are duplicated into the range you selected, and the Auto Fill Options button appears below the filled content. You can click the Auto Fill Options button to

▶ **VOCABULARY**
filling

fill handle

TIP

Be aware that you can fill data only when the destination cells are adjacent to the original cell.

open the menu shown in **Figure 3–3**. You choose whether you want to copy both the cell's formatting and the cell's contents (the default), only the cell's contents, or only the cell's formatting.

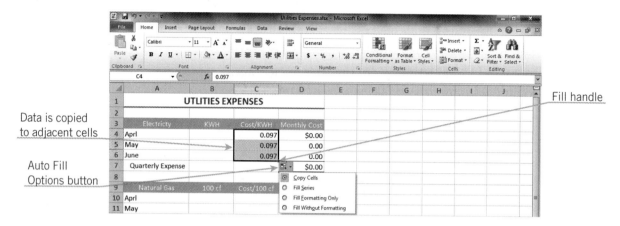

FIGURE 3–3   Auto Fill Options menu

You can also use the fill handle to continue a series of text items, numbers, or dates. For example, you might want to enter column labels of months, such as January, February, March, and so on, or row labels of even numbers, such as 2, 4, 6, and so forth. First, enter data in at least two cells to establish the pattern you want to use. Then, select the cells that contain the series pattern. Finally, drag the fill handle over the range of cells you want to fill. Excel enters appropriate data in the cells to continue the pattern.

Step-by-Step 3.3

1. Click cell **C4**, type **.097** to record the cost of electricity, and then press the **Enter** button ✓ on the Formula Bar. The cost of electricity for all three months is $0.097 per kilowatt hour. You want the amount entered in cell C4 to be entered in cells C5 and C6.

2. Point to the **fill handle** in the lower-right corner of cell C4. The pointer changes to a black cross **+**.

3. Click and drag the **fill handle** down to cell **C6**, and then release the mouse button. The contents of C4 are copied to cells C5 and C6.

4. Click cell **C10**, type **1.72** to record the cost per 100 cubic feet of natural gas, and then press the **Enter** button ✓ on the Formula Bar.

5. Click and drag the **fill handle** in the lower-right corner of cell C10 down to cell **C12**, and then release the mouse button. The data from cell C10 is copied to cells C11 and C12.

6. In cell C16, type **1.98** to record the cost per 1000 gallons of water, and then press the **Enter** button ✓ on the Formula Bar.

7. Click and drag the **fill handle** in the lower-right corner of cell C16 down to cell **C18**, and then release the mouse button. The data from cell C16 is copied to cells C17 and C18.

8. In column B, enter the utility usage data shown in **Figure 3–4**. The monthly costs in column D are calculated based on the data you entered.

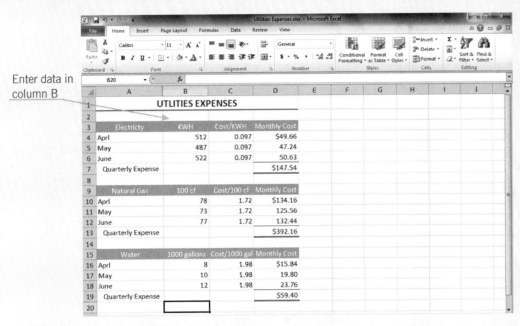

FIGURE 3–4
Utility usage data

Enter data in column B

9. Save the workbook, and leave it open for the next Step-by-Step.

Inserting and Deleting Rows, Columns, and Cells

As you build a worksheet, you may need to add rows or columns to store more data. Sometimes, you may need to remove a row or column of data. At other times, you may need to insert or delete specific cells. On the Home tab of the Ribbon, the Cells group includes buttons for inserting and deleting rows, columns, and cells.

Inserting Rows and Columns

To insert a row, click the row heading to select the row where you want the new row to appear. Then, click the Insert button in the Cells group on the Home tab. A blank row is added, and the existing rows shift down. To insert a column, click the column heading to select the column where you want the new column to appear. Then, click the Insert button in the Cells group. A blank column is added, and the existing columns shift to the right. The Insert Options button appears so you can choose to format the inserted row or column with the same formatting as the row or column on either side or clear the formatting.

TIP

If you select more than one row or column, the same number of rows or columns you selected is inserted in the worksheet.

Deleting Rows and Columns

The process for deleting a row or column is similar to the process for inserting one. First, click the row or column heading of the row or column you want to delete. Then, in the Cells group on the Home tab, click the Delete button. The selected row or column disappears, removing all its data and formatting. The existing rows shift up, or the existing columns shift left.

If you accidentally delete the wrong column or row, you can click the Undo button on the Quick Access Toolbar to restore the data. You can click the Redo button on the Quick Access Toolbar to cancel the Undo action.

Inserting and Deleting Cells

When entering a long column of data, it is not unusual to discover an omitted number near the top of the column. Rather than moving the existing data to make room for entering the omitted data, you can insert a new, blank cell. First, select the cell where you want to insert the new cell. Then, in the Cells group on the Home tab, click the Insert button arrow, and then click Insert Cells. The Insert dialog box appears, as shown in **Figure 3–5**. In this dialog box, you choose whether to shift the existing cells down or to the right.

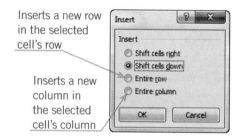

Inserts a new row in the selected cell's row

Inserts a new column in the selected cell's column

FIGURE 3–5   Insert dialog box

Another common problem is entering a number twice in a long column of data. To eliminate the duplicate data and reposition the rest of the data correctly, you can delete the cell that contains the duplicate value. First, select the cell you want to delete. Then, in the Cells group on the Home tab, click the Delete button arrow, and then click Delete Cells. The Delete dialog box appears so you can choose whether to shift the remaining cells up or to the left.

Step-by-Step 3.4

1. Click the **row 3** row heading. Row 3 is selected.

2. On the Home tab, in the Cells group, click the **Insert** button. A new, blank row appears as row 3. The original row 3 becomes row 4.

3. In cell B3, enter **Units Used**. In cell C3, enter **Unit Cost**. In cell D3, enter **Billed**. Select the range **B3:D3**, and then apply the **20% - Accent3** cell style to the range.

4. Click the **column B** column heading. Column B is selected.

5. On the Home tab, in the Cells group, click the **Insert** button. A new, blank column appears as column B. The original column B becomes column C and picks up the formatting used in column B.

6. Click cell **B3**. On the Home tab, in the Cells group, click the **Delete** button arrow, and then click **Delete Sheet Columns**. Column B is deleted, and the remaining columns shift left.

7. Click the **row 4** row heading. Row 4 is selected.

8. In the Cells group, click the **Delete** button. Row 4 disappears, and the remaining rows shift up.

9. On the Quick Access Toolbar, click the **Undo** button [image]. Row 4 reappears in the worksheet.

10. Click cell **B18**. In the Cells group, click the **Insert** button arrow, and then click **Insert Cells**. The Insert dialog box appears, as shown in Figure 3–5.

11. Click the **Shift cells down** option button, if it is not selected. Click **OK**. The data in the range B18:B19 shifts to the range B19:B20. Cell B18 is still the active cell.

12. On the Home tab, in the Cells group, click the **Delete** button arrow, and then click **Delete Cells**. The Delete dialog box appears.

13. Click the **Shift cells up** option button, if it is not selected. Click **OK**. The data in the range B19:B20 shifts back to the range B18:B19.

14. Save the workbook, and leave it open for the next Step-by-Step.

Freezing Panes in a Worksheet

Often a worksheet includes more data than you can see on the screen at one time. As you scroll the worksheet, titles and labels at the top or side of the worksheet might shift out of view, making it difficult to identify the contents of particular columns. For example, the worksheet title *Utilities Expenses* in the previous Step-by-Step might have scrolled off the screen when you were working in the lower part of the worksheet.

You can view two parts of a worksheet at once by freezing panes. When you *freeze panes*, you select which rows and/or columns of the worksheet remain visible on the screen as the rest of the worksheet scrolls. For example, you can freeze the row or column titles so they appear on the screen no matter where you scroll in the

▶ **VOCABULARY**
freeze panes

TECHNOLOGY CAREERS

Business managers use Excel worksheets in a variety of ways. For example, human resource managers use worksheets to conduct performance reviews and to manage employee records. Production managers use worksheets to track machine production efficiency and to keep machine maintenance records.

worksheet. As shown in **Figure 3–6**, rows 1, 2, and 3 are frozen so they remain on-screen even when you scroll down to row 16 (hiding rows 4 through 15).

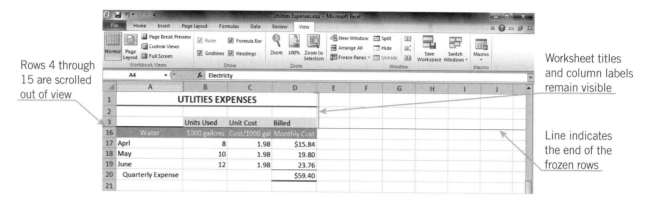

FIGURE 3–6   Worksheet with rows 1 through 3 frozen

When you freeze panes in a worksheet, the rows and columns that remain locked on screen depend on the location of the active row, column, or cell. **Table 3–1** describes the different selection options. On the View tab of the Ribbon, in the Window group, click the Freeze Panes button, and then click Freeze Panes. A black line appears between the frozen and unfrozen panes of the worksheet.

TABLE 3–1   Freeze panes options

TO FREEZE	DO THE FOLLOWING
Rows	Select the first row below the row(s) you want to freeze
Columns	Select the first column to the right of the column(s) you want to freeze
Rows and columns	Select the first cell below and to the right of the row(s) and column(s) you want to freeze

When you want to unlock all the rows and columns to allow them to scroll, you need to unfreeze the panes. On the View tab of the Ribbon, in the Window group, click the Freeze Panes button, and then click Unfreeze Panes. The black line disappears, and all rows and columns are unfrozen.

Splitting a Worksheet Window

You might want to view different parts of a large worksheet at the same time. *Splitting* divides the worksheet window into two or four panes that you can scroll independently. This enables you to see different parts of a worksheet at the same time. Splitting is particularly useful in a large worksheet when you want to copy data from one area to another. You can click in one pane and scroll the worksheet as needed while the other part of the worksheet remains in view in a different pane.

▶ VOCABULARY
split

You can split the worksheet window into horizontal panes, as shown in **Figure 3–7**, vertical panes, or both. Select a row to split the window into horizontal panes. Select a column to split the worksheet into vertical panes. Select a cell to split the worksheet into both horizontal and vertical panes. Then, on the View tab of the Ribbon, in the Window group, click the Split button. The Split button remains selected, and a split bar separates the panes you created. If you want to resize the panes, drag the split bar. When you want to return to a single pane, click the Split button again.

> **EXTRA FOR EXPERTS**
>
> You can use the mouse to add, resize, and remove panes. Drag the split box above the vertical scroll bar down to create horizontal panes. Drag the split box that appears to the right of the horizontal scroll bar to the left to create vertical panes. Drag a split bar to resize the panes. Double-click a split bar to remove it.

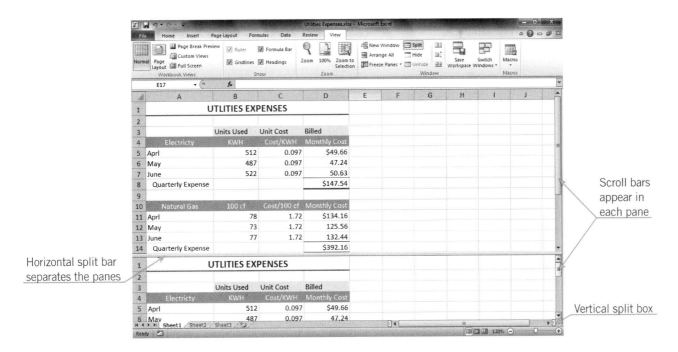

FIGURE 3–7 Worksheet window split into horizontal panes

Step-by-Step 3.5

1. Click cell **A4**.

2. Click the **View** tab on the Ribbon, and then locate the **Window** group. This group contains the buttons for freezing and splitting panes.

3. Click the **Freeze Panes** button, and then click **Freeze Panes**. The title and column headings in rows 1 through 3 are locked. A black line appears between rows 3 and 4.

4. Scroll the worksheet down until row **16** is at the top of the worksheet window. The worksheet title and column headings remain locked at the top of the screen, even as other rows scroll out of view, as shown in Figure 3–6.

5. On the View tab, in the Window group, click the **Freeze Panes** button, and then click **Unfreeze Panes**. The title and column headings are no longer frozen.

6. Click the **row 15** row heading.

7. On the View tab, in the Window group, click the **Split** button. A split bar appears above row 15, dividing the worksheet into two horizontal panes.

8. Click in the lower pane and scroll up to row **1**. The same part of the worksheet appears in both panes, as shown in Figure 3–7.

9. Double-click the **split bar**. The split is removed, and worksheet is displayed again one pane.

10. Save the workbook, and leave it open for the next Step-by-Step.

Checking Spelling in a Worksheet

An important step in creating a professional workbook is to correct any misspellings. Typographical errors can be distracting and can cause others to doubt the accuracy of the rest of the workbook's content. To help track down and correct spelling errors in a worksheet, you can use the Spelling command, which checks the spelling in the entire active worksheet against the dictionary that comes with Microsoft Office. To check the spelling in a worksheet, click the Review tab on the Ribbon, and then, in the Proofing group, click the Spelling button. The Spelling dialog box appears, as shown in **Figure 3–8**, and highlights the first potential spelling error shown in the Not in Dictionary box.

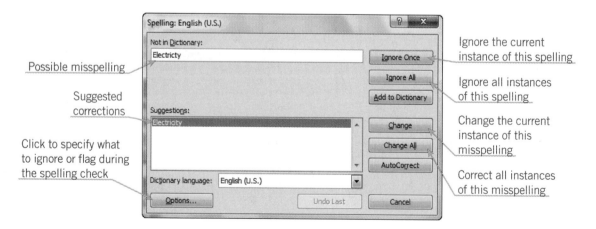

FIGURE 3–8   Spelling dialog box

The Spelling dialog box provides many ways to deal with a possible misspelling. If the word is mistyped, you can correct the spelling yourself or click the correct word in the Suggestions box. Then, click Change to replace the current instance of the misspelling with the correct word, or click Change All to replace every instance of the misspelling. If the word is correct (as often happens with company and product names), you can click Ignore to move to the next potential spelling error without making a change to the word, or click Ignore All to skip every instance of this word in the worksheet. After you have addressed all the possible misspellings in the worksheet, a dialog box appears to let you know that the spelling check is complete for the entire sheet.

Be aware that the spelling checker is not foolproof. The default spelling options are to ignore words that are capitalized, contain numbers, or are Internet addresses. As a final check, you should proofread the worksheet for any misspellings that the spelling checker ignored or missed. You might find words that are spelled correctly, but used incorrectly (such as *they're*, *their*, and *there*, or *hour* and *our*). In addition, you might discover a missing word (*and* or *the*, for instance). This final check helps to ensure that your worksheet is free from errors.

EXTRA FOR EXPERTS

If Excel incorrectly flags a word that you use frequently as a misspelling, you can add the word to a custom dictionary that resides on your computer by clicking the Add to Dictionary button. If the misspelling is a typo you make often, you can select the correct word in the Suggestions box, and then click the AutoCorrect button. Excel will automatically correct this mistake whenever you type it.

Step-by-Step 3.6

1. Press the **Ctrl+Home** keys. Cell A1 is the active cell in the worksheet.

2. Click the **Review** tab on the Ribbon, and then locate the **Proofing** group. The Spelling button is located here.

3. Click the **Spelling** button. The Spelling dialog box appears, as shown in Figure 3–8. The word *Electricty* is identified as a misspelled word. One correction appears in the Suggestions box.

4. In the Suggestions box, click **Electricity** if it is not selected, and then click **Change**. The spelling of the word in the worksheet is corrected, and *Aprl* appears in the dialog box as the next possible misspelled word.

5. In the Suggestions box, click **April**, if it is not selected, and then click **Change All**. All three instances of this misspelling are corrected, and *cf* appears in the Not in Dictionary box as the next possible misspelling. However, *cf* is being used as an abbreviation for cubic feet, so you will ignore all instances of this abbreviation in the worksheet.

6. Click **Ignore All**. A dialog box appears, indicating the spelling check is complete for the entire sheet. (If the spelling checker flags other possible misspellings, change or ignore them as necessary, until the dialog box appears.)

7. Click **OK**.

8. Proofread the worksheet. In cell A1, the word *UTLITIES* is misspelled. The spelling checker did not flag this word because the word is capitalized.

9. Click cell **A1**, and then, in the Formula Bar, click after *UT* to place the insertion point.

10. Type **I** to insert the missing letter in the word, and then press the **Enter** key.

11. Save the workbook, and leave it open for the next Step-by-Step.

Preparing a Worksheet for Printing

So far, you have worked in *Normal view*, which is the best view for entering and formatting data in a worksheet. Excel has other views as well. *Page Layout view* shows how the worksheet will appear on paper, which is helpful when you prepare a worksheet for printing. Excel has many options for changing how a worksheet appears on a printed page.

Setting Margins

The *margin* is the blank space around the top, bottom, left, and right sides of a page. The margin settings determine how many of a worksheet's columns and rows fit on a printed page. You can increase (widen) the margins in a worksheet to create extra blank space for jotting notes on the printed copy. Or, you can decrease (narrow) the margins in a worksheet when you want to print more columns and rows on a page. To change the margins of a worksheet, click the Page Layout tab on the Ribbon, and then, in the Page Setup group, click the Margins button. You can then choose among three preset margins—Normal (the default), Wide, and Narrow, as shown in **Figure 3–9**.

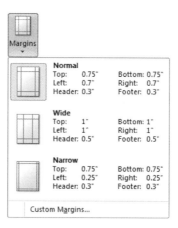

FIGURE 3–9　Margins menu

Changing the Page Orientation

You can print worksheets using different orientations to best display the data. Worksheets printed in portrait orientation are longer than they are wide. In contrast, worksheets printed in landscape orientation are wider than they are long. By default, Excel is set to print pages in portrait orientation. Many worksheets, however, include more columns of data than fit on pages in portrait orientation. These pages look better and are easier to understand when printed in landscape orientation. You can change the orientation of the worksheet by clicking the Page Layout tab on the Ribbon, and then, in the Page Setup group, clicking the Orientation button. As shown in **Figure 3–10**, you can then click Portrait or Landscape on the menu.

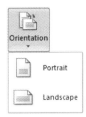

FIGURE 3–10   Orientation menu

Setting the Print Area

When you print a worksheet, Excel assumes that you want to print all of the data entered in the worksheet. If you want to print only a portion of the data in a worksheet, you need to set the print area. The *print area* consists of the cells and ranges designated for printing. For example, you might want to print only the range A1:A19, which shows the utility and month data, and the range D3:D19 (billed amount). To do this, first select the range. Then, click the Page Layout tab on the Ribbon. In the Page Setup group, click the Print Area button, and then click Set Print Area. Each time you print the worksheet, only the cells in the print area appear on the page. You must clear the print area to print the entire worksheet again. In the Page Setup group on the Page Layout tab, click the Print Area button, and then click Clear Print Area.

A print area can include multiple ranges and/or nonadjacent cells. For example, you might want to print the utility and month data as well as the billed amount. To do so, select the cells and ranges you want to print, and then set the print area. The selected cells and ranges will print until you clear the print area.

Inserting, Adjusting, and Deleting Page Breaks

When a worksheet or the print area doesn't fit on one printed page, you can use a page break to indicate where the next page begins. Excel inserts an *automatic page break* whenever it runs out of room on a page. You can also insert a *manual page break* to start a new page. To insert a manual page break, select the row below where you want to insert a horizontal page break, or select the column to the left of where you want to insert a vertical page break. Then, click the Breaks button in the Page Setup group on the Page Layout tab, and then click Insert Page Break.

▶ **VOCABULARY**

print area

automatic page break

manual page break

📖 EXTRA FOR EXPERTS

You can center the print area on the printed page. On the Page Layout tab, click the Page Setup Dialog Box Launcher. Click the Margins tab. In the Center on page section, check Horizontally to center the print area between the left and right margins and/or check Vertically to center it between the top and bottom margins. Click OK.

▶ **VOCABULARY**
Page Break Preview
scale

The simplest way to adjust page breaks in a worksheet is in *Page Break Preview*, as shown in **Figure 3–11**. On the status bar, click the Page Break Preview button to switch the worksheet to this view. Dashed lines appear for automatic page breaks, and solid lines appear for manual page breaks. You can drag any page break to a new location.

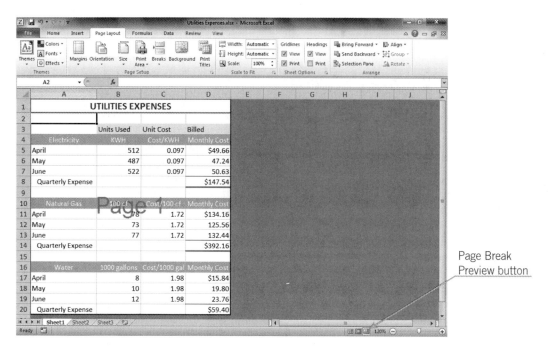

FIGURE 3–11   Page Break Preview

When you no longer need a manual page break any longer, you can delete it. Click below or to the left of the page break you want to remove. Click the Page Layout tab on the Ribbon. In the Page Setup group, click the Breaks button, and then click Remove Page Break.

Scaling to Fit

Scaling resizes a worksheet to print on a specific number of pages. The Scale to Fit group on the Page Layout tab contains three options for resizing a worksheet, as shown in **Figure 3–12**. You can fit the worksheet on the number of pages you specify for its width or height. Just click the Width arrow or the Height arrow, and then select the maximum pages for the printed worksheet's width or height. Another option is to set the percentage by which you want to shrink or enlarge the worksheet on the printed page. Click the Scale arrows to increase or decrease the percentage.

FIGURE 3–12   Scale to Fit group on the Page Layout tab

Choosing Sheet Options

By default, gridlines, row numbers, and column letters appear in the worksheet—but not on the printed page—to help you enter and format data. You can choose to show or hide gridlines and headings in a worksheet or on the printed page. The Sheet Options group, shown in **Figure 3–13**, contains check boxes for viewing and printing gridlines and headings. Check and uncheck the boxes as needed.

FIGURE 3–13   Sheet Options group on the Page Layout tab

Specifying Print Titles

Print titles are designated rows and/or columns in a worksheet that are printed on each page. Specified rows are printed at the top of each page. Specified columns are printed on the left of each page. To set print titles, click the Page Layout tab on the Ribbon, and then, in the Page Setup group, click the Print Titles button. The Page Setup dialog box appears with the Sheet tab displayed, as shown in **Figure 3–14 A**. Click the Collapse button next to the Rows to repeat at top box to shrink the dialog box, as shown in **Figure 3–14 B**. Click the row or rows to use as the print title. Then, click the Expand button to restore the dialog box to its full size. You use the same process to select columns to repeat at left. Click OK to add the print titles to the worksheet.

> **VOCABULARY**
> **print titles**

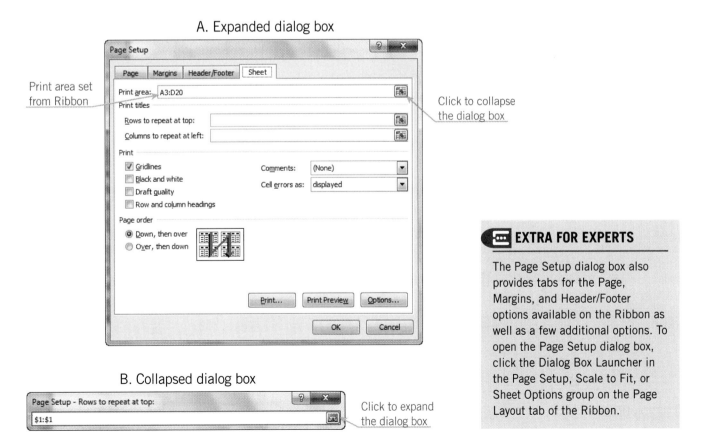

FIGURE 3–14   Sheet tab in the Page Setup dialog box

> **EXTRA FOR EXPERTS**
>
> The Page Setup dialog box also provides tabs for the Page, Margins, and Header/Footer options available on the Ribbon as well as a few additional options. To open the Page Setup dialog box, click the Dialog Box Launcher in the Page Setup, Scale to Fit, or Sheet Options group on the Page Layout tab of the Ribbon.

Step-by-Step 3.7

1. Click the **Page Layout** tab on the Ribbon. This tab contains many commands for preparing a worksheet for printing.

2. In the Page Setup group, click the **Margins** button to open the menu shown in Figure 3–9, and then click **Wide**. The margins are set to one inch on all sides. A dashed line, indicating an automatic page break, appears after column F.

3. On the Page Layout tab, in the Page Setup group, click the **Orientation** button to open the menu shown in Figure 3–10, and then click **Landscape**. The automatic page break moves to after column J, indicating that the printed workbook will be wider than it is tall.

4. Select the range **A3:D20**.

5. On the Page Layout tab, in the Page Setup group, click the **Print Area** button, and then click **Set Print Area**. Only the selected range will print on the page.

6. On the Page Layout tab, in the Scale to Fit group, click the **Scale** up arrow, shown in Figure 3–12, six times until **130** appears in the box. The printed data will be enlarged to take up more of the page.

7. On the Page Layout tab, in the Sheet Options group, click the **Gridlines Print** check box to insert a check mark. The gridlines will be printed on the page.

8. On the Page Layout tab, in the Page Setup group, click the **Print Titles** button. The Page Setup dialog box appears, as shown in Figure 3–14 A.

9. On the Sheet tab, in the Print titles section, click the **Collapse** button on the Rows to repeat at top box.

10. In the worksheet, click **row 1** row heading as the row to repeat at the top of each printed page. The row reference is added to the dialog box, as shown in Figure 3–14 B.

11. In the collapsed Page Setup dialog box, click the **Expand** button .

12. Click **OK**.

13. Press the **Ctrl+Home** keys. Cell A1 becomes the active cell.

14. Save the workbook, and leave it open for the next Step-by-Step.

Inserting Headers and Footers

> **VOCABULARY**
> **header**
>
> **footer**

Headers and footers are useful for adding identifying text to a printed page. A *header* is text that is printed in the top margin of each page, as shown in **Figure 3–15**. A *footer* is text that is printed in the bottom margin of each page. Text that is commonly included in a header or footer is your name, the page number, the current date, the workbook file name, and the worksheet name. Headers and footers are each divided into three sections, which you can use to organize the text.

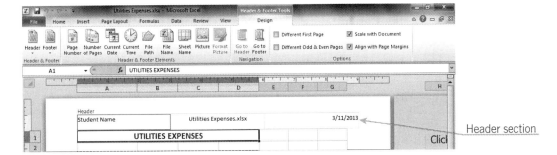

FIGURE 3–15 Completed Header section

To create a header or footer for a printed worksheet, click the Insert tab on the Ribbon, and then in the Text group, click the Header & Footer button. The worksheet switches to Page Layout view, and the Header & Footer Tools Design tab includes groups for working with headers and footers. The insertion point is in the center header box, but you can easily move to the left or right section by clicking a different box. Type the text you want to enter, or click a button in the Header & Footer Elements group on the Design tab. To enter a preset header or footer, in the Header & Footer group on the Design tab, click the Header or Footer button, and then click the header or footer you want to use. Click anywhere in the worksheet to close the headers and footers.

> **TIP**
>
> You can enter, edit, delete, and format the text in each header and footer section the same way you do for text in worksheet cells.

Step-by-Step 3.8

1. Click the **Insert** tab on the Ribbon, and then locate the **Text** group.

2. Click the **Header & Footer** button. The worksheet changes to Page Layout view. The insertion point is in the center header box.

3. On the Design tab, in the Header & Footer Elements group, click the **File Name** button. The code *&[File]* appears in the center header box.

4. Press the **Tab** key to move to the right header box. The code *&[File]* in the center header box is replaced with *Utilities Expenses.xlsx*, which is the current file name of the workbook. Remember, if your computer is not set to show file extensions, you see *Utilities Expenses* in the center header box.

5. On the Design tab, in the Header & Footer Elements group, click the **Current Date** button. The code *&[Date]* appears in the right header box.

6. Press the **Tab** key to move the insertion point to the left header box. The code *&[Date]* in the right header box is replaced with the current date.

7. In the left header box, type your name. The header is complete, as shown in Figure 3–15.

8. On the Design tab, in the Navigation group, click the **Go to Footer** button. The insertion point moves to the left footer box.

9. Click the center footer box.

10. On the Design tab, in the Header & Footer Elements group, click the **Page Number** button. The code *&[Page]* appears in the center footer box. After you move the insertion point out of the center footer box, the actual page number will appear.

11. Click the worksheet to close the headers and footers. Press the **Ctrl+Home** keys to make cell A1 the active cell. The worksheet appears in Page Layout view, as shown in **Figure 3–16**, giving a good sense of how it will be printed on the page.

FIGURE 3–16
Worksheet in Page Layout view

Column and row headings will not be printed

Print title

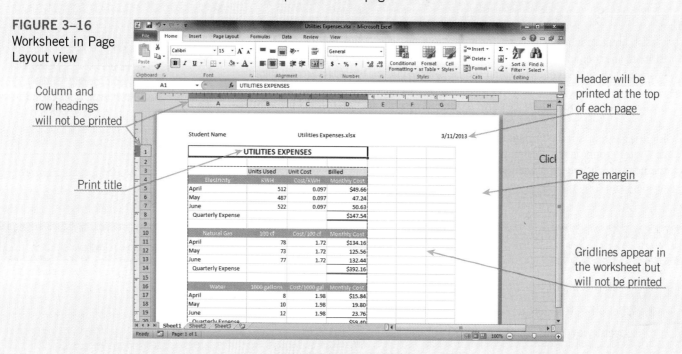

Header will be printed at the top of each page

Page margin

Gridlines appear in the worksheet but will not be printed

12. Save the workbook.

13. Click the **File** tab to open Backstage view. In the navigation bar, click **Print**. A preview of the printed worksheet and buttons to access many of the page layout settings are displayed, as shown in **Figure 3–17**.

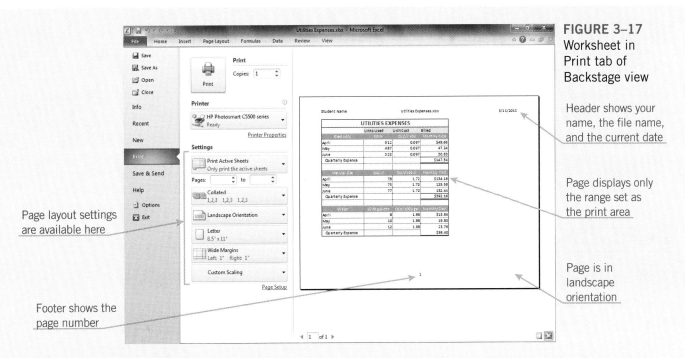

FIGURE 3–17
Worksheet in
Print tab of
Backstage view

Header shows your
name, the file name,
and the current date

Page displays only
the range set as
the print area

Page is in
landscape
orientation

Page layout settings
are available here

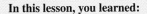

Footer shows the
page number

14. On the Print tab, click the **Print** button, and then close the workbook.

The worksheet is printed.

SUMMARY

In this lesson, you learned:

- You can copy or move data to another part of the worksheet. You can use the Copy, Cut, and Paste buttons, the drag-and-drop method, and the fill handle to copy and move data in a worksheet. These tools save time by eliminating the need to retype data.

- As you build a worksheet, you may need to insert a row or column to enter more data, or delete a row or column of unnecessary data. You can also insert or delete specific cells within a worksheet.

- When a worksheet becomes large, the column or row labels can scroll out of view as you work on other parts of the worksheet. To keep selected rows and columns on the screen as the rest of the worksheet scrolls, you can freeze panes.

- Splitting a large worksheet enables you to view and work in different parts of a worksheet at once, in two or four panes that you can scroll independently.

- You can check a worksheet for possible misspellings and correct them using the Spelling dialog box.

- When you are ready to print a worksheet, switching from Normal view to Page Layout view can be helpful. You can modify how a worksheet appears on the printed page by increasing or decreasing the margins, changing the page orientation, designating a print area, inserting page breaks, scaling, showing or hiding gridlines and headings, and specifying print titles.

- Headers and footers are useful for adding identifying text at the top and bottom of the printed page. Common elements include your name, the page number, the current date, the workbook file name, and the worksheet name.

■ VOCABULARY REVIEW

Define the following terms:

automatic page break	header	Page Layout view
copy	manual page break	paste
cut	margin	print area
fill handle	Normal view	print titles
filling	Office Clipboard (Clipboard)	scale
footer	Page Break Preview	split
freeze panes		

■ REVIEW QUESTIONS

TRUE / FALSE

Circle T if the statement is true or F if the statement is false.

T F   **1.** When you paste data into cells with existing data, the pasted data replaces the existing data.

T F   **2.** The Fill commands are available only when you are copying data to cells adjacent to the original cell.

T F   **3.** Deleting a row or column moves the data in that row or column to the adjacent row or column.

T F   **4.** Splitting creates two, three, or four panes in the worksheet.

T F   **5.** The spelling checker might not find all the misspellings or incorrectly used words in a worksheet.

WRITTEN QUESTIONS

Write a brief answer to each of the following questions.

1. What key do you press to copy data using the drag-and-drop method?

2. How do you paste multiple copies of data that has been copied to the Clipboard?

3. What should you do if you accidentally delete a column or row?

4. How do you keep the titles and column labels of a worksheet on the screen, no matter where the worksheet is scrolled?

5. What is the difference between a header and a footer?

FILL IN THE BLANK

Complete the following sentences by writing the correct word or words in the blanks provided.

1. _____ removes a cell or range from its original location in the worksheet.

2. _____ shows how the worksheet will appear on paper.

3. The _____ is the blank space around the top, bottom, left and right sides of a page.

4. The _____ consists of the cells and ranges designated for printing.

5. _____ are designated rows and/or columns in a worksheet that are printed on each page.

■ PROJECTS

If you have a SAM 2010 user profile, your instructor may have assigned an autogradable version of the indicated project. If so, log into the SAM 2010 Web site at *www.cengage.com/sam2010* to download the instruction and start files.

PROJECT 3–1

Match the correct command in Column 2 to the action indicated in Column 1.

Column 1

1. You are tired of typing repetitive data.

2. A portion of the worksheet would be more useful in another area of the worksheet.

3. You forgot to type a row of data in the middle of the worksheet.

4. You no longer need a certain column in the worksheet.

5. Column headings scroll out of view while you are working in the worksheet.

6. You want to be sure that all words are spelled correctly in the worksheet.

7. Your boss requests a printed copy of your worksheet.

8. You need to print only a selected area of the worksheet.

Column 2

_____ A. Fill or Copy

_____ B. Cut, Paste

_____ C. Insert Sheet Rows

_____ D. Delete Sheet Columns

_____ E. Print

_____ F. Print Area

_____ G. Freeze Panes

_____ H. Spelling

SAM PROJECT 3–2

1. Open the **Assets.xlsx** workbook from the drive and folder where your Data Files are stored.

2. Save the workbook as **Assets Statement** followed by your initials.

3. Insert a column to the left of column B.

4. Change the width of column A to 45.00 characters.

5. Move the contents of the range D3:D16 to the range B3:B16.

6. Change the width of columns B and C to 10.00 characters.

7. Indent the contents of A9, A13, and A16.

8. Underline the contents of B3:C3.

9. Check the spelling in the worksheet, and then proofread the worksheet to correct any errors the spelling checker missed. (*Hint:* You will need to make three corrections with the spelling checker and one correction by proofreading.)

10. Insert a footer that includes your name in the left footer box and the current date in the right footer box.

11. Save, preview, and print the worksheet, and then close the workbook.

PROJECT 3–3

1. Open the **Trade.xlsx** workbook from the drive and folder where your Data Files are stored.

2. Save the workbook as **Trade Balance** followed by your initials.

3. Freeze rows 1 through 6.

4. Check the spelling of the countries listed in the worksheet. (*Hint*: You will need to make four corrections.)

5. Change the orientation of the worksheet to portrait.

6. Scale the worksheet to 80% of its original size.

7. Change the margins to Wide.

8. In cell A5, enter your name.

9. Save, preview, and print the worksheet, and then close the workbook.

PROJECT 3–4

1. Open the **Inventory.xlsx** workbook from the drive and folder where your Data Files are stored.

2. Save the workbook as **Inventory Purchase** followed by your initials.

3. Organize the worksheet so inventory items are grouped by supplier, as shown below. Be sure to insert suitable headings and format them appropriately. Some of the data is out of order and needs to be moved.

Item	Product Code	Quantity
Mega Computer Manufacturers		
Mega X-39 Computers	X-39-25879	24
Mega X-40 Computers	X-40-25880	18
Mega X-41 Computers	X-41-25881	31
Xenon Paper Source		
Xenon Letter Size White Paper	LT-W-45822	70
Xenon Letter Size Color Paper	LT-C-45823	16
Xenon Legal Size White Paper	LG-W-45824	20
Xenon Legal Size Color Paper	LG-C-45825	7
MarkMaker Pen Company		
MarkMaker Black Ball Point Pens	MM-Bk-43678	100
MarkMaker Blue Ball Point Pens	MM-Bl-43677	120
MarkMaker Red Ball Point Pens	MM-R-43679	45

4. The following inventory item was excluded from the worksheet. Add the item below the MarkMaker Red Ball Point Pens row by using the Fill command and then editing the copied data.

Item	Product Code	Quantity
MarkMaker Green Ball Point Pens	MM-G-43680	35

5. Delete the following item.

Item	Product Code	Quantity
Mega X-39 Computers	X-39-25879	24

6. Change the page orientation to landscape.

7. Hide the gridlines from view.

8. Insert a header that includes your name in the center header box and the current date in the right header box.

9. Save, preview, and print the worksheet, and then close the workbook.

PROJECT 3–5

1. Open the **Time.xlsx** workbook from the drive and folder where your Data Files are stored.

2. Save the workbook as **Time Sheet** followed by your initials.

3. Delete rows 4 and 5.

4. Enter the following data in rows 13 through 16 in the time record.

Date	From	To	Admin.	Meetings	Phone	Work Description
9-Oct	8:15 AM	12:00 PM	1.75		2.50	Staff meeting and called clients
10-Oct	7:45 AM	11:30 AM	2.00		1.75	Paperwork and called clients
11-Oct	7:45 AM	11:30 AM			3.75	Called clients
13-Oct	8:00 AM	12:00 PM	2.50		1.50	Mailed flyers and met w/KF

5. Freeze rows 1 through 7 in the worksheet.

6. Insert a blank row above row 16. Use Auto Fill to enter the formula in cell D16. Enter the following information:

Date	From	To	Admin.	Meetings	Phone	Work Description
12-Oct	7:45 AM	11:30 AM	2.00		1.75	Paperwork and called clients

7. Change the orientation of the worksheet to landscape.

8. In the range B1:D1, enter your first name, middle initial, and last name, replacing the data already in that range. Save the workbook.

9. Preview the worksheet in Backstage view. Click the Zoom to Page button in the lower-right corner of the window to zoom in to see the total hours worked.

10. Print the worksheet, and then close the workbook.

PROJECT 3–6

1. Open the **Chemistry.xlsx** workbook from the drive and folder where your Data Files are stored.

2. Save the workbook as **Chemistry Grades** followed by your initials.

3. Merge and center the range A1:H1. Merge and center the range A2:H2.

4. Insert a column between the current columns A and B.

5. In the range B3:B9, enter the following data:

Cell	Data
B3	First Name
B4	Max
B5	Aiden
B6	Cindy
B7	Raul
B8	Alicia
B9	Mika

6. Change the worksheet to landscape orientation.

7. Switch to Page Layout view. Click in the left header box and type your name.

8. Go to the footer, and insert *Page 1* in the center footer box. (*Hint*: On the Header & Footer Tools Design tab, in the Header & Footer group, click the Footer button, and then click Page 1.)

9. Save, preview, and print the worksheet, and then close the workbook.

PROJECT 3–7

1. Open the **Club.xlsx** workbook from the drive and folder where your Data Files are stored.

2. Save the workbook as **Club Equipment** followed by your initials.

3. Bold and center the column headings in row 2.

4. Insert a row above row 3.

5. Freeze the column headings in row 2.

6. Insert a row above row 8, and then, in cell A8, enter **Bats**.

7. Copy cell E4 to the range E5:E11.

8. Format the Cost (D4:D11) and Total (E4:E12) columns as currency with two decimal places.

9. In the Sport and Cost columns, enter the following data, and then widen the columns as needed to display all of the data:

Item	Sport	Cost
Basketballs	**Basketball**	32
Hoops	**Basketball**	60
Backboards	**Basketball**	135
Softballs	**Softball**	8
Bats	**Softball**	45
Masks	**Softball**	55
Volleyballs	**Volleyball**	35
Nets	**Volleyball**	155

10. In the Quantity column, enter the following data:

Basketballs	5	Bats	8
Hoops	2	Masks	2
Backboards	2	Volleyballs	7
Softballs	25	Nets	1

11. You have $1,785 to spend on equipment. Use any remaining cash to purchase as many basketballs as possible. Increase the number of basketballs and watch the dollar amount in the total. You should use $1,780 and have $5 left over.

12. In cell A16, enter **Prepared by:** followed by your name.

13. Change the worksheet to landscape orientation.

14. Save, preview, and print the worksheet, and then close the workbook.

PROJECT 3–8

1. Open the **Creston.xlsx** workbook from the drive and folder where your Data Files are stored.

2. Save the workbook as **Creston Pool** followed by your initials.

3. Move data as needed to better reorganize the worksheet.

4. Format the worksheet in an appropriate and appealing way.

5. Set appropriate margins and page orientation.

6. Check the spelling in the worksheet, and then proofread the worksheet to correct any errors the spelling checker missed. (*Hint:* You will need to make three corrections with the spelling checker and one correction by proofreading.)

7 Insert your name, the workbook file name, and the current date in the appropriate header and footer boxes.

8. Save, preview, and print the worksheet, and then close the workbook.

■ CRITICAL THINKING

ACTIVITY 3–1

As a zoo employee, you have been asked to observe a chimpanzee's behavior during a three-day period. You need to record the number of minutes the animal displays certain behaviors while the zoo is open to visitors. Create a worksheet to record the number of minutes that the chimpanzee participates in the following behaviors during each of the three days.

■ Sleeping

■ Eating

■ Walking

■ Sitting

■ Playing

Format the worksheet to make it attractive and easy to read. Change margins, orientation, and other page setup options to prepare the worksheet for printing. Include appropriate headers and footers, including at least your name in one of the boxes. Save, preview, and print the workbook.

LESSON 4

Entering Worksheet Formulas

■ OBJECTIVES

Upon completion of this lesson, you should be able to:

- Enter and edit formulas.
- Distinguish between relative, absolute, and mixed cell references.
- Use the point-and-click method to enter formulas.
- Use the Sum button to add values in a range.
- Preview a calculation.
- Display formulas instead of results in a worksheet.
- Manually calculate formulas.

■ VOCABULARY

absolute cell reference

formula

manual calculation

mixed cell reference

operand

operator

order of evaluation

point-and-click method

relative cell reference

Sum button

You can use the numerical data in a worksheet to perform mathematical calculations. Rather than add specific numbers, you can use cell references in equations to make the calculation more flexible. As these equations become more complex, you will need to keep in mind the order of evaluation to be sure you obtain the intended results. You can create equations using the keyboard or the mouse. To enter common calculations quickly, you can use the Sum button. These mathematical calculations are what make Excel such a powerful tool for both personal and business use.

What Are Formulas?

One of the main advantages of Excel is that you can use numbers entered in cells to make calculations in other cells. The equation used to calculate values based on numbers entered in cells is called a *formula*. Each formula begins with an equal sign (=). The results of the calculation appear in the cell in which the formula is entered. The formula itself appears in the Formula Bar. For example, if you enter the formula =8+6 in cell A1, the value 14 appears in the cell, and the formula =8+6 appears in the Formula Bar when cell A1 is the active cell, as shown in **Figure 4–1**.

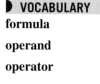

▶ **VOCABULARY**

formula

operand

operator

Formula in the active cell appears in the Formula Bar

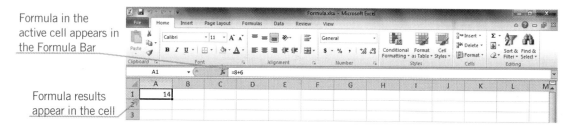

Formula results appear in the cell

FIGURE 4–1   Formula and formula results

Entering a Formula

Worksheet formulas consist of two components: operands and operators. An *operand* is a constant (text or number) or cell reference used in a formula. An *operator* is a symbol that indicates the type of calculation to perform on the operands, such as a plus sign (+) for addition. **Table 4–1** shows the different mathematical operators you can use in formulas. Consider the formula =B3+5. In this formula, the cell reference B3 and the constant 5 are operands, and the plus sign (+) is an operator. This formula tells Excel to add the value in cell B3 to the value 5. After you finish typing a formula in a cell, you enter it by pressing the Enter key or the Tab key or by clicking the Enter button on the Formula Bar.

TABLE 4–1   Mathematical operators

OPERATOR	OPERATION	EXAMPLE	MEANING
+	Addition	B5+C5	Adds the values in cells B5 and C5
−	Subtraction	C8–232	Subtracts 232 from the value in cell C8
*	Multiplication	D4*D5	Multiplies the value in cell D4 by the value in cell D5
/	Division	E6/4	Divides the value in cell E6 by 4
^	Exponentiation	B3^3	Raises the value in cell B3 to the third power

In editing mode, each cell reference in a formula appears in a specific color. The corresponding cell in the worksheet is outlined in the same color. You can change a cell reference in a formula by dragging the outlined cell to another location in the worksheet. You can also change which cells are included in a reference by dragging any corner of the colored outline to resize the selected range.

Step-by-Step 4.1

1. Open the **Formula.xlsx** workbook from the drive and folder where your Data Files are stored.

2. Save the workbook as **Formula Practice** followed by your initials.

3. Click cell **C3**. You'll enter a formula in this cell.

4. Type **=A3+B3** and then press the **Enter** key. The formula result 479 appears in the cell. Cell C4 is the active cell.

5. In cell C4, type **=A4–B4** and then press the **Enter** key. The formula result –147 appears in the cell. Cell C5 is the active cell.

6. In cell C5, type **=A5*B5** and then press the **Enter** key. The formula result 13166 appears in the cell. Cell C6 is the active cell.

7. In cell C6, type **=A6/B6** and then press the **Enter** key. The formula result 18 appears in the cell. Compare your results to **Figure 4–2**.

> **TIP**
>
> You can type cell references in uppercase (A1) or lowercase (a1) letters.

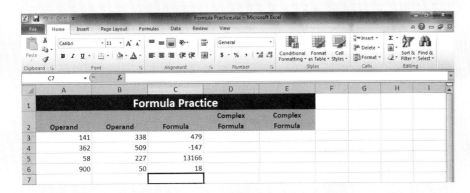

FIGURE 4–2
Formulas entered in worksheet

8. Save the workbook, and leave it open for the next Step-by-Step.

Order of Evaluation

Formulas can include more than one operator. For example, the formula =C3*C4+5 includes two operators and performs both multiplication and addition to calculate the value in the cell. The sequence used to calculate the value of a formula is called the *order of evaluation*.

Formulas are evaluated in the following order:

1. Contents within parentheses are evaluated first. You can use as many sets of parentheses as you want. The innermost set of parentheses is evaluated first.

2. Mathematical operators are evaluated in the order shown in **Table 4–2**.

3. If two or more operators have the same order of evaluation, the equation is evaluated from left to right. For example, in the formula =20–15–2, first the number 15 is subtracted from 20, then 2 is subtracted from the difference (5).

TABLE 4–2   Order of evaluation

ORDER OF EVALUATION	OPERATOR	SYMBOL
First	Exponentiation	^
Second	Positive or negative	+ or −
Third	Multiplication or division	* or /
Fourth	Addition or subtraction	+ or −

Step-by-Step 4.2

1. Click cell **D3**, and then type **=(A3+B3)*20**. This formula adds the values in cells A3 and B3, and then multiplies the result by 20.

2. Press the **Tab** key. The formula results in the value 9580, which appears in cell D3. Cell E3 is the active cell.

3. In cell E3, type **=A3+B3*20**. This formula is the same as the one you entered in cell D3, but without the parentheses. The lack of parentheses changes the order of evaluation and the resulting value.

4. Press the **Enter** key. The formula in cell E3 results in the value 6901. This differs from the formula results in cell D3 because Excel multiplied the value in cell B3 by 20 before adding the value in cell A3. In cell D3, Excel added the values in cells A3 and B3, and then multiplied the sum by 20.

5. Save the workbook, and leave it open for the next Step-by-Step.

Editing Formulas

If you attempt to enter a formula with an incorrect structure in cell, Excel opens a dialog box that explains the error and provides a possible correction. You can accept that correction or choose to correct the formula yourself. For example, if you enter a formula with an opening parenthesis but no closing parenthesis, a dialog box appears, as shown in **Figure 4–3**, indicating that Excel found an error and proposing a correction that adds a closing parenthesis to the formula. Click Yes to accept the proposed correction. Click No to see a description of the error in another dialog box, and then click OK to return to the formula. You can correct the formula by editing it directly in the cell or by clicking in the Formula Bar.

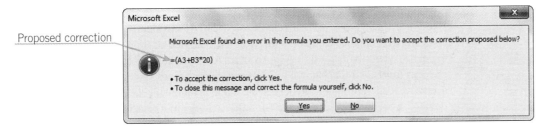

FIGURE 4–3   Formula error message

Although Excel checks the formula for the correct structure, it does not check the formula for the correct values or cell references. If you discover that you need to make a correction, you can edit the formula. Click the cell with the formula you want to edit. Press the F2 key or double-click the cell to enter editing mode or click in the Formula Bar. Move the insertion point as needed to edit the entry. Then, press the Enter key or click the Enter button on the Formula Bar to enter the formula.

Step-by-Step 4.3

1. Click cell **E3**. The formula is displayed in the Formula Bar.

2. In the Formula Bar, click after = (the equal sign).

3. Type **(** (an opening parenthesis). You will intentionally leave out the closing parenthesis.

4. Press the **Enter** key. The dialog box shown in Figure 4–3 appears, indicating that Excel found an error and offers a possible correction.

5. Read the message, and then click **No**. You will correct the error yourself. A dialog box appears, describing the specific error Excel found, as shown in **Figure 4–4**.

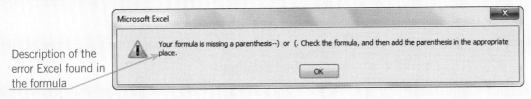

FIGURE 4–4
Formula error
description message

6. Read the message, and then click **OK**.

7. Move the insertion point in the Formula Bar between the 3 and the *.

8. Type **)** (a closing parenthesis).

9. Press the **Enter** key. The value in cell E3 changes to 9580.

10. Save the workbook, and leave it open for the next Step-by-Step.

Comparing Relative, Absolute, and Mixed Cell References

Excel has three types of cell references: relative, absolute, and mixed. A *relative cell reference* adjusts to its new location when copied or moved to another cell. For example, when the formula =A3+A4 is copied from cell A5 to cell B5, the formula changes to =B3+B4, as shown in **Figure 4–5**. How does Excel know how to change a relative cell reference? It creates the same relationship between the cells in the new location. In other words, the formula =A3+A4 in cell A5 instructs Excel to add the two cells directly above it. When you move this formula to another cell, such as cell B5, Excel uses that same instruction: to add the two cells directly above the cell with the formula. Notice that only the cell references change; the operators remain the same.

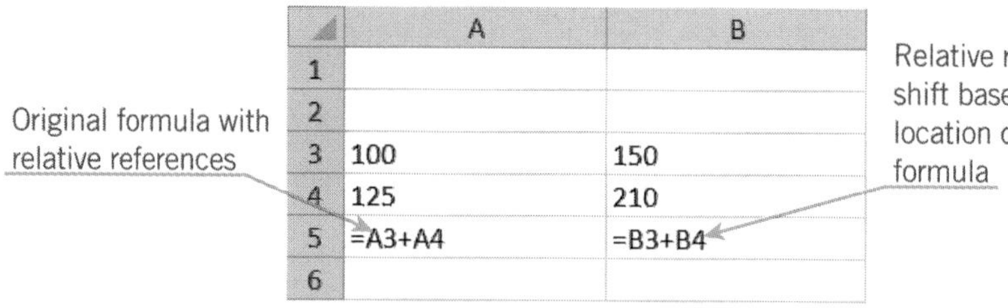

Original formula with relative references

Relative references shift based on new location of copied formula

	A	B
1		
2		
3	100	150
4	125	210
5	=A3+A4	=B3+B4
6		

FIGURE 4–5 Relative cell references

Absolute cell references do not change when copied or moved to a new cell. To create an absolute cell reference, you insert a dollar sign ($) before the column letter and before the row number. For example, when the formula =$A$3+$A$4 in cell A5 is copied to cell B7, the formula remains unchanged, as shown in **Figure 4–6**.

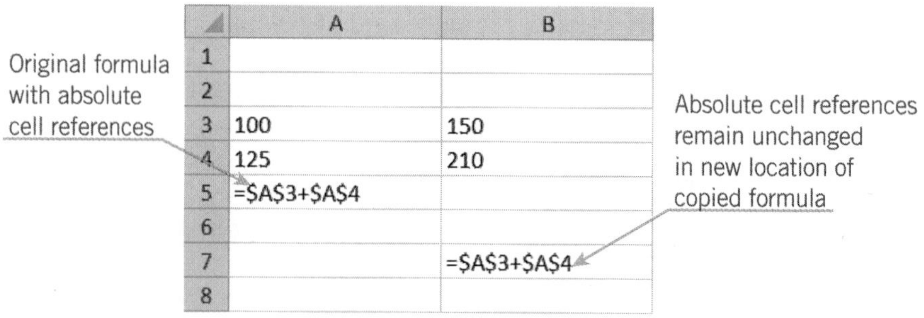

Original formula with absolute cell references

Absolute cell references remain unchanged in new location of copied formula

	A	B
1		
2		
3	100	150
4	125	210
5	=$A$3+$A$4	
6		
7		=$A$3+$A$4
8		

FIGURE 4–6 Absolute cell references

TECHNOLOGY CAREERS

Engineers use Excel worksheets to perform complex calculations in areas such as construction, transportation, and manufacturing. For example, Excel worksheets are used to fit equations to data, interpolate between data points, solve simultaneous equations, evaluate integrals, convert units, and compare economic alternatives.

Cell references that contain both relative and absolute references are called *mixed cell references*. When formulas with mixed cell references are copied or moved to another cell, the row or column references preceded by a dollar sign do not change; the row or column references not preceded by a dollar sign adjust to match the cell to which they are moved. As shown in **Figure 4–7**, when the formula =A$3+A$4 is copied from cell A5 to cell B7, the formula changes to =B$3+B$4.

▶ **VOCABULARY**
mixed cell reference

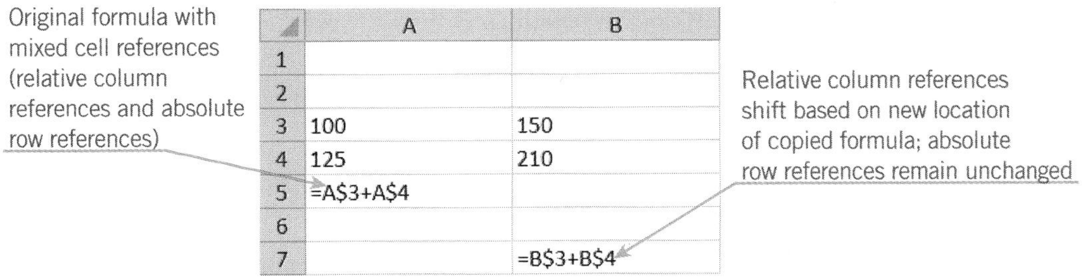

Original formula with mixed cell references (relative column references and absolute row references)

◢	A	B
1		
2		
3	100	150
4	125	210
5	=A$3+A$4	
6		
7		=B$3+B$4

Relative column references shift based on new location of copied formula; absolute row references remain unchanged

FIGURE 4–7   Mixed cell references

Step-by-Step 4.4

1. Click cell **D3**. The formula =(A3+B3)*20 (shown in the Formula Bar) contains only relative cell references.

2. Drag the fill handle to cell **D4** to copy the formula from cell D3 to cell D4.

3. Click cell **D4**. The value in cell D4 is 17420, and the formula in the Formula Bar is =(A4+B4)*20. The operators in the formula remain the same, but the relative cell references change to reflect the new location of the formula.

4. Click cell **D5**, type =$A$3*($B$3–200) and then press the **Enter** key. The value in cell D5 is 19458. The formula contains absolute cell references, which are indicated by the dollar signs that precede the row and column references.

5. Copy the formula in cell **D5** to cell **E6**. The value in cell E6 is 19458, the same as in cell D5.

6. Click cell **D5** and look at the formula in the Formula Bar.

EXTRA FOR EXPERTS

You can press the F4 key to change a cell reference from a relative reference to an absolute reference to a mixed reference with an absolute row to a mixed reference with an absolute column and back to a relative reference.

7. Click cell **E6** and look at the formula in the Formula Bar. The formula in cell D5 is exactly the same as the formula in cell E6 because the formula you copied from cell D5 contains absolute cell references.

8. Click cell **E4**, type **=$A$4+B4** and then press the **Enter** key. This formula contains both relative and absolute cell references. The value in cell E4 is 871.

9. Copy the formula in cell **E4** to cell **E5**, and then click cell **E5**. The relative cell reference B4 changes to B5, but the absolute reference $A$4 stays the same. The value in cell E5 is 589.

10. Copy the formula in cell **E5** to cell **D6**. The relative cell reference B5 changes to A6, but the absolute reference $A$4 stays the same. The value in cell D6 is 1262.

11. Click cell **A8**, and then enter your name. Save, preview, print, and close the workbook.

Creating Formulas Quickly

So far, you have created formulas by typing the formula or editing an existing formula. You can also create formulas quickly by using the point-and-click method and the Sum button.

Using the Point-and-Click Method

▶ **VOCABULARY**
point-and-click method

Earlier, you constructed formulas by typing the entire formula directly in a worksheet cell. You can include cell references in a formula by using the *point-and-click method* to click each cell rather than typing a cell reference. The point-and-click method is particularly helpful when you need to enter long formulas that contain multiple cell references.

To use the point-and-click method, simply click the cell instead of typing its cell reference. For example, to enter the formula =A3+B3 with the point-and-click method, click the cell in which you want to enter the formula, press =, click cell A3, press +, click cell B3, and then press the Enter key.

Step-by-Step 4.5

▶ **TIP**

A flashing colored border indicates that you can replace the current reference in the formula by clicking another cell or selecting a range. When the border stops flashing, the cell reference is "locked," and you must select the reference in the formula to replace it.

1. Open the **Juice.xlsx** workbook from the drive and folder where your Data Files are stored.

2. Save the workbook as **Juice Sales** followed by your initials.

3. Click cell **F6**, type **=(** to begin the formula, and then click cell **B6**. A flashing blue border surrounds cell B6 to indicate it is selected, and its cell reference in the formula is also blue.

4. Type *****. The flashing border disappears, but the cell border and reference remain blue.

5. Click cell **C6**. A flashing green border appears around cell C6, and its cell reference in the formula is the same color.

6. Type **)+(** and then click cell **D6**. The cell border and reference in the formula are purple.

7. Type ***** and then click cell **E6**. The cell border and reference in the formula are red. **Figure 4–8** shows the color-coded formula and cell references.

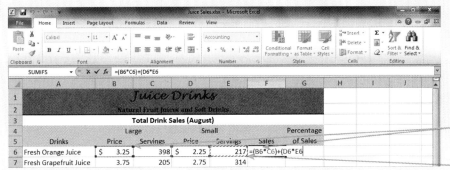

FIGURE 4–8
Color-coded formula

Each cell reference in the formula is color-coded to match the selected cell border

Flashing border around selected cell

8. Type **)** and then press the **Enter** button ✓ on the Formula Bar. The value $1,781.75 appears in cell F6.

9. Use the fill handle to copy the formula in cell F6 to the range **F7:F11**. Click cell **F12** to deselect the range. All the monthly sales are calculated for each type of drink, as shown in **Figure 4–9**.

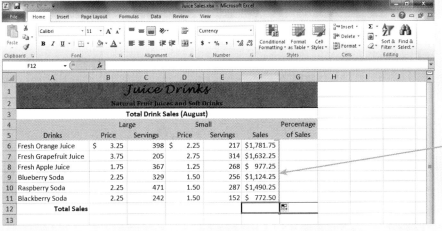

FIGURE 4–9
Monthly drink sales

Monthly sales for each type of drink

10. Save the workbook, and leave it open for the next Step-by-Step.

Using the Sum Button

Worksheet users frequently need to add long columns or rows of numbers. The *Sum button*, located in the Editing group on the Home tab of the Ribbon, makes this operation simple. To use the Sum button, click the cell where you want the total

▶ **VOCABULARY**
Sum button

to appear, and then click the Sum button. Excel scans the worksheet to determine the most logical adjacent column or row of cells with numbers to add. An outline appears around the range it suggests, and the range reference appears in the active cell. If you want to add the numbers in a different range, drag to select those cells. Press the Enter key to complete the formula. The active cell displays the sum.

The Sum button enters a formula with the SUM function, which is a shorthand way to specify adding numbers in a range. The SUM function that adds the numbers in the range D5:D17, for example, is =SUM(D5:D17). Functions are discussed in greater detail in the next lesson.

Step-by-Step 4.6

1. Make sure cell **F12** is the active cell.

2. On the Home tab, in the Editing group, click the **Sum** button Σ. The suggested range F6:F11 is outlined. The formula =SUM(F6:F11) appears in the Formula Bar and cell F12. See **Figure 4–10**.

FIGURE 4–10
SUM function in the formula

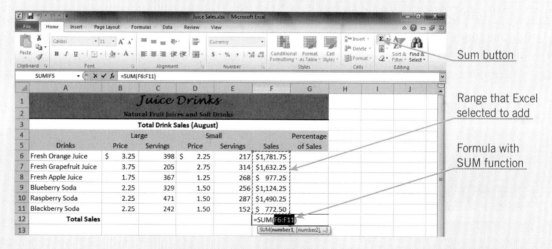

3. Verify that the range **F6:F11** is the selected range. Press the **Enter** key. The range is deselected and the formula results of $7,778.25 appear in cell F12, which is the sum of the numbers in column F.

4. Click cell **G6**, and then type **=**.

5. Click cell **F6**, and then type **/**.

6. Click cell **F12**, press the **F4** key to change the cell reference (F12) to an absolute reference ($F$12). You used an absolute reference to cell F12 because you want the cell reference to remain unchanged when you copy it to the rest of the range.

7. Press the **Enter** button ✓ on the Formula Bar. The formula results 22.91% appear in cell G6.

8. Copy the formula in cell G6 to the range **G7:G11**. The Percentage of Sales is entered for all of the drinks.

9. Click cell **G12**. On the Home tab, in the Editing group, click the **Sum** button **Σ**. Press the **Enter** key. The total percentage of sales is 100.0%. See **Figure 4–11**.

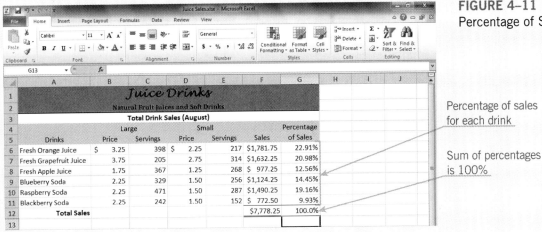

FIGURE 4–11
Percentage of Sales calculated

Percentage of sales for each drink

Sum of percentages is 100%

10. Save the workbook, and leave it open for the next Step-by-Step.

Previewing Calculations

When you select a range that contains numbers, the status bar shows the results of common calculations for the range, without you having to enter a formula. By default, these calculations display the average value in the selected range, a count of the number of values in the selected range, and a sum of the values in the selected range. For ranges that contain only text values, the status bar displays a count of the number of values in the range. You can also customize Excel to display a numerical count, minimum value, and maximum value for the selected range. **Table 4–3** describes each of these options.

TABLE 4–3   Summary calculation options for the status bar

CALCULATION	DESCRIPTION
Average	Displays an average of the values in the selected range
Count	Lists how many cells in the selected range contain values
Numerical Count	Lists how many of the cells in the selected range contain numbers
Minimum	Shows the smallest number in the selected range
Maximum	Shows the largest number in the selected range
Sum	Adds all the numbers in the selected range

To display the default calculations in the status bar, just select a range. You can change which summary calculations appear in the status bar. Right-click the status bar to open the Customize Status Bar menu shown in **Figure 4–12**. Options that are preceded by a check mark appear in the status bar. Options without a check mark are hidden. You can choose which calculations you want to show or hide. Click a checked option to hide it, or click an unchecked option to show it. Press Esc to close the menu. The checked summary calculations appear in the status bar for selected ranges until you change the displayed options.

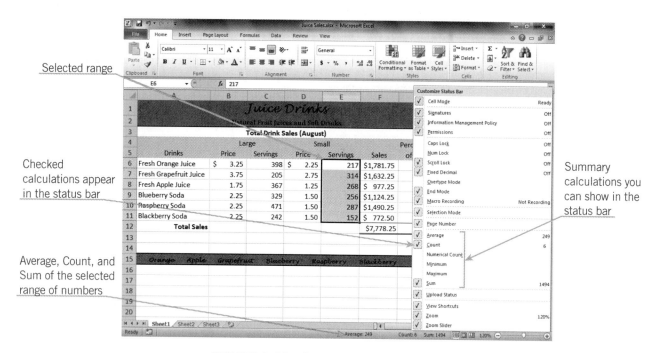

FIGURE 4–12   Customize Status Bar menu

Step-by-Step 4.7

You can use the summary calculations in the status bar to confirm that the same formula in the worksheet is correct. Cell F12 contains the SUM function formula that adds the values in the range F6:F11. To confirm the formula is correct and the results are accurate, select the range F6:F11, then compare the Sum value in the status bar with the value in cell F12. The sum in the status bar should equal the value in cell F12.

1. Select the range **E6:E11**. Summary calculations for the small servings appear in the status bar, showing an Average of 249, a Count of 6, and a Sum of 1494.

2. Right-click the **status bar**. The Customize Status Bar menu appears, as shown in Figure 4–12.

3. Click **Minimum**. A check mark precedes Minimum on the menu, and the menu remains open so you can click additional options. The fewest number of small drinks served, 152, appears in the status bar. Depending on where you right-clicked, this or another calculation in the status bar might be covered by the shortcut menu.

4. Click **Minimum** to hide the calculation from the status bar, and then press the **Esc** key to close the menu.

5. Select the range **F6:F11**. Summary calculations for the sales appear in the status bar, showing an Average of $1,296.38, a Count of 6, and a Sum of $7,778.25.

6. Click cell **A13** to deselect the range.

7. Save the workbook, and leave it open for the next Step-by-Step.

Showing Formulas in the Worksheet

In previous Step-by-Steps, you viewed formulas in the Formula Bar or directly in the worksheet cells as you typed or edited the formulas. After you enter the formulas, the cells show the formula results rather than the formulas. Typically, the formula result is what you want to see. However, when creating a worksheet with many formulas, you may find it simpler to organize formulas and detect formula errors when all formulas are displayed in their cells. To do this, click the Formulas tab on the Ribbon, and then, in the Formula Auditing group, click the Show Formulas button. The formulas replace the formula results in the worksheet. If a cell does not contain a formula, the data entered in the cell remains displayed. The Show Formulas button remains selected until you click it again to redisplay the formula results. It can be helpful to print the worksheet showing formulas for reference.

> **TIP**
>
> You can also switch between showing formulas and showing formula results in a worksheet by pressing the Ctrl+` keys (the grave accent ` key is located above the Tab key on most standard keyboards).

Calculating Formulas Manually

Excel calculates formula results when you enter the formula and recalculates the results whenever the cells used in that formula change. If a worksheet contains many formulas, the calculation and recalculation process can take a long time. When you need to edit a worksheet with many formulas, you can specify *manual calculation*, which lets you determine when Excel calculates the formulas.

    The Formulas tab on the Ribbon contains all the buttons you need when working with manual calculations. To switch to manual calculation, click the Calculation Options button in the Calculation group, and then click Manual. When you want to calculate the formula results for the entire workbook, click the Calculate Now button. To calculate the formula results for only the active worksheet, click the Calculate Sheet button. To return to automatic calculation, click the Calculation Options button, and then click Automatic.

> ▶ **VOCABULARY**
> **manual calculation**

Step-by-Step 4.8

1. Click the **Formulas** tab on the Ribbon. In the Formula Auditing group, click the **Show Formulas** button. All formulas appear in the worksheet cells instead of the formula results.

2. Scroll to the right as needed so that columns F and G appear on the screen and you can see the formula results.

3. On the Formulas tab, in the Calculation group, click the **Calculation Options** button. A menu of options appears, as shown in **Figure 4–13**.

FIGURE 4–13
Worksheet with
formulas displayed

Button is a toggle;
click it again to
redisplay the
formula results

Text and numbers
remain unchanged

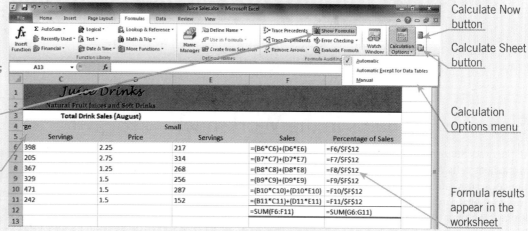

Calculate Now
button

Calculate Sheet
button

Calculation
Options menu

Formula results
appear in the
worksheet

4. Click **Manual**. Automatic calculation is turned off.

5. Press the **Ctrl+`** keys. The formula results reappear.

6. Click cell **C6**, and then enter **402**. Click cell **C7**, and then enter **220**. Click cell **C10**, and then enter **305**. The worksheet values change, but Excel does not recalculate the formula results.

7. On the Formulas tab, in the Calculation group, click the **Calculate Sheet** button ▦ while watching the worksheet. Excel recalculates the formulas when you click the button. For example, the total sales amount in cell F12 is now $7,474.00.

8. On the Formulas tab, in the Calculation group, click the **Calculation Options** button, and then click **Automatic**.

9. Insert a header with your name in the left section and the current date in the right section.

10. Save, preview, print, and close the workbook.

TIP

You can also press the Shift+F9 keys to calculate the values in the worksheet.

SUMMARY

In this lesson, you learned:

■ Formulas are equations used to calculate values and display them in a cell. Formulas can include values referenced in other cells of the worksheet. Each formula begins with an equal sign and contains at least two operands and one operator.

■ Formulas can include more than one operator. The order of evaluation determines the sequence used to calculate the value of a formula.

■ When you enter a formula with an incorrect structure, Excel can correct the error for you, or you can choose to edit it yourself. To edit a formula, click the cell with the formula and then make changes in the Formula Bar. You can also double-click a formula and then edit the formula directly in the cell.

- Relative references adjust to a new location when copied or moved to another cell. Absolute references do not change, regardless of where they are copied or moved. Mixed references contain both relative and absolute references.

- Formulas can be created quickly using the point-and-click method. With this method, you insert a cell reference in a formula by clicking a cell rather than typing its column letter and row number.

- The Sum button in the Editing group on the Home tab inserts a formula with the SUM function, which adds the value of cells in a specified range.

- The status bar shows a preview of common formulas, such as Average, Count, and Sum, when you select a range of cells. You can choose which formula previews to show or hide in a worksheet by right-clicking the status bar.

- You can view the formulas in a worksheet, instead of the formula results, by clicking the Show Formulas button in the Formula Auditing group on the Formulas tab.

- Excel calculates formula results in a worksheet when you enter the formula, and recalculates the results whenever the values in the cells used in that formula change. When you need to edit a worksheet with many formulas and don't want formulas to recalculate automatically, you can click the Calculation Options button in the Calculation group on the Formulas tab, and then click Manual. When you want to calculate the formula results for the current worksheet, click the Calculate Sheet button.

■ VOCABULARY REVIEW

Define the following terms:

absolute cell reference

formula

manual calculation

mixed cell reference

operand

operator

order of evaluation

point-and-click method

relative cell reference

Sum button

REVIEW QUESTIONS

TRUE / FALSE

Circle T if the statement is true or F if the statement is false.

T   F   **1.**   An operator is a constant or cell reference used in formulas.

T   F   **2.**   In a formula, multiplication is performed before subtraction.

T   F   **3.**   In a formula, operations within parentheses are performed after operations outside parentheses.

T   F   **4.**   An absolute reference does not change when the formula is copied or moved to another cell.

T   F   **5.**   Manual calculation lets you control when Excel calculates formula results.

WRITTEN QUESTIONS

Write a brief answer to each of the following questions.

1. In a worksheet formula, which operator has the highest priority in the order of evaluation?

2. What type of cell reference will not adjust to its new location when it is copied or moved to another cell?

3. Write an example of a formula that contains a mixed cell reference.

4. Explain how to enter the formula =C4+B5+D2 in cell D3 using the point-and-click method.

5. How do you display formulas instead of formula results in a worksheet?

FILL IN THE BLANK

Complete the following sentences by writing the correct word or words in the blanks provided.

1. The equation used to calculate values based on numbers entered in cells is called a(n) _____.

2. The sequence used to calculate the value of a formula is called the _____.

3. The cell reference D4 is an example of a(n) _____ cell reference.

4. Default summary calculations for a selected range appear in the _____.

5. _____ calculation lets you control when Excel calculates the formulas in a worksheet.

PROJECTS

If you have a SAM 2010 user profile, your instructor may have assigned an autogradable version of the indicated project. If so, log into the SAM 2010 Web site at *www.cengage.com/sam2010* to download the instruction and start files.

PROJECT 4–1

Match the letter of the worksheet formula in Column 2 to the description of the worksheet operation performed by the formula in Column 1.

Column 1

_____ 1. Adds the values in cells A3 and A4

_____ 2. Subtracts the value in cell A4 from the value in cell A3

_____ 3. Multiplies the value in cell A3 by 27

_____ 4. Divides the value in cell A3 by 27

_____ 5. Raises the value in cell A3 to the 27th power

_____ 6. Divides the value in cell A3 by 27, and then adds the value in cell A4

_____ 7. Divides the value in cell A3 by the result of 27 plus the value in cell A4

_____ 8. Multiplies the value in cell A3 by 27, and then divides the product by the value in cell A4

_____ 9. Divides 27 by the value in cell A4, and then multiplies the result by the value in cell A3

_____ 10. Raises the value in A3 to the 27th power, and then divides the result by the value in A4

Column 2

A.   =A3/(27+A4)

B.   =A3/27+A4

C.   =A3^27/A4

D.   =(A3*27)/A4

E.   =A3*(27/A4)

F.   =A3^27

G.   =A3+A4

H.   =A3–A4

I.   =A3/27

J.   =A3*27

SAM PROJECT 4–2

1. Open the **Zoo.xlsx** workbook from the drive and folder where your Data Files are stored.

2. Save the workbook as **Zoo Invoice** followed by your initials.

3. In cells D6, D7, D8, and D9, enter formulas that multiply the values in column B by the values in column C.

4. In cell D10, enter a formula to sum the totals in the range D6:D9.

5. In cell D11, enter a formula to calculate an 8% sales tax of the subtotal in cell D10.

6. In cell D12, enter a formula to add the subtotal and sales tax.

7. Change the worksheet to manual calculation.

8. Format the range D6:D12 in the Accounting number format. The worksheet is ready to accept customer data.

9. A customer purchases two tiger T-shirts, three dolphin T-shirts, one sweatshirt, and four coffee mugs. Enter these quantities in column C and recalculate the values.

10. Insert a footer with your name in the left section and the current date in the right section.

11. Save the workbook, preview and print the worksheet, and then close the workbook.

PROJECT 4–3

1. Open the **Operation.xlsx** workbook from the drive and folder where your Data Files are stored.

2. Save the workbook as **Operation Results** followed by your initials.

3. Enter formulas in the specified cells that perform the operations listed below. After you enter each formula, write the resulting value in the space provided.

Resulting Value	Cell	Operation
a. _____	C3	Add the values in cells A3 and B3.
b. _____	C4	Subtract the value in cell B4 from the value in cell A4.
c. _____	C5	Multiply the value in cell A5 by the value in cell B5.
d. _____	C6	Divide the value in cell A6 by the value in cell B6.
e. _____	B7	Sum the values in the range B3:B6.
f. _____	D3	Add the values in cells A3 and B3, and then multiply by 3.
g. _____	D4	Add the values in cells A3 and A4, and then multiply by cell B3.
h. _____	D5	Copy the formula in cell D4 to cell D5.
i. _____	D6	Subtract the value in cell B6 from the value in cell A6, and then divide by 2.
j. _____	D7	Divide the value in cell A6 by 2, and then subtract the value in cell B6.

4. In cell A1, enter your name. Save, preview, print, and close the workbook.

PROJECT 4-4

1. Open the **Investment.xlsx** workbook from the drive and folder where your Data Files are stored.

2. Save the workbook as **Investment Record** followed by your initials.

3. In cells D6 through D8, enter formulas to calculate the values of the stocks. The formulas should multiply the number of shares in column B by the price of the shares in column C.

4. In cells D10 and D11, enter formulas to calculate the values of the mutual funds. As with the stocks, the formulas should multiply the number of shares in column B by the price of the shares in column C.

5. In cell D12, enter a formula that sums the values in cells D4 through D11. Format cell D12 with a Top and Double Bottom Border.

6. In cell E4, enter the formula **=D4/$D$12**. This formula determines the percentage of each investment value with respect to the total investment value.

7. Copy the formula in cell E4 to the ranges E6:E8 and E10:E11. Notice that the absolute reference to cell D12 in the formula remains unchanged as you copy the formula.

8. In cell E12, enter a formula that sums the percentages in cells E4 through E11. Format cell E12 with a Top and Double Bottom Border.

9. Insert a footer with your name in the left section, the file name in the center section, and the current date in the right section.

10. Save, preview, and print the workbook.

11. Save the workbook as **Investment Record Updated** followed by your initials.

12. Change the worksheet to manual calculation in preparation for updating the investment values.

13. Enter the following updated share price amounts in the appropriate cells:

Investment	Price
MicroCrunch Corp.	$17.25
Ocean Electronics, Inc.	$21.75
Photex, Inc.	$12.25
Prosperity Growth Fund	$ 6.50
Lucrative Mutual Fund	$24.00

14. Perform the manual calculation.

15. Save, preview, print, and close the workbook.

PROJECT 4-5

1. Open the **Mackenzie.xlsx** workbook from the drive and folder where your Data Files are stored.

2. Save the workbook as **Mackenzie Development** followed by your initials.

3. In cell D5, enter a formula that multiplies the square footage in cell B5 by the value per square foot in cell C5.

4. In cell D6, enter a formula that multiplies the number of bathrooms in cell B6 by the value per bathroom in cell C6.

5. In cell D7, enter a formula that multiplies the number of car garages in cell B7 by the value per car garage in cell C7.

6. In cell D8, enter a formula that calculates the increase in value in cell C8 if 1 is entered in cell B8.

7. In cell D9, enter a formula that calculates the increase in value in cell C9 if 1 is entered in cell B9.

8. In cell D10, use the Sum button to calculate the sum of the numbers in the range D5:D9.

9. A potential buyer inquires about the estimated price of a home with the following specifications:

Square Footage:	**2000**
Number of Bathrooms:	**3**
Number of Car Garage:	**2**
On a Cul-de-Sac?	**No**
With a Swimming Pool?	**Yes**

In the range B5:B9, enter this data to determine the estimated home cost.

10. Insert a footer with your name in the left section and the current date in the right section.

11. Save, preview, print, and close the workbook.

■ CRITICAL THINKING

ACTIVITY 4–1

You have been offered three jobs, each with a different salary. You know the gross pay (the amount before taxes), but not the net pay (the amount you receive after taxes have been taken out). Assume you will have to pay 10% income tax and 7% Social Security tax. Develop a worksheet with formulas to calculate your net pay. The format should be similar to that shown in **Figure 4–14**.

Your worksheet should include the following:

■ In the range C7:C9, formulas that multiply the gross pay in column B by the 10% income tax.

■ In the range D7:D9, formulas that multiply the gross pay in column B by the 7% Social Security tax.

■ In the range E7:E9, formulas that subtract the amounts in columns C and D from the amount in column B.

Format the worksheet appropriately and attractively. Insert a header with your name and the current date. Save, preview, print, and close the workbook.

ACTIVITY 4–2

One of the most difficult aspects of working with formulas in a worksheet is getting them to calculate the proper value when you copy and move them into other cells. Copying and moving formulas requires an understanding of the differences between relative and absolute cell references. Research the differences between absolute and relative cell references in the Excel Help system. Write a brief explanation of the differences in your own words, and give an example of a situation in which you would use each type of cell reference. List the name(s) of the Help topics you used for reference.

	A	B	C	D	E
1	Potential Net Pay				
2					
3	Income Tax	10%			
4	Social Security Tax	7%			
5					
6	Job Offer	Gross Pay	Income Tax	Social Security Tax	Net Pay
7	1	$24,500			
8	2	$26,200			
9	3	$27,100			
10					

FIGURE 4–14   Format for net pay worksheet

Estimated Time:
2 hours

LESSON 5

Using Functions

■ OBJECTIVES

Upon completion of this lesson, you should be able to:

- Identify the parts of a function.
- Enter formulas with functions.
- Use functions to solve mathematical problems.
- Use functions to solve statistical problems.
- Use functions to solve financial problems.
- Use logical functions to make decisions with worksheet data.
- Use functions to insert times and dates in a worksheet.
- Use text functions to format and display cell contents.

■ VOCABULARY

argument
date and time functions
financial functions
Formula AutoComplete
function
logical functions
mathematical functions
statistical functions
text functions
trigonometric functions

In the previous lesson, you created formulas that used cell references and constants. A formula can also contain a function. Functions often simplify formulas that are long or complex. Excel includes functions to perform complex calculations in specialized areas of mathematics, including statistics, logic, trigonometry, accounting, and finance. Function formulas are also used to display and determine dates and times. You will work with all these different types of functions in this lesson.

What Are Functions?

▶ **VOCABULARY**

function

argument

A *function* is a shorthand way to write an equation that performs a calculation. For example, the SUM function adds values in a range of cells. A formula with a function has three parts: an equal sign, a function name, and for most functions at least one argument, as shown in **Figure 5–1**. The equal sign identifies the cell contents as a formula. The function name identifies the operation to be performed. The *argument* is the value the function uses to perform a calculation, including a number, text, or a cell reference that acts as an operand. The argument follows the function name and is enclosed in parentheses. If a function contains more than one argument, commas separate the arguments.

$$=SUM(F6:F11)$$

Equal sign   Function name   Argument

FIGURE 5–1   Parts of a function

In the previous lesson, you used the Sum button to enter a formula with the SUM function, =SUM(F6:F11). The equal sign specifies that the cell entry is a formula. The function name SUM identifies the operation. Parentheses enclose the argument, which is the range of cells to add—in this case, cells F6 through F11. The function provides a simpler and faster way to enter the formula =F6+F7+F8+F9+F10+F11.

Entering Formulas with Functions

To enter a formula with a function, you need to do the following. First, start the formula with an equal sign. Second, select or enter the function you want to use. Third, select or enter the arguments. Finally, enter the completed formula. The results appear in the cell.

Because Excel includes so many functions, the best way to select a function is to use the Insert Function dialog box. To open the Insert Function dialog box, click the Insert Function button on the Formula Bar. From this dialog box, you can browse all of the available functions to select the one you want. First, click a category in the Or select a category box, and then click the function you want in the Select a function box. A brief description of the selected function appears near the bottom of the dialog box, as shown in **Figure 5–2**. Click OK. The Function Arguments dialog box then appears.

▶ **TIP**

If you know the function you want to enter, you can click the appropriate category button in the Function Library group on the Formulas tab of the Ribbon, click the function you want in the menu that appears, and then enter the arguments in the Function Arguments dialog box.

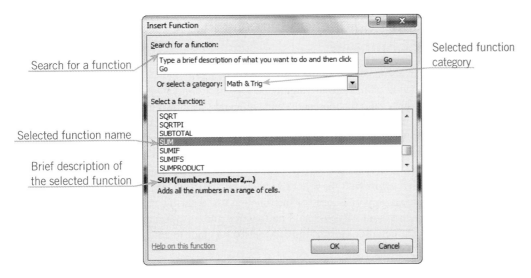

FIGURE 5–2   Insert Function dialog box

The Function Arguments dialog box, shown in **Figure 5–3**, provides a description of each argument you need to enter for the selected function. When an argument requires a cell or range, you can choose one of two ways to enter the reference. You can type the range directly in the appropriate argument box of the Function Arguments dialog box. Or, you can click in the appropriate argument box and then select the cell or range directly in the worksheet. When you select a range in the worksheet, the dialog box shrinks to show only the title bar and the argument box, so you can see more of the worksheet. It expands to the full size when you release the mouse button. You can also click the Collapse Dialog Box button on the right side of an argument box to shrink the dialog box so only its title bar and the argument box are displayed, and then click the Expand Dialog Box button to return the Function Arguments dialog box to its full size. After all the arguments are complete, click OK. The function is entered in the active cell.

EXTRA FOR EXPERTS

You can also use the Insert Function dialog box to find a specific function. In the Search for a function box, type a brief description of what you want to do. Then, click Go. A list of functions that match the description appears in the Select a function box. Double-click the appropriate function to open the Function Arguments dialog box.

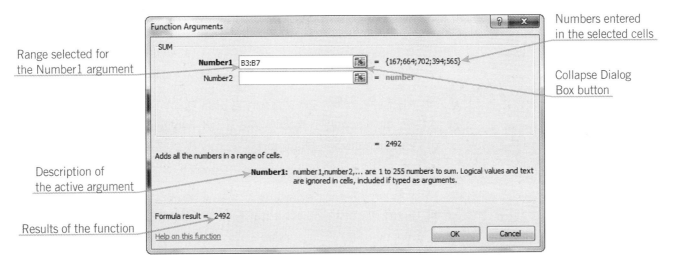

FIGURE 5–3   Function Arguments dialog box

Entering a Function Directly in a Cell Using Formula AutoComplete

You can also enter a formula with a function directly in a cell by typing an equal sign, the function name, and the argument. *Formula AutoComplete* helps you enter a formula with a valid function name and arguments, as shown in **Figure 5–4**. As you begin to type the function name, a list of function names appears below the active cell. The functions listed match the letters you have typed. For example, when you type *=s*, all functions that begin with the letter *s* appear in the list box, such as SEARCH, SECON, and SERISSUM. When you type *=su*, the list narrows to show only functions that begin with the letters *su*, such as SUBSTITUTE, SUBTOTAL, and SUM. Continue typing until you see the function you want. Then, double-click the name of the function you want to use. The function and its arguments appear in a ScreenTip below the cell. You can use the ScreenTip as a guide to enter the necessary arguments.

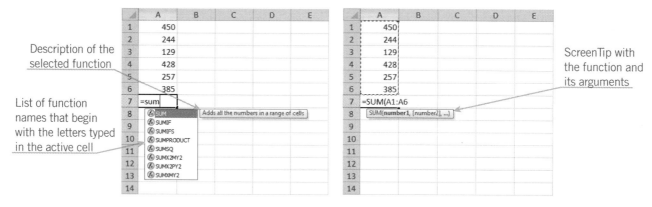

Description of the selected function

List of function names that begin with the letters typed in the active cell

ScreenTip with the function and its arguments

FIGURE 5–4   Formula AutoComplete

Step-by-Step 5.1

1. Open the **Functions.xlsx** workbook from the drive and folder where your Data Files are stored.

2. Save the workbook as **Functions Worksheet** followed by your initials.

3. Click cell **B10**.

4. On the Formula Bar, click the **Insert Function** button f_x. The Insert Function dialog box appears.

5. Next to the Or select a category box, click the **arrow**, and then click **Math & Trig**.

6. Scroll down the **Select a function** list, and then click **SUM**. The SUM function and a description of its purpose appear below the Select a function box, as shown in Figure 5–2.

7. Click **OK**. The Function Arguments dialog box appears with a range reference selected in the Number1 box. The Number1 argument is the range of cells whose values you want to add. Excel tried to "guess" which cells you want to add. You want to add a different range.

8. In the worksheet, select the range **B3:B7**. The Function Arguments dialog box collapses when you click a cell in the worksheet and expands when you release the mouse button. The value that will appear in cell B10, 2492, appears below the SUM function section and at the bottom of the dialog box, as shown in Figure 5–3.

9. Click **OK**. The formula in cell B10 is =SUM(B3:B7). The formula appears in the Formula Bar, and the results of the formula (2492) appear in cell B10.

10. Save the workbook, and leave it open for the next Step-by-Step.

> **TIP**
>
> You can also enter the formula with the SUM function in cell B10 by typing =*SUM(B3:B7)* or clicking the Sum button in the Editing group on the Home tab.

Types of Functions

Excel provides many functions you can use in formulas. Each function has a different purpose. The functions are organized by category, such as Math & Trig, Statistical, Financial, Logical, Date & Time, and Text. The next sections introduce some of the most common functions in each of these categories.

Mathematical and Trigonometric Functions

Mathematical functions and *trigonometric functions* manipulate quantitative data in a worksheet. Some mathematical operations, such as addition, subtraction, multiplication, and division, do not require functions. However, mathematical and trigonometric functions are particularly useful when you need to determine values such as logarithms, factorials, sines, cosines, tangents, and absolute values.

You already used a mathematical and trigonometric function when you created a formula with the SUM function. **Table 5–1** describes two other mathematical functions, the square root and rounding functions, as well as one trigonometric function, the natural logarithm. Notice that the rounding operation requires two arguments, which are separated by a comma.

> ▶ **VOCABULARY**
> **mathematical functions**
> **trigonometric functions**

TABLE 5–1 Commonly used mathematical and trigonometric functions

FUNCTION	RETURNS
SQRT(number)	The square root of the number in the argument. For example, =SQRT(C4) returns the square root of the value in cell C4.
ROUND(number,num_digits)	The number in the first argument rounded to the number of decimal places designated in the second argument. For example, =ROUND(14.23433,2) returns 14.23, which rounds the number in the first argument to two decimal places. If the second argument is a negative number, the first argument is rounded to the left of the decimal point. For example, =ROUND(142.3433,–2) returns 100.
LN(number)	The natural logarithm of a number. For example, =LN(50) returns 3.912023.

Step-by-Step 5.2

1. Click cell **B11**. On the Formula Bar, click the **Insert Function** button. The Insert Function dialog box appears.

2. Next to the Or select a category box, click the **arrow**, and then click **Math & Trig**, if it is not already selected.

3. Click the **Select a function** box, and then press the **S** key five times until *SQRT* is selected. Read the description of the function.

4. Click **OK**. The Function Arguments dialog box appears. Read the description of the argument.

5. In the Number box, type **B10**. You want to calculate the square root of the value in cell B10, which is 2492, as shown to the right of the Number box. The number that will appear in cell B11, 49.9199359, appears under the function and at the bottom of the dialog box next to Formula result =, as shown in **Figure 5–5**.

FIGURE 5–5
SQRT function argument

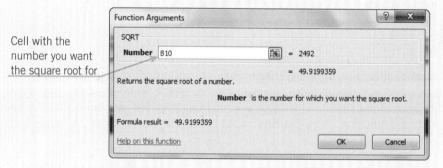

6. Click **OK**. The formula entered in cell B11 is =SQRT(B10), which calculates the square root of the value in cell B10—2492—and results in the value 49.9199359.

7. Click cell **B12**. On the Formula Bar, click the **Insert Function** button. The Insert Function dialog box appears with Math & Trig selected in the Or select a category box.

8. Click the **Select a function** box, and then press the **R** key five times to select ROUND.

9. Read the function's description. Click **OK**. The Function Arguments dialog box appears.

10. Read the description of the first argument. In the Number box, type **B11**.

11. Press the **Tab** key to place the insertion point in the Num_digits box. Read the description of the second argument.

12. Type **2**. The formula results appear below the function and at the bottom of the dialog box, as shown in **Figure 5–6**.

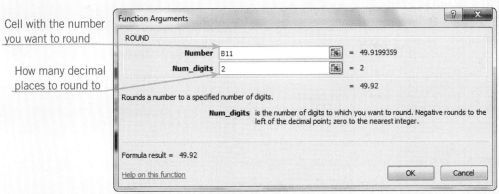

Cell with the number you want to round

How many decimal places to round to

FIGURE 5–6
ROUND function arguments

13. Click **OK**. The formula in cell B12 is =ROUND(B11,2), which rounds the value in cell B11 to two digits, displays the results of 49.92.

14. Save the workbook, and leave it open for the next Step-by-Step.

Statistical Functions

Statistical functions are used to describe quantities of data. For example, statistical functions can determine the average, standard deviation, or variance of a range of data. Statistical functions can also determine the number of values in a range, the largest value in a range, and the smallest value in a range. **Table 5–2** describes some of the statistical functions available in Excel. All the statistical functions contain a range for the argument. You can include multiple ranges by entering additional arguments. The range is the body of numbers the statistics will describe.

▶ **VOCABULARY**
statistical functions

TABLE 5–2 Commonly used statistical functions

FUNCTION	RETURNS
AVERAGE(number1,number2...)	The average (or mean) of the range; for example, =AVERAGE(E4:E9) returns the average of the numbers in the range E4:E9
COUNT(value1,value2...)	The number of cells in the range that contain numbers; for example, =COUNT(D6:D21) returns 16 if all the cells in the range contain numbers
COUNTA(value1,value2...)	The number of cells in the range that are not empty; for example, =COUNT(B4:B15) returns 11 if all the cells in the range contain data
MAX(number1,number2...)	The largest number in the range
MIN(number1,number2...)	The smallest number in the range
STDEV.P(number1,number2...)	The estimated standard deviation of the numbers in the range
VAR.P(number1,number2...)	The estimated variance of the numbers in the range

Step-by-Step 5.3

1. Click cell **B15**. On the Formula Bar, click the **Insert Function** button . The Insert Function dialog box appears. You want to find the average of values in the range B3:B7.

2. Next to the Or select a category box, click the **arrow**, and then click **Statistical**. The Statistical functions appear in the Select a function box.

3. In the Select a function box, click **AVERAGE**, and then click **OK**. The Function Arguments dialog box appears.

4. Next to the Number1 box, click the **Collapse Dialog Box** button. The Function Arguments dialog box shrinks to its title bar and Number1 box.

5. In the worksheet, drag to select the range **B3:B7**. The range reference appears in the Number1 box, as shown in **Figure 5–7**.

FIGURE 5–7
Collapsed Function
Arguments dialog box

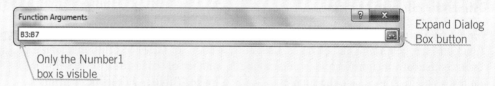

Only the Number1 box is visible

Expand Dialog Box button

6. Click the **Expand Dialog Box** button. The Function Arguments dialog box expands to its full size, as shown in **Figure 5–8**.

FIGURE 5–8
Expanded Function
Arguments dialog box

Selected range in the Number1 box

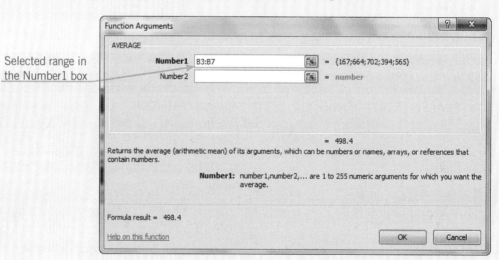

7. Click **OK**. The average of the values in the range B3:B7, which is 498.4, appears in cell B15.

8. Click cell **B16**. On the Formula Bar, click the **Insert Function** button. You want to find how many cells in the range B3:B7 contain numbers.

9. In the Or select a category box, click **Statistical**, if it is not already selected. In the Select a function box, double-click **COUNT**. The Function Arguments dialog box appears.

10. In the Value1 box, enter **B3:B7**, and then click **OK**. The number of cells in the range B3:B7 that contain numbers is 5.

11. Click cell **B17**, and then enter **=MAX(B3:B7)**. The largest number in the range B3:B7 is 702.

12. Click cell **B18**, and then enter **=MIN(B3:B7)**. The smallest number in the range B3:B7 is 167.

13. Click cell **B19**, and then enter **=STDEV.P(B3:B7)**. The standard deviation of the range B3:B7 is 196.9960406.

14. Click cell **B20**, and then enter **=VAR.P(B3:B7)**. The variance of the range B3:B7 is 38807.44.

15. Save the workbook, and leave it open for the next Step-by-Step.

Financial Functions

Financial functions are used to analyze loans and investments. Some commonly used financial functions are future value, present value, and payment, which are described in **Table 5–3**. Note that for these functions to return the correct value, the payment and the interest rate must have the same time period. For example, the payment period is usually expressed in months, whereas interest rates are commonly expressed in years. So, if the payment period is monthly, you must divide the annual interest rate by 12 to determine the monthly rate.

▶ **VOCABULARY**
financial functions

TABLE 5–3 Commonly used financial functions

FUNCTION	RETURNS
FV(rate,nper,pmt,pv,type)	The future value of an investment based on equal payments (third argument), at a fixed interest rate (first argument), for a specified number of periods (second argument). (The fourth and fifth arguments for the present value of the investment and the timing of the payments are optional.) For example, =FV(.08,5,−100) determines the future value of five $100 payments earning an 8% interest rate at the end of five years.
PV(rate,nper,pmt,fv,type)	The present value of a loan or an investment based on equal payments (third argument), at a fixed interest rate (first argument), for a specified number of payments (second argument). (The fourth and fifth arguments for the future value of the investment and the timing of the payments are optional.) For example, =PV(.1,5,−500) displays the current value of five payments of $500 at a 10% interest rate.
PMT(rate,nper,pv,fv,type)	The equal payments needed to repay a loan (third argument), at a fixed interest rate (first argument), in a specified number of periods (second argument). (The fourth and fifth arguments for the future value of the loan and the timing of the payments are optional.) For example, =PMT(.01,36,10000) displays the monthly payment needed to repay a $10,000 loan at a 1% monthly interest rate (12% annual interest rate divided by 12 months), for 36 months (three years multiplied by 12 months).

Scientists use Excel workbooks to help them as they conduct research. They record collected data in worksheets. Then they use statistical function formulas to analyze experimental results.

Step-by-Step 5.4

1. Click cell **B24**, and then enter **.015**. The annual interest rate of 1.5% appears in the cell.

2. Click cell **B25**, and then enter **6**, which is the number of payment periods—one payment each year for six years.

3. Click cell **B26**, and then enter **–250**. The annual payment of $(250.00) appears in the cell.

> **TIP**
>
> A negative number indicates a payment; a positive number indicates income. In this case, you use a negative number because you are making a payment to the bank.

4. Click cell **B27**. On the Formula Bar, click the **Insert Function** button ⨍ₓ. In the Insert Function dialog box, next to the Or select a category box, click the **arrow**, and then click **Financial**. In the Select a function box, click **FV**. Click **OK**.

5. In the Rate box, type **B24**, the cell with the annual interest rate. In the Nper box, type **B25**, the cell that contains the number of payment periods. In the Pmt box, type **B26**, the cell that contains the annual payment amount. See **Figure 5–9**.

FIGURE 5–9
FV function arguments

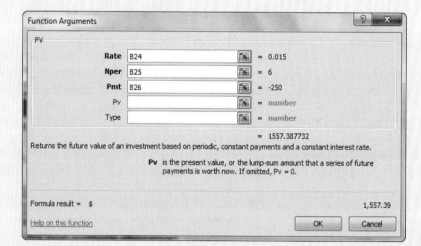

6. Click **OK**. As you can see in cell B27, the amount in the savings account will have grown to $1,557.39 after six years.

7. Click cell **B29**, and then enter **2.5**. The annual interest rate of 2.5% appears in the cell.

8. Click cell **B30**, and then enter **8**, which is the number of payment periods—one payment each year for eight years.

9. Click cell **B31**, and then enter **–210**. The annual payment of $(210.00) appears in the cell. (Remember, a negative number indicates a payment; a positive number indicates income. In this case, you use a negative number because you are making a payment.)

10. Click cell **B32**, and then enter **=PV(B29,B30,B31)** using Formula AutoComplete to help you enter the function accurately. The delayed payments are more profitable because the present value, $1,505.73, is greater than the immediate lump sum of $1,200.

11. Click cell **B34**, and then enter **1**. The monthly interest rate of 1.0% appears in the cell.

12. Click cell **B35**, and then enter **=5*12** to determine the number of monthly payment periods (the number of years, 5, multiplied by 12 months). The number of monthly payment periods, 60, appears in the cell.

13. Click cell **B36**, and then enter **6000**, which is the amount of the loan (the principal amount).

14. Click cell **B37**, and then enter **=PMT(B34,B35,B36)**, using Formula AutoComplete to help you enter the function accurately. The monthly payment ($133.47) appears in the cell in red. The parentheses around the number indicate that it is a negative number, and a payment.

TIP

The monthly interest rate is determined by dividing the annual interest rate by 12 months. In this case, the annual interest rate of 12% divided by 12 months equals 1%, which you entered in cell B34.

15. Click cell **B38**, and then enter **=(B37*B35)+B36** to determine the interest you will pay over the life of the loan. The formula multiples the monthly payment returned by the PMT function in cell B37 by the number of monthly payments stored in cell B35, and then adds the loan amount in cell B36. Because the payments are negative, you need to add the loan amount to calculate the difference between the total payments and the total principal. Under the conditions of this loan, you will pay a total of $2,008.00 in interest over the life of the loan, as shown in **Figure 5–10**.

FIGURE 5–10
Financial functions

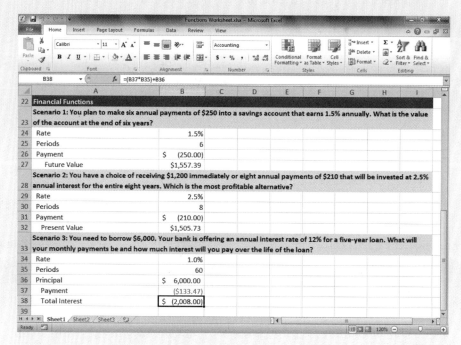

16. Insert a header with your name and the current date. Save, print, and close the workbook.

Logical Functions

▶ **VOCABULARY**
logical functions

Logical functions, such as the IF function, display text or values if certain conditions exist. In the IF function, the first argument sets a condition for comparison, called a *logical test*. The second argument determines the value that appears in the cell if the logical test is true. The third argument determines the value that appears in the cell if the logical test is false.

For example, a teacher might use the IF function to determine whether a student has passed or failed a course. The formula =IF(C4>60,"PASS","FAIL") returns *PASS* if the value in cell C4 is greater than 60; otherwise the formula returns *FAIL*.

Table 5–4 describes the IF, AND, OR, NOT, and IFERROR functions.

 TIP

You must use quotation marks to enclose the text you want the IF function to return in the second and third arguments. For example, =IF(B10<100,"Low Result","High Result").

TABLE 5–4 Commonly used logical functions

FUNCTION	RETURNS
IF(logical_test,value_if_true,value_if_false)	One value if the condition in the logical test is true, and another value if the condition in the logical test is false; for example, =IF(2+2=4, "Over", "Under") returns *Over*
AND(logical1,logical2,...)	TRUE if all of the arguments are true, and FALSE if any or all of the arguments are false; for example, =AND(1+1=2,1+2=3) returns *TRUE*, but =AND(1+1=2,1+2=4) returns *FALSE*
OR(logical1,logical2,...)	TRUE if any of the arguments are true, and FALSE if none of the arguments is true; for example, =OR(1+1=2,1+2=3) returns *TRUE*, and =OR(1+1=2,1+2=4) returns *TRUE*, but =OR(1+1=3,1+2=4) returns *FALSE*
NOT(logical)	TRUE if the argument is false, and FALSE if the argument is true; for example, =NOT(2+2=1) returns *TRUE*, but =NOT(2+2=4) returns *FALSE*
IFERROR(value,value_if_error)	The formula results if the first argument contains no error, and the specified value if the argument is incorrect; for example, =IFERROR(2+2=1, "Error in calculation") returns *Error in calculation*

Step-by-Step 5.5

1. Open the **Reynolds.xlsx** workbook from the drive and folder where your Data Files are stored.

2. Save the workbook as **Reynolds Optical** followed by your initials.

3. Click cell **D6**, and then type **=IF(B6<5,22.5,0)**. This formula returns 22.50 (the shipping fee) if the quantity in cell B6 is less than 5. If the quantity in cell B6 is not less than 5, then the formula returns 0.

4. Press the **Enter** key. This order has no shipping fee because the order quantity is six, more than the five cartons needed for free shipping.

5. Copy the formula in cell **D6** to the range **D7:D15**, and then click cell **A18**. The shipping fee is calculated for all the orders, as shown in **Figure 5–11**.

FIGURE 5–11
Shipping fee calculated with the IF function

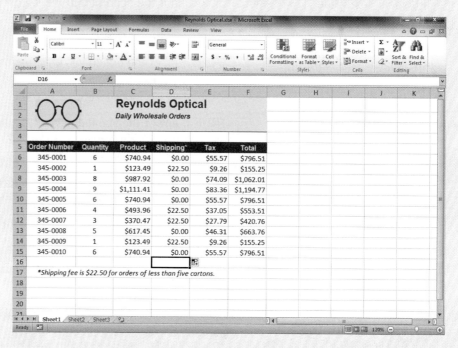

6. Insert a footer that includes your name and the current date. Save, print, and close the workbook.

Date and Time Functions

▶ **VOCABULARY**

date and time functions

Functions can also be used to insert dates and times in a worksheet. For example, *date and time functions* can be used to convert serial numbers to a month, a day, or a year. A date function can also be used to insert the current date or the current date and time. **Table 5–5** describes the DATE, NOW, and TODAY functions.

TABLE 5–5   Commonly used date and time functions

FUNCTION	RETURNS
DATE(year,month,day)	The date specified in the year, month, and day arguments, which are entered as numbers. For example, =DATE(2013,5,23) returns 5/23/2013.
NOW()	The current date and time based on the computer's date and time settings. For example, =NOW() returns the current date and time, such as 5/23/2013 22:05. This function has no arguments.
TODAY()	The current date based on the computer's date setting and formatted as a date. For example, =TODAY() returns the current date, such as 5/23/2013. This function has no arguments.

Text Functions

Text functions are used to format and display cell contents. A text function can be used to convert text in a cell to all uppercase or lowercase letters. Text functions can also be used to repeat data contained in another cell. These functions are described in **Table 5–6**. Note that if you enter text instead of a cell reference in the argument, the text must be enclosed within quotation marks.

▶ **VOCABULARY**

text functions

TABLE 5–6   Commonly used text functions

FUNCTION	OPERATION
PROPER(text)	Converts the first letter of each word in the specified cell to uppercase and the rest to lowercase.
LOWER(text)	Converts all letters in the specified cell to lowercase.
UPPER(text)	Converts all letters in the specified cell to uppercase.
SUBSTITUTE(text,old_text,new_text,instance_num)	Replaces existing text (the second argument) in a specified cell (the first argument) with new text (the third argument). If you omit the optional fourth argument, instance_num, every occurrence of the text is replaced. For example, =SUBSTITUTE(C2,"Income","Revenue") replaces every instance of the word *Income* in cell C2 with the word *Revenue*.
REPT(text,number_times)	Repeats the text (first argument) in the specified cell a specified number of times (second argument). For example, =REPT(B6,3) repeats the text in cell B6 three times.

Step-by-Step 5.6

1. Open the **Finances.xlsx** workbook from the drive and folder where your Data Files are stored.

2. In cell **A1**, replace the word *NAME* with your name.

3. In cell **B13**, enter **=NOW()**. The current date and time appear in the cell.

4. Click cell **B13**. On the Home tab, in the Number group, click the **Number Format arrow**, and then click **General**. The date changes to the serial number Excel uses to express the current date and time.

5. On the Home tab, in the Number group, click the **Number Format arrow**, and then click **Short Date**. The date changes to the form 5/23/2013.

6. On the Quick Access Toolbar, click the **Undo** button 🔄 twice. The current date and time in cell B13 return to their original format.

7. Click cell **B14**. You want to repeat the text in cell A1 in cell B14.

8. Click the **Formulas** tab on the Ribbon. In the Function Library group, click the **Text** button, and then click **REPT**. The Function Arguments dialog box appears.

9. In the Text box, enter **A1**. In the Number_times box, enter **1**. The contents of cell A1 will be repeated once in cell B14.

10. Click **OK**. The title in cell A1 is repeated in cell B14.

11. Save the workbook using the contents of cell B14 as the file name. Your screen should look similar to **Figure 5–12**.

FIGURE 5–12
Date & Time and
Text functions

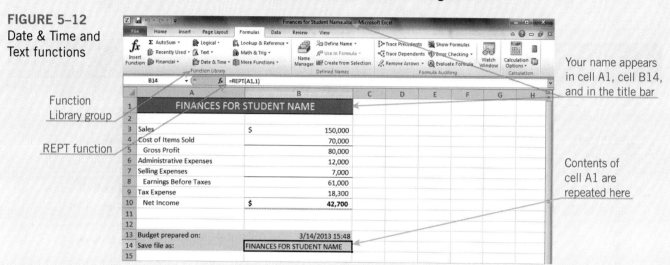

12. Print and close the workbook.

SUMMARY

In this lesson, you learned:

- A function is a shorthand way to write an equation that performs a calculation. A formula with a function has three parts: an equal sign, a function name, and for most functions one argument, which acts as an operand.

- The best way to select a function is from the Insert Function dialog box. The Function Arguments dialog box provides a description of each argument you enter for the function.

- When you type a formula with a function directly in a worksheet cell, Formula AutoComplete helps you enter a formula with a valid function name and arguments.

- Functions can be used to perform mathematical, statistical, financial, and logical operations. They can also be used to insert and calculate dates and times and to format text.

■ VOCABULARY REVIEW

Define the following terms:

argument
date and time functions
financial functions
Formula AutoComplete

function
logical functions
mathematical functions

statistical functions
text functions
trigonometric functions

◼ REVIEW QUESTIONS

TRUE / FALSE

Circle T if the statement is true or F if the statement is false.

T   F   **1.**   Formulas with functions have three parts: an equal sign, a function name, and usually an argument.

T   F   **2.**   The argument identifies the function to be performed.

T   F   **3.**   You select the function you want to use in the Function Arguments dialog box.

T   F   **4.**   The COUNTA function returns the number of cells in the range identified in the argument that contain data.

T   F   **5.**   The OR function displays one value if the specified condition is true and a different value if the condition is false.

WRITTEN QUESTIONS

Write a brief answer to each of the following questions.

1. What is a function?

2. Write the formula with a function that would add all the values in cells D6, D7, and D8.

3. Explain what happens when you click the Insert Function button on the Formula Bar.

4. What does the SQRT function return?

5. What does the TODAY function return?

FILL IN THE BLANK

Complete the following sentences by writing the correct word or words in the blanks provided.

1. The _____ is (are) enclosed in parentheses in a formula with a function.

2. The _____ dialog box specifies arguments to be included in the function.

3. _____ functions manipulate quantitative data in a worksheet.

4. _____ functions are used to analyze loans and investments.

5. _____ functions display text or values if certain conditions exist.

■ PROJECTS

If you have a SAM 2010 user profile, your instructor may have assigned an autogradable version of the indicated project. If so, log into the SAM 2010 Web site at *www.cengage.com/sam2010* to download the instruction and start files.

PROJECT 5–1

Write the appropriate formula to perform each of the described operations. Refer to Tables 5–1 through 5–6 to help you determine the function and its arguments.

_____ 1. Add all the values in the range F14:F42.

_____ 2. Determine the largest value in the range J45:J102.

_____ 3. Determine the average of the values in the range L29:L40.

_____ 4. Determine the smallest value in the range X14:X92.

_____ 5. Determine the standard deviation of the values in the range K4:K33.

_____ 6. Determine the yearly payments on a $4,500 loan at 8% for 7 years.

_____ 7. Determine the value of a savings account at the end of 5 years, after making five yearly payments of $475 each and earning 3%.

_____ 8. Round the value in cell E3 to the tenths place.

_____ 9. Determine the present value of a pension plan that will pay you 20 yearly payments of $7,000 each; the current rate of return is 7.5%.

_____ 10. Determine the square root of 375.

_____ 11. Determine the variance of the values in the range G9:G35.

_____ 12. Determine how many cells in the range H7:H24 contain numbers.

SAM PROJECT 5–2

1. Open the **National.xlsx** workbook from the drive and folder where your Data Files are stored.

2. Save the workbook as **National Bank** followed by your initials.

3. In cell B12, enter the PMT function to calculate the yearly payment for borrowers. The lending rate will be entered in cell B8, the term of the loan will be entered in cell B10, and the loan principal (or present value) will be entered in cell B6. (The formula results are *#NUM!*, indicating a number error because you haven't entered data in the argument's cell references yet.)

4. A potential borrower inquires about the payments on a $6,500 loan for four years. The current lending rate is 6%. Determine the yearly payment on the loan. (The number in cell B12 is a negative number because this amount must be paid.)

5. Insert a header with your name and the current date.

6. Print the portion of the worksheet that pertains to the loan (the range A2:C15) to give to the potential borrower.

7. In cell B25, enter the FV function to calculate the future value of periodic payments for depositors. The interest rate will be entered in cell B23, the term of the payments will be entered in cell B21, and the yearly payments will be entered in cell B19. (The formula results show *$0.00*, because you haven't entered data in the argument's cell references yet.)

8. A potential depositor is starting a college fund for her child. She inquires about the value of yearly deposits of $2,575 at the end of 18 years. The current interest rate is 4.5%. Determine the future value of the deposits. (Remember to enter the deposit as a negative number because the depositor must pay this amount.)

9. Print the portion of the worksheet that pertains to the investment (the range A15:C27) to give to the potential depositor.

10. Save and close the workbook.

PROJECT 5–3

1. Open the **Exam.xlsx** workbook from the drive and folder where your Data Files are stored.

2. Save the workbook as **Exam Scores** followed by your initials.

3. In cell B25, enter a formula with a function to determine the number of students who took the examination.

4. In cell B26, enter a formula with a function to determine the average exam grade.

5. In cell B27, enter a formula with a function to determine the highest exam grade.

6. In cell B28, enter a formula with a function to determine the lowest exam grade.

7. In cell B29, enter a formula with a function to determine the standard deviation of the exam grades.

8. Format cells B26 and B29 to display two digits to the right of the decimal.

9. Insert a header with your name and the current date. Save, print, and close the workbook.

PROJECT 5–4

The Tucson Coyotes have just completed seven preseason professional basketball games. Coach Patterson will soon be entering a press conference in which he is expected to talk about the team's performance for the upcoming season. Coach Patterson wants to be well informed about player performance before entering the press conference.

Part 1

1. Open the **Coyotes.xlsx** workbook from the drive and folder where your Data Files are stored.

2. Save the workbook as **Coyotes Stats** followed by your initials.

3. In cell J6, enter a function that adds the values in the range B6:I6.

4. Copy the formula in cell J6 to the range J7:J12.

5. In cell J19, enter a function that adds the values in the range B19:I19.

6. Copy the formula in cell J19 to the range J20:J25.

7. In cell B13, enter a function that averages the game points in the range B6:B12.

8. In cell B14, enter a function that calculates the standard deviation of the game points in the range B6:B12.

9. In cell B15, enter a function that counts the number of cells that contain data in the range B6:B12.

10. Copy the formulas in the range B13:B15 to the range C13:I15.

11. In cell B26, enter a function that averages the rebounds in the range B19:B25.

12. In cell B27, enter a function that calculates the standard deviation of the rebounds in the range B19:B25.

13. In cell B28, enter a function that counts the number of cells that contain data in the range B19:B25.

14. Copy the formulas in the range B26:B28 to the range C26:I28.

15. Insert a footer with your name and the current date. Save and print the workbook, and leave it open.

Part 2

Based on the Coyotes Stats workbook you prepared, indicate in the blanks the names of the players who are likely to be mentioned in the following interview. When you have finished filling in the blanks, close the workbook.

Reporter: You have had a very successful preseason. Three players seem to be providing the leadership needed for a winning record.

Patterson: Basketball teams win by scoring points. It's no secret that we rely on (1) _____, (2) _____, and (3) _____ to get those points. All three average at least 10 points per game.

Reporter: One player seems to have a problem with consistency.

Patterson: (4) _____ has his good games and his bad games. He is a young player and we have been working with him. As the season progresses, I think you will find him to be a more reliable offensive talent.

(*Hint*: One indication of consistent scoring is the standard deviation. A high standard deviation might indicate high fluctuation of points from game to game. A low standard deviation might indicate that the scoring level is relatively consistent.)

Reporter: What explains the fact that (5) _____ is both an effective scorer and your leading rebounder?

Patterson: He is a perceptive player. When playing defense, he is constantly planning how to get the ball back to the other side of the court.

Reporter: Preseason injuries can be heartbreaking. How has this affected the team?

Patterson: (6) _____ has not played since being injured in the game against Kansas City. He is an asset to the team. We are still waiting to hear from the doctors whether he will be back soon.

Reporter: It is the end of the preseason. That is usually a time when teams make cuts. Of your healthy players, (7) _____ is the lowest scorer. Will you let him go before the beginning of the regular season?

Patterson: I don't like to speculate on cuts or trades before they are made. We'll just have to wait and see.

PROJECT 5–5

1. Open the **Golf.xlsx** workbook from the drive and folder where your Data Files are stored.

2. Save the workbook as **Golf Tryouts** followed by your initials. A player must average a score of less than 76 to qualify for the team.

3. In cell I5, enter a function that displays *Made* if the average score in cell H5 is less than 76 and *Cut* if the score is not less than 76. (*Hint*: The IF function has three arguments. The first argument is the logical test that determines whether the value in cell H5 is less than 76. The second argument is the text that appears if the statement is true. The third argument is the text that appears if the statement is false. Because the items to be displayed are words rather than numbers, they must be entered within quotation marks.)

4. Copy the formula from cell I5 to the range I6:I16.

5. In cell B21, enter a function that displays today's date.

6. Click cell B22, and then enter your name.

7. Save, print, and close the workbook.

PROJECT 5–6

1. Open the **Xanthan.xlsx** workbook from the drive and folder where your Data Files are stored.

2. Save the workbook as **Xanthan Promotion** followed by your initials.

3. In cell B7, enter **75** as the supervisor rating of leadership potential. In cell B8, enter **80** as the supervisor rating of understanding of duties. In cell B9, enter **90** as the supervisor rating of willingness to work hard.

4. In cell B12, enter a function that determines the average of the values in the range B7:B10.

5. Format cell B12 in the Number format with no decimal places.

6. In cell B13, enter an IF function that displays *Promotion* if the average score in cell B12 is greater than or equal to 80 and *No Promotion* if the average score is less than 80.

7. Format the contents of cell B13 as bold and centered.

8. In cell B10, enter each of the following test scores, one at a time, and watch the average score: **70**, **78**, **82**, **85**, and **90**. Which scores will result in a promotion?

9. Insert a footer with your name and the current date. Save, print, and close the workbook.

■ CRITICAL THINKING

ACTIVITY 5–1

You are considering purchasing a car and want to compare prices offered by different dealerships. Some dealerships have cars that include the accessories you want; others need to add the accessories for an additional price. Prepare a worksheet similar to the one shown in **Figure 5–13**.

Perform the following operations to provide information that will be useful to making the car purchase decision.

■ In the range D3:D7, enter formulas that add the values in column B to the values in column C.

■ In cell D9, enter a function that determines the highest price in the range D3:D7.

■ In cell D10, enter a function that determines the lowest price in the range D3:D7.

■ In cell D11, enter a function that determines the average price in the range D3:D7.

	A	B	C	D
1	**Price Comparison by Dealership**			
2	Dealer	Base Price	Accessories	Total
3	Bernalillo New and Used	$ 19,900	$ 1,600	
4	Los Alamos Auto	$ 23,050	$ 2,300	
5	Mountain Auto Sales	$ 26,000	$ 2,200	
6	Sandia Car Sales	$ 27,900	$ 1,200	
7	Truchas Truck & Auto	$ 26,500	$ 3,000	
8				
9			Highest Price	
10			Lowest Price	
11			Average Price	

FIGURE 5–13

ACTIVITY 5–2

The Insert Function dialog box contains a Search for a function box, as shown in **Figure 5–14**. When you enter a brief description of what you want to do and click Go, Excel will list functions best suited for the task you want to perform.

Suppose you are preparing a large worksheet in which all cells in a range should contain data. You want to enter a function near the end of a range that displays the number of cells in the range that are blank. If a number other than zero appears as the function result, you will know that you must search for the cell or cells that are empty and enter the appropriate data.

Create a new workbook, and then open the Insert Function dialog box. Enter a description in the Search for a function box that will find a function to count the number of empty cells in a range. If more than one function is suggested, click each function in the Select a function box and read the description of the function that appears below the box. Which function is most appropriate to complete this task?

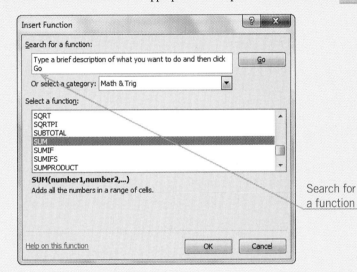

FIGURE 5–14

ACTIVITY 5–3

A manufacturing company prepares a budget each month. At the end of the month, the Accounting Department prepares a report similar to the one shown in **Figure 5–15**, which compares the actual amount spent to the budgeted amount.

Write an IF function you can use to draw attention to an item that exceeded its budget.

	A	B	C	D
1	**Manufacturing Expense Report**			
2		**Budget**	**Actual**	**Variance**
3	Labor	$64,000	$72,000	($8,000)
4	Raw Material A	$48,000	$47,900	$100
5	Raw Material B	$39,750	$42,000	($2,250)
6	Overhead	$125,000	$122,750	$2,250
7				

FIGURE 5–15

LESSON 6

Enhancing a Worksheet

■ OBJECTIVES

Upon completion of this lesson, you should be able to:

- Sort and filter data in a worksheet.
- Apply conditional formatting to highlight data.
- Hide worksheet columns and rows.
- Insert a shape, SmartArt graphic, picture, and screenshot in a worksheet.
- Use a template to create a new workbook.
- Insert a hyperlink in a worksheet.
- Save a workbook in a different file format.
- Insert, edit, and delete comments in a worksheet.
- Use the Research task pane.

■ VOCABULARY

ascending sort

comment

conditional formatting

descending sort

filter

filter arrow

hyperlink

object

picture

Research task pane

screen clipping

screenshot

shape

SmartArt graphic

sort

template

There are many ways to enhance the appearance of a workbook. You can arrange the data in a meaningful order, display only the data related to a specific question, or highlight data that meets certain criteria. You can hide rows or columns to help focus attention on specific data or results. You can add shapes, graphics, and pictures to a worksheet. You can use a template to create many worksheets with the same basic structure. You can add a link to a worksheet that jumps to another part of the worksheet, another file, or a Web site. You can save a workbook in a different format, making it available in other programs or versions of Excel. Finally, you can add comments to worksheet cells to document their contents. You will learn to do all these tasks in this lesson.

Sorting Data

Data entry often occurs in an order that is not necessarily best for understanding and analysis. *Sorting* rearranges data in a more meaningful order. For example, you might want to sort a list of names in alphabetical order. In an *ascending sort*, data with letters is arranged in alphabetical order (A to Z), data with numbers is arranged from smallest to largest, and data with dates is arranged from earliest to latest. The reverse order occurs in a *descending sort*, which arranges data with letters from Z to A, data with numbers from largest to smallest, and data with dates from oldest to newest. When you sort data contained in columns of a worksheet, Excel does not include the column headings.

To sort data, you first click a cell in the column you want to sort. Click the Data tab on the Ribbon. In the Sort & Filter group, click the Sort A to Z button for an ascending text sort or click the Sort Z to A button for a descending text sort. The button names change depending on what type of data you selected for sorting. For numerical data, the buttons are Sort Smallest to Largest and Sort Largest to Smallest. For date and time data, the buttons are Sort Oldest to Newest and Sort Newest to Oldest.

You can sort by more than one column of data. For example, you might want to sort a list of names in alphabetical order by last name and then within last names by first name. In this case, you need to create a sort with different levels of criteria. The last name is the first-level sort and the first name is the second-level sort. You set up a sort with multiple levels in the Sort dialog box, which is shown in **Figure 6–1**. To open the Sort dialog box, click the Sort button in the Sort & Filter group on the Data tab of the Ribbon. You set up the first-level sort by selecting the column to use in the Sort by row in the Sort dialog box. The Column box indicates the column that will be used for the first-level sort, such as Last Name. The Sort On box indicates the type of data to be sorted, which is usually Values. If data is formatted with different font or fill colors, you can sort the data by color. The Order box specifies whether the sort is ascending or descending. To create an additional sort level, such as for the First Name column, click Add Level. The Then by row is added to the dialog box. You set up the second-level (and each next-level) sort by selecting the sort column, the data type, and the sort order, just as you did for the first-level sort. After creating all the sort levels, click OK. The data is rearranged in the order you specified.

TIP

The Sort commands are also available on the Home tab of the Ribbon and on a shortcut menu. On the Home tab, in the Editing group, click the Sort & Filter button to open a menu with the Sort commands. Or, right-click a cell in the column you want to sort, and then point to Sort on the shortcut menu to open a submenu of Sort commands. In either case, click the appropriate Sort command.

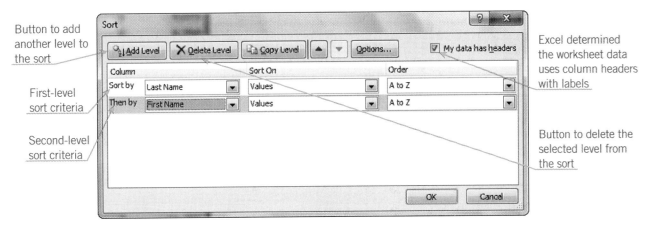

Button to add another level to the sort

First-level sort criteria

Second-level sort criteria

Excel determined the worksheet data uses column headers with labels

Button to delete the selected level from the sort

FIGURE 6–1   Sort dialog box

Step-by-Step 6.1

1. Open the **Salary.xlsx** workbook from the drive and folder where your Data Files are stored.

2. Save the workbook as **Salary List** followed by your initials.

3. Click cell **D4**. Clicking any cell in column D indicates that you want to sort by the Salary data in column D.

4. Click the **Data** tab on the Ribbon, and then locate the **Sort & Filter** group. This group includes the buttons for sorting in ascending or descending order and opening the Sort dialog box.

5. In the Sort & Filter group, click the **Sort Smallest to Largest** button. The data in the range A4:D29 is sorted in ascending order by the numerical values in column D.

6. On the Data tab, in the Sort & Filter group, click the **Sort** button. The Sort dialog box appears. The sort you just created appears as the first-level sort in the Sort by row.

7. In the Column column, click the **Sort by arrow**, and then click **Last Name**. Notice that the column headings from the Salary data appear in the Sort by list. Values is already selected in the Sort On column.

8. In the Order column, click the **arrow**, and then click **A to Z**, if it is not already selected.

9. Click **Add Level**. A Then by row is added so you can specify the second-level sort.

10. In the Column column, click the **Then by arrow**, and then click **First Name**. Values is already selected in the Sort On box.

11. In the Order column, click the **arrow**, and then click **A to Z**, if it is not already selected. Your Sort dialog box should match Figure 6–1.

12. Click **OK**. The data is sorted by last name and then by first name, as shown in **Figure 6–2**.

FIGURE 6–2
Data sorted by last name and then by first name

Sort buttons

Then data is sorted in alphabetical order by first name

Data is sorted first in alphabetical order by last name

Three employees with the last name *Brown* are sorted in alphabetical order by their first names

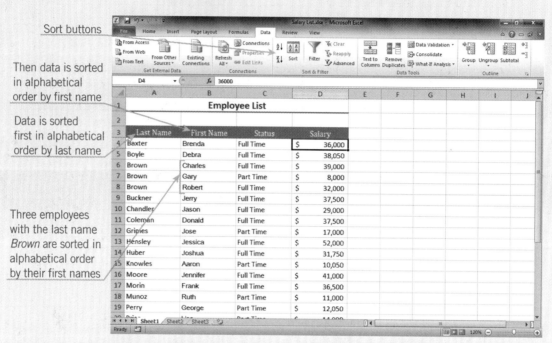

13. Save the workbook, and leave it open for the next Step-by-Step.

Filtering Data

TIP

The Filter commands are also available on the Home tab of the Ribbon and on a shortcut menu. On the Home tab, in the Editing group, click the Sort & Filter button to access the Filter commands. Or, right-click the cell in the column you want to filter, and then point to Filter on the shortcut menu to open a submenu of Filter commands. In either case, click the appropriate command.

Filtering displays a subset of data that meets certain criteria and temporarily hides the rows that do not meet the specified criteria. For example, you could filter a list of employees to show only those employees who work full time. The rows that contain part-time employees are then hidden, but these employees are not deleted from the worksheet.

You can filter by value, by criteria, or by color. On the Data tab of the Ribbon, in the Sort & Filter group, click the Filter button. *Filter arrows* appear in the lower-right corners of the cells with column labels. When you click a filter arrow, the AutoFilter menu for that column appears, as shown in **Figure 6–3**. The AutoFilter menu displays a list of all the values that appear in that column along with additional criteria and color filtering options. When you select one of the values, the filter is applied to the data to display only those rows in the worksheet in which that value is entered in the filtered column.

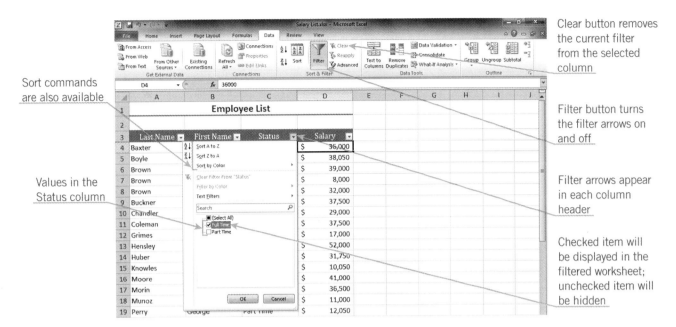

Sort commands are also available

Values in the Status column

Clear button removes the current filter from the selected column

Filter button turns the filter arrows on and off

Filter arrows appear in each column header

Checked item will be displayed in the filtered worksheet; unchecked item will be hidden

FIGURE 6–3   AutoFilter menu

The Number, Text, and Data AutoFilters provide different filtering options. For example, you can use comparison operators, such as equals, between, and begins with, to select data. You can also filter numbers based on their relative values, such as the top 10, above average, or below average. If you select the Top 10 number filter, the Top 10 AutoFilter dialog box appears, as shown in **Figure 6–4**. In the Top 10 AutoFilter dialog box, you can choose to show the largest (top) or smallest (bottom) values in the column. For example, you might show the rows with the 10 largest values in that column of the worksheet. However, you can change the specifications in the dialog box to show a different number of items or a percentage, such as the Bottom 50 Items or the Top 10 Percent.

TIP

Unlike sorting, filtering does not rearrange the order of the data, although you can sort the data that is filters. If you copy, format, and print data that is filtered, only the visible data are affected. If data is formatted with different font or fill colors, you can filter the data by color.

The rank of items to show

The number of items or percentages to show

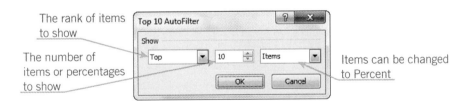

Items can be changed to Percent

FIGURE 6–4   Top 10 AutoFilter dialog box

When a column is filtered, the filter arrow icon changes from ⬚ to ⬚. When you want to see all the data in a worksheet again, you can restore all the rows by clearing the filter. Click the filter arrow, and then click the Clear Filter From command or click the Clear button in the Sort & Filter group on the Data tab of the Ribbon. To hide the filter arrows, click the Filter button in the Sort & Filter group.

EXTRA FOR EXPERTS

You can apply more than one filter to data to further limit the subset of data. For example, you might filter an employee list to show all part-time employees, and then filter the list of part-time employees to show only employees with salaries of greater than $10,000.

Step-by-Step 6.2

1. Click cell **C4**.

2. On the Data tab, in the Sort & Filter group, click the **Filter** button. Filter arrows appear on cells A3 through D3, which are the cells with the column labels.

3. In cell C3, click the **filter arrow**. The AutoFilter menu appears.

4. Click the **(Select All)** check box. All of the column values are deselected.

5. Click the **Full Time** check box. The Part Time check box remains deselected on the AutoFilter menu, as shown in Figure 6–3.

6. Click **OK**. The list of employees is filtered to show only the full-time workers. All of the part-time employees are hidden.

7. In cell D3, click the **filter arrow**. You'll add a second filter to show the 10 full-time employees who earn the highest salaries.

8. On the AutoFilter menu, point to **Number Filters**, and then click **Top 10**. The Top 10 AutoFilter dialog box appears, as shown in Figure 6–4.

9. Click **OK**. The worksheet is filtered to show the 10 employees who work full time and earn the highest salaries.

10. Insert a footer that includes your name and the current date. Save and print the workbook. Switch to Normal view.

11. Click the **Data** tab on the Ribbon. In the Sort & Filter group, click the **Clear** button. The filter is removed from the worksheet, and all of the employees are visible.

12. On the Data tab, in the Sort & Filter group, click the **Filter** button. The filter arrows disappear from the cells with the column labels.

13. Save the workbook, and leave it open for the next Step-by-Step.

Applying Conditional Formatting

Conditional formatting changes the appearance of cells that meet a specified condition. Conditional formatting helps you analyze and understand data by highlighting cells that answer a question, such as "Which employees have worked for the company for more than three years?" The Highlight Cells Rules format cells based on comparison operators such as greater than, less than, between, and equal to. You can also highlight cells that contain specific text, a certain date, or even duplicate values. The Top/Bottom Rules format cells based on their rank, such as the top 10 items, the bottom 15%, or those that are above average compared to the rest of the values in the range. You specify the number of items or the percentage to include.

To add conditional formatting, select the range you want to analyze. On the Home tab, in the Styles group, click the Conditional Formatting button, point to Highlight Cells Rules or Top/Bottom Rules, and then click the condition you want. In the dialog box that appears, enter the appropriate criteria, select the formatting you want, and then click OK. The conditional formatting is applied to the selected range. To remove the conditional formatting, click the Conditional Formatting button, point to Clear Rules, and then click Clear Rules from Selected Cells or Clear Rules from Entire Sheet.

▶ **VOCABULARY**
Conditional formatting

TIP

If you update the data in a range, the conditional formatting changes to reflect the new values. Consider a worksheet that conditionally formats employee salaries to highlight the top five salaries. If an employee receives a raise that changes her salary rank from sixth to fifth, this employee's salary is conditionally formatted and the employee's salary previously ranked as fifth is cleared of conditional formatting.

Step-by-Step 6.3

1. Select the range **D4:D29**. These cells contain the salaries for each of the 26 employees.

2. Click the **Home** tab on the Ribbon. In the Styles group, click the **Conditional Formatting** button. The Conditional Formatting menu appears.

3. Point to **Top/Bottom Rules**. The Top/Bottom Rules submenu appears, as shown in **Figure 6–5**.

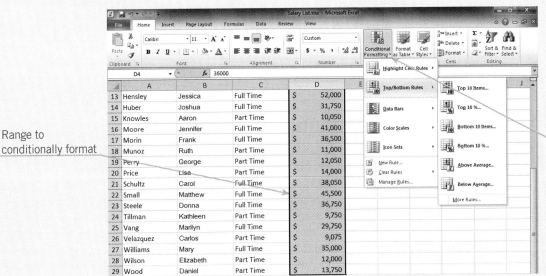

Range to conditionally format

FIGURE 6–5
Top/Bottom Rules submenu on the Conditional Formatting menu

Button to open the Conditional Formatting menu

4. Click **Top 10 Items**. The Top 10 Items dialog box appears, as shown in **Figure 6–6**.

FIGURE 6–6
Top 10 Items
dialog box

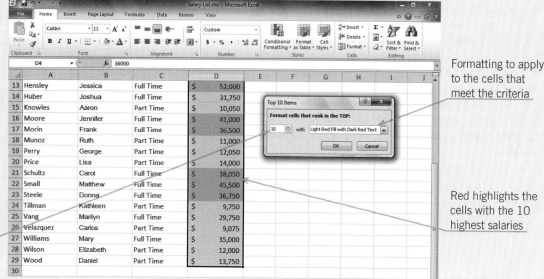

Number of cells to format

Formatting to apply to the cells that meet the criteria

Red highlights the cells with the 10 highest salaries

5. Type **5** in the left box to reduce the number of salaries to the top five.

6. Click **OK**. The five highest salaries appear in red text on a red background.

7. On the Home tab, in the Styles group, click the **Conditional Formatting** button.

8. On the Conditional Formatting menu, point to **Top/Bottom Rules**, and then click **Bottom 10 Items**. The Bottom 10 Items dialog box appears.

9. Type **5** in the left box, click the **arrow**, and then click **Yellow Fill with Dark Yellow Text**.

10. Click **OK**. Click any cell in column E to deselect the range. The five lowest salaries appear in yellow text on a yellow background.

11. Save, print, and close the workbook. Leave Excel open for the next Step-by-Step.

TIP

You can also display and hide selected rows and columns using the Ribbon. Click the Home tab. In the Cells group, click the Format button. On the Format menu that appears, in the Visibility section, point to Hide & Unhide. Use the commands on the submenu that opens to hide or unhide (display) the selected rows, columns, or sheet.

Hiding Columns and Rows

Hiding a row or column temporarily removes it from view. Hiding rows and columns enables you to use the same worksheet to view different data. For example, you can hide monthly data and display only the total values. To hide data, select the rows or columns you want to hide, and then right-click the selection. On the shortcut menu that appears, click Hide to remove the selection from view in the worksheet. You can repeat this process to hide as many rows and columns in the worksheet as you like. Hidden rows and columns remain out of sight until you redisplay them. To display hidden data, select the row or column on each side of the hidden rows or columns you want to redisplay. Right-click the selection, and then click Unhide on the shortcut menu.

Step-by-Step 6.4

1. Open the **Titus.xlsx** workbook from the drive and folder where your Data Files are stored.

2. Save the workbook as **Titus Oil** followed by your initials.

3. Select columns **B** through **G**. You'll hide the monthly data for the oil wells.

4. Right-click the selected columns. On the shortcut menu that appears, click **Hide**. Columns B through G are hidden.

5. Click cell **I1** to deselect the range. The worksheet shows the six-month production total for each well in the field, as shown in **Figure 6–7**.

Columns B through G are hidden

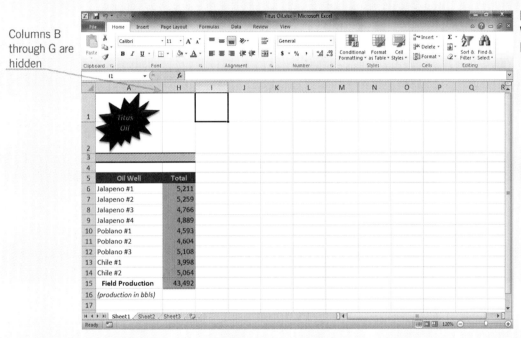

FIGURE 6–7
Worksheet with hidden columns

6. Insert a footer with your name and the current date. Save and print the workbook. Return to Normal view.

7. Select columns **A** and **H**. These columns surround the hidden columns.

8. Right-click the selected columns. On the shortcut menu that appears, click **Unhide**. Columns B through G reappear.

9. Select rows **6** through **14**. You'll hide individual oil well data, leaving only the monthly totals.

10. Right-click the selected rows, and then click **Hide** on the shortcut menu. Rows 6 through 14 are hidden.

11. Click cell **A19** to deselect the range. The worksheet shows only the field production totals for each month. Save and print the workbook.

12. Select rows **5** and **15**. These rows surround the hidden rows.

13. Right-click the selected rows, and then click **Unhide** on the shortcut menu. Rows 6 through 14 reappear in the worksheet. Click cell **A4** to deselect the rows.

14. Save the workbook, and leave it open for the next Step-by-Step.

Adding a Shape to a Worksheet

Shapes, such as rectangles, circles, arrows, lines, flowchart symbols, and callouts, can help make a worksheet more informative. For example, you might use a rectangle or circle to create a corporate logo. Or, you might use a callout to explain a value in the worksheet. Excel has a gallery of shapes you can use.

Inserting a Shape

To open the Shapes gallery, click the Insert tab on the Ribbon, and then, in the Illustrations group, click the Shapes button. In the Shapes gallery that appears, as shown in **Figure 6–8**, click the shape you want to insert. The pointer changes to a crosshair, which you click and drag in the worksheet to draw the shape. The shape is inserted in the worksheet.

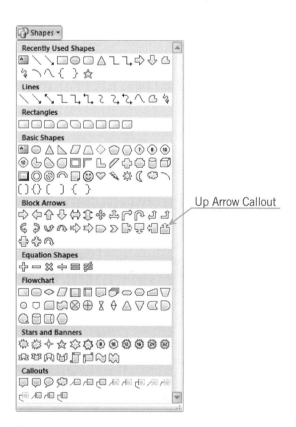

FIGURE 6–8   Shapes gallery

Modifying a Shape

Shapes are inserted in the worksheet as objects. An *object* is anything that appears on the screen that you can select and work with as a whole, such as a shape, picture, or chart. When the shape is selected, the Drawing Tools appear on the Ribbon and contain the Format tab, as shown in **Figure 6–9**. You use the tools on the Format tab to modify the shape. For example, you can change the shape's style, fill, and outline as well as add special effects, such as shadows. You can also move and resize the selected shape.

▶ **VOCABULARY**
object

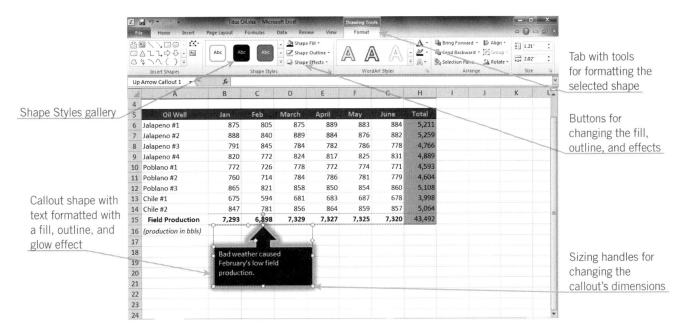

FIGURE 6–9   Formatted shape in the worksheet

Deleting an Object

When you no longer need a shape or any other object in a worksheet, you can delete it. First click the object to select it. Then press the Delete key. The object is removed from the worksheet.

Step-by-Step 6.5

1. Click the **Insert** tab on the Ribbon. In the Illustrations group, click the **Shapes** button. The Shapes gallery appears, as shown in Figure 6–8.

2. In the Block Arrows section, click the **Up Arrow Callout** button ⬆ (the last button in the second row). The pointer changes shape to a crosshair ✛.

3. Click and drag from cell **B17** to cell **E20**, and then release the mouse button. A callout with a light blue background and dark blue outline is inserted in the worksheet, with the upper-left corner in cell B17 and the lower-right corner in cell E20. The Format tab appears under Drawing Tools on the Ribbon.

4. Type **Bad weather caused February's low field production.** (including the period). The text is inserted in the callout.

5. Point to the lower-right sizing handle until the pointer changes to the diagonal resize pointer ⬉, and then drag left to column D and down to row 22. The callout is narrower but longer.

6. Point to the callout to display the four-headed move pointer ⬩, and then drag the callout until its arrow points to the bottom of cell **C15**. The callout points to the correct cell and remains selected.

7. On the Format tab, in the Shape Styles group, click the **Shape Fill** arrow. A color palette appears.

8. In the Theme Colors section, click **Black, Text 1** (the second color in the first row). The callout background color changes to black.

9. On the Format tab, in the Shape Styles group, click the **Shape Outline** arrow. A color palette appears.

10. In the Standard Colors section, click **Orange** (the third color). The line around the callout changes to orange.

11. On the Format tab, in the Shape Styles group, click the **Shape Effects** button.

12. On the Shapes Effects menu, point to **Glow**. In the Glow Variations section, click **Red, 11 pt glow, Accent color 2** (the second effect in the third row). The callout is formatted as shown in Figure 6–9.

13. Click any cell in the worksheet to deselect the shape. The Format tab disappears from the Ribbon.

14. Save the workbook, and leave it open for the next Step-by-Step.

Adding a SmartArt Graphic to a Worksheet

SmartArt graphics enhance worksheets by providing a visual representation of information and ideas. SmartArt graphics are often used for organizational charts, flowcharts, and decision trees.

Inserting a SmartArt Graphic

To insert a SmartArt graphic, click the SmartArt button in the Illustrations group on the Insert tab. The Choose a SmartArt Graphic dialog box appears, as shown in **Figure 6–10**. You can select from a variety of layouts, including list, matrix, and pyramid. Click the SmartArt graphic you want to use in the center pane and read its description in the right pane. Click OK to insert the graphic in the worksheet as an object.

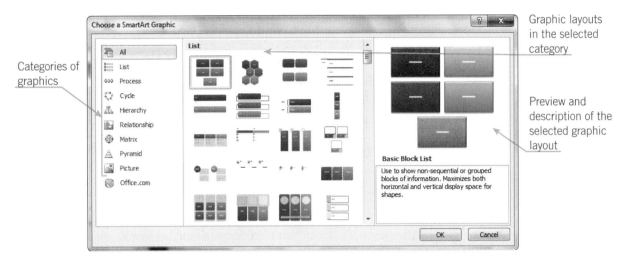

FIGURE 6–10   Choose a SmartArt Graphic dialog box

Modifying a SmartArt Graphic

When the SmartArt graphic is selected, SmartArt Tools appear on the Ribbon and contain the Design and Format tabs, as shown in **Figure 6–11**. You use the tools on the Design tab to select a layout, apply a style, and select the layout's color. The Format tab has tools to modify the shapes used in the selected layout by changing the shape, size, fill color, and outline color, as well as tools to apply shape styles and special effects such as shadows. You can also move and resize the selected shapes.

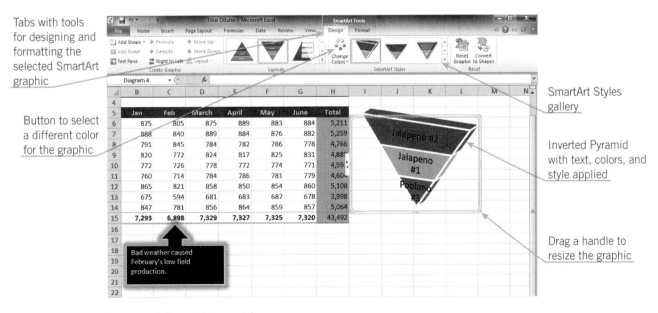

FIGURE 6–11   Formatted SmartArt graphic

Step-by-Step 6.6

1. Click the **Insert** tab on the Ribbon. In the Illustrations group, click the **SmartArt** button. The Choose a SmartArt Graphic dialog box appears, as shown in Figure 6–10.

2. In the left pane, click **Pyramid**.

3. In the center pane, click **Inverted Pyramid** (the second graphic). A preview and description appears in the right pane.

4. Click **OK**. The SmartArt graphic appears in the worksheet, on top of the data. The SmartArt Tools appear on the Ribbon.

5. Type **Jalapeno #2**. The text appears in the top level of the pyramid.

6. Click **[Text]** in the second level of the pyramid, and then type **Jalapeno #1**. Click **[Text]** in the bottom level of the pyramid, and then type **Poblano #3**.

7. Click within the selection box to deselect the text box, but keep the SmartArt graphic selected. Drag the lower-right sizing handle up until the graphic is about four columns wide and nine rows high.

8. If the Type your text here box to the left of the SmartArt graphic is open, click the **Close** button ⊠.

9. Position the pointer on the selection box to change it to the move pointer ⬆️. Drag the **selection box** until its upper-left corner is in cell I6. The pyramid covers the range I6:L14.

10. On the Design tab, in the SmartArt Styles group, click the **Change Colors** button. A gallery of color options appears.

11. In the Colorful section, click **Colorful – Accent Colors** (the first color option). Each of the top three oil well producers is a different color in the pyramid.

12. On the Design tab, in the SmartArt Styles group, click the **More** button ⏷. The gallery of SmartArt Quick Styles appears.

13. Point to each style to see its Live Preview. In the 3-D section, click **Brick Scene** (the second style in the second row). The pyramid changes to reflect the Quick Style, as shown in Figure 6–11.

14. Save, print, and close the workbook. Leave Excel open for the next Step-by-Step.

Adding a Picture to a Worksheet

▶ **VOCABULARY**
picture

You can use a picture to make the appearance of a worksheet more attractive. A *picture* is a digital photograph or other image file. Some organizations like to include their corporate logo on worksheets. Pictures can also be used to illustrate data in a worksheet. For instance, you might want to insert a picture of each product in an inventory list.

Inserting a Picture

You can insert a picture in a worksheet by using a picture file or by using the Clip Art task pane. If you have access to the Internet, you can also download pictures from Office.com to insert in your worksheets.

To insert a picture from a file, click the Picture button in the Illustrations group on the Insert tab of the Ribbon. The Insert Picture dialog box, which looks and functions like the Open dialog box, appears. Go to the drive or folder that contains the picture file, and then double-click the picture file you want to use.

The Clip Art task pane provides a wide variety of clip art, photographs, movies, and sounds that you can insert in a worksheet. To access the Clip Art task pane, click the Clip Art button in the Illustrations group on the Insert tab of the Ribbon. The Clip Art task pane appears on the right side of the program window, as shown in **Figure 6–12**. In the Search for box, type a brief description of the clip you want to find, and then click Go. Clips that match the search words appear in the results box. Click an image to insert it in the worksheet.

Brief description of the clip you want to find

The types of files you want to find—clip art, photographs, movies, and/or sounds

Search results; click a clip to insert it in the workbook

FIGURE 6–12   Clip Art task pane

> **TIP**
>
> You can place a background pattern or picture in a worksheet. On the Page Layout tab, in the Page Setup group, click the Background button. In the Sheet Background dialog box, select the picture you want in the background of the worksheet, and then click Insert.

> **WARNING**
>
> All images are protected by copyright law. You cannot download and use a picture you find on a Web site without permission. Contact the copyright holder to obtain permission. Some Web sites offer free images for noncommercial use. Others offer images you purchase for a fee.

Modifying a Picture

A picture is inserted in the workbook as an object. As with shapes, you can move, resize, or format the picture to fit your needs. When you click a picture to select it, the Picture Tools Format tab appears on the Ribbon. The Format tab contains tools to edit and format the picture. The tools in the Adjust group enable you to change a picture's appearance, such as its brightness, contrast, color, and background. The Picture Styles group includes the Picture Styles gallery as well as tools to change the picture's shape and border, and effects such as shadows and rotation. The Size group includes the Crop button, which you use to cut out parts of the picture you do not want to use, and options to change the picture's size.

Step-by-Step 6.7

1. Open the **Beautiful.xlsx** workbook from the drive and folder where your Data Files are stored.

2. Save the workbook as **Beautiful Blooms** followed by your initials.

3. Click the **Insert** tab on the Ribbon. In the Illustrations group, click the **Picture** button. The Insert Picture dialog box appears.

4. Click the **Tulips.jpg** file from the drive and folder where your Data Files are stored. This file contains the picture you want to insert.

5. Click the **Insert** button. The tulips picture is inserted in the worksheet. The Picture Tools Format tab appears on the Ribbon.

6. On the Format tab, in the Adjust group, click the **Remove Background** button. The Background Removal tab appears on the Ribbon, and all areas of the background to be removed are purple, as shown in **Figure 6–13**.

FIGURE 6–13
Picture background marked for removal

Button to apply the background changes

Drag a sizing handle to change background removal area

Purple area will be removed

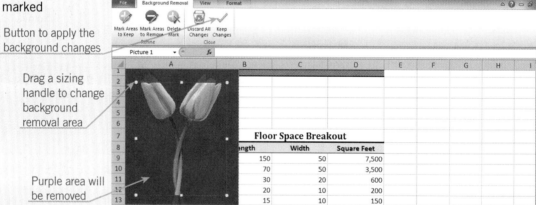

7. Drag the top-middle resize handle up so that all of the flowers are visible.

8. On the Background Removal tab, in the Close group, click the **Keep Changes** button. The picture's background is removed, leaving only the flowers.

9. Drag the lower-right sizing handle up to the bottom of row 6. The picture resizes proportionally and covers the range A1:A6.

10. On the Format tab, in the Picture Styles group, click the **More** button. The gallery of Picture Styles appears.

11. Point to different picture styles to see the Live Preview, and then click **Snip Diagonal Corner, White** (the third style in the third row). The overall style of the picture changes to include a gray background and a white border with the upper-right and lower-left corners clipped.

12. Position the pointer on the picture to change it to the move pointer ✛. Drag the picture until its upper-left corner is in cell A2. The picture covers the range A2:A7, as shown in **Figure 6–14**.

Button to remove picture's background

Buttons for changing the brightness, contrast, and color

Picture with background removed and style applied

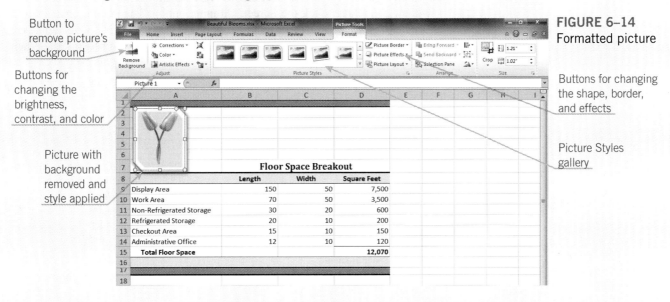

FIGURE 6–14
Formatted picture

Buttons for changing the shape, border, and effects

Picture Styles gallery

13. Click the right side of cell **A1** to select that cell and deselect the picture.

14. Save the workbook, and leave it open for the next Step-by-Step.

Adding a Screenshot or Screen Clipping to a Worksheet

A *screenshot* is a picture of all or part of something you see on your monitor, such as a Word document, an Excel workbook, a photograph, or a Web page. When you take a screenshot, you can include everything visible on your monitor or a *screen clipping*, which is the area you choose to include. The screenshot is added to the worksheet as a picture object that you can resize and modify like any other picture. When you take a screenshot or screen clipping, the original file is not changed.

▶ **VOCABULARY**
screenshot

screen clipping

To take a screenshot, first open the file or Web page that you want to use. Then, switch to Excel and click the Insert tab on the Ribbon. In the Illustrations group, click the Screenshot button. The Screenshot gallery appears, as shown in **Figure 6–15**. To include the entire program window, click the appropriate thumbnail in the Available Windows section of the Screenshot gallery. To choose part of a window to include, click the Screen Clipping option. The pointer changes to a crosshair shape, and the first program window becomes available. Click and drag to select the portion of the window you want to include in the screenshot. When you release the mouse button, the selected portion is added to your worksheet as a picture object.

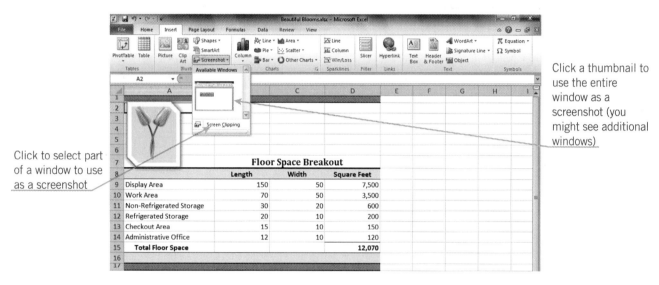

Click to select part of a window to use as a screenshot

Click a thumbnail to use the entire window as a screenshot (you might see additional windows)

FIGURE 6–15   Screenshot gallery

Step-by-Step 6.8

1. Open the **Logo.docx** document from the drive and folder where your Data Files are stored.

2. Switch to the **Beautiful Blooms** workbook.

3. In Excel, click the **Insert** tab on the Ribbon. In the Illustrations group, click the **Screenshot** button. The Screenshot gallery appears, as shown in Figure 6–15.

4. In the Screenshot gallery, click **Screen Clipping**. The Excel program window is minimized, the Word program window displaying the Logo document is activated and dimmed, and the pointer changes to a crosshair ✛.

5. Click just above the upper-left corner of the logo, drag to the lower-right corner of the logo, and then release the mouse button. The logo is copied from the document, the Excel program window becomes active, and a copy of the logo is added as a picture object in the worksheet.

6. Move the pointer to the **Beautiful Blooms** picture so it changes to a move pointer, and then drag the picture so the upper-right corner is in the upper-right corner of cell D2. Release the mouse button. Your screen should look similar to **Figure 6–16**.

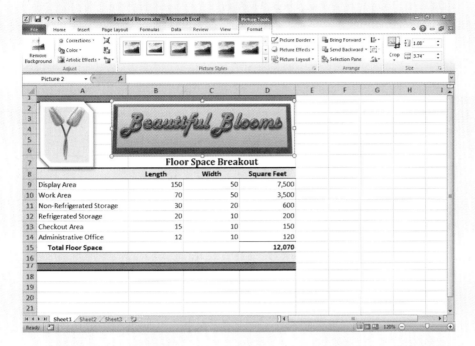

FIGURE 6–16
Screen clipping inserted in the worksheet

7. Close the Logo document.

8. Insert a footer with your name and the current date.

9. Save, print, and close the workbook. Leave Excel open for the next Step-by-Step.

Using a Template

Templates are predesigned workbook files that you can use as the basis or model for new workbooks. The template includes all the parts of a workbook that will not change, such as text labels, formulas, and formatting. You save a copy of the template as a workbook and enter the variable data. You can use a template again and again, entering different data in each new workbook you create from the template. For example, suppose your employer asks you to submit a weekly time sheet. Each week you use the same worksheet format, but the number of hours and dates you enter in the worksheet change. You can use a template to save the portion of the worksheet that is the same every week. Then, each week, you can create a new workbook based on the template and add the data for the current week.

▶ **VOCABULARY**
template

TIP

Each time you download a template from Office.com, Microsoft verifies that the version of the Office software on your computer is genuine. Depending on your setup, you might see a message explaining this feature.

Excel includes a variety of templates, which you access from the New tab in Backstage view, as shown in **Figure 6–17**. The Home templates are template files stored on your computer. The Office.com Templates, which are available when your computer is connected to the Internet, are organized by categories, such as Budgets, Forms, and Invoices. Click a template category to display the templates available for that category. Click a template to display a preview and description of the selected template in the right pane. To open a new workbook based on the selected template, click the Create button or the Download button. Templates have the file extension .xltx to differentiate them from regular Excel workbook files. After you open a workbook based on a template file, you need to save it with a descriptive name to the appropriate location.

Option to access sample templates on your computer

Templates installed on your computer

Categories of templates available on Office.com if your computer is connected to the Internet (yours might differ)

Preview of the selected template

Button to create a new workbook based on the selected template (changes to Download if the template is on Office.com)

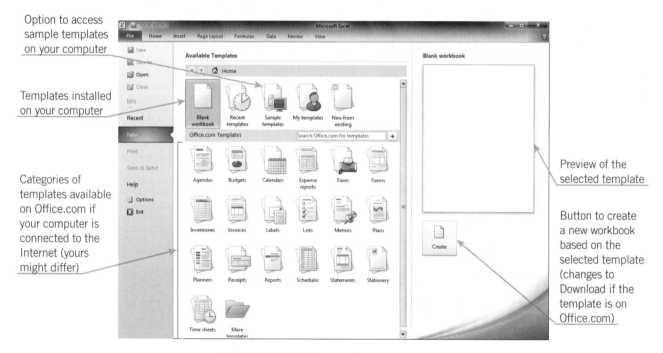

FIGURE 6–17   New tab in Backstage view

You can also create a workbook based on an existing file. Click the New from existing button. The New from Existing Workbook dialog box, which looks and functions like the Open dialog box, appears. Select the workbook you want to use as the basis for another workbook, and then click Create New. A copy of the selected workbook appears in the program window. You can modify the file as needed, and then save the workbook with an appropriate name and location, without overwriting the original workbook.

Step-by-Step 6.9

1. Click the **File** tab on the Ribbon, and then, in the navigation bar, click **New**. The New tab appears, as shown in Figure 6–17.

2. In the Home templates section, click **Sample templates**. A list of templates installed on your computer appears in the Available Templates pane.

3. In the Sample templates list, click **Time Card**. A preview of the Time Card template appears in the right pane.

4. Click the **Create** button. A workbook based on the Time Card template appears in the program window. The default name of the workbook is *Time Card1*.

5. Save the workbook as **Time Card** followed by your initials.

6. Zoom the worksheet to **85%** so you can see the entire width of the time card.

7. In cell **C7**, enter your name.

8. Click cell **C16**, and then enter **5/25/2013** as the week ending date. The dates for the specified week appear in the range C21:C27, the Date column in the time card.

9. Click cell **D21**, and then enter **7**. The total hours for the day appear in cell H21, and the total regular hours for the week appear in cell D28.

10. Click cell **D29**, and then enter **12.5**. The rate of $12.50 per hour for regular hours is entered. The total regular pay for the day appears in cell D30, and the total pay for the week appears in cell H30.

11. Click cell **E21**, and then enter **1.5**. The total hours for the day in cell H21 are updated to include the overtime hours, and the total overtime hours for the week appear in cell E28.

12. Click cell **E29**, and then enter **18.75**. The rate of $18.75 per hour for overtime hours is entered. The total overtime pay for the day appears in cell E30, and the updated total pay for the week appears in cell H30. Your worksheet should look similar to **Figure 6–18**.

Formula entered in workbook template

Formula enters the appropriate dates based on the week ending date you entered

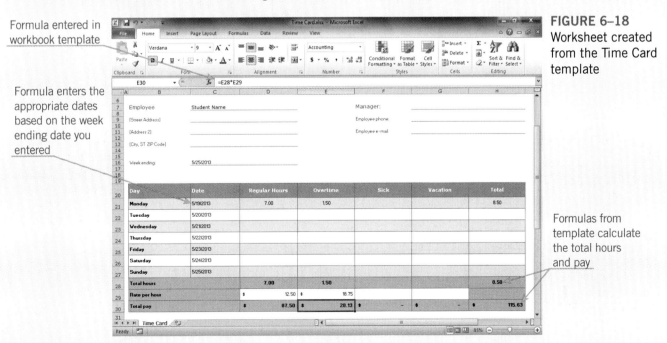

FIGURE 6–18
Worksheet created from the Time Card template

Formulas from template calculate the total hours and pay

13. Save, print, and close the workbook. Leave Excel open for the next Step-by-Step.

▶ **VOCABULARY**
hyperlink

TIP

You can enter a custom ScreenTip that appears when a user points to a hyperlink. In the Insert Hyperlink dialog box, click ScreenTip. In the Set Hyperlink ScreenTip dialog box that appears, type the text in the ScreenTip text box, and then click OK. Use the Insert Hyperlink dialog box to finish creating the hyperlink, and then click OK.

Inserting a Hyperlink

A *hyperlink* is a reference that opens a Web page, a file, a specific location in the current workbook, a new document, or an e-mail address when you click it. A hyperlink usually appears as text in a cell, but you can also use an object, such as a picture, as a hyperlink. For example, you can create a hyperlink in a worksheet to open a workbook that contains the source data for information used in the current worksheet. You can also create a hyperlink to open a company's Web page using the company's logo picture.

Creating a Hyperlink

To create a hyperlink, first click the cell or object that you want to use for the hyperlink. On the Insert tab of the Ribbon, in the Links group, click the Hyperlink button. The Insert Hyperlink dialog box appears, as shown in **Figure 6–19**. Type the file name or Web page address in the Address box, and then click OK. The hyperlink is added to the worksheet.

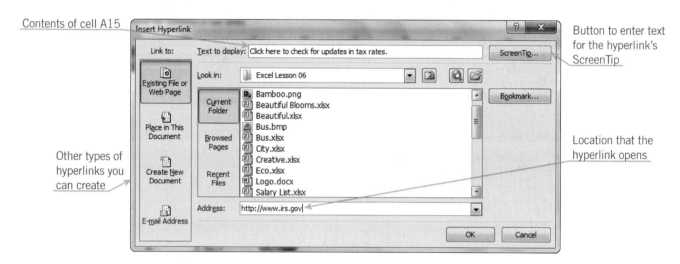

FIGURE 6–19 Insert Hyperlink dialog box

Using a Hyperlink

When you point to a hyperlink, the pointer appears as a hand. To use the hyperlink, click the cell or object. If you created a hyperlink to a file, a program starts and opens the file when you click the hyperlink. If you created a hyperlink to a Web page, your Web browser starts and opens the Web page when you click the hyperlink.

TIP

The worksheet cell is the hyperlink, not the contents entered in that cell. If the contents extend beyond the cell's border, the hyperlink will not work if the user clicks the text that extends into the next cell. The actual cell must be clicked.

Editing a Hyperlink

You can edit a hyperlink to change its displayed text, ScreenTip, the location it opens. Click the cell or object with the hyperlink, and then click the Hyperlink button in the Links group on the Insert tab. The Edit Hyperlink dialog box appears, and looks and functions just like the Insert Hyperlink dialog box. In addition, it contains the Remove Link button, which you can click to delete the hyperlink from the cell or object without changing the cell's contents or the object.

Step-by-Step 6.10

1. Open the **Tax.xlsx** workbook from the drive and folder where your Data Files are stored.

2. Save the workbook as **Tax Estimate** followed by your initials.

3. Click cell **A15**. You will use this cell as the hyperlink to open the Web site for the Internal Revenue Service (IRS).

4. Click the **Insert** tab on the Ribbon. In the Links group, click the **Hyperlink** button. The Insert Hyperlink dialog box appears.

5. In the Address box, type **www.irs.gov**. This is the Web site you want to open when a user clicks the hyperlink. Excel inserts *http://* before the Web address, as shown in Figure 6–19.

6. Click **OK**. Cell A15 is a hyperlink with blue and underlined text, which is a common format for indicating a hyperlink.

7. Point to **cell A15**. The pointer changes to 🖑 and the default ScreenTip appears, as shown in **Figure 6–20**.

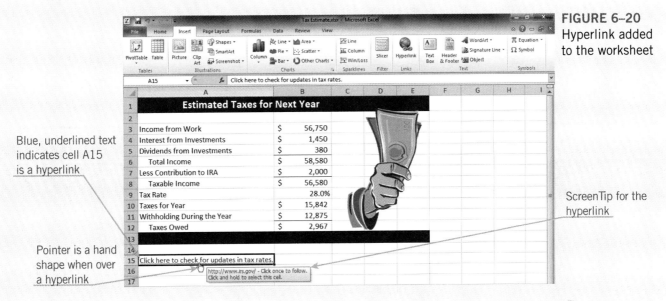

Blue, underlined text indicates cell A15 is a hyperlink

Pointer is a hand shape when over a hyperlink

ScreenTip for the hyperlink

FIGURE 6–20
Hyperlink added to the worksheet

8. If your computer is connected to the Internet, click cell **A15**. Your browser starts and opens the home page for the IRS. If your computer is not connected to the Internet, continue with Step 10.

9. Close your browser and return to the worksheet.

10. Insert a header with your name and the current date.

11. Save, print, and close the workbook. Leave Excel open for the next Step-by-Step.

Saving a Workbook in a Different Format

Excel workbooks can be saved in different file formats so that they can be opened in other programs. For example, if you want to share data with a coworker or friend who uses an earlier version of Excel, you can save your Excel file in a format that is readable by Excel 2003. You can also save the file in a format that can be viewed as a Web page on the Internet. **Table 6–1** describes some of the different formats in which you can save a workbook.

TABLE 6–1   Common file formats in which to save workbooks

FILE TYPE	DESCRIPTION	FILE EXTENSION
CSV (Comma delimited)	Data separated by commas	.csv
Excel Template	File used to create other similar files	.xltx
Formatted Text (Space delimited)	Data separated by spaces	.prn
Microsoft Excel 97-2003	Data created in an earlier version of Excel	.xls
Text (Tab delimited)	Data separated by tabs	.txt
Single File Web Page	File to be displayed on the Internet	.mht, .mhtml
Web Page	File to be displayed on the Internet	.htm, .html
XML Data	Data in Extensible Markup Language	.xml

Step-by-Step 6.11

1. Open the **Travel.xlsx** workbook from the drive and folder where your Data Files are stored.

2. Open the Save As dialog box. In the File name box, type **Travel Expenses 2003** followed by your initials.

3. Click the **Save as type** button. A list of file types you can use to save the workbook appears. Click **Excel 97-2003 Workbook (*.xls)**. You will save the Excel 2010 workbook in a format that Excel 2003 and earlier versions can open.

4. Click **Save**. The Microsoft Excel – Compatibility Checker dialog box appears, as shown in **Figure 6–21**, listing elements of the workbook that are not supported by earlier versions of Excel. In this case, some of the formatting in the current worksheet cannot be saved in the earlier file format. These formats will be converted to the earlier format.

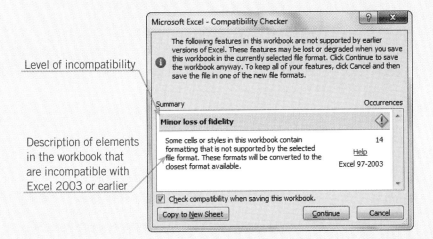

FIGURE 6–21
Microsoft Excel – Compatibility Checker dialog box

5. Click **Continue**. The dialog box closes and the workbook is saved as a file that can be opened in Excel 2003 and earlier versions. Close the **Travel Expenses 2003** workbook.

6. Open the **Travel.xlsx** workbook from the drive and folder where your Data Files are stored. Open the Save As dialog box. In the File name box, type **Travel Expenses** followed by your initials.

7. Click the **Save as type** button, and then click **Single File Web Page**. The Save As dialog box expands to show additional options.

8. Click **Change Title**. The Enter Text dialog box appears. In the Page title box, type **Expense Report for Sales Staff**, and then click **OK**. The page title will appear in the title bar of the browser.

9. Click **Publish**. The Publish as Web Page dialog box appears. Click the **Choose** arrow, and then click **Items on Sheet1**, if it is not already selected.

10. Click **Change**. The Set Title dialog box appears. Press the **Delete** key to delete the text in the Title box, and then click **OK**. You do not want the same text to appear in both the browser title bar and the browser window centered over the worksheet content.

11. In the File name box, change the file name to **Travel Expenses Web** followed by your initials. The full path shows the drive and folders in which the file will be saved.

12. Click the **Open published web page in browser** check box, if it is not already checked. The Publish as Web Page dialog box should match **Figure 6–22**.

FIGURE 6–22
Publish as Web Page
dialog box

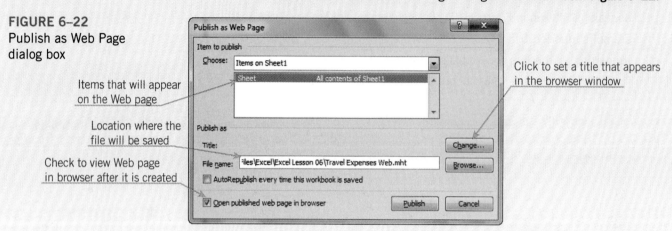

Items that will appear on the Web page

Location where the file will be saved

Check to view Web page in browser after it is created

Click to set a title that appears in the browser window

13. Click **Publish**. The Web page appears in your browser, as it would if it were published on the Web. If you use Internet Explorer as your Web browser, your screen should look similar to **Figure 6–23**.

FIGURE 6–23
Web page in Internet Explorer

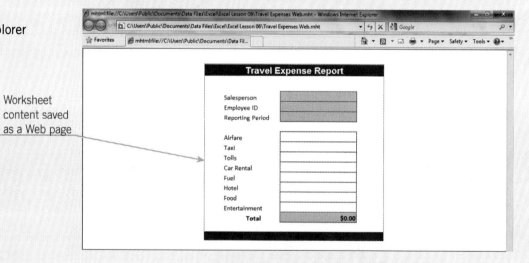

Worksheet content saved as a Web page

14. Close the browser. Save the workbook as **Travel Expenses** followed by your initials, and leave it open for the next Step-by-Step.

Working with Comments

A *comment* is a note attached to a cell that you can use to explain or identify information contained in the cell. For example, you might use comments to provide the full text of abbreviations entered in cells. You might also use comments to explain the calculations in cells that contain formulas, or to provide feedback to others without altering the worksheet structure. For example, a supervisor might use comments to offer suggestions to an employee on how to improve the worksheet format.

Inserting a Comment

All of the comments tools are located on the Review tab of the Ribbon in the Comments group. The New Comment button inserts a comment in the active cell. A comment box appears to the right of the selected cell with the user name followed by a colon at the top of the box. Type the comment, and then click outside the comment box to close it. A red triangle appears in the upper-right corner of the cell to indicate that it contains a comment. The comment box appears whenever you point to the cell that contains it. It disappears when you move the pointer to another cell.

Editing and Deleting a Comment

To edit a comment, click the cell that contains the comment. Then click the Edit Comment button in the Comments group on the Review tab. Edit the text as usual. To delete a comment, click the cell that contains the comment. Then click the Delete button in the Comments group on the Review tab. The comment is removed from the cell.

▶ **VOCABULARY**
comment

TIP

You can show or hide all the comments in a worksheet by toggling the Show All Comments button in the Comments group. Use the Previous and Next buttons to move between comments in the worksheet.

Step-by-Step 6.12

1. Click cell **A4**. You want to add a comment to this cell.

2. Click the **Review** tab on the Ribbon. In the Comments group, click the **New Comment** button. The comment box appears to the right of the active cell. Your name (or another user's name, depending on your settings in Excel) appears in the comment box.

3. In the comment box, type the following comment: **Please change to Employee Number**.

4. Click cell **A13**. The comment box for cell A4 disappears, and a small red triangle appears in the upper-right corner of cell A4 to indicate that the cell contains a comment.

5. On the Review tab, in the Comments group, click the **New Comment** button.

EXTRA FOR EXPERTS

The user name in the comment box matches the user name entered for that copy of Excel. To change the user name, click the File tab, and then click Options in the navigation bar. The Excel Options dialog box appears with the General options displayed. In the Personalize your copy of Microsoft Office section, in the User name box, type the name you want to appear in comments. Click OK.

6. In the comment box, type the following comment: **The per diem maxi-mum is $50**.

7. Click cell **A16**. The comment box for cell A13 disappears, and a small red triangle appears in the upper-right corner of cell A13, indicating that the cell contains a comment.

8. Point to cell **A13**. The cell comment appears, as shown in **Figure 6–24**.

FIGURE 6–24
Comments added to the worksheet

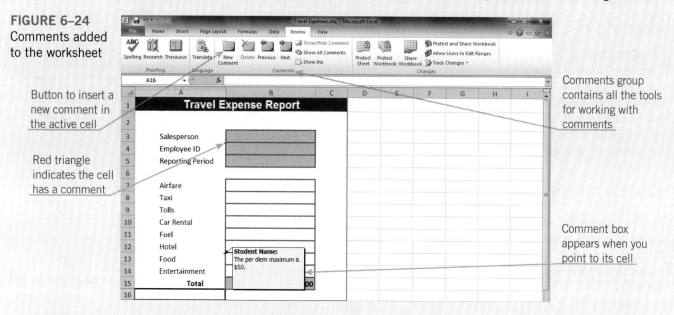

Button to insert a new comment in the active cell

Red triangle indicates the cell has a comment

Comments group contains all the tools for working with comments

Comment box appears when you point to its cell

9. Click cell **B3**, and then enter your name.

10. Save, print, and close the workbook. Leave Excel open for the next Step-by-Step.

Using the Research Task Pane

The *Research task pane* provides access to information typically found in references such as dictionaries, thesauruses, and encyclopedias. In Excel, the Research task pane also provides numerical data typically used in a worksheet, such as statistics or corporate financial data.

To open the Research task pane, click the Review tab on the Ribbon, and then, in the Proofing group, click the Research button. The Research task pane appears along the right side of the program window. In the task pane, select a reference book, a research site, or a business and financial site, and then search for a subject or topic. Your computer must be connected to the Internet to use the Research task pane.

Step-by-Step 6.13

1. Open the **Stock.xlsx** workbook from the drive and folder where your Data Files are stored.

2. Save the workbook as **Stock Quotes** followed by your initials.

3. In cell A2, enter the current date.

4. Click the **Review** tab on the Ribbon. In the Proofing group, click the **Research** button. The Research task pane appears on the right side of the program window.

5. In the Search for box, type **AMZN**.

6. Click the **All Reference Books** arrow, and then click **MSN Money Stock Quotes**. The search results appear in the task pane. The Last amount is the most recent price for that stock.

7. Click cell **C5**, and then enter the amount that appears for *Last*. The current price is entered in cell C5. Excel returns the total value in cell E5 by multiplying the value in cell C5 by the value in cell D5.

8. On the Research task pane, in the Search for box, type **HD**. Click the **Start searching** button ⊡. The most recent price for The Home Depot stock appears in the search results box.

9. Click cell **C6**, and then enter the Last amount. The current price is entered in cell C6, and the value amounts are calculated.

⊸— WARNING

If your computer is not connected to the Internet, you can read but not complete Steps 5 through 10. Enter the values shown in Figure 6–25 in the range C5:C9 in your worksheet. Then, continue with Step 11.

◖ TIP

You can change which reference books and research sites are available from the Research task pane. Click the Research options link at the bottom of the task pane, check and uncheck services as needed, and then click OK.

10. Repeat the process in Steps 7 and 8 to find the current prices for the ticker symbols INTC, JNJ, and MSFT, and enter the Last amounts in the range C7:C9. Your worksheet should be similar to **Figure 6–25**. The actual amounts in the Price and Value columns will differ because they are based on the most recent stock prices.

FIGURE 6–25
Research
task pane

Button to toggle the
Research task pane
open and closed

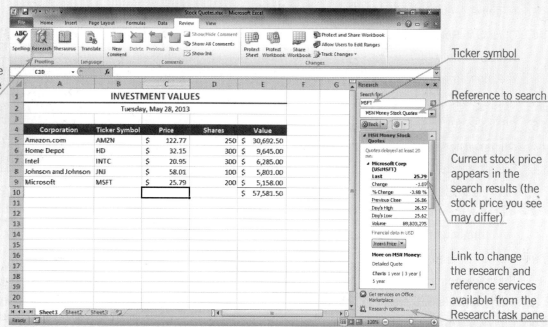

Ticker symbol

Reference to search

Current stock price
appears in the
search results (the
stock price you see
may differ)

Link to change
the research and
reference services
available from the
Research task pane

11. On the Review tab, in the Proofing group, click the **Research** button. The Research task pane closes.

12. Insert a header with your name and the current date. Save, print, and close the workbook, and then close Excel.

SUMMARY

In this lesson, you learned:

- Sorting rearranges worksheet data in ascending or descending alphabetical, numerical, or chronological order. Filtering displays a subset of data in a worksheet that meets specific criteria.

- Conditional formatting formats worksheet data by changing the appearance of cells that meet a specified condition, such as a comparison or rank.

- Hiding rows and/or columns lets you use the same worksheet to view different data. You can unhide the hidden rows and columns at any time.

- Shapes, such as rectangles, circles, arrows, lines, flowchart symbols, and callouts, can help make a worksheet more informative. Excel has a gallery of shapes you can insert.

- SmartArt graphics enhance worksheets by providing visual representations of information and ideas. Excel has a variety of SmartArt graphics you can use and customize.

- Pictures can make a worksheet's appearance more attractive. You can insert a picture from a file or use the Clip Art task pane to search for pictures. You can also use the Screenshot tool to insert a picture of an entire program window or a screen clipping of a part of a window's contents.

- Templates are predesigned workbook files that can be used as the basis or model when creating a new workbook. A template includes all parts of the workbook that will not change, such as labels, formulas, and formatting.

- You can use a cell or an object to create hyperlinks to another Web page, another file, a specific location in the current workbook, a new document, or an e-mail address.

- You can save a workbook in a different file format, so it can be opened in other programs or in an earlier version of Excel.

- Comments are notes that are added to cells to provide additional information or feedback about that cell's contents. The Research task pane provides access to information typically found in references such as dictionaries, thesauruses, and encyclopedias. In Excel, it also provides numerical data, such as current stock prices.

■ VOCABULARY REVIEW

Define the following terms:

ascending sort	hyperlink	screenshot
comment	object	shape
conditional formatting	picture	SmartArt graphic
descending sort	Research task pane	sort
filter	screen clipping	template
filter arrow		

■ REVIEW QUESTIONS

TRUE / FALSE

Circle T if the statement is true or F if the statement is false.

T F **1.** Sorting always arranges data in a worksheet with the smallest values listed first.

T F **2.** Filtering reorganizes data so it appears in a different order.

T F **3.** Hiding deletes a row or column from a worksheet.

T F **4.** Inserting a comment in a cell does not affect the results of a formula contained in that cell.

T F **5.** Excel workbooks can be saved in other file formats.

MATCHING

Match the correct term in Column 2 to its description in Column 1.

Column 1

_____ 1. Workbook used as a model to create other workbooks

_____ 2. Changes the look of cells that meet a specific condition

_____ 3. Organizes data in a more meaningful order

_____ 4. A cell or picture that opens another location or file, an e-mail address, a new document, or a Web page when clicked

_____ 5. Displays a subset of data that meet certain criteria

_____ 6. A message that explains or identifies information in a cell

Column 2

A. Filter

B. Comment

C. Conditional formatting

D. Hyperlink

E. Sorting

F. Template

FILL IN THE BLANK

Complete the following sentences by writing the correct word or words in the blanks provided.

1. A(n) _____ sort arranges data with numbers from highest to lowest.

2. Highlighting cells based on their rank, such as the top 10 items, is an example of _____ formatting.

3. A(n) _____ is anything that appears on the screen that you can select and work with as a whole, such as a shape, picture, or chart.

4. A(n) _____ is an area of a program window that you can insert in a workbook as object.

5. The _____ task pane provides access to information typically found in dictionaries, thesauruses, and encyclopedias.

▪ PROJECTS

If you have a SAM 2010 user profile, your instructor may have assigned an autogradable version of the indicated project. If so, log into the SAM 2010 Web site at *www.cengage.com/sam2010* to download the instruction and start files.

PROJECT 6–1

1. Open the **Zoom.xlsx** workbook from the drive and folder where your Data Files are stored. Save the workbook as **Zoom Salaries** followed by your initials. The worksheet contains the annual salaries and ratings of Level 10 employees.

2. Sort the data in the range A6:E20 by the Performance Rating in descending numerical order (largest to smallest).

3. In cell F5, enter **Salary Category** as the label.

4. In cell F6, enter the following formula to indicate the employee's salary category (low or high) based on his or her annual salary: **=IF(D6<36001,"Low","High")**.

5. Copy the formula in cell F6 to the range F7:F20.

   The Level 10 management is concerned that employee salaries do not reflect the annual performance ratings. If salaries are allocated based on annual ratings, employees with higher performance ratings should appear near the top of the worksheet and have *High* in the Salary Category column. Employees with lower ratings should appear near the bottom of the worksheet and have *Low* in the Salary Category column. When a salary does not reflect the employee's annual rating, the salary category in column F might appear to be out of place.

6. Insert a comment in the Employee ID column for each employee you think is underpaid explaining why you believe that employee is underpaid based on the data in the worksheet.

7. Apply conditional formatting to the Annual Salary column to highlight the top five annual salaries with light red fill with dark red text.

8. Insert a header with your name and the current date. Save, print, and close the workbook.

SAM PROJECT 6–2

1. Open the **Top.xlsx** workbook from the drive and folder where your Data Files are stored. Save the workbook as **Top Films** followed by your initials.

2. Conditionally format the data to highlight the top 10 highest grossing films using a green fill with dark green text. Column D contains the number of dollars that the film grossed.

3. Conditionally format the data to highlight the bottom 10 lowest grossing films using a yellow fill with dark yellow text.

4. Sort the data by Gross in descending order (largest to smallest). Make a note of which movie has the largest gross.

5. Sort the data by Release Date in ascending order (oldest to newest) and then by Film in ascending order (A to Z).

6. Add a left arrow callout in columns E and F pointing to the highest grossing film. Enter the text **Top grossing movie of all time!** in the callout.

7. Insert a header with your name and the current date. Make sure the callout will print on the same page as the file data. Save, print, and close the workbook.

PROJECT 6–3

1. Open the **City.xlsx** workbook from the drive and folder where your Data Files are stored. Save the workbook as **City Facts** followed by your initials.

2. Click cell B2 and turn on the filter arrows.

3. Run the following AutoFilters to answer the following questions. Remember to restore the records after each filter by clearing the filter.

Column	AutoFilter	Criterion
B	Top 10	4 items
C	Top 10	Bottom 4 items
D	Top 10	10 percent
G	Equals	0

  A. What are the four largest cities in the United States?

  B. What are the four cities in the United States with the coldest average January temperatures?

  C. What cities are in the top 10% of the average highest July temperatures?

  D. How many of the 30 largest cities are at sea level (have altitudes of 0)?

4. Save and close the workbook.

PROJECT 6–5

1. Start Excel. In Backstage view, on the New tab, display the Sample templates installed on your computer. Create a new workbook based on the **Billing Statement** template.

2. Save the workbook as **Roberts Statement** followed by your initials.

3. Zoom the worksheet so you can see the entire statement, if it is not already in view.

4. Enter the following data in the worksheet.

Cell	Data
B1	(your name)
C8	15679
C10	EX6-5
F2	(504) 555-8796
F3	(504) 555-8797
F8	**Anita Roberts**
F9	**4509 Lumpton Road**
F10	**New Orleans, LA 70135**
F11, F12	(delete cell contents)
B15	**10/8/13**
C15	**Event Planning**
D15	**013**
E15	**Graduation Party**
F15	**325**
G15	**50**

5. Save, print, and close the workbook.

PROJECT 6–4

1. Open the **Eco.xlsx** workbook from the drive and folder where your Data Files are stored. Save the workbook as **Eco Container** followed by your initials.

2. Hide columns B through E to remove the quarterly data from view.

3. Unhide columns B through E to restore the quarterly data.

4. Hide rows 7 through 14 to remove the regional data from view.

5. Insert a header with your name and the current date. Print the worksheet.

6. Unhide rows 7 through 14 to restore the regional data.

7. Insert the **Bamboo.png** picture from the drive and folder where your Data Files are stored.

8. Using the sizing handles, resize the bamboo picture to an appropriate size and then drag the picture to an attractive position on the worksheet.

9. Format the picture using the color, artistic effect, picture style, or picture effects of your choice.

10. Preview the workbook and change the page orientation if needed so that the worksheet prints on one page.

11. Save, print, and close the workbook.

PROJECT 6–6

1. Open the **Bus.xlsx** workbook from the drive and folder where your Data Files are stored. Save the workbook as **Bus Records** followed by your initials.

2. On the Insert tab, in the Illustrations group, click the Picture button. The Insert Picture dialog box appears.

3. Insert the **Bus.bmp** picture from the drive and folder where your Data Files are stored.

4. Use the Dialog Box Launcher in the Size group on the Picture Tools Format tab to open the Format Picture dialog box.

5. In the Scale section, in the Height box, type **41%**. Click Close.

6. Drag the picture so that it fits within the range E1:E3.

7. Remove the picture background so that only the bus remains in the picture. You need to drag the sizing handles so that the entire bus is visible, leaving only the background marked to delete.

8. Add a Glow picture effect, using Orange, 18 pt glow, Accent color 6.

9. Insert a header with your name and the current date. Save, print, and close the workbook.

PROJECT 6–7

1. Open the **Creative.xlsx** workbook from the drive and folder where your Data Files are stored. Save the workbook as **Creative Cubicle** followed by your initials.

2. In cell D8, insert the following comment: **Shut down for two hours for maintenance**.

3. In cell D9, insert the following comment: **Production time increased by two hours to make up for maintenance on Machine 102**.

4. In cell G9, insert the following comment: **Shut down for major repairs**.

5. Insert a cube shape in the upper-left corner of the workbook.

6. On the Drawing Tools Format tab, in the Size group, enter **0.5"** in the Shape Height box and the Shape Width box.

7. Change the shape fill color to Orange, Accent 6.

8. Change the shape effect so the 3-D Rotation is Off Axis 1 Right.

9. Copy and paste the cube shape, and then drag the copy so it overlaps the lower-right corner of the first cube.

10. Insert a header with your name and the current date. Save, print, and close the workbook.

■ CRITICAL THINKING

ACTIVITY 6–1

Additional clip art is available on Office.com. You can access the site by clicking *Find more on Office.com content* in the Clip Art task pane. If you have Internet access, search for the following clip art items:

- Lion
- Valentine heart
- Doctor
- Cactus

Copy each clip art item to a blank worksheet. Resize and format each item using effect and options that you choose.

ACTIVITY 6–2

SmartArt graphics are a simple way to present hierarchical information or relationships, such as for a team, club, school, family, or organization. For example, your school probably has a principal, teachers, and students. In a worksheet, insert a SmartArt graphic to illustrate at least three levels of that hierarchy. Format the SmartArt graphic appropriately.

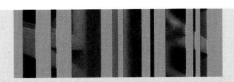

LESSON 7

Working with Multiple Worksheets and Workbooks

■ OBJECTIVES

Upon completion of this lesson, you should be able to:

■ Move between worksheets in a workbook.

■ Rename worksheets and change the sheet tab color.

■ Reposition, hide and unhide, and insert and delete worksheets.

■ Create cell references to other worksheets.

■ Create 3-D references.

■ Print all or part of a workbook.

■ Arrange multiple workbooks in the program window.

■ Move and copy worksheets between workbooks.

■ VOCABULARY

3-D reference

destination

source

worksheet range

When you have a lot of data to manage, you can organize that data in multiple worksheets or even in multiple workbooks. To work effectively, you need to know how to move between worksheets, rename worksheets, and change their sheet tab colors. You will find it helpful to reorder, hide, and insert or delete worksheets. You can also create cell references to other worksheets or to other workbooks, which means you can share data between worksheets and workbooks. You can print all or part of a workbook, and display more than one workbook at the same time. You can also move or copy worksheets from one workbook to another. You'll learn all these skills in this lesson.

Moving Between Worksheets

A workbook is a collection of worksheets. Each worksheet within the workbook is identified with a sheet tab that appears at the bottom of the workbook window. The name of the worksheet appears on the sheet tab. Unless you rename the worksheets, they are identified with the default names *Sheet1*, *Sheet2*, and so on, as shown in **Figure 7–1**.

Sheet tabs for the inactive worksheets

Sheet tab for the active worksheet

Tab scrolling buttons

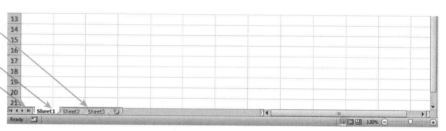

FIGURE 7–1   Default sheet tabs in a workbook

To view a specific worksheet, simply click its sheet tab. The worksheet that appears in the workbook window is called the active worksheet (or active sheet). The active sheet has a white sheet tab. If you don't see the sheet tab for the worksheet you want to display, use the tab scrolling buttons to display the sheet tab.

Identifying Worksheets

To better identify worksheets and their contents, you can give them more descriptive names. You can also change the color of each sheet tab.

Renaming a Worksheet

Although you can use the default worksheet names (*Sheet1*, *Sheet2*, and so on), a good practice is to use descriptive names to help identify the contents of each worksheet. For example, the worksheet name *Quarter 1 Budget* is a better reminder of a worksheet's contents than *Sheet1*. To rename a worksheet, double-click its sheet tab. The worksheet name in the sheet tab is selected. Type a new name for the worksheet, and then press the Enter key.

TIP

To rename a worksheet, you can also right-click its sheet tab, and then click Rename on the shortcut menu. Type a new name, and then press the Enter key.

Changing the Color of a Sheet Tab

Another way to categorize worksheets is by changing the color of the sheet tabs. For example, a sales manager might use different colors to identify each sales region. To change the sheet tab color, right-click the sheet tab you want to change, point to Tab Color on the shortcut menu, and then click the color you want for that sheet tab.

Step-by-Step 7.1

1. Open the **Crystal.xlsx** workbook from the drive and folder where your Data Files are stored. Save the workbook as **Crystal Sales** followed by your initials.

2. Click the **Sheet3** sheet tab. The Sheet3 worksheet appears as the active sheet. This worksheet summarizes the sales data stored in the other worksheets.

3. Double-click the **Sheet3** sheet tab. The worksheet name is highlighted.

4. Type **Corporate**, and then press the **Enter** key. The name *Corporate* appears on the third sheet tab.

5. Double-click the **Sheet1** sheet tab to make Sheet1 the active sheet and to highlight the worksheet name, type **Western**, and then press the **Enter** key. The Sheet1 worksheet is renamed as *Western*.

6. Rename the Sheet2 worksheet as **Eastern**. Rename the Sheet4 worksheet as **Northern**.

7. Right-click the **Corporate** sheet tab, and then point to **Tab Color**. A palette of colors appears, as shown in **Figure 7–2**.

Command to rename the selected sheet tab

Command to change the tab color for the selected sheet tab

Command to remove color from the selected sheet tab

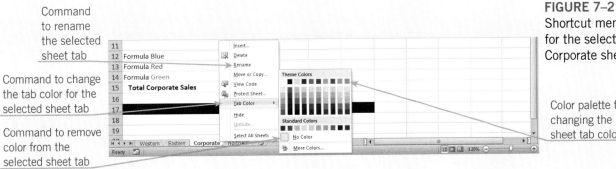

FIGURE 7–2
Shortcut menu for the selected Corporate sheet tab

Color palette for changing the sheet tab color

8. In the Theme Colors section, click **Black, Text 1** (the second color in the first row). A black line appears at the bottom of the Corporate sheet tab.

9. Click the **Northern** sheet tab. The Northern worksheet becomes the active sheet, and you can see the black sheet tab for the Corporate worksheet.

10. Right-click the **Northern** sheet tab, point to **Tab Color** to open the color palette, and then, in the Theme Colors section, click **Orange, Accent 6** (the last color in the first row).

11. Right-click the **Western** sheet tab, point to **Tab Color**, and then click **Aqua, Accent 5** (the ninth color in the first row).

12. Right-click the **Eastern** sheet tab, point to **Tab Color**, and then, in the Theme Colors section, click **Purple, Accent 4** (the eighth color in the first row).

13. Click the **Corporate** sheet tab. The Corporate worksheet is active, and the colored sheet tabs are visible for the regional worksheets, as shown in **Figure 7–3**.

FIGURE 7–3
Renamed and colored sheet tabs

Color is a shaded line when the sheet tab is selected

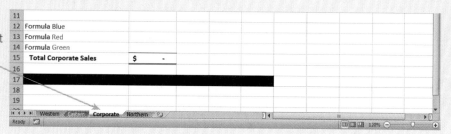

14. Save the workbook, and leave it open for the next Step-by-Step.

Managing Worksheets Within a Workbook

Often, data and analysis are best organized on multiple worksheets. For example, you can enter financial data for each quarter of the year in four different worksheets, and then summarize the annual data in a fifth worksheet. Another common workbook organization is to place sales data for each sales territory or region in its own worksheet, and then summarize the total sales in another worksheet.

Repositioning a Worksheet

To make it simpler to find information, you can position worksheets in a logical order, such as placing a summary worksheet first, followed by the worksheets that contain the data being summarized. You can reposition a worksheet by dragging its sheet tab to a new location. A placement arrow indicates the new location, as shown in **Figure 7–4**. When you release the mouse button, the worksheet moves to that position.

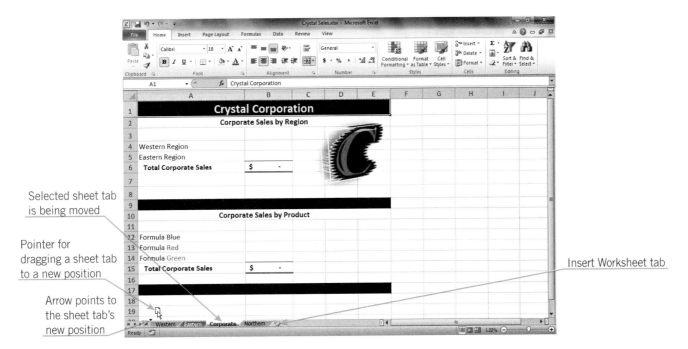

Selected sheet tab is being moved

Pointer for dragging a sheet tab to a new position

Arrow points to the sheet tab's new position

Insert Worksheet tab

FIGURE 7–4 Sheet tab being repositioned

Hiding and Unhiding a Worksheet

Some workbooks include many worksheets. Some workbooks might contain data you do not need to see, but still want to save, such as a list of employee names or data from past months. You can keep the sheet tabs organized by hiding the worksheets you do not need to view. Right-click the worksheet you want to hide, and then click Hide on the shortcut menu. To unhide a worksheet, right-click any sheet tab, and then click Unhide on the shortcut menu. The Unhide dialog box appears, as shown in **Figure 7–5**. Click the worksheet you want to unhide, and then click OK.

Worksheet hidden in the active workbook

FIGURE 7–5 Unhide dialog box

Inserting and Deleting Worksheets

By default, each workbook contains three worksheets. You can always add or delete worksheets as needed to accommodate your data. To insert a blank worksheet, click the Insert Worksheet tab next to the existing sheet tabs. A new worksheet is added to the right of the last worksheet. After adding it, you can drag the new worksheet to the position you want. Another option is to click the sheet tab of the worksheet that will *follow* the new sheet. On the Home tab of the Ribbon, in the Cells group, click the Insert button arrow, and then click Insert Sheet. A new worksheet is inserted to the right of the sheet you selected.

Deleting a worksheet permanently removes it and all its contents from the workbook. You cannot undo the action. To delete a worksheet, click the sheet tab for the worksheet you want to remove. On the Home tab of the Ribbon, in the Cells group, click the Delete button arrow, and then click Delete Sheet. If the worksheet is blank, the worksheet is permanently removed from the workbook without confirmation. If the worksheet contains data, a dialog box appears to confirm that you want to delete the worksheet, as shown in **Figure 7–6**. Click Delete to continue the action, or click Cancel to leave the worksheet in the workbook. After clicking Delete, you cannot undo the action.

TIP

You can also right-click a sheet tab, click Delete on the shortcut menu, and then click Delete in the message box to delete a worksheet.

FIGURE 7–6   Message that appears when deleting a worksheet

Step-by-Step 7.2

1. Click and drag the **Corporate** sheet tab to the left until the arrow points to the left of the Western sheet tab, as shown in Figure 7–4.

2. Release the mouse button. The sheet tab for the Corporate worksheet is first.

3. Right-click the **Northern** sheet tab, and then click **Hide** on the shortcut menu. The Northern worksheet and its sheet tab are hidden.

4. Right-click any sheet tab, and then click **Unhide** on the shortcut menu. The Unhide dialog box appears, as shown in Figure 7–5, listing the name of the hidden worksheet in the workbook.

5. Click **Northern**, if it is not already selected, and then click **OK**. The Northern worksheet and its sheet tab reappear.

6. Make sure the Northern worksheet is the active sheet.

7. On the Home tab of the Ribbon, in the Cells group, click the **Delete button arrow**, and then click **Delete Sheet**. A dialog box appears warning that data may exist in the worksheet selected for deletion, as shown in Figure 7–6.

8. Click **Delete**. The Northern worksheet is deleted, and its sheet tab no longer appears at the bottom of the worksheet.

9. Save the workbook, and leave it open for the next Step-by-Step.

Consolidating Workbook Data

In some cases, you might need several worksheets to solve one numerical problem. For example, a business that has several divisions might keep the financial results of each division in a separate worksheet. Then another worksheet might combine those results to show summary results for all divisions.

Creating Cell References to Other Worksheets

Rather than retyping data and formulas on multiple worksheets, you can create a reference to existing data and formulas in other places. For example, you could use this type of reference to display regional sales totals on a summary sheet. The location of the data being referenced is the *source*. The location where the data will be used is the *destination*.

To display data or formula results from one worksheet in another worksheet in the same workbook, you use a formula in the format shown in **Figure 7–7**. First, click the destination cell where you want to display the data or formula results from another worksheet. Type an equal sign to begin the formula. Click the sheet tab for the worksheet that contains the source cell or source range you want to reference, and then click the source cell or select the source range to include it in the formula. Finally, press the Enter key to complete the formula. For example, the reference *Sheet2!B3* refers to the value contained in cell B3 on Sheet2 and the reference *Sheet2!A1:C3* refers to the values contained in the range A1:C3 on Sheet2.

▶ **VOCABULARY**

source

destination

3-D reference

> **TIP**
>
> The contents of a source cell appear in the destination cell. Any change you make to the source cell also changes the value in the destination cell.

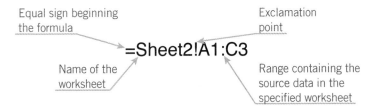

FIGURE 7–7 Formula with a reference to another worksheet

Creating 3-D References

A *3-D reference* is a reference to the same cell or range in multiple worksheets that you use in a formula. You can use 3-D references to incorporate data from other worksheets into the active worksheet. You can use a 3-D reference with 18 different functions, including SUM, AVERAGE, COUNT, MIN, MAX, and PRODUCT. For example, you might want to enter the SUM function in a summary worksheet to add several numbers contained in other worksheets, such as with quarterly or regional sales data. In general, to use 3-D references, worksheets should have the same organization and structure.

A 3-D reference includes the worksheet range, an exclamation point, and a cell or range, as shown in the formula in **Figure 7–8**. A *worksheet range* is a group of adjacent worksheets. In a worksheet range, as in a cell range, a colon separates the names of the first worksheet and the last worksheet in the group. An exclamation mark separates the worksheet range from its cell or range reference. For example, the reference *Sheet2:Sheet4!B3* refers to the values contained in cell B3 on Sheet2, Sheet3, and Sheet4 and the reference *Sheet2:Sheet4!A1:C3* refers to the values contained in the range A1:C3 on Sheet2, Sheet3, and Sheet4.

FIGURE 7–8   Formula with a 3-D reference

Because a worksheet range is a group of adjacent worksheets, moving a worksheet into the range or removing a worksheet from the range affects the formula results. In the 3-D reference *Sheet2:Sheet4!B3*, if you move Sheet1 so it is positioned between Sheet3 and Sheet4, the value in cell B3 of Sheet1 is also included in the 3-D reference.

Table 7–1 gives other examples of formulas with worksheet and 3-D references.

TABLE 7–1   Formulas that reference other worksheets

FORMULA	DESCRIPTION
=Sheet4!D9	Displays the value from cell D9 in the Sheet4 worksheet
=Sheet1!D10+Sheet2!D11	Adds the value from cell D10 in the Sheet1 worksheet and the value from cell D11 in the Sheet2 worksheet
=SUM(Sheet2!D10:D11)	Adds the values from cells D10 and D11 in the Sheet2 worksheet
=SUM(Sheet2:Sheet4!D12)	Adds the value from cell D12 in the Sheet2, Sheet3, and Sheet4 worksheets

TECHNOLOGY CAREERS

Excel workbooks are extremely useful in areas of business that have a quantitative orientation, such as accounting and finance. In accounting, formulas are used to build financial statements. Financial officers in corporations use worksheets to project sales and control costs.

Step-by-Step 7.3

1. Click the **Corporate** sheet tab. You will enter formulas in this worksheet that reference cells in the Western and Eastern worksheets.

2. Click cell **B4**, and then type = to begin the formula.

3. Click the **Western** sheet tab. The worksheet name and an exclamation mark are added to the formula in the Formula Bar, which is *=Western!*. The Western worksheet appears in the workbook window so you can select a cell or range.

4. Click cell **B6**. The cell address is added to the reference in the Formula Bar, which is *=Western!B6*. The Western worksheet remains visible so you can select additional cells.

5. Press the **Enter** key. The formula is entered, and the Corporate worksheet is active again. The formula result $525,367 appears in cell B4.

6. In the Corporate worksheet, click cell **B5**, if it is not the active cell. Type = to begin the formula. Click the **Eastern** sheet tab, and then click cell **B6**. The formula *=Eastern!B6* appears in the Formula Bar. Press the **Enter** key. The formula is entered in cell B5 of the Corporate worksheet, displaying the result $521,001.

7. In the Corporate worksheet, click cell **B12**. Type = to begin the formula. Click the **Western** sheet tab, and then click cell **B3**. The formula *=Western!B3* appears in the Formula Bar.

8. Type + to enter the operator, click the **Eastern** sheet tab, and then click cell **B3**. The formula *=Western!B3+Eastern!B3* appears in the Formula Bar.

9. Press the **Enter** key. The formula is entered in cell B12 of the Corporate worksheet, which shows the formula result $306,744.

10. In the Corporate worksheet, click cell **B13**, if it is not already selected, and then type **=SUM(** to begin the formula.

11. Click the **Western** sheet tab, press and hold the **Shift** key, and then click the **Eastern** sheet tab. Release the **Shift** key. The formula with the worksheet range reference *=SUM('Western:Eastern'!* appears in the Formula Bar.

12. Click cell **B4**, and then press the **Enter** key. The cell reference is added to the 3-D reference in the formula, which is *=SUM('Western:Eastern'!B4)*. The formula result $551,399, which adds the values in cell B4 in the Eastern and Western worksheets, appears in cell B13.

13. Copy the formula in cell B13, and then paste the formula into cell B14. The value in cell B15 is the same as the value in cell B6, as shown in **Figure 7–9**.

FIGURE 7–9
Data summarized on one worksheet

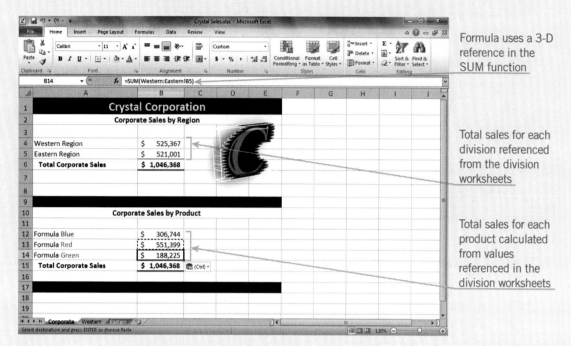

Formula uses a 3-D reference in the SUM function

Total sales for each division referenced from the division worksheets

Total sales for each product calculated from values referenced in the division worksheets

14. Save the workbook, and leave it open for the next Step-by-Step.

Printing a Workbook

So far, you have printed an active worksheet or selected areas of an active worksheet. You can also print an entire workbook, selected worksheets, or selected areas of a workbook. You designate the portion of the workbook to print on the Print tab in Backstage view, as shown in **Figure 7–10**. These options are described in **Table 7–2**.

Print the active worksheets in the workbook

Print all of the worksheets in the workbook, regardless of which are active

Print all of the cells selected in the workbook

Print all the contents of the active worksheets instead of the print areas

Header will show your name and the current date

Range A4:B6 in the Corporate worksheet

Each range prints on a separate page

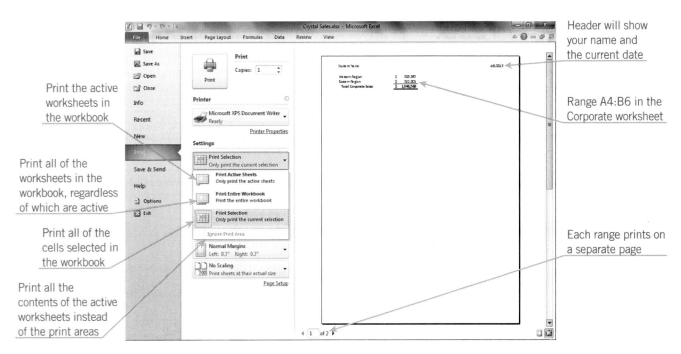

FIGURE 7-10 Print tab in Backstage view

TABLE 7-2 Print options

OPTION	DESCRIPTION
Print Active Sheets	Prints worksheet displayed in the workbook window, or a group of selected worksheets (Ctrl key +click sheet tabs to select multiple worksheets)
Print Entire Workbook	Prints all of the worksheets in the workbook
Print Selection	Prints the adjacent or nonadjacent ranges selected within a single worksheet
Ignore Print Area	Prints the entire worksheet, regardless of what print area is set for that worksheet

Printing Nonadjacent Selections of a Worksheet

You have already learned how to set a print area for a specific range in a worksheet. However, at times you might want to print more than one part of a worksheet on a page. For example, you might want to print the top and bottom sections of a worksheet, but not the middle section. To do this, you need to select multiple ranges in the worksheet.

To select more than one cell or range in a worksheet, select the first cell or range, hold down the Ctrl key, select each additional cell or range, and then release the Ctrl key. You can set the print area to include the nonadjacent range, and then print the active sheet as usual. Another alternative is to click Print Selection in the Settings section on the Print tab.

Printing More Than One Worksheet

When a workbook includes multiple worksheets, you will often want to print more than one worksheet at a time. To print all of the worksheets in the workbook, click Print Entire Workbook in the Settings section on the Print tab. To print specific worksheets in a workbook, you must first select the worksheets. To select multiple worksheets in a workbook, hold down the Ctrl key as you click the sheet tab of each worksheet you want to include in the group, and then release the Ctrl key (this method is referred to as Ctrl+click). In the Settings section on the Print tab, click Print Active Sheets.

Step-by-Step 7.4

1. Insert a header with your name and the current date.

2. In the Corporate worksheet, select the range **A4:B6**.

3. Hold down the **Ctrl** key, select the range **A12:B15**, and then release the **Ctrl** key. A nonadjacent range is selected in the Corporate worksheet.

4. Click the **File** tab on the Ribbon. In the navigation bar, click **Print**. The Print tab appears.

5. In the Settings section, click the top button. Point to **Print Selection** in printing options, as shown in Figure 7–10.

6. Click **Print Selection**. The range A4:B6 will print on page 1 and the range A12:B15 will print on page 2, as shown in the preview.

7. Click the **Print** button. The selected areas are printed.

8. Click the **Western** sheet tab, hold down the **Ctrl** key, click the **Eastern** sheet tab, and then release the **Ctrl** key. The two sheet tabs are selected.

9. Click the **File** tab on the Ribbon. In the navigation bar, click **Print**. The Print tab appears.

10. In the Settings section, click the top button, and then click **Print Active Sheets**. The Print tab shows a preview the selected worksheets.

11. Click the **Print** button. The worksheets with the data for each region are printed on separate pages.

12. Save and close the workbook. Leave Excel open for the next Step-by-Step.

Working with Multiple Workbooks

So far, you have worked with worksheets in the same workbook. Sometimes you might want to use data from worksheets in different workbooks. You can view these worksheets on the screen by arranging the workbooks. If you want to use the data from a worksheet in one workbook in another workbook, you can move or copy the worksheet to the new workbook.

Arranging Workbooks

Arranging lets you view more than one workbook on the screen at the same time. To arrange all the open workbooks, click the View tab on the Ribbon. In the Window group, click the Arrange All button. The Arrange Windows dialog box appears, as shown in **Figure 7–11**. Click the arrangement that you want to use to view the workbooks: Tiled, Horizontal, Vertical, or Cascade.

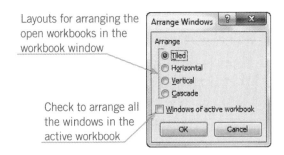

Layouts for arranging the open workbooks in the workbook window

Check to arrange all the windows in the active workbook

FIGURE 7–11   Arrange Windows dialog box

You can tell which workbook is active by looking at its title bar. The active workbook has a gray title bar, an Excel program icon in the upper-left corner, sizing buttons, and scroll bars. To make a workbook active, click its title bar or click anywhere in the worksheet. All of the buttons and commands on the Ribbon are available as usual.

Moving and Copying Worksheets Between Workbooks

When you need to include a worksheet from one workbook in another workbook, you can copy or move the worksheet. Right-click the sheet tab of the worksheet you want to move or copy, and then click Move or Copy on the shortcut menu. The Move or Copy dialog box appears. Click the To book arrow and click the workbook where you want to move or copy the selected worksheet. After you select the destination workbook, the names of all of its worksheets appear in the Before sheet box. Click the worksheet that you want to appear after the copied or moved worksheet. If you want to move the worksheet, click OK. If you want to copy the worksheet, click the Create a copy check box, and then click OK.

TIP

To move or copy multiple worksheets, first select the worksheets you want to move or copy, and then move or copy the worksheets as usual.

Step-by-Step 7.5

1. Open the **Annual.xlsx** workbook from the drive and folder where your Data Files are stored. Save the workbook as **Annual Income** followed by your initials.

2. Open the **March.xlsx** workbook from the drive and folder where your Data Files are stored. Save the workbook as **March Income** followed by your initials.

3. Click the **View** tab on the Ribbon. In the Window group, click the **Arrange All** button. The Arrange Windows dialog box appears, as shown in Figure 7–11.

4. Click the **Horizontal** option button, and then click **OK**. Both workbooks appear in the workbook window, as shown in **Figure 7–12**.

FIGURE 7–12
Workbooks arranged horizontally

Active workbook has an icon, a gray title bar, sizing buttons, and scroll bars

Inactive workbook has a white title bar and no scroll bars

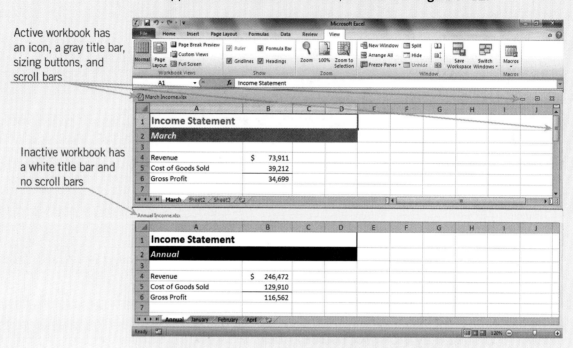

5. In the March Income workbook, right-click the **March** sheet tab, and then click **Move or Copy** on the shortcut menu. The Move or Copy dialog box appears.

6. Click the **To book** arrow, and then click **Annual Income.xlsx**. The worksheets in the Annual Income workbook appear in the Before sheet box.

7. In the Before sheet box, click **April** so the March worksheet will follow the February worksheet.

8. Click the **Create a copy** check box. The dialog box settings should appear similar to those in **Figure 7–13**.

FIGURE 7–13
Move or Copy dialog box

Workbook you want to copy a worksheet to

Worksheet you want to appear after the copied workbook

Check to copy rather than move the worksheet

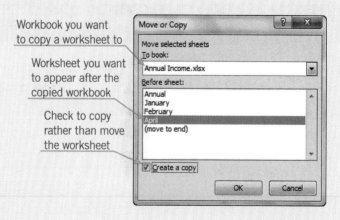

9. Click **OK**. A copy of the March worksheet appears in the Annual Income workbook before the April worksheet.

10. Click in the **March Income** workbook to make it the active workbook, and then on the title bar of the March Income workbook, click the **Close Window** button 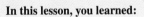 to close the workbook.

11. Click the **Maximize** button ◻ on the title bar of the Annual Income workbook. The workbook expands to fill the window.

12. Click the **Annual** tab. Notice that the totals that were updated include the values from the March worksheet because of the 3-D references in the formulas.

13. Click the **Annual** sheet tab, hold down the **Shift** key, click the **April** sheet tab, and then release the **Shift** key to select all the worksheets in the workbook. Insert a header with your name and the current date. The header appears on all the worksheets.

14. Click the **File** tab to open Backstage view. On the navigation bar, click **Print**. On the Print tab, in the Settings section, click the top button, and then click the **Print Entire Workbook**. Click the **Print** button. Save and close the workbook.

SUMMARY

In this lesson, you learned:

- Sheet tabs identify the names of worksheets. You click a sheet tab to make a worksheet the active sheet.

- You can rename worksheets with more descriptive names to better identify them. You can also change the color of the sheet tabs.

- Data is often best organized in multiple worksheets. You can drag a sheet tab to a new position to organize the worksheets in a more logical order. You can hide worksheets from view and then unhide them when needed. You can also insert and delete worksheets to accommodate the data.

- Rather than retyping data, you can create references to cells or ranges in another worksheet. You can also create formulas with 3-D references to the same cell or range in multiple worksheets.

- You can print entire workbooks, active worksheets, or selections in one or more worksheets.

- Arranging multiple workbooks in the workbook window lets you view their contents at the same time. Worksheets can be moved or copied from one workbook to the location you specify in the same or another workbook.

◼ VOCABULARY REVIEW

Define the following terms:

3-D reference   source   worksheet range
destination

■ REVIEW QUESTIONS

TRUE / FALSE

Circle T if the statement is true or F if the statement is false.

T   F   **1.**   Hiding a worksheet permanently removes it from the workbook.

T   F   **2.**   You can insert a worksheet in a workbook as needed to accommodate your data.

T   F   **3.**   When you create a reference to a cell in another worksheet, the location where the data will be used is the source.

T   F   **4.**   A worksheet range is a group of adjacent worksheets.

T   F   **5.**   In addition to printing an active worksheet or selected areas of an active worksheet, you can also print an entire workbook, selected worksheets, or selected areas of a workbook.

MATCHING

Match the correct formula result in Column 2 to its formula in Column 1.

Column 1

1. =Sheet2!D10
2. =Sheet2!D10+Sheet3!D11
3. =SUM(Sheet2:Sheet4!D10)
4. =SUM(Sheet2!D10:D11)
5. =Sheet3!D10+Sheet3!D11

Column 2

A. Inserts the value in cell D10 of the Sheet2 worksheet

B. Adds the values in cells D10 and D11 of the Sheet3 worksheet

C. Adds the values in cells D10 and D11 of the Sheet2 worksheet

D. Adds the values in cell D10 of the Sheet2 worksheet and cell D11 of the Sheet3 worksheet

E. Adds the values in cell D10 in the Sheet2, Sheet3, and Sheet4 worksheets

FILL IN THE BLANK

Complete the following sentences by writing the correct word or words in the blanks provided.

1. A(n) _____ is a collection of worksheets.

2. The worksheet that appears in the workbook window is the _____.

3. _____ identify worksheets within a workbook and appear at the bottom of the workbook window.

4. You can create formulas with _____ to the same cell or range in multiple worksheets.

5. _____ multiple workbooks in the workbook window lets you view their contents at the same time.

PROJECTS

If you have a SAM 2010 user profile, your instructor may have assigned an autogradable version of the indicated project. If so, log into the SAM 2010 Web site at *www.cengage.com/sam2010* to download the instruction and start files.

PROJECT 7–1

1. Open the **Rain.xlsx** workbook from the drive and folder where your Data Files are stored. Save the workbook as **Rain Records** followed by your initials.

2. Move the Sheet2 worksheet to the left of the Sheet3 worksheet.

3. Rename the worksheets and change the sheet tab colors as listed below:

Worksheet	New Name	Tab Color
Sheet1	**Annual**	Aqua, Accent 5
Sheet2	**January**	Aqua, Accent 5, Lighter 80%
Sheet3	**February**	Aqua, Accent 5, Lighter 60%
Sheet4	**March**	Aqua, Accent 5, Lighter 40%

4. Delete the Sheet5 worksheet.

5. In the Annual worksheet, in cell B3, display the total rainfall recorded in the January worksheet in cell B34.

6. In the Annual worksheet, in cell B4, display the total rainfall recorded in the February worksheet in cell B31.

7. In the Annual worksheet, in cell B5, display the total rainfall recorded in the March worksheet in cell B34.

8. Insert a header with your name and the current date in the Annual worksheet, and then save the workbook.

9. Print the Annual worksheet, and then close the workbook.

SAM PROJECT 7–2

1. Open the **Vote.xlsx** workbook from the drive and folder where your Data Files are stored. Save the workbook as **Vote Tally** followed by your initials.

2. Rename the worksheets and change the sheet tab colors as listed below:

Worksheet	New Name	Tab Color
Sheet1	**District 5**	Red
Sheet2	**P107**	Yellow
Sheet3	**P106**	Purple
Sheet4	**P105**	Green

3. Delete the Sheet5 worksheet.

4. Reposition the worksheets so they appear in the following order from left to right: District 5, P105, P106, and P107.

5. In the District 5 worksheet, in cell D7, enter a formula that adds the values in cell C5 of each of the precinct worksheets.

6. In the District 5 worksheet, in cell D9, enter a formula that adds the values in cell C7 of each of the precinct worksheets.

7. In the District 5 worksheet, in cell D11, enter a formula that adds the values in cell C9 of each of the precinct worksheets.

8. In the District 5 worksheet, in cell D13, enter a formula that adds the values in cell C11 of each of the precinct worksheets.

9. Insert a header with your name and the current date in the District 5 worksheet, and then save the workbook.

10. Print the District 5 worksheet, and then close the workbook.

PROJECT 7–3

1. Open the **Alamo.xlsx** workbook from the drive and folder where your Data Files are stored. Save the workbook as **Alamo Industries** followed by your initials.

2. Change the sheet tab colors as listed below:

Worksheet	Tab Color
Consolidated	Green
Alamogordo	Orange
Artesia	Light Blue

3. In the Consolidated worksheet, in cell D6, enter a formula that adds the values in cell B6 of the Alamogordo and Artesia worksheets.

4. In the Consolidated worksheet, in cell D7, enter a formula that adds the values in cell B7 of the Alamogordo and Artesia worksheets.

5. In the Consolidated worksheet, in cell D9, enter a formula that adds the values in cell B9 of the Alamogordo and Artesia worksheets.

6. In the Consolidated worksheet, in cell D10, enter a formula that adds the values in cell B10 of the Alamogordo and Artesia worksheets.

7. Insert a header with your name and the current date in the Consolidated worksheet, and then save the workbook.

8. Print all of the worksheets in the workbook, and then close the workbook.

PROJECT 7–4

1. Open the **Delta.xlsx** workbook from the drive and folder where your Data Files are stored. Save the workbook as **Delta Circuitry** followed by your initials.

2. Reposition the worksheets so they appear in the following order from left to right: Year, January, February, and March.

3. Change the worksheet tab colors as listed below:

Worksheet	Tab Color
Year	Red
January	Purple, Accent 4
February	Orange, Accent 6
March	Blue, Accent 1

4. In the Year worksheet, in cells B5, B6, and B7, display the total January monthly production for Circuits 370, 380, and 390. These values are recorded in the January worksheet in the range F4:F6.

5. In the Year worksheet, in cells C5, C6, and C7, display the total February monthly production for each circuit. These values are recorded in the February worksheet in the range F4:F6.

6. In the Year worksheet, in cells D5, D6, and D7, display the total March monthly production for each circuit. These values are recorded in the March worksheet in the range F4:F6.

7. Insert a header with your name and the current date in the Year worksheet, and then save the workbook.

8. Print the Year worksheet, and then close the workbook.

■ CRITICAL THINKING

ACTIVITY 7–1

Suppose you manage a local clothing store chain. Each of the chain's three stores has sent you a workbook in the same format that contains inventory data. You want to use the data you received to create a summary workbook with totals from all three stores. Use Excel Help to find out how you can create an external reference to a cell or range in another workbook. Write a brief description of your findings.

LESSON 8

Working with Charts

■ OBJECTIVES

Upon completion of this lesson, you should be able to:

- Identify the types of charts you can create in Excel.
- Create an embedded chart in a worksheet and move a chart to a chart sheet.
- Update a data source.
- Choose a chart layout and style.
- Create a 3-D chart.
- Display and hide chart elements.
- Format and modify a chart.
- Create sparklines.

■ VOCABULARY

axis

chart

chart area

chart layout

chart sheet

chart style

column chart

data label

data marker

data series

data source

data table

embedded chart

exploded pie chart

legend

line chart

pie chart

plot area

scatter chart

sparkline

▶ **VOCABULARY**
chart

A *chart* is a graphical representation of data. Charts make the data in a worksheet easier to understand by providing a visual picture of the data. For example, the left side of the worksheet shown in Figure 8–1 shows the populations of three major American cities over a 25-year time period. You might be able to detect the population changes by carefully examining the table. However, the population changes in each city are easier to see when the data is illustrated in a chart, such as the one shown on the right side of the worksheet in **Figure 8–1**. In this lesson, you will learn how to create, edit, and format charts.

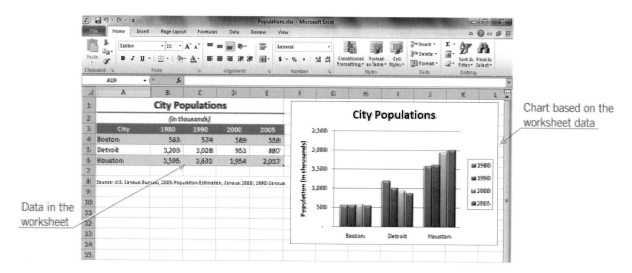

FIGURE 8–1   Worksheet data and chart

Comparing Chart Types

You can create a variety of charts in Excel. Each chart type works best for certain types of data. In this lesson, you will create four of the most commonly used charts: a column chart, a line chart, a pie chart, and a scatter chart. These charts as well as several other types of charts are available in the Charts group on the Insert tab on the Ribbon, as shown in **Figure 8–2**.

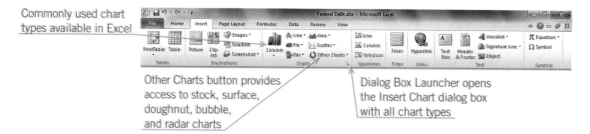

FIGURE 8–2   Charts group on the Insert tab

Column Chart

A *column chart* uses bars of varying heights to illustrate data in a worksheet. It is useful for showing relationships among categories of data. For example, the column chart in Figure 8–1 has one vertical bar to represent the population of each city in four different years. The bars show how the population of one city compares to populations of other cities.

Line Chart

A *line chart* is similar to a column chart, but it uses points connected by a line instead of bars. A line chart is ideal for illustrating trends over time. For example, the line chart shown in **Figure 8–3** illustrates the federal budget debt from 1995 to 2009. The vertical *axis* represents the federal budget debt in billions of dollars, and the horizontal axis shows the years. The line chart makes it easy to see that the federal budget debt has increased over time. A line chart can include multiple lines to compare two or more sets of data. For example, you could use a second line to chart the tax revenue received during the same time period.

▶ **VOCABULARY**
column chart

line chart

axis

TIP

Businesses often use column, bar, and line charts to illustrate growth over several periods. For example, a column chart can illustrate the changes in yearly production or income over a 10-year period.

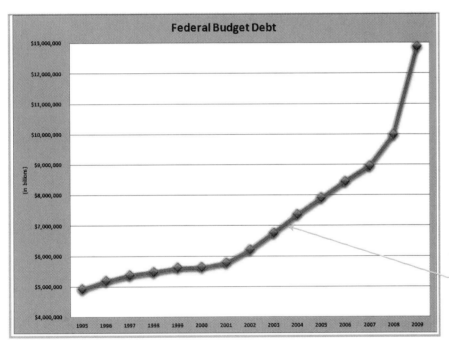

Ideal for illustrating trends of data over time

FIGURE 8–3   Line chart

Pie Chart

A *pie chart* shows the relationship of parts to a whole. Each part is shown as a "slice" of the pie. For example, **Figure 8–4** shows a pie chart that illustrates the grades earned by students in a class. Each slice represents one letter grade, and its size corresponds to the number of students who earned that grade.

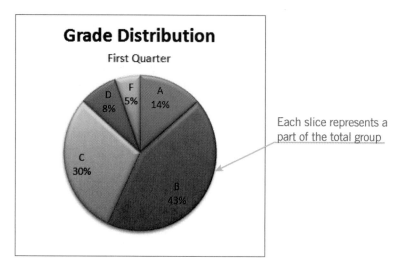

TIP

Businesses often use pie charts to indicate the magnitude of certain expenses in comparison to other expenses. Pie charts are also used to illustrate a company's market share in comparison to its competitors'.

FIGURE 8–4   Pie chart

You can pull one slice or multiple slices away from the pie to distinguish them, creating an *exploded pie chart*. This is helpful when you want to emphasize a specific part of the pie.

Scatter Chart

A *scatter chart*, sometimes called an XY chart, shows the relationship between two categories of data, such as a person's height and weight. One category is represented on the vertical axis, and the other category is represented on the horizontal axis. Because the data points on a scatter chart are not related to each other, they are usually not connected to each other with a line, like they are in a line chart. For example, **Figure 8–5** shows a scatter chart with one data point for each of 12 individuals, based on the person's height and weight. In most cases, a taller person tends to weigh more than a shorter person. However, because some people are underweight and others are overweight, you cannot use a line to represent the relationship between height and weight.

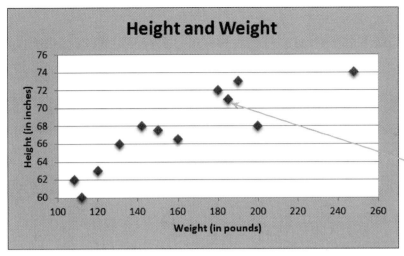

FIGURE 8–5   Scatter chart

Creating a Chart

The process for creating a chart is similar no matter which chart type you want to create. First, you select the data you want to use for the chart. Second, you select a chart type. Finally, you select the chart location. In this section, you will create a column chart.

Selecting the Data to Chart

Charts are based on data. In Excel, the chart data, called the *data source*, is stored in a range of cells in the worksheet. When you select the data source for a chart, you should also include the text you want to use as labels in the chart. You can also choose whether to chart more than one series of data. A *data series* is a group of related information in a column or row of a worksheet that is plotted on the chart.

▶ **VOCABULARY**
data source
data series

Selecting a Chart Type

The next step is to select the type of chart you want to create, such as a column, pie, or line chart. Each chart type has a variety of subtypes you can choose from. The chart types are available on the Insert tab in the Charts group. You can click the button for a specific chart type and then select the subtype you want. The Insert Chart dialog box, shown in **Figure 8–6**, provides access to all of the chart types and subtypes. You open the Insert Chart dialog box by clicking the Dialog Box Launcher in the Charts group on the Insert tab.

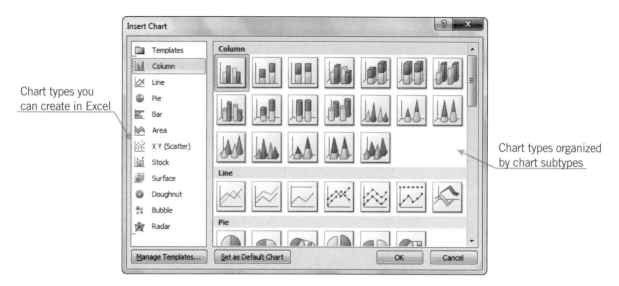

Chart types you can create in Excel

Chart types organized by chart subtypes

FIGURE 8–6   Insert Chart dialog box

Choosing the Chart Location

After you select a chart type and subtype, the chart is inserted in the center of the worksheet, as shown in **Figure 8-7**. This is called an ***embedded chart***. When a chart is selected, the Chart Tools appear on the Ribbon with three tabs: Design, Layout, and Format. Also, a selection box with sizing handles appears around the chart. The embedded chart can be viewed at the same time as the data from which it is created. When you print the worksheet, the chart is also printed.

Chart Tools appear on the Ribbon when the chart is selected

Data source for the column chart

Selection box appears around the selected column chart

Button to move the chart between an embedded chart in a worksheet and a chart sheet

Corner sizing handle

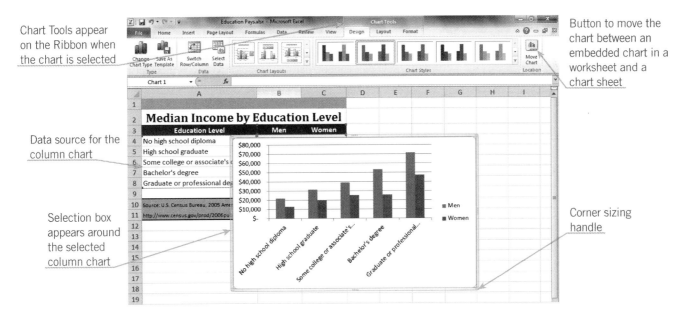

FIGURE 8–7 Embedded chart

An embedded chart might cover the data source or other information in the worksheet. You can quickly move and resize the embedded chart so it fits better within the worksheet. You move an embedded chart by dragging the selected chart by its selection box to a different part of the worksheet. You resize an embedded chart by dragging one of the sizing handles, which are indicated by the dots at the corners and sides of the selected chart.

You can move an embedded chart to a *chart sheet*, which is a separate sheet in a workbook that stores a chart. A chart sheet does not contain worksheet cells, data, or formulas. A chart sheet displays the chart without its data source, and is convenient when you plan to create more than one chart from the same data or want to focus on the chart rather than its underlying data.

EXTRA FOR EXPERTS

You can keep a chart's height and width in the same proportion as you resize it by pressing Shift as you drag a corner sizing handle.

VOCABULARY

chart sheet

TIP

You can rename a chart sheet like any other worksheet. Right-click its sheet tab, and then click Rename on the shortcut menu. Type a descriptive name for the chart sheet, and then press the Enter key.

TIP

Embedded charts are useful when you want to print a chart next to the data the chart illustrates. When a chart will be displayed or printed without the data used to create the chart, a separate chart sheet is usually more appropriate.

To move an embedded chart to a chart sheet, click the Chart Tools Design tab on the Ribbon. Then, in the Location group, click the Move Chart button. The Move Chart dialog box appears, as shown in **Figure 8–8**. You can choose to move the chart to a new chart sheet that you name or to any worksheet in the workbook as an embedded chart. You can use the same process to move a chart from a chart sheet to any worksheet as an embedded chart.

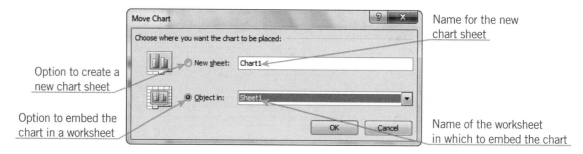

FIGURE 8–8   Move Chart dialog box

Step-by-Step 8.1

1. Open the **Education.xlsx** workbook from the drive and folder where your Data Files are stored. Save the workbook as **Education Pays** followed by your initials. Column A contains education levels, and columns B and C contain the median incomes of men and women for each corresponding education level.

2. Select the range **A3:C8**. This is the data you want to chart.

3. Click the **Insert** tab on the Ribbon. In the Charts group, click the **Column** button. A gallery of available column chart subtypes appears.

4. In the 2-D Column section, point to **Clustered Column** (the first chart in the first row). A ScreenTip appears with a description of the selected chart: *Clustered Column. Compare values across categories by using vertical rectangles.*

5. Click the **Clustered Column** button. The 2-D clustered column chart is embedded in the worksheet. A selection box with sizing handles appears around the chart, as shown in Figure 8–7.

6. Point to the selection box. The pointer changes to the move pointer ⬩. Drag the selected chart so that the upper-left corner of the chart is in cell A13. The chart is repositioned in the worksheet.

7. Drag the lower-right sizing handle to cell **D26**. The chart is sized to cover the range A13:D26.

8. On the Ribbon, click the **Design** tab, if it is not already selected.

9. In the Location group, click the **Move Chart** button. The Move Chart dialog box appears, as shown in Figure 8–8.

10. Click the **New sheet** option button. The text in the New sheet box is selected so you can type a descriptive name for the chart sheet.

11. In the New sheet box, type **Column**.

12. Click **OK**. The embedded chart moves to a chart sheet named *Column*, as shown in **Figure 8–9**. The chart illustrates the value of education in attaining higher income. The columns get higher on the right side of the chart, indicating that those who stay in school are rewarded with higher incomes.

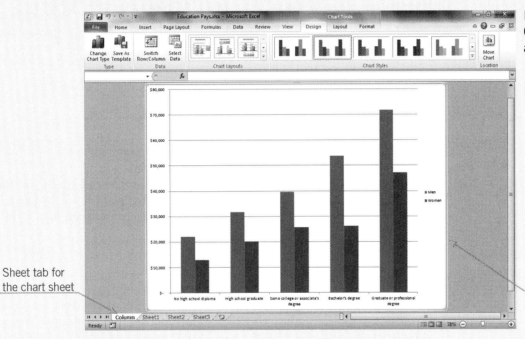

FIGURE 8–9
Column chart sheet added to workbook

Sheet tab for the chart sheet

Selected chart in the chart sheet

13. Save the workbook, and leave it open for the next Step-by-Step.

Updating a Data Source

Charts are based on the data stored in a worksheet. If you need to change the data in the worksheet, the chart is automatically updated to reflect the new data. You switch between a chart sheet and a worksheet by clicking the appropriate sheet tabs.

Step-by-Step 8.2

1. Click the **Sheet1** sheet tab. This worksheet with the data source appears.

2. Click cell **A5**, and then enter **High school diploma**.

3. Click the **Column** sheet tab to display the chart sheet. The label for the second column reflects the edit you made to the data source.

4. Save the workbook, and leave it open for the next Step-by-Step.

Designing a Chart

▶ VOCABULARY
legend

Most charts include some basic elements, such as a title and *legend*, which you can choose to include or hide. You can also choose a chart style and layout to give the chart a cohesive design. Finally, you can add labels and other elements to make the chart easier to understand and interpret and more attractive.

Selecting Chart Elements

Charts are made up of different parts, or elements. **Figure 8–10** identifies some common chart elements, which are described in **Table 8–1**. Not all elements appear in every type of chart. For example, a pie chart does not have axes. Also, you can choose which chart elements to use in a chart.

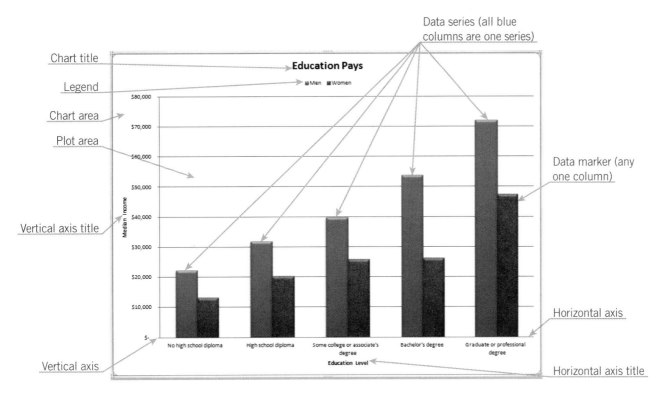

FIGURE 8–10   Chart elements

TABLE 8–1   Chart elements

ELEMENT	DESCRIPTION
Chart area	The entire chart and all other chart elements
Plot area	The area that displays the graphical representation of data
Data series	Related information in a worksheet column or row that is plotted on a chart; many charts can include more than one data series
Data marker	A symbol (such as a bar, line, dot, slice, and so forth) that represents a single data point or value from the corresponding worksheet cell
Data label	Text or numbers that provide additional information about a data marker, such as the value from the worksheet cell (not shown in Figure 8–10)
Axes	Lines that establish a relationship between data in a chart; most charts have a horizontal x-axis and a vertical y-axis
Titles	Descriptive labels that identify the contents of the chart and the axes
Legend	A list that identifies the patterns, symbols, or colors used in a chart
Data table	A grid that displays the data plotted in the chart (not shown in Figure 8–10)

The quickest way to select a chart element is to click it. You can tell that you are clicking the correct element by first pointing to the element to display a ScreenTip with its name. A selected chart element is surrounded by a selection box. You can also use the Ribbon to select chart elements. When the chart is selected, click the Format tab or the Layout tab on the Ribbon. In the Current Selection group, click the arrow next to the Chart Elements box. A menu of chart elements for the selected chart appears. Click the name of the element you want to select.

After you select a chart element, you can modify it. For example, you can select the chart title or an axis title, and then enter new text for the title. You can also use the standard text formatting tools to change the font, font size, font color, and so forth of the selected title.

Choosing a Chart Layout and Style

▶ **VOCABULARY**

chart layout

chart style

You can quickly change a chart's appearance by applying a layout and style. A *chart layout* specifies which elements are included in a chart and where they are placed. **Figure 8–11** shows the chart layouts available for column charts. For example, the legend appears above, below, to the right of, or to the left of the chart in different layouts.

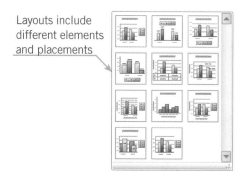

Layouts include different elements and placements

FIGURE 8–11   Chart Layouts gallery for column charts

A *chart style* formats the chart based on the colors, fonts, and effects associated with the workbook's theme. **Figure 8–12** shows the chart styles available for column charts.

Styles include different colors and effects

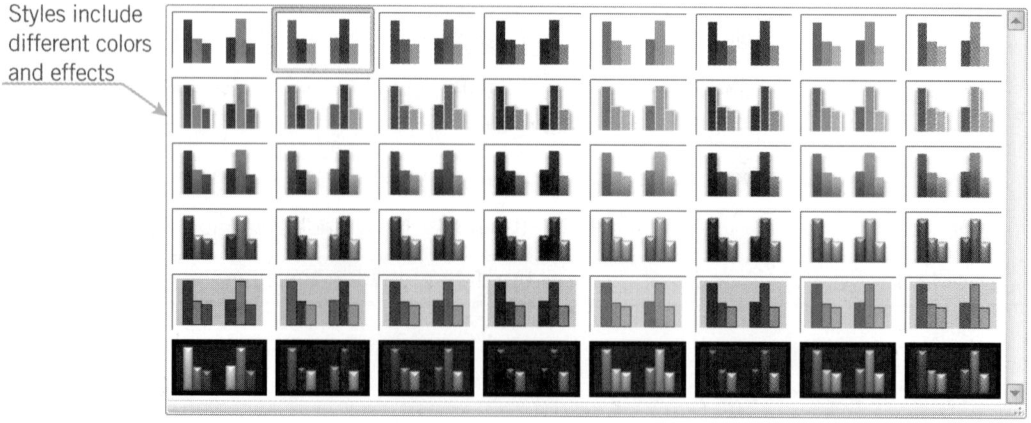

FIGURE 8–12   Chart Styles gallery for column charts

You can quickly choose a layout and style for a selected chart from the Ribbon. Click the Design tab on the Ribbon. In the Chart Layouts group, click the chart layout you want to use. In the Chart Styles group, click the chart style you want to use.

Arranging Chart Elements

You can modify a chart's appearance by displaying and hiding specific chart elements and rearranging where they are positioned. For example, you can choose when and where to display the chart title, axis titles, legend, *data labels*, *data table*, axes, gridlines, and the *plot area*. First, select the chart. Then click the Layout tab on the Ribbon. The Labels, Axes, and Background groups on the Layout tab contain buttons for each chart element. Finally, use the commands on the appropriate button to display that element in a particular location in the *chart area* or hide it.

> **VOCABULARY**
> **data label**
> **data table**
> **plot area**
> **chart area**

Step-by-Step 8.3

1. On the Ribbon, click the **Design** tab, if it is not already selected.

2. In the Chart Layouts group, click the **More** button ⬇. The Chart Layouts gallery appears, as shown in Figure 8–11.

3. Click **Layout 9** (the third layout in the third row). Placeholders for the chart title and axes titles are added to the chart.

4. Click the **Chart Title** to select it. Type **Education Pays**, and then press the **Enter** key. The chart title is updated.

5. Click the vertical **Axis Title** to select it, type **Median Income**, and then press the **Enter** key.

6. Click the horizontal **Axis Title** to select it, type **Education Level**, and then press the **Enter** key.

7. On the Design tab, in the Chart Styles group, click the **More** button ⬇. The Chart Styles gallery appears, as shown in Figure 8–12.

8. Click **Style 26** (the second style in the fourth row). The chart changes to match the selected style.

9. On the Ribbon, click the **Layout** tab.

10. On the Layout tab, in the Labels group, click the **Legend** button. A gallery appears with different placement options for the legend.

11. Click **Show Legend at Top**. The legend moves to below the chart title, as shown in Figure 8–10.

12. On the Ribbon, click the **Insert** tab. In the Text group, click the **Header & Footer** button. The Page Setup dialog box appears with the Header/Footer tab active. Click the **Custom Header** button. The Header dialog box opens.

> **TIP**
>
> You can delete a selected chart by pressing Delete. You can delete chart sheets by right-clicking the sheet tab for the chart sheet, and then clicking Delete on the shortcut menu.

13. In the Left section box, type your name. Click in the **Right section** box, and then click the **Insert Date** button 🗓. Click the **OK** button in each dialog box. The header is added to the chart sheet.

14. Save the workbook, print the chart sheet, and close the workbook. Leave Excel open for the next Step-by-Step.

Creating a 3-D Chart

▶ **VOCABULARY**

data marker

A pie chart shows the relationship of a part to a whole. Each part is shown as a "slice" of the pie. The slices are different colors to distinguish each *data marker*. Pie charts, as with many chart types, can be two-dimensional (2-D) or three-dimensional (3-D). When you select the chart style, click a 3-D chart subtype to create a 3-D chart.

Step-by-Step 8.4

1. Open the **Great.xlsx** workbook from the drive and folder where your Data Files are stored. Save the workbook as **Great Plains** followed by your initials.

2. Select the range **A5:B8**. This range contains the data that shows the sales for each product segment.

3. Click the **Insert** tab on the Ribbon. In the Charts group, click the **Pie** button.

4. In the 3-D Pie section, click **Pie in 3-D** (the first chart in the row). A 3-D pie chart is embedded in the worksheet.

5. On the Ribbon, click the **Design** tab, if the tab is not already selected. In the Chart Layouts group, click the **More** button ⏷. The Chart Layouts gallery appears.

6. Click **Layout 1** (the first layout in the first row). The legend disappears, and each slice of the pie shows the label and the percentage of the whole it comprises.

7. In the chart, click the **Chart Title**, type **Annual Sales by Segment**, and then press the **Enter** key. The new chart title is entered above the chart.

8. Move and resize the chart to fit within the range **D1:H9**. The 3-D pie chart, shown in **Figure 8–13**, illustrates that soybeans account for the largest percentage of annual sales.

> **EXTRA FOR EXPERTS**
>
> To create an exploded pie chart, select one of the 2-D or 3-D exploded pie chart subtypes. Or, you can click the data markers in an existing pie chart to select the series, click the slice you want to explode, and then drag the selected slice away from the pie.

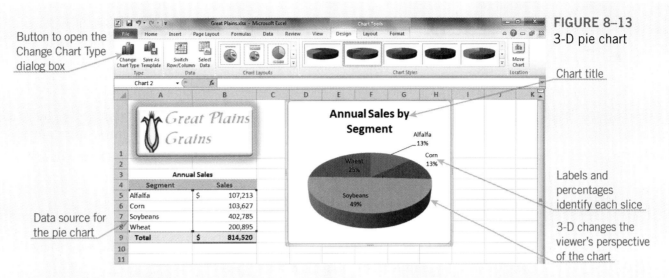

FIGURE 8–13
3-D pie chart

Button to open the Change Chart Type dialog box

Chart title

Data source for the pie chart

Labels and percentages identify each slice

3-D changes the viewer's perspective of the chart

9. Click cell **A11** to deselect the pie chart.

10. Insert a header with your name and the current date, and then print the worksheet.

11. Save and close the workbook. Leave Excel open for the next Step-by-Step.

Formatting and Modifying a Chart

Scatter charts are sometimes called XY charts because they place data points between the x-axis and the y-axis. Scatter charts can be harder to design because you must designate which data should be used on each axis.

Step-by-Step 8.5

1. Open the **Coronado.xlsx** workbook from the drive and folder where your Data Files are stored. Save the workbook as **Coronado Foundries** followed by your initials.

2. Select the range **B5:B15**. Press and hold the **Ctrl** key, select the range **D5:D15**, and then release the **Ctrl** key. This nonadjacent range contains the data you want to chart.

3. Click the **Insert** tab on the Ribbon. In the Charts group, click the **Scatter** button. In the Scatter section, click **Scatter with only Markers** (the first chart in the first row). The scatter chart is embedded in the worksheet.

4. On the Ribbon, click the **Layout** tab. In the Labels group, click the **Chart Title** button, and then click **Above Chart**. The chart title appears above the scatter chart and is selected.

5. Type **June Production and Scrap Report**, and then press the **Enter** key.

6. On the Layout tab, in the Labels group, click the **Axis Titles** button, point to **Primary Horizontal Axis Title**, and then click **Title Below Axis**. The axis title appears below the horizontal axis and is selected.

7. Type **Units Produced**, and then press the **Enter** key. The horizontal axis title is updated.

8. On the Layout tab, in the Labels group, click the **Axis Titles** button, point to **Primary Vertical Axis Title**, and then click **Rotated Title**. The axis title is rotated along the vertical axis and is selected.

9. Type **Units of Scrap**, and then press the **Enter** key. The vertical access title is updated.

10. Click the **Legend** to select it, and then press the **Delete** key. The legend is removed from the chart.

11. Right-click the **chart area** of the selected chart, and then click **Move Chart** on the shortcut menu. The Move Chart dialog box appears.

12. Click the **New sheet** option button. In the New sheet box, type **Scatter Chart**.

13. Click **OK**. The scatter chart appears on a new chart sheet. The chart illustrates that factories with larger production tend to generate more scrap.

14. Save the workbook, and leave it open for the next Step-by-Step.

Formatting a Chart

The Chart Tools provide a simple way to create professional-looking charts. However, you might want to fine-tune a chart's appearance to better suit your purposes. For example, you might want to change the color of a data marker or the scale used for the axis. To make changes to an element's fill, border color, border style, shadow, 3-D format, alignment, and so forth, you need to open its Format dialog box. The Format dialog box for each chart element contains options for editing specific characteristics of that element.

To access the Format dialog box for a chart element, select the chart element you want to edit. Then, on the Format tab on the Ribbon, in the Current Selection group, click the Format Selection button. The Format dialog box for the selected element appears. You can also right-click the element you want to edit, and then click the corresponding Format command on the shortcut menu.

Step-by-Step 8.6

1. On the Ribbon, click the **Format** tab.

2. In the Current Selection group, click the **Chart Elements arrow** to open a menu of elements on the selected chart, and then click **Horizontal (Value) Axis**.

3. In the Current Selection group, click the **Format Selection** button. The Format Axis dialog box appears with the Axis Options active, as shown in **Figure 8–14**.

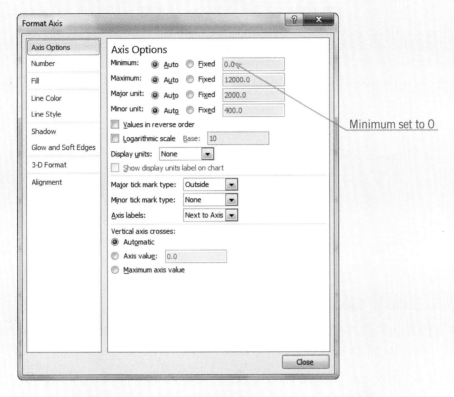

FIGURE 8–14
Format Axis dialog box for the horizontal (value) axis

4. Next to Minimum, click the **Fixed** option button. In the Minimum Fixed box, select the current value, and then type **4000**. The x-axis ranges from 4,000 to 12,000 units produced.

5. Click **Close**. The section of the chart to the left of 4,000 on the x-axis, which did not have any data points, disappears.

6. Point to the **Vertical (Value) Axis** on the chart. The ScreenTip appears, confirming that the correct element will be selected.

7. Click the **Vertical (Value) Axis** on the chart, right-click the selected axis, and then click **Format Axis** on the shortcut menu. The Format Axis dialog box appears with the Axis Options active.

8. Next to Maximum, click the **Fixed** option button. In the Maximum Fixed box, select the current value, and then type **250**.

9. Click **Close**. The section of the chart above 250 on the y-axis, which did not have any data points, disappears.

10. Point to the **Chart Area**. Verify that the ScreenTip reads *Chart Area*. Click the **Chart Area** to select it. See **Figure 8–15**.

FIGURE 8–15
Scatter chart

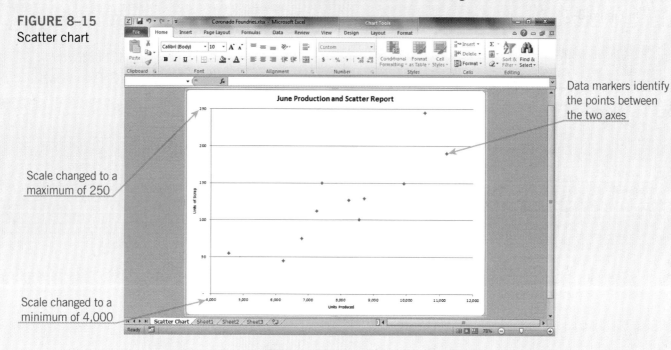

Data markers identify the points between the two axes

Scale changed to a maximum of 250

Scale changed to a minimum of 4,000

11. Insert a header with your name and the current date, and then print the chart sheet.

12. Save and close the workbook. Leave Excel open for the next Step-by-Step.

Editing and Formatting Chart Text

You might want to change a chart title's font or color to make a chart more attractive and interesting. You use the standard text formatting tools to make changes to the fonts used in the chart.

Step-by-Step 8.7

1. Open the **Red.xlsx** workbook from the drive and folder where your Data Files are stored. Save the workbook as **Red Cross** followed by your initials.

2. Click the **Bar Chart** sheet tab. The bar chart illustrates the operating expenses for each year.

3. Click **American Red Cross** to select the chart title.

4. Click to the right of the last **s** in the title. The insertion point appears at the end of the title.

5. Press the **Enter** key. The insertion point is centered under the first line of the title.

6. Type **Operating Expenses**, and then click the **Chart Area**. The chart resizes to accommodate the second line of the title.

7. Click the **Horizontal (Value) Axis** to select it.

8. Click the **Home** tab on the Ribbon. In the Font group, click the **Font Size arrow**, and then click **10**. The font size of the horizontal axis labels changes to 10 points.

9. Click the **Vertical (Category) Axis** to select it.

10. On the Home tab, in the Font group, click the **Font Size arrow**, and then click **10**. The font size of the vertical axis labels changes to 10 points.

11. Save the workbook, and leave it open for the next Step-by-Step.

Changing the Chart Type

You can change the chart type or subtype at any time. Select the chart, and then on the Design tab, in the Type group, click the Change Chart Type button. The Change Chart Type dialog box appears, and includes the same options as the Insert Chart Type dialog box. The only difference is that the chart type and subtype you select update the selected chart instead of creating a new chart.

 TIP

Not all charts are interchangeable. For example, data suitable for a pie chart is often not logical in a scatter chart. However, most line charts are easily converted into column or bar charts.

Step-by-Step 8.8

1. On the Ribbon, click the **Design** tab.

2. In the Type group, click the **Change Chart Type** button. The Change Chart Type dialog box appears with the Bar chart type selected.

3. In the Line section, click **Line with Markers** (the fourth line chart subtype).

4. Click **OK**. The bar chart changes to a line chart with markers.

5. Rename the chart sheet as **Line Chart**. **Figure 8–16** shows the chart with the new chart type and style.

FIGURE 8–16
Line chart

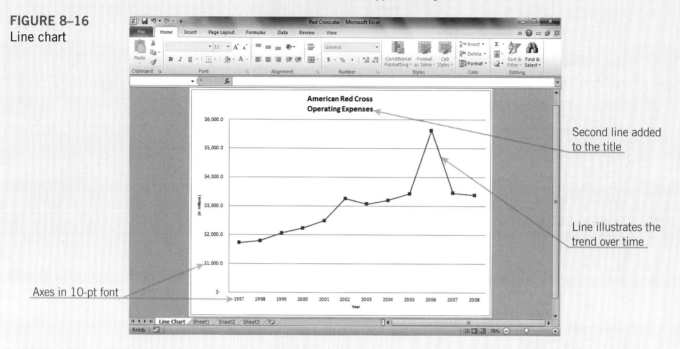

Axes in 10-pt font

Second line added to the title

Line illustrates the trend over time

6. Insert a header with your name and the current date, and then print the chart sheet.

7. Save the workbook, and leave it open for the next Step-by-Step.

Inserting Sparklines

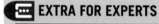
Sparklines are mini charts that you can insert into a cell. They are useful for highlighting patterns or trends in data. **Figure 8–17** shows examples of the three types of sparklines you can create: line, column, and win/loss. A line sparkline is a line chart that appears within one cell. A column sparkline is a column chart that appears within one cell. A win/loss sparkline inserts a win/loss chart, which tracks gains and losses, within one cell.

	A	B	C	D	E
1	**Sparklines**				
2	Line				
3	Revenue	$ 1,203	$ 1,028	$ 951	$ 887
4					
5	Column				
6	Units Sold	1595	1631	1954	2017
7					
8	Win/Loss				
9	Value	102	175	(75)	25
10					

FIGURE 8–17   Examples of line, column, and win/loss sparklines

To create a sparkline, first select the range where you want to insert the spar-kline. In the Sparklines group on the Insert tab, click the button corresponding to the type of sparkline you want to create. The Create Sparklines dialog box appears, as shown in **Figure 8–18**. You select the cells that contain the data you want to chart with the sparkline. Click Create. A sparkline for each data series appears in a sepa-rate worksheet cell in the location range you selected.

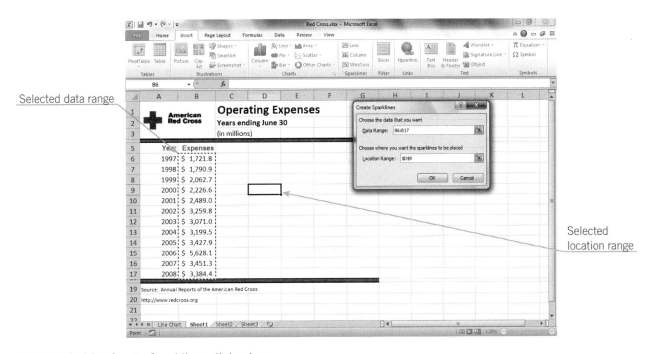

Selected data range

Selected location range

FIGURE 8–18   Create Sparklines dialog box

After you create sparklines, you can modify them, using tools on the Design tab. You can show a variety of data markers on the sparklines, including the high and low points, negative point, first and last points, and all data points. These options are available in the Show group. You can change the appearance of a sparkline by selecting a style from the Style gallery, or using the Sparkline Color button or the Marker Color button to choose new colors for the sparkline or data markers, respectively. You can also change the sparkline type from one type to another using the buttons in the Type group.

Step-by-Step 8.9

1. Click the **Sheet1** sheet tab. This is the worksheet with the data.

2. Click cell **D9**. This cell is where you want the sparkline to appear.

3. Click the **Insert** tab on the Ribbon.

4. In the Sparklines group, click the **Line** button. The Create Sparklines dialog box appears.

5. Make sure the insertion point is in the Data Range box, and then select the range **B6:B17** in the worksheet. This range contains the data you want to chart in the sparkline. The Create Sparklines dialog box should look like Figure 8–18.

6. Click **OK**. The line sparkline inserted in cell D9 shows how expenses have continually increased, with a sharp spike in a recent year.

7. Select the range **D9:G11**.

8. Click the **Home** tab on the Ribbon. In the Alignment group, click the **Merge and Center** button ⊞. The line sparkline increases to fill the merged cell, making it easier to see.

9. On the Ribbon, click the **Design** tab. The Design tab appears on the Ribbon when a sparkline is selected, and contains options for formatting the sparkline.

10. In the Show group, click the **High Point** check box, the **Low Point** check box, and the **Markers** check box. Data markers are added to each data point. The markers for the high and low points are a different color than the rest of the data points. See **Figure 8–19**.

FIGURE 8–19
Line sparkline

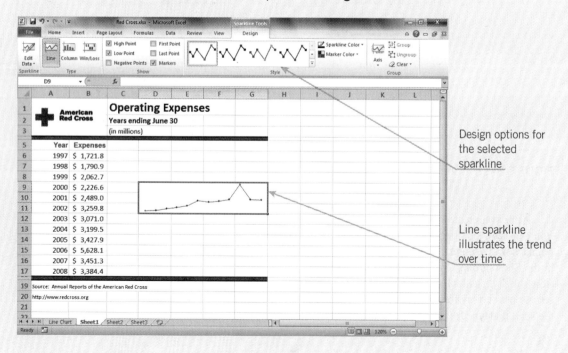

Design options for the selected sparkline

Line sparkline illustrates the trend over time

11. On the Design tab, in the Type group, click the **Column** button. The line sparkline changes to a column sparkline. The bars for the high and low points have different colors. Because a column sparkline doesn't have data points, it doesn't have any markers on it. See **Figure 8–20**.

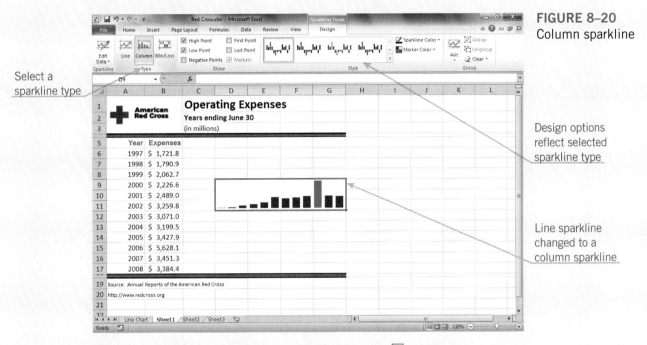

Select a sparkline type

FIGURE 8–20
Column sparkline

Design options reflect selected sparkline type

Line sparkline changed to a column sparkline

12. On the Design tab, in the Style group, click the **More** button. In the Style gallery, click **Sparkline Style Dark #3** (the third style in the fifth row). The bar colors in the sparkline are updated with colors from Sparkline Style Dark #3.

13. Insert a header with your name and the current date, and then print the worksheet.

14. Save and close the workbook.

SUMMARY

In this lesson, you learned:

- A chart is a graphical representation of data. You can create several types of worksheet charts, including column, line, pie, and scatter charts.

- Charts can be embedded within a worksheet or created on a chart sheet.

- The process for creating a chart is the same for all chart types. Select the data for the chart. Select a chart type. Move, resize, and format the chart as needed.

- Charts are made up of different parts, or elements. You can apply a chart layout and a chart style to determine which elements appear in the chart, where they appear, and how they look.

- If the data in a chart's data source is changed in the worksheet, the chart is automatically updated to reflect the new data.

- You can fine-tune a chart by clicking a chart element and then opening its Format dialog box. You can also edit and format the chart text, using the standard text formatting tools.

- You can change the type of chart in the Change Chart Type dialog box.

- Sparklines are mini charts you can insert into a worksheet cell to show a pattern or trend. The three types of sparklines are line, column, and win/loss.

VOCABULARY REVIEW

Define the following terms:

axis	data label	legend
chart	data marker	line chart
chart area	data series	pie chart
chart layout	data source	plot area
chart sheet	data table	scatter chart
chart style	embedded chart	sparkline
column chart	exploded pie chart	

REVIEW QUESTIONS

TRUE / FALSE

Circle T if the statement is true or F if the statement is false.

T   F   **1.**   Charts are a graphical representation of data.

T   F   **2.**   An embedded chart can be moved and resized.

T   F   **3.**   A sparkline is a mini chart that is inserted within a cell.

T   F   **4.**   When the data source changes, charts created from that data do not change.

T   F   **5.**   After you create a chart, you can change the chart type or subtype.

FILL IN THE BLANK

Complete the following sentences by writing the correct word or words in the blanks provided.

1. A(n) _____ chart is represented by a circle divided into portions.

2. A group of related information in a column or row of a worksheet that is plotted on a chart is a(n) _____.

3. A(n) _____ chart is inserted on the same sheet as the data being charted.

4. In a chart, the _____ shows the patterns or symbols that identify the different types of data.

5. A(n) _____ specifies which elements are included in a chart and their locations.

MATCHING

Match the correct chart type in Column 2 to its description in Column 1.

Column 1

1. Shows the relationship of parts to a whole.

2. Shows the relationship between two categories of data, creating data points that are unrelated to each other

3. Illustrates trends over time

4. Shows relationships among categories of data

5. Tracks gains or losses

Column 2

A. Column chart

B. Line chart

C. Pie chart

D. Scatter chart

E. Win/loss sparkline

■ PROJECTS

If you have a SAM 2010 user profile, your instructor may have assigned an autogradable version of the indicated project. If so, log into the SAM 2010 Web site at *www.cengage.com/sam2010* to download the instruction and start files.

PROJECT 8–1

1. Open the **Largest.xlsx** workbook from the drive and folder where your Data Files are stored. Save the workbook as **Largest Cities** followed by your initials.

2. Select the data in the range A5:B14, and then insert an embedded column chart using the 2-D clustered column style.

3. Move the chart to a chart sheet named **Column Chart**.

4. Apply Layout 6 and Style 29 to the chart. Delete the Series 1 Data Labels from the chart if it appears over the Jakarta column.

5. Enter the chart title as **10 Largest Cities in the World**.

6. Enter the vertical axis title as **Population in Millions**.

7. Insert a header with your name and the current date, and then print the chart sheet. Save and close the workbook.

SAM PROJECT 8–2

1. Open the **Concession.xlsx** workbook from the drive and folder where your Data Files are stored. Save the workbook as **Concession Sales** followed by your initials.

2. Select the range H5:H10, and then create line sparklines for the data range B5:E10.

3. Show high point markers on the line sparklines, and format them with Sparkline Style Dark #3.

4. Insert a header with your name and the current date. Print the worksheet.

5. Using the data in the range A4:E10, create an embedded 2-D clustered column chart.

6. Move the chart to a chart sheet named **Column Chart**.

7. Apply the Layout 1 chart layout to the chart. Apply the Style 34 chart style to the chart.

8. Change the chart title to **Concession Sales**. Change the font size of the chart title to 24 points.

9. Add the following rotated vertical axis title: **Sales in Dollars**. Change the font size of the axis title to 14 points.

10. Change the font size of the horizontal and vertical axis labels to 12 points and make them bold.

11. Move the legend to above the chart. Change the font size of the legend to 12 points.

12. Right-click the plot area of the chart, and then click Format Plot Area on the shortcut menu. In the Format Plot Area dialog box that appears, click the Solid fill option button. Click the Color button, and then click White, Background 1, Darker 15% (the first color in the third row). Click Close.

13. Which product(s) has decreased in sales over the last four games? Which product(s) has increased in sales over the last four games?

14. Insert a header with your name and the current date. Print the chart sheet. Save and close the workbook.

PROJECT 8–3

1. Open the **Run.xlsx** workbook from the drive and folder where your Data Files are stored. Save the workbook as **Run Times** followed by your initials.

2. Using the data in the range A5:B14, insert an embedded line chart with markers in the worksheet.

3. Apply chart Style 39.

4. In the range A5:A14, delete the word **Week**, leaving only the week number.

5. Add a horizontal axis title below the axis with the text **Week**.

6. Add a rotated vertical axis with the text **Time in Minutes**.

7. Do not include a chart title or legend in the chart.

8. Resize and move the chart to fill the range C4:K19.

9. Insert a header with your name and the current date. Print the worksheet with the embedded chart, and then save and close the workbook.

PROJECT 8–5

1. Open the **Cash.xlsx** workbook from the drive and folder where your Data Files are stored. Save the workbook as **Cash Surplus** followed by your initials.

2. Using the data in the range A6:B13, create an embedded pie chart using the Pie in 3-D style.

3. Move the chart to a chart sheet named **3-D Pie Chart**.

4. Choose the chart layout that includes a chart title and data labels with percentages, but does not include a legend.

5. Change the chart title to **Where We Spend Our Money**.

6. Apply the Style 26 chart style.

7. Change the font size of the chart title to 24 points.

8. Change the font size of the data labels to 14 points.

9. Based on the chart, in which area(s) does the family spend the most?

10. Insert a header with your name and the current date. Print the chart sheet. Save and close the workbook.

PROJECT 8–4

1. Open the **McDonalds** workbook from the drive and folder where your Data Files are stored. Save the workbook as **McDonalds Report** followed by your initials.

2. Using the data in the range A3:B6, create an embedded pie chart using the Pie in 3-D style.

3. Apply the Layout 6 chart layout and the Style 18 chart style.

4. Enter the chart title **Total Restaurants**.

5. Show the legend at the top of the chart.

6. Move the chart to a chart sheet named **Pie Chart**.

7. Format the font sizes of the chart title to 28 points, the data labels (showing the slice percentages) to 18 points, and the legend to 14 points.

8. Insert a header with your name and the current date. Print the chart sheet. Save and close the workbook.

PROJECT 8–6

1. Open the **Study.xlsx** workbook from the drive and folder where your Data Files are stored. Save the workbook as **Study and Grades** followed by your initials.

2. Using the data in the range B4:C21, create an embedded scatter chart with only markers.

3. Move the chart to a chart sheet named **Scatter Chart**.

4. Apply the Layout 4 chart layout to the chart.

5. Add the following chart title above the chart: **Relationship Between Study Time and Test Grades**.

6. Add the following horizontal axis title below the axis: **Hours of Study**.

7. Add the following rotated vertical axis title: **Test Grades**.

8. Change the font size of the chart title to 20 points.

9. Change the font size of the axis titles to 14 points.

10. Delete the legend.

11. Format the vertical axis so its minimum value is fixed at 50.

12. What relationship, if any, does the chart show between test grades and study time?

13. Insert a header with your name and the current date. Print the chart sheet. Save and close the workbook.

PROJECT 8–7

1. Open the **Starburst.xlsx** workbook from the drive and folder where your Data Files are stored. Save the workbook as **Starburst Growth** followed by your initials.

2. Using the data in the range A5:F7, create an embedded 2-D line chart with markers.

3. Move the chart to a chart sheet named **Line Chart**.

4. Apply the Layout 1 chart layout to the chart. Apply the Style 32 chart style to the chart.

5. Change the chart title to **Starburst Software Net Revenues and Net Income**.

6. Change the vertical axis title to **(Dollars in Millions)**.

7. Show the legend at the top of the chart.

8. Have the company's net revenues decreased, increased, or remained stable?

9. Insert a header with your name and the current date. Print the chart sheet.

10. Press and hold the Ctrl key as you drag and drop the sheet tab for the Line Chart chart sheet directly to the right of the Line Chart sheet tab to make a copy. Rename the copied chart sheet **Clustered Column Chart**.

11. Change the chart type to a clustered column chart.

12. Print the chart sheet. Save and close the workbook.

PROJECT 8–8

1. Open the **Chico.xlsx** workbook from the drive and folder where your Data Files are stored. Save the workbook as **Chico Temperatures** followed by your initials.

2. Using the data in the range A3:M5, create an embedded 2-D line chart with markers.

3. Move the chart to a chart sheet named **Line Chart**.

4. Apply the Layout 5 chart layout to the chart. Apply the Style 28 chart style to the chart.

5. Change the chart title to **Average Temperatures in Chico, California**.

6. Change the vertical axis title to **Temperatures in Fahrenheit**.

7. On the Ribbon, click the Layout tab. In the Current Selection group, use the Chart Elements arrow to select Series "High" in the chart.

8. Click the Format Selection button to open the Format Data Series dialog box. Make the following changes:
   a. Click Marker Fill to display the options. Click the Solid fill option button. Click the Color button, and then click Dark Red in the Standard Colors section.
   b. Click Line Color to display the options. Click the Solid line option button. Click the Color button, and then click Dark Red in the Standard Colors section.
   c. Click Marker Line Color to display the options. Click the Solid line option button. Click the Color button, and then click Dark Red in the Standard Colors section if necessary.

9. Click Close to close the Format Data Series dialog box.

10. On the Layout tab, in the Current Selection group, use the Chart Elements arrow to select Series "Low" in the chart.

11. Click the Format Selection button to open the Format Data Series dialog box. Make the following changes:
   a. Click Marker Fill to display the options. Click the Solid fill option button. Click the Color button, and then click Blue in the Standard Colors section.
   b. Click Line Color to display the options. Click the Solid line option button. Click the Color button, and then click Blue in the Standard Colors section.
   c. Click Marker Line Color to display the options. Click the Solid line option button. Click the Color button, and then click Blue in the Standard Colors section if necessary.

12. Click Close to close the Format Data Series dialog box.

13. Insert a header with your name and the current date. Print the chart sheet. Save and close the workbook.

■ CRITICAL THINKING

ACTIVITY 8–1

For each scenario, which chart type would be the most appropriate to illustrate the data? Justify your answer.

Scenario 1. A scientist has given varying amounts of water to 200 potted plants. Over 35 days, the height of the plant and the amount of water given to the plant are recorded in a worksheet. What is the best chart type to illustrate the connection between water and plant growth?

Scenario 2. A corporation developed a new product last year. A manager in the corporation recorded the number of units sold each month. He noticed that sales in summer months were much higher than sales in winter months. What chart type can he use to illustrate this trend to other sales managers?

Scenario 3. Students entering a high school come from five middle schools. The principal has recorded the name of the middle school and the number of students from each middle school. What chart type can she use to show which middle schools supply significantly more students than other middle schools?

ACTIVITY 8–2

You recently opened Sounds Good CDs, a store that buys and sells used CDs and DVDs. As a small business owner, you are responsible for budgets and inventory. Initially, you manually tracked the inventory and budget data in a notebook. Now that the business is growing, this method has become too cumbersome. You decide to transfer the data into an electronic format.

In a new workbook, create and format one worksheet to track inventory and one worksheet to track the budget. Both worksheets should contain the name of your store—Sounds Good CDs—and a title describing the data.

For the inventory worksheet, include (a) the title of the CD or DVD, (b) the artist, (c) the quantity of each, and (d) the cost per item. Enter the data shown in **Figure 8–21** in the worksheet. Rename the worksheet as **Inventory**.

Title	Artist	Quantity	Cost
Nerve Net	Brian Eno	4	$ 6.95
Thursday Afternoon	Brian Eno	2	$ 7.95
Geometry	Robert Rich	3	$ 5.95
On This Planet	Steve Roach	3	$ 8.95
Possible Planet	Steve Roach	5	$ 6.95

FIGURE 8–21

The budget worksheet records the expected income and expenses for the month. Include rows for (a) sales revenue, (b) purchases of CDs, (c) rent expense, (d) utilities expense, (e) tax expense, and (f) net income. Include columns for (a) actual amounts and (b) budgeted amounts. Then, enter the data shown in **Figure 8–22**.

	Actual	Budgeted
Sales Revenue	$ 14,875	$ 12,950
Purchases of CDs	6,500	5,800
Rent	975	975
Utilities	425	425
Taxes	817	667
Net Income		

FIGURE 8–22

For the Actual Net Income, enter a formula that subtracts the purchases and expenses from revenue. For the Budgeted Net Income, enter a formula that subtracts the purchases and expenses from revenue. Rename the worksheet as **Budget**.

Insert column sparklines in the range D6:D10 based on the data in the range B6:C10. Change the last point marker color to a different color than the first point marker color.

Using the data you entered in the Budget worksheet, create an embedded chart that compares the actual and budgeted values in each category. Use an appropriate chart type. Choose which chart elements to display, where they should be located, and how the chart is formatted.

For both worksheets, insert a header with your name and the current date, and then print the worksheets.

EXCEL UNIT REVIEW

Introductory Microsoft Excel

■ REVIEW QUESTIONS

TRUE / FALSE

Circle T if the statement is true or F if the statement is false.

T F **1.** The active cell reference appears in the Formula Bar.

T F **2.** To select a group of cells, you must click each cell individually until all cells in the range are selected.

T F **3.** The Save As dialog box appears every time you save a worksheet.

T F **4.** The formula =$B$4+C9 contains an absolute cell reference.

T F **5.** After you edit the data source in the worksheet, the chart is also updated to reflect the changes.

MATCHING

Match the description in Column 2 with the text position function in Column 1.

Column 1	Column 2
_____ 1. Wrapping	A. Displays cell contents on multiple lines
_____ 2. Orientation	B. Aligns the text to the right, left, or center
_____ 3. Indenting	C. Combines several cells into one and places the contents in the middle of the cell
_____ 4. Alignment	D. Moves the text several spaces to the right or left
_____ 5. Merge and Center	E. Displays text at an angle, vertically, up, or down

FILL IN THE BLANK

Complete the following sentences by writing the correct word or words in the blanks provided.

1. A(n) _____ cell reference changes when copied or moved.

2. _____ formatting is used to highlight cells that meet specific criteria.

3. The _____ function adds a range of numbers in a worksheet.

4. A(n) _____ chart uses wedges in a circle to represent values in a worksheet.

5. The _____ contains information that is printed at the top of every page.

MATCHING

Match the correct result in Column 2 to the formula in Column 1. Assume the following values appear in the worksheet:

Cell	Value
B2	5
B3	6
B4	4
B5	7

Column 1

_____ 1. =10+B5

_____ 2. =B2*B4

_____ 3. =(B3+B4)/B2

_____ 4. =AVERAGE(B3:B4)

_____ 5. =SUM(B2:B5)

Column 2

A. 22

B. 20

C. 17

D. 5

E. 2

 PROJECTS

PROJECT 1

1. Open the **Gas.xlsx** workbook from the drive and folder where your Data Files are stored. Save the workbook as **Gas Sales** followed by your initials.

2. Format cell A1 with the Title cell style. Format the range A2:A3 with bold.

3. Change the width of column A to 15. Change each of the widths of columns B through D to 12.

4. Merge and center the range A1:D1.

5. In cell B2, enter the current date, and then apply the Long Date format.

6. Merge and center the range B2:D2.

7. In cell B3, enter **3:55 PM** for time, and then apply the Time format.

8. Merge and center the range B3:D3.

9. Format the text in the range A2:D3 in 12-point Cambria.

10. Wrap the text in cell C5.

11. Format range A5:D5 with the Accent 1 cell style, and then bold and center the text in the cells.

12. Format the range B6:B9 in the Number format with a comma separator and no decimal places.

13. Format the range C6:D9 in the Currency format.

14. In cell B10, use the SUM function to add the total number of gallons sold, and then format the cell with the Total cell style.

15. In cell D10, use the SUM function to add the total sales, and then format the cell with the Total cell style. Click cell A12. **Figure UR–1** shows the completed worksheet.

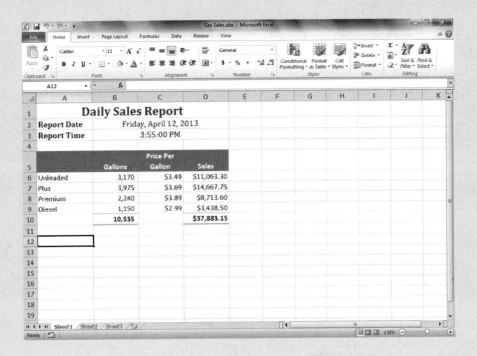

FIGURE UR-1

16. Insert a header with your name and the current date. Save, print, and close the workbook.

PROJECT 2

1. Open the **Organic.xlsx** workbook from the drive and folder where your Data Files are stored. Save the workbook as **Organic Financials** followed by your initials.

2. Format the company name and other headings in bold. Format the company name in a larger font than the rest of the text in the financial statement.

3. Merge and center each of the first four rows across columns A and B.

4. Separate the headings from the body of the financial statement by one row.

5. Resize the columns so you can view all of their contents.

6. Format the first (Revenue) and last (Net income) numbers in the financial statement to display dollar signs and thousands separators, but no decimal places.

7. Format all the other numbers to include a thousands separator but no dollar sign and no decimal places. Compare your worksheet to **Figure UR–2**.

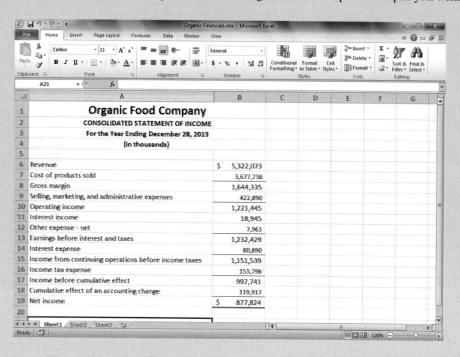

FIGURE UR–2

8. Format the worksheet to make it visually attractive and appealing, such as by adding borders, font colors, fill colors, alignments, cell styles, and so forth as appropriate.

9. Insert a header with your name and the current date. Save, print, and close the workbook.

PROJECT 3

1. Open the **Club.xlsx** workbook from the drive and folder where your Data Files are stored. Save the workbook as **Club Members** followed by your initials.

2. Sort the range A2:B16 by the values in column B in order from largest to smallest.

3. Resize the columns as needed to so that all the content is displayed.

4. Format the worksheet title with the Title cell style to distinguish it from the other text in the workbook.

5. Enter the text **Exceptional and Outstanding Members** in a new row above the row for Susan Estes, and then format the text in bold and italic.

6. Enter the text **Exceptional Members** in a new row above the row for Susan Estes, and then format the text in bold.

7. Enter the text **Outstanding Members** in a new row above the row for Jose Santos, and then format the text in bold.

8. Enter the text **Other Active Members** in a new row above the row for Mohamed Abdul, and then format the text in bold and italic.

9. Delete the row with Allen Tse.

10. Format the numbers in column B using the Number format with a thousands separator and no decimal places. Your worksheet should look similar to **Figure UR–3**.

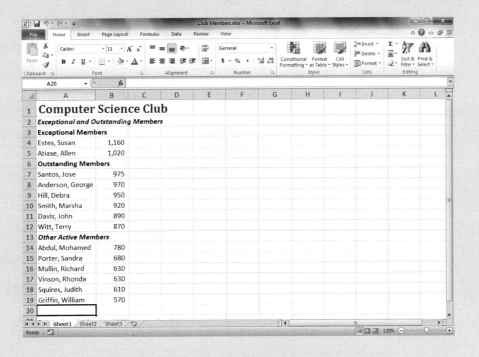

FIGURE UR-3

11. Format the worksheet using cell styles, alignments, font styles, colors, and so forth to make the worksheet visually appealing.

12. Insert a header with your name and the current date. Save, print, and close the workbook.

PROJECT 4

1. Open the **CompNet.xlsx** workbook from the drive and folder where your Data Files are stored. Save the workbook as **CompNet Expenses** followed by your initials.

2. Create an embedded Pie in 3-D chart based on the data in the range A12:B17. Move the chart to chart sheet named **Expenses Chart**.

3. Apply the chart layout that includes a chart title above the chart and labels and percentages on the slices.

4. Apply the Style 10 chart style.

5. Enter **Expenses for 2013** as the chart title, and then change the font size to 24 points.

6. Change the font size of the data labels to 11 points. Compare your worksheet with **Figure UR–4**.

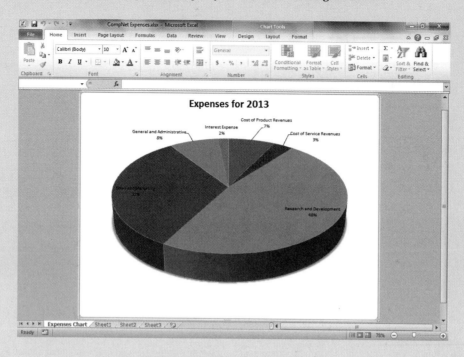

FIGURE UR–4

7. Based on the chart, what is the largest expense category? What is the smallest expense category?

8. Insert a header with your name and the current date. Save, print, and close the workbook.

■ SIMULATION

You work at the Java Internet Café, which has been open only a few months. The café serves coffee, other beverages, and pastries, and offers Internet access. Seven computers are set up on tables along the north side of the store. Customers can come in, have a cup of coffee and a pastry, and browse the Web.

Your manager asks you to create a menu of coffee prices and computer prices. You will do this by integrating Microsoft Excel and Microsoft Word.

JOB 1

1. Create a new workbook. Save the workbook as **Coffee Prices** followed by your initials.

2. Enter the data shown in **Figure UR–5** in the worksheet.

	A	B	C	D	E
1	Coffee Prices				
2					
3	House coffee	2		Café latte	3.5
4	Refills	0.5		Cappucino	3.5
5	Espresso	2.75		Café breve	3.25
6	Extra shot	0.55		Café con panna	3.75
7					

FIGURE UR–5

3. Change the widths of columns A and D to 20. Change the widths of columns B and E to 10. Change the width of column C to 4.

4. Left-align the data in columns B and E.

5. Indent and italicize the text in cells A4 and A6.

6. Change the font of all data to Arial, 12 points.

7. Format the data in columns B and E as Currency.

8. Merge and center the range A1:E1. Change the font of the text in the merged cell A1 to Arial, 14 points. Format the merged cell A1 with a bottom border.

9. Hide the gridlines from view. Save the workbook. Copy the data in the range A1:E6.

10. Start Word and open the **Java.docx** document from the drive and folder where your Data Files are stored. Save the document as **Java Menu** followed by your initials.

11. On a blank line below the *Menu* heading, center the blank line, and then paste a link to the worksheet data you copied. On the Home tab, in the Clipboard group, click the Paste button arrow to open the Paste menu, and then click Paste Special. The Paste Special dialog box appears. In the Paste Special dialog box, click the Paste link option button, and then click Microsoft Excel Worksheet Object, as shown in **Figure UR-6**. Click OK.

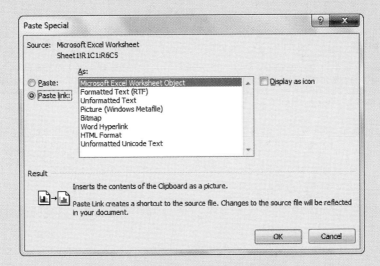

FIGURE UR-6

12. Switch to Excel, and then open the **Computer.xlsx** workbook from the drive and folder where your Data Files are stored. Save the workbook as **Computer Prices** followed by your initials.

13. Copy the data in the range A1:C13.

14. Switch to the **Java Menu** document.

15. On a blank line after the Coffee Prices menu items, center the line if it is not already centered, and then paste a link to the worksheet data you copied. On the Home tab, in the Clipboard group, click the Paste button arrow to open the Paste menu, and then click Paste Special. In the Paste Special dialog box, click the Paste link option button, click Microsoft Excel Worksheet Object, and then click OK.

16. Insert your name and the current date in the blank line of the footer.

17. Preview the document. Adjust the placement of data if necessary so that all data fits on one page.

18. Save, print, and close the **Java Menu** document.

19. Close the **Coffee Prices** and **Computer Prices** workbooks without saving changes.

JOB 2

The menu you created has been very successful. However, your manager asks you to make a few changes.

1. Open the **Coffee Prices** and **Computer Prices** workbooks you saved in Job 1.

2. Edit the **Coffee Prices** and **Computer Prices** workbooks as shown in **Figure UR-7**.

Java Internet Café

2001 Joliet Avenue
Boulder, CO 80302-2001
303.555.JAVA
JavaCafe@cybershop.com

Java Internet Café offers customers high-speed Internet access as well as free Wi-Fi. Bring your own computer or use one of ours. Each of our computers has a special interface to help new users get started. Enjoy one of our specialty coffees as you check your email or surf the Web! Ask your server to help you get started.

Menu

Coffee Prices

House coffee	$2.00		Café latte	$3.50
Refills	$0.50 .75		Cappucino	$3.50
Espresso	$2.75 3.00		Café breve	$3.25
Extra shot	$0.55		Café con panna	$3.75

Computer Prices

Workstation with Internet/Email	$8.00/hour
After the first hour, charges	
accrue by the minute only.	
Use of Webcam	$2.00/session Free
Print (black and white)	$0.25/page
Print (color)	$0.50/page
Print color photo paper (4x6)	$1.00/page
High resolution scanning	$2.00/page
Photocopy (black and white)	$0.25/page
Photocopy (color)	$0.50/page
Fax ʌ (*domestic only*)	$2.00/first page
	$0.50/each additional page

Sit back, sip your coffee, and surf the web.

FIGURE UR–7

3. Save and close the **Coffee Prices** and **Computer Prices** workbooks.

4. Open the **Java Menu** document you created in Job 1.

5. Update the document when prompted because you revised the linked files since you saved and closed the Java Menu document.

6. Make the correction in the footer, as shown in Figure UR–7.

7. Save the document as **Java Menu Revised** followed by your initials.

8. Print and close the document.

Estimated Time for Unit:
20.5 hours

ADVANCED

MICROSOFT EXCEL UNIT

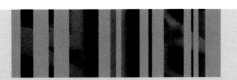

LESSON 9

Applying Advanced Formats to Worksheets

■ OBJECTIVES

Upon completion of this lesson, you should be able to:

- Create custom number formats.
- Use conditional formatting rules.
- Create conditional formatting formulas.
- Format tables.
- Create custom AutoFilters.
- Apply themes.
- Switch banded rows and columns.
- Add or delete rows and columns in tables.
- Add totals to tables.

■ VOCABULARY

conditional formatting formulas

custom AutoFilter

banded columns

banded rows

tables

themes

Introduction

Microsoft Excel comes equipped with a number of advanced tools and features that empower you to create professional-looking spreadsheets using advanced formatting techniques, such as tables, themes, and conditional formatting. In this lesson, you will learn how to apply advanced features to data in a worksheet. You will also learn about custom AutoFilters.

Creating Custom Number Formats

Occasionally you may need to apply a number format that is not already predefined in the existing number formats. For example, the date format Year-Month, which would display a date in the format 2014-March, is not one of the formats available in Excel. You can create your own format by selecting the Custom category in the Format Cells dialog box.

Formats are composed of codes. These codes are simply strings of characters that represent the actual data, such as *m* for *month*, *d* for *day*, and *y* for *year*. You can easily create your own codes by assembling these characters in a certain order. **Table 9–1** describes the various character codes you can select.

TABLE 9–1   Format codes

FORMAT CODE	WHAT IT MEANS
0	Placeholder for a digit. A zero will appear if there is not another number available.
#	Placeholder for a digit. Nothing will appear if there is not another number available..
; (semicolon)	Divides the parts of the format code.
$	Puts a dollar sign with the number at the same location it appears in the format code.
%	Puts a percent sign with the number at the same location it appears in the format code.
, (comma)	Puts a comma with the number at the same location it appears in the format code.
. (decimal)	Puts a decimal with the number at the same location it appears in the format code.
M or m	Used for months in dates or for minutes in time.
D or d	Used for days.
Y or y	Used for years.
H or h	Used for hours.
S or s	Used for seconds.
: (colon)	Used to separate hours, minutes, and seconds.

Step-by-Step 9.1

1. Open the **Customer** file from the drive and folder where your Data Files are stored.

2. Save the workbook as **Customer List**, followed by your initials.

3. Select the range **E4:E22**.

4. On the Ribbon, click the **Home** tab. In the Cells group, click the **Format** button, and then click **Format Cells**.

5. If necessary, click the **Number** tab in the Format Cells dialog box.

6. Select **Custom** from the Category list box.

7. Highlight the text in the Type text box, and then type **yyyy-mm**. (Entering *y* four times represents the complete year number—hence, the year will be displayed as 2014. Entering *m* twice represents the month as two digits, such as 02 for February.) Your dialog box should appear similar to **Figure 9–1**.

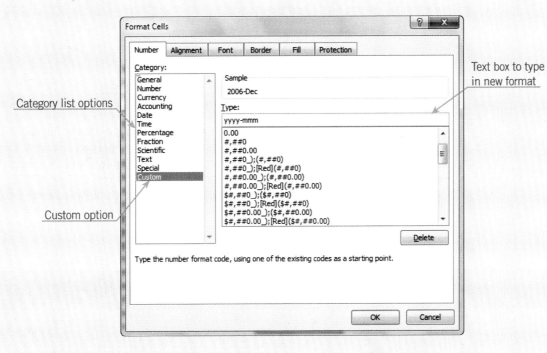

FIGURE 9–1
Custom format in Format Cells dialog box

Category list options

Custom option

Text box to type in new format

8. Click **OK** and then look at your dates. Next, you will modify the custom format you just created.

9. Verify that the range E4:E22 is still selected, click the **Format** button, and then click **Format Cells**.

10. Select **Custom** from the Category list box, if necessary, and then click the custom format you just created. Type one more **m** in the Type text box so your final format is yyyy-mmm.

11. Click **OK** and then view the results. Notice that the day of the month is abbreviated with three letters, as shown in **Figure 9–2**.

FIGURE 9–2
Custom date format

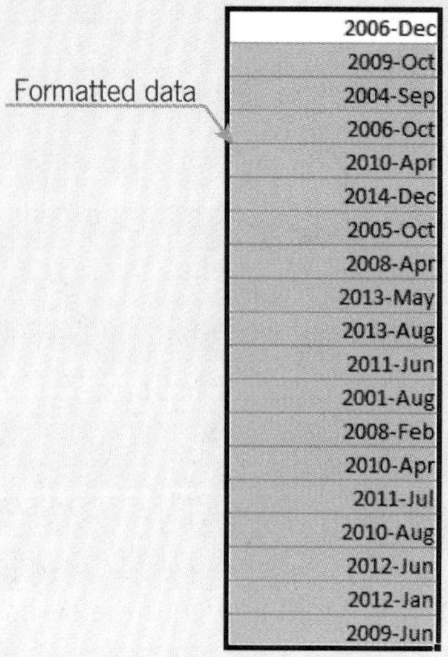

Formatted data →

2006-Dec
2009-Oct
2004-Sep
2006-Oct
2010-Apr
2014-Dec
2005-Oct
2008-Apr
2013-May
2013-Aug
2011-Jun
2001-Aug
2008-Feb
2010-Apr
2011-Jul
2010-Aug
2012-Jun
2012-Jan
2009-Jun

12. Save, print, and close the workbook.

Using Conditional Formatting Rules

Conditional formatting applies a font, border, or pattern to worksheet cells when certain conditions exist in those cells. For example, you might want to highlight products that are your top sellers. By applying conditional formats and criteria, you can then view the cell formats to see which cells met the condition. Before you start entering the conditional formatting rules, you will need to select the range of data where you want Excel to apply the formats. You can select from a wide variety of formats available in the New Formatting Rule dialog box.

EXTRA FOR EXPERTS

You can remove conditional formatting rules by clicking the Styles group on the Home tab, clicking the Conditional Formatting button arrow, and then clicking Clear Rules.

Step-by-Step 9.2

1. Open the **Employee** file from the drive and folder where your Data Files are stored.

2. Save the workbook as **Employee List** followed by your initials.

3. Select the range **I4:I21**. These cells contain the hourly wage rates for each of the hourly employees.

4. On the Ribbon, click the **Home** tab. In the Styles group, click the **Conditional Formatting** button.

5. Click **New Rule** on the Conditional Formatting menu. The New Formatting Rule dialog box opens, as shown in **Figure 9–3**.

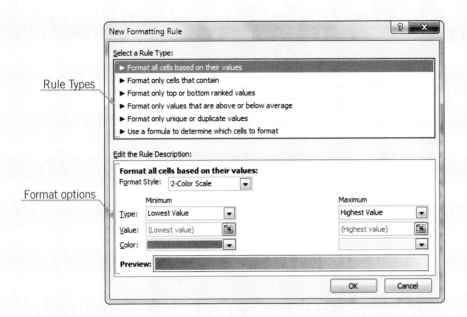

FIGURE 9–3
New Formatting Rule
dialog box

6. Click the **Format only values that are above or below average** option.

7. Click the **Format values that are** menu arrow and then select **below**.

8. Click the **Format** button to display the Format Cells dialog box.

9. Click the **Fill** tab to shown the fill colors, and then select the blue color in the middle of the top row.

10. Click **OK** to close the Format Cells dialog box.

11. Click **OK** to close the New Formatting Rule dialog box and display the formatted cells. Check to see if the formats were applied correctly. You will now clear these formats for the next exercise.

12. On the Home tab in the Styles group, click the **Conditional Formatting** button, point to **Clear Rules**, and then click **Clear Rules from Entire Sheet**.

13. Leave the workbook open for the next Step-by-Step.

Creating Conditional Formatting Formulas

The conditional formatting you applied in the previous exercise uses options that are available in the New Formatting Rule dialog box. However, sometimes the option you need is not available. You would then need to create your own conditional format rule based on a formula called a *conditional formatting formula*. For example, you might want to find all of the values in a selected range that are greater than an amount located in that range. You might have a cell in the selected range with an amount of $500, and you want to find out how many other cells in this range have an amount greater than $500. In addition, if the amount in this cell changes to $600, you want the same conditional formatting to appear without having to enter another formula.

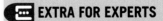
VOCABULARY
conditional formatting formula

EXTRA FOR EXPERTS

You can create a custom format for your conditional format by clicking the Format button in the New Formatting Rule dialog box.

Step-by-Step 9.3

1. Select the range **I4:I21**, which contains the hourly wages.

2. On the Ribbon, click the **Home** tab. In the Styles group, click the **Conditional Formatting** button.

3. Click **New Rule** on the Conditional Formatting menu. The New Formatting Rule dialog box opens.

4. Click the **Use a formula to determine which cells to format** option.

5. Click in the **Format values where this formula is true** text box.

6. Type **=I4<$I$4** in the text box, as shown in **Figure 9–4**.

FIGURE 9–4
New Formatting Rule dialog box with formula entered

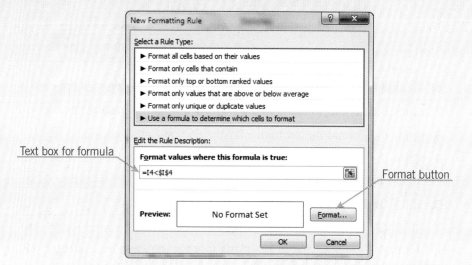

7. Click the **Format** button to display the Format Cells dialog box.

8. Click the **Fill** tab to show the fill colors, and then click the orange color in the top row.

9. Click **OK** to close the Format Cells dialog box.

10. Click **OK** to close the New Formatting Rule dialog box and display the formatted cells. View the formats based on the condition you entered, as shown in **Figure 9–5**.

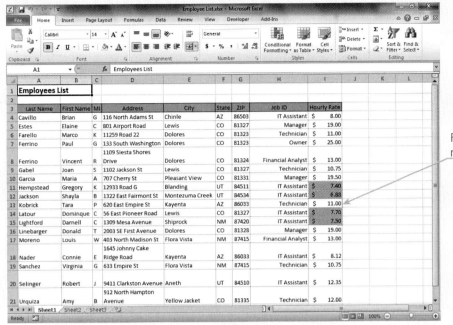

FIGURE 9–5
Conditional
formatting applied

Formatted cells
met criteria

11. Save, print, and close the workbook.

Formatting Tables

After entering data into a worksheet, the design of the worksheet can enhance the appearance of the data. *Tables* provide professional presentation features for displaying worksheet data. Formatting tables works best when there are not any existing background colors. You should also be sure that there are no blank columns

▶ **VOCABULARY**
tables

or rows. Excel offers quite a variety of table formats in the Table Format gallery shown in **Figure 9–6**.

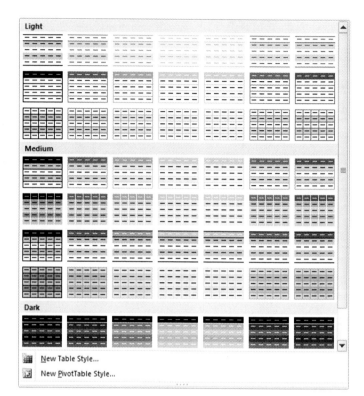

FIGURE 9–6   Table Format gallery

After you select a format for your table, the Table Tools Design tab appears on the Ribbon. AutoFilters are automatically added to the data when you format data as a table.

Step-by-Step 9.4

1. Open the **Tool** file from the drive and folder where your Data Files are stored.

2. Save the workbook as **Tool Sales** followed by your initials. Notice that the text in the worksheet has very basic formatting. The column headings simply have a bold format applied.

3. Click any cell in the range.

4. On the Home tab in the Styles group, click the **Format as Table** button to display the Table Format gallery.

5. Select the **Table Style Medium 2** option, which is the second table in the first row of the Medium group. The Format As Table dialog box opens with the range =$A$3:$F$15 displayed.

6. Click **OK**. The table formats are displayed as shown in **Figure 9–7**. *Note*: If this range did not appear in the Format as Table dialog box, you could type this range in the Where is the data for your table text box and then click OK.

FIGURE 9–7
Formatted table

7. Reduce the column widths for columns B and C so that these column headings are displayed in two rows in the same cell. Next, you will add formats to the worksheet title so that it blends better with the table formats.

8. Click **cell A1**, and then, on the Home tab in the Styles group, click the **Cell Styles** button.

9. In the Themed Cell Styles section of the Cell Styles gallery, click **20% Accent1**, which is the first option in this grouping.

10. In the Font group, click the **Bold** button **B** to add bold formatting to the text in cell A1.

11. Save, print, and leave the workbook open for the next Step-by-Step.

EXTRA FOR EXPERTS

To convert a table back to a normal range, but keep the data and table style formatting, click anywhere in the table. Click the Design tab on the Ribbon, then click the Convert to Range option in the Tools group. Click Yes when asked if you want to convert the table to a normal range.

Creating Custom AutoFilters

The *Custom AutoFilter* is a feature that lets you display only cells that meet specific criteria. Excel has predefined filters for numbers such as Greater Than, Less Than, Above Average, and Below Average, as shown on the AutoFilter Number list options in **Figure 9–8**.

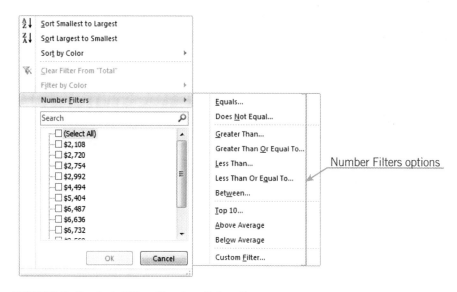

FIGURE 9–8   AutoFilter Number list options

If the filtered data is text, the Text Filter options are Equals, Does Not Equal, Begins With, Ends With, Contains, Does Not Contain, and Custom Filters. Sometimes you may need to filter for number data that is not already defined in the Number Filters menu. For example, you may want to filter a range of data that requires two filters, such as Greater Than and Less Than. In this case, you need to create a custom AutoFilter.

Step-by-Step 9.5

1. Click the **Filter** arrow, located next to the title, for the Total column.

2. Click the **(Select All)** check box. All the columns are now deselected.

3. Point to **Number Filters**, and then click **Custom Filter**. The Custom AutoFilter dialog box opens.

4. In the top row of the Custom AutoFilter dialog box, click the **down arrow** under Total and then select **is greater than**.

5. Click in the text box at the top-right in the Custom AutoFilter dialog box and then type **5000**. You could select an option from the list, but typing the exact number into the text field gives you more control over the filter process.

6. In the second row, click the **down arrow** in the left text box and select **is less than**.

7. Click in the text box to the right of the second row and then type **7000**. Excel will find the totals that are in the range of greater than 5000 and less than 7000. Your dialog box should resemble the one shown in **Figure 9–9**.

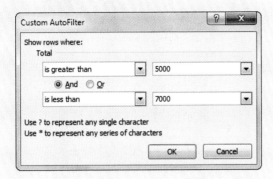

FIGURE 9–9
Custom AutoFilter dialog box

8. Click **OK**. If necessary, increase the size of the chart so that the names appear. The results of the filtering will be displayed, as shown in **Figure 9–10**.

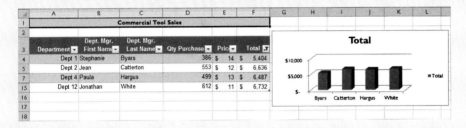

FIGURE 9–10
Results of Custom AutoFilter

9. Save, print, and close the workbook.

Applying Themes

Themes are a simple way to make your worksheet appear more professional. With themes, you can have borders, background colors, shading, and graphic effects applied instantly to an entire workbook. Several themes are available with Excel 2010, and each theme has a specific look. The themes that are loaded with Excel 2010 are located in the Theme gallery, as shown in **Figure 9–11**.

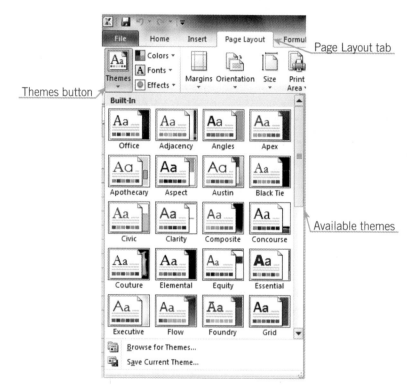

FIGURE 9–11   Theme Gallery

Theme formats apply to your entire workbook with the exception of very few objects, such as an embedded object. So, if you change a theme in one worksheet, all other worksheets will appear with the same theme. In addition, the same themes that you apply in Excel are also available in other Microsoft Office applications, such as Word, PowerPoint, and Access. Before you apply a theme, you need to add some basic formatting to the data, such as a table format, so that Excel knows how to apply the theme to your worksheet.

Step-by-Step 9.6

1. Open the **Themes** file from the drive and folder where your Data Files are stored.

2. Save the workbook as **Applied Themes** followed by your initials.

3. On the Ribbon, click the **Page Layout** tab. In the Themes group, click the **Themes** button. The Theme gallery displays.

4. Move the pointer over the various theme options in the Theme gallery to view the different formats.

5. Click the **Austin** theme to change the formats in your worksheet.

6. Click the **Customer Returns** worksheet tab to view this worksheet. Notice that the Austin theme is also applied to this worksheet.

7. Click the **Themes** button, and then select the **Hardcover** theme. View the new formats in your worksheet.

8. Click **cell A1**. Then, on the Home tab in the Font group, click the **Fill Color** button arrow and then select a fill color that will coordinate with the Hardcover theme.

9. Click the **Customer Purchases** worksheet and then select cell A1, or any cell in the column headings. On the Home tab in the Editing group, click the **Sort & Filter** button arrow, and then click **Filter**. The AutoFilters should now be removed, as shown in **Figure 9–12**.

AutoFilters removed

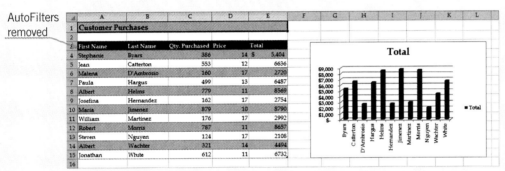

FIGURE 9–12
AutoFilters removed from theme

10. Save the workbook and leave it open for the next Step-by-Step.

Switching Banded Rows and Columns

When you create a table, the rows and columns appear with different formats. Typically, one row will have a lighter format, and the adjacent row will have a darker format. This type of formatting is referred to as banding. For example, if you choose a theme that includes the color blue, you would have one row in a white or light blue and the next row in a darker blue. The following row will appear with the lighter row again. These same formats appear in columns. Excel refers to the row format as **banded rows** and the column format as **banded columns**. You have the option to switch between banded rows and banded columns. These options are available on the Table Tools Design tab, which appears after you add table formatting as shown in **Figure 9–13**.

▶ **VOCABULARY**
banded rows

banded columns

FIGURE 9–13   Table Tools Design tab on Ribbon

Step-by-Step 9.7

1. Save the workbook as **Applied Themes 2**.

2. In the Themes workbook, select any cell within the data.

3. On the Ribbon, click the **Table Tools Design** tab. In the Table Style Options group, notice that the Banded Rows check box is selected and the Banded Columns check box is not selected, as shown in Figure 9–13.

4. Click the **Banded Rows** check box to deselect it. Notice how the heavy shading in alternating rows is removed.

5. Click the **Banded Columns** check box to select it. Your table should now appear with alternating columns shaded, as shown in **Figure 9–14**.

FIGURE 9–14
Banded columns

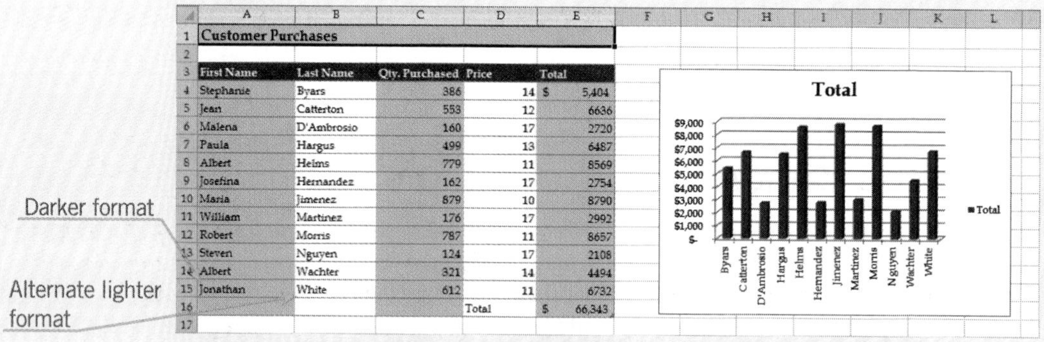

Darker format

Alternate lighter format

6. Click the **Customer Returns** worksheet tab. Note that while themes are applied to the entire workbook, individual formatting features, such as banded rows and columns, are unique to the worksheet in which they were applied.

7. Save, print, and close the workbook.

Adding or Deleting Rows and Columns in Tables

When you apply banded rows or banded columns to a table, you will want the same formatting to appear if you need to add or delete a column or row. To keep the table formatting intact, it is best to use the commands on the Insert and Delete menus in the Cells group on the Home tab.

After selecting a range within a table where you want a new row or column to appear, click the Insert button arrow in the Cells group on the Home tab and you will see the available menu commands as shown in **Figure 9–15**.

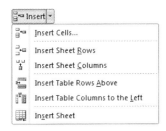

FIGURE 9–15   Insert menu options

Selecting the Insert Table Rows Above command inserts a row in the table above the selected range. Also, notice that you can insert a column to the left of a selected column. These commands are also available when you right-click a selection in the table.

> **TIP**
>
> You can type in any cell next to the column on the right side of the table and the column formats will automatically appear in this column after you press Enter.

> **TIP**
>
> If the last cell in the lower-right corner of a table is selected, you can press Tab to create a new, formatted row.

Step-by-Step 9.8

1. Open the **Team** file from the drive and folder where your Data Files are stored.

2. Save the workbook as **Team List** followed by your initials.

3. Select the range **B9:D9**. You will insert a new row in the table.

4. On the Home tab in the Cells group, click the **Insert** button arrow and then click **Insert Table Row Above**.

5. Click a cell outside the table to view the formatting.

6. Type **23487**, **Basketball**, and **BASK-2** into cells **B9:D9** respectively.

7. Click in **cell E9**, type **Jan-2014**, and then press **Enter**. Notice how Column E is now formatted the same as Column D. Next, you will delete a row.

8. Select range **B12:E12**.

9. On the Home tab in the Cells group, click the **Delete** button and then click **Delete Table Rows**.

Compare your table to **Figure 9–16**.

FIGURE 9–16
Revised table

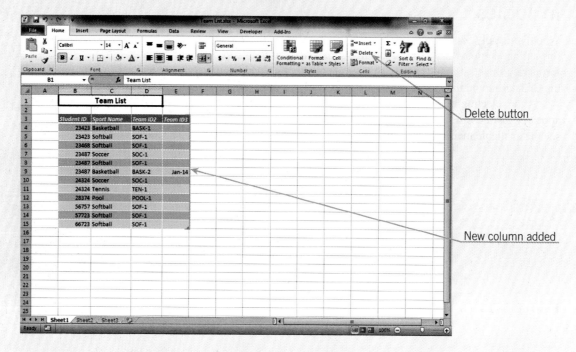

Delete button

New column added

10. Save, print, and close the workbook.

Adding Totals to Tables

After formatting data as a table, you may want to add totals to the rows or columns of data. Excel recognizes data that is formatted as a table and retains the format when you add totals on the bottom row of the table or next to the far-right column. To add totals to rows in a table, you type a new column heading next to the far-right column heading and press Enter. Or, you can type a formula next to the last cell in the top row of data underneath where the column heading would appear. When you press Enter, Excel automatically enters this formula for each of the remaining rows in the table. Excel also gives you the option to add a total row at the bottom of a column in a table by selecting Total Row in the Table Style Options group on the Design tab. Excel will add a total to the bottom of the column at the far-right side of the table. You can also select another function from the Functions list that appears on the new row.

Step-by-Step 9.9

1. Open the **Bakery** file from the drive and folder where your Data Files are stored.

2. Save the workbook as **Bakery Sales** followed by your initials.

3. Click **cell D3**, type **Totals**, and then press **Enter**. Notice how the new Column D is formatted exactly like the rest of the table, as shown in **Figure 9–17**. You will use this column to add totals to the table.

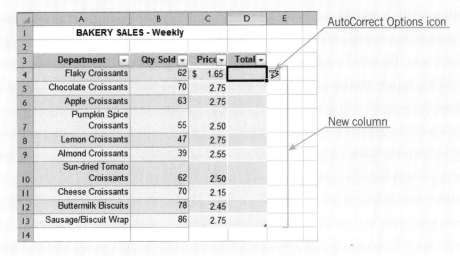

AutoCorrect Options icon

New column

FIGURE 9–17
Table with new column

4. In cell D4, type = (equal sign) to start a formula.

5. Click **B4**.

6. Type * (asterisk) for multiplication.

7. Click **cell C4** and then press **Enter**. Column D now contains column totals throughout the table.

8. On the Ribbon, click the **Design** tab.

9. In the Table Style Options group, click the **Total Row** check box. Excel adds a row with a formula that sums the row totals.

10. Click **cell D14**, click the **down arrow** to display the Function list, and then click **Average**. The total function changes to show the average function for the column. The average sales amount now appears in cell D14.

11. To change the Average function back to the Sum function, click **D14**, click the **down arrow**, and then click **Sum** from the Function list. Next, you will change the text color for the new row so that it is easier to read.

12. Select **A14:D14**.

13. On the Home tab, in the Font group, click the **Font Color** arrow and then click **Black, Text 1, Lighter 5%** located in the bottom row of the Theme colors. The completed table should appear as shown in **Figure 9–18**.

FIGURE 9–18
Table with totals added

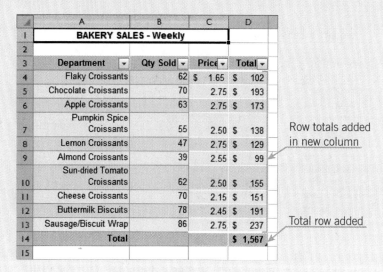

14. Save, print, and close the workbook.

SUMMARY

In this lesson, you learned:

- You can create a custom number format and apply it to data in the worksheet cells.

- Conditional formatting rules enable you to highlight data that meets specific criteria.

- Conditional formatting formulas let you highlight data based on the criteria you enter in the formula.

- Formatting data and text as a table applies various professional formats and filters.

- Custom AutoFilters give you the option to apply specific filters based on criteria entered into the custom AutoFilter dialog box.

- Themes let you apply a formatting scheme throughout the workbook, thereby eliminating the time-consuming task of applying individual formats in each worksheet.

- You can select and change banded rows and banded columns in a table.

- You can add a total row and total column in a table.

■ VOCABULARY REVIEW

Define the following terms:

conditional formatting formulas	banded columns	tables
Custom AutoFilter	banded rows	themes

■ REVIEW QUESTIONS

TRUE / FALSE

Circle T if the statement is true or F if the statement is false.

T   F   1. You can apply a theme to a worksheet that does not have any formatting.

T   F   2. Filters are automatically applied when you format data as a table.

T   F   3. You can add a SUM function at the top of a total column in a table, and when you press [Enter], the formula is copied to the remaining cells in the column.

T   F   4. The SUM function is the only function available for a total row or column.

T   F   5. Both conditional formatting rules and conditional formatting formulas apply formats to cells that meet only one specific criterion.

FILL IN THE BLANK

Complete the following sentences by writing the correct word or words in the blanks provided.

1. The format character _____ is used for months in a format code.

2. _____ applies a font, border, or pattern to worksheet cells when certain conditions exist in those cells.

3. After basic formatting is applied to the worksheet data, _____ let you add borders, background colors, shading, and graphic effects instantly to an entire workbook.

4. The format character _____ is used for hours in a format code.

5. AutoFilters are automatically added to the data when you format data as a(n) _____.

WRITTEN QUESTIONS

Write a brief answer to the following questions.

1. What is the difference between the following date codes: *yyyy-mmm-dd* and *mmmm-yyyy*?

2. Explain the process to enter a formula for conditional formatting.

3. How would you add a theme to worksheet data that does not have any formatting?

4. Explain the process for creating a Custom AutoFilter.

5. How would you add a column with totals to a table?

■ PROJECTS

If you have a SAM 2010 user profile, your instructor may have assigned an autogradable version of the indicated project. If so, log into the SAM 2010 Web site at *www.cengage.com/sam2010* to download the instruction and start files.

PROJECT 9–1

1. Open the **Team – Revised** file from the drive and folder where your Data Files are stored.

2. Save the workbook as **Team Assignments** followed by your initials.

3. Create a custom number format that changes the date formats in column F to Jan-15. Do not add a year to the format since all the team assignments are in 2014.

4. Format the worksheet title, the column headings, and column D with a light gray background color.

5. Save, print, and close the workbook.

SAM PROJECT 9–2

1. Open the **Store Lease Dates** file from the drive and folder where your Data Files are stored.

2. Save the workbook as **Store Lease Dates Information** followed by your initials.

3. Add table formatting of your choice to the data.

4. Create a custom AutoFilter for the Lease Date column that filters the data within the date range 6/15/2014 through 12/31/2014.

5. Format the worksheet title font using the same color and formatting as the table column headings.

6. Save, print, and close the workbook.

PROJECT 9–3

1. Open the **Coach Assignment** file from the drive and folder where your Data Files are stored.

2. Save the workbook as **Coach Assignment Information** followed by your initials.

3. Add table formatting to your worksheet. Select a style that includes background shading in the cells.

4. Remove the filters.

5. Apply a theme to your worksheet.

6. Remove the banded row formatting.

7. Add banded column formatting.

8. Save, print, and close the workbook.

PROJECT 9–4

1. Open the **Home Sales** file from the drive and folder where your Data Files are stored.

2. Save the workbook as **Home Sales – 2014** followed by your initials.

3. Add conditional formatting to the Total column that formats sales greater than 1,500,000.

4. Use a custom format for the conditional formatting that highlights the cell with a yellow cell background (fill) color.

5. Change the conditional formatting to highlight cells with sales over 1,750,000. Use the same yellow fill color.

6. Save, print, and close the workbook.

■ CRITICAL THINKING

ACTIVITY 9–1

You are the new manager of the New Internet Products Corporation. After reviewing workbooks created by the former manager, you decide to enhance the data contained in the files by applying different formatting features.

1. Open the **Trendy Resort** file from the drive and folder where your Data Files are stored, and then save it as **Trendy Resort Projected Sales** followed by your initials.

2. Format the First Year worksheet using the formatting features you learned about in this lesson. Apply a conditional format to the projected sales data, and use conditional formatting to highlight those projected sales figures that exceed $60,000 for any month and any division. Format the title and subtitle as desired.

3. Save and print the worksheet in landscape orientation so all the data fits on one page, then close the workbook.

ACTIVITY 9–2

1. Open the **Budget** file from the drive and folder where your Data Files are stored, and then save it as **Proposed Budget** followed by your initials.

2. Format the data as a table with a dark text color.

3. Add a column for department totals and a total row.

4. Format the headings with a similar color as the formatted table.

5. Save and print the worksheet in landscape orientation so all the data fits on one page, then close the workbook.

LESSON 10

Using Advanced Chart Features

■ OBJECTIVES

Upon completion of this lesson, you should be able to:

- Switch rows and columns in charts.
- Add a data table to a chart.
- Add data labels to data markers.
- Create sparklines.
- Design combination charts.
- Construct a gauge chart.
- Create a chart template.
- Apply a chart template.

■ VOCABULARY

chart floor

chart template

combination chart

data labels

data markers

data point

data series

data table

gauge chart

horizontal gridlines

primary axis

secondary axis

sparklines

vertical gridlines

x-axis

y-axis

Introduction

Charts are a great solution for presenting data in Excel graphically. Charts are simple to make and format. You can quickly change one type of chart to another if you need to show data in a different perspective. Excel has many chart formatting features that you can apply to a chart to make it a professional representation of the data. In this lesson, you will learn how to apply advanced chart features to charts.

Understanding How Charts Are Created

Charts are created from data in a worksheet. This data is typically arranged in columns and rows. **Figure 10–1** shows an example of data that will be used to create a chart. The rows contain data for different types of pizza. The columns show the pizza sales by month.

Columns show monthly pizza sales

Rows show types of pizza

▲	A	B	C	D	E	F	G
1			Byar's Pizza Franchise				
2			Quarterly Report				
3							
4		**April**	**May**	**June**			
5	*Cheese*	$ 15,000.00	$ 16,545.00	$ 17,000.00			
6	*Pepperoni*	15,750.00	17,550.00	19,250.00			
7	*Sausage*	9,000.00	10,150.00	11,225.00			
8	*Veggie*	3,450.00	5,555.00	7,000.00			
9	*Anchovy*	1,500.00	1,400.00	1,300.00			
10	**Total**	**$44,700.00**	**$51,200.00**	**$55,775.00**			
11							
12							

FIGURE 10–1   Worksheet with columns and rows of data

The type of chart you choose determines how the data in the rows and columns will appear in the chart. For example, the pizza data in this example was plotted as a Line chart, as shown in **Figure 10–2**. Notice that the types of pizza are placed on the horizontal axis, and the monthly sales are placed on the vertical axis. The horizontal axis is called the *x-axis*, and the vertical axis is called the *y-axis*. Each line of data in the chart is a *data series*.

▶ **VOCABULARY**

x-axis

y-axis

data series

Line data series
for April

Y-axis shows
dollar amounts

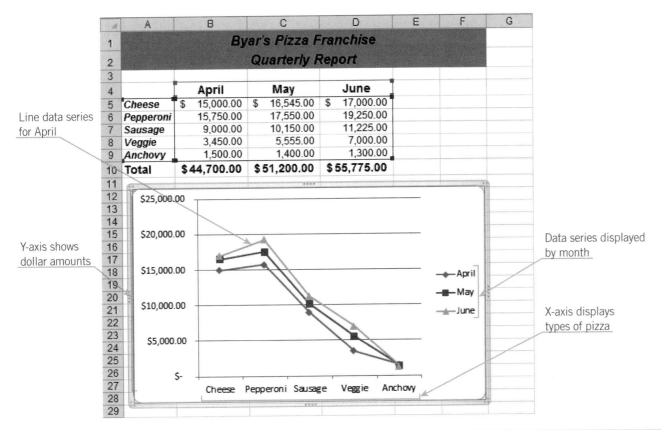

Data series displayed
by month

X-axis displays
types of pizza

FIGURE 10–2   Line chart created from worksheet data

EXTRA FOR EXPERTS

When creating a chart, do not
select the data totals when selecting the data for the chart. Because
the totals are typically much larger
numbers than the data itself, the
chart would not display the data
series accurately.

Switching Rows and Columns in Charts

After creating a chart, you may find that you want to switch the order of how chart data is displayed. You can do this using the Switch Row/Column button on the Design tab. In **Figure 10–3**, the pizza data has been switched so that the x-axis displays the months and the data series shows the sales amount for each type of pizza.

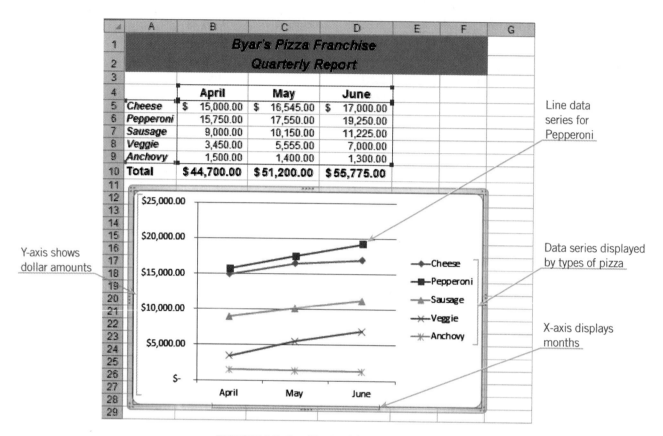

FIGURE 10–3   Chart with rows and columns switched

Step-by-Step 10.1

1. Open the **Byars Pizza** file from the drive and folder where your Data Files are stored.

2. Save the workbook as **Byars Pizza Sales**, followed by your initials. You will use the data in the worksheet to create a chart.

3. Select the range **A4:D9**.

4. On the Ribbon, click the **Insert** tab.

5. In the Charts group, click the **Line** button, and then click the **Line with Markers** button, the first 2-D Line chart in the second row.

6. Move the chart by clicking the Selection box around the chart and dragging it to **A11:F27**, then compare your screen to **Figure 10–4**.

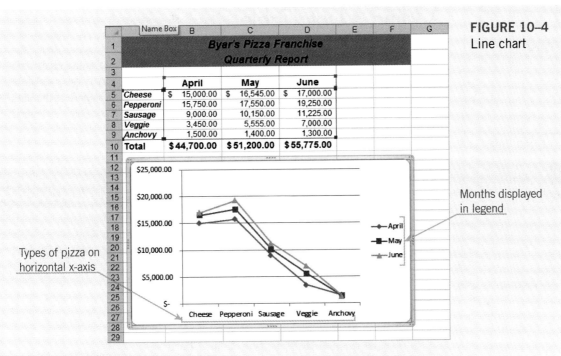

FIGURE 10–4
Line chart

Months displayed in legend

Types of pizza on horizontal x-axis

7. On the Ribbon, click the **Design** tab and then in the Data group, click the **Switch Row/Column** button. Notice how the horizontal axis shows the months and the vertical axis shows the sales by pizza type, as shown in **Figure 10–5**.

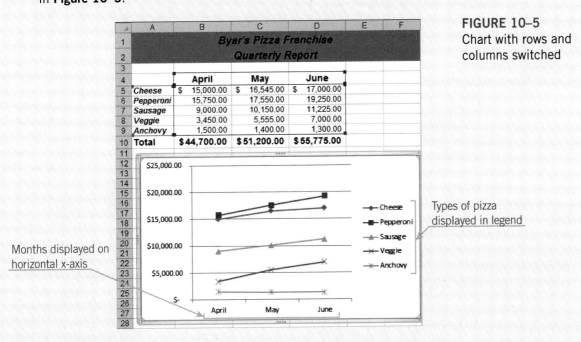

FIGURE 10–5
Chart with rows and columns switched

Types of pizza displayed in legend

Months displayed on horizontal x-axis

8. Save the workbook and leave it open for the next Step-by-Step.

Adding a Data Table

▶ **VOCABULARY**
data table

A *data table* displays the data used to create a chart. It appears below the chart. The data table lets you quickly view the worksheet data while looking at the chart data series. The data table feature is especially useful when your chart is on a separate sheet in the workbook. You can choose to have the legend appear as part of the data table rather than having the legend displayed in a separate part of the chart. A legend is a list that shows the colors and symbols used in a chart.

Step-by-Step 10.2

1. Verify that the chart is selected.

2. On the Ribbon, click the **Design** tab, if it is not already selected. You will first move the chart to a new sheet.

3. In the Location group, click the **Move Chart** button.

4. In the Move Chart dialog box, click the **New sheet** option button.

5. In the New sheet text box, type **Sales Chart**.

6. Click **OK**. The chart moves to a new sheet named Sales Chart.

7. On the Layout tab in the Labels group, click **Data Table** and then click **Show Data Table with Legend Keys**. Your chart appears as shown in **Figure 10–6**.

FIGURE 10–6
Chart with data table and legend

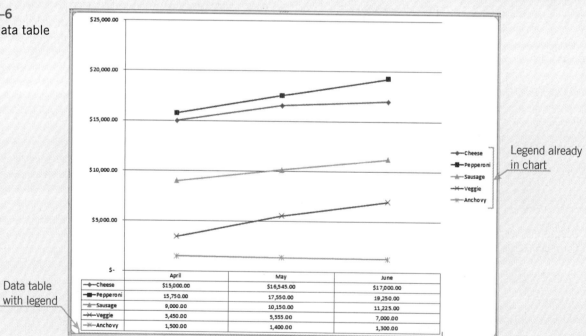

8. Click the legend on the right side of the chart and then press **Delete**. Since the data table has a legend, you no longer need the original legend.

9. On the Layout tab in the Labels group, click **Chart Title**, and then click **Above Chart** to add a chart title. The chart title appears above the line chart and is selected. When you start typing the chart title, your text will replace this text and the title you type will be displayed.

10. Type **Byars Pizza Sales** for the chart title, and then press **Enter**. The chart title appears above the chart as shown in **Figure 10–7**.

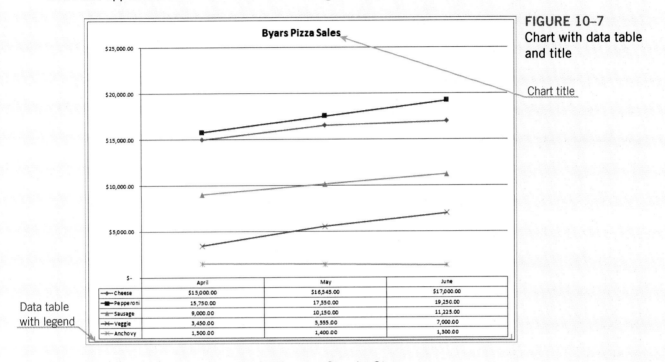

FIGURE 10–7
Chart with data table and title

11. Save the workbook and leave it open for the next Step-by-Step.

Adding Data Labels to Data Series

A *data label* can appear as numbers or text next to each data marker in the data series. The *data markers* represent where the actual data would be in the chart. For example, you might have a range of data in the worksheet with 500, 1500, and 1000 in the data range. In a line chart, the line would start at 500 and a line segment would be drawn to 1500. Another line segment would be drawn from 1500 to 1000. Each

▶ **VOCABULARY**
data label

data marker

▶ **VOCABULARY**
data point

place where the line segments start or stop is a ***data point*** and can be displayed with a data marker. Adding data labels allows you to see the value for each data marker in the chart. An example of a chart with data labels is shown in **Figure 10–8**.

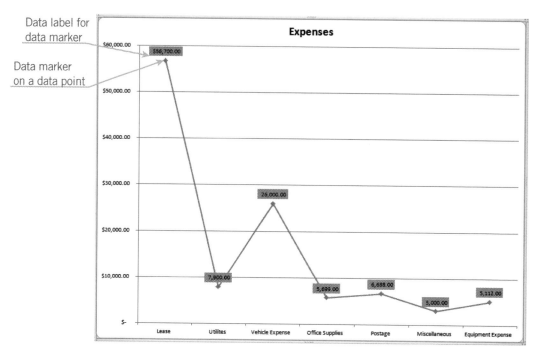

Data label for
data marker

Data marker
on a data point

FIGURE 10–8   Chart with data labels

You can place the data labels to the left, right, top, or bottom of the data points. Data label features, such as color and border outlines, can be changed.

Step-by-Step 10.3

1. With the Sales Chart sheet selected, click the **Layout** tab on the Ribbon, if necessary.

2. In the Layout group, click the **Data Labels** button and then click **Above**. The labels display above the line series; however, some of the labels run into the line markers, so you decide to try another option.

3. Click the **Data Labels** button again and then click **Left**. You will now format the labels.

4. Click any one of the data labels that you just added.

5. Click **Data Labels**, and then click **More Data Label Options**.

6. In the Format Data Labels dialog box, click the **Fill** option on the left side, as shown in **Figure 10–9**.

Click to display
Fill options

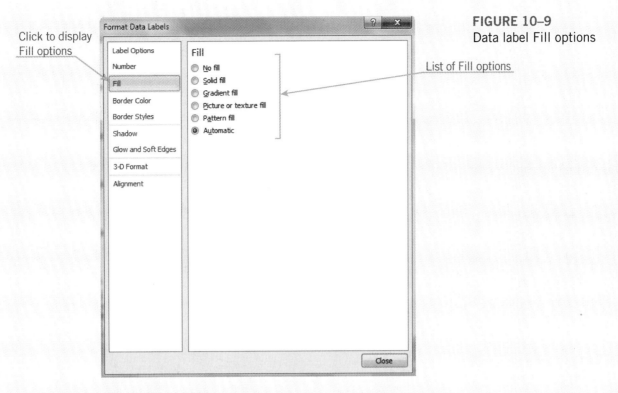

FIGURE 10–9
Data label Fill options

List of Fill options

7. Click the **Solid fill** option button on the right side of the dialog box.

8. Click the **Color** arrow and then choose the **Red, Accent 2, Lighter 40%** option.

9. Click **Close**.

10. Repeat Steps 4–9 to apply the same color format to the remaining data labels. Your completed chart should resemble the one shown in **Figure 10–10**.

FIGURE 10–10
Completed chart with data labels

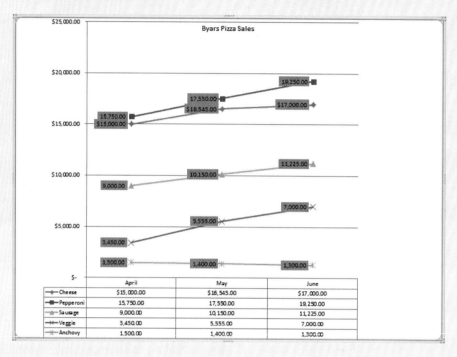

EXTRA FOR EXPERTS

You can copy and paste formats from one label to another using the Format Painter feature. Select a label that has the formats you want to copy, then click the Format Painter button in the Clipboard group on the Home tab. Click the Format Painter over the label that you want to apply the formatting to. The text's format changes to the new format. You can double-click the Format Painter button to keep it selected. This is useful when you want to format multiple labels. Click it again to turn it off.

11. Save, print, and close the workbook.

Creating Sparklines

VOCABULARY
sparkline

A new feature introduced in Excel 2010 is the addition of sparklines. A *sparkline* is a miniature chart that can be displayed in a single row or column of data. You can also create these small charts for each row or column of data within a worksheet. Sparklines are displayed next to the data they represent. Since sparklines are so compact, you can fit them on several adjacent rows or columns of data. After you create sparklines, you can add data markers. You can have the high, low, first, and last points on a sparkline display with data markers. If you select the Markers feature, all data points on the sparklines will be highlighted. You can format sparklines easily using colors and styles.

Excel has three types of sparklines: Line, Column, and Win/Loss. An example of each is shown in **Figure 10–11**.

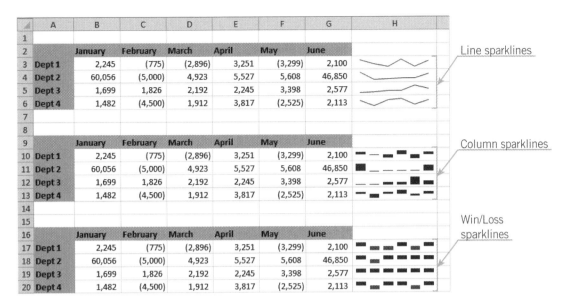

Line sparklines

Column sparklines

Win/Loss
sparklines

FIGURE 10–11 Types of sparklines

Step-by-Step 10.4

1. Open the **College Book** file from the drive and folder where your Data Files are stored.

2. Save the workbook as **College Book Sales**, followed by your initials.

3. Select **B4:G12**.

4. On the Ribbon, click the **Insert** tab and then in the Sparklines group, click **Line**. The Create Sparklines dialog box opens, as shown in **Figure 10–12**. In the Create Sparklines dialog box, you select the cell or range of cells where the sparklines will appear.

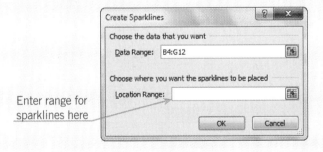

Enter range for
sparklines here

FIGURE 10–12
Create Sparklines dialog box

5. Move the Create Sparklines dialog box out of the way, if necessary, so that you can select the range **H4:H12**. When you release the mouse button, the selected range appears in the Location Range text box.

6. Click **OK**, then compare your worksheet to **Figure 10–13**. Next, you will make Column H wider so that you can see more detail on the sparklines.

FIGURE 10–13
Worksheet with sparklines added

	A	B	C	D	E	F	G	H
1				College Book Sales				
2								
3		January	February	March	April	May	June	
4	Department 01	2,245	775	2,896	3,251	3,299	2,100	⌇
5	Department 02	60,056	4,103	4,923	5,527	5,608	46,850	⌇
6	Department 03	1,699	1,826	2,192	2,245	3,398	2,577	⌇
7	Department 04	1,482	4,500	1,912	3,817	2,525	2,113	⌇
8	Department 05	2,555	2,747	7,200	4,961	5,015	3,204	⌇
9	Department 06	20,900	4,625	5,550	6,450	4,900	4,165	⌇
10	Department 07	2,231	2,398	2,878	4,302	2,200	1,955	⌇
11	Department 08	7,500	1,576	1,891	2,231	1,800	2,542	⌇
12	Department 09	2,114	2,273	2,727	2,900	1,699	2,345	⌇
13								
14								

Sparklines

7. Right-click the **Column H** heading, then click **Column Width** from the shortcut menu. Type **25** in the Column width box and then click **OK**.

8. Select the range **H4:H12** that contains the sparklines.

9. Click the **Design** tab and then, in the Show group, click the **High Point** check box.

10. In the Style group, click the **Marker Color** button arrow, point to **High Point**, and then select **Red** for the data marker color.

11. In the Style group, click the **More** arrow to display the available styles for the sparklines.

12. Position the mouse pointer over Sparkline Style Accent 5, Darker 25% to see the Live Preview of this style in the chart. Then, click to select it. Your completed worksheet should resemble **Figure 10–14**.

> **TIP**
>
> You can also click in a column cell, click Format in the Cells group on the Home tab, and then click Column Width to change the width of a column.

FIGURE 10–14
Sparklines with style and high point markers

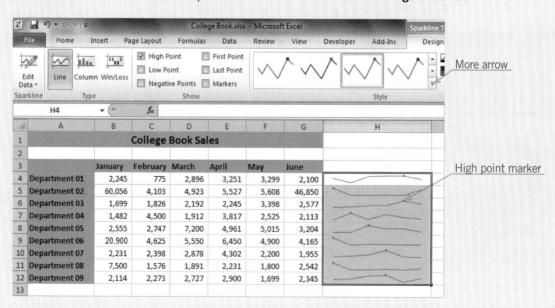

More arrow

High point marker

13. Save, print, and close the workbook.

Creating a Combination Chart

You can create a chart that shows data on two y-axes for the purpose of showing different data. This type of chart is called a **combination chart**. For example, you may have data that shows rainfall amounts measured in inches over several months. Then, you may want to also show the percentage change between the rainfall amounts. You now have two different types of data series: one expressed in inches and the other as percentages. In Excel, you can create a chart that shows both data series in one chart. The y-axis on the left side of the chart is called the **primary axis**. The y-axis on the right side of the chart is called the **secondary axis**. **Figure 10–15** shows a combination chart that displays rainfall in inches and the change in rainfall in percentages. The primary axis displays the rainfall in inches, and the secondary axis displays the percentage change in rainfall.

▶ **VOCABULARY**

combination chart

primary axis

secondary axis

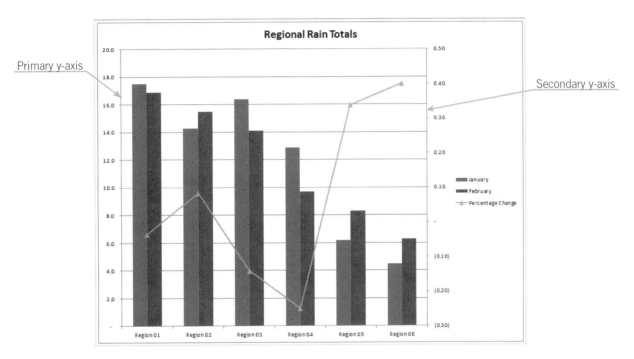

FIGURE 10–15 Combination chart

When making a chart with two y-axes, you will need to use two-dimensional, or 2-D data series. The legend will show the format for each series so that you can identify them in the chart.

Step-by-Step 10.5

1. Open the **Rain Totals** file from the drive and folder where your Data Files are stored.

2. Save the file as **Rain Totals Change** followed by your initials.

3. Select the range **A5:C11**, then press and hold **Ctrl** as you select the nonadjacent range **E5:E11** by dragging from E5 to E11.

4. Press **F11** to create a chart on its own sheet.

5. Double-click the **Chart 1** sheet tab, then type **Rain Chart** to change the chart sheet tab name. The chart is displayed in **Figure 10–16**.

FIGURE 10–16
Rain Totals chart with one y-axis

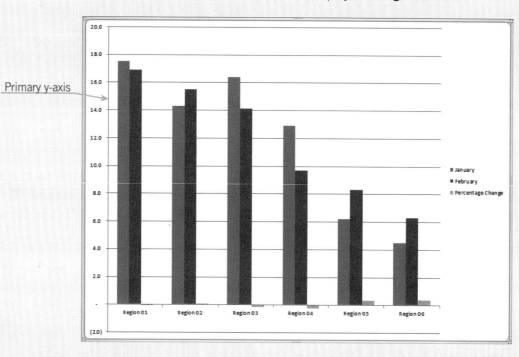

6. Right-click any data marker for the Percentage Change series, then click **Change Series Chart Type**.

7. In the Change Chart Type dialog box, click the **Line** category on the left, and then click the **Line with Markers** chart type. See **Figure 10–17**.

EXTRA FOR EXPERTS

To instantly create a chart in its own chart sheet, simply select the range of data you want in the chart and press F11. Excel generates a chart with column data series. You can then, if necessary, enhance the chart features.

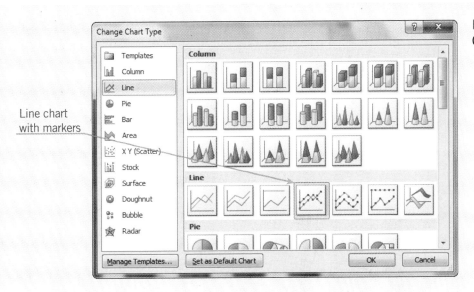

FIGURE 10–17
Change Chart Type dialog box

8. Click **OK** to close the Change Chart Type dialog box. Notice the legend displays the new line series type for Percentage Change.

9. Click any line data series marker to select the entire series.

10. On the Ribbon, click the **Format** tab and then in the Current Selection group, click **Format Selection** to display the Format Data Series dialog box.

11. In the Format Data Series dialog box, verify that the Series Options category is selected on the left, and then click the **Secondary Axis** option button on the right-side. The dialog box should appear as shown in **Figure 10–18**.

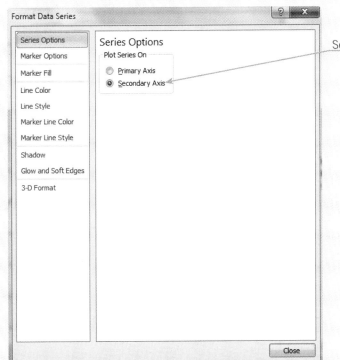

FIGURE 10–18
Format Data Series dialog box

12. Click the **Close** button to close the Format Data Series dialog box. Then, click the **Layout** tab, click **Chart Title**, and then click **Above Chart** to add a title to the chart.

13. Type **Regional Rain Totals** for the chart title, then deselect the title. Your completed chart should appear as shown in **Figure 10–19**.

FIGURE 10–19
Completed combination chart

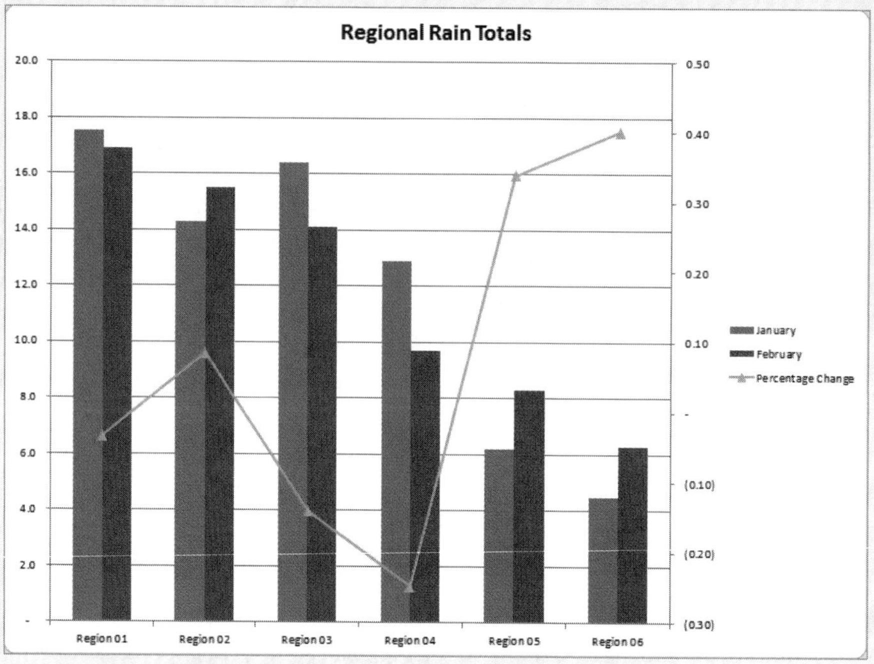

14. Save and close the workbook.

Creating Gauge Charts

A **gauge chart**, or progress chart, shows the amount of progress accomplished toward a goal. For example, you may belong to an organization that promotes walking for better health. The organization might have a goal to collect $50,000 in donations during a specific period of time. A gauge chart shows how much money has been collected from donations as a percentage of the goal. For example, if $20,329 has been collected, about 41 percent of the goal is met. You can show this progress in a gauge chart.

The chart in **Figure 10–20** shows that the donation goal is entered into cell B19, and cell B18 shows the total of cells B5:B16. The percentage is calculated by dividing the donation total by the donation goal. In a gauge chart, the chart is based on one cell of data: the percentage shown in cell B21.

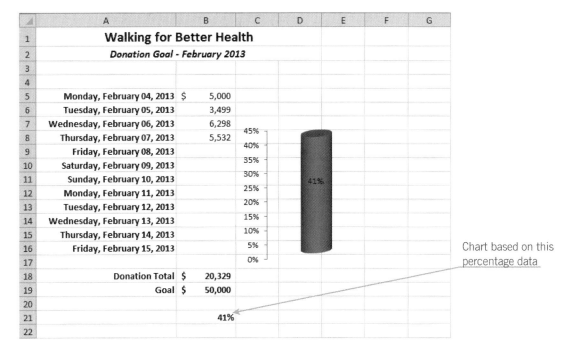

FIGURE 10-20 Gauge chart

As additional amounts are entered in the donation range, the percentage figure shown in cell B21 will increase. In a gauge chart, it is helpful to show this percentage in the chart. Other chart elements, such as the gridlines, legend, and chart floor, can be removed. Chart gridlines are the horizontal and vertical lines within the chart itself and are called *horizontal gridlines* and *vertical gridlines*. The *chart floor* is the foundation, or base, of a 3-D chart.

> **VOCABULARY**
> **horizontal gridlines**
> **vertical gridlnes**
> **chart floor**

Step-by-Step 10.6

1. Open the **Donation** file from the drive and folder where your Data Files are stored, and then save the workbook as **Donation Goal**, followed by your initials. You will calculate the percentage of donations received for an animal rescue shelter.

2. Select **cell B21** and then type the formula **=B18/B19** to calculate the percentage of donations received based on the goal. Next, you will create a cylinder chart to display the percentage.

3. Select **cell B21**, and then click the **Insert** tab. In the Charts group, click **Column**, and then click **Clustered Cylinder**.

4. Move and resize the chart to fit within the range **D5:H21**, as shown in **Figure 10–21**. Next you will remove chart elements so that only the cylinder data series is displayed.

FIGURE 10–21
Gauge chart moved
and resized

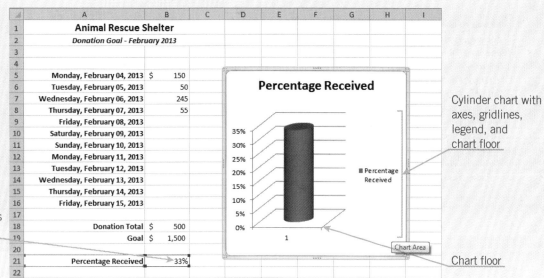

Chart based on this
percentage data

Cylinder chart with
axes, gridlines,
legend, and
chart floor

Chart floor

5. Click the **Layout** tab, then in the Axes group, click **Axes**, point to **Primary Horizontal Axis**, and then click **None** to remove the horizontal chart axis. Click **Axes** again, point to **Primary Vertical Axis**, and then click **None** to remove the vertical chart axis.

6. In the Legends group, click **Legend** and then click **None** to remove the legend.

7. In the Axes group, click **Gridlines**, point to **Primary Horizontal Gridlines**, and then click **None** to remove the horizontal chart gridline. Click **Gridlines** again, point to **Primary Vertical Gridlines**, and then click **None** to remove the vertical gridlines. The chart floor is the final chart feature to be removed.

8. In the Background group, click **Chart Floor**, and then select **None**. The chart floor is removed. Next, you will add the percentage value to the column.

9. In the Labels group, click **Data Labels**, and then click **More Data Label Options**. In the Format Data Labels dialog box, click **Number** on the left and then click **Percentage** in the Category list.

10. Double-click the value in the Decimal places text box, then type **0** (zero) so that there are no decimal places in the percentage. Click **Close** to close the dialog box.

11. Drag the percentage data label to the middle of the cylinder.

12. On the Ribbon, click the **Home** tab. In the Font group, click the **Font Size** buttton arrow, click **16**, and then click the **Bold** button.

13. Select **cell B9**, type **210**, and then press **Enter** to see how the progress increases in the chart. The percentage should now be 47%, as shown in **Figure 10–22**.

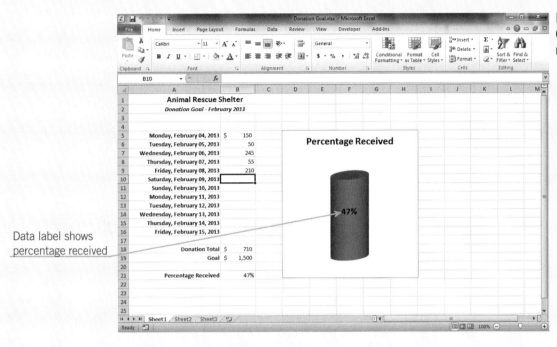

Data label shows percentage received

FIGURE 10–22
Gauge chart reflecting change

14. Save, print, and close the workbook.

Creating Chart Templates

Excel has a variety of chart styles and formats that you can apply to a chart. You may find, however, that you tend to make the same changes to charts to fit a specific professional design. If so, you can create a ***chart template*** by creating a chart and adding the formats and settings that are unique to the charts you want to create. You then save the chart as a template. When you create your next chart, you can simply select the chart, apply your chart template, and the features will be instantly applied. Chart templates are saved in the same default location as the preformatted chart templates.

Step-by-Step 10.7

1. Open the **College Clothing** file from the drive and folder where your Data Files are stored, then save the workbook as **College Clothing Sales**, followed by your initials.

2. Select the range **A5:G16**, and then press **F11** to create a chart in its own sheet.

3. Click the **Design** tab and then, in the Chart Styles group, click the **More** arrow (the bottom arrow in the Chart Styles group) to display the Chart Styles gallery.

4. Select **Style 26**.

5. Click the **Layout** tab, then in the Axes group, click **Axes**, point to **Primary Horizontal Axis**, and then click **More Primary Horizontal Axis Options**. The Format Axis dialog box opens, as shown in **Figure 10–23**.

FIGURE 10–23
Format Axis dialog box

Click feature to display options for that feature

Options displayed for selected feature

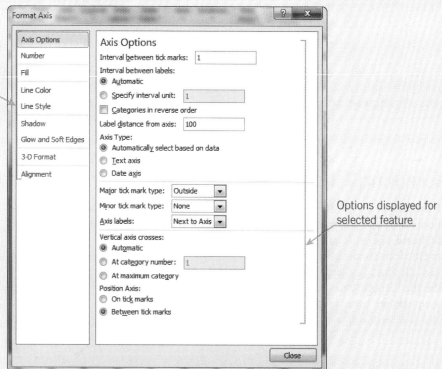

6. In the Format Axis dialog box, click **Alignment** on the left.

7. In the **Custom Angle** text box, type **45** to add a 45° angle to the text, and then click **Close** to close the dialog box.

8. In the Labels group, click **Chart Title**, click **Above Chart**, type **University Sales**, and then press **Enter.**

9. Verify that the chart title is still selected, and then click the **Home** tab. In the Font group, click the **Font Color** arrow button and then click **Dark Blue, Text 2, Lighter 40%.**

10. Click the **Design tab**, and then in the Type group, click **Save As Template** to open the Save Chart Template dialog box, as shown in **Figure 10–24**.

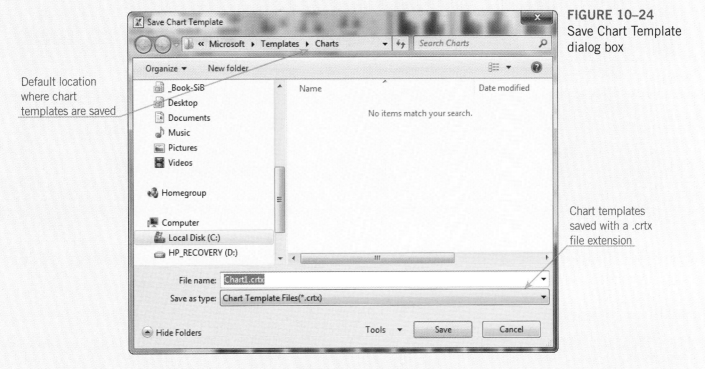

FIGURE 10–24
Save Chart Template dialog box

Default location where chart templates are saved

Chart templates saved with a .crtx file extension

11. In the File name text box, type **Business Chart Template** followed by your initials.

12. Click **Save**. The chart template is now ready to use.

13. Save and close the workbook.

Applying a Chart Template

After creating a chart template, you can apply it to new charts that you create. Applying a chart template to a chart will save you time because you will not need to change each chart feature individually. The chart template applies all the chart elements in the template at one time.

Step-by-Step 10.8

1. Open the **University Expenses** file from the drive and folder where your Data Files are stored, then save it as **University Expenses Chart** followed by your initials.

2. Select **A5:M10**.

3. On the Ribbon, click the **Insert** tab, then in the Charts group, click the **Charts dialog box** launcher to display the Insert Chart dialog box as shown in **Figure 10–25**.

FIGURE 10–25
Insert Chart dialog box

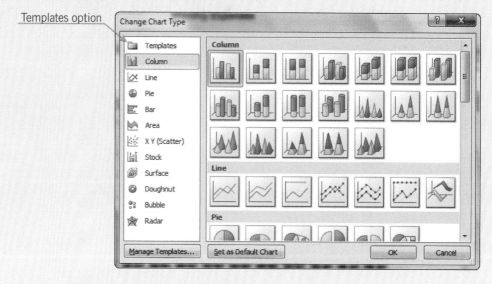

4. Click **Templates** to display the available templates as shown in **Figure 10–26**.

FIGURE 10–26
Insert Chart dialog box with Templates selected

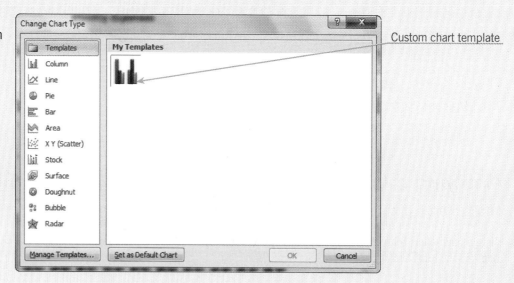

5. Click the chart icon under **My Templates**.

6. Click **OK** to close the Insert Chart dialog box. The Business Chart template is applied to your chart.

7. Move and resize the chart to fit within the range **C13:L34**.

8. Click the chart title, type **Monthly Expenses Chart**, and then click outside the chart title to deselect it. The completed chart should appear as shown in **Figure 10–27**.

FIGURE 10–27
Chart template applied

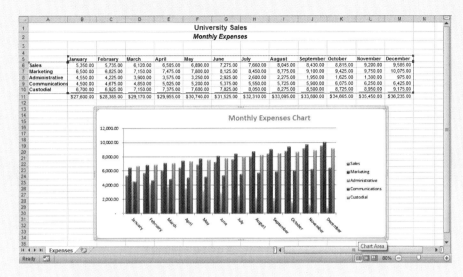

9. Save, print, and close the workbook.

SUMMARY

In this lesson, you learned:

- You can switch rows and columns of data in a chart.
- A data table that shows the data used to create a chart can be added to the chart.
- Data labels can be added to data markers in a data series.
- A sparkline is a miniature chart that can be displayed in a single row or column of data.

- You can design a combination chart that has two y-axes.
- You can construct gauge charts that show progress towards a goal.
- A chart template can be created for a chart design that will be used repeatedly.
- Chart templates can be applied to charts after they are created.

■ VOCABULARY REVIEW

Define the following terms:

chart floor
chart template
combination chart
data labels
data markers

data series
data table
gauge chart
horizontal gridlines
primary axis

secondary axis
sparklines
vertical gridlines
x-axis
y-axis

■ REVIEW QUESTIONS

TRUE / FALSE

Circle T if the statement is true or F if the statement is false.

T   F   **1.**   Data labels display the chart data and are shown below the chart.

T   F   **2.**   Sparklines can display a Line, Column, or Win/Loss chart for each row of data in a worksheet.

T   F   **3.**   Data labels can only be placed to the left or right of the data series.

T   F   **4.**   In a chart with two y-axes, the y-axis on the left is referred to as the primary axis and the y-axis on the right side is called the secondary axis.

T   F   **5.**   A gauge chart shows the amount of progress toward a goal.

FILL IN THE BLANK

Complete the following sentences by writing the correct word or words in the blanks provided.

1. A(n) _____ shows the data used to create the chart and is shown below the chart.

2. _____ can appear as numbers or text next to each data marker in the data series.

3. A(n) _____ is a miniature chart.

4. A(n) _____ includes specific chart formatting that may be applied to other charts after you create them.

5. The _____ is considered the foundation of the chart and is located at the base of the chart.

WRITTEN QUESTIONS

Write a brief answer to the following questions.

1. Explain the process to create a chart template.

2. What are the key features of a gauge chart?

3. Explain the process to switch rows and columns of data in a chart.

4. Explain the difference between a data table and a data label.

5. How would you create Line sparklines in a worksheet?

PROJECTS

If you have a SAM 2010 user profile, your instructor may have assigned an autogradable version of the indicated project. If so, log into the SAM 2010 Web site at *www.cengage.com/sam2010* to download the instruction and start files.

PROJECT 10–1

1. Open the **Income** file from the drive and folder where your Data Files are stored. Save the workbook as **Income Statement** followed by your initials.

2. Create a chart in its own worksheet based on the expenses in range A10:B16.

3. Delete the legend.

4. Add the chart title **2013 Expenses** above the chart.

5. Add data labels for the Outside End location.

6. Save, print, and close the workbook.

PROJECT 10–3

1. Open the **Pie Sales** file from the drive and folder where your Data Files are stored, and then save it as **Pie Sales First Quarter 2013** followed by your initials.

2. Create a chart in its own worksheet based on the first quarter pie sales. You will need to select nonadjacent ranges to create the chart.

3. Switch the columns and rows so that the months appear on the x-axis and the sales amounts appear on the y-axis.

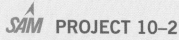 PROJECT 10–2

1. Open the **Projected Earnings** file from the drive and folder where your Data Files are stored, and then save the file as **Projected Earnings by Department** followed by your initials.

2. Add Line sparklines for each row in column H.

3. Change the sparkline color to red.

4. Add High Point markers to the sparklines.

5. Add Low Point markers to the sparklines.

6. Save and close the workbook.

4. Add a chart title above the chart with the text **First Quarter 2013 Pie Sales**.

5. Add a data table with a legend key.

6. Delete the legend on the right side of the chart.

7. Save and close the workbook.

◼ CRITICAL THINKING

ACTIVITY 10–1

You are the assistant manager of a college bookstore. You would like to impress the store manager with your Excel skills. She asks you to create charts based on quarterly sales. You ask her what type of formatting she would like to see in the charts, and you then create a chart template including these features.

1. Open the **College** file from the drive and folder where your Data Files are stored, and then save it as **College Bookstore** followed by your initials.

2. Create a column chart in a chart sheet named **First Quarter**. Format the chart with the colors of your choice.

3. Add **First Quarter Sales** as a title for the chart.

4. Add a data table with a legend key to the chart.

5. Add data labels at the outside end of the markers in the data series.

6. Decide whether the legend should be removed.

7. Save the chart features as a template with the name **Quarterly Sales** followed by your initials.

8. Save and print the worksheet in landscape orientation and so all the data fits on one page, then close the workbook.

ACTIVITY 10–2

You are a real estate broker and owner of GMRE Real Estate. You prefer to view your listings graphically in a chart. You use Excel to create your chart.

1. Open the **GMRE Real Estate** file from the drive and folder where your Data Files are stored to create the chart.

2. Save the workbook as **GMRE Real Estate Listings** followed by your initials.

3. Create a column chart using the data in the **Address**, **City**, **State**, and **Sales Price** columns.

4. Add data labels in the center of the data markers.

5. Change the chart sheet name to **Listings Chart**.

6. Save and close the file.

LESSON 11

Improving Data Accuracy

■ OBJECTIVES

Upon completion of this lesson, you should be able to:

- Use advanced sorting.
- Add subtotals to worksheet data.
- Create a validation rule.
- Enter data in a validation range.
- Circle invalid data.
- Improve data entry accuracy using drop-down lists.
- Convert text to columns.
- Combine text.
- Use a Watch Window.

■ VOCABULARY

concatenation

data validation

delimiter

destination range

grand total

subtotal

validation range

validation rule

Watch Window

Introduction

In this lesson, you will learn about several Excel features that enable you to work efficiently and accurately with worksheet data. The Subtotal feature instantly adds a formula that totals the worksheet data to a cell. The Subtotal feature also formats the worksheet in an outline, which lets you automatically display or hide data. This feature will save you time and increase your productivity.

You will also learn how you can use the Data Validation feature to set rules about how data can be entered. Adding data validation to your worksheet cells helps you monitor the accuracy of the data that's being entered. Excel places circles around any invalid data using the Circle Invalid Data feature. You can also create drop-down lists from which you can select data to control the type of data entered in cells.

In addition, you will learn two new data options: one for combining data and another for separating data. With the first option, you learn how to increase accuracy by letting Excel combine data using a process called *concatenation*. The second option, Convert Text to Columns, separates data for you, rather than you having to retype it yourself.

Finally, Excel offers a Watch Window feature that enables you to view data from one worksheet while you enter or view data in another worksheet. Using a Watch Window lets you view two sets of data at once for convenience. To use any of these accuracy features, you first need to make sure your data is sorted with precision.

▶ **VOCABULARY**
concatenation

Advanced Sorting

You learned how to sort data in ascending order, A to Z, and descending order, Z to A. This method works well for simple alphabetical and numeric data. For all other types of data, such as dates, you'll find you need more options for sorting data. Excel offers a variety of sorting options, and you can create custom sorting options. You can also sort multiple columns of data at one time.

In this next Step-by-Step, you will first sort text in alphabetical order and then using different sort levels, such as Division. In addition, you will learn how to sort data based on four sort levels.

Step-by-Step 11.1

1. Open the **New Lock** file from the drive and folder where your Data Files are stored.

2. Save the workbook as **New Lock Sales**, followed by your initials.

3. Click in any cell under a column heading, and then click the **Data** tab on the Ribbon.

4. In the Sort & Filter group, click the **Sort** button. The Sort dialog box opens, as shown in **Figure 11–1**. For the first sort level, you will sort the column data for division.

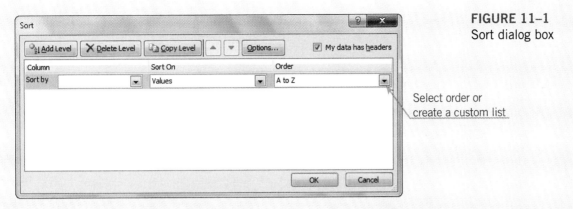

FIGURE 11–1
Sort dialog box

5. In the Sort dialog box, click the **Sort by** arrow, and then click **Division**. A division is an area where a company's regional sales offices are located. You will now sort the column data by month.

6. In the Sort dialog box, click the **Add Level** button. Click the **Then by** arrow, and then click **Month**.

7. Click the **Order** arrow, then click **Custom List** to view the custom list of sort options. The Custom Lists dialog box opens.

8. In the Custom Lists dialog box, click **January, February, March, April**, and then click **OK** to close the dialog box.

9. Click the **Add Level** button, click the **Then by** arrow, and then click **Last Name** to add another level of sorting.

10. Repeat Step 9 to add another level to the Sort dialog box for **First Name**. Your dialog box should appear similar to **Figure 11–2**.

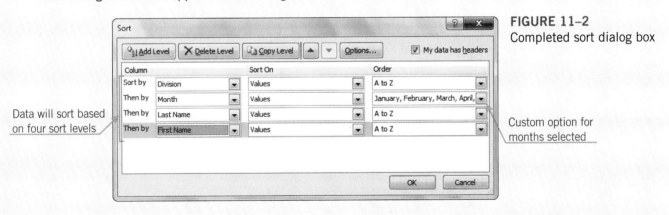

FIGURE 11–2
Completed sort dialog box

11. Click **OK** to sort the data, then view the worksheet data based on the sort options you entered, as shown in **Figure 11–3**.

FIGURE 11–3
Data sorted based on four sort levels

Data first sorted by Division

	A	B	C	D	E
1		**New Lock Corporation**			
2		**Employee Sales**			
3					
4	**Division**	**Month**	**Sales**	**Last Name**	**First Name**
5	East	January	$ 69,306	Baines	Bill
6	East	January	$ 138,639	Clavell	Fugi
7	East	January	$ 49,484	Gebal	Barbara
8	East	January	$ 69,750	Hassell	Sue
9	East	February	$ 72,217	Baines	Bill
10	East	February	$ 144,461	Clavell	Fugi
11	East	February	$ 51,562	Gebal	Barbara
12	East	February	$ 72,680	Hassell	Sue
13	East	March	$ 78,717	Baines	Bill
14	East	March	$ 157,463	Clavell	Fugi
15	East	March	$ 56,202	Gebal	Barbara
16	East	March	$ 79,221	Hassell	Sue
17	North	January	$ 162,457	Crawford	Katie
18	North	January	$ 164,576	Khorjin	Fugi
19	North	February	$ 169,280	Crawford	Katie
20	North	February	$ 171,488	Khorjin	Fugi
21	North	March	$ 184,515	Crawford	Katie
22	North	March	$ 186,922	Khorjin	Fugi
23	South	January	$ 53,208	Dominquez	Gary
24	South	January	$ 39,802	Gonzalez	Lisa
25	South	January	$ 101,222	Hernandez	Sally
26	South	January	$ 193,400	Holder	Howard
27	South	January	$ 179,862	Hussam	Ali
28	South	January	$ 75,001	Welch	JoAnne
29	South	February	$ 55,443	Dominquez	Gary

Sheet1 Sheet2 Sheet3

Months sorted based on the order that months occur during the year

12. Save, print, and leave the workbook open for the next Step-by-Step.

Adding Subtotals

You can add formulas to a worksheet that instantly calculate totals within the worksheet data using Excel's Subtotal feature.

A *subtotal* is the total of only specific parts of the data. The *grand total* is the total for all the data.

The Subtotal feature is useful when you want to view totals in the worksheet data but you don't want formulas permanently entered into the worksheet at that time. The Subtotal feature quickly calculates subtotals and grand totals, but they can be removed when you're finished viewing or printing the data. **Figures 11–4** and **11–5** show the location of inventory items in a craft store. These items are stored in aisles on the east and west side of the store. Figure 11–4 shows the worksheet before subtotals are calculated, and Figure 11–5 shows the worksheet with subtotals applied. Notice how subtotals appear after each department.

▶ **VOCABULARY**
subtotal

grand total

Store Aisle Location	Shelf Location	Item No.	Description	Quantity in Stock	Cost	Total Cost in Inventory
			Arts & Crafts, Inc.			
			Inventory			
East - 3A	4L	12-223	Paint - Blue	45	$ 0.99	$ 44.55
East - 3A	4L	12-295	Paint - White	35	$ 0.99	$ 34.65
East - 3A	4L	12-230	Paint - Green	39	$ 0.99	$ 38.61
East - 3A	7L	12-305	Paint - Yellow	25	$ 0.99	$ 24.75
East - 3A	6L	12-231	Paint - Purple	45	$ 0.99	$ 44.55
East - 3A	7L	12-307	Paint - Light Yellow	25	$ 0.99	$ 24.75
East - 4A	9R	15-223	Varnish - Clear	26	$ 3.99	$ 103.74
East - 4A	9R	15-993	Varnish - Satin	3	$ 3.99	$ 11.97
East - 4A	9R	15-152	Varnish - Extra Gloss	15	$ 3.99	$ 59.85
East - 4A	10R	15-223	Varnish - Almost Clear	26	$ 3.99	$ 103.74
East - 4A	10R	15-998	Varnish - Gold Satin	24	$ 3.99	$ 95.76
East - 5A	5L	12-259	Paint - Eggshell	35	$ 0.99	$ 34.65
East - 5A	5L	12-237	Paint - Light Green	39	$ 0.99	$ 38.61
West - 1B	11R	50-116	16" Wicker Basket	14	$ 1.99	$ 27.86
West - 1B	13R	50-120	20" Wicker Basket	21	$ 2.39	$ 50.19
West - 1B	12R	50-117	17" Wicker Basket	17	$ 1.99	$ 33.83
West - 2B	14R	50-121	21" Wicker Basket	18	$ 2.59	$ 46.62

FIGURE 11–4 Data before subtotals applied

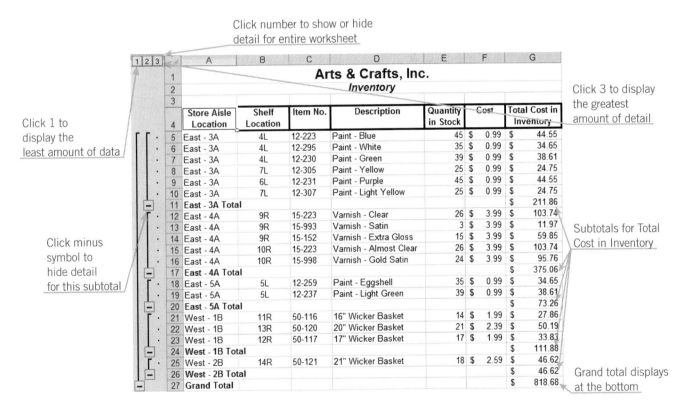

Click number to show or hide detail for entire worksheet

Click 1 to display the least amount of data

Click minus symbol to hide detail for this subtotal

Click 3 to display the greatest amount of detail

Subtotals for Total Cost in Inventory

Grand total displays at the bottom

FIGURE 11–5 Data after subtotals applied

When you use the Subtotal feature, you will need to decide where you want the subtotals to be placed in the worksheet data. For example, if you have columns of inventory data by store aisle, as in Figure 11–4, you can have inventory subtotals placed after each aisle. Be sure to sort the data first so that the items for the subtotal are grouped together.

When you add subtotals to a worksheet, the worksheet is displayed in an outline format. The outline format makes viewing the subtotals easier. In the outline format, you can click the minus button (–) to collapse or hide the data. You click the plus button (+) to expand or redisplay the data.

Notice in Figure 11–5 that the numbers 1, 2, and 3 also appear in the outline. These numbers let you display as much or as little data as you want for the entire worksheet. Selecting 1 only displays the grand total. Selecting 2 only shows the subtotals with no other data, and selecting 3 displays all the worksheet data.

To add subtotals, you select the Subtotal button to display the available options you can select in the Subtotal dialog box, as shown in **Figure 11–6**.

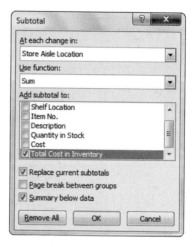

FIGURE 11–6   Subtotal dialog box

The options available in the Subtotal dialog box are described in **Table 11–1**.

TABLE 11–1   Options in the Subtotal dialog box

OPTION	DESCRIPTION
At each change in	This option lets you select the column of data that will determine how data is grouped for subtotaling.
Use function	Selecting this option lets you select the summary calculation to be performed. You may choose Sum, Average, Count, Min, Max, Product, or one of several statistical calculations.
Add subtotal to	This option determines in which column the subtotal will be placed.
Replace current subtotals	When subtotals already exist, using this option replaces existing subtotals.
Page break between groups	Selecting this option creates a page break between each group subtotal.
Summary below data	This option inserts subtotals and a grand total below the detailed data.
Remove All	Selecting this option removes subtotals from data.

Step-by-Step 11.2

1. Click **cell A4** or any cell with a column heading.

2. On the Ribbon, click the **Data** tab, and then in the Outline group, click the **Subtotal** button.

3. Click the **list arrow** below "At each change in", then click **Division** to have subtotals placed after each division. Next, you will select the Sum option to total the data.

4. Click the **Use function** list arrow and then click **Sum**.

5. In the Add subtotal to section, click each marked check box to remove all check marks from the list.

6. In the Add subtotal to section, click the **Sales** check box to add a check mark, and then compare your Subtotal dialog box to **Figure 11–7**.

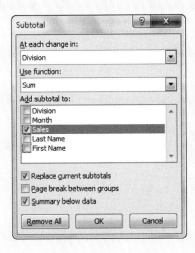

FIGURE 11–7
Completed Subtotal dialog box

7. Click **OK** to close the Subtotal dialog box, and then widen the columns to view the subtotals, if necessary.

8. In the Outline pane on the left side of the workbook data, click **2** so that only the Division subtotals appear, as shown in **Figure 11–8**.

Level 2 selected to display the Division totals only

Click plus symbols to redisplay data

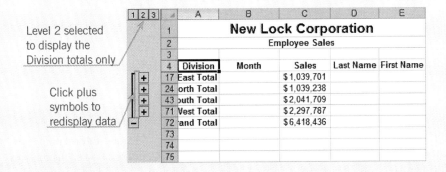

FIGURE 11–8
Data with only Division subtotals displayed

EXTRA FOR EXPERTS

To remove subtotals from the data, click any cell with data. Click the Subtotal button and then click Remove All in the Subtotal dialog box.

9.   In the Outline pane, click **1** to display only the grand total.

10. In the Outline pane, click **3** to display all the data with the subtotals.

11. In the Outline pane, click the **minus symbol (–)** next to East Total. Notice how the data for the East division is collapsed, but the data and totals for the other divisions are still displayed.

12. Save, print, and close the workbook.

Creating a Data Validation Rule

▶ VOCABULARY

data validation

validation rule

validation range

When you or someone else will be adding or changing data to the same worksheet, you may want to use the *Data Validation* feature to ensure that the data is entered as accurately as possible. Adding a *validation rule* allows you to set parameters for worksheet cells where values will be entered. For example, an inventory sheet may contain cells with cost values. If you know that the costs for the products are always within a certain range of values, you can define this range of values in the Settings tab of the Data Validation dialog box. The range of cells that you select to apply the validation rule is called the *validation range*.

You can also create an input message that displays when a cell in the validation range is selected. When the cell is selected, the input message appears stating how the data should be entered or what values are acceptable. Using the Error Alert tab in the Data Validation dialog box, you can create an error alert that appears when a value you enter does not fall within the range.

Several style options are available for the Error Alert tab in the Data Validation dialog box, as shown in **Figure 11–9**.

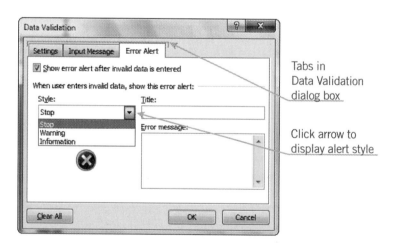

FIGURE 11–9   Data Validation dialog box

The available style options are the Stop style, Warning style, and Information style. If the Stop style is selected in the Error Alert tab, you will not be allowed to enter any value that does not meet the criteria. Choosing the Warning style displays a warning dialog box but allows the data to be entered. The Information style option also allows data to be entered but simply displays an information box with a message that the data entered is invalid.

Step-by-Step 11.3

1. Open the **Fan Fair** file from the drive and folder where your Data Files are stored, and then save the workbook as **Fan Fair Inventory**, followed by your initials. You will now add a validation rule to a range of cells.

2. Select **E6:E21**.

3. On the Ribbon, click the **Data** tab, and then in the Data Tools group, click the **Data Validation** button to open the Data Validation dialog box.

4. In the Data Validation dialog box, click the **Allow** list arrow and then click **Decimal**. Selecting Decimal will allow the user to enter a dollar amount with two decimals.

5. Click the **Data** list arrow and then click **between**, if necessary.

6. Click in the **Minimum** box, and then type **4.00**. 4.00 is the minimum amount that may be entered.

7. Click in the **Maximum** box, and then type **17.00**. 17.00 is the maximum amount that may be entered. The completed Settings tab in the Data Validation dialog box should appear as shown in **Figure 11–10**. You will now enter an input message for the data validation.

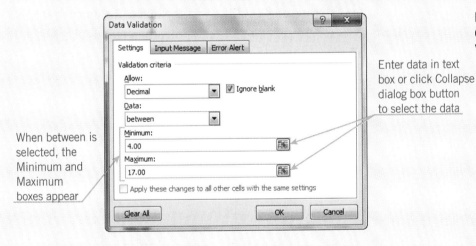

FIGURE 11–10
Completed Settings tab in Data Validation dialog box

8. Click the **Input Message** tab in the Data Validation dialog box, click in the Title text box, and then type **Data Entry Requirement**.

> **TIP**
>
> When the exact amounts that you want to enter in the Data Validation dialog box are in the worksheet, you can click the Collapse dialog box button and then select the cell with the amount.

9. Click in the **Input message** text box and then type **Enter an amount between $4.00 and $17.00**. The completed Input Message tab is shown in **Figure 11–11**.

FIGURE 11–11
Completed Input Message tab in Data Validation dialog box

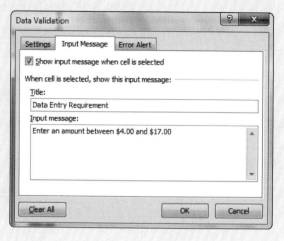

10. Click the **Error Alert** tab. This tab allows you to add an error message if an incorrect amount of data is entered.

11. Click the **Style** list arrow and then click **Warning**.

12. In the Title text box, type **Incorrect Data Entered**.

13. Click in the **Error message** text box and then type **The amount entered must be between $4.00 and $17.00**, as shown in **Figure 11–12**.

FIGURE 11–12
Completed Error Alert tab in Data Validation dialog box

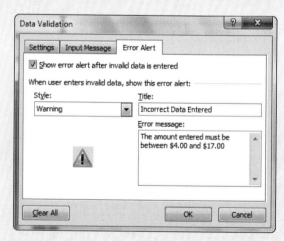

14. Click **OK** to close the Data Validation dialog box.

15. Save the workbook and leave it open for the next Step-by-Step.

Entering Data into a Validation Range

After you select a range and enter a validation rule for the validation range, the data entered into this range is monitored. If the data is invalid, a message will appear to let you know what is wrong. The error message gives you the option to select No or

Continue. Select No if you do not want to enter the data, and select Continue to enter the data. In this next Step-by-Step, you will enter data in the validation range.

Step-by-Step 11.4

1. Click **cell E6**. Notice the input message that appears when you select the cell, as shown in **Figure 11–13**.

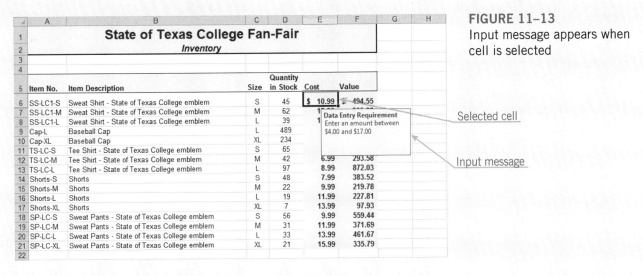

FIGURE 11–13
Input message appears when cell is selected

2. Type **20.00** into cell E6 and then press **Enter**. The error message appears as shown in **Figure 11–14**.

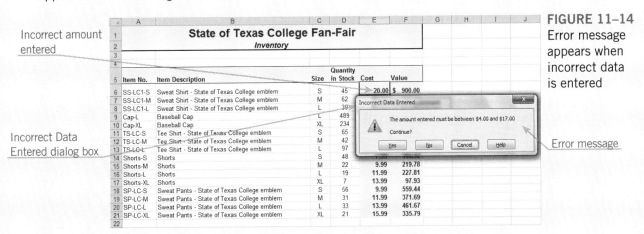

FIGURE 11–14
Error message appears when incorrect data is entered

3. In the Incorrect Data Entered dialog box, click **No,** type **11.99** in cell E6, and then press **Enter**. The amount is now entered into the cell.

4. Save the workbook and leave it open for the next Step-by-Step.

Circling Invalid Data

In addition to using data validation to specifically detail the valid data that should be entered, you can use the Circle Invalid Data feature to have circles drawn around data that does not meet the data validation requirements. The circles act as a visual reminder of which cells contain invalid data.

Step-by-Step 11.5

1. Save the workbook as **Fan Fair Inventory – 2**, followed by your initials.

2. Click **cell E7**, type **122.99**, and then press **Enter**.

3. Click **Yes** to continue.

4. Click **cell E18**, type **99.99**, and then press **Enter**.

5. Click **Yes** to continue. Two cells now have data outside the validation range of $4.00 and $17.00.

6. On the Ribbon, click the **Data** tab. In the Data Tools group, click the **Data Validation** button arrow, and then click **Circle Invalid Data**. Red circles appear, around cells E7 and E18, as shown in **Figure 11–15**.

FIGURE 11–15
Invalid data appears with a circle

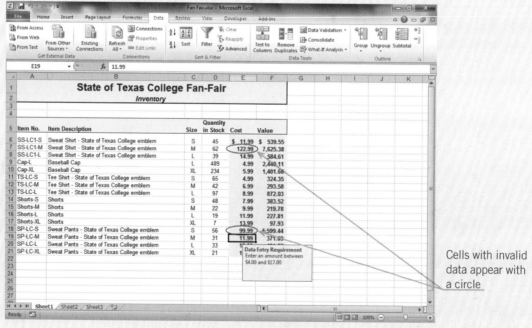

Cells with invalid data appear with a circle

7. Click in **cell E7**, type **13.99**, and then press **Enter** to correct the first validation error.

8. In cell E18, type **9.99**, and then press **Enter**. Notice that the circles are now gone.

9. Save, print, and close the workbook.

Adding a Drop-Down List for Selections

To further increase data accuracy, you can add drop-down lists that display specific selections from which you can choose. Drop-down lists are very useful when only specific data can be entered into a cell. To create a drop-down list, it is easier if you first create a range of cells that has the selections that should appear in the list. For example, if you have a range of cells in which you only want specific areas (such as north, south, east, or west) to appear, you can create a list with only these selections. This list can be created in another worksheet. Then, you will enter the cell range with the list information in the Data Validation dialog box.

When you select a cell with the data validation, an arrow appears to the right of the cell. You can then click the arrow to display the list.

Step-by-Step 11.6

1. Open the **Arts & Crafts** file from the drive and folder where your Data Files are stored, then save the workbook as **Arts & Crafts Inventory**, followed by your initials. You will now add a drop-down list to a range of cells.

2. Select **A5:A50**. Because you have selected additional cells below the existing data, several more rows of data may be added.

3. On the Ribbon, click the **Data** tab, and then in the Data Tools group, click **Data Validation**.

4. In the Data Validation dialog box, click the **Settings** tab, click the **Allow** list arrow, and then click **List**.

5. Click the **Collapse dialog box** button 📉.

6. Click the **Locations in Store** worksheet tab. The store aisle locations appear, as shown in **Figure 11–16**.

FIGURE 11–16
Store aisle locations

7. Select cells **A2:A6**, as shown in **Figure 11–17**. The data in the five cells will serve as the five choices in the drop-down list.

Click Expand dialog box button to restore Data Validation dialog box

FIGURE 11–17
Collapsed Data Validation dialog box

8. Click the **Expand dialog box** button ⬚ to restore the Data Validation dialog box, and then compare your dialog box to **Figure 11–18**.

FIGURE 11–18
Completed Settings tab in the Data Validation dialog box

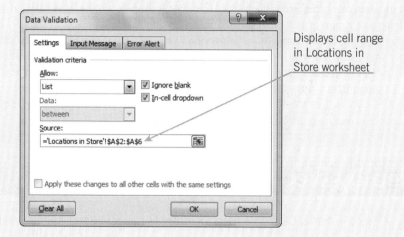

Displays cell range in Locations in Store worksheet

9. In the Data Validation dialog box, click the **Input Message** tab to add an input message.

10. Click in the **Input Message** text box and then type **Click arrow to select value from the list**.

11. Click **OK** to close the Data Validation dialog box.

12. Click in **cell A22**, and then click the list arrow to display the list of store aisle locations, as shown in **Figure 11–19**.

FIGURE 11–19
Store Aisle Location data validation list

List displays valid selections

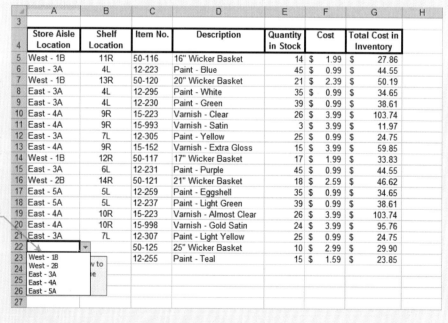

13. Click **West – 2B** in the data validation list.

14. Save, print, and close the workbook.

Converting Text to Columns

The Convert Text to Columns feature is a great method for separating data in a worksheet, such as first and last names. By letting Excel separate the data for you, rather than you typing the data yourself, accuracy is significantly improved.

The Convert Text to Columns Wizard provides a step-by-step process to help you choose how to separate your data. You will need to choose whether you want to separate the data based on a delimiter or fixed width. A *delimiter* is a character, such as a comma, space, or a tab, used to separate data. Using a delimiter works best if your data has a similar format, such as *firstname lastname*, where a space separates the text. The Fixed Width option lets you mark the exact place where the data will be split, such as after 15 characters. When you apply the Fixed Width option, cells will be split at the exact location you specify, even if that is not where you want all the data to split.

After you define how you want to separate the data, you will need to enter a destination range. The *destination range* is the location in the worksheet where the separated data will be placed.

▶ **VOCABULARY**
delimiter
destination range

Step-by-Step 11.7

1. Open the **Computer Training Students** file from the drive and folder where your Data Files are stored, and then save the workbook as **Computer Training Students List** followed by your initials. You will insert two columns to make room for the students' first names and last names.

2. Drag to select any cells in columns **C** and **D**.

3. On the Ribbon, click the **Home** tab. In the Cells group, click the **Insert Cells** button arrow, and then click **Insert Sheet Columns**. Now that you made room for the names, the first names will appear in Column C and the last names will appear in Column D. Next, you will split the data.

4. Select **B2:B25**.

5. On the Ribbon, click the **Data** tab, and then in the Data Tools group, click the **Text to Columns** button. The Convert Text to Columns Wizard opens, as shown in **Figure 11–20**.

FIGURE 11–20
Convert Text to Columns
Wizard – Step 1 of 3

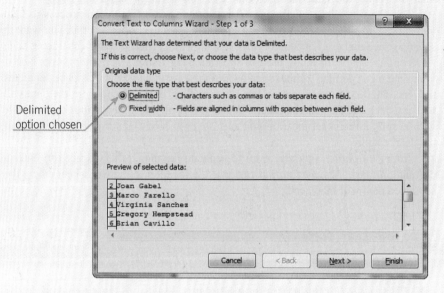

6. Click the **Delimited** option button, if necessary, and then click **Next**.

7. In the Convert Text to Columns – Step 2 of 3 dialog box, click the **Space** check box to indicate that you would like a space to separate the first name and the last name.

8. Verify that the remaining check boxes are not checked, and then compare your screen to **Figure 11–21**.

FIGURE 11–21
Convert Text to Columns Wizard –
Step 2 of 3

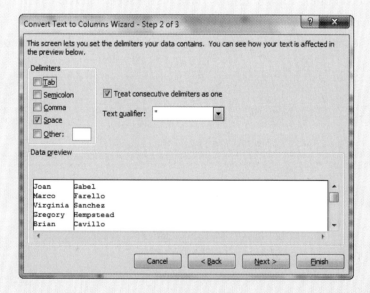

9. Click **Next** to display the Convert Text to Columns – Step 3 of 3 dialog box, and then click the **Text** option button in the Column data format section.

10. Click the **Collapse dialog box button** and then select **C2:D25** to select the range for the last names.

11. Click the **Expand dialog box button** 🔲 to redisplay the dialog box, and then compare your dialog box to **Figure 11–22**.

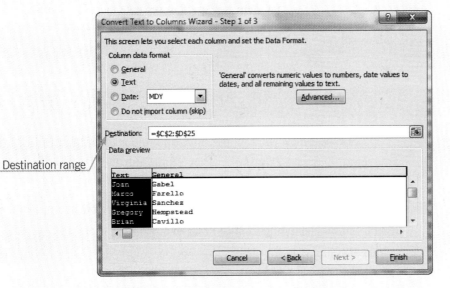

Destination range

FIGURE 11–22
Convert Text to Columns
Wizard – Step 3 of 3

12. Click **Finish**.

13. Click **cell C1**, type **First Name**, press **[Tab]** to select cell D1, and then type **Last Name**.

Your converted data should appear as displayed in **Figure 11–23**.

FIGURE 11–23
Converted data

	Student Number	Student Name	First Name	Last Name	Address	City	State	ZIP
1								
2	1001	Joan Gabel	Joan	Gabel	1102 Jackson Street	Lewis	CO	81327
3	1002	Marco Farello	Marco	Farello	11259 Road 22	Dolores	CO	81323
4	1003	Virginia Sanchez	Virginia	Sanchez	633 Empire Street	Flora Vista	NM	87415
5	1004	Gregory Hempstead	Gregory	Hempstead	12933 Road G	Blanding	UT	84511
6	1005	Brian Cavillo	Brian	Cavillo	116 North Adams Street	Chinle	AZ	86503
7	1006	Cynthia Jones	Cynthia	Jones	755 Cherry Street	Pleasant View	CO	81331
8	1007	Anthony Laporte	Anthony	Laporte	620 East Empire Street	Kayenta	AZ	86033
9	1008	Tara Kobrick	Tara	Kobrick	620 East Empire Street	Kayenta	AZ	86033
10	1009	Darnell Lightford	Darnell	Lightford	1309 Mesa Avenue	Shiprock	NM	87420
11	1010	Louis Moreno	Louis	Moreno	403 North Madison Street	Flora Vista	NM	87415
12	1011	Paul Ferrino	Paul	Ferrino	133 South Washington	Dolores	CO	81323
13	1012	Richard Conlee	Richard	Conlee	307 Memorial Drive	Kirtland	NM	87417
14	1013	Connie Nader	Connie	Nader	1645 Johnny Cake Ridge Road	Kayenta	AZ	86033
15	1014	Robert Selinger	Robert	Selinger	9411 Clarkston Avenue	Aneth	UT	84510
16	1015	Rachel Thompson	Rachel	Thompson	623 South Hampton Way	Farmington	NM	87499
17	1016	Shayla Jackson	Shayla	Jackson	1322 East Fairmont Street	Montezuma Creek	UT	84534
18	1017	Amy Urquiza	Amy	Urquiza	912 North Hampton Avenue	Yellow Jacket	CO	81335
19	1018	Thomas White	Thomas	White	322 South Cripple Creek Avenue	Aneth	UT	84510
20	1019	Dora Langston	Dora	Langston	1155 NE Highland Parkway	Shiprock	NM	87420
21	1020	Dominque Latour	Dominque	Latour	56 East Pioneer Road	Lewis	CO	81327
22	1021	Maria Garcia	Maria	Garcia	707 Cherry Street	Pleasant View	CO	81331
23	1022	Donald Linebarger	Donald	Linebarger	1998 SE First Avenue	Dolores	CO	81328
24	1023	Vincent Ferrino	Vincent	Ferrino	1109 Siesta Shores Drive	Dolores	CO	81324
25	1024	Elaine Estes	Elaine	Estes	801 Airport Road	Lewis	CO	81327

14. Save, print, and close the workbook.

Combining Text

Separating first and last names into separate cells makes it easier to sort the columns with the data by last name and then by first name. However, there may be times when you want the first name and last name combined as one value in a single cell. For example, you may need the first and last name in one cell when merging Excel data to create letters in Microsoft Word.

To join the values of cells together, you use the Concatenate function. The Concatenate function combines the text from two or more cells into one cell.

You can also add other text, such as spaces, into the Concatenate function. For example, you may want to add a space when you are putting first name and last name together in a single cell so that there is a space to separate them. To add text, you include the text, such as a space, between quotation marks. For example, to add a space, you would enter " " into the Concatenate function.

Step-by-Step 11.8

1. Open the **Employees** file from the drive and folder where your Data Files are stored, and save the workbook as **Employees List**, followed by your initials.

2. Click any cell in Column D. You are going to add a new column where the employees' combined first and last names will be placed.

3. On the Ribbon, click the **Home** tab. In the Cells group, click the **Insert Cells** button arrow and then click **Insert Sheet Columns**.

4. Click in **cell D4**. This cell is the first cell in which the combined text will be placed. On the Ribbon, click the **Formulas** tab, and then in the Function Library group, click the **Insert Function** button. The Insert Function dialog box opens, as shown in **Figure 11–24**.

FIGURE 11–24
Insert Function dialog box

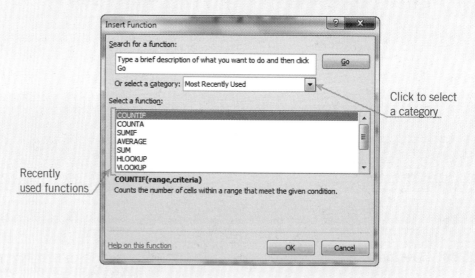

5. Click the **Or select a category** list arrow, and then click **Text**.

6. In the Select a function section, click **CONCATENATE**, and then click **OK** to display the Function Arguments dialog box.

7. In the Function Arguments dialog box, type **A4** in the Text1 text box.

8. Click in the **Text2** text box and then type " " (quote space quote) to add a space between the first name and middle initial.

9. In the Text3 text box, type **B4**.

10. Click in the Text4 text box and type " " (quote space quote) to add a space between middle initial and last name, then type **C4** in the Text5 text box. The completed dialog box should appear as shown in **Figure 11–25**.

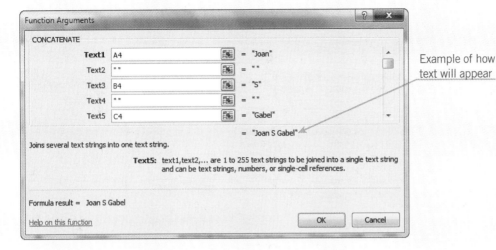

FIGURE 11–25
Completed Function
Arguments dialog box

Example of how
text will appear

11. Click **OK** to close the Function Arguments dialog box.

12. Click **cell D4**, point to the **Fill handle** in the lower-right corner of cell D4, and then drag the **Fill handle** down to cell D27. Next, you will increase the width of column D to display the complete name.

13. Increase the column width, if necessary. Click in any cell outside of column D so you can view the results. The completed worksheet should appear as shown in **Figure 11–26**.

FIGURE 11–26
Concatenated data
in worksheet

Column with
concatenated data

	A	B	C	D	E	F	G	H
3	First Name	Middle Initial	Last Name		Address	City	State	ZIP
4	Joan	S	Gabel	Joan S Gabel	1102 Jackson Street	Lewis	CO	81327
5	Marco	K	Farello	Marco K Farello	11259 Road 22	Dolores	CO	81323
6	Virginia	G	Sanchez	Virginia G Sanchez	633 Empire Street	Flora Vista	NM	87415
7	Gregory	K	Hempstead	Gregory K Hempstead	12933 Road G	Blanding	UT	84511
8	Brian	G	Cavillo	Brian G Cavillo	116 North Adams Street	Chinle	AZ	86503
9	Cynthia	Z	Jones	Cynthia Z Jones	755 Cherry Street	Pleasant View	CO	81331
10	Anthony	L	Laporte	Anthony L Laporte	620 East Empire Street	Kayenta	AZ	86033
11	Tara	P	Kobrick	Tara P Kobrick	620 East Empire Street	Kayenta	AZ	86033
12	Darnell	C	Lightford	Darnell C Lightford	1309 Mesa Avenue	Shiprock	NM	87420
13	Louis	W	Moreno	Louis W Moreno	403 North Madison Street	Flora Vista	NM	87415
14	Paul	G	Ferrino	Paul G Ferrino	133 South Washington	Dolores	CO	81323
15	Richard	P	Conlee	Richard P Conlee	307 Memorial Drive	Kirtland	NM	87417
16	Connie	E	Nader	Connie E Nader	1645 Johnny Cake Ridge Road	Kayenta	AZ	86033
17	Robert	J	Selinger	Robert J Selinger	9411 Clarkston Avenue	Aneth	UT	84510
18	Rachel	O	Thompson	Rachel O Thompson	623 South Hampton Way	Farmington	NM	87499
19	Shayla	B	Jackson	Shayla B Jackson	1322 East Fairmont Street	Montezuma Creek	UT	84534
20	Amy	B	Urquiza	Amy B Urquiza	912 North Hampton Avenue	Yellow Jacket	CO	81335
21	Thomas	M	White	Thomas M White	322 South Cripple Creek Avenue	Aneth	UT	84510
22	Dora	V	Langston	Dora V Langston	1155 NE Highland Parkway	Shiprock	NM	87420
23	Dominque	C	Latour	Dominque C Latour	56 East Pioneer Road	Lewis	CO	81327
24	Maria	A	Garcia	Maria A Garcia	707 Cherry Street	Pleasant View	CO	81331
25	Donald	T	Linebarger	Donald T Linebarger	1998 SE First Avenue	Dolores	CO	81328
26	Vincent	R	Ferrino	Vincent R Ferrino	1109 Siesta Shores Drive	Dolores	CO	81324
27	Elaine	C	Estes	Elaine C Estes	801 Airport Road	Lewis	CO	81327

14. Save, print, and close the workbook.

Adding a Watch Window

You can add cells of data into a Watch Window if you want to be able to view the data while working in another worksheet. The *Watch Window* lets you view the data that you specify, as shown in **Figure 11–27**.

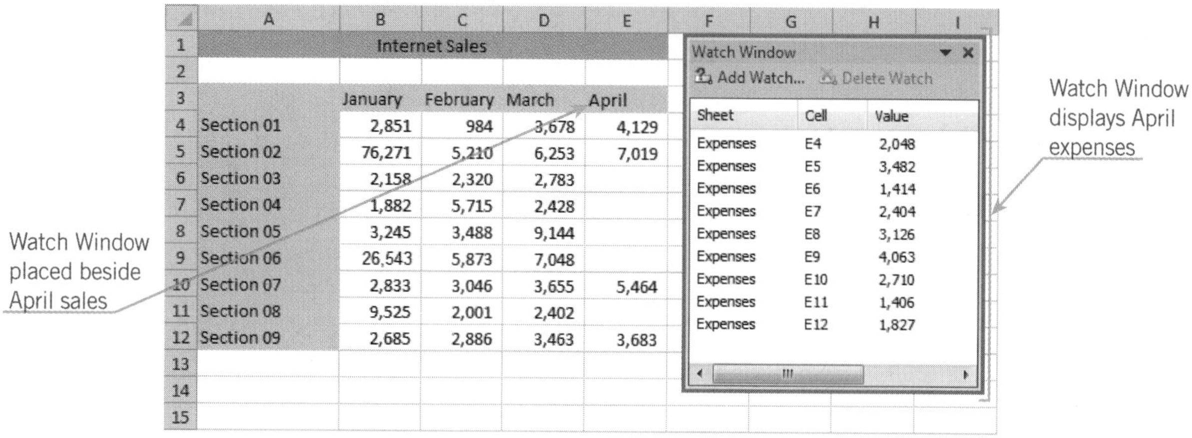

FIGURE 11–27   Worksheet with Watch Window

In this example, the data in the Watch Window is located on a worksheet named Expenses. The Watch Window shows the cell number and the value for the cell. By placing the Watch Window next to sales, you will be able to see when the sales amount is greater than the expenses for each section. And, when sales are greater than expenses, that section should have a profit.

The Watch Window remains visible regardless of which worksheet you are using in the workbook, and it remains open while the workbook is open. When you reopen the Watch Window, it will display the range of data you previously selected.

When the Watch Window first appears, it will include workbook name, worksheet name, cell range name (if any), cell name, value, and formula (if any). In the Watch Window, you can hide the column headings by dragging the right side of the column heading to the left until the column heading is no longer visible.

Step-by-Step 11.9

1. Open the **College Book Sales** file from the drive and folder where your Data Files are stored, then save the workbook as **College Book Sales and Expenses**, followed by your initials.

2. Click the **Expenses** worksheet tab to view the department expenses, as shown in **Figure 11–28**. You will now create a Watch Window for expenses.

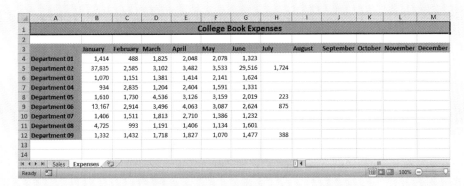

FIGURE 11–28
Expenses worksheet

3. On the Ribbon, click the **Formulas** tab, and then in the Formula Auditing group, click the **Watch Window** button. The Watch Window appears, as shown in **Figure 11–29**.

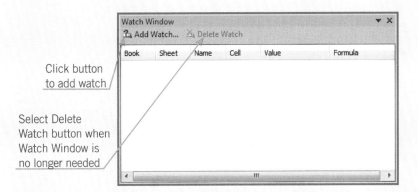

FIGURE 11–29
Watch Window

4. In the Watch Window, click the **Add Watch** button to display the Add Watch dialog box. This dialog box is where you select the cell or cells that you want displayed in the Watch Window.

5. Select the range **H4:H12**. The data in these cells will be visible in the Watch Window. The completed Add Watch dialog box opens, as shown in **Figure 11–30**.

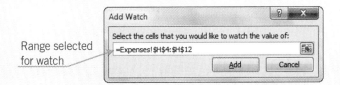

FIGURE 11–30
Add Watch dialog box

6. Click the **Add** button. The Watch Window displays the workbook name, worksheet name, name of cell (if a name was created), and cell name. You will need to increase the size of the Watch Window to view all the values. See **Figure 11-31**.

FIGURE 11-31
Watch Window needs
to be expanded

Cell amounts
not displayed

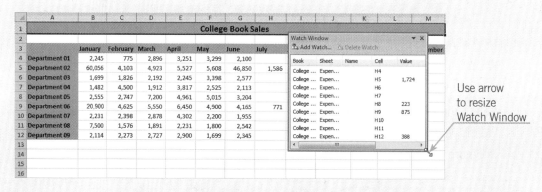

Task Pane
Options arrow

7. Click the **Sales** worksheet tab. Notice that the Watch Window remains open. You will now resize the Watch Window and move it next to Column H. If you were going to enter July sales data, this would allow you to view July expenses as you enter July sales data.

8. On the Watch Window, click the **Task Pane Options** arrow, and then click **Size**. The mouse pointer becomes a double-arrow pointer, as shown in **Figure 11-32**.

FIGURE 11-32
Resizing the
Watch Window

Use arrow
to resize
Watch Window

9. Drag the **arrow** pointer to resize the window, then click the mouse button when the window is the desired size. You will now decrease the size of the columns so that only the Cell and Value columns appear in the Watch Window.

10. Place your mouse pointer over the right side of the column heading for Book and drag it to the left until it is no longer displayed.

11. Decrease the size of the Sheet, Name, and Formula columns until they are no longer displayed.

12. Drag the window next to column H, as shown in **Figure 11-33**.

EXTRA FOR EXPERTS

If you want to change the cells displayed in the Watch Window, click in the first cell in the window and then Shift + Click on the last cell. Then, click the Delete Watch button. You can then add another range to the Watch Window by selecting the Add Watch button.

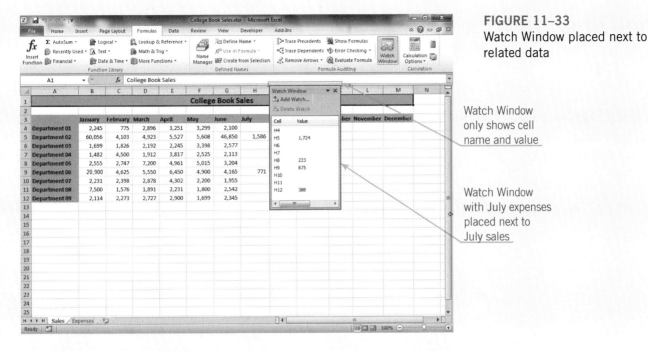

FIGURE 11–33
Watch Window placed next to related data

Watch Window only shows cell name and value

Watch Window with July expenses placed next to July sales

13. Save and close the workbook.

SUMMARY

In this lesson, you learned:

- You can use advanced sorting features to organize worksheet data.

- Adding subtotals to worksheet data lets you instantly view totals in the worksheet.

- Adding a validation rule to a range improves accuracy when data is entered.

- When you enter data in a validation range, you can create input and error messages for the range.

- You can choose to have the Data Validation feature place circles around invalid data.

- You can improve data entry accuracy with drop-down lists.

- Rather than retyping data, you can use the Convert Text to Columns feature to separate data from one cell into multiple cells.

- Text from multiple cells can be combined into one cell using the Concatenate feature.

- The Watch Window lets you view data from one worksheet while you work in other worksheets.

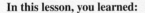 VOCABULARY REVIEW

Define the following terms:

concatenation	destination range	validation range
data validation	grand total	validation rule
delimiter	subtotal	Watch Window

■ REVIEW QUESTIONS

TRUE / FALSE

Circle T if the statement is true or F if the statement is false.

T   F   **1.**   To separate data from one cell into multiple cells, you use the Concatenate function.

T   F   **2.**   If you want to view data from one worksheet while you are working in another one, you could use the Watch Window.

T   F   **3.**   The Data Validation feature offers the ability to create a drop-down list from which you can select data.

T   F   **4.**   You can use the Subtotal feature to quickly add subtotals and a grand total to columns of worksheet data.

T   F   **5.**   The only way to tell if invalid data is entered into a validation range is to look for an error message.

FILL IN THE BLANK

Complete the following sentences by writing the correct word or words in the blanks provided.

1. When a worksheet is in the outline view when using subtotals, the minus symbol lets you _____ data and the plus symbol lets you _____ data.

2. The _____ feature is used to separate data from one cell into multiple cells.

3. To display data from one worksheet while you are entering data into another worksheet, you would use the _____ feature.

4. The type of message that explains how or what data should be entered when you select a cell is called a(n) _____ message.

5. On the Error Alert tab in the Data Validation dialog box, if the _____ style is selected, you will not be allowed to enter a value that does not meet the criteria.

WRITTEN QUESTIONS

Write a brief answer to the following questions.

1. Explain the process for combining text, such as a person's name, from multiple cells into one cell.

2. Explain the three styles that are available on the Error Alert tab in the Data Validation dialog box.

3. Write a brief description of the process to combine a date that is separated into three cells (one for month, one for date, and one for year) into one cell.

4. Describe how you would show more or less detail of a worksheet after adding subtotals to worksheet data.

5. List at least four types of information displayed in the Watch Window.

■ PROJECTS

If you have a SAM 2010 user profile, your instructor may have assigned an autogradable version of the indicated project. If so, log into the SAM 2010 Web site at *www.cengage.com/sam2010* to download the instruction and start files.

PROJECT 11–1

1. Open the **Pharmacy** file from the drive and folder where your Data Files are stored, and save the workbook as **Pharmacy Refills**, followed by your initials.

2. Sort the data by Prescription Number and then by Refill Date.

3. Add subtotals to the data and use the Count function at each change in Prescription Number. Add the count to the Prescription Number column.

4. Save, print, and close the workbook.

SAM PROJECT 11–2

1. Open the **Pacific Sales** file from the drive and folder where your Data Files are stored and then save the workbook as **Pacific Sales by Employee**, followed by your initials.

2. Use the Concatenate formula to join the first name and last name of the employees together in Column F. Separate the first name and last name with a space.

3. Use the Data Validation feature to add a drop-down list to cells F68:F500 that provides a list of the 21 employees. *Note*: You might want to create a list of the employees on another worksheet, so you can select this range in the Data Validation dialog box.

4. Enter **Employee Name** as the column title in cell F4.

5. Create an input message for the validation range F68:F500 that does not have a title, but does indicate that employees should be selected from the list.

6. Create an error alert for the validation range F68:F500. Use the Stop style option so only employees in the list may be entered into the cells. Add the word **Error** as the title and add the text **You may only enter employees from the provided list** as the error message.

7. Test a cell in the validation range to see if the input message and drop-down list display accurately.

8. Save, print, and close the workbook.

PROJECT 11–3

1. Open the **Local Dept Sales** file from the drive and folder where your Data Files are stored.

2. Save the workbook as **Local Dept Sales and Expenses**, followed by your initials.

3. Add a Watch Window to the Expenses worksheet that displays the June Sales data.

4. Resize the Watch Window to display the amounts.

5. Save and close the workbook.

■ CRITICAL THINKING

ACTIVITY 11–1

In a new Excel workbook, create a data list of large household items. Include columns for item categories, item names, year purchased, and the estimated value of the item. Format the data as desired. Use the Subtotal feature to show and hide various levels of data. Save the workbook as **Household Inventory**, followed by your initials. An example of household inventory is shown in **Figure 11–34**.

ACTIVITY 11–2

Create a workbook with data relevant to your life that requires a Watch Window. Think of two sets of information that would be helpful to see at the same time. For example, you might want to create two schedules of games for two different sports that you play to see if there are any conflicts. Or you might want to create a list of calorie counts for approved diet foods and another worksheet that keeps track of the food you eat daily. Use two worksheets in your workbook and save the workbook as **Watch Window**, followed by your initials.

	A	B	C	D
1	**Household Inventory**			
2				
3	R	Name	Year Purchased	Estimated Value
4	Electronics	Computer	2012	$ 3,000
5	Electronics	Printer	2012	$ 1,500
6	Electronics	Television	2014	$ 2,000
7	Electronics	Stereo System	2014	$ 1,500
8	Electronics	Speakers	2014	$ 750
9	**Electronics Total**			$ 8,750
10	Furniture	Living Room Couch	2010	$ 3,000
11	Furniture	Living Room Chairs	2010	$ 2,500
12	Furniture	Bedroom 1 Suite	2012	$ 5,250
13	Furniture	Bedroom 2 Suite	2013	$ 3,500
14	Furniture	Bedroom 3 Suite	2014	$ 2,750
15	Furniture	Armoire	2009	$ 3,000
16	Furniture	Dining Room Table	2009	$ 1,500
17	Furniture	Buffet	2009	$ 2,000
18	**Furniture Total**			$ 23,500
19	Appliances	Stove	2010	$ 1,200
20	Appliances	Double Oven	2010	$ 1,500
21	Appliances	Refrigerator	2010	$ 1,000
22	Appliances	Dishwasher	2010	$ 750
23	Appliances	Freezer	2010	$ 700
24	**Appliances Total**			$ 5,150
25	**Grand Total**			$ 37,400

FIGURE 11–34   Example of household inventory worksheet

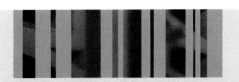

LESSON 12

Creating PivotTables and PivotCharts

■ OBJECTIVES

Upon completion of this lesson, you should be able to:

- Create a PivotTable.
- Sort and filter PivotTable data.
- Modify a PivotTable.
- Change value calculations and formats.
- Update data and refresh the PivotTable.
- Create a PivotChart.
- Filter a PivotChart.
- Modify a PivotChart.
- Add a slicer to a PivotTable.

■ VOCABULARY

child

parent

pivot

PivotChart

PivotTable

slicer

Introduction

Excel offers a unique method for changing the way data can be displayed using the PivotTable feature. A PivotTable lets you rearrange worksheet data so you can analyze it in a variety of ways. You can also create a PivotChart to graphically display the PivotTable. Excel 2010 has a new feature called the slicer. The slicer, which looks like a free-floating note pad, includes column headings that you click to filter data in a PivotTable. The slicer is easy to use, professional in appearance, and prints with the PivotTable.

Creating a PivotTable

VOCABULARY

PivotTable

pivot

A *PivotTable* looks like an ordinary table; however, the data in a PivotTable can be rearranged and summarized in different ways so that you can view the data from various perspectives. Your worksheet typically has columns and rows of related data. Sometimes you might want to change the order of this data, so you can look at it differently.

As its name suggests, a PivotTable lets you *pivot* or rearrange the data. You can place the PivotTable in the same worksheet as the data used to create the PivotTable, or you can place the PivotTable in its own worksheet. After the PivotTable is created, you can continue to rearrange it.

When you create a PivotTable, you do not need to use all of the data in the worksheet; you can select only the data you want to view. The data that you choose needs to have column headings. Any blank columns or blank rows need to be removed from the worksheet data.

For example, you may have a worksheet with data for students applying for student loans. This data might include columns for Last Name, First Name, Class Level, Major, Grade Point Average, and Student Loan Amount. Using a PivotTable, you could rearrange the data in many different ways. You could quickly reorganize the data by Class Level and Student Loan Amount in an easy-to-read format. You might also want to see the total of all student loans.

To rearrange the data, you drag the column headings into the Report Filter, Column Labels, Row Labels, and Values areas in the PivotTable Field List dialog box. Doing so rearranges the worksheet data into a PivotTable based on your selections, as shown in **Figure 12–1**.

Available fields
display on the left
side of dialog box

PivotTable
layout area

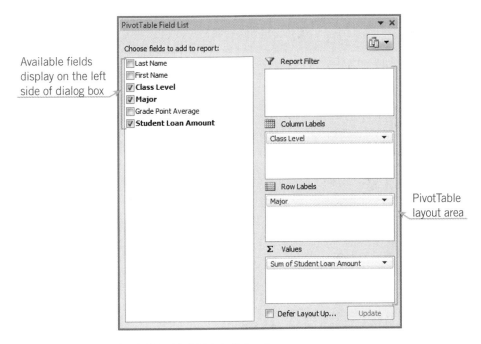

FIGURE 12–1   PivotTable Field List dialog box

Based on this example, the various Class Levels (Freshman, Sophomore, Junior, and Senior) will appear as column headings. The Majors, such as Finance, Education, and History, will display on the rows. The sum of Student Loan Amounts will show as the values.

In this next Step-by-Step, you will create a PivotTable based on student loan information.

Step-by-Step 12.1

1. Open the **Student Loans** file from the drive and folder where your Data Files are stored.

2. Save the workbook as **Student Loans - 2014**, followed by your initials. The worksheet contains student loan data, as shown in **Figure 12–2**. You will use the data to create a PivotTable in a new worksheet.

FIGURE 12–2
Worksheet data for PivotTable

Worksheet data to be used in PivotTable →

Column headings will appear as fields →

Last Name	First Name	Class Level	Major	Grade Point Average	Student Loan Amount
	Madison College				
	Student List				
Aannestad	JoAnne	Junior	History	2.7	$ 2,500
Alkier	Sallye	Freshman	Finance	2.6	$ 445
Ascot	Ali	Junior	Education	4.0	$ -
Bennett	Jack	Junior	Finance	2.6	$ -
Buescher	David	Sophomore	Chemistry	3.0	$ 3,244
Caldwell	Jack	Senior	Music	3.1	$ 1,450
Coats	Grace	Senior	Economics	3.7	$ 200
Conlee	Howard	Sophomore	Finance	3.4	$ 2,778
Cortez	Lisa	Senior	Economics	3.8	$ 623
D'Ambrosio	David	Freshman	Music	3.2	$ 757
Estes	Stephanie	Freshman	Biology	3.8	$ 5,138
Feraco	Gary	Senior	History	3.0	$ 775
Ferrino	Howard	Sophomore	History	3.5	$ -
Gabel	Grace	Freshman	Finance	2.3	$ 1,450
Garcia	Bryce	Freshman	Business	3.4	$ 11,000
Gattis	Lilly	Junior	Economics	3.4	$ 1,490
Hargus	Joy	Junior	Finance	2.7	$ 1,358
Hernandez	Brian	Senior	Music	3.1	$ 1,850
Hernandez	Cynthia	Sophomore	History	3.1	$ 9,000
Jackson	Anthony	Senior	Finance	3.7	$ 450
Johnson	Darnell	Junior	Biology	2.5	$ 2,569
Johnson	Tara	Junior	Finance	2.3	$ 775
Kobrick	Louis	Sophomore	Education	3.6	$ -

Students

Ready

3. Select **cell A4** or any cell in the worksheet data, so that Excel knows where the data for the PivotTable is located.

4. On the Ribbon, click the **Insert** tab, and then click the **PivotTable** button in the Tables group. The Create PivotTable dialog box opens.

5. Verify that **A4:F60** appears in the Table/Range text box. Note that you could also change the range if you wanted.

6. Select the **New Worksheet** option button, if necessary, then click **OK**. The PivotTable Field List dialog box appears on the right side of the worksheet and the PivotTable pane is shown on the left, as seen in **Figure 12–3**.

TIP

You can also choose to place the PivotTable in the existing worksheet by clicking the Existing Worksheet option button in the Create PivotTable dialog box.

Drag field from list to layout area

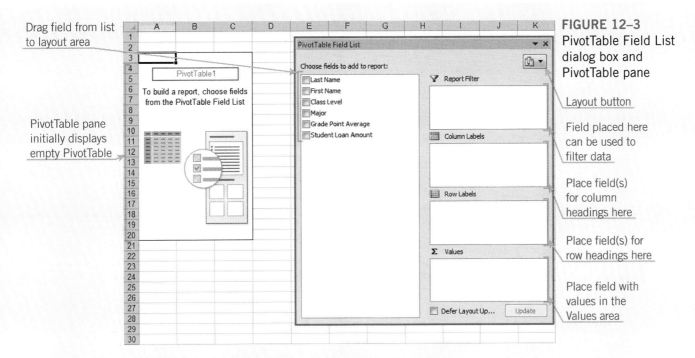

PivotTable pane initially displays empty PivotTable

FIGURE 12–3
PivotTable Field List dialog box and PivotTable pane

Layout button

Field placed here can be used to filter data

Place field(s) for column headings here

Place field(s) for row headings here

Place field with values in the Values area

7. At the upper-right corner of the PivotTable Field List dialog box, click the **Layout button** , then click **Fields Section and Areas Section Side by Side**. There are five possible ways to view the layout of the PivotTable Field List.

8. In the PivotTable Field List dialog box, place the mouse pointer over **Major** and drag it into the **Row Labels** area. Notice how the PivotTable begins to form in the pane to the left as you drag column headings into the PivotTable Field List dialog box. See **Figure 12–4**.

Row Labels appear in PivotTable pane

Check mark indicates field used in layout area

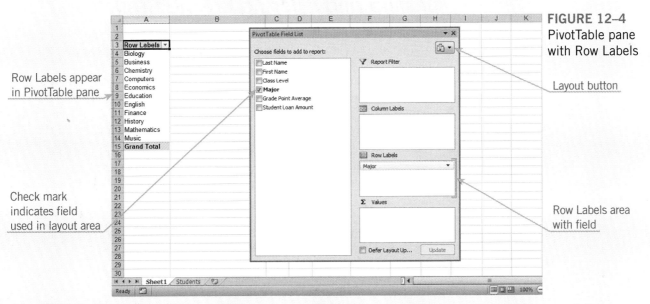

FIGURE 12–4
PivotTable pane with Row Labels

Layout button

Row Labels area with field

9. Drag **Class Level** to the **Column Labels** area.

10. Drag **Student Loan Amount** to the **Values** area. Your PivotTable Field List dialog box and PivotTable pane should resemble **Figure 12–5**.

FIGURE 12–5
PivotTable Field List
dialog box and
PivotTable pane

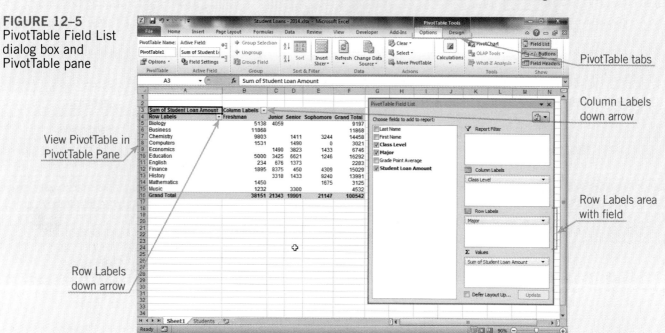

PivotTable tabs

Column Labels
down arrow

View PivotTable in
PivotTable Pane

Row Labels area
with field

Row Labels
down arrow

11. If necessary, click the **Options** tab on the Ribbon, and then click the **Field List** button in the Show group to close the PivotTable Field List.

12. Save the workbook and leave it open for the next Step-by-Step.

Sorting and Filtering PivotTable Data

After you create the PivotTable, you can sort and filter the data to provide additional ways to analyze it. The sort and filter options are displayed when you click the Column Labels down arrow or the Row Labels down arrow on the PivotChart.

You can select a sort option to sort the data in ascending order, from A to Z, or in descending order, from Z to A. Numbers would sort lowest to highest in ascending order and highest to lowest in descending order. When you filter data, the data you want to show is displayed and the rest of the data is hidden. The sort and filter options for Column Labels are shown in **Figure 12–6**.

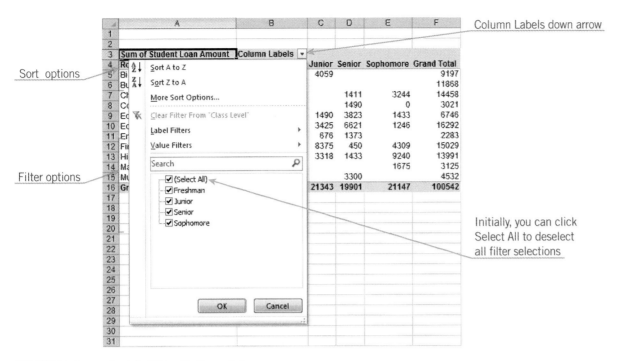

FIGURE 12–6   Sort & Filter Options list

To deselect all of the filter selections, you click Select All. Then, you can click the selection or selections you want to use in the filter.

After you sort or filter the data, a graphic, like a ScreenTip, appears when you place your mouse pointer over the Column Labels and Row Labels down arrows. This graphic lets you know how the data is sorted and filtered. In the next Step-by-Step, you will first filter data and then sort it.

Step-by-Step 12.2

1. In cell B3, click the **down arrow** next to the Column Labels heading.

2. Click the **Select All** check box to remove the check marks from the Class Level check boxes. You are going to filter the data to view only the Junior and Senior class levels.

3. Click the **Junior** and **Senior** check boxes to select them.

4. Click **OK** to view the filtered results, as shown in **Figure 12–7**.

FIGURE 12–7
Filtered PivotTable

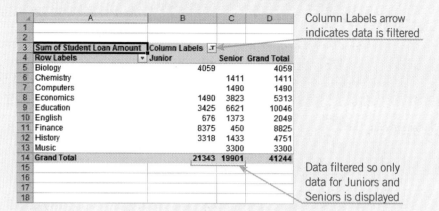

Column Labels arrow
indicates data is filtered

Data filtered so only
data for Juniors and
Seniors is displayed

5. In cell A4, click the **Row Labels** down arrow.

6. In the Sort & Filter list, select **Sort Z to A**. You want to view the Majors in a descending order alphabetically.

7. In cell A4, place the mouse pointer over the down arrow and notice that a graphic appears, letting you know that Class Level is filtered and Major is sorted Z to A, as shown in **Figure 12–8**.

FIGURE 12–8
Filtered and sorted PivotTable

Majors sorted in
descending order

Graphic shows how
the PivotTable is
filtered and sorted

Row Labels arrow
indicates data is sorted

8. Save the workbook and leave it open for the next Step-by-Step.

Modifying the PivotTable

After you create the PivotTable, you can continue to rearrange the data. To change the location of rows and columns, you simply need to redisplay the PivotTable Field List dialog box and shift the order of the fields. You can also add additional levels of detail. For example, you can add two fields, such as Major and Last Name, to an area of the PivotTable Field List, such as Row Labels. The modified PivotTable will display the student's last name under his or her major.

When you add levels of fields, Outline buttons appear in the PivotTable so that you can show or hide these levels. Clicking the minus symbol hides the data, and clicking the plus sign displays the data.

Step-by-Step 12.3

1. If necessary, click the **Options** tab, and then click the **Field List** button in the Show group to display the PivotTable Field List dialog box.

2. Drag the **Last Name** field so that it is below Major in the Row Labels area. The student's last name is now displayed beneath their major, as shown in **Figure 12–9**.

Outline symbols are displayed with multiple fields

Last Name of student appears under his or her major

Click minus symbol to hide detail that is displayed under Education

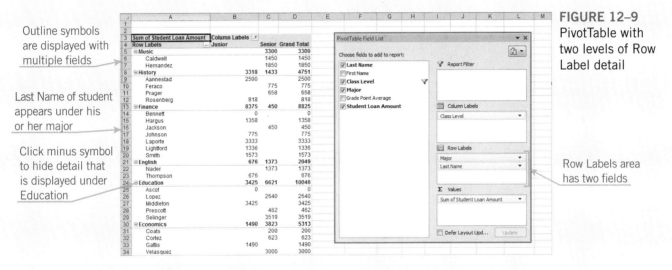

Row Labels area has two fields

FIGURE 12–9
PivotTable with two levels of Row Label detail

3. Click the **Field List** button in the Show group to close the PivotTable Field List dialog box. You will now change the sort order on Major.

4. In cell A4, click the **Row Labels** down arrow, and then click **Sort A to Z**.

5. Click the **Field Headers** button in the Show group to remove the Row Labels and Column Labels field headers. The modified PivotTable appears as shown in **Figure 12–10**.

FIGURE 12–10
Sorted PivotTable
without field headers

Row Labels header no longer displayed

Column Labels header no longer displayed

Sorted in ascending order by Major and then by student's Last Name

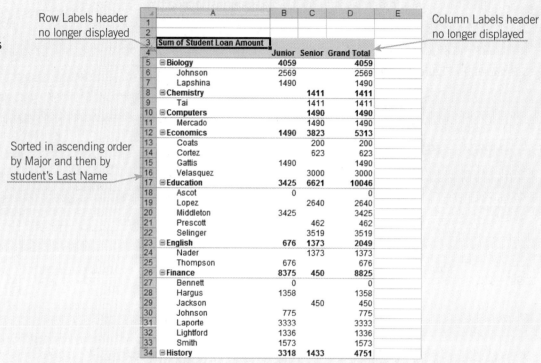

	A	B	C	D	E
1					
2					
3	Sum of Student Loan Amount				
4		Junior	Senior	Grand Total	
5	⊟Biology	4059		4059	
6	Johnson	2569		2569	
7	Lapshina	1490		1490	
8	⊟Chemistry		1411	1411	
9	Tai		1411	1411	
10	⊟Computers		1490	1490	
11	Mercado		1490	1490	
12	⊟Economics	1490	3823	5313	
13	Coats		200	200	
14	Cortez		623	623	
15	Gattis	1490		1490	
16	Velasquez		3000	3000	
17	⊟Education	3425	6621	10046	
18	Ascot	0		0	
19	Lopez		2640	2640	
20	Middleton	3425		3425	
21	Prescott		462	462	
22	Selinger		3519	3519	
23	⊟English	676	1373	2049	
24	Nader		1373	1373	
25	Thompson	676		676	
26	⊟Finance	8375	450	8825	
27	Bennett	0		0	
28	Hargus	1358		1358	
29	Jackson		450	450	
30	Johnson	775		775	
31	Laporte	3333		3333	
32	Lightford	1336		1336	
33	Smith	1573		1573	
34	⊟History	3318	1433	4751	

6. Save the workbook and leave it open for the next Step-by-Step.

Changing Formats and Value Calculation

When you first create a PivotTable, the numbers are brought in, but their formats are not. You may want to change the format of the PivotTable data so the people viewing it will know that the data are dollar amounts, percentages, or just numbers with a comma to separate thousands. For example, if someone looks at the data in a PivotTable and sees 3.79, they will not know if it is $3.79, 3.79%, or just 3.79. Adding formats to the values will help them know what the values represent.

In addition, you may want to calculate the data differently, such as a percentage of the total amount. You can change how the values in a PivotTable are displayed and calculated by choosing the Calculations button in the Calculations group and selecting Show Values As. Then, you choose an option in the Show Values As list, as shown in **Figure 12–11**.

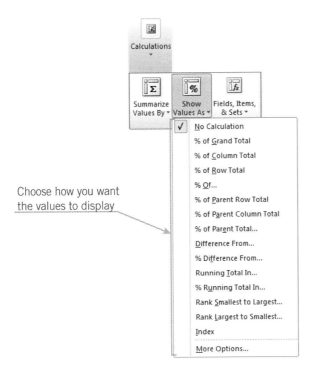

FIGURE 12–11   Show Values As list

You can quickly change the format and calculation by redisplaying the Show Values As list and selecting another option. Or, you can select No Calculation to return the PivotTable format back to how it looked when you first created it.

You can also create your own calculation using any of the options that end with an ellipsis (…). The Parent options refer to data that has more than one level of detail. When there is more than one level, the main row heading is referred to as the *parent* and the level of detail below this level is the *child*.

▶ **VOCABULARY**
parent
child

Step-by-Step 12.4

1. Select **B5:D42**.

2. Click the **Home** tab and then click the **Comma Style** button in the Number group.

3. To remove the decimal places, click the **Decrease Decimal** button twice.

4. Click any cell in the PivotTable that contains numerical data.

5. Click the **Options** tab, click the **Calculations** button, select the **Show Values As** button arrow in the Calculations group, and then click **% of Grand Total**.

6. Click the **minus symbol** next to Biology to hide the student last name data below the major. Notice that the minus symbol is now a plus symbol, as shown in **Figure 12–12**.

FIGURE 12–12
Values as a percentage of grand total

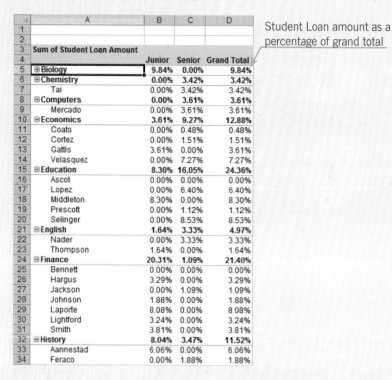

Student Loan amount as a percentage of grand total

	A	Junior	Senior	Grand Total
3	Sum of Student Loan Amount			
5	⊞ Biology	9.84%	0.00%	9.84%
6	⊟ Chemistry	0.00%	3.42%	3.42%
7	Tai	0.00%	3.42%	3.42%
8	⊟ Computers	0.00%	3.61%	3.61%
9	Mercado	0.00%	3.61%	3.61%
10	⊟ Economics	3.61%	9.27%	12.88%
11	Coats	0.00%	0.48%	0.48%
12	Cortez	0.00%	1.51%	1.51%
13	Gattis	3.61%	0.00%	3.61%
14	Velasquez	0.00%	7.27%	7.27%
15	⊟ Education	8.30%	16.05%	24.36%
16	Ascot	0.00%	0.00%	0.00%
17	Lopez	0.00%	6.40%	6.40%
18	Middleton	8.30%	0.00%	8.30%
19	Prescott	0.00%	1.12%	1.12%
20	Selinger	0.00%	8.53%	8.53%
21	⊟ English	1.64%	3.33%	4.97%
22	Nader	0.00%	3.33%	3.33%
23	Thompson	1.64%	0.00%	1.64%
24	⊟ Finance	20.31%	1.09%	21.40%
25	Bennett	0.00%	0.00%	0.00%
26	Hargus	3.29%	0.00%	3.29%
27	Jackson	0.00%	1.09%	1.09%
28	Johnson	1.88%	0.00%	1.88%
29	Laporte	8.08%	0.00%	8.08%
30	Lightford	3.24%	0.00%	3.24%
31	Smith	3.81%	0.00%	3.81%
32	⊟ History	8.04%	3.47%	11.52%
33	Aannestad	6.06%	0.00%	6.06%
34	Feraco	0.00%	1.88%	1.88%

7. Click the **minus symbols** next to Chemistry, Computers, Economics, Education, English, Finance, History, and Music to hide all of the last names. Your modified PivotTable should appear as shown in **Figure 12–13**.

FIGURE 12–13
All majors with collapsed data

Plus signs appear when data is collapsed

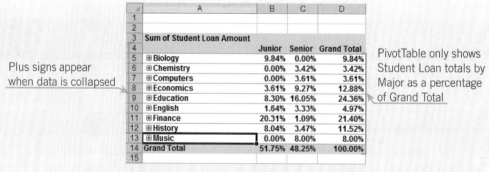

	A	Junior	Senior	Grand Total
3	Sum of Student Loan Amount			
5	⊞ Biology	9.84%	0.00%	9.84%
6	⊞ Chemistry	0.00%	3.42%	3.42%
7	⊞ Computers	0.00%	3.61%	3.61%
8	⊞ Economics	3.61%	9.27%	12.88%
9	⊞ Education	8.30%	16.05%	24.36%
10	⊞ English	1.64%	3.33%	4.97%
11	⊞ Finance	20.31%	1.09%	21.40%
12	⊞ History	8.04%	3.47%	11.52%
13	⊞ Music	0.00%	8.00%	8.00%
14	Grand Total	51.75%	48.25%	100.00%

PivotTable only shows Student Loan totals by Major as a percentage of Grand Total

8. Right-click the **worksheet tab** and then select **Rename** from the shortcut menu to rename the worksheet with the PivotTable.

9. Type **PivotTable**, and then press **Enter** to display the new worksheet name.

10. Save the workbook and leave it open for the next Step-by-Step.

Updating Data and Refreshing the PivotTable

The data used to create the PivotTable can be changed; however, the data in the PivotTable will not be updated to reflect this change until you click the Refresh button. Once you click the Refresh button, located in the Data group on the Options tab, the PivotTable data is updated to reflect the changes to the worksheet data.

Step-by-Step 12.5

1. View the percentage in cell C6 of the PivotTable. The current percentage for senior chemistry majors is 3.42%.

2. Click the **Students** worksheet tab to view the worksheet data.

3. Select **cell F52**.

4. Type **14,111** and then press **Enter**.

5. Click the **PivotTable** worksheet tab, and then click any cell in the PivotTable. Notice the percentage in cell C6 is still 3.42%.

6. Click the **Options** tab, and in the Data group, click the **Refresh** button to refresh the PivotTable data. The percentage in cell C6 is now 26.16%, as shown in **Figure 12–14**.

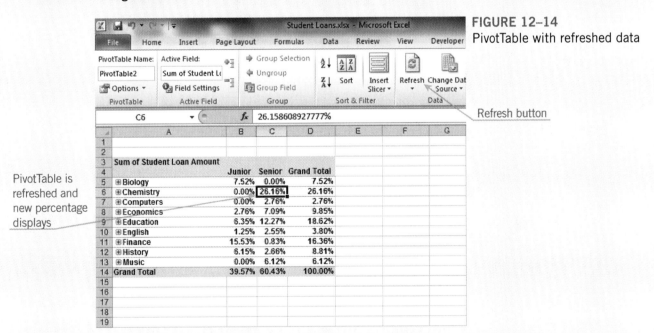

FIGURE 12–14
PivotTable with refreshed data

7. Save and print the PivotTable worksheet, then close the workbook.

Creating a PivotChart

Not only can you rearrange the data in a worksheet by creating PivotTables, you can create a visual representation of this data in a **PivotChart**. When you create a PivotChart with worksheet data, a PivotTable is created at the same time. If you have already created a PivotTable, you can create a PivotChart based on the PivotTable.

▶ **VOCABULARY**
PivotChart

The PivotTable and PivotChart are linked. If a change is made to the PivotTable, the associated PivotChart changes as well. If changes are made to the PivotChart, the PivotTable reflects this change too.

Each PivotChart type (with the exception of pie charts) typically has two axes: a horizontal axis and a vertical axis. The horizontal axis usually plots the categories along the bottom of the chart. The vertical axis usually plots values, such as dollar amounts, along the left side of the chart.

Step-by-Step 12.6

1. Open the **Discount Internet** file from the drive and folder where your Data Files are stored.

2. Save the file as **Discount Internet Sales** followed by your initials.

3. Select **cell A4** or any cell in the worksheet data.

4. On the Ribbon, click the **Insert** tab, click the **PivotTable** button arrow in the Tables group, and then click **PivotChart**.

5. If necessary, type or select **A4:E67** in the Table/Range text box. Make sure the New Worksheet option button is selected and then click **OK**. The PivotTable Field List dialog box opens with an empty PivotTable and PivotChart, as shown in **Figure 12–15**.

FIGURE 12–15
PivotTable Field List for PivotTable and PivotChart

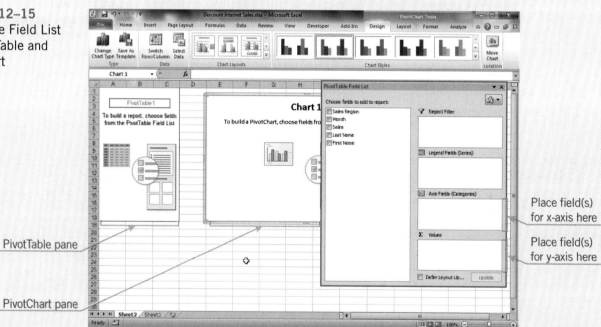

6. In the PivotTable Field List dialog box, place the mouse pointer over **Sales Region** and drag it into the **Axis Fields** area to have each Sales Region appear on the horizontal axis.

7. Next, drag **Sales** to the **Values** area so that the dollar amount will display in the chart and dollars will show on the vertical axis.

8. Drag **Month** to the **Axis Fields** area below Sales Region to add months along with the sales region on the horizontal axis. The PivotTable Field List dialog box, PivotTable, and PivotChart should appear as shown in **Figure 12–16**.

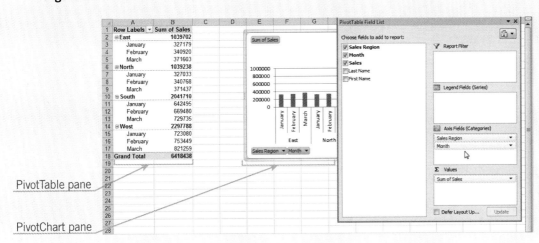

PivotTable pane

PivotChart pane

FIGURE 12–16
PivotTable and
PivotChart

9. Click the **Analyze** tab and then in the Show/Hide group, click the **Field List** button to close the PivotTable Field List dialog box.

10. Save the workbook and leave it open for the next Step-by-Step.

Filtering the PivotChart

Just as you can filter PivotTable data, you can filter PivotChart data as well. You may want to filter a PivotChart so that less data appears in the chart. For example, your chart may include the twelve months on the horizontal axis, and you may want to view the chart with only one month of data. When you filter the PivotChart, the same filtered data appears in the PivotTable. Chart filters are located in the chart itself. In the next Step-by-Step, you will first reformat the PivotTable data. Then, you will filter the chart.

Step-by-Step 12.7

1. Select **B2:B18** to reformat the values.

2. Click the **Home** tab, and in the Number group, click the **Comma Style** button 🔲.

3. With the range still selected, click the **Decrease Decimal** button in the Number group twice to remove the decimals from the numbers. Notice how the data in the chart is also reformatted. See **Figure 12–17**.

FIGURE 12–17
Reformatted
PivotTable and
PivotChart

Formatted data also
appears in chart

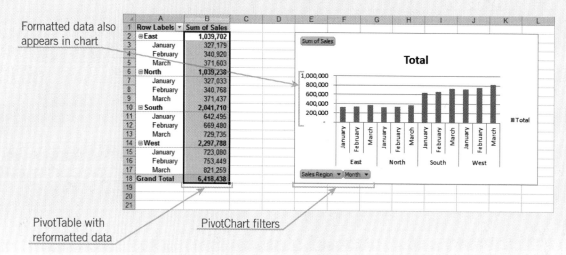

PivotTable with
reformatted data

PivotChart filters

4. Click the **Month** down arrow in the PivotChart to display the sort and filter options.

5. Click the **Select All** check box to remove the filter arrows for months, so that you can filter by a certain month or a couple of months.

6. Click the **January** check box, and then click **OK**. Now only sales for January are displayed in the PivotTable and PivotChart, as shown in **Figure 12–18**.

FIGURE 12–18
Filtered PivotChart
and PivotTable

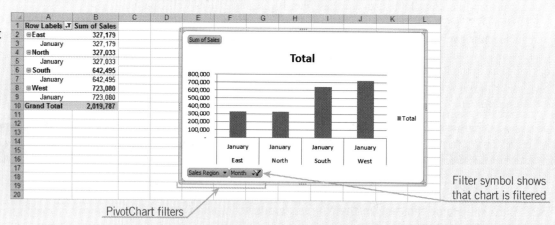

Filter symbol shows
that chart is filtered

PivotChart filters

7. Click the **Month** down arrow, click the **Select All** check box, and then click **OK** to redisplay the months.

8. To filter by Sales Region so only a specific region or regions are displayed, click the **Sales Region** down arrow. Then click the **Select All** check box to deselect it.

9. Click the **South** check box to select it, and then click **OK**. Your PivotTable and PivotChart should appear as shown in **Figure 12–19**.

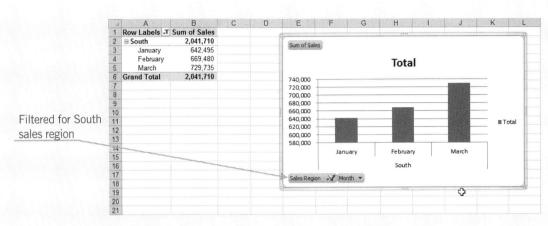

FIGURE EX–19
Completed PivotTable
and PivotChart

Filtered for South
sales region

10.   Save the workbook and leave it open for the next Step-by-Step.

Modifying the PivotChart

PivotCharts can be modified just like ordinary Excel charts. For example, you can
change the chart type and add chart styles. When the PivotChart is selected, additional tabs appear on the Ribbon. These tabs are designated for making changes to
the PivotChart. You will now change the PivotTable chart type and chart style.

Step-by-Step 12.8

1.   Click the **PivotChart** to select it.

2.   On the Ribbon, click the **Design** tab and then in the Type group, click
     the **Change Chart Type** button so that you can change the chart type.

3.   In the Change Chart Type dialog box, click **Column** on the left, if neces-
     sary, and then click the **3-D Clustered Column** chart in the first row. See
     Figure 12–20.

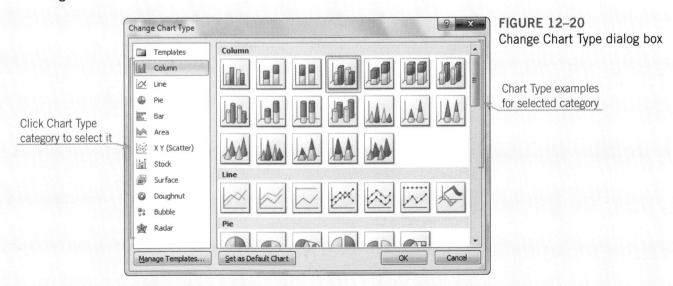

FIGURE 12–20
Change Chart Type dialog box

Chart Type examples
for selected category

Click Chart Type
category to select it

4. Click **OK** to close the Change Chart Type dialog box.

5. On the Design tab, in the Chart Styles group, click the **More** button arrow ⬇ to display the Chart Styles, as shown in **Figure 12–21**.

FIGURE 12–21
Chart styles

Click any chart style to select it

Style 14

Bottom row in Chart Styles has dark background color

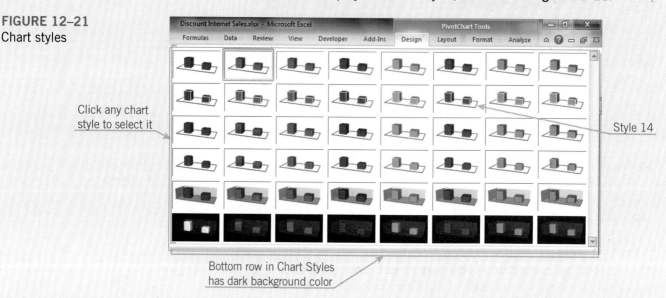

6. Select **Style 14** in the second row of the Chart Style options. Your chart should appear as shown in **Figure 12–22**.

FIGURE 12–22
PivotChart with new style applied

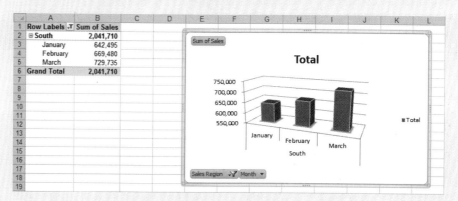

7. Save, print the worksheet with the PivotTable and PivotChart, and then close the workbook.

Using the Slicer

▶ **VOCABULARY**
slicer

The *slicer* is a new feature in Excel 2010. It is a visual control that looks like a note pad. Clicking selections on the slicer lets you filter your data in a PivotTable. A slicer acts like a filter, but it is easier to use. The slicer can be placed next to the PivotTable and remains visible so that selections can be easily accessed. By keeping the slicer displayed, you can hide and display data by clicking items in the slicer.

Each field (column of data) in the PivotTable can have its own slicer to filter data for the column. When an item is highlighted in the slicer, only the data for that item is displayed. In **Figure 12–23**, only December is highlighted, so only December data is displayed in the PivotTable.

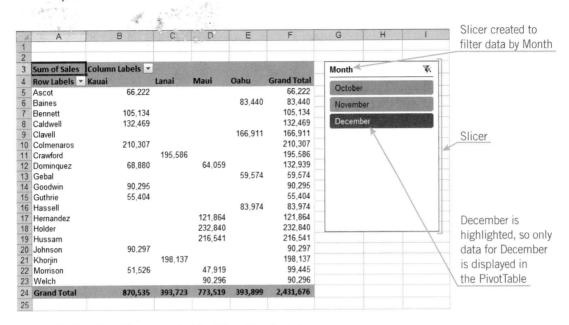

FIGURE 12–23   Slicer created to filter Month data

When a slicer is first displayed, it appears with a basic design. However, you can choose another style for the slicer on the Options tab. For example you may want the slicer to appear with similar colors as your worksheet The slicer will print when you print the worksheet. If you do not want the slicer to print, you can drag it out of the print range or right-click it and choose Remove from the shortcut menu.

Step-by-Step 12.9

1. Open the **Division Sales** file from the drive and folder where your Data Files are stored.

2. Save the file as **Division Sales for Hawaii** followed by your initials.

3. Click the **PivotTable worksheet** tab to view the PivotTable.

4. Select **cell A3** or any cell in the PivotTable.

5. On the Ribbon, click the **Options** tab and then click **Insert Slicer** in the Sort & Filter group. The Insert Slicers dialog box opens, as shown in **Figure 12–24**.

FIGURE 12–24
Insert Slicers dialog box

Select the fields you want to insert a slicer for

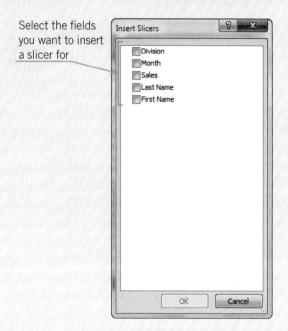

6. Click the **Month** check box to have a slicer appear for the months in the PivotTable.

7. Click **OK**. Next, you will move the slicer next to the PivotTable.

8. Place your mouse pointer over the Month slicer and drag it to the side of the PivotTable. When the slicer is first displayed, all of the items are selected, as shown in **Figure 12–25**.

FIGURE 12–25
PivotTable and slicer

PivotTable with all data displayed

Slicer to filter Month data

Grand Total for all sales

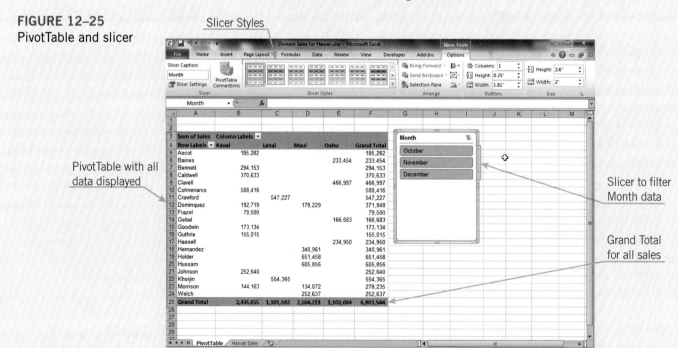

9. On the Month slicer, click **October**. Only sales for October are displayed in the PivotTable, as shown in **Figure 12–26**.

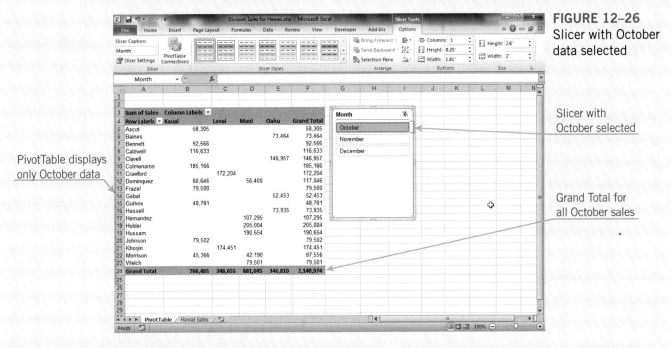

FIGURE 12–26
Slicer with October data selected

PivotTable displays only October data

Slicer with October selected

Grand Total for all October sales

10. Press and hold **Shift** and then click **November** on the Month slicer to view sales for both October and November. Now, two months of data are displayed in the PivotTable.

11. Verify that the Month slicer is selected, and then, on the Options tab, click the **More** button ⬇ in the Slicer Styles group. The Slicer Styles appear as shown in **Figure 12–27**.

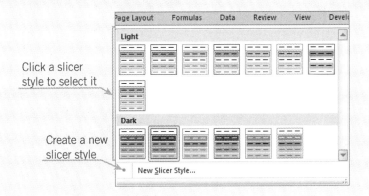

Click a slicer style to select it

Create a new slicer style

FIGURE 12–27
Slicer styles

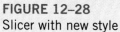

12.   Select **Slicer Style Dark 2**, as shown in **Figure 12–28**.

FIGURE 12–28
Slicer with new style

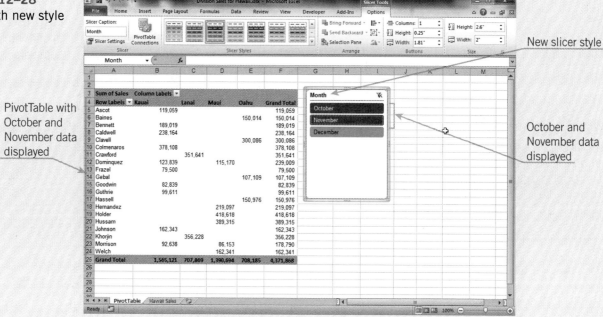

13.   Save, print the worksheet with the PivotTable and the slicer, and then close the workbook.

SUMMARY

In this lesson, you learned:

■   You can create PivotTables based on worksheet data.

■   You can sort and filter PivotTable data.

■   After a PivotTable is created, it can be modified.

■   You can change formats and value calculations in a PivotTable.

■   After you update worksheet data that was used to create a PivotTable, you need to refresh the PivotTable to display the changes.

■   PivotCharts can be created with PivotTables.

■   PivotCharts can be filtered.

■   After a PivotChart is created, it can be modified.

■   Adding a slicer to a PivotTable lets you filter data.

■ VOCABULARY REVIEW

Define the following terms:

child
parent

pivot
PivotChart

PivotTable
slicer

■ REVIEW QUESTIONS

TRUE / FALSE

Circle T if the statement is true or F if the statement is false.

T   F   **1.**   You can place the PivotTable in the same worksheet as the data used to create the PivotTable or on a separate worksheet in the workbook.

T   F   **2.**   You can change the layout of a PivotTable after it has been created using the PivotTable Field List.

T   F   **3.**   Excel automatically creates a PivotTable when you create a PivotChart.

T   F   **4.**   A slicer can be used to filter data in a PivotTable.

T   F   **5.**   PivotTables can be filtered, but a PivotChart cannot be filtered.

FILL IN THE BLANK

Complete the following sentences by writing the correct word or words in the blanks provided.

1. If data that was used to create a PivotTable is changed, you update the PivotTable by clicking the _____ button.

2. Data in a PivotTable can be filtered using the filter buttons in the Field Header cells or by using the _____.

3. The design of a slicer can be changed by selecting a(n) _____.

4. To collapse data in a PivotTable that has multiple row headings, you click the _____.

5. To remove the filter arrows in the Sort & Filter list, you click the _____ check box.

WRITTEN QUESTIONS

Write a brief answer to the following questions.

1. After a PivotTable has been created, how would you rearrange it to view another perspective of the data?

2. If you make changes to the data that is used to create a PivotTable, how do you update the data in the PivotTable?

3. What is the purpose of a slicer?

4. Explain how you would filter a PivotChart.

5. Explain how you would change the chart style for a PivotChart.

■ PROJECTS

If you have a SAM 2010 user profile, your instructor may have assigned an autogradable version of the indicated project. If so, log into the SAM 2010 Web site at *www.cengage.com/sam2010* to download the instruction and start files.

PROJECT 12–1

You will create a PivotTable that shows the total sales amounts of products in each of two stock areas.

1. Open the P K Industries file from the drive and folder where your Data Files are stored, and save it as **P K Industries Analysis** followed by your initials.

2. Create a PivotTable with the following setup:

    Column Labels: **Stock Area**

    Row Labels: **Item #**

    Values: **Total Product Value in Inventory**

3. Add a currency format with two decimal places to the product values. (Adjust the column widths if necessary.)

4. Remove the Field Headers.

5. Change the name of the worksheet with the PivotTable to **Stock Area Analysis**.

6. Print the PivotTable. Save and close the workbook.

PROJECT 12–3

You will create a PivotTable that shows employee sales by region.

1. Open the Virginia Sales file from the drive and folder where your Data Files are stored, and save it as **Virginia Sales by Region** followed by your initials.

2. Create a PivotTable on a new worksheet with the following setup:

    Column Labels: **Region**

    Row Labels: **Employee**

    Values: **Sales**

 **PROJECT 12–2**

You will create a PivotTable that shows grade point averages for students by their last name.

1. Open the Spelling Bee file from the drive and folder where your Data Files are stored, and save it as **Spelling Bee Groups** followed by your initials.

2. Create a PivotTable with the following setup:

    Column Labels: **Competition Group**

    Row Labels: **State**

                   Last Name

                   First Name

    Values: **Fees Still Due**

3. Add a slicer to filter on **Competition Group**.

4. Select 1 in the slicer so that only data for Competition Group 1 will be displayed in the PivotTable.

5. Change the PivotTable worksheet name to **Competition Groups**.

6. Print the PivotTable with the slicer.

7. Save and close the workbook.

3. Close the PivotTable Field List.

4. Print the PivotTable.

5. Save and close the workbook.

■ CRITICAL THINKING

ACTIVITY 12–1

You are the manager for a production company. You will be giving a presentation to the company owner this afternoon, and you want to create a PivotChart and PivotTable that show the total electricity costs for each of the departments.

1. Open the Electricity file from the drive and folder where your Data Files are stored, and save it as **Electricity Usage** followed by your initials.

2. Create a PivotChart that shows **Departments** on the horizontal axis and **Usage** as the Value.

3. Change the chart type to a three-dimensional column.

4. Format the usage numbers to a comma style with one decimal place.

5. Print the PivotTable and PivotChart.

6. Save and close the workbook.

ACTIVITY 12–2

Using Excel's Help system, find information on how you can turn off the Grand Totals for Rows and Columns in a PivotTable. Write a brief explanation of this procedure.

LESSON 13

Using Powerful Excel Functions

■ OBJECTIVES

Upon completion of this lesson, you should be able to:

- Use the COUNT and COUNTA functions.
- Utilize the COUNTBLANK function to count blank cells.
- Use the Subtotal function with filtered data.
- Create a named range.
- Use a named range in a function.
- Use a SUMIF function.
- Search for data using VLOOKUP.
- Search for data using HLOOKUP.

■ VOCABULARY

condition

criteria

function number

lookup table

Introduction

Excel offers a variety of powerful tools that allow you to increase your productivity by using functions to count, sum, and locate specific information. This lesson discusses a number of these extremely useful functions. First, you will count numerical data in a range using the COUNT function. Counting data is important if you are doing such tasks as a head count of employees or volunteers. Next, you will count cells that have text with the COUNTA function. To count the number of cells without content, you will use the COUNTBLANK function.

Once again, you will use the Subtotal function. But, this time, you will expand its capabilities by counting filtered cells. You'll learn about the SUMIF function that is used to total only cells that meet a certain condition. To save time when you enter functions, you will learn how to name ranges of data.

Finally, you will see the advantage of using LOOKUP functions to find data. LOOKUP functions find data in a lookup table. The VLOOKUP function locates data when it is displayed vertically in the lookup table. The HLOOKUP function finds data when it is displayed horizontally in the lookup table. You will explore each of these features in this lesson.

Using COUNTA versus COUNT

Excel provides two functions for counting cells: one for counting cells with numeric data and another for counting cells with text. To find the total number of cells that have numeric data, you use the COUNT function. To count cells with text, you use the COUNTA function. The COUNTA function can count cells if they contain text or a combination of text and numbers. In the next Step-by-Step, you will use the COUNT function to count the total of numeric values in a column and the COUNTA function to count the number of cells in a column that have text.

Step-by-Step 13.1

1. Open the **Antique Class** file from the drive and folder where your Data Files are stored.

2. Save the workbook as **Antique Class Enrollment**, followed by your initials. You will first use the COUNT function to count the number of cells with numeric data.

3. Click **cell E36**.

4. Type the function **=COUNT(E5:E34)** and then press **Enter**. Excel shows a count of 30. See **Figure 13–1**.

FIGURE 13–1
COUNT function counts
numeric data

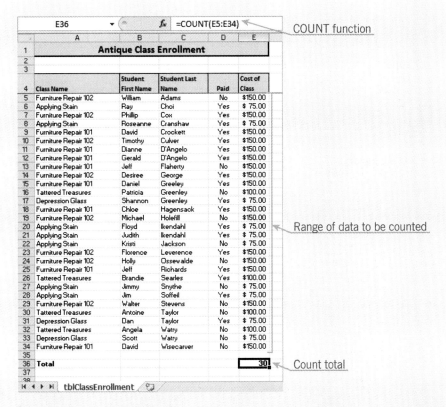

5. Click cell **C36**.

6. Type the function **=COUNT(C5:C34)** and press **Enter**. Notice how 0 appears as the result, because cells C5:C36 contain no numeric data. Next, you will use the COUNTA function.

7. Click cell **C36**.

8. Type the function **=COUNTA(C5:C34)** and then press **Enter**. The number 30, which is the count of students in the class and is textual data, appears in the cell, as shown in **Figure 13-2**.

FIGURE 13-2
COUNTA function counts cells with text

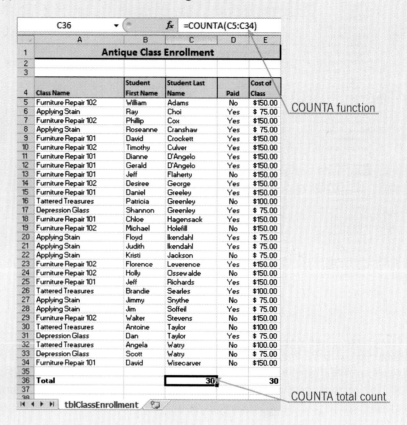

9. Save, print, and close the workbook.

Using COUNTBLANK

The COUNTBLANK function counts the number of cells that do not have any numbers or text entered in them. You may want to count blank cells to see how many cells do not contain data.

For example, you might have a worksheet that has a list of volunteers for each day of the week. Volunteers enter the number of hours they can work in any given day. On the days that a volunteer will not be working, the cell is left blank. So, if you want to see how many open volunteer slots you have for a certain day, you could use the COUNTBLANK function to count the empty cells. Then, if you see that one of the days has quite a few blanks, you could call other volunteers to see if they might be able to help.

In the next Step-by-Step, the library has a list of 24 volunteers. They need 12 volunteers working per day at the library. If the day of the week has more than 12 blanks, you will need to contact more volunteers to see if they might be able to help.

Step-by-Step 13.2

1. Open the **Library Volunteers** file from the drive and folder where your Data Files are stored.

2. Save the workbook as **Library Volunteers – June 2014**, followed by your initials. The library needs 12 volunteers working per day. You need to find the days that do not have enough volunteers.

3. Click **cell C31**.

4. Type the function **=COUNTBLANK(C6:C29)** and then press **Enter** to view the result. You will now copy the formula to the rest of the cells.

5. Click in **cell C31**. Place your mouse pointer over the fill handle in the lower-right corner of this cell, and then click and drag to cell **I31**. The COUNTBLANK function is now copied to each of these cells. Notice that Tuesday, Wednesday, and Thursday do not have enough volunteers, as shown in **Figure 13–3**.

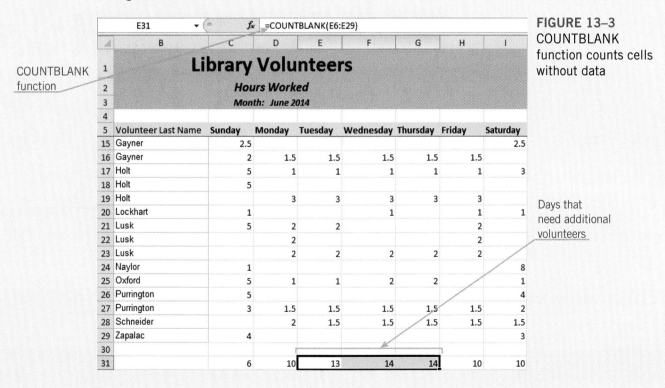

FIGURE 13–3
COUNTBLANK function counts cells without data

COUNTBLANK function

Days that need additional volunteers

| E31 | fx | =COUNTBLANK(E6:E29) |

	B	C	D	E	F	G	H	I
1		**Library Volunteers**						
2		**Hours Worked**						
3		**Month: June 2014**						
4								
5	**Volunteer Last Name**	**Sunday**	**Monday**	**Tuesday**	**Wednesday**	**Thursday**	**Friday**	**Saturday**
15	Gayner	2.5						2.5
16	Gayner	2	1.5	1.5	1.5	1.5	1.5	
17	Holt	5	1	1	1	1	1	3
18	Holt	5						
19	Holt		3	3	3	3	3	
20	Lockhart	1			1		1	1
21	Lusk	5	2	2			2	
22	Lusk		2				2	
23	Lusk		2	2	2	2	2	
24	Naylor	1						8
25	Oxford	5	1	1	2	2		1
26	Purrington	5						4
27	Purrington	3	1.5	1.5	1.5	1.5	1.5	2
28	Schneider		2	1.5	1.5	1.5	1.5	1.5
29	Zapalac	4						3
30								
31		6	10	13	14	14	10	10

6. Save, print, and close the workbook.

Counting Filtered Cells Using the Subtotal Function

The Subtotal function is quite powerful and provides additional summing capabilities. When you used the Subtotal function previously by clicking the Subtotal button on the Data tab, data was summed within the data range to give you subtotals and a grand total.

The Subtotal function can also be used to count, sum, or average filtered data. When you filter data, sometimes you may want to count the number of filtered cells in a column. After the data is filtered, only the cells for the item you filtered will be displayed; the other cells will be hidden. If you use the COUNT function, it will count all cells in the column whether they are hidden or not. Using the Subtotal function lets you count only cells that are displayed.

The Subtotal function is =SUBTOTAL (function number, data range). The *function number* is a number that represents a calculation. The function number lets you control the calculation that the Subtotal function performs, such as sum, count, or average. A list of commonly used Subtotal function numbers and the calculations they perform is shown in **Table 13–1**.

▶ **VOCABULARY**

function number

TABLE 13–1   Commonly used Subtotal function numbers

FUNCTION NUMBER	WHAT IT CALCULATES
1	AVERAGE
2	COUNT
3	COUNTA
4	MAX
5	MIN
9	SUM

Even though the function is Subtotal, the function number tells Excel what to do with the range of data. When you used the Subtotal function previously, Excel used function number 9. This function number is included when you click the Subtotal button, because it calculates the subtotals within the data and gives you a grand total, which is a very useful feature. You will now use the Subtotal function to count filtered data.

Step-by-Step 13.3

1. Open the **Class Enrollment** file from the drive and folder where your Data Files are stored.

2. Save the workbook as **Class Enrollment Totals**, followed by your initials. You will use the data to create a count of the number of students enrolled in classes.

3. Click **cell A4** or any cell under a column heading.

4. On the Ribbon, click the **Data** tab, and then click the **Filter** button in the Sort & Filter group.

5. In cell A4, click the **filter arrow**.

6. Click the **(Select All)** check box. All of the columns are now deselected.

7. Click the **4** check box and then click **OK**. The list of classes is filtered to show only Class Number 4.

8. Select **cell B46**, type the function **=SUBTOTAL(2,B5:B44)**, and then press **Enter**. Notice how all of the cells in column B are counted, showing that nine students are enrolled in Class Number 4. See **Figure 13–4**.

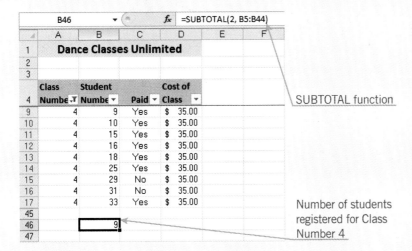

FIGURE 13–4
SUBTOTAL function counts displayed cells

SUBTOTAL function

Number of students registered for Class Number 4

9. Save, print, and close the workbook.

Creating Named Ranges

When you use functions, you usually type in a range of cells, such as =SUM(A5:A40). Rather than typing this range, you can give the range a meaningful name and use it in the function. For example, if the range of data, A5:A40, is the data for the month of April, you could name this range April. Then, you could enter this name in the function as =SUM(April). Named ranges are helpful if you need to use a range in several functions. You just need to remember the name of the range rather than the beginning and ending cell names.

If you want to use a name range with two words, you will need to use an underscore (_), rather than a space, to separate the words. Excel does not accept spaces in named ranges. In the next Step-by-Step, you will name two ranges of data.

Step-by-Step 13.4

1. Open the **Student Gymnastics** file from the drive and folder where your Data Files are stored.

2. Save the workbook as **Student Gymnastics - Paid**, followed by your initials.

3. Select the range **B5:B44**.

4. Click in the **Name Box** located to the far left on the formula bar. Notice how the cell name in the Name Box becomes highlighted.

5. Type **Paid**, press **Enter**, and then compare your screen to **Figure 13–5**.

FIGURE 13–5
Name Box with name entered

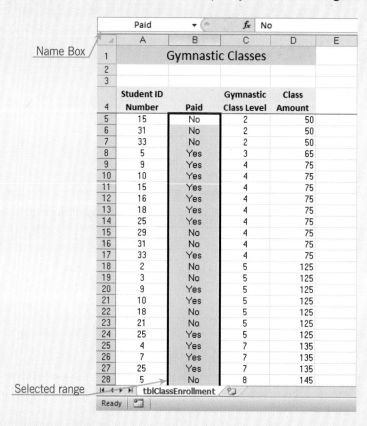

6. Select the range **D5:D44**.

7. Click in the **Name Box** and then type **Amount**.

8. Press **Enter**.

9. Save the workbook and leave it open for the next Step-by-Step.

Using a Named Range in a Function

After you name a range, Excel remembers that name. You select a named range by clicking the Name Box down arrow and then selecting the named range that you want to include in a function. The named range then becomes highlighted in the worksheet. Using named ranges in functions is convenient because you can enter the range name instead of the cell names. If you update the range, such as by adding new cells to it, the results of the formula that use the range will be updated as well. As you are typing the range name into the formula, a border appears around the cells to help you confirm whether you are entering the correct range name.

Step-by-Step 13.5

1. Click **cell D46**.

2. Type **=SUM(Amount)**. This function will total the data in the Amount column.

3. Press **Enter**. The result, $4,910, is the total of the class amounts.

4. Add an accounting number format without decimal places to cell D46. Your screen should appear as shown in **Figure 13–6**.

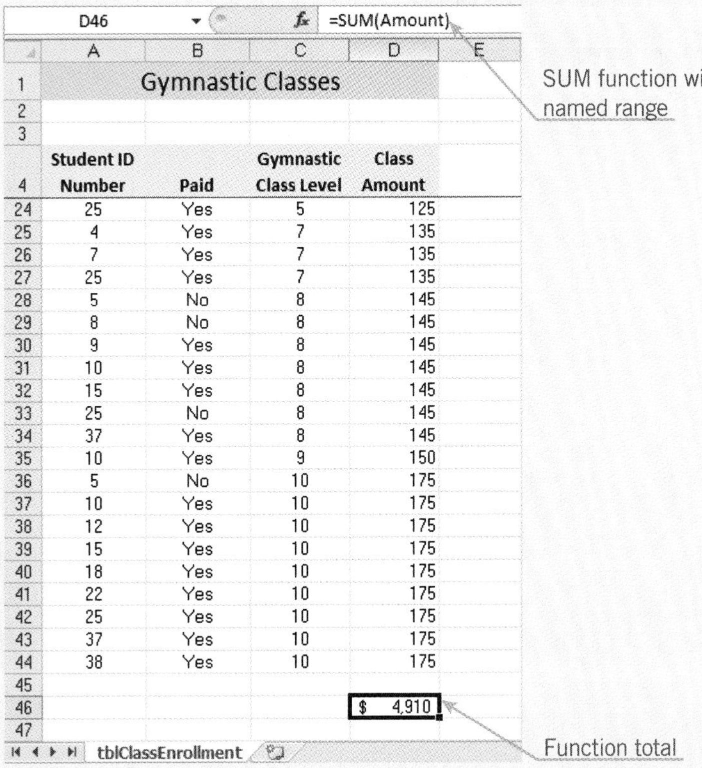

	D46			fx	=SUM(Amount)	
	A	B	C	D	E	
1		Gymnastic Classes				
2						
3						
4	Student ID Number	Paid	Gymnastic Class Level	Class Amount		
24	25	Yes	5	125		
25	4	Yes	7	135		
26	7	Yes	7	135		
27	25	Yes	7	135		
28	5	No	8	145		
29	8	No	8	145		
30	9	Yes	8	145		
31	10	Yes	8	145		
32	15	Yes	8	145		
33	25	No	8	145		
34	37	Yes	8	145		
35	10	Yes	9	150		
36	5	No	10	175		
37	10	Yes	10	175		
38	12	Yes	10	175		
39	15	Yes	10	175		
40	18	Yes	10	175		
41	22	Yes	10	175		
42	25	Yes	10	175		
43	37	Yes	10	175		
44	38	Yes	10	175		
45						
46				$ 4,910		
47						

tblClassEnrollment

SUM function with named range

Function total

FIGURE 13–6
Function with named range

5. Save the workbook and leave it open for the next Step-by-Step.

Using the SUMIF Function

You have previously used the SUM function to get the total amount for data in a range of cells. The SUM function quickly calculates the total when you click the SUM button on the Home tab. The SUMIF function is another form of the SUM function. The SUMIF function will only total data that meets a certain condition. In other words, data will be included in the total if the condition is true.

A *condition* is a requirement that needs to be met. *Criteria* are the conditions you are searching for in a data range. For example, you might have a list of students who signed up for gymnastics classes. If they paid for the class, a Yes is entered in the cell next to their student ID number. If they did not pay, the word No is shown. The conditions for this example are either yes or no; either they have paid or not. So when you enter criteria into the function, you select one of these conditions. Excel will then search the data range for cells that match the criteria.

The SUMIF function is =SUMIF(range,criteria,sum_range). Range refers to the cells of data that you want Excel to use when it searches for the criteria. Criteria are the information that Excel will look for in the range. If data in the range matches the criteria, Excel will then look to the sum_range. The data in the sum_range that is located in the same row as data in the range will be included in the total.

An example of a SUMIF function is shown in **Figure 13–7**.

> **VOCABULARY**
>
> **condition**
>
> **criteria**

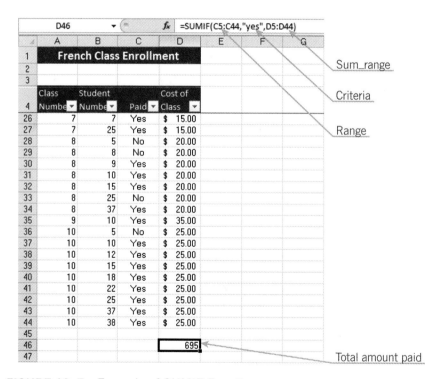

FIGURE 13–7   Example of SUMIF Function

In this next Step-by-Step, you will calculate the total amount students have paid for their classes. Only the amounts actually paid by students, indicated by a "yes" next to their name, will be included in the sum. Since the criteria for the function are text, you will need to use quote marks, as in "yes". You can also use named ranges in the SUMIF function.

Step-by-Step 13.6

1. Click **cell D48**.

2. Type the function **=SUMIF(Paid,"yes",Amount)**. Notice how borders appear around the named ranges as you type them into the formula.

3. Press **Enter**. You see that $3,500 has been collected from students who have paid for their classes.

4. Add an accounting number format without decimal places to **cell D48**. See **Figure 13-8**. Next, you will add text in column A to show the difference between the two totals.

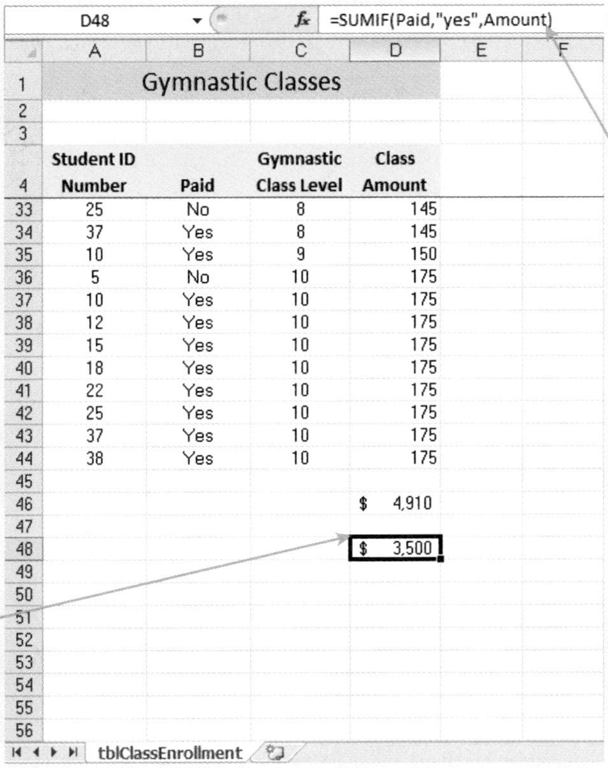

	D48			f_x	=SUMIF(Paid,"yes",Amount)	
	A	B	C	D	E	F
1		Gymnastic Classes				
2						
3						
4	**Student ID Number**	**Paid**	**Gymnastic Class Level**	**Class Amount**		
33	25	No	8	145		
34	37	Yes	8	145		
35	10	Yes	9	150		
36	5	No	10	175		
37	10	Yes	10	175		
38	12	Yes	10	175		
39	15	Yes	10	175		
40	18	Yes	10	175		
41	22	Yes	10	175		
42	25	Yes	10	175		
43	37	Yes	10	175		
44	38	Yes	10	175		
45						
46				$ 4,910		
47						
48				$ 3,500		
49						
50						
51						
52						
53						
54						
55						
56						

H ◀ ▶ H   tblClassEnrollment

Borders appear around the named ranges as you type them in the formula

FIGURE 13–8
SUMIF function using named ranges

SUMIF function with named range

5. Select **cell A46**, then type **Total Class Amount**.

6. Select **cell A48**, then type **Total Paid**.

7. Select **cells A46** and **A48**, then select the **Home** tab and in the Alignment group, click the **Align Text Left** button. Click in **cell A49** and view the results. Compare your screen to **Figure 13–9**.

FIGURE 13–9
SUMIF function results

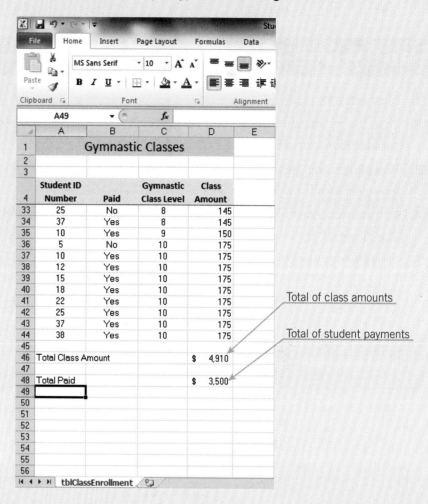

8. Save, print, and close the workbook.

Creating a VLOOKUP Function

LOOKUP functions allow you to find data that already exists rather than looking for the data yourself. This feature is very useful when you need to make a decision based on a range of data. For example, suppose you had several levels of Spanish classes and each level had a different cost. Rather than trying to figure out the cost of the class, you can let Excel look up and determine the cost for you. The range of data with the class costs is called the lookup table. A ***lookup table*** is the range of data you create in either a vertical or horizontal format, which Excel will use to match against the criteria. In this case, a lookup table with a vertical format is used for the class level. When the class level is located in the lookup table, this amount is entered into the cell for the cost of that class.

> **VOCABULARY**
> **lookup table**

You use the VLOOKUP function when the range of data, or lookup table, is listed vertically in columns. When you use the VLOOKUP function, you will need to enter information into the Function Arguments dialog box. You will enter the Lookup_value, the Table_array, and the Col_index_num. The Lookup_value is the value that Excel will look for in the first column of the lookup table. Table_array is the range of cells for the lookup table. The final information Excel needs for the function is the column number from the table. The column number is the column in the lookup table that has the data you want to bring from the table into the cell with the function. An example of a LOOKUP function is shown in **Figure 13–10**.

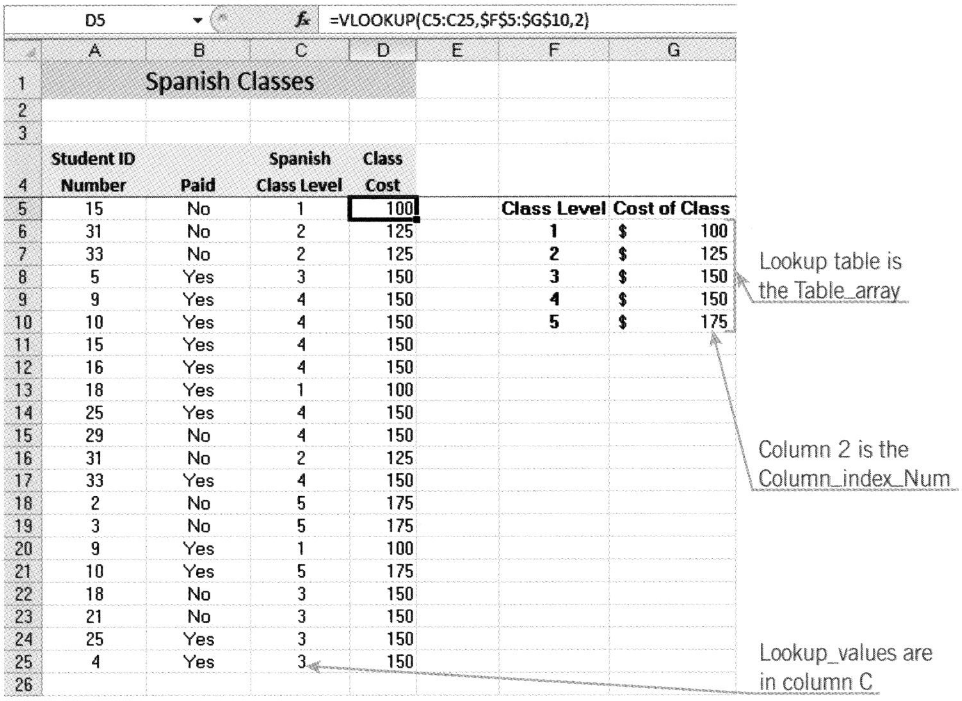

	D5		▼	*fx*	=VLOOKUP(C5:C25,$F$5:$G$10,2)	
	A	B	C	D	E	F	G
1		**Spanish Classes**					
2							
3							
4	**Student ID Number**	**Paid**	**Spanish Class Level**	**Class Cost**			
5	15	No	1	100		**Class Level**	**Cost of Class**
6	31	No	2	125		1	$ 100
7	33	No	2	125		2	$ 125
8	5	Yes	3	150		3	$ 150
9	9	Yes	4	150		4	$ 150
10	10	Yes	4	150		5	$ 175
11	15	Yes	4	150			
12	16	Yes	4	150			
13	18	Yes	1	100			
14	25	Yes	4	150			
15	29	No	4	150			
16	31	No	2	125			
17	33	Yes	4	150			
18	2	No	5	175			
19	3	No	5	175			
20	9	Yes	1	100			
21	10	Yes	5	175			
22	18	No	3	150			
23	21	No	3	150			
24	25	Yes	3	150			
25	4	Yes	3	150			
26							

Lookup table is the Table_array

Column 2 is the Column_index_Num

Lookup_values are in column C

FIGURE 13–10   Example of VLOOKUP function

In Figure 13–10, the cost of the Spanish classes needed to be entered in column D, the Class Cost column. The VLOOKUP function matched the Class Level in column C to the table with class costs in cells F6:G10. The correct class cost was then placed into the cells in column D.

Step-by-Step 13.7

1. Open the **PCI Sales** file from the drive and folder where your Data Files are stored. Save the workbook as **PCI Sales Bonuses**, followed by your initials. Next, you will name the ranges to be used in the VLOOKUP function.

2. Select the range **E6:E11**, click in the **Name Box**, type **Total_Sales**, and then press **Enter**.

3. Select the range **H6:I12**, click in the **Name Box**, type **Bonus_Table**, and then press **Enter**.

4. Select **cell F6**.

5. Click the **Formulas** tab, and then click the **Lookup & Reference** arrow button in the Function Library group. The Lookup & Reference list is displayed, as shown in **Figure 13–11**.

FIGURE 13–11
Lookup & Reference list

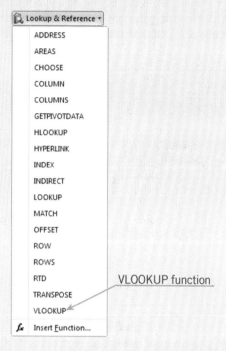

VLOOKUP function

6. Click **VLOOKUP** from the list. The Function Arguments dialog box for VLOOKUP opens, as shown in **Figure 13–12**.

FIGURE 13–12
Function arguments for
VLOOKUP dialog box

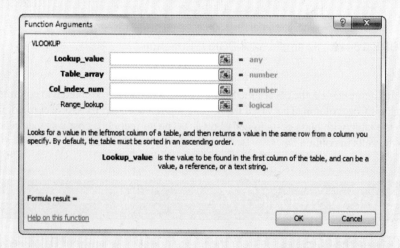

7. Click in the **Lookup_value** text box, and then type **Total_Sales** to find the sales amount for each salesperson. You will now enter the range for the bonus table.

8. Click in the **Table_array** text box and then type **Bonus_Table**.

9. Click in the **Col_index_num** text box, and then type **2** to indicate which column in the bonus table should be searched for the bonus amount. The bonus column, which is the second column in the bonus table, contains the data to be entered into cell F6. The completed dialog box should appear as shown in **Figure 13–13**.

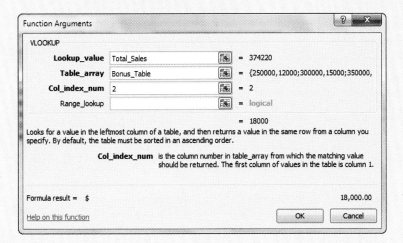

FIGURE 13–13
Completed Function Arguments for VLOOKUP dialog box

10. Click **OK**.

11. To copy the formula in cell F6 to cells F7:F11, place your mouse pointer over the **fill handle** in the lower-right corner of cell F6, and then click and drag to cell **F11**. Your completed worksheet should appear as shown in **Figure 13–14**.

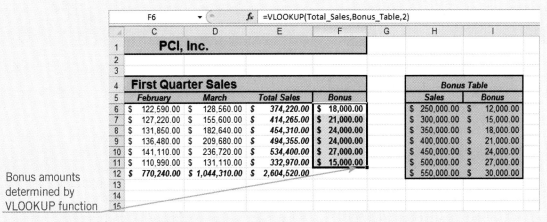

Bonus amounts determined by VLOOKUP function

FIGURE 13–14
Worksheet with VLOOKUP results

12. Print the worksheet. Save and close the workbook.

Using the HLOOKUP Function

You learned that a VLOOKUP function looks in the lookup table when the table is arranged vertically in columns. Use the HLOOKUP function when the data in the lookup table is listed horizontally in rows.

When you use the HLOOKUP function, you will need to enter the Lookup_value, Table_array, and the Row_index_num information into the Function Argument dialog box. For the Lookup_value, you will need to specify what to look for in the lookup table. Table_array is the range of cells for the lookup table. You will also need the row number from the table that has the data you want returned to the cell with the HLOOKUP function. An example of an HLOOKUP function is shown in **Figure 13–15**.

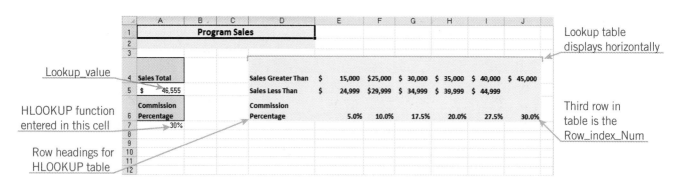

FIGURE 13–15   Example of HLOOKUP function

In this figure, the salespersons receive a commission based on their total amount of sales. The commission is shown as a percentage. For example, if the salesperson made $25,500 in sales, he or she would get a 10 percent commission, or $2,550. The commission percentage appears in cell A7. The HLOOKUP function matches the sales amount in cell A5 to the sales and commission lookup table located in cells E4:J6. Notice how the table is displayed horizontally.

Step-by-Step 13.8

1. Open the Booth file from the drive and folder where your Data Files are stored. Save the workbook as **Booth Sales**, followed by your initials.

2. Click **cell A7**.

3. Click the **Formulas** tab, and then click the **Lookup & Reference** button arrow in the Function Library group.

4. Click **HLOOKUP** from the list. The Function Arguments dialog box for HLOOKUP opens.

5. Click in the **Lookup_value** text box, and then type **A5** to find the commission percentage. You will now enter the range for the bonus table.

6. Click in the **Table_array** text box and then type **$E$4:$J$6**.

7. Click in the **Row_index_num** text box and then type **3**. Row 3 is the commission percentage row, which is the third row in the table. The completed dialog box should appear as shown in **Figure 13–16**.

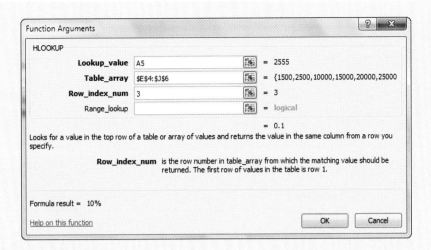

FIGURE 13–16
Function Arguments for
HLOOKUP dialog box

8. Click **OK**.

9. Click **cell A5**.

10. Type **2555** and then press **Enter**. A 10% commission percentage appears in cell A7. See **Figure 13–17**.

HLOOKUP
determined
percentage rate
based on sales total

FIGURE 13–17
Worksheet with
HLOOKUP results

11. Save, print, and close the workbook.

SUMMARY

In this lesson, you learned:

- The COUNT function counts cells with numeric data and the COUNTA function counts cells with text or a combination of text and numbers.

- You can use COUNTBLANK to count cells without any data.

- The SUBTOTAL function can be used to count filtered data.

- You can name a range of data.

- A named range can be used in a function.

- The SUMIF function totals data that meet a certain condition.

- You can use the VLOOKUP function to find data that is displayed vertically in a lookup table.

- You can use the HLOOKUP function to find data that is displayed horizontally in a lookup table.

■ VOCABULARY

Define the following terms:

condition   function number   lookup table
criteria

■ REVIEW QUESTIONS

TRUE / FALSE

Circle T if the statement is true or F if the statement is false.

T   F   **1.**   VLOOKUP locates data in a range that displays data vertically.

T   F   **2.**   The COUNTA function is used to count data in a filtered list.

T   F   **3.**   The SUMIF function totals all cells in a range.

T   F   **4.**   Named ranges cannot be used in functions.

T   F   **5.**   The Subtotal function is used to count blank cells.

FILL IN THE BLANK

1. A(n)_____ is a requirement that needs to be met.

2. The _____ function is used to count filtered data.

3. The _____ function will calculate only cells that meet a certain requirement.

4. To count blank cells, you would use the _____ function.

5. If you have a lookup table that is displayed vertically, you would use the _____ function.

WRITTEN QUESTIONS

Write a brief answer to the following questions.

1. What is the difference between the VLOOKUP function and the HLOOKUP function?

2. Explain the difference between the COUNT and COUNTA functions.

3. Explain what the 1, 2, 3, and 9 function numbers calculate when used with the Subtotal function.

4. Explain how you would count cells that do not have any data, such as text or numbers.

5. If you use a range of cells frequently, explain what you could do to make entering this range into a function easier to remember.

■ PROJECTS

If you have a SAM 2010 user profile, your instructor may have assigned an autogradable version of the indicated project. If so, log into the SAM 2010 Web site at *www.cengage.com/sam2010* to download the instruction and start files.

PROJECT 13–1

1. Open the **Spanish Class** file from the drive and folder where your Data Files are stored. Save the workbook as **Spanish Class Costs**, followed by your initials.

2. Add a VLOOKUP function to cell D5 that looks at the Spanish Class Level in column C, compares it to the table data in cells F6:G10, and returns the appropriate cost to cell D5.

3. Copy the formula to the remaining cells in column D.

4. Save, print, and close the workbook.

PROJECT 13–3

1. Open the **Bonus** file from the drive and folder where your Data Files are stored. Save the workbook as **Bonus for Sports**, followed by your initials.

2. Create a HLOOKUP formula in cell **A7** that will look at the amount of sales entered into cell A5, compare it to the HLOOKUP table, and enter the correct percentage in cell A7.

3. Select cell **A5** and type **67,500**.

4. View the percentage result in cell A7.

5. Save, print, and close the workbook.

SAM PROJECT 13–2

1. Open the **Chinese Class** file from the drive and folder where your Data Files are stored. Save the workbook as **Chinese Class Enrollment**, followed by your initials.

2. Add AutoFilters to the columns.

3. Filter the Class Number column for class 5.

4. In cell A46, use the Subtotal function to count the number of students in class 5.

5. Save, print, and close the workbook.

CRITICAL THINKING

ACTIVITY 13–1

Your boss at Houston Eastern/Central Oil asks you to create a LOOKUP function in the company's sales report indicating the commission percentage based on program manager sales. Open the **Sales** file from the drive and folder where your Data Files are stored, and then save the workbook as **Sales Commissions** followed by your initials. The data file includes the company sales commission report. You decide to create an HLOOKUP function that will calculate the sales commission percentage based on the amount of sales that are entered into cell A5. By adding this function, your boss can quickly let the program managers know their commission rate. You test the HLOOKUP to see if the correct commission percentage is returned for the sales total of $46,555.

ACTIVITY 13–2

As the new manager of the local library, you discover that the previous manager used the CHOOSE function instead of a LOOKUP function. You decide to research the CHOOSE function to see if it would work better for looking up values vertically. Create a document explaining the result of your research and save it as a Word document with the file name **CHOOSE Function**, followed by your initials.

LESSON 14

Creating and Using Macros

■ OBJECTIVES

Upon completion of this lesson, you should be able to:

- Understand macros.
- Review macro security settings.
- Record a macro.
- Save a macro as a macro-enabled workbook.
- Run a macro.
- Edit a macro.
- Create a button.
- Align and format a button.
- Open a macro-enabled workbook.

■ VOCABULARY

button

code

macro

virus

Introduction

A *macro* automates a common, repetitive task you perform in Excel, thereby saving valuable time. In this lesson, you will learn how to create macros. You will then run the macro, which means to have the macro perform the automated task. You will also learn how to make changes to a macro and how to add a macro to a button that can be clicked to run the macro.

Understanding Macros

A macro simply records a series of steps that you do frequently, such as formatting text. For example, you may want to format all worksheet titles using the same font, size, color, and alignment. Continuously repeating these steps can be time consuming. Macros can simplify repetitive tasks. When you create a macro, Excel records the selections you make on the Ribbon as well as the keystrokes you use. Visual Basic for Applications (or VBA) is the program used to create macros. VBA is a programming language that is embedded into applications such as Excel.

When a macro is being recorded, all of the selections you make are translated into code. *Code* is simply the macro actions formatted in easy-to-read sentences, just like text in a book.

Before you record a macro, it is important to review and understand macro security settings.

Reviewing Macro Security Settings

Macros are susceptible to a virus attack. A *virus* is a computer program that is designed to reproduce by copying itself and attaching to other programs in a computer. Viruses can cause extreme damage to data on your computer. If a virus attaches itself to a macro, it can cause damage when you run the macro. To help protect your data from the corruption caused by a virus hidden in a macro, you can set one of four macro security levels in Excel: *Disable all macros without notification*, *Disable all macros with notification*, *Disable all macros except digitally signed macros*, and *Enable all macros*. The Disable all macros with notification option is the default setting unless you choose another. **Table 14–1** explains each setting in detail.

TABLE 14–1   Macro security level options

MACRO SECURITY LEVEL OPTIONS	DESCRIPTION
Disable all macros without notification	Disables harmful content, but does not notify you.
Disable all macros with notification	Harmful content will be disabled and a notification appears on the Message Bar, just below the Ribbon, letting you know that the macro is disabled unless you click the Enable Content button on the Message Bar.
Disable all macros except digitally signed macros	Only macros that are digitally signed and come from a trusted source will be executed.
Enable all macros	Allows all macros to run and does not offer any protection.

► VOCABULARY

macro

code

virus

As a best practice, you should set the security level in Excel to Disable all macros with notification or Disable all macros except digitally signed macros. In the next Step-by-Step, you will view the macro settings currently set for Excel.

Step-by-Step 14.1

1. Start Excel, click the File tab on the Ribbon, then click the Options button. The Excel Options dialog box opens, as shown in **Figure 14–1**. You choose macro security level settings in the Trust Center section of the Excel Options dialog box.

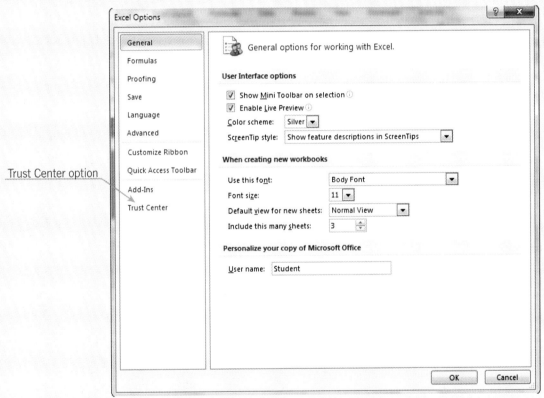

Trust Center option

FIGURE 14–1
Excel Options
dialog box

2. In the Excel Options dialog box, click **Trust Center** on the left and then click the **Trust Center Settings** button on the right.

3. Click **Macro Settings** on the left to display the macro settings, as shown in **Figure 14–2**. Notice that the default setting is on. Now that you have viewed the settings, you will close the dialog boxes.

FIGURE 14–2
Trust Center dialog box

Macro Settings

Macro Settings
options

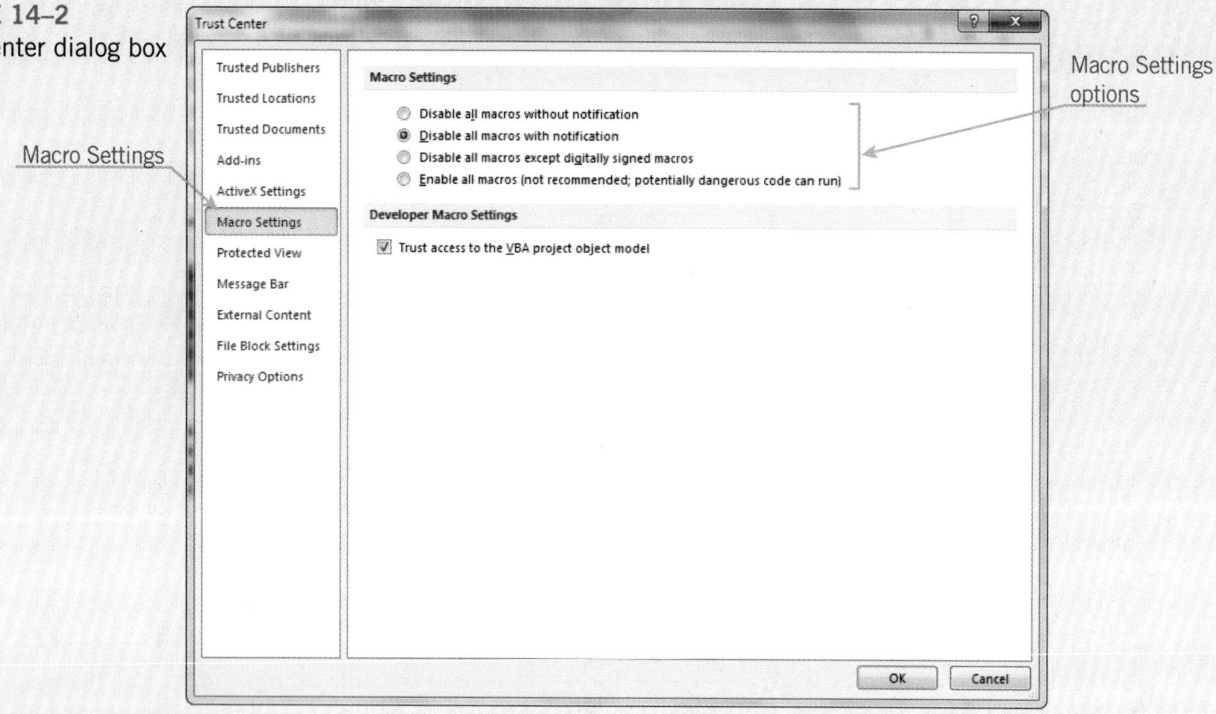

4. In the Trust Center dialog box, click **OK**.
5. In the Excel Options dialog box, click **OK**.

EXTRA FOR EXPERTS

Macro settings can also be viewed by clicking the Developer tab on the Ribbon, then clicking the Macro Security button in the Code group.

Recording a Macro

To begin recording a macro, you click the Record Macro button in the Code group on the Developer tab. Once you choose options in the Record Macro dialog box and close it, the macro records every task you do in Excel. The options in the Record Macro dialog box are described in **Table 14–2**.

TABLE 14–2   Record Macro dialog box options

RECORD MACRO OPTIONS	DESCRIPTION
Macro name	Enter an easily identifiable name for the macro. The first character of the macro name must be a letter. Other characters can be letters, numbers, or an underscore. Since spaces cannot be used in the name, an underscore can be used to separate words.
Shortcut key	Assign a key or keys that will be used in combination with the Ctrl key to run a macro. This setting is optional. Try to avoid using letters already assigned to shortcut keys, such as Ctrl+C, which is used to copy data.
Store macro in	From the drop-down list, you can select to store the macro in This Workbook so it is available when the current workbook is opened. You can also choose to store the macro in the Personal Macro Workbook, which makes it available any time you use Excel. Or, you can store the macro in a new workbook.
Description	Create a brief description of the macro to use for future reference. Entering a description is optional.

In the next Step-by-Step, you will record a macro that applies formats to worksheet data.

Step-by-Step 14.2

1. Open the **School Budget** file from the drive and folder where your Data Files are stored. Click the **First Semester** worksheet tab, if necessary.

2. On the Ribbon, click the **Developer** tab and then click the **Record Macro** button in the Code group. The Record Macro dialog box opens, as shown in **Figure 14–3**.

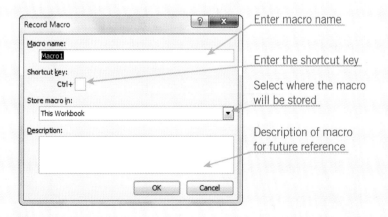

FIGURE 14–3
Record Macro dialog box

3. In the Record Macro dialog box, type **Formats** in the Macro name text box.

4. Click in the **Shortcut key** text box, press and hold the **Shift** key, and then press **F**. The shortcut key for the Formats macro will be Ctrl+Shift+F.

5. Click in the **Description** text box and then type **Adds text format and cell background colors**. The completed dialog box should appear as shown in **Figure 14–4**.

FIGURE 14–4
Completed Record Macro dialog box

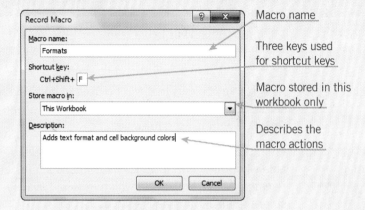

Macro name

Three keys used for shortcut keys

Macro stored in this workbook only

Describes the macro actions

6. Click **OK** to close the Record Macro dialog box. Notice that the Record Macro button changed to the Stop Recording button on the Developer tab in the Code group because Excel is now recording everything you do.

7. Select the range **A4:A9**.

8. Click the **Home** tab, and then click the **Bold** button **B** in the Font group.

9. Click the **Fill Color** button arrow, and then choose **Red, Accent 2, Lighter 40%**.

10. Select the range **A12:A15**.

11. Click the **Bold** button **B** in the Font group, click the **Fill Color** button arrow, and then choose **Yellow**.

12. Select the range **B4:B15**.

13. In the Number group, click the **Comma Style** button. The Comma Style format will add decimal places and a comma to separate thousands.

14. Click the **Developer** tab, and then click the **Stop Recording** button in the Code group. The worksheet shows the formatting options you chose. See **Figure 14–5**. Leave the workbook open for the next Step-by-Step.

FIGURE 14–5
First Semester worksheet with formats applied

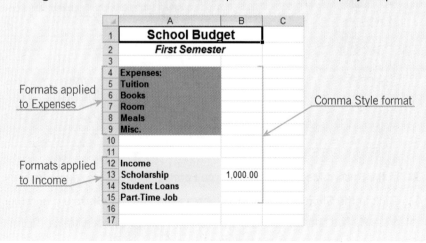

Formats applied to Expenses

Formats applied to Income

Comma Style format

Saving a Workbook as a Macro-Enabled Workbook

A workbook that is saved in Excel is saved in the default format with the file extension .xlsx. If you want to save a workbook that has a macro, you will need to save it with the .xlsm file extension in the Save dialog box. The file extension .xlsm is used for a macro-enabled workbook. A macro-enabled workbook lets you save the macro in the workbook and then run the macro. You can also save an ordinary Excel workbook as a macro-enabled workbook using the Save As command.

In the next Step-by-Step, you will save the workbook as a macro-enabled workbook.

Step-by-Step 14.3

1. In the School Budget workbook, click the **File** tab and click **Save As**.

2. In the Save As dialog box, click after the *t* in School Budget in the File name text box, press the **Spacebar**, and then type **First Year** followed by your initials. The file name should be School Budget First Year.

3. Click the **Save as type** list arrow to display the available file types, as shown in **Figure 14–6**.

Macro-Enabled Workbook file type .xlsm

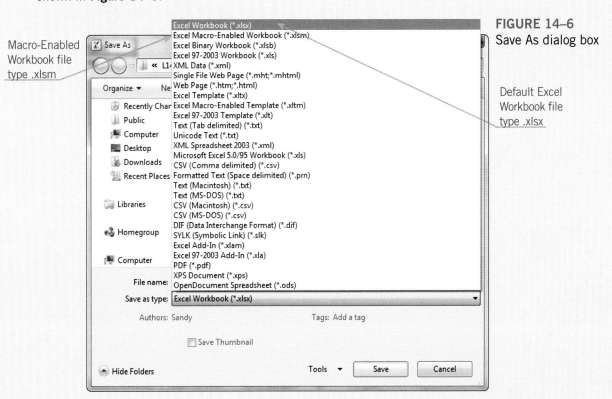

FIGURE 14–6
Save As dialog box

Default Excel Workbook file type .xlsx

4. Click **Excel Macro-Enabled Workbook (*.xlsm)**.

5. Click **Save** to close the Save As dialog box.

6. Leave the workbook open for the next Step-by-Step. In the next Step-by-Step, you will run the macro to apply the same formatting to the other worksheets.

Running a Macro

After a macro is created, it is ready to use. Excel provides different ways to run a macro. You can use a shortcut key combination if you created one in the Record Macro dialog box. Or, on the Developer tab in the Code group, you can select the Macros button. When you select the Macros button, the Macro dialog box appears. You then click the macro you want and click the Run button. You will now run the Formats macro to apply the same formatting used in the First Semester worksheet to the remaining worksheets in the workbook.

Step-by-Step 14.4

1. Click the **Second Semester** worksheet tab to display the data as it currently appears as shown in **Figure 14–7**.

FIGURE 14–7
Second Semester worksheet

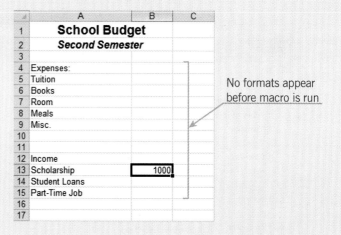

No formats appear
before macro is run

2. Press **Ctrl+Shift+F**. The formats you recorded in the macro are applied to the Second Semester worksheet, as shown in **Figure 14–8**.

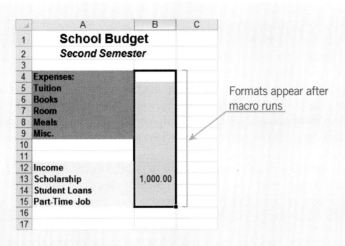

FIGURE 14–8
Second Semester worksheet with formats applied

Formats appear after macro runs

3. Click the **Third Semester** worksheet tab.

4. On the Ribbon, click the **Developer** tab, and then click the **Macros** button in the Code group.

5. Make sure the Formats macro is selected and then click **Run**.

6. Click the **Fourth Semester** worksheet tab.

7. Press **Ctrl+Shift+F**. All four worksheets now have the same formatting.

8. Save the workbook and leave it open for the next Step-by-Step.

EXTRA FOR EXPERTS

You can assign a combination of keys, such as Ctrl+Q or Ctrl+Shift+F to the macro. Then, when you are ready to run the macro, press the key combination assigned to the macro and Excel will execute the recorded tasks.

Editing a Macro

After you run a macro, you may want to make changes to it. Macros are easy to edit, once you become familiar with working with the code in VBA. To edit a macro, you need to make changes to the code. Modifying code is similar to modifying text in a Microsoft Word document. You can type text into the code and use the Delete, Backspace, and Enter keys as well as the Copy and Paste commands. An example of the code used in a macro is shown in **Figure 14–9**.

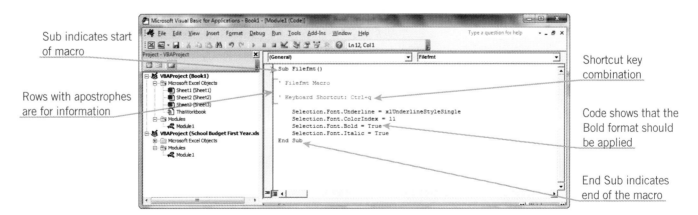

FIGURE 14–9   Example of a macro in VBA code

The code word *Sub* appears at the top of the macro, indicating the start of the macro. Under Sub, the descriptions of the macro, which are preceded with an apostrophe to differentiate them from the actual macro, are listed. In this case, the code shows the name of the macro and the shortcut key combination, Ctrl+Q, used to run the macro. The tasks that make up the macro are listed next. The next rows of code show the formats used. You use True or False to describe if the format is turned on or off. For example, the row Selection.Font.Bold = True means that the macro will apply the bold format to a selected cell. If you do not want the bold format, you would delete the word True and type False. Finally, the code *End Sub* signals the end of the macro.

When you edit a macro, you will need to run the macro again for the changes to be applied in the workbook. In the next Step-by-Step, you will edit the Formats macro by adding the Italic format to the text.

Step-by-Step 14.5

1. In the Code group, click the **Macros** button. The Formats macro is displayed in the Macro dialog box, as shown in **Figure 14–10**.

FIGURE 14–10
Macro dialog box

Select macro to edit

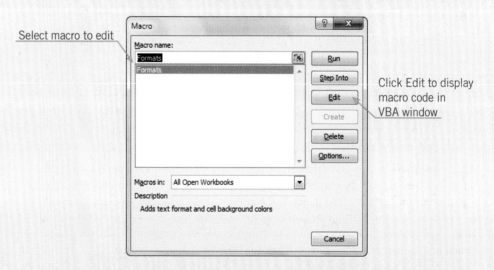

Click Edit to display macro code in VBA window

2. Verify that the Formats macro is highlighted, then click the **Edit** button. The Microsoft Visual Basic for Applications window opens, as shown in **Figure 14–11**. You will add the Italic format to the macro.

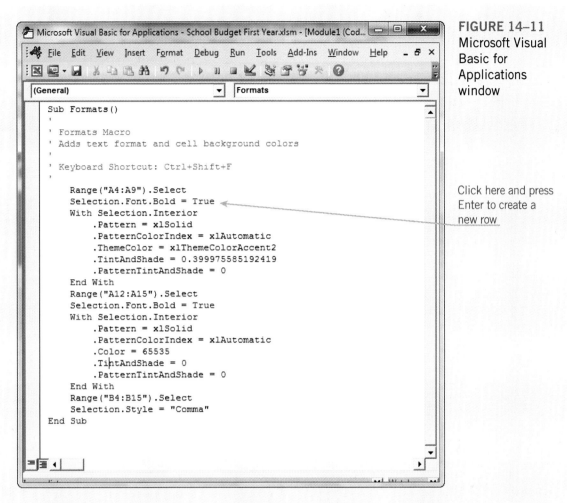

FIGURE 14–11
Microsoft Visual
Basic for
Applications
window

3. Click at the end of the first line: **Selection.Font.Bold=True**, then press
Enter to make room for a new row of code.

4. Type **Selection.Font.Italic=True**, then compare your new macro code to **Figure 14–12**.

FIGURE 14–12
Making edits to the Formats macro

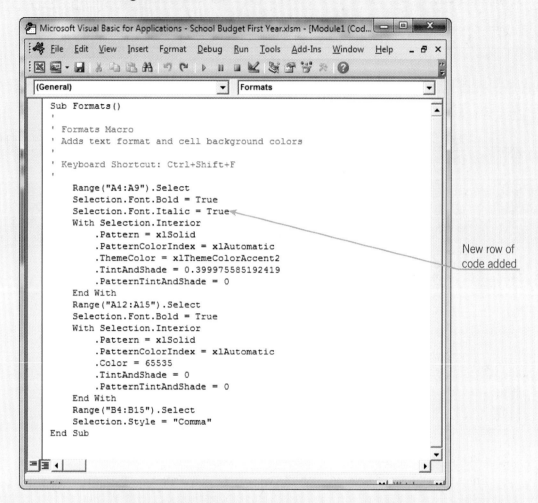

```
Sub Formats()
'
' Formats Macro
' Adds text format and cell background colors
'
' Keyboard Shortcut: Ctrl+Shift+F
'
    Range("A4:A9").Select
    Selection.Font.Bold = True
    Selection.Font.Italic = True
    With Selection.Interior
        .Pattern = xlSolid
        .PatternColorIndex = xlAutomatic
        .ThemeColor = xlThemeColorAccent2
        .TintAndShade = 0.399975585192419
        .PatternTintAndShade = 0
    End With
    Range("A12:A15").Select
    Selection.Font.Bold = True
    With Selection.Interior
        .Pattern = xlSolid
        .PatternColorIndex = xlAutomatic
        .Color = 65535
        .TintAndShade = 0
        .PatternTintAndShade = 0
    End With
    Range("B4:B15").Select
    Selection.Style = "Comma"
End Sub
```

New row of code added

5. In the Microsoft Visual Basic for Applications window, click the **Save** button 🖫 on the toolbar.

6. Click the **View Microsoft Excel** button 🗷 on the toolbar to return to the Excel worksheet.

7. Click the **Fourth Semester** worksheet.

8. Press **Ctrl+Shift+F**, then compare your screen to **Figure 14–13**. The Formats macro is applied to the text and includes the updated Italic format.

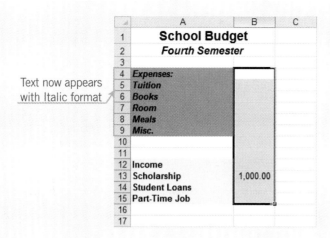

FIGURE 14–13
Fourth Semester worksheet with
new formats

9. Apply the Formats macro to the **First Semester**, **Second Semester**, and **Third Semester** worksheets.

10. Save and close the workbook.

11. Close the Microsoft Visual Basic for Applications window by clicking the Close button ☒ in the upper-right corner of the window.

Creating a Button

Excel has many types of Form Controls that allow you to create items that would go on a form, such as a check box, scroll bar, and button. A *button* is called a control because it controls the actions that are assigned to it. When you create a button, you are asked to assign a macro to it. When you click the button, the macro will run.

> VOCABULARY
> **button**

You create a button by first choosing the Button form control and then drawing the button where you want it to appear in the worksheet. When you release the mouse button, the Assign Macro dialog box opens, prompting you to select the macro you want assigned to the button. You will draw two buttons in the worksheet and assign macros to them.

Step-by-Step 14.6

1. Open the **Pet Store** file from the drive and folder where your Data Files are stored. Save the workbook as a macro-enabled workbook with the file name **Pet Store Inventory**, followed by your initials.

2. On the Ribbon, click the **Developer** tab, if necessary. In the Controls group, click the **Insert** arrow button to display the available controls.

3. Click the **Button (Form Control)**, which is the first control in the top row.

4. Using **Figure 14–14** as a guide, hold the left mouse button down and then drag to create a button in cells A1:A3, which is the approximate size as the one shown. Release the mouse button. The Assign Macro dialog box opens, as shown in **Figure 14–15**.

FIGURE 14–14
Approximate size of button

Location of first button

FIGURE 14–15
Assign Macro dialog box

Select macro for button

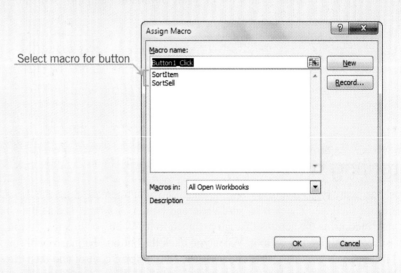

5. Click **SortItem**, and then click **OK**. The button appears, as shown in **Figure 14–16**. Next, you will change the name of the button to a more meaningful name. To edit button text, you must right-click the button and choose Edit Text.

FIGURE 14–16
Worksheet with button

Selection handles indicate that the button can be resized

Button added to worksheet

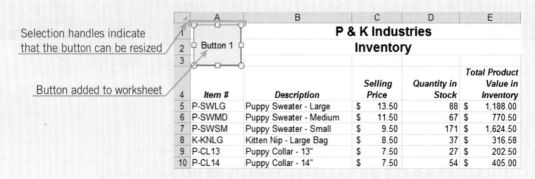

6. With the mouse pointer over the button, right-click the **button**, and then select **Edit Text** from the shortcut menu.

7. Highlight the existing text, press **Delete**, and then type **Sort by Item#**.

8. Click outside the button to view the results, and then test the button by clicking it. The worksheet data should be sorted by Item #. Next, you will create another button for the SortSell macro.

9. In the Controls group, click the **Insert** button and then click the **Button (Form Control)**. Draw another button of the same size to the right of the Sort by Item# button.

10. Click **SortSell** in the Assign Macro dialog box, and then click **OK**.

11. Right-click the new button and then click **Edit Text**.

12. Highlight the existing text, press **Delete**, and then type **Sort by Selling Price**.

13. Click outside the button to view the results. Compare your buttons to **Figure 14–17**. In the next Step-by-Step, you will align and resize the buttons.

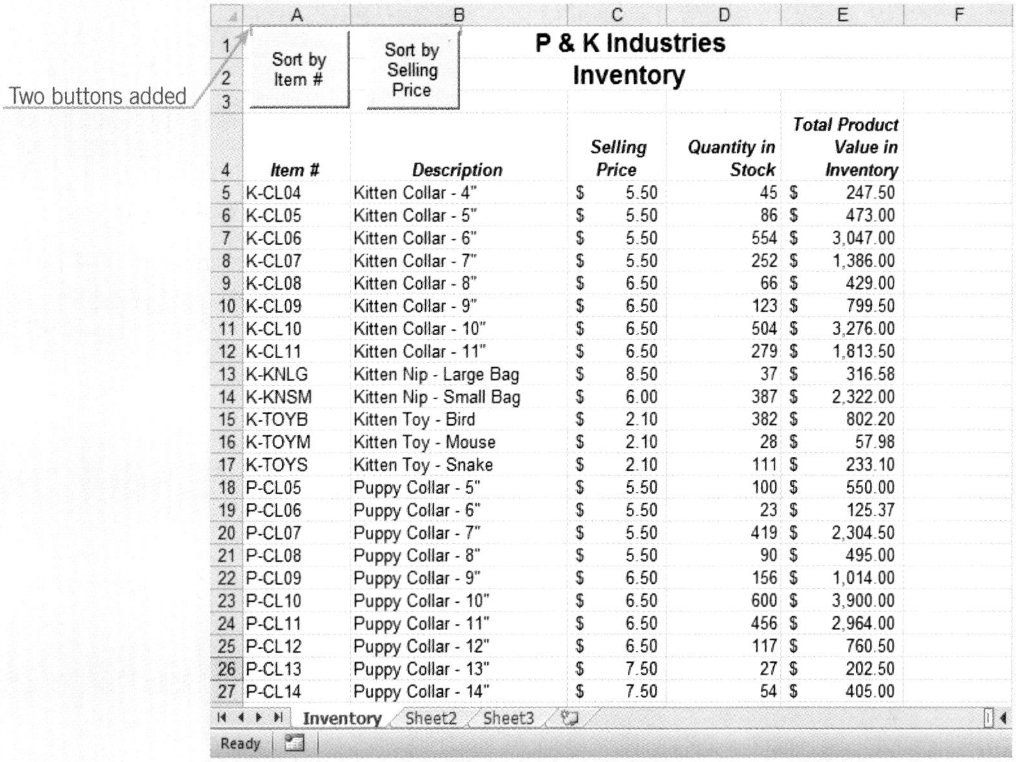

Two buttons added

⊿	A	B	C	D	E	F
1	Sort by Item #	Sort by Selling Price	**P & K Industries**			
2			**Inventory**			
3						
4	*Item #*	*Description*	*Selling Price*	*Quantity in Stock*	*Total Product Value in Inventory*	
5	K-CL04	Kitten Collar - 4"	$ 5.50	45	$ 247.50	
6	K-CL05	Kitten Collar - 5"	$ 5.50	86	$ 473.00	
7	K-CL06	Kitten Collar - 6"	$ 5.50	554	$ 3,047.00	
8	K-CL07	Kitten Collar - 7"	$ 5.50	252	$ 1,386.00	
9	K-CL08	Kitten Collar - 8"	$ 6.50	66	$ 429.00	
10	K-CL09	Kitten Collar - 9"	$ 6.50	123	$ 799.50	
11	K-CL10	Kitten Collar - 10"	$ 6.50	504	$ 3,276.00	
12	K-CL11	Kitten Collar - 11"	$ 6.50	279	$ 1,813.50	
13	K-KNLG	Kitten Nip - Large Bag	$ 8.50	37	$ 316.58	
14	K-KNSM	Kitten Nip - Small Bag	$ 6.00	387	$ 2,322.00	
15	K-TOYB	Kitten Toy - Bird	$ 2.10	382	$ 802.20	
16	K-TOYM	Kitten Toy - Mouse	$ 2.10	28	$ 57.98	
17	K-TOYS	Kitten Toy - Snake	$ 2.10	111	$ 233.10	
18	P-CL05	Puppy Collar - 5"	$ 5.50	100	$ 550.00	
19	P-CL06	Puppy Collar - 6"	$ 5.50	23	$ 125.37	
20	P-CL07	Puppy Collar - 7"	$ 5.50	419	$ 2,304.50	
21	P-CL08	Puppy Collar - 8"	$ 5.50	90	$ 495.00	
22	P-CL09	Puppy Collar - 9"	$ 6.50	156	$ 1,014.00	
23	P-CL10	Puppy Collar - 10"	$ 6.50	600	$ 3,900.00	
24	P-CL11	Puppy Collar - 11"	$ 6.50	456	$ 2,964.00	
25	P-CL12	Puppy Collar - 12"	$ 6.50	117	$ 760.50	
26	P-CL13	Puppy Collar - 13"	$ 7.50	27	$ 202.50	
27	P-CL14	Puppy Collar - 14"	$ 7.50	54	$ 405.00	

Inventory / Sheet2 / Sheet3

Ready

FIGURE 14–17
Worksheet with both buttons added

14. Click the buttons one at a time to test the macros, save the workbook, and leave it open for the next Step-by-Step.

Aligning and Formatting Buttons

When you create several buttons in one workbook, aligning them can be difficult. Fortunately, Excel gives you an easy way to align and resize buttons. Since buttons have macros associated with them, you cannot click a button to select it without running the macro assigned to it.

To select a button with an assigned macro, you right-click the button. A shortcut menu appears. If you do not want any of the selections from the shortcut menu, click outside the menu to remove it from view. To select another button, press and hold Shift, and then right-click the other button. With more than one button selected, the Format tab appears on the Ribbon. The Format tab has options that let you make changes to the buttons, such as aligning buttons by their tops, bottoms, left sides, right sides, or centers.

You can also right-click a button and choose Format Control from the shortcut menu. The Format Control dialog box opens so you can make changes to the text format. When more than one object is selected, Format Object displays on the shortcut menu instead of Format Control. In the next Step-by-Step, you will align and change the text format for the buttons.

Step-by-Step 14.7

1. Place your mouse pointer over either button, then right-click to select it.

2. Place your mouse pointer over the other button, press and hold **Shift**, and then right-click the other button to select both buttons.

3. Click the **Format** tab and then click the **Align** button arrow in the Arrange group. The alignment options appear, as shown in **Figure 14–18**.

FIGURE 14–18
Alignment options

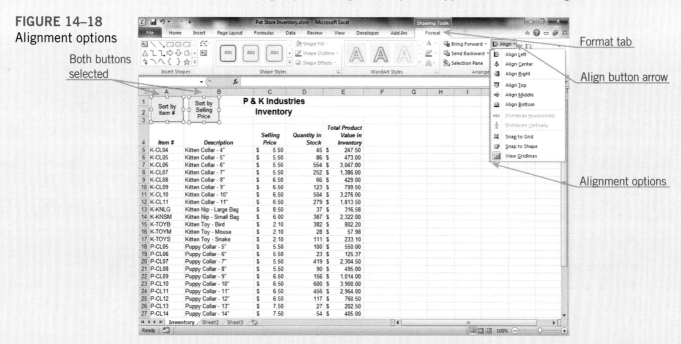

4. Click **Align Top** to align the buttons by their top edges. The tops of the buttons are the same distance from the top of the worksheet.

5. With both buttons still selected, right-click a button and then click **Format Object** from the shortcut menu. The Format Control dialog box opens, as shown in **Figure 14–19**.

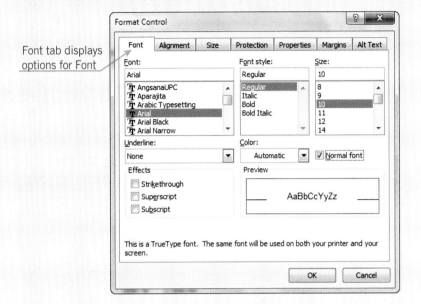

FIGURE 14–19
Format Control dialog box

6. In the Font Style list, click **Bold**.

7. Click the **Color** arrow, then click **Blue** located in the second row.

8. Click **OK** to close the Format Control dialog box. Your buttons appear with bold blue text. Compare your screen to **Figure 14–20**.

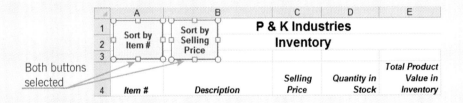

FIGURE 14–20
Aligned and formatted buttons

9. Click outside the buttons to deselect them.

10. Save and close the workbook.

Opening a Macro-Enabled Workbook

When you open a workbook with macros, a security warning appears on the Message Bar. The message lets you know that the macros have been disabled. This warning is displayed whenever the Disable all macros with notification option is chosen in the Macro Settings section of the Trust Center. To enable the macros, click the Enable Content button on the Message Bar. In the next Step-by-Step, you will open a macro-enabled workbook, enable the workbook macros, and run the macro that adds total functions to the data.

Step-by-Step 14.8

1. Open **Month End** from the drive and folder where your Data Files are stored. The security warning appears on the Message Bar, as shown in **Figure 14–21**.

FIGURE 14–21
Message Bar with security warning

Message Bar

Click Enable Content to enable the macros

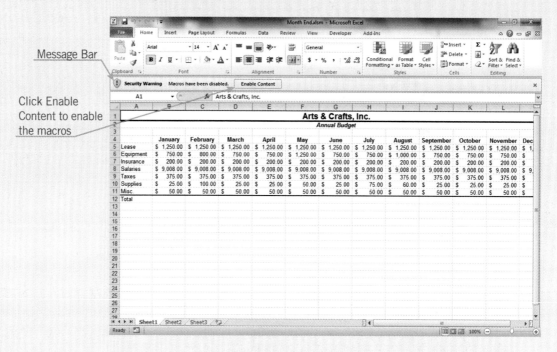

2. Save the workbook as **Month End Budget**, followed by your initials.

3. Click the **Enable Content** button.

4. Click the **Developer** tab, and then click the **Macros** button in the Code group.

5. Verify that the **Totals** macro is selected, and then click the **Run** button.

6. Click in **cell A1** to view the results of the Total function applied to each of the columns, as shown in **Figure 14–22**.

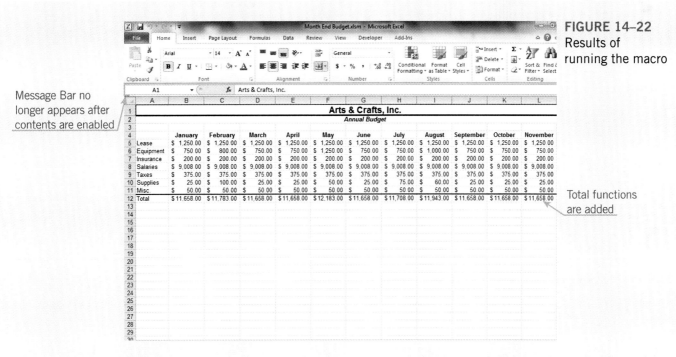

FIGURE 14–22
Results of running the macro

Message Bar no longer appears after contents are enabled

Total functions are added

7. Save and close the workbook.

SUMMARY

In this lesson, you learned:

- Macros can automate frequently used tasks.
- You can review and change macro security settings.
- You can record a macro.
- A workbook can be saved as a macro-enabled workbook.
- After a macro is created, you can run the macro.

- If changes need to be made to a macro, you can edit the macro.
- Buttons are a type of form control that have a macro assigned to them.
- Buttons can be aligned and formatted.
- When you open a macro-enabled workbook, you can enable the workbook contents and run any macros in the workbook.

 VOCABULARY REVIEW

Define the following terms:

button   macro   virus
code

 REVIEW QUESTIONS

TRUE / FALSE

Circle T if the statement is true or F if the statement is false.

T   F   **1.**   Macros can automate frequently used tasks.

T   F   **2.**   To run a macro, you can only use the shortcut keys assigned to the macro.

T   F   **3.**   When you create a macro, Excel translates the macro into Visual Basic for Applications code.

T   F   **4.**   Once you run a macro, it cannot be edited.

T   F   **5.**   When you open a macro-enabled workbook, you click Enable Content so the macros will work.

FILL IN THE BLANK

1. The programming language that is embedded into Excel for macros is called _____.

2. To save a workbook with a macro, you save it in the _____ file format.

3. Since clicking a button runs a macro, to change the text formats on a button, you need to _____ the button to select it.

4. If you want to stop recording a macro, you can select the Stop Recording button on the Developer tab or the Stop Recording button on the _____.

5. A(n) _____ is called a control because it controls the actions that are assigned to it.

WRITTEN QUESTIONS

Write a brief answer to the following questions.

1. What is a macro?

2. Explain how you would edit a macro.

3. Explain how to create a button.

4. How do you edit text that appears on the button?

5. How do you return to your worksheet from the Microsoft Visual Basic for Applications window?

■ PROJECTS

If you have a SAM 2010 user profile, your instructor may have assigned an autogradable version of the indicated project. If so, log into the SAM 2010 Web site at *www.cengage.com/sam2010* to download the instruction and start files.

PROJECT 14–1

1. Open the **Arts and Crafts** file from the drive and folder where your Data Files are stored.

2. Save the workbook as a macro-enabled workbook with the file name **Arts and Crafts Expenses**, followed by your initials.

3. Create a macro that inserts a blank column to the left of whichever cell is selected when the macro is run. Name the macro **Insert_Column** and assign a shortcut key of your choice.

4. Run the macro to be certain it works.

5. Print the worksheet.

6. Save and close the workbook.

SAM PROJECT 14–2

1. Open the **College Budget** file from the drive and folder where your Data Files are stored.

2. Save the workbook as a macro-enabled workbook with the file name **College Budget – Annual**, followed by your initials.

3. In the First Year worksheet, record a macro named **Blue_Format** without using shortcut keys. The macro should include the following formats:
   - Aqua, Accent 5, Lighter 40% cell background to cells **B4:G4**
   - Aqua, Accent 5, Lighter 60% cell background to cells **A5:A11**
   - Aqua, Accent 5, Lighter 40% cell background to cells **B12:G12**

4. Click the Second Year worksheet tab.

5. Create a button in cells D1:D2 and assign the Blue_Format macro to the button.

6. Click the button to apply the formats to the Second Year worksheet. Edit the button text to read **Add formats** using a bold font.

7. Save and print the workbook.

8. Close the workbook.

PROJECT 14–3

1. Open the **College Book** workbook from the drive and folder where your Data Files are stored.

2. Select Enable Contents.

3. Save the workbook in its macro-enabled workbook file type, and save the file as **College Book Sales**, followed by your initials.

4. Edit the **File_format** macro to include bold format to cells **A4:A12**.

5. Run the macro.

6. Print the worksheet.

7. Save and close the workbook.

■ CRITICAL THINKING

ACTIVITY 14–1

You are preparing an Excel worksheet for your company's year-end close. Open the **Project Sales** workbook from the drive and folder where your Data Files are stored and save it as a macro-enabled workbook with the file name **Project Sales Totals**, followed by your initials. Create a macro that totals each month's expenses and places them in row 18. Print the worksheet when you are done. Save and close the workbook.

ACTIVITY 14–2

Think of a macro you could write in Excel that could be applied to a document for your personal use. For example, think of your weekly schedule at your job, earnings, salary increases, or savings plans. Write the purpose of your macro and what it would accomplish for you.

LESSON 15

Working with Auditing and Analysis Tools

■ OBJECTIVES

Upon completion of this lesson, you should be able to:

- Use the Trace Precedents feature.
- Use the Trace Dependents feature.
- Use the Trace Error feature.
- Check for errors in functions.
- Perform a what-if analysis using the Goal Seek feature.
- Create a scenario.
- View the scenario summary.
- Consolidate data.
- Create a one-way data table.

■ VOCABULARY

audit

consolidating

dependent

precedent

Scenario Manager

tracer arrow

Introduction

Excel offers a number of tools that give you the ability to check for accuracy in formulas, solve problems with formulas, and analyze existing data. Using the auditing features such as Trace Precedents, Trace Dependents, and Trace Error, you can check for potential problems in cells that are used in a formula. The Trace Precedents feature finds the cells that are used in the function. The Trace Dependents feature looks for formulas that use data in a selected cell. The Trace Error feature locates cells that are used in the formula to assist in identifying the source of the error. To locate errors with formulas or functions, you can use the Error Checking tool.

You use the Goal Seek feature when you need to know the value required to arrive at a specific goal. The Scenario Manager is useful when you want to find out the result of a scenario based on changing data in several cells. Finally, you can use the Data Table feature when you want to project the results of a function in several cells, not just the one cell containing the function.

Using Trace Precedents

▶ **VOCABULARY**

audit

precedent

tracer arrow

When you **audit** something, you are checking it for accuracy. When you look at a function in Excel to see if it is correct, you are doing an audit of that function. Excel's auditing feature, Trace Precedents, finds the cells that are used in the function. **Precedents** refer to cells that supply the values used in a function.

The Trace Precedents feature is useful if you want to confirm that the cells you intended to use in the function are in fact used by the function or if the result of a function does not look correct. Using this feature can help you locate the source of a problem.

For example, if you click a cell that has a SUM function and then click the Trace Precedents button, the cells that are used in this function are surrounded by a border. An arrow called a **tracer arrow** is drawn to the cell with the SUM function, as shown in **Figure 15–1**.

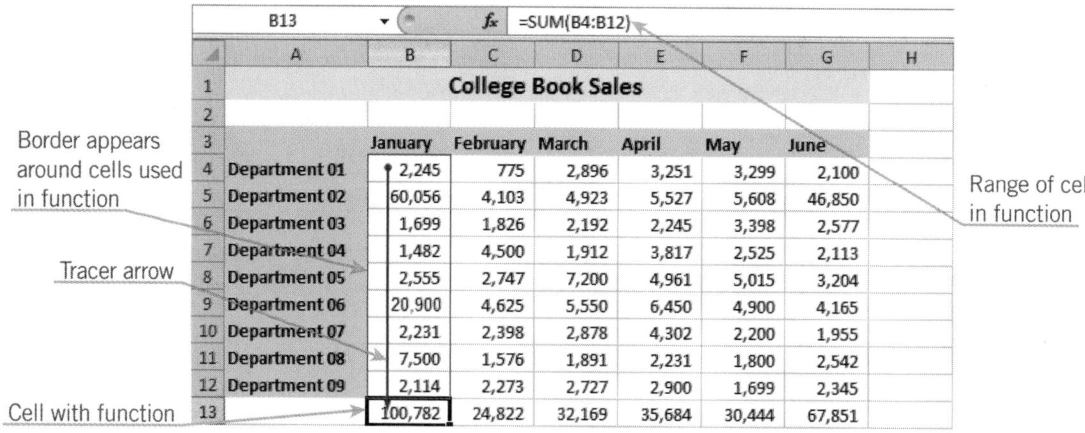

FIGURE 15–1   Example of trace precedents

If the precedent cells are in a range of cells in the same row or column, a border is placed around them. When you print the worksheet, the tracer arrows in your worksheet will print as well. However, when you save the file, the tracer arrows are removed.

Step-by-Step 15.1

1. Open the **Grades** file from the drive and folder where your Data Files are stored.

2. Save the workbook as **History Grades**, followed by your initials. The workbook includes test grades for a history test.

3. Click cell **E19**. This cell has the function that averages the test scores. You want to check the function for accuracy.

4. Click the **Formulas** tab, then click the **Trace Precedents** button in the Formula Auditing group. The range of cells used in the function has a border. A tracer arrow displays from cell B6 and points to cell E19, as shown in **Figure 15–2**.

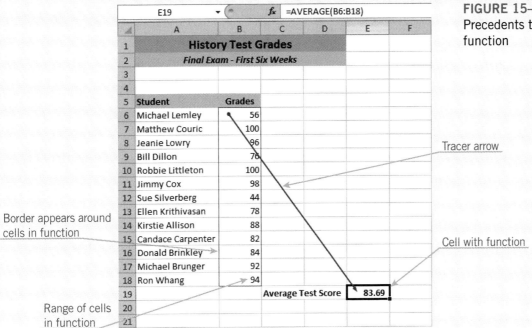

FIGURE 15–2
Precedents traced for Average function

5. Print the worksheet.

6. In the Formula Auditing group, click the **down arrow** next to the Remove Arrows button and select **Remove Precedent Arrows** from the list.

7. Save the workbook and leave it open for the next Step-by-Step.

EXTRA FOR EXPERTS

Remember, a formula is typed in by the user and can be simple, such as =B5 + B6. Functions are shown next to parentheses and require arguments, such as =SUM(B5:B6).

Using Trace Dependents

The Trace Dependents feature works by locating formulas and/or functions that depend on the value in a selected cell. For example, if you select a cell containing data and then click the Trace Dependents button, a tracer arrow is drawn from the selected cell, called the *dependent*, pointing to the cell with the function. In other words, the function depends on the data in the selected cell to calculate the answer. You may find that several functions depend on the data in the selected cell and, in that case, you will have several tracer arrows drawn from that cell to the various functions.

After you click the Trace Dependents or Trace Precedents buttons, you can remove the tracer arrows by clicking the Remove Arrows button in the Formula Auditing group. The Remove Arrows button gives you the option to remove the Trace Dependents tracer arrows, the Trace Precedents tracer arrows, or all the tracer arrows. In the next Step-by-Step, you will add Trace Dependents tracer arrows and then remove them.

▶ **VOCABULARY**
dependent

Step-by-Step 15.2

1. Click **cell B7.** You could select any cell with data to see if it is used in a function.

2. In the Formula Auditing group, click the **Trace Dependents** button. The Trace Dependents tracer arrow points to cell E19 with the function.

3. Click **cell B15**.

4. Click the **Trace Dependents** button. Both cells B7 and B15 have tracer arrows that point to the cell with the function, as shown in **Figure 15–3**.

FIGURE 15–3
Average function depends on cells with tracer arrows

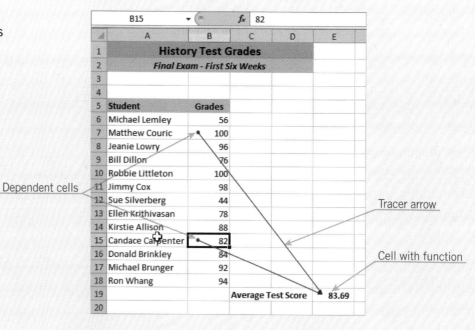

5. Print the worksheet.

6. Save and close the workbook.

Using Trace Error

Sometimes when you are entering formulas or functions, you may notice that an error displays instead of the result of the formula or function. For example, if you enter an Average function in a cell but #DIV/0! appears instead, the calculation includes an error. The #DIV/0! error indicates that either the function is dividing by a zero or that cells used in the function have missing data. To locate the source of the error, you click the cell with the error and then click the Trace Error command. Once the error is traced, you can make changes to the data to correct the error.

In addition, Excel displays an information icon next to the cell with the error status. When you click the icon, a list containing the error and options for resolving the error appears. The error found using Trace Error is highlighted in the list. Divide by Zero Error is an example of a possible error. Seeing the error helps you fix the error in the cell. If you want more assistance, you can select Help on this Error from the list to access the Help feature in Excel. In the next Step-by-Step, you will trace errors found when an Average function was copied.

Step-by-Step 15.3

1. Open the **Book Sales** file from the drive and folder where your Data Files are stored.

2. Save the workbook as **Yearly Book Sales**, followed by your initials.

3. Click **cell G14**. This cell contains an error. Next you will use the Trace Error feature to find the problem.

4. In the Formula Auditing group, click the **Error Checking** button arrow, and then click **Trace Error**. The cells used in the formula are surrounded by a border, and a tracer arrow points from these cells to the function in cell G14, as shown in **Figure 15–4**. Notice the information icon that appears next to the function.

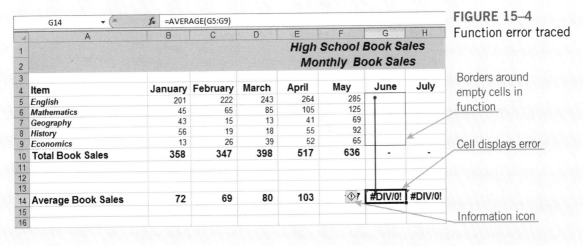

FIGURE 15–4
Function error traced

Borders around empty cells in function

Cell displays error

Information icon

5. Click the **information icon** arrow to display the information list, as shown in **Figure 15–5**. The Divide by Zero Error is highlighted, providing information about the error. Next, you will trace the error for adjacent cells that also show an error.

FIGURE 15–5
Information list

6. Select **cell H14**.

7. Click the **Error Checking** arrow button, and then click **Trace Error**. The cells used in this function are surrounded by a border. You realize that this error occurs not because the Average function is averaging zeros, which would not result in an error. Instead, you see that Columns G and H contain no data. You will now enter zeros in the cells that are used by the function.

8. Select **cell G5**, type **0**, and then press **Enter**.

9. Type **0** in cells **G6:G9** and then save the workbook to remove the tracer arrows.

10. Type **0** in cells **H5:H9**. Compare your completed worksheet to **Figure 15–6**.

FIGURE 15–6
Corrected worksheet

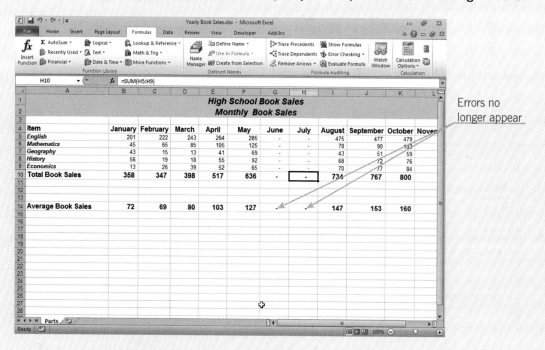

11. Save and close the workbook.

Checking for Errors

The Trace Error feature is helpful when you are just tracing one cell for an error. The Error Checking feature is a better choice when your worksheet has lots of data and you want Excel to check all of the formulas and functions in the worksheet for potential problems. When an error is located, the Error Checking dialog box gives you information about the error. In this dialog box, you can choose to show the calculation steps to help identify where the problem occurs. If no errors are found, a dialog box lets you know that the error check for the worksheet is complete.

Step-by-Step 15.4

1. Open the **Auto Parts** file from the drive and folder where your Data Files are stored.

2. Save the workbook as **Auto Parts Sales**, followed by your initials.

3. Click the **Formulas** tab, then in the Formula Auditing group, click the **Error Checking** button arrow, and then click **Error Checking**. The Error Checking dialog box opens, letting you know that an error occurred with the AVERAGE function in cell N14. You may need to move the dialog box out of the way so that you can see the function with the border in cell N14. See **Figure 15–7**.

Shows cell with error

Potential problem with function

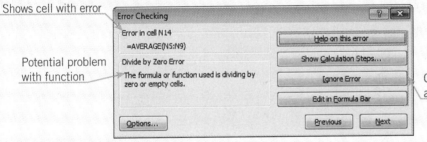

FIGURE 15–7
Error Checking dialog box

Click buttons to display additional options

4. In the Error Checking dialog box, click the **Show Calculation Steps** button to open the Evaluate Formula dialog box. In the Evaluate Formula dialog box, the function is displayed in the Evaluation box, as shown in **Figure 15–8**. You decide to continue to evaluate the function to see more information about the error.

Indicates problem when function performs calculation

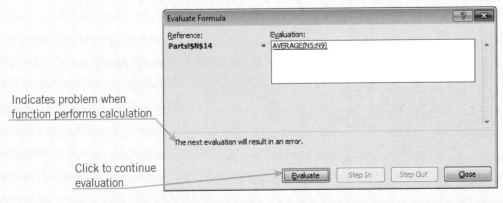

FIGURE 15–8
Evaluate Formula dialog box

Click to continue evaluation

5. Click the **Evaluate** button. The Evaluation box now shows the results of the function when calculated. See **Figure 15–9**.

FIGURE 15–9
Evaluation box when function is evaluated

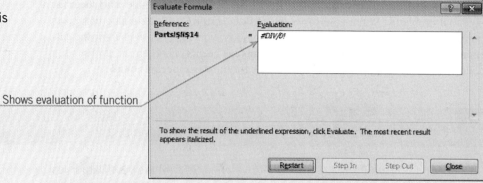

Shows evaluation of function

6. Close the Evaluate Formula dialog box.

7. Click the **Next** button to see if the worksheet contains any additional errors. A message box appears letting you know that no additional errors were found and the error check is complete. See **Figure 15–10**.

FIGURE 15–10
Message box

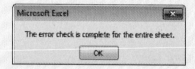

8. Click **OK** to close the message box.

9. Select **cell N14**, if necessary, and then press **Delete** to delete the formula that should not be in this cell.

10. Save and close the workbook.

Performing a What-if Analysis Using the Goal Seek Feature

Functions and formulas usually perform mathematical calculations using known values. Sometimes, however, you may know the result (the goal), but you don't necessarily know the values needed to arrive at the goal. For example, you may want to save $15,000 for your first year of college that starts five years from now. You need to know how much to save each month in order to meet this goal. The **Goal Seek** feature finds the unknown value you need in order to accomplish your goal.

The Goal Seek feature is referred to as a "what-if" analysis tool. In other words, "What if I want to save $15,000 in five years, how much do I need to save each month?" When you use Goal Seek, you will be asked for some information in the Goal Seek dialog box, shown in **Figure 15–11**.

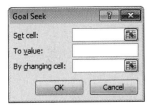

FIGURE 15–11   Goal Seek dialog box

In the Set cell text box, you enter the cell containing the function that Excel uses to find the answer. Next, enter the desired goal in the To value text box. In the By changing cell text box, you enter the cell where you want the answer displayed.

Step-by-Step 15.5

1. On the Ribbon, click the **File** tab, click **New**, and then double-click **Blank workbook**. You will use a new workbook for this Step-by-Step. Save the workbook as **College Fund Goal**, followed by your initials.

2. Click **cell C5**. Because this is a blank worksheet, you can select any cell in which to enter the formula. You will enter a formula that finds out how much money you need to save each month for five years in order to save $15,000.

3. Type **=A5*12*5** and then press **Enter**. This formula takes the unknown monthly savings amount in cell A5 and multiplies it by 12 payments per year for 5 years. Cell A5 is chosen at random; you could choose another cell to accomplish the same goal.

4. Select **cell C5**, and then click the **Data** tab.

5. In the Data Tools group, click the **What-If Analysis** arrow button, and then click **Goal Seek**. You should see cell C5 in the Set cell text box, as shown in **Figure 15–12**.

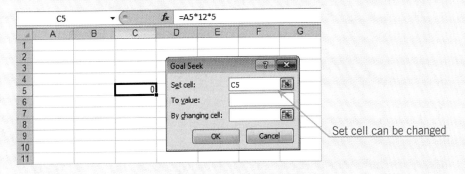

FIGURE 15–12
The Goal Seek dialog box

6. Click in the **To value** text box, then type **15000**. This is the goal value, the amount of money you wish to save. Notice that you do not need to enter the comma, but it is okay if you do.

7. Click in the **By changing cell** text box, and then type **A5**. This cell will show the goal seek solution. The completed dialog box should appear as shown in **Figure 15–13**.

FIGURE 15–13
Completed Goal Seek dialog box

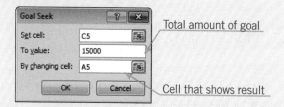

8. Click **OK**. The Goal Seek Status dialog box opens to let you know that it has found a solution, as shown in **Figure 15–14**.

FIGURE 15–14
Goal Seek Status dialog box

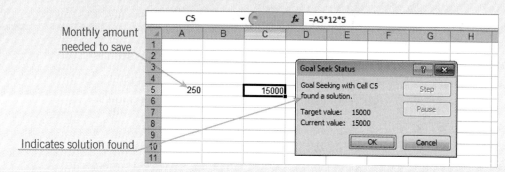

9. Click **OK** to close the Goal Seek Status dialog box. Next you will use Goal Seek to find out how much money needs to be saved each month if you need $17,500 for the first year of college.

10. Click the **What-If Analysis** arrow button, and then click **Goal Seek**.

11. Verify that cell C5 is still displayed in the Set cell text box, click in the **To value** text box, and then type **17500**.

12. Press **Tab** to move to the By changing cell text box, and then type **A5**. Click **OK**, then compare your screen to **Figure 15–15**.

FIGURE 15–15
Completed Goal Seek Status dialog box with new value

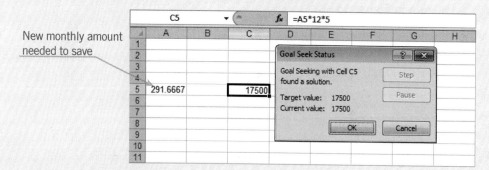

13. Click **OK** to close the Goal Seek Status dialog box, and then click in **cell A5**.

14. Click the **Home** tab, and then click the **Accounting Number Format** button $ in the Number group to apply the currency format with two decimal places.

15. Save and close the workbook.

Creating Scenarios

Another type of "what-if" analysis is the Scenario feature. When you use Goal Seek, it focuses on changing one cell of data. By comparison, the *Scenario Manager* performs a "what-if" analysis that lets you change several cells of data.

Scenarios are sometimes used to view various changes in expenses. For example, some of your expenses may increase while others may decrease. You can create a scenario based on expenses increasing and another scenario based on expenses decreasing. Using scenarios to view these changes lets you see how much more or how much less money you or your company will make in the future. When you create scenarios, you need to give the scenario a name, such as Best Case for the decrease in expenses or Worst Case for the increase in expenses. In addition, you may want to create a scenario with the original data so you can refer back to it.

▶ **VOCABULARY**
Scenario Manager

Step-by-Step 15.6

1. Open the **Blooming Yards** file from the drive and folder where your Data Files are stored, and then save the workbook as **Blooming Yards Income and Expenses**, followed by your initials.

2. Click the **Data** tab. In the Data Tools group, click the **What-If Analysis** button arrow, and then click **Scenario Manager**. The Scenario Manager dialog box opens, as shown in **Figure 15–16**. Notice that it does not show any scenarios yet. You will now add one.

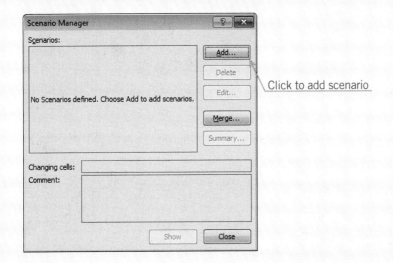

FIGURE 15–16
Scenario Manager dialog box

3. Click the **Add** button to display the Add Scenario dialog box, as shown in **Figure 15–17**. Notice that you can select the Prevent changes check box in the Add Scenario dialog box to avoid unwanted changes to the scenarios, such as someone opening the workbook and editing the scenarios.

FIGURE 15–17
Add Scenario dialog box

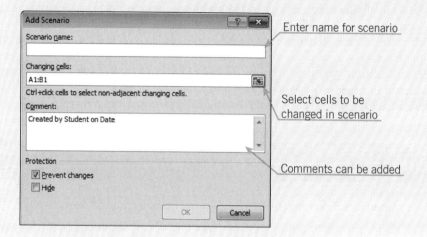

4. In the Scenario name text box, type **Current Expenses**.

5. Press **Tab** to move to the Changing cells text box, then type **B10:B17**. You select this range of cells because they are the actual expenses related to planting trees and flowers.

6. Click **OK**. The values you entered in the Changing cells text box appear in the Scenario Values dialog box, as displayed in **Figure 15–18**. Values in the other cells in the range are displayed as well.

FIGURE 15–18
Scenario Values dialog box

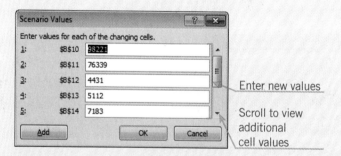

7. Click **OK**. The current expenses are saved, and the Scenario Manager dialog box opens.

8. Click **Add**.

9. In the Scenario name text box, type **Best Case Scenario**, then click **OK**.

10. In the text box next to $B$10 type **85000**, press **Tab** to move to the text box next to $B$11, and then type **70000**. This scenario will show us what would happen if the Flowers expense went down to $85,000 and the Fruit/Vegetables expense decreased to $70,000.

11. Click **OK** to close the Scenarios Values dialog box. The Best Case Scenario is completed.

12. Click **Add**. In the Scenario name text box, type **Worst Case Scenario**, and then click **OK**.

13. In the text box next to $B$10 type **105000**, press **Tab** to move to the next text box, type **85000**, and then click **OK** to close the Scenario Values dialog box. This scenario will show what would happen if expenses increased. The Scenario Manager dialog box should appear as shown in **Figure 15–19**.

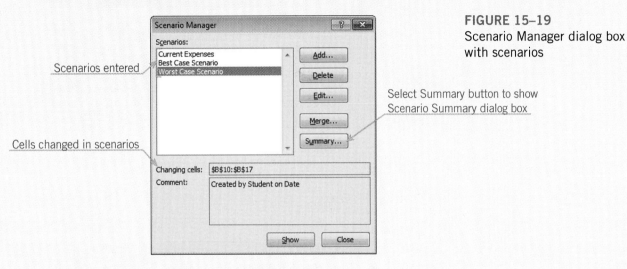

FIGURE 15–19
Scenario Manager dialog box with scenarios

14. Leave the workbook open for the next Step-by-Step.

Viewing the Scenario Summary

After you've created scenarios, the Scenario Manager lets you view them in a formatted report on a separate worksheet. Excel automatically names the new worksheet *Scenario Summary* and applies formatting to the data. Each time you request a scenario summary, Excel creates a new worksheet that includes the data currently in the worksheet.

Step-by-Step 15.7

1. In the Scenario Manager dialog box, click the **Summary** button. The Scenario Summary dialog box opens, as shown in **Figure 15–20**.

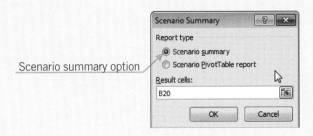

FIGURE 15–20
Scenario Summary dialog box

2. With the Scenario summary option button selected, click **OK** to display the Scenario Summary. Compare your screen to **Figure 15–21**. Next, you will change some of the current values.

FIGURE 15–21
Scenario Summary
worksheet

Shows current
values in
Financial Statement
worksheet

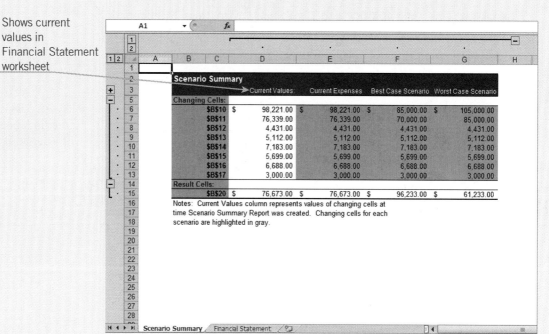

3. Click the **Financial Statement** worksheet tab. You will now change data in the worksheet and then create a new scenario summary.

4. Select **cell B17** and then type **500**.

5. Select **cell B14**, type **5345**, and then press **Enter**.

6. On the Data tab in the Data Tools group, click the **What-If Analysis** button arrow, and then click **Scenario Manager**.

7. Click the **Summary** button.

8. Click **OK**. The new Scenario Summary worksheet appears as shown in **Figure 15–22**. Notice that the data you revised in the worksheet is shown in this scenario summary.

Revised values in
Financial Statement
worksheet appear in
Current Values

Scenario Summary
displays with
Outline buttons

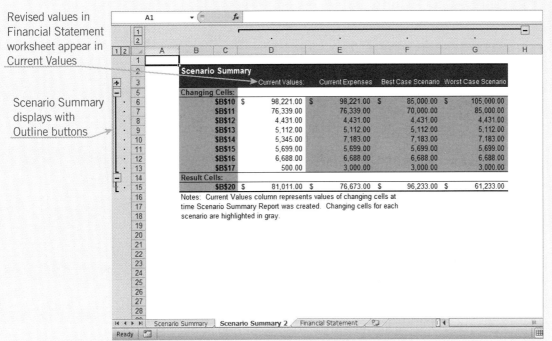

FIGURE 15–22
New Scenario
Summary worksheet

9. Save, print, and close the workbook.

Consolidating Data

To consolidate means to combine or unite. In Excel, *consolidating* involves bringing data from several worksheets together into one worksheet. You can choose various functions to use when consolidating, such as Sum, Average, or Count, just to name a few. You can consolidate data from several worksheets in the same workbook or between several workbooks.

The Consolidate feature is very flexible. The data that you consolidate does not need to be in the exact location in each of the worksheets. In the Consolidate dialog box, you can select the cells you want to consolidate, or, if you named the ranges, you can enter the range names.

You also choose the function you want to use, such as SUM, to consolidate data. In the next Step-by-Step, you will consolidate data from three worksheets into one worksheet so that you can see the totals.

▶ **VOCABULARY**
consolidating

Step-by-Step 15.8

1. Open the **Coastal Sales** file from the drive and folder where your Data Files are stored, and then save the workbook as **Coastal Sales – First Quarter**, followed by your initials. The workbook has four worksheets: First Quarter Sales, January, February, and March. You will add the data from the monthly worksheets into the First Quarter Sales worksheet. In each of the monthly worksheets, the range C5:C25 has been named using the month name.

2. Click the **First Quarter Sales** worksheet tab, then select **B5:B25**.

3. Click the **Data** tab, and then click the **Consolidate** button in the Data Tools group. The Consolidate dialog box opens, as shown in **Figure 15–23**.

FIGURE 15–23
Consolidate dialog box

Select function for consolidation

Type range name in Reference text box

Click Add button to add range for consolidation

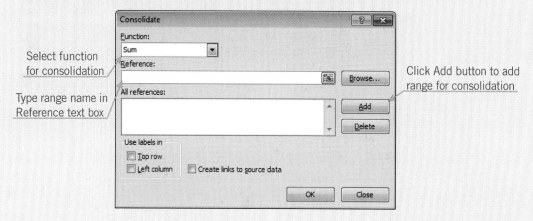

4. In the Reference text box, type **January**, and then click the **Add** button.

5. In the Reference text box, type **February**, and then click the **Add** button.

6. In the Reference text box, type **March**, click the **Add** button, and then compare your screen to **Figure 15–24**.

FIGURE 15–24
Completed Consolidate dialog box

Ranges added

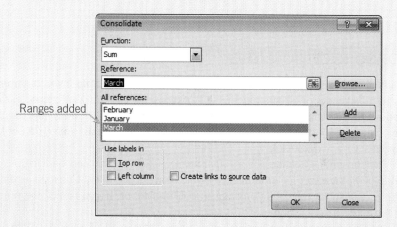

7. Click **OK** to close the Consolidate dialog box, then view the consolidated totals in the First Quarter Sales worksheet shown in **Figure 15–25**.

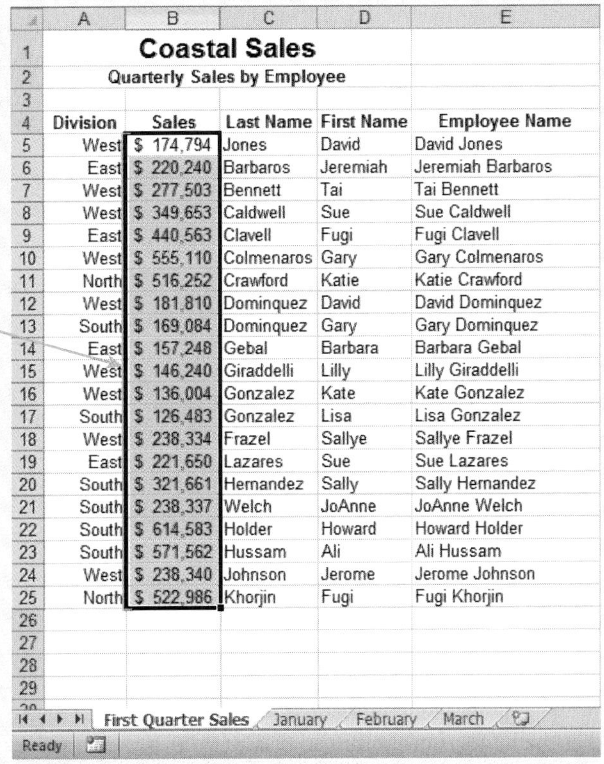

	A	B	C	D	E
1	**Coastal Sales**				
2	Quarterly Sales by Employee				
3					
4	**Division**	**Sales**	**Last Name**	**First Name**	**Employee Name**
5	West	$ 174,794	Jones	David	David Jones
6	East	$ 220,240	Barbaros	Jeremiah	Jeremiah Barbaros
7	West	$ 277,503	Bennett	Tai	Tai Bennett
8	West	$ 349,653	Caldwell	Sue	Sue Caldwell
9	East	$ 440,563	Clavell	Fugi	Fugi Clavell
10	West	$ 555,110	Colmenaros	Gary	Gary Colmenaros
11	North	$ 516,252	Crawford	Katie	Katie Crawford
12	West	$ 181,810	Dominquez	David	David Dominquez
13	South	$ 169,084	Dominquez	Gary	Gary Dominquez
14	East	$ 157,248	Gebal	Barbara	Barbara Gebal
15	West	$ 146,240	Giraddelli	Lilly	Lilly Giraddelli
16	West	$ 136,004	Gonzalez	Kate	Kate Gonzalez
17	South	$ 126,483	Gonzalez	Lisa	Lisa Gonzalez
18	West	$ 238,334	Frazel	Sallye	Sallye Frazel
19	East	$ 221,650	Lazares	Sue	Sue Lazares
20	South	$ 321,661	Hernandez	Sally	Sally Hernandez
21	South	$ 238,337	Welch	JoAnne	JoAnne Welch
22	South	$ 614,583	Holder	Howard	Howard Holder
23	South	$ 571,562	Hussam	Ali	Ali Hussam
24	West	$ 238,340	Johnson	Jerome	Jerome Johnson
25	North	$ 522,986	Khorjin	Fugi	Fugi Khorjin
26					
27					
28					
29					

Total of data from other worksheets now in First Quarter Sales worksheet

First Quarter Sales / January / February / March

Ready

FIGURE 15–25
Consolidated data in First Quarter Sales worksheet

EXTRA FOR EXPERTS

If you are consolidating data from multiple workbooks, you can select the Create links to source data check box in the Consolidate dialog box. This option automatically updates combined data. Whenever data changes in one workbook, the combined data is updated.

8. Save, print, and close the workbook.

Creating a One-Way Data Table

A one-way data table uses one function to change cells that use this function. For example, you may have a PMT function that finds the monthly payment of a car loan. To find the payment amount, you need certain information, such as the amount owed on the car, the interest rate, and the number of months for the loan. You can then use the PMT function to find out how much the loan payment will be each month.

You may want to find out how much the monthly payment would be if you reduced the number of months used to pay for the car. Your monthly payment would increase, but the interest you would save might be worth it, if you can afford the new monthly payment amount. Using a data table, you can instantly calculate the new monthly payment. An example of a one-way data table is shown in **Figure 15–26**.

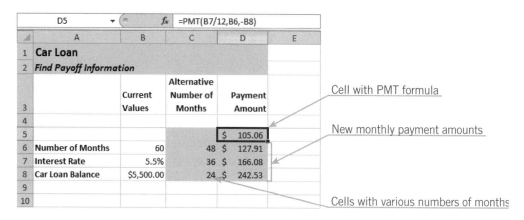

FIGURE 15–26   Example of a one-way data table

Notice that the payment function is in cell D5. The payment function works by using the number of months in cell B6, the interest rate in cell B7, and the car loan balance in cell B8 to calculate the monthly payment shown in cell D5. To change the number of months, you would enter this data into the cells next to the original values. In this example, you enter the new months in cells C6:C8. Notice that the function needs to be placed one column over and one row up from the new data. All of the cells with data that will be used in the data table need to be filled with a color. Excel only recognizes cells with color fills as part of the data table

Step-by-Step 15.9

1. Open the **Credit Card** file from the drive and folder where your Data Files are stored.

2. Save the workbook as **Credit Card Payoff**, followed by your initials.

3. Click **cell D5** and view the payment function. Notice that the function uses the number of months in cell B6. You will now enter the additional number of months to pay off the credit card.

4. Select **cell C6**, type **48**, and then press **Enter**.

5. Type **36** in cell C7, and then press **Enter**.

6. Type **24** in cell C8, and then press **Enter**. You will now add a fill color to the range that you want to use in the data table.

7. Select **C5:D8**.

8. Click the **Home** tab, click the **Fill Color** button arrow in the Font group, and then click **Dark Blue, Text 2, Lighter 80%**, (the fourth color in the second row). Your worksheet should resemble **Figure 15–27**.

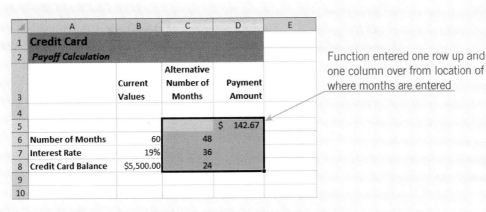

FIGURE 15–27
Worksheet formatted for data table

9. Click the **Data** tab, click the **What-If Analysis button** in the Data Tools group, and then click **Data Table**. The Data Table dialog box opens, as shown in **Figure 15–28**.

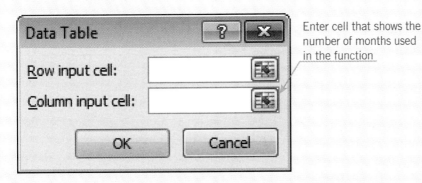

FIGURE 15–28
Data Table dialog box

10. Click in the **Column input cell** text box, and then type **B6**.

11. Click **OK** to close the Data Table dialog box. See **Figure 15–29**.

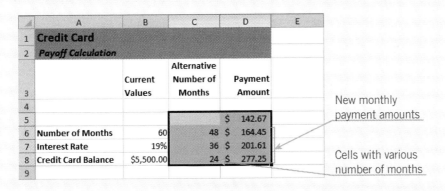

FIGURE 15–29
Worksheet with data table results

12. Click cell **C8**, type **12**, and then press **Enter**. Notice the payment amount in D8 changes to $506.86.

13. Save, print, and close the workbook.

SUMMARY

In this lesson, you learned:

- The Trace Precedents feature finds the cells that are used in the function.

- The Trace Error feature locates cells that are used in a formula to assist in identifying the source of an error.

- The Trace Dependents button works by locating formulas or functions that depend on the value in a selected cell.

- If a cell containing a formula has an error, the Trace Error feature displays the cells used in the formula.

- You can check for errors throughout an entire worksheet, using the Error Checking feature.

- The Goal Seek feature can perform a "what-if" analysis based on a single function.

- The Scenario Manager performs a "what-if" analysis and lets you view the results based on changing several cells of data.

- You can view scenarios in the scenario summary.

- Data from multiple worksheets can be totaled using the Consolidate feature.

- A one-way data table shows various results for a function within a range of cells.

■ VOCABULARY REVIEW

Define the following terms:

audit

consolidating

dependent

precedent

Scenario Manager

tracer arrow

■ REVIEW QUESTIONS

TRUE / FALSE

Circle T if the statement is true or F if the statement is false.

T   F   **1.** Consolidating data involves combining values from several worksheets together and showing the total of these values in another worksheet.

T   F   **2.** You can only create one scenario for a set of values.

T   F   **3.** If you select a cell with data and click the Trace Dependents button, Excel will draw an arrow from the selected cell pointing to the cell with the function that references that cell.

T   F   **4.** To check all formulas and functions in a workbook, you use the Error Checking option.

T   F   **5.** Goal Seek helps you find a value to meet a goal.

FILL IN THE BLANK

1. If you want to use a "what-if" analysis tool to find a value for a single cell of data, you use the _____ feature.

2. To do a "what-if" analysis that focuses on changing several cells of data, you would use the _____ feature.

3. To locate the source of an error in a function, you could click in the cell with the function and then click the _____ tool.

4. If you want to check for problems in all the formulas and functions in a workbook, you use the _____ feature.

5. A(n) _____ uses one function to produce results in several cells.

WRITTEN QUESTIONS

Write a brief answer to the following questions.

1. What is the difference between Trace Error and Error Checking?

2. What is the purpose of Goal Seek?

3. What can the Scenario Manager feature show you?

4. Explain the difference between consolidating data in one workbook versus consolidating data using several workbooks.

5. Explain the term audit.

■ PROJECTS

If you have a SAM 2010 user profile, your instructor may have assigned an autogradable version of the indicated project. If so, log into the SAM 2010 Web site at *www.cengage.com/sam2010* to download the instruction and start files.

PROJECT 15–1

1. Open the **Supplies** file from the drive and folder where your Data Files are stored.

2. Save the workbook as **Office Supplies**, followed by your initials.

3. Search all the formulas and functions for potential errors.

4. If errors are found, correct them.

5. Save and close the workbook.

SAM PROJECT 15–2

1. Open the **International Sales** file from the drive and folder where your Data Files are stored.

2. Save the workbook as **International Sales Financials**, followed by your initials.

3. Create a scenario showing the current values.

4. Create a scenario that shows the values of the current expenses. For the changing cells, type the range **B10:B16**.

5. Create another scenario named **Increased Lease and Utilities Expense**. Enter the following expenses into the scenario:

   B10 (Lease): 75000

   B11 (Utilities): 9000

6. Create another scenario named **Decreased Lease and Utilities Expense**. Enter the following expenses into the scenario:

   B10 (Lease): 45000

   B11 (Utilities): 7000

7. Click the Summary button and create a scenario summary.

8. Save and close the workbook.

PROJECT 15–3

1. Click the File tab, click New, and then double-click Blank workbook. Save the workbook as **Down Payment Goal**, followed by your initials.

2. Select cell C5.

3. Type **=A5*12*10** and then press Enter. This formula takes the unknown monthly savings amount in cell A5 and multiplies it by 12 payments per year for 10 years.

4. Select cell C5, and on the Data tab, in the Data Tools group, click the What-If Analysis button, and then click Goal Seek.

5. Click in the To value text box, then type **25000**. This is the goal value.

6. Click in the By changing cell box, then type **A5**. This cell will show the Goal Seek solution.

7. Click OK.

8. Add the Accounting Number Format to cells A5 and C5.

9. Save and close the workbook.

■ CRITICAL THINKING

ACTIVITY 15–1

1. Open the **Trees and Landscaping** file from the drive and folder where your Data Files are stored.

2. Save the workbook as **Trees and Landscaping Financials**, followed by your initials.

3. Create a scenario named **Increased Sales** that increases the income for Trees Planted.

4. Create another scenario that shows a decrease in income in Trees Planted, then assign an appropriate name to the scenario.

5. Create a scenario summary that shows the current values, the increased income, and the decreased income.

6. Save and close the workbook.

ACTIVITY 15–2

1. Think of a data table you could create in Excel that could be applied to a document you use for personal use. For example, you may want to pay off your student loans or you may want to refinance your loans at a lower interest rate. Create the data table in Excel and save it as **Payoff**, followed by your initials.

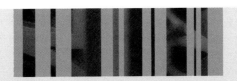

LESSON 16

Protecting, Tracking, and Sharing Workbooks

■ OBJECTIVES

Upon completion of this lesson, you should be able to:

- Add password protection to a worksheet.
- Remove password protection from a worksheet.
- Add password protection to a workbook.
- Remove password protection from a workbook.
- Enable the Track Changes feature.
- Change a workbook with tracked changes.
- Accept or reject tracked changes.
- Disable the Track Changes feature.
- Create a shared workbook.
- Modify a shared workbook.

■ VOCABULARY

case sensitive

decrypt

disable

enable

encrypt

password

shared workbook

Introduction

To protect your Excel data from unwanted changes, you can add password protection to worksheets and workbooks. Adding password protection to the entire workbook prevents anyone who does not know the password from opening or viewing the file. If you add password protection to individual worksheets, only the people who know the password can make changes to them.

If you want to keep track of the changes made in a workbook, you can enable the Track Changes feature. Then, when a change is made, Excel will record the date and time of the change, the person who made the change, the previous entry in the cell, and the changed entry in the cell. As you review the changes, you can accept or reject each change.

Shared workbooks allow you to work in the same workbook with other users at the same time. The Track Changes feature is also available with shared workbooks.

Adding Password Protection to a Worksheet

When you have a worksheet that several people have access to, you run the risk of unwanted changes, whether a user makes them intentionally or accidentally. To prevent changes to a worksheet, you can protect it with a password.

A *password* refers to a sequence of characters, known only by you, that is required for access to the file. Passwords are *case sensitive*. In other words, if a password contains capital letters, you will need to enter the password using the same capital letters. In this next Step-by-Step, you will password-protect a worksheet.

▶ **VOCABULARY**

password

case sensitive

Step-by-Step 16.1

1. Open the **State College** file from the drive and folder where your Data Files are stored.

2. Save the workbook as **State College Inventory**, followed by your initials.

3. On the Ribbon, click the **Review** tab, and then click the **Protect Sheet** button in the Changes group. The Protect Sheet dialog box opens, as shown in **Figure 16–1**.

FIGURE 16–1
Protect Sheet dialog box

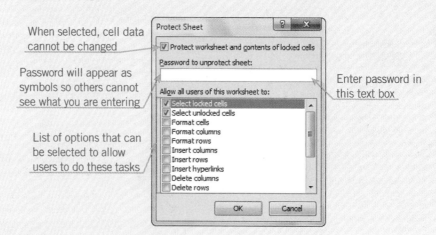

When selected, cell data cannot be changed

Password will appear as symbols so others cannot see what you are entering

List of options that can be selected to allow users to do these tasks

Enter password in this text box

4. In the Password to unprotect sheet text box, type **Cat**.

5. Click **OK** to close the Protect Sheet dialog box. You are prompted to confirm your password by typing it again in the Confirm Password dialog box, as shown in **Figure 16–2**.

Reenter password in this text box

FIGURE 16–2
Confirming password

6. In the Reenter password to proceed text box, type **Cat**.

7. Click **OK** to close the Confirm Password dialog box. On the Review tab, notice that the Unprotect Sheet button is available since protection is applied to the worksheet.

8. Select **cell D10**, type **3**. Notice that a message box appears letting you know that the cell you are trying to change is protected. See **Figure 16–3**.

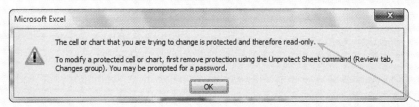

FIGURE 16–3
Protection warning message box

Message indicates that cell cannot be changed

9. Click **OK** to close the message box, and then select the **Home** tab. Notice how most of the buttons are not available, indicating that changes cannot be made to the worksheet.

10. Right-click **cell A5**, and then select **Clear Contents** from the shortcut menu. The message box appears.

11. Click **OK** to close the message box.

12. Click the **Insert Worksheet** button [icon] next to the Inventory worksheet.

13. In the new worksheet, select **cell A5**, type **500**, and then press **Enter**. A message box does not appear since this worksheet is not protected.

14. Save the workbook and leave it open for the next Step-by-Step.

Removing Password Protection from a Worksheet

When a worksheet is password protected, changes cannot be made to it. If you need to change data or other information on the worksheet, you will need to remove the password protection. When you are finished making the changes, you can add the password protection to the worksheet again. Next, you will remove password protection from the worksheet.

Step-by-Step 16.2

1. Click the **Inventory** worksheet tab.

2. Click the **Review** tab, and then click the **Unprotect Worksheet** button in the Changes group. The Unprotect Sheet dialog box is shown in **Figure 16–4**.

FIGURE 16–4
Unprotect Sheet dialog box

Enter password in this text box

3. In the Password text box, type **Cat** and then click **OK**.

4. Select **cell D10**, type **350**, and then press **Enter**. The worksheet is unprotected so you are able to make changes to it. Compare your worksheet to **Figure 16–5**.

FIGURE 16–5
Unprotected worksheet with change

	A	B	C	D	E	F
1		**State College Fan-Fair**				
2		*Inventory*				
3						
4						
5	Item No.	Item Description	Size	Quantity in Stock	Cost	Value
6	SS-LC1-S	Sweat Shirt - State College College emblem	S	45	$ 10.99	$ 494.55
7	SS-LC1-M	Sweat Shirt - State College College emblem	M	62	$ 12.99	$ 805.38
8	SS-LC1-L	Sweat Shirt - State College College emblem	L	39	$ 14.99	$ 584.61
9						$ -
10	Cap-L	Baseball Cap	L	350	$ 4.99	$1,746.50
11	Cap-XL	Baseball Cap	XL	234	$ 5.99	$1,401.66
12						$ -
13	TS-LC-S	Tee Shirt - State College College emblem	S	65	$ 4.99	$ 324.35
14	TS-LC-M	Tee Shirt - State College College emblem	M	42	$ 6.99	$ 293.58
15	TS-LC-L	Tee Shirt - State College College emblem	L	97	$ 8.99	$ 872.03
16						$ -
17	Shorts-S	Shorts	S	48	$ 7.99	$ 383.52
18	Shorts-M	Shorts	M	22	$ 9.99	$ 219.78
19	Shorts-L	Shorts	L	19	$ 11.99	$ 227.81
20	Shorts-XL	Shorts	XL	7	$ 13.99	$ 97.93
21						$ -
22	SP-LC-S	Sweat Pants - State College College emblem	S	56	$ 9.99	$ 559.44
23	SP-LC-M	Sweat Pants - State College College emblem	M	31	$ 11.99	$ 371.69
24	SP-LC-L	Sweat Pants - State College College emblem	L	33	$ 13.99	$ 461.67
25	SP-LC-XL	Sweat Pants - State College College emblem	XL	21	$ 15.99	$ 335.79
26						

Cell D10 changed

5. Save and close the workbook.

Adding Password Protection to a Workbook

To prevent a workbook from being opened by an unauthorized person, you can password-protect a workbook. If someone tries to open a password-protected workbook, he or she will be first prompted to enter the password in a dialog box. If the password is not entered correctly, the workbook will not open. Passwords for a workbook are case sensitive; they must be entered exactly as when they were created.

When you password-protect a workbook, you are encrypting the file. *Encrypting* means that the information in the file is scrambled. Therefore, if an unauthorized person tries to pry into the file, they will only see unreadable text and symbols. You may have seen news reports in which unauthorized individuals use their computer knowledge to gain unauthorized access to a person's file. Using passwords will help prevent this from happening.

To make sure you have access to a protected file in case you lose the password, you should create an unprotected backup of the file and store it in another location.

▶ **VOCABULARY**
encrypting

Step-by-Step 16.3

1. Open the **Employee** file from the drive and folder where your Data Files are stored.

2. Save the workbook as **Employee List**, followed by your initials.

3. Click the **File** tab and then click **Info**, if necessary. The Protect Workbook button is located in the Info section of the File window, as shown in **Figure 16–6**.

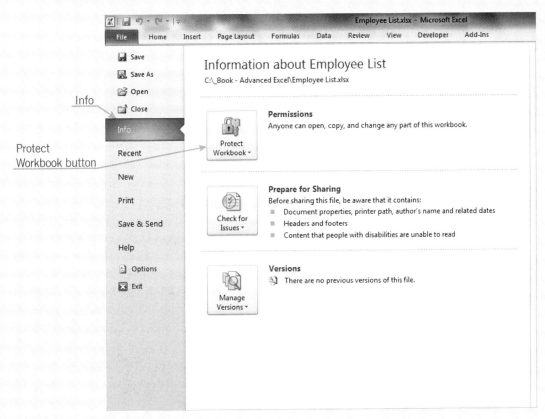

FIGURE 16–6
Info section of the File window

4. Click the **Protect Workbook** button to display the workbook protection options, as shown in **Figure 16–7**.

FIGURE 16–7
Protect Workbook options

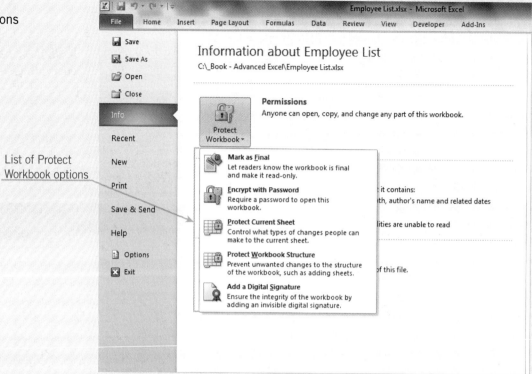

List of Protect Workbook options

5. Click the **Encrypt with Password** option to display the Encrypt Document dialog box.

6. In the Password text box, type **Cat** and then press **Enter**.

7. In the Confirm Password dialog box, type **Cat** in the Reenter password text box, and then press **Enter**. The workbook is now password protected.

8. Save and close the workbook.

Removing Password Protection from a Workbook

If you need to let others access a password-protected workbook, you can remove the password protection without giving out the password. When you remove the password protection, you are *decrypting* the workbook, or removing the encryption. If you want to be sure that the original file is not changed, you can create a copy of the workbook and remove the password from the copied file. Then, you still have the original password-protected workbook.

In this next Step-by-Step, you will open the password-protected workbook and save the file with another filename so you still have a copy of the workbook with a password. Then, you will remove the password from the new file.

▶ **VOCABULARY**
decrypting

Step-by-Step 16.4

1. Open the **Employee List** file and notice that the Password dialog box opens, as shown in **Figure 16–8**.

Enter password in this text box

FIGURE 16–8
Password dialog box

2. In the Password text box, type **Cat** and then click **OK**.

3. Save the workbook as **Employee List – Revised**, followed by your initials.

4. Click the **File** tab and then select **Info**, if necessary. Notice that a message appears under Permissions showing that a password is required to open this workbook.

5. Click the **Protect Workbook** button, and then click **Encrypt with Password**. The Encrypt Document dialog box opens, as shown in **Figure 16–9**. The encrypted password is shown in the Password text box.

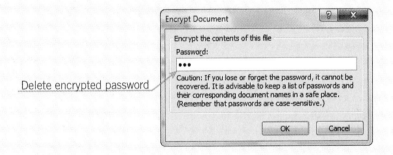

Delete encrypted password

FIGURE 16–9
Encrypt Document dialog box

6. Highlight the password in the Password text box, and then press [**Delete**].

7. Click **OK** to close the Encrypt Document dialog box.

8. On the File tab, click **Save**.

9. Close the workbook.

10. Open the **Employee List – Revised** workbook. Notice that you are not asked for a password.

11. Save and close the workbook.

> **EXTRA FOR EXPERTS**
>
> If you do not want any more changes made to a workbook, you can mark it as final. When you mark a workbook as final, the workbook opens as a read-only file. To mark a workbook as final, click the File tab, click Info, click the Protect Workbook button, and then click Mark as Final.

Enabling the Track Changes Feature

The Track Changes feature shows changes made to an Excel worksheet. When Track Changes is enabled, cells that have been changed appear with a border. Also, Excel identifies the name of the person who made the change and the date of the change. The border will appear around the changed cells until the file is closed. When the file is reopened, the border does not appear, but Excel still keeps a history of the changes. If the Track Changes feature is enabled, it makes the workbook a shared file. When a file is shared, several people can make changes to the workbook at the same time.

The advantage of tracking changes is that you can go back and review the changes in the workbook. And, as you review the changes, you can accept or reject each change. You *enable* the Track Changes feature by clicking the Track changes while editing check box in the Highlight Changes dialog box. In the dialog box, you can choose *When* (when should changes be tracked), *Who* (whose changes should be tracked), and *Where* (which range of cells should be tracked) options. You can also choose whether you want the changes to be highlighted on the screen or listed on a new sheet.

▶ **VOCABULARY**

enable

Step-by-Step 16.5

1. Open the **Water Usage** file from the drive and folder where your Data Files are stored, and then save the workbook as **Water Usage by Department**, followed by your initials.

2. On the Ribbon, click the **Review** tab.

3. In the **Changes** group, click the **Track Changes** button arrow, and then click **Highlight Changes**.

   The Highlight Changes dialog box opens, as shown in **Figure 16–10**.

FIGURE 16–10
Highlight Changes dialog box

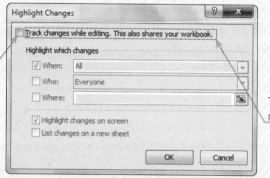

When selected, changes to cell data will be tracked

Tracking changes also makes the workbook shared

4. In the Highlight Changes dialog box, click the **Track changes while editing** check box to select it. Notice that the workbook will be shared when you select this option.

5. If necessary, click the **arrow** to the right of the When text box, and then click **All**, as shown in **Figure 16–11**. All changes made to the workbook will be tracked.

FIGURE 16–11
Options for when to highlight changes

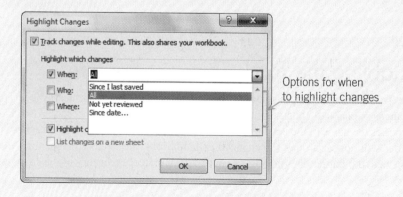

Options for when to highlight changes

6. Click the **Who** check box, then verify that the option is set to Everyone.

7. Click the **Where** check box.

8. Click the **Collapse dialog box** button 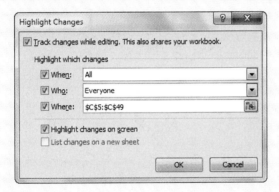 next to the Where text box.

9. Select the range **C5:C49**.

10. Click the **Expand dialog box** button to return to the Highlight Changes dialog box.

11. Click the **Highlight changes on screen** check box, if necessary, and then compare your dialog box to **Figure 16–12**. Selecting this option will display a triangle in the upper-left corner and a border around each cell that has been changed.

FIGURE 16–12
Completed Highlight Changes dialog box

12. Click **OK** to close the Highlight Changes dialog box.

13. You may receive a message that this action will now save the workbook and asking if you want to continue. Click **OK**. Notice that the word Shared appears on the Excel title bar after the filename.

14. Save the workbook and leave it open for the next Step-by-Step.

Making Changes in a Workbook with Tracked Changes

When you see a cell with a border around it, you know that a change has been made. If you place your mouse pointer over the highlighted cell, a callout will appear showing the date, time, original cell data, changed data for the cell, and the name of the person who made the change. Excel does not track changes to worksheet names and formats applied to cells or data. For this next Step-by-Step, you will change data in two cells in the worksheet with the Track Changes feature enabled.

Step-by-Step 16.6

1. Select **cell C5**.

2. Type **654.3**, and then press **Enter**.

3. In cell C6, type **595.9** and then press **Enter**.

4. Select **C10**, type **640.0**, and then press **Enter**. Compare your screen to **Figure 16–13**.

FIGURE 16–13
Worksheet with tracked changes

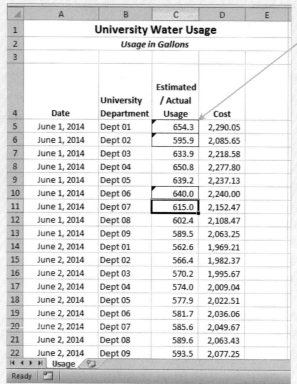

Cells with edited data appear with a border

	A	B	C	D	E
1		**University Water Usage**			
2		*Usage in Gallons*			
3					
4	Date	University Department	Estimated / Actual Usage	Cost	
5	June 1, 2014	Dept 01	654.3	2,290.05	
6	June 1, 2014	Dept 02	595.9	2,085.65	
7	June 1, 2014	Dept 03	633.9	2,218.58	
8	June 1, 2014	Dept 04	650.8	2,277.80	
9	June 1, 2014	Dept 05	639.2	2,237.13	
10	June 1, 2014	Dept 06	640.0	2,240.00	
11	June 1, 2014	Dept 07	615.0	2,152.47	
12	June 1, 2014	Dept 08	602.4	2,108.47	
13	June 1, 2014	Dept 09	589.5	2,063.25	
14	June 2, 2014	Dept 01	562.6	1,969.21	
15	June 2, 2014	Dept 02	566.4	1,982.37	
16	June 2, 2014	Dept 03	570.2	1,995.67	
17	June 2, 2014	Dept 04	574.0	2,009.04	
18	June 2, 2014	Dept 05	577.9	2,022.51	
19	June 2, 2014	Dept 06	581.7	2,036.06	
20	June 2, 2014	Dept 07	585.6	2,049.67	
21	June 2, 2014	Dept 08	589.6	2,063.43	
22	June 2, 2014	Dept 09	593.5	2,077.25	

Usage

Ready

5. Save and close the workbook. You will reopen the workbook in the next step to see how the file opens and remembers the history of tracked changes.

Accepting or Rejecting Tracked Changes

As you review changes made to cells, you can accept or reject the changes. The Accept or Reject Changes dialog box will show the name of the person who made the change, the date and time of the change, the cell name, the original data in the cell, and the changed data. You can accept or reject each change one at a time or you can accept or reject all changes at once. In this next Step-by-Step, you will accept and reject changes.

Step-by-Step 16.7

1. Reopen the **Water Usage by Department** file.

2. Click the **Review** tab, on the Review tab, click the **Track Changes** arrow button, and then click **Accept/Reject Changes** in the Changes group. The Select Changes to Accept or Reject dialog box opens, as shown in **Figure 16–14**.

Lets you view all changes not yet reviewed

FIGURE 16–14
Select Changes to Accept or Reject dialog box

3. Verify that *Not yet reviewed* is located in the When text box, and then click **OK**. The Accept or Reject Changes dialog box opens, as shown in **Figure 16–15**. The first change that appears is the change to cell C5.

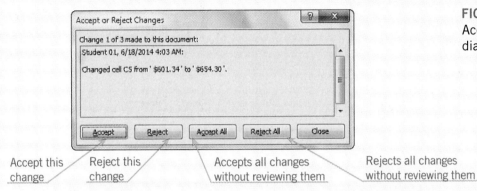

FIGURE 16–15
Accept or Reject Changes dialog box

Accept this change   Reject this change   Accepts all changes without reviewing them   Rejects all changes without reviewing them

4. Click the **Accept** button to accept the first change. The dialog box now shows the change made to cell C6.

5. Click the **Accept** button to accept the second change. The dialog box now shows the change made to cell C10. You realize that you do not need the change in cell C10.

6. Click the **Reject** button. The Accept or Reject Changes dialog box closes. Compare your screen to **Figure 16–16**.

FIGURE 16–16
Worksheet after reviewing changes

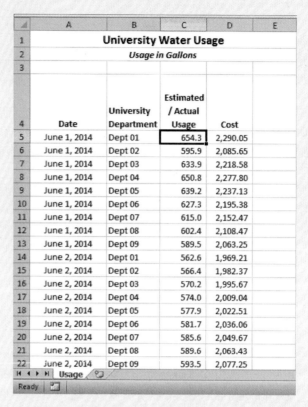

	A	B	C	D	E
1		**University Water Usage**			
2		*Usage in Gallons*			
3					
4	Date	University Department	Estimated / Actual Usage	Cost	
5	June 1, 2014	Dept 01	654.3	2,290.05	
6	June 1, 2014	Dept 02	595.9	2,085.65	
7	June 1, 2014	Dept 03	633.9	2,218.58	
8	June 1, 2014	Dept 04	650.8	2,277.80	
9	June 1, 2014	Dept 05	639.2	2,237.13	
10	June 1, 2014	Dept 06	627.3	2,195.38	
11	June 1, 2014	Dept 07	615.0	2,152.47	
12	June 1, 2014	Dept 08	602.4	2,108.47	
13	June 1, 2014	Dept 09	589.5	2,063.25	
14	June 2, 2014	Dept 01	562.6	1,969.21	
15	June 2, 2014	Dept 02	566.4	1,982.37	
16	June 2, 2014	Dept 03	570.2	1,995.67	
17	June 2, 2014	Dept 04	574.0	2,009.04	
18	June 2, 2014	Dept 05	577.9	2,022.51	
19	June 2, 2014	Dept 06	581.7	2,036.06	
20	June 2, 2014	Dept 07	585.6	2,049.67	
21	June 2, 2014	Dept 08	589.6	2,063.43	
22	June 2, 2014	Dept 09	593.5	2,077.25	

Usage

Ready

7. Save the workbook and leave it open for the next Step-by-Step.

Disabling the Track Changes Feature

▶ **VOCABULARY**
disable

If you decide that you no longer need to track changes in the workbook, you can disable the Track Changes feature. When you *disable* Track Changes, the workbook will no longer be shared. Before you disable the Track Changes feature, you should make sure all the changes are reviewed, accepted, or rejected since all change history will be removed when you disable this feature. You will now disable the Track Changes feature from the workbook.

Step-by-Step 16.8

1. In the Changes group, click the **Track Changes** button arrow, and then click **Highlight Changes**.

2. In the Highlight Changes dialog box, click the **Track changes while editing** check box to deselect it.

3. Click **OK** to close the Highlight Changes dialog box. A message box appears letting you know selecting this option will remove the workbook from shared use, as shown in **Figure 16–17**.

Message indicates that workbook will no longer be shared and change history will be lost

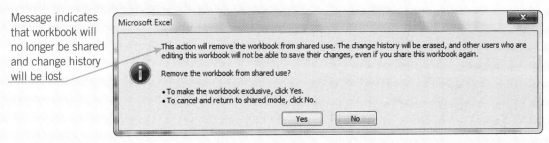

FIGURE 16–17
Message about removing workbook from shared use

4. Click **Yes**. Notice that the word Shared is no longer in the Excel title bar.

5. Save and close the workbook.

Creating a Shared Workbook

The Share Workbook feature allows several people to work in a workbook simultaneously. For example, an airline company may have several employees that need to view a workbook containing reservation rate information. Allowing multiple employees to view and make changes to a workbook at one time helps to maximize efficiency and productivity.

With a ***shared workbook***, changes made by multiple users are tracked. You can then choose to accept or reject these changes. If a conflict occurs from different people making changes to the same cell, Excel provides a prompt that enables you to resolve the conflict by choosing which change you want to keep. You enable the Share Workbook feature using the Share Workbook dialog box.

▶ **VOCABULARY**
shared workbook

The Advanced tab in the Share Workbook dialog box, shown in **Figure 16–18**, gives you several options for managing workbook changes. These options are described in **Table 16–1**.

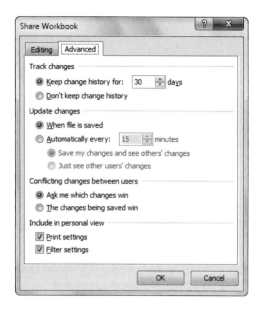

FIGURE 16–18   Advanced tab settings in the Share Workbook dialog box

TABLE 16–1   Advanced options in the Share Workbook dialog box

OPTION	DESCRIPTION
Track changes	You can choose to keep a history of changes made to the shared file or select the option so no history of changes will be kept.
Update changes	Allows you to update changes automatically when the file is saved or based on the minutes you enter, such as update changes every 15 minutes.
Conflicting changes between users	The Ask me which changes win option displays the Resolve Conflict dialog box so that you may see which changes caused a conflict. You can then decide which changes to keep. The second option automatically keeps the changes made within the file being saved.
Include in personal view	Allows you to keep your personal print options, such as page breaks, as well as any filter settings.

In the next Step-by-Step, you will enable a workbook to be shared.

Step-by-Step 16.9

1. Open the **Airline Rates** file from the drive and folder where your Data Files are stored.

2. Save the workbook as **Airline Rates Shared**, followed by your initials.

3. Click the **Review** tab, and then click the **Share Workbook** button in the Changes group. The Share Workbook dialog box opens, as shown in **Figure 16–19**.

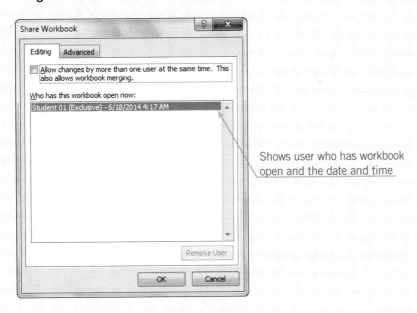

Shows user who has workbook open and the date and time

FIGURE 16–19
Share Workbook dialog box

4. Click the **Allow changes by more than one user at the same time** check box to select it.

5. Click the **Advanced** tab.

6. In the Update changes section, click the **Automatically every 15 minutes** option button to select it.

7. Click **OK** to close the Share Workbook dialog box. A message box appears letting you know that the workbook will now be saved.

8. Click **OK** to save the workbook and close the message box.

9. Leave the workbook open for the next Step-by-Step.

Modifying a Shared Workbook

When you make changes to a shared workbook, Excel keeps track of the changes. However, the changes are not marked with a border as they are when the Track Changes feature is used.

For this next Step-by-Step, you will edit data in the workbook. You will save and close the workbook, and then reopen the workbook. By saving, closing, and reopening the shared workbook, you will be pretending to be another user opening and making changes to the workbook. After making changes, you will save the workbook and then go through the process of reviewing, accepting, and rejecting changes.

Step-by-Step 16.10

1. Click cell **C10**.

2. Type **300**, and then press the **Tab** key to move to cell D10.

3. Type **600**, and then press **Enter**.

4. With cell **C11** selected, type **80**, and then press **Enter**.

5. Save and close the workbook.

6. Reopen the **Airline Rates Shared** workbook.

7. Select cell **D11**, type **145**, and then press **Enter**.

8. Save the workbook, and then compare your worksheet to **Figure 16–20**.

FIGURE 16–20
Shared workbook with changes

	A	B	C	D	E
1		Stay in the Air Airlines			
2		Rate Table			
3					
4					
5	Flight From	Flight To	One-Way Fare	Round-Trip Fare	
6	Seattle	Dallas	$ 172.00	$ 215.00	
7	Dallas	New Orleans	$ 79.00	$ 120.00	
8	New Orleans	Atlanta	$ 112.00	$ 200.00	
9	Atlanta	Houston	$ 213.00	$ 400.00	
10	Houston	San Francisco	$ 300.00	$ 600.00	
11	San Francisco	Los Angeles	$ 80.00	$ 145.00	
12	Los Angeles	Chicago	$ 220.00	$ 220.00	
13	Chicago	New York	$ 215.00	$ 360.00	
14	New York	Chicago	$ 172.00	$ 299.00	
15	Dallas	Sacramento	$ 225.00	$ 425.00	
16	San Francisco	Sacramento	$ 75.00	$ 150.00	
17	Dallas	Houston	$ 75.00	$ 150.00	
18	Phoenix	Los Angeles	$ 175.00	$ 330.00	
19	New York	Phoenix	$ 335.00	$ 575.00	
20	Seattle	Chicago	$ 240.00	$ 385.00	
21	Chicago	Los Angeles	$ 225.00	$ 395.00	
22	Kansas City	Houston	$ 118.00	$ 212.00	
23	Salt Lake City	New York	$ 198.00	$ 375.00	
24	Augusta	Philadelphia	$ 98.00	$ 176.00	
25	Miami	Dallas	$ 196.00	$ 355.00	
26	Los Angeles	New York	$ 300.00	$ 575.00	
27					

9. On the Review tab in the Changes group, click the **Track Changes** button arrow and then click **Accept/Reject Changes**.

10. Make sure the **When** check box is selected with the **Not yet reviewed option** selected, and then click **OK** to start reviewing the changes. The Accept or Reject Changes dialog box shows the first cell where a change was made, including the date and time the change was made as well as the amount in the cell before the change was made. See **Figure 16–21**.

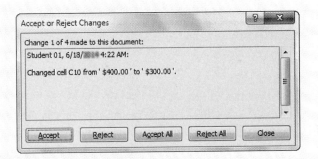

FIGURE 16–21
Accept or Reject Changes
dialog box

11. Click **Accept** to accept the change.

12. Click **Accept** to accept the next change.

13. Click **Reject** twice to reject the changes in cells C11 and D11, then compare your screen to **Figure 16–22**.

FIGURE 16–22
Worksheet with shared changes completed

	A	B	C	D	E
1		**Stay in the Air Airlines**			
2		*Rate Table*			
3					
4					
5	**Flight From**	**Flight To**	**One-Way Fare**	**Round-Trip Fare**	
6	Seattle	Dallas	$ 172.00	$ 215.00	
7	Dallas	New Orleans	$ 79.00	$ 120.00	
8	New Orleans	Atlanta	$ 112.00	$ 200.00	
9	Atlanta	Houston	$ 213.00	$ 400.00	
10	Houston	San Francisco	$ 300.00	$ 600.00	
11	San Francisco	Los Angeles	$ 79.00	$ 113.00	
12	Los Angeles	Chicago	$ 220.00	$ 220.00	
13	Chicago	New York	$ 215.00	$ 360.00	
14	New York	Chicago	$ 172.00	$ 299.00	
15	Dallas	Sacramento	$ 225.00	$ 425.00	
16	San Francisco	Sacramento	$ 75.00	$ 150.00	
17	Dallas	Houston	$ 75.00	$ 150.00	
18	Phoenix	Los Angeles	$ 175.00	$ 330.00	
19	New York	Phoenix	$ 335.00	$ 575.00	
20	Seattle	Chicago	$ 240.00	$ 385.00	
21	Chicago	Los Angeles	$ 225.00	$ 395.00	
22	Kansas City	Houston	$ 118.00	$ 212.00	
23	Salt Lake City	New York	$ 198.00	$ 375.00	
24	Augusta	Philadelphia	$ 98.00	$ 176.00	
25	Miami	Dallas	$ 196.00	$ 355.00	
26	Los Angeles	New York	$ 300.00	$ 575.00	
27					
28					

14. Save and close the workbook.

SUMMARY

In this lesson, you learned:

- You can add password protection to a worksheet to prevent unwanted changes.

- When password protection is no longer needed, you can remove it from a worksheet.

- You can add password protection to an entire workbook.

- A password can be removed from the workbook.

- You can track changes in a workbook by enabling the Track Changes feature.

- The Track Changes feature keeps a history of the changes made.

- You can accept or reject tracked changes.

- If you no longer need to track changes, you can disable the Track Changes feature.

- Several users can use the same workbook at the same time with the Share Workbook feature enabled.

- You can make changes to a shared workbook.

■ VOCABULARY

Define the following terms:

case sensitive   enable   password
decrypt   encrypt   shared workbook
disable

■ REVIEW QUESTIONS

TRUE / FALSE

Circle T if the statement is true or F if the statement is false.

T   F   **1.**   When a worksheet is password protected, the worksheet cannot be viewed.

T   F   **2.**   After password protection is added to a workbook, it cannot be removed.

T   F   **3.**   If the Track Changes feature is enabled, a border appears around cells that are changed.

T   F   **4.**   You can accept or reject tracked changes.

T   F   **5.**   If several users need to view and make changes to a workbook at the same time, you can enable the Share Workbook feature.

FILL IN THE BLANK

Complete the following sentences by writing the correct word or words in the blanks provided.

1. A(n) _____ is a sequence of characters, known only to you, that is required for access to a file if it is protected.

2. Passwords are _____, which means that if a password is CAT, it cannot be entered as "cat" or "Cat".

3. When you password-protect a workbook, you are _____ the workbook data so that if an unauthorized person tries to pry into the file, they will see only unintelligible symbols.

4. If a workbook is shared, you will see the word _____ appear in the Excel title bar.

5. When the Track Changes feature is enabled, a(n) _____ appears around a cell when a change is made to it.

WRITTEN QUESTIONS

Write a brief answer to the following questions.

1. Explain the features of a workbook with the Track Changes features enabled.

2. Explain the benefits of creating a shared workbook.

3. Explain what is meant by the term case sensitive.

4. Explain how you would remove password protection from a workbook.

5. Explain why you might want to reject a change when using Track Changes.

■ PROJECTS

If you have a SAM 2010 user profile, your instructor may have assigned an autogradable version of the indicated project. If so, log into the SAM 2010 Web site at *www.cengage.com/sam2010* to download the instruction and start files.

PROJECT 16–1

1. Open the **Cost and Sales** file from the drive and folder where your Data Files are stored.

2. Save the workbook as **Cost and Sales Prices**, followed by your initials.

3. Add password protection to the Inventory worksheet using the password **Dog5**.

4. Click any cell in the worksheet and try to make a change. You should see a message box letting you know that the worksheet is protected.

5. Click OK to close the message box.

6. Save and close the workbook.

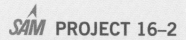 **PROJECT 16–2**

1. Open the **Best Diamonds** file from the drive and folder where your Data Files are stored.

2. Save the workbook as **Best Diamonds List**, followed by your initials.

3. Enable the Track Changes features using All for When and Everyone for Who.

4. Click OK to save the workbook.

5. Click cell B9, type **3300**, and then press Enter.

6. Click cell B16, type **7350**, and then press Enter.

7. Click the Track Changes button, and then click Accept/Reject Changes. If necessary, click OK to save the workbook.

8. Reject the change in cell B9.

9. Accept the change in B16.

10. Save and close the workbook.

PROJECT 16–3

1. Open the **New York College** file from the drive and folder where your Data Files are stored.

2. Save the workbook as **New York College Sports**, followed by your initials.

3. Add password protection to the workbook with the password **Kitten**.

4. Save and close the workbook.

5. Open the **New York College Sports** workbook.

6. Enter the password so you can view the file.

7. Click cell D6, type **50**, and then press Enter.

8. Save and close the workbook.

■ CRITICAL THINKING

ACTIVITY 16–1

Hobby Store is a company owned by two brothers. As the company's accountant, you make changes to the product costs and quantities on a regular basis. Both brothers want to review your changes. You decide to open the **Hobby Store** file and use the Track Changes feature. You've just received the price changes as shown below.

CELL	CHANGE
F8	1.99
E22	40

Turn on the Track Changes feature and then make these changes. When you are done, print the worksheet. Save the workbook as **Hobby Store Inventory**, followed by your initials.

ACTIVITY 16–2

You want to create a shared workbook for people on your office project team. Using Excel's Help system, explain if it is possible to create a shared workbook on a computer network.

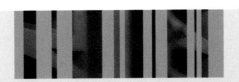

LESSON 17

Importing and Exporting Data

■ OBJECTIVES

Upon completion of this lesson, you should be able to:

- Import data from Microsoft Access.
- Import a text file.
- Use the Document Inspector.
- Save a file as a PDF document.
- Export a file to SkyDrive.
- Use signature lines.

■ VOCABULARY

delimited

export

fixed width

import

signature line

SkyDrive

Introduction

▶ **VOCABULARY**

import

export

Excel offers the ability to import and export data. *Importing* refers to bringing data from other programs, such as Access or Word, into an Excel workbook. *Exporting* refers to taking Excel data from a workbook and sending it to another program or to the Web. Before you export data, you may want to save the file as a PDF (Portable Document File). When the workbook is saved as a PDF, it can be viewed without having to install Excel to open it.

In Excel, you can hide comments and columns or rows of data, which allows you to present specific information to different audiences. Before you send a workbook to other individuals or export it to the Web, you can use the Document Inspector to find any hidden information and then choose whether to remove it from the workbook.

To share a workbook with others on the Web, you can export the file to the Web. Microsoft provides 25GB of free space on the Web for each individual who creates a SkyDrive account. In this lesson, you will also learn about signature lines. Signature lines provide security for a file. They inform users that the file format is final and cannot be changed, and that a signature is required on the signature line.

Importing Data from Microsoft Access

Microsoft Access is a database program included in some versions of Microsoft Office. Access is used to store large amounts of data and provides for easy viewing and printing of data. If you use Access, you may want to bring the data from Access into Excel so that you can add formulas and analyze the data. Excel works well with Access data and provides an easy method for importing data from an Access database into an Excel workbook. The next Step-by-Step takes you through the process of importing Access data into Excel.

Step-by-Step 17.1

1. Start Excel, and then create a new workbook.
2. On the Ribbon, click the **Data** tab, and then click the **From Access** button in the Get External Data group. The Select Data Source dialog box opens, as shown in **Figure 17–1**.

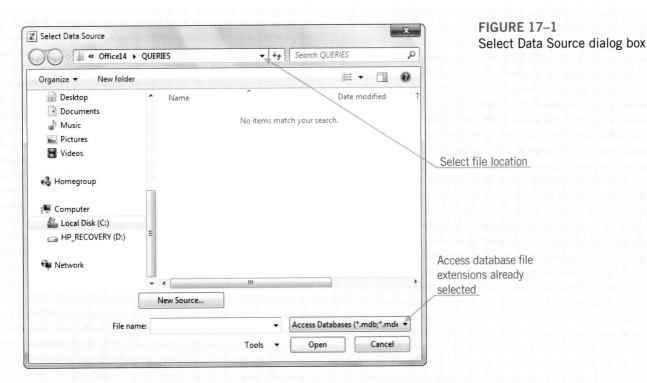

FIGURE 17–1
Select Data Source dialog box

3. Navigate to the drive and folder where you store your Data Files, click **Customer.accdb**, and then click **Open**. The Import Data dialog box opens, as shown in **Figure 17–2**. The Import Data dialog box offers options for viewing the imported data.

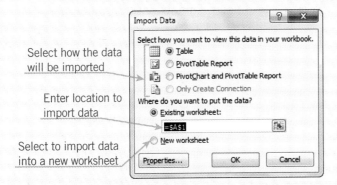

FIGURE 17–2
Import Data dialog box

4. Accept the default option (Table) and then click **OK** to import the data. The data appears in the worksheet in the form of a table with AutoFilters. See **Figure 17–3**.

FIGURE 17–3
Imported
Access data

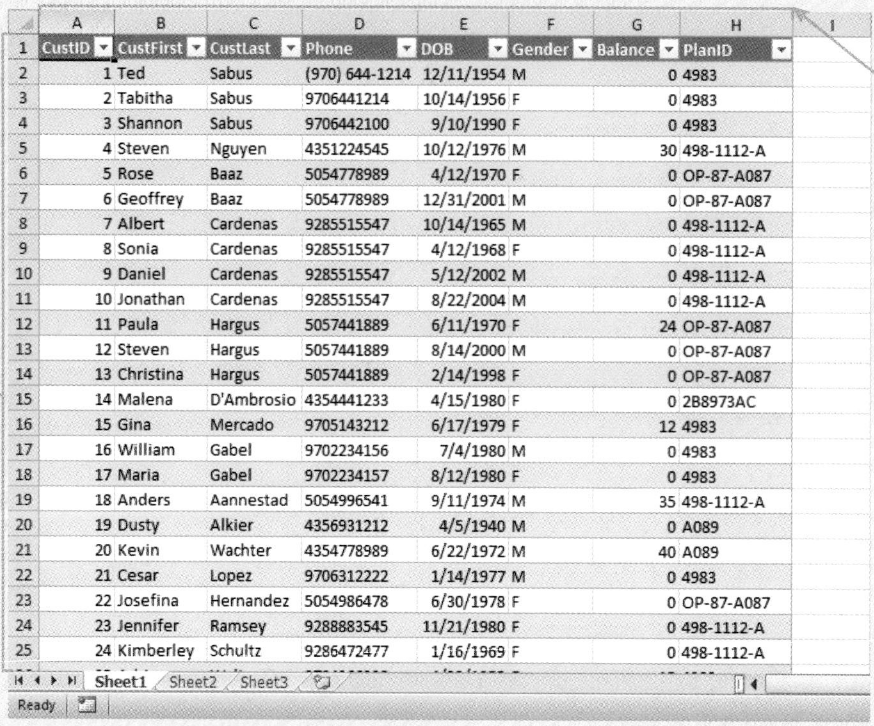

Data imported as a table

AutoFilters added to imported data

	CustID	CustFirst	CustLast	Phone	DOB	Gender	Balance	PlanID
1	CustID	CustFirst	CustLast	Phone	DOB	Gender	Balance	PlanID
2	1 Ted	Sabus	(970) 644-1214	12/11/1954	M		0	4983
3	2 Tabitha	Sabus	9706441214	10/14/1956	F		0	4983
4	3 Shannon	Sabus	9706442100	9/10/1990	F		0	4983
5	4 Steven	Nguyen	4351224545	10/12/1976	M		30	498-1112-A
6	5 Rose	Baaz	5054778989	4/12/1970	F		0	OP-87-A087
7	6 Geoffrey	Baaz	5054778989	12/31/2001	M		0	OP-87-A087
8	7 Albert	Cardenas	9285515547	10/14/1965	M		0	498-1112-A
9	8 Sonia	Cardenas	9285515547	4/12/1968	F		0	498-1112-A
10	9 Daniel	Cardenas	9285515547	5/12/2002	M		0	498-1112-A
11	10 Jonathan	Cardenas	9285515547	8/22/2004	M		0	498-1112-A
12	11 Paula	Hargus	5057441889	6/11/1970	F		24	OP-87-A087
13	12 Steven	Hargus	5057441889	8/14/2000	M		0	OP-87-A087
14	13 Christina	Hargus	5057441889	2/14/1998	F		0	OP-87-A087
15	14 Malena	D'Ambrosio	4354441233	4/15/1980	F		0	2B8973AC
16	15 Gina	Mercado	9705143212	6/17/1979	F		12	4983
17	16 William	Gabel	9702234156	7/4/1980	M		0	4983
18	17 Maria	Gabel	9702234157	8/12/1980	F		0	4983
19	18 Anders	Aannestad	5054996541	9/11/1974	M		35	498-1112-A
20	19 Dusty	Alkier	4356931212	4/5/1940	M		0	A089
21	20 Kevin	Wachter	4354778989	6/22/1972	M		40	A089
22	21 Cesar	Lopez	9706312222	1/14/1977	M		0	4983
23	22 Josefina	Hernandez	5054986478	6/30/1978	F		0	OP-87-A087
24	23 Jennifer	Ramsey	9288883545	11/21/1980	F		0	498-1112-A
25	24 Kimberley	Schultz	9286472477	1/16/1969	F		0	498-1112-A

Sheet1 / Sheet2 / Sheet3

Ready

5. Save the workbook as **Access Import**, followed by your initials.
6. Close the workbook.

Importing Text Data

You can import text into an Excel worksheet. In Excel, you can change the fonts, formats, and analyze the imported data. Text formats that can be imported into Excel include .txt, .csv, or .prn.

When you import text, the Text Import Wizard opens and walks you through steps to import the data. In the first step of the Text Import Wizard, you need to identify the type of data in the imported file as delimited or fixed width. **Delimited** data is separated by a tab, semicolon, comma, or space. **Fixed width** data is separated at the same place in each cell, such as after 15 characters. If you select the Delimited option, you need to select which character will be used to separate the columns in Step 2. In the final step of the Text Import Wizard, you select the format for the imported data. Selecting General will convert the number values to a number format, date values to dates, and the remaining text data will be brought in as text. You can also choose to import everything as text, or if all the data are dates, you can select the Date format option. In this next Step-by-Step, you will import text that is in a .txt file format and then make changes to the data after it is imported.

▶ **VOCABULARY**
delimited

fixed width

Step-by-Step 17.2

1. Start Excel, and then create a new workbook.

2. Click the **Data** tab, and then click the **From Text** button in the Get External Data group. The Import Text File dialog box opens, as shown in **Figure 17–4**.

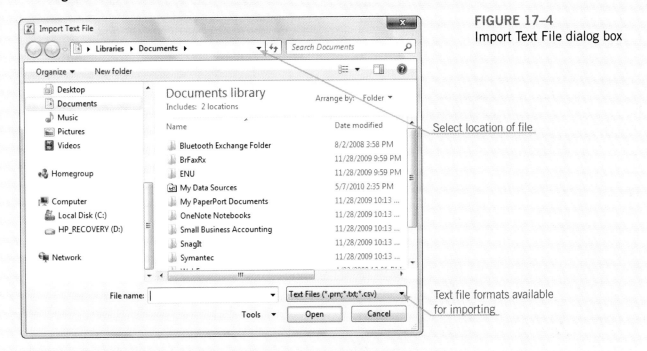

FIGURE 17–4
Import Text File dialog box

3. Navigate to the drive and folder where you store your Data Files, click **Pacific Sales.txt**, and then click **Import**. The Text Import Wizard – Step 1 of 3 dialog box opens, as shown in **Figure 17–5**. The wizard recognizes the imported data as delimited.

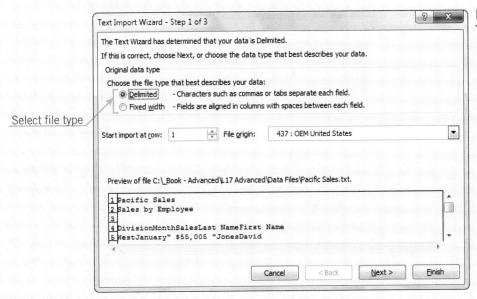

FIGURE 17–5
Text Import Wizard – Step 1 of 3

4. Leave the Delimited option button selected and then click **Next**. The Text Import Wizard – Step 2 of 3 dialog box appears, as shown in **Figure 17–6**. The wizard recognizes that the data is separated by tabs.

FIGURE 17–6
Text Import Wizard – Step 2 of 3

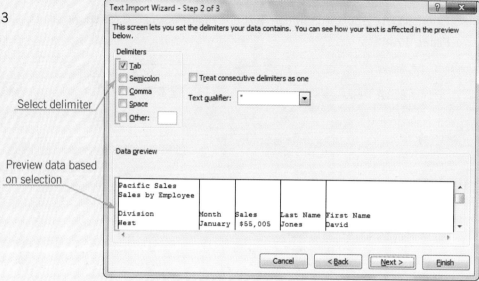

5. Leave the Tab check box selected and then click **Next**. The Text Import Wizard – Step 3 of 3 dialog box opens, as shown in **Figure 17–7**.

FIGURE 17–7
Text Import Wizard – Step 3 of 3

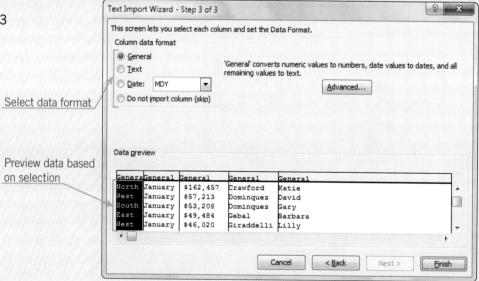

6. In the Text Import Wizard – Step 3 of 3 dialog box, click the **General** option button, if necessary, and then click **Finish**. The Import Data dialog box opens. You can choose to import the data into the cell you specify in the existing worksheet or in a new worksheet.

7. In the Import Data dialog box, click **OK**.

8. Select **C5:C67**.

9. Click the **Home** tab, and in the Number group, click the **Accounting Number Format** button.

10. Save the workbook as **Text Import** followed by your initials, and then close the file.

Using the Document Inspector

Before you export a workbook, you may want to use the Document Inspector to locate possible hidden and personal information. The Document Inspector then gives you the option to delete this information. Hidden data occurs for many reasons and is typical of workbooks that are shared among several people. Hidden data may be in comments, rows, columns, or even entire worksheets. Personal information could be the author's name or title. It might also include company information that you may not want others to see, such as the company name or manager's name. The Document Inspector first offers a checklist of items it will inspect, and then offers you the ability to delete those items from the workbook. For the next Step-by-Step, you will inspect a workbook yourself and then use the Document Inspector to find hidden data and delete this information.

Step-by-Step 17.3

1. Open the **Students** file from the drive and folder where your Data Files are stored.

2. Save the workbook as **Computer Students**, followed by your initials. You will look for comments and hidden information and then use the Document Inspector to create a checklist of items to inspect.

3. Select **cell H8**. Notice that cell H8 has a triangle in the upper-right corner indicating that this cell has a comment.

4. Click the **Review** tab and then click the **Show/Hide Comment** button. The comment will remain visible as you select another cell.

5. To look for hidden worksheets, right-click the **Students** worksheet tab and then click **Unhide** from the shortcut menu. Notice that a worksheet named College Bound Students is hidden, as shown in **Figure 17–8**.

Hidden worksheet

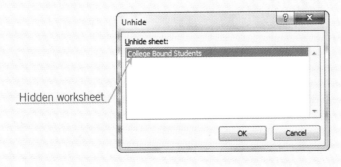

FIGURE 17–8
Unhide dialog box

6. Click **Cancel** to close the Unhide dialog box and keep the College Bound Students worksheet hidden.

7. Click the **File** tab and then click **Print** to view a print preview of the worksheet. Excel automatically adds a page header with the worksheet name and page footer with the page number, as shown in **Figure 17–9**. Information in page headers and footers is another item searched by the Document Inspector.

FIGURE 17–9
Print preview shows header
and footer

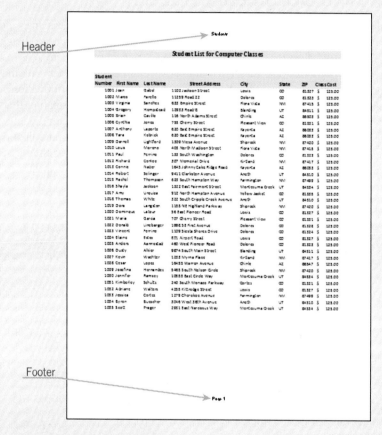

8. On the File tab, click **Info**.

9. Click the **Check for Issues** button. The Check for Issues options display as shown in **Figure 17–10**.

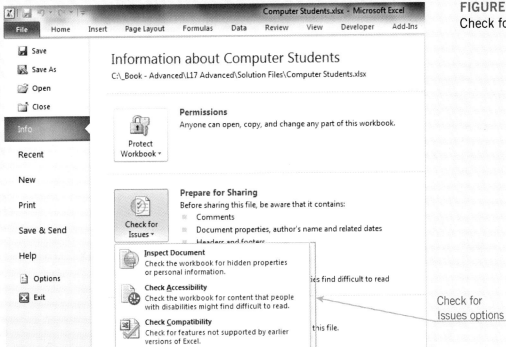

FIGURE 17–10
Check for Issues options

10. Click **Inspect Document**. You may be prompted to save the file before the Document Inspector dialog box opens. The Document Inspector dialog box opens, as shown in **Figure 17–11**. In this dialog box, you can add and remove check marks in order to define what you would like to search for with the Document Inspector.

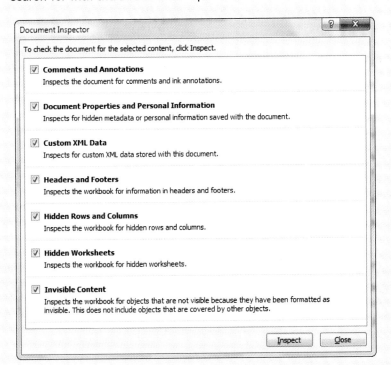

FIGURE 17–11
Document Inspector dialog box

11. Leave all the options selected and then click the **Inspect** button. The Document Inspector returns the search results in a new window, as shown in **Figure 17–12**. In the following steps, you will remove each of these items from the workbook.

FIGURE 17–12
Document Inspector results

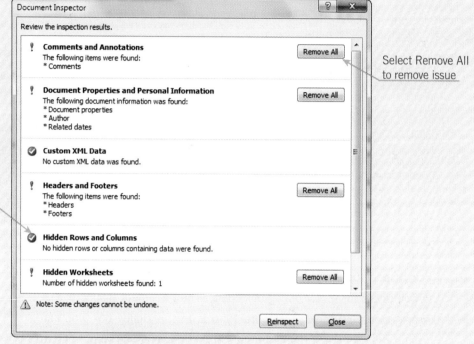

Select Remove All to remove issue

Check mark indicates that no hidden rows or columns containing data were found

12. Click the **Remove All** button next to **Comments and Annotations**. All comments and annotations are removed from the workbook.

13. Click the **Remove All** button next to **Document Properties and Personal Information** and then again for **Headers and Footers**. The Document Inspector dialog box updates automatically.

FIGURE 17–13
Document Inspector after
removing issues

14. Click **Close** to close the Document Inspector dialog box, click the **Home**
    tab, and then verify that the comment in cell H8 is removed.

15. Save your work and leave the workbook open for the next Step-by-Step.

Saving a File as a PDF or an XPS Document

PDF stands for portable document format. When a worksheet is saved as a PDF, it
can be viewed without the reader needing to install Excel. All of the fonts, formats,
and images used in Excel are preserved in the PDF. If the worksheet or workbook
is saved in PDF format, it can be e-mailed or uploaded to a Web site. The XPS format was developed by Microsoft and is similar to PDF. XPS also retains the exact
look of the Excel document and protects it from being changed. The main difference
between the PDF and the XPS is that the PDF is accessible to more people because it
is available on most platforms. PDF files can be viewed in Adobe Acrobat or Adobe
Reader. If you do not have Adobe Reader on your computer, you can download it at
no cost from the Adobe Web site. The XPS format can only be read on some platforms. To save an Excel workbook as a PDF or as an XPS, you click the File tab,
click Save & Send, and then click the Create PDF/XPS Document button. In the next
Step-by-Step, you will save a file as a PDF and then view the file in Adobe Reader.

Step-by-Step 17.4

1. Click the **File** tab and then click **Save & Send**. The Save & Send options are displayed, as shown in **Figure 17–14**.

FIGURE 17–14
File tab with Save & Send options

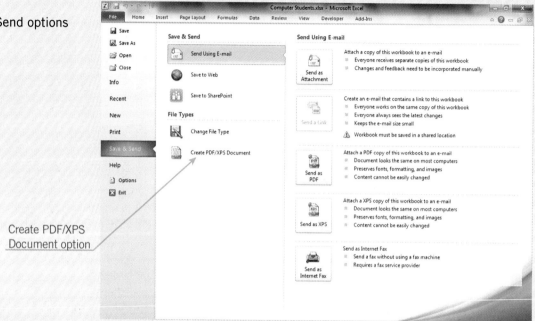

Create PDF/XPS
Document option

2. Click the **Create PDF/XPS Document** option, then click the **Create PDF/ XPS button**.

3. The Publish as PDF or XPS dialog box opens, as shown in **Figure 17–15**.

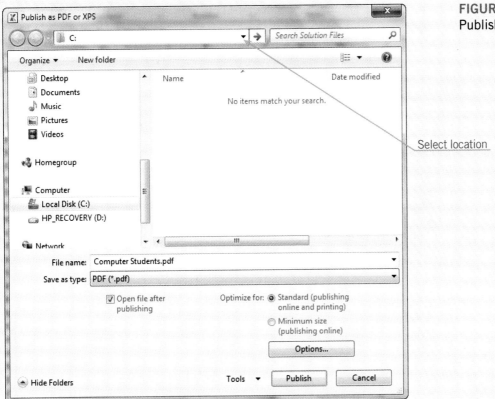

FIGURE 17–15
Publish as PDF or XPS dialog box

4. Verify that the **Open file after publishing** check box is selected (located under Save as type), and then click the **Publish** button. The PDF file opens in Adobe Reader, as shown in **Figure 17–16**. Notice that the file does not display comments, headers, or footers because you removed them using the Document Inspector.

FIGURE 17–16
PDF file displayed

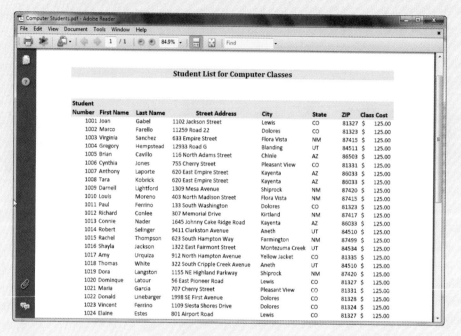

5. Click **File** on the Adobe Reader menu bar, and then click **Exit** to close the file.

6. Save the workbook and leave it open for the next Step-by-Step.

Exporting a File to SkyDrive

If you need to share your files so that other individuals can view them, you might want to consider placing the files on the Web. Microsoft offers 25 GB of online Web storage for free using the *SkyDrive* program. SkyDrive allows you to access and share files online with friends, family members, or co-workers. To access SkyDrive, you must have a Windows Live account.

After you export or upload a file to your SkyDrive account, the file can then be shared and accessed. The file can be downloaded by others from SkyDrive and edited. When the file is downloaded, it opens in Protected View, but it can be edited by clicking the Enable Editing button. If you are concerned about protecting the workbook from being viewed by unauthorized individuals, you can add password protection to the workbook in Excel. In this next Step-by-Step, you will create a SkyDrive account, upload a file to SkyDrive, and then download the file from SkyDrive to your computer.

▶ **VOCABULARY**
SkyDrive

Step-by-Step 17.5

1. Click the **File** tab, and then click **Save & Send**. In the center pane, click **Save to Web**. Your screen should look similar to **Figure 17–17**.

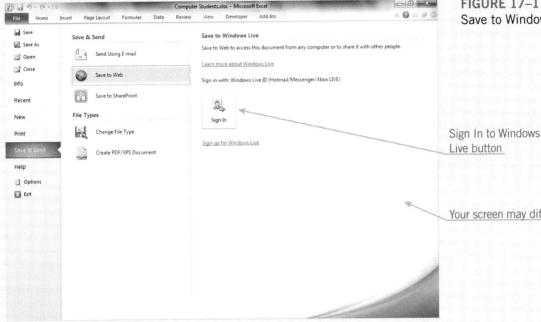

FIGURE 17–17
Save to Windows Live screen

Sign In to Windows Live button

Your screen may differ

2. If you have a Windows Live ID, click the **Sign In** button, enter your ID and password, and then click **OK**. If you do not have an account, click the **Sign up for Windows Live** link and follow the instructions to create a new account. After you access Windows Live, your screen should appear similar to **Figure 17–18**.

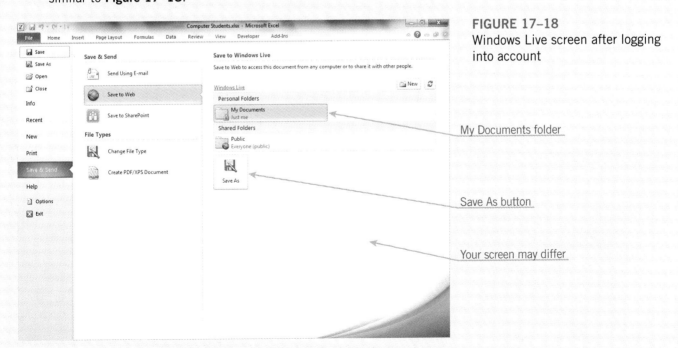

FIGURE 17–18
Windows Live screen after logging into account

My Documents folder

Save As button

Your screen may differ

3. Click the **My Documents** folder to select it, and then click the **Save As** button. The Save As dialog box opens, as shown in **Figure 17–19**.

FIGURE 17–19
Save As dialog box

Filename that will appear in SkyDrive

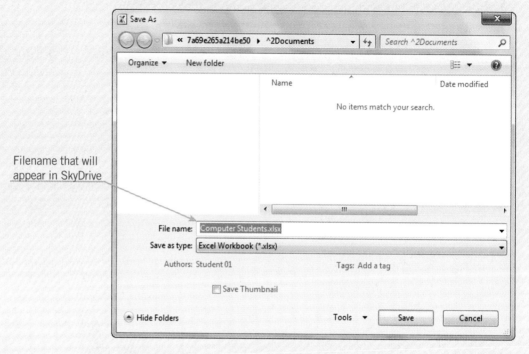

4. Leave the filename as it appears and then click **Save**. The workbook is now available on SkyDrive.

5. Close the workbook. You will now go to the SkyDrive Web site and locate the file.

6. Using your browser, go to **skydrive.live.com**. You should still be signed in.

7. Click the **My Documents** folder and then click the **Computer Students** workbook.

8. If necessary, click the **View** link located above the workbook. Your workbook should appear similar to **Figure 17–20**.

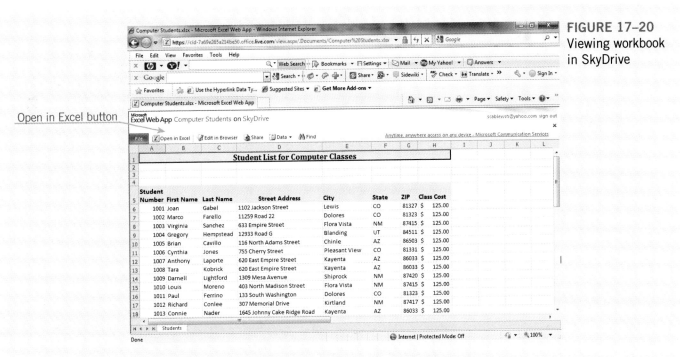

FIGURE 17–20
Viewing workbook
in SkyDrive

Open in Excel button

9. Click the **Open in Excel** button. A message appears indicating that some files may be harmful to your computer.

10. Click **OK** to close the message box.

11. If necessary, enter your Windows Live ID and password, and then click **OK**. The workbook is now open in Excel as a read-only file. See **Figure 17–21**.

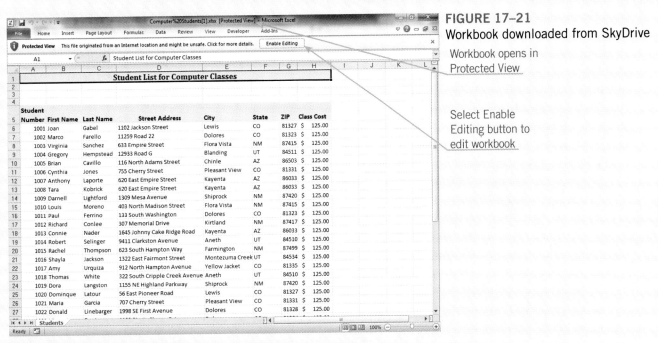

FIGURE 17–21
Workbook downloaded from SkyDrive

Workbook opens in
Protected View

Select Enable
Editing button to
edit workbook

12. Close all open workbooks and then close the browser window.

▶ **VOCABULARY**
signature line

Using a Signature Line

A *signature line* is a security feature that you add to a workbook file so that someone else can sign, or verify, the information. This can be useful if you want to verify the authenticity of a file coming from someone else. You can even have the signature line dated. Also, you can create your own signature file to verify that it came from you. The signature file can be created using the Signature Services from the Office Marketplace at a small cost, or you can create a graphic file, such as a .jpg or .tif file.

Once a signature line has been added, the file is saved as a Read-Only file. Then, the person who has an authorized signature can sign the signature line. Any changes made to the workbook after it is signed will result in the signature being removed, and you will not be able to sign the document again. Likewise, if you try to save the workbook with a different name, the signature line will show the words *Invalid signature* above the signature line. In this next Step-by-Step, you will add a signature line to a workbook file. Then, you will open the file and add the signature of the person verifying the workbook data.

Step-by-Step 17.6

1. Open the **Income** file from the drive and folder where your Data Files are stored and then save the workbook as **Income Statement**, followed by your initials.

2. Select **cell A25** and then click the **Insert** tab.

3. In the Text group, click the **Signature Line** button. A message box displays a disclaimer that Microsoft is not legally responsible for warranty of digital signatures.

4. Click **OK**. The Signature Setup dialog box opens, as shown in **Figure 17–22**.

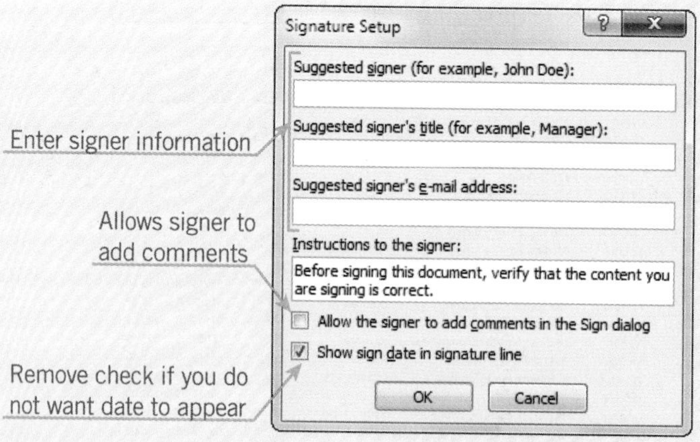

FIGURE 17–22
Signature Setup dialog box

Enter signer information

Allows signer to add comments

Remove check if you do not want date to appear

Signature Setup

Suggested signer (for example, John Doe):

Suggested signer's title (for example, Manager):

Suggested signer's e-mail address:

Instructions to the signer:
Before signing this document, verify that the content you are signing is correct.

☐ Allow the signer to add comments in the Sign dialog
☑ Show sign date in signature line

OK   Cancel

5. In the **Suggested signer** text box, type **Angelina Tarrant**.

6. Click in the **Suggested signer's title** text box, type **Manager**, and then click the **Allow the signer to add comments in the Sign dialog** check box.

7. Click in the **Instructions to the signer** box, type **Verify the income and expenses are correct**, and then click the **Show sign date in signature line** check box to deselect it. Compare your screen to **Figure 17–23**.

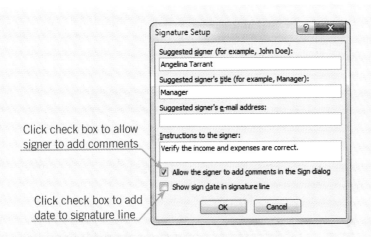

Click check box to allow signer to add comments

Click check box to add date to signature line

FIGURE 17–23
Completed Signature Setup dialog box

8. Click **OK**. The signature line appears in the worksheet.

9. Save the **Income Statement** file, then save the workbook again as **Income Statement for Verification**, followed by your initials.

10. Close the workbook and then reopen the workbook. Notice the yellow information bar above the formula bar, as shown in **Figure 17–24**.

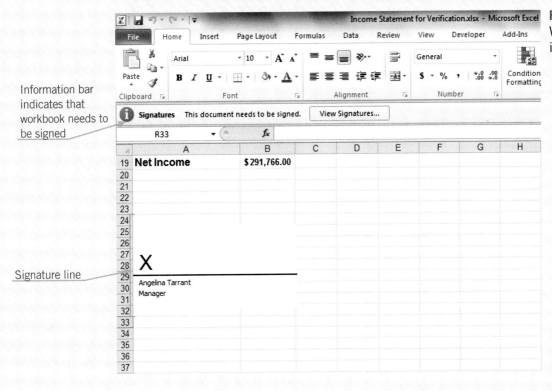

Information bar indicates that workbook needs to be signed

Signature line

FIGURE 17–24
Worksheet with information bar

11. Right-click the **signature placeholder** and then click **Sign**. Click **OK** to accept the disclaimer. The Sign dialog box opens, as shown in **Figure 17–25**.

FIGURE 17–25
Sign dialog box

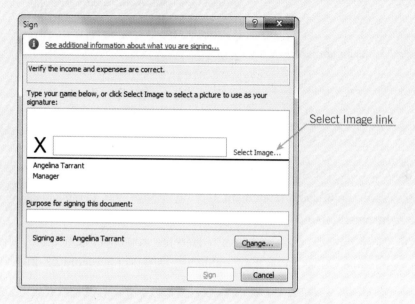

12. Click the **Select Image** link, navigate to your Data Files folder, select the **Angelina Tarrant signature.tif file**, and then click **Select**.

13. Click in the **Purpose for signing the document** text box, and then type **Income and Expenses are correct**. The signature appears in the Sign dialog box, as shown in **Figure 17–26**.

FIGURE 17–26
Sign dialog box with signature

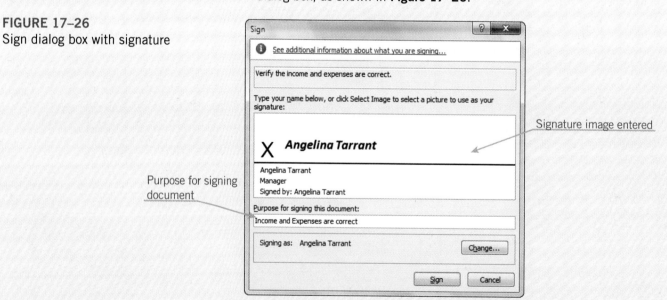

14. Click the **Sign** button. The Signature Confirmation message box appears.

15. Click **OK**. The information bar shows that the workbook is marked as complete. See **Figure 17–27**.

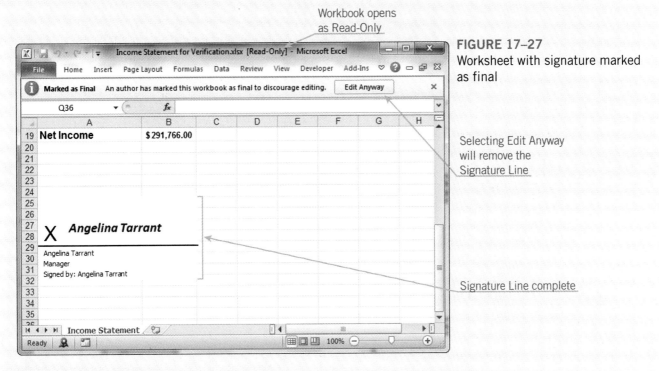

Workbook opens as Read-Only

FIGURE 17–27
Worksheet with signature marked as final

Selecting Edit Anyway will remove the Signature Line

Signature Line complete

16. Close the workbook.

SUMMARY

In this lesson, you learned:

- Data from Microsoft Access can be imported into Excel.
- Text files in the .txt, .csv, and .prn formats can be imported in Excel.
- The Document Inspector locates hidden or sensitive information and lets you keep or remove the data.

- Saving a workbook as a PDF puts the file in a format that can be sent via e-mail, and the document can be viewed without the viewer needing to install Excel.
- An Excel workbook can be exported to SkyDrive.
- Using signature lines adds security to a file so the file cannot be changed without the signature being removed.

 VOCABULARY

Define the following terms:

delimited

export

fixed width

import

signature line

SkyDrive

REVIEW QUESTIONS

TRUE / FALSE

Circle T if the statement is true or F if the statement is false.

T   F   **1.** Workbooks with a signature line can be saved with another filename without removing the signature line.

T   F   **2.** An Excel workbook can be exported to the Web.

T   F   **3.** Importing data refers to bringing data from another program into Excel.

T   F   **4.** Saving an Excel workbook in a PDF file format allows others to view the file without needing to install Excel.

T   F   **5.** Text data cannot be imported into an Excel workbook.

FILL IN THE BLANK

1. Microsoft provides 25GB of free Web space if you create an account in a program called _____.

2. When you send a workbook to another program or to the Web, you are said to be _____ the file.

3. You can use the _____ _____ to locate hidden comments, rows, and columns.

4. To bring data from another program into Excel, you need to _____ the data.

5. If you try to save a workbook that has a signature line with another filename, the signature line will be _____.

WRITTEN QUESTIONS

Write a brief answer to the following questions.

1. Explain the difference between importing and exporting data.

2. Explain the process for exporting a workbook to SkyDrive.

3. Explain the purpose of the Document Inspector.

4. What is the benefit of saving an Excel workbook as a PDF document?

5. Explain how to import a text file into an Excel workbook.

■ PROJECTS

If you have a SAM 2010 user profile, your instructor may have assigned an autogradable version of the indicated project. If so, log into the SAM 2010 Web site at *www.cengage.com/sam2010* to download the instruction and start files.

PROJECT 17–1

1. Start a new Excel workbook.

2. Import **Doctors.accdb** from the drive and folder where your Data Files are stored.

3. Save the workbook as **Doctors Import**.

4. Use the ClinicID AutoFilter to filter for ClinicID 8.

5. Save and close the workbook.

SAM PROJECT 17–2

1. Open the **Regional Managers** file from the drive and folder where your Data Files are stored.

2. Save the workbook as **Regional Managers Weekly Sales**, followed by your initials. You will now look for hidden information using the Document Inspector.

3. Remove the document properties and personal information.

4. Remove the headers and footers.

5. Remove the hidden worksheets. Leave the rows and columns hidden.

6. Save and close the workbook.

PROJECT 17–3

1. Open the **Household** file from the drive and folder where your Data Files are stored.

2. Create a PDF file from the workbook with the filename **Household Addresses**.

3. Close the workbook.

4. Open the PDF file.

5. Print the PDF file.

6. Close the PDF file.

CRITICAL THINKING

ACTIVITY 17–1

1. Locate the text file **Arts and Crafts** in the drive and folder where your Data Files are stored, and then import the file into a new workbook. Save the workbook as **A&C Imported File**, followed by your initials.

2. Examine the data and think of at least one formula that you could add to the workbook.

3. Add any formats that you think will enhance the appearance of the worksheet.

4. Print the sheet and then close the workbook.

ACTIVITY 17–2

1. You have imported a text file into Excel that contains the names, ID numbers, and salaries of all employees at your company. You know that you would like the imported data to change if any modifications are made to it in the original file. Use Excel's Help system to find information on updating or refreshing imported data. Explain how you would proceed.

UNIT REVIEW

Advanced Microsoft Excel

■ REVIEW QUESTIONS

TRUE / FALSE

Circle T if the statement is true or F if the statement is false.

T F **1.** Themes enable you to apply borders, background colors, shading, and graphic effects instantly to an entire workbook.

T F **2.** When you format data as a table, AutoFilters are automatically added to the data.

T F **3.** Protection may be added to worksheets, or to an entire workbook.

T F **4.** If you use the Subtotals feature to place subtotals within worksheet data, they cannot be removed.

T F **5.** An Excel workbook may be shared and accessed with external users by uploading the file to SkyDrive.

T F **6.** A sparkline is a miniature chart that is displayed on its own sheet in a workbook.

T F **7.** To improve data accuracy when entering repetitive data, you can create a drop-down list with the data from which to select.

T F **8.** A VLOOKUP function finds data in the lookup table when a table is arranged horizontally in columns.

T F **9.** Creating a macro is a way to automate some of the common, repetitive tasks you perform in Excel, thereby saving valuable time.

T F **10.** If #DIV/0! appears in a cell instead of the results of a formula, you need to delete the formula since it cannot be repaired.

FILL IN THE BLANK

Complete the following sentences by writing the correct word or words in the blanks provided.

1. _____ applies a font, border, or pattern to worksheet cells when certain conditions exist in those cells.

2. Adding a(n) _____ below a chart lets you view the worksheet data while looking at the chart data series.

3. To join the values of cells together, you use the _____ function.

4. The data in a(n) _____ can be rearranged and summarized in different ways so that you can view the data from various perspectives.

5. The _____ function counts the number of cells that do not have any numbers or text entered in them.

6. The file extension used for a macro-enabled workbook is _____.

7. You can use the _____ feature when your worksheet has lots of data and you want Excel to check all of the formulas and functions in the worksheet for potential problems.

8. To prevent a workbook from being opened by an unauthorized person, you can add a(n) _____ to the workbook.

9. _____ refers to bringing data from other programs, such as Access, into an Excel workbook.

10. Before you export a workbook, you may want to use the _____ to locate possible hidden information in the workbook.

MULTIPLE CHOICE

Select the best response for each of the following statements.

1. In a custom number format that has month, day, and year, you use a _____ to represent the month.

   A. d

   B. y

   C. m

   D. 0

2. The horizontal axis at the bottom of a chart is the _____.

   A. X-axis

   B. Y-axis

   C. Z-axis

   D. U-axis

3. A _____ can appear as numbers or text next to each data marker in the data series.

   A. data point

   B. data list

   C. data axis

   D. data label

4. The _____ feature is a great method for separating data in a worksheet, such as first and last names.

   A. Concatenate

   B. Text Table

   C. Convert Text to Columns

   D. Data Marker

5. A _____ is a visual control that looks like a notepad; clicking selections on it lets you filter data in a PivotTable.

   A. sparkline

   B. slicer

   C. Pivot Note

   D. chart

6. A _____ lets you add a signature to a workbook and marks the workbook as final.

   A. signature line

   B. password

   C. PivotChart

   D. Data Note

7. The _____ function can count cells if they contain text or numbers.

   A. COUNT

   B. SUBTOTAL

   C. COUNTA

   D. SUM

8. The _____ function will only total data that meets a certain condition.

   A. Concatenate

   B. COUNTA

   C. COUNTA

   D. SUMIF

9. The _____ function locates data when it is displayed vertically in the lookup table.

   A. VLOOKUP

   B. HLOOKUP

   C. PivotTable

   D. Filter

10. If several people need to work on a workbook at the same time, you can create a _____ workbook.

   A. shared

   B. PivotChart

   C. themed

   D. table-style

■ PROJECTS

PROJECT 1

The annual sales for each employee at New Western are recorded in a workbook. You decide to add a PivotTable and PivotChart to the workbook so that you can view the data in different ways.

1. Open the **New Western** file from the drive and folder where your Data Files are stored.

2. Save the workbook as **New Western Sales** followed by your initials.

3. Create a PivotTable and Pivot Chart in a new worksheet with the following information:

   Axis Fields: **Division**

   　　　　　　　Last Name

   Values:　　**Sales**

4. Decrease the font size on the X-axis until all of the names are displayed.

5. Format the Total column with the Comma Style and no decimal places.

6. Change the worksheet name for the PivotTable and PivotChart to **Sales Table**.

7. Filter the PivotChart so that only the Northwest division is displayed.

8. Save, print, and close the workbook.

PROJECT 2

The expenses for your three years of law school are recorded in a workbook. You want to create a macro that will add formats to each worksheet in the workbook.

1. Open the **Law School** file from the drive and folder where your Data Files are stored.

2. Save the workbook as a macro-enabled workbook with the filename **Law School Budget** followed by your initials.

3. Create a macro named **Formats** with the shortcut key **Ctrl + F** to add formats to the worksheets as follows:

   a.　The worksheet title should be **Bold, Font Size - 16**, and **Dark Blue, Text 2, Darker 25%**.

   b.　The worksheet subtitle should be **Bold, Font Size - 12, Italic, Dark Blue, Text 2, Lighter 40%**.

   c.　The ranges **A6:A12** and **B5:L5** should have **Dark Blue, Text 2, Darker 25%** font.

   d.　Add totals to the bottom of the month columns.

4. Use the macro to add the formats to each worksheet in the workbook.

5. Save, print, and close the workbook.

PROJECT 3

The Imports file is an income statement. You will create a scenario for store lease, store utilities, and shipping expense variances.

1. Open the **Imports** file from the drive and folder where your Data Files are stored.

2. Save the workbook as **Imports Unlimited** followed by your initials.

3. Create a scenario named **Current Expenses** using the expenses currently in the Income Statement worksheet.

4. Create a scenario named **Increased Expenses**. Enter the following expenses into the scenario:

   Cell **B10** (Store Lease): **83500**

   Cell **B11** (Store Utilities): **26000**

   Cell **B12** (Shipping Expenses): **8500**

5. Create a scenario named **Decreased Expenses**. Enter the following expenses into the scenario:

   Cell **B10** (Store Lease): **45000**

   Cell **B11** (Store Utilities): **20000**

   Cell **B12** (Shipping Expenses): **6000**

6. Print the **Scenario Summary** worksheet.

7. Save and then close the workbook.

PROJECT 4

1. Open the **Corporate** file from the drive and folder where your Data Files are stored.

2. Save the workbook as **Corporate Tees** followed by your initials.

3. Enter a formula in cell **D19** that will calculate the total of the order based on the quantity of tee shirts purchased multiplied by the price.

4. Enable the Track Changes feature to highlight all changes.

5. Enter the following information into the worksheet:

   Cell **B8**:   235

   Cell **B10**:   **Susan Williams**

   Cell **B11**:   **630 North Shore Blvd.**

   Cell **B19**:   5

6. Enter the following information into the worksheet:

   Cell **B8**:   **236**

   Cell **B10**:   **Juan Lopez**

   Cell **B11**:   **444 Southlake**

   Cell **B19**:   **2**

7. Open the Select Changes to Accept or Reject dialog box, and then review and accept the changes.

8. Print the worksheet.

9. Save and close the workbook.

■ CRITICAL THINKING

JOB 1

You are figuring out how much money to save each month for family trips. The monthly amount that needs to be saved will help you determine which trips best fit your budget. You decide to use Goal Seek to find the monthly savings amount for each trip.

1. Open the **Trip Planning** file from the drive and folder where your Data Files are stored.

2. Save the workbook as **Trip Planning Estimates** followed by your initials.

3. You think that the trip to Disneyland will take two years of savings, the trip to Alaska will take four years of savings, and the trip to Costa Rica will take five years of savings. Enter formulas in cells **C4**, **C6**, and **C8** that can be used with Goal Seek to find the monthly payment amount. (*Hint:* You would enter a formula in C4 such as =B4*2*12.)

4. Use Goal Seek to find the monthly payment amount for the trip to Disneyland if it costs $4,000.

5. Use Goal Seek to find the monthly payment amount for the trip to Alaska if it costs $5,000.

6. Use Goal Seek to find the monthly payment amount for the trip to Costa Rica if it costs $7,500.

7. Print the worksheet and save the workbook.

8. Close the workbook.

JOB 2

You are the Inventory Supervisor for a college bookstore. To ensure that your assistants enter correct information into the inventory workbook, you decide to add data validation to the workbook. You will also add drop-down lists to the Item # and Description columns to save time and increase accuracy.

1. Open the **Discount Inventory** file from the drive and folder where your Data Files are stored.

2. Save the workbook as **Discount Interior Inventory** followed by your initials.

3. Add data validation for both the Item # column and the Description column starting in row 65 through row 100. (*Hint*: You should have 17 items for each drop-down list.)

4. To test the drop-down lists, select cell B65, then select W-SWMD.

5. Select cell C65, then select Wallpaper Border – Small.

6. Save and print the Inventory worksheet.

7. Close the workbook.

APPENDIX A

Computer Concepts

The Computer: An Overview

A computer is a machine that is used to store, retrieve, and manipulate data. A computer takes *input*, uses instructions to *process* and *store* that data, and then produces *output*. You enter the data into the computer through a variety of input devices, such as a keyboard or mouse. The processor processes the data to produce information. Information is output presented in many ways such as an image on a monitor, printed pages from a printer, or sound through speakers. Computer *software* is stored instructions or programming that runs the computer. *Memory* inside the computer stores the programs or instructions that run the computer as well as the data and information. Various *storage devices* are used to transfer or safely store the data and information on *storage media*.

A *computer system* is made up of components that include the computer, input, and output devices. Computer systems come in many shapes, sizes, and configurations. The computer you use at home or in school is often called a *personal computer*. *Desktop computers* often have a 'computer case' or a *system unit*, which contains processing devices, memory, and some storage devices. **Figure A–1** shows a typical desktop computer. Input devices such as the mouse or pointing device, and keyboard are attached to the system unit by cables or wires. Output devices, such as the monitor (display device), speakers, and printer are also attached to the system unit by cables or wires. *Wireless technology* makes it possible to eliminate wires and use the airwaves to connect devices. *Laptop* or *notebook* computers have all the essential parts: the keyboard, pointing device, and display device all in one unit. See **Figure A–2** for a typical notebook computer.

FIGURE A–1   A desktop computer system

FIGURE A–2   A laptop computer

When learning about computers, it is helpful to organize the topics into a discussion about the hardware and the software, and then how the computer processes the data.

Computer Hardware

The physical components, devices, or parts of the computer are called *hardware*. Computer hardware includes the essential components found on all computers such as the central processing unit (CPU), the monitor, the keyboard, and the mouse. Hardware can be divided into categories: Input devices, processors, storage devices, and output devices. ***Peripheral devices*** are additional components, such as printers, speakers, and scanners that enhance the computing experience. Peripherals are not essential to the computer, but provide additional functions for the computer.

Input Devices

There are many different types of input devices. You enter information into a computer by typing on a keyboard or by pointing, clicking, or dragging a mouse. A ***mouse*** is a handheld device used to move a pointer on the computer screen. Similar to a mouse, a ***trackball*** has a roller ball that turns to control a pointer on the screen. Tracking devices, such as a ***touchpad***, are an alternative to the trackball or mouse. Situated on the keyboard of a laptop computer, they allow you to simply move and tap your finger on a small electronic pad to control the pointer on the screen.

Tablet PCs allow you to input data by writing directly on the computer screen. Handwriting recognition technology converts handwritten writing to text. Many computers have a microphone or other ***sound input device*** which accepts speech or sounds as input and converts the speech to text or data. For example, when you telephone a company or bank for customer service, you often have the option to say your requests or account number. That is ***speech recognition technology*** at work!

Other input devices include scanners and bar code readers. You can use a ***scanner*** to convert text or graphics from a printed page into code that a computer can process. You have probably seen ***bar code readers*** being used in stores. These are used to read bar codes, such as the UPC (Universal Product Code), to track merchandise or other inventory in a store. See **Figure A–3**.

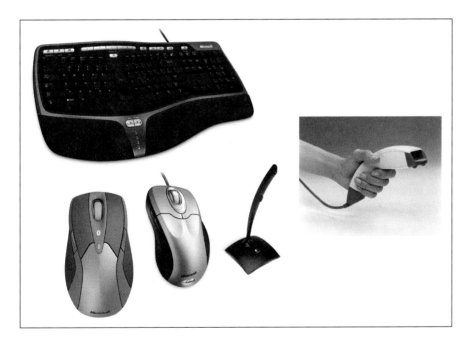

FIGURE A–3   Examples of input devices

Processing Devices

Processing devices are mounted inside the system unit of the computer. The *motherboard* is where the computer memory and other vital electronic parts are stored. See **Figure A–4**. The *central processing unit* (**CPU**) is a silicon chip that processes data and carries out instructions given to the computer. The CPU is stored on the motherboard of the computer. The *data bus* includes the wiring and pathways by which the CPU communicates with the peripherals and components of the computer.

FIGURE A–4   A motherboard

Storage Devices

Computers have to store and retrieve data for them to be of any use at all. Storage devices are both input and output devices. A *storage medium* holds data. Storage media include hard drives, tape, memory cards, solid state flash drives, CDs, and DVDs. A *storage device* is the hardware that stores and retrieves data from a storage medium. Storage devices include hard drives, card readers, tape drives, and CD and DVD drives.

Storage devices use magnetic, optical, or solid state technologies. Magnetic storage uses magnetic fields to store data and can be erased and used over and over again. Optical technology uses light to store data. Optical storage media use one of three technologies: read-only (ROM), recordable (R), or rewritable (RW). Solid state storage uses no moving parts and can be used over and over again. There are advantages and disadvantages to each technology.

Most computers have more than one type of storage device. The main storage device for a computer is the *hard drive* that is usually inside the system unit. Hard drives use magnetic storage. The hard drive reads and writes data to and from a round magnetic platter, or disk. **Figure A–5** shows a fixed storage unit. It is not removable from the computer.

FIGURE A–5 An internal hard drive

External and removable hard drives that can plug into the USB port on the system unit are also available. External drives offer flexibility; allowing you to transfer data between computers easily. See **Figure A–6**. At the time this book was written, typical hard drives for a computer system that you might buy for your personal home use range from 500 gigabytes (GB) to 2 terabytes.

FIGURE A–6 An external hard drive

The *floppy disk drive* is older technology that is no longer available on new computers. Some older computers still have a floppy disk drive which is mounted in the system unit with access to the outside. A floppy disk is the medium that stores the data. You put the floppy disk into the floppy disk drive so the computer can read and write the data. The floppy disk's main advantage was portability. You can store data on a floppy disk and transport it for use on another computer. A floppy disk can hold up to 1.4MB (megabytes) of information. A Zip disk is similar to a floppy disk. A *Zip disk* is also an older portable disk technology that was contained in a plastic sleeve. Each disk held 100MB or 250MB of information. A special disk drive called a *Zip drive* is required to read and write data to a Zip disk.

Optical storage devices include the **CD drive** or **DVD drive** or *Blu-ray drive.* CDs, DVDs, and **Blu-ray drive (BD)** use optical storage technology. See **Figure A–7**.

FIGURE A–7   A CD/DVD/Blu-ray drive

These drives are typically mounted inside the system unit, although external versions of these devices are also available. Most new computers are equipped with CD/DVD burners. That means they have read and write capabilities. You use a CD/DVD drive to read and write CDs and DVDs. A **CD** is a compact disc, which is a form of optical storage. Compact discs can store 700 MB of data. These discs have a great advantage over other forms of removable storage as they can hold vast quantities of information—the entire contents of a small library, for instance. They are also fairly durable. Another advantage of CDs is their ability to hold graphic information, including moving pictures, with the highest quality stereo sound. A **DVD** is also an optical disc that looks like a CD. It is a high-capacity storage device that can contain up to 4.7GB of data, which is a seven-fold increase over a CD. There are two variations of DVDs that offer even more storage—a 2-layer version with 9.4GB capacity and double-sided discs with 17GB capacity. A DVD holds 133 minutes of data on each side, which means that two two-hour full-length feature movies can be stored on one disc. Information is encoded on the disk by a laser and read by a CD/DVD drive in the computer. ***Blu-ray discs (BD)*** offer even more storage capacity. These highest-capacity discs are designed to record full-length high-definition feature films. As of this writing, a BD can store upwards of 35GB of data. Special Blu-ray hardware, including disc players available in gaming systems and Blu-ray burners, are needed to read Blu-ray discs.

A CD drive only reads CDs, a DVD drive can read CDs and DVDs, a Blu-ray drive reads BDs, CDs, and DVDs. CD/DVD/BD drives look quite similar, as do the discs. See **Figure A–8**.

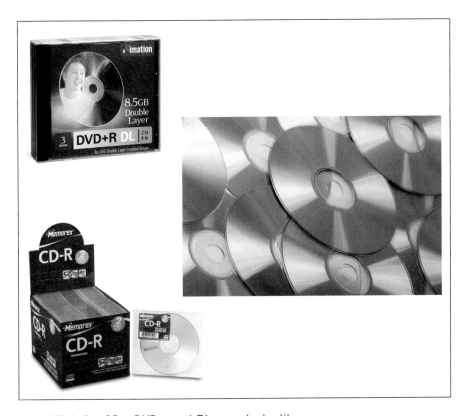

FIGURE A–8   CDs, DVDs, and Blu-rays look alike

APPENDIX A

Solid state storage is another popular storage technology. A **_USB flash drive_** is a very portable small store device that works both as a drive and medium. It plugs directly into a USB port on the computer system unit. You read and write data to the flash drive. See **Figure A–9**.

FIGURE A–9   A flash drive

Solid state card readers are devices that can read solid state cards. Solid state storage is often used in cameras. See **Figure A–10**.

FIGURE A–10   Solid state card and card reader

Magnetic tape is a medium most commonly used for backing up a computer system, which means making a copy of files from a hard drive. Although it is relatively rare for data on a hard drive to be completely lost in a crash (that is, for the data or pointers to the data to be partially or totally destroyed), it can and does happen. Therefore, most businesses and some individuals routinely back up files on tape. If you have a small hard drive, you can use DVDs or CD-ROMs or solid state storage such as a flash drive or memory card to back up your system. **Figure A–11** shows a tape storage system.

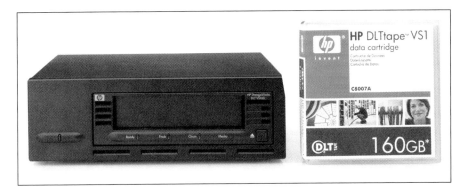

FIGURE A–11   Tape storage system

Output Devices

The *monitor* on which you view your computer work is an output device. It provides a visual representation of the information stored in or produced by your computer. The typical monitor for today's system is a flat-screen monitor similar to a television. Computer monitors typically use *LCD technology*. LCD stands for Liquid Crystal Display. See **Figure A–12**. LCD monitors provide a very sharp picture because of the large number of tiny dots, called *pixels*, which make up the display as well as its ability to present the full spectrum of colors. *Resolution* is the term that tells you how clear an image will be on the screen. Resolution is measured in pixels. A typical resolution is 1024 × 768. A high-quality monitor may have a resolution of 1920 × 1080, or 2560 × 1440 or higher. Monitors come in different sizes. The size of a monitor is determined by measuring the diagonal of the screen. Laptops have smaller monitors than desktop computers. A laptop monitor may be 13", 15", or 17". Desktop monitors can be as large as 19"–27" or even larger.

FIGURE A–12   An LCD monitor

Printers are a type of output device. They let you produce a paper printout of information contained in the computer. Today, most printers use either inkjet or laser technology to produce high-quality print. Like a copy machine, a *laser printer* uses heat to fuse a powdery substance called *toner* to the page. *Ink-jet printers* use a spray of ink to print. Laser printers give the sharpest image and often print more pages per minute (ppm) than ink-jet printers. Ink-jet printers provide nearly as sharp an image, but the wet printouts can smear when they first are printed. Most color printers, or photo printers for printing photographs, are ink-jet printers. Color laser printers are more costly. These printers allow you to print information in a full array of colors, just as you see it on your monitor. See **Figure A–13**.

FIGURE A–13   Printers

Laptop or Notebook Computer

A *laptop computer*, also called a *notebook computer*, is a small folding computer that can literally fit in a person's lap or in a backpack. Within the fold-up case of a laptop is the CPU, data bus, monitor (built into the lid), hard drive (sometimes removable), USB ports, CD/DVD drive, and trackball or digital tracking device. The advantage of the laptop is its portability—you can work anywhere because you can use power either from an outlet or from the computer's internal, rechargeable batteries. Almost all laptops have wireless Internet access built into the system. The drawbacks are the smaller keyboard, smaller monitor, smaller capacity, and higher price, though some laptops offer full-sized keyboards and higher quality monitors. As technology allows, storage capacity on smaller devices is making it possible to offer laptops with as much power and storage as a full-sized computer. See **Figure A–14**.

FIGURE A–14   Laptop computers

Personal Digital Assistants (PDA) and Smartphones

A *Personal Digital Assistant (PDA)* is a pocket-sized electronic organizer that helps you to manage addresses, appointments, expenses, tasks, and memos. If you own a cell phone, chances are it is a *Smartphone* and it can do more than just make and receive phone calls. Today, many handheld devices, such as cell phones and Personal Digital Assistants include features such as a full keypad for text messaging and writing notes, e-mail, a browser for Web access, a calendar and address book to manage contacts and appointments, a digital camera, radio, and digital music player. Most handheld devices also include software for games, financial management, personal organizer, GPS, and maps. See **Figure A–15**.

FIGURE A–15 Smartphones

The common input devices for PDAs and some Smartphones include touch-sensitive screens that accept input through a stylus pen or small keyboards that are either built in to the device or available as software on the screen. Data and information can be shared with a Windows-based or Macintosh computer through a process called synchronization. By placing your handheld in a cradle or through a USB port attached to your computer, you can transfer data from your PDA's calendar, address book, or memo program into your computer's information manager program and vice versa. The information is updated on both sides, making your handheld device a portable extension of your computer.

How Computers Work

All input, processing, storage, and output devices function together to make the manipulation, storage, and distribution of data and information possible. Data is information entered into and manipulated or processed within a computer. Processing includes computation, such as adding, subtracting, multiplying, and dividing; analysis planning, such as sorting data; and reporting, such as presenting data for others in a chart or graph. This next section explains how computers work.

Memory

Computers have two types of memory—RAM and ROM. **RAM**, or ***random access memory***, is the silicon chips in the system unit that temporarily store information when the computer is turned on. RAM is what keeps the software programs up and running and provides visuals that appear on your screen. You work with data in RAM up until you save it to a storage media such as a hard disk, CD, DVD, or solid state storage such as flash drive.

Computers have sophisticated application programs that include a lot of graphics, video, and data. In order to run these programs, computers require a lot of memory. Therefore, computers have a minimum of 512MB of RAM. Typical computers include between 2GB and 4GB of RAM to be able to run most programs. Most computer systems are expandable and you can add on RAM after you buy the computer. The more RAM available for the programs, the faster and more efficiently the machine will be able to operate. RAM chips are shown in **Figure A–16**.

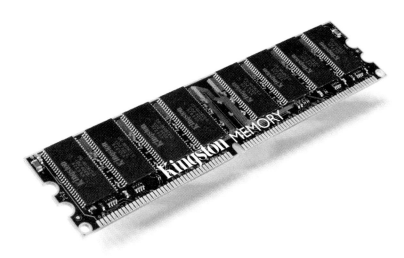

FIGURE A–16   RAM chips

ROM, or *read-only memory*, is the memory that stays in the computer when it is turned off. It is ROM that stores the programs that run the computer as it starts or "boots up." ROM holds the instructions that tell the computer how to begin to load its operating system software programs.

Speed

The speed of a computer is measured by how fast the computer processes each instruction. There are several factors that affect the performance of a computer: the speed of the processor, or the *clock speed*, the *front side bus speed*—the speed of the bus that connects the processor to main memory—the speed in which data is written and retrieved from the hard drive or other storage media, and the speed of the graphics card if you are working on programs that use a lot of graphic images. These all factor into a computer's performance.

The speed of a computer is measured in *megahertz (MHz)* and *gigahertz (GHz)*. Processor speed is part of the specifications when you buy a computer. For example, to run Windows 7 on a computer, you need a processor that has 1 gigahertz (GHz) or faster 32-bit (x86) or 64-bit (x64) processor. Processors are sold by name and each brand or series has its own specifications. Processor manufacturers include AMD, Intel, and Motorola.

Networks

Computers have expanded the world of communications. A *network* is defined as two or more computers connected to share data. *LANs (local area networks)* connect computers within a small area such as a home, office, school, or building. Networks can be wired or wireless. The *Internet* is the largest network in the world connecting millions of computers across the globe. Using the Internet, people can communicate across the world instantly.

Networks require various communication devices and software. *Modems* allow computers to communicate with each other by telephone lines. Modem is an acronym that stands for "MOdulator/DEModulator." Modems convert data in bytes to sound media in order to send data over the phone lines and then convert it back to bytes after receiving data. Modems operate at various rates or speeds. *Network cards* in the system unit allow computers to access networks. A *router* is an electronic device that joins two or more networks. For example, a home network can use a router and a modem to connect the home's LAN to the Internet. A *server* is the computer hardware and software that "serves" the computers on a network. Network technology is sometimes called "client-server." A personal computer that requests data from a server is referred to as a *client*. The computer that stores the data is the *server*. On the Internet, the computer that stores Web pages is the *Web server*. **Figure A–17** shows a network diagram.

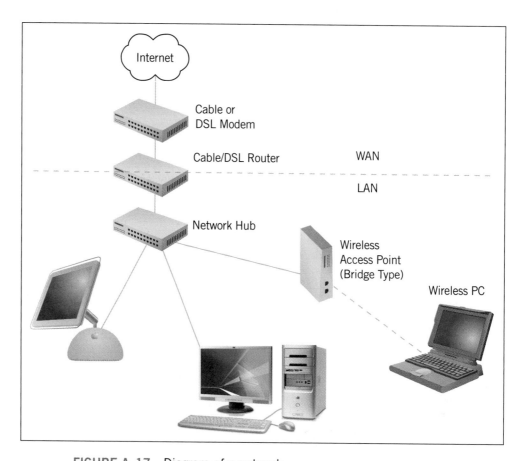

FIGURE A–17   Diagram of a network

Networks have certain advantages over stand-alone computers: they allow communication among the computers; they allow smaller capacity computers to access the larger capacity of the server computers on the network; they allow several computers to share peripherals, such as one printer; and they can make it possible for all computers on the network to have access to the Internet.

Connect to the Internet

To connect to the Internet you need to subscribe to an *Internet Service Provider (ISP)*. There are several technologies available. Connection speeds are measured in bits per second. Upload speeds are slower than download speeds. *Dial-up* is the oldest, and the slowest Internet access technology that is offered by local telephone companies. To get access to the Internet, your computer has to dial out through a phone line. Many people have moved to *always-on connection technologies*. The computer is always connected to the Internet if you turn the computer on, so you don't have to dial out. These always-on faster technologies, known as a *Digital Subscriber Line (DSL)*, include cable connections, satellites, and fiber optic. They are offered by telephone and cable television companies, as well as satellite service providers. It can be noted that satellite Internet access is the most expensive and dialup is the cheapest. DSL is through phone lines. **Table A–1** shows a brief comparison of these technologies based on the time this book was written and average speed assessments.

TABLE A–1 Comparing average Internet access options

FEATURE	SATELLITE	DSL	CABLE	FIBER OPTIC
Max. High Speed	Download speeds ranging anywhere from 768 Kbps up to 5.0 Mbps	Download speed 10 Mbps/ upload speed 5 Mbps	Download speed 30 Mbps/ upload speed 10 Mbps	Download speed 50 Mbps/ upload speed 20 Mbps
Access is through	Satellite dish	Existing phone line	Existing TV cable	Fiber-optic phone lines
Availability	Available in all areas; note that satellite service is sensitive to weather conditions	Generally available in populated areas	Might not be available in rural areas	Might not be available in all areas as fiber-optic lines are still being installed in many areas

Software

A *program* is a set of instructions that the computer uses to operate. *Software* is the collection of programs and other data input that tells the computer how to run its devices, how to manipulate, store, and output information, and how to accept the input you give it. Software fits into two basic categories: systems software and applications software. A third category, network software, is really a type of application.

Systems Software

The *operating system* is the main software or *system software* that runs a computer and often defines the type of computer. There are two main types or platforms for personal computers. The Macintosh computer, or Mac, is produced by Apple Computer, Inc. and runs the Mac operating system. The PC is a Windows-based computer produced by many different companies, but which runs the Microsoft Windows operating system.

Systems software refers to the operating system of the computer. The operating system is a group of programs that is automatically copied in from the time the computer is turned on until the computer is turned off. Operating systems serve two functions: they control data flow among computer parts, and they provide the platform on which application and network software work—in effect, they allow the "space" for software and translate its commands to the computer. The most popular operating systems in use today are the Macintosh operating system, MAC OS X and several different versions of Microsoft Windows, such as Windows XP, Windows Vista, or Windows 7. See **Figure A–18** and **Figure A–19**.

FIGURE A–18   Windows 7 operating system

FIGURE A–19 Mac OS

Since its introduction in the mid-1970s, Macintosh has used its own operating system, a graphical user interface (GUI) system that has evolved over the years. The OS is designed so users "click" with a mouse on pictures, called icons, or on text to give commands to the system. Data is available to you in the WYSIWYG (what-you-see-is-what-you-get) format; that is, you can see on-screen what a document will look like when it is printed. Graphics and other kinds of data, such as spreadsheets, can be placed into text documents. However, GUIs take a great deal of RAM to keep all of the graphics and programs operating.

The original OS for IBM and IBM-compatible computers (machines made by other companies that operate similarly) was DOS (disk operating system). It did not have a graphical interface. The GUI system, Windows™, was developed to make using the IBM/IBM-compatible computer more "friendly." Today's Windows applications are the logical evolution of GUI for IBM and IBM-compatible machines. Windows is a point-and-click system that automatically configures hardware to work together. You should note, however, that with all of its abilities comes the need for more RAM, or a system running Windows will operate slowly.

Applications Software

When you use a computer program to perform a data manipulation or processing task, you are using applications software. Word processors, databases, spreadsheets, graphics programs, desktop publishers, fax systems, and Internet browsers are all applications software.

Network Software

A traditional network is a group of computers that are hardwired (connected together with cables) to communicate and operate together. Today, some computer networks use RF (radio frequency) wireless technology to communicate with each other. This is called a *wireless network*, because you do not need to physically hook the network together with cables. In a typical network, one computer acts as the server, controlling the flow of data among the other computers, called nodes, or clients on the network. Network software manages this flow of information.

History of the Computer

Though various types of calculating machines were developed in the nineteenth century, the history of the modern computer begins about the middle of the last century. The strides made in developing today's personal computer have been truly astounding.

Early Development

The ENIAC, or Electronic Numerical Integrator and Computer, (see **Figure A–20**) was designed for military use in calculating ballistic trajectories and was the first electronic, digital computer to be developed in the United States. For its day, 1946, it was quite a marvel because it was able to accomplish a task in 20 seconds that normally would take a human three days to complete. However, it was an enormous machine that weighed more than 20 tons and contained thousands of vacuum tubes, which often failed. The tasks that it could accomplish were limited, as well.

FIGURE A–20   The ENIAC

From this awkward beginning, however, the seeds of an information revolution grew. The invention of the silicon chip in 1971, and the release of the first personal computer in 1974, launched the fast-paced information revolution in which we now all live and participate.

Significant dates in the history of computer development are listed in **Table A–2**.

TABLE A–2   Milestones in the development of computers

YEAR	DEVELOPMENT
1948	First electronically stored program
1951	First junction transistor
1953	Replacement of tubes with magnetic cores
1957	First high-level computer language
1961	First integrated circuit
1965	First minicomputer
1971	Invention of the microprocessor (the silicon chip) and floppy disk
1974	First personal computer (made possible by the microprocessor)

The Personal Computer

The PC, or personal computer, was mass marketed by Apple beginning in 1977, and by IBM in 1981. It is this desktop device with which people are so familiar and which, today, contains much more power and ability than did the original computer that took up an entire room. The PC is a small computer (desktop size or less) that uses a microprocessor to manipulate data. PCs may stand alone, be linked together in a network, or be attached to a large mainframe computer. See **Figure A–21**.

FIGURE A–21   An early IBM PC

Computer Utilities and System Maintenance

Computer operating systems let you run certain utilities and perform system maintenance to keep your computer running well. When you add hardware or software, you make changes in the way the system operates. With Plug and Play, most configuration changes are done automatically. The *drivers*, software that runs the peripherals, are installed automatically when your computer identifies the new hardware. When you install new software, many changes are made to the system automatically that determine how the software starts and runs.

In addition, you might want to customize the way the new software or hardware works with your system. You use *utility software* to make changes to the way hardware and software works. For example, you can change the speed at which your mouse clicks, how quickly or slowly keys repeat on the keyboard, and the resolution of the screen display. Utilities are included with your operating system. If you are running Windows XP, Windows Vista, or Windows 7, the Windows Control Panel provides access to the many Windows operating system utilities. **Figure A–22** shows the System and Security utilities in the Control Panel for Windows 7.

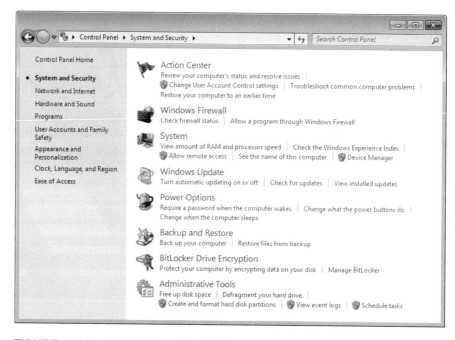

FIGURE A–22   Control Panel for Windows 7

Virus and Spyware Protection

Certain maintenance should be performed regularly on computers. *Viruses* are malicious software programs that can damage the programs on your computer causing the computer to either stop working or run slowly. These programs are created by people, called *hackers*, who send the programs out solely to do harm to computers. Viruses are loaded onto your computer without your knowledge and run against your wishes. *Spyware* is also a form of a program that can harm your computer. There are utilities and programs called *antispyware* and *antivirus* programs that protect your computer from spyware and viruses.

You should install and update your antivirus and spyware protection software regularly, and scan all new disks and any incoming information from online sources for viruses. Some systems do this automatically; others require you to install software to do it.

Disk Maintenance

From time to time, you should run a program that scans or checks the hard drive to see that there are not bad sectors (areas) and look for corrupted files. Optimizing or defragmenting the hard disk is another way to keep your computer running at its best. Scanning and checking programs often offers the option of "fixing" the bad areas or problems, although you should be aware that this could result in data loss.

Society and Computers

The electronic information era has had global effects and influenced global change in all areas of people's lives including education, government, society, and commerce. With the changes of this era have come many new questions and responsibilities. There are issues of ethics, security, and privacy.

Ethics

When you access information—whether online, in the workplace, or via purchased software—you have a responsibility to respect the rights of the person or people who created that information. Digital information, text, images, and sound are very easy to copy and share, however, that does not make it right to do so. You have to treat electronic information with respect. Often images, text, and sound are copyrighted. *Copyright* is the legal method for protecting the intellectual property of the author—the same way as you would a book, article, or painting. For instance, you must give credit when you copy information from the Web or another person's document.

If you come across another person's personal information, you must treat it with respect. Do not share personal information unless you have that person's permission. For example, if you happen to pass a computer where a person left personal banking information software open on the computer or a personal calendar available, you should not share that information. If e-mail comes to you erroneously, you should delete it before reading it.

When you use equipment that belongs to your school, a company for which you work, or others, here are some rules you should follow:

1. Do not damage computer hardware.

2. Do not add or remove equipment without permission.

3. Do not use an access code or equipment without permission.

4. Do not read others' e-mail.

5. Do not alter data belonging to someone else without permission.

6. Do not use the computer for play during work hours or use it for personal profit.

7. Do not access the Internet for nonbusiness related activities during work hours.

8. Do not install or uninstall software without permission.

9. Do not make unauthorized copies of data or software or copy company files or procedures for personal use.

10. Do not copy software programs to use at home or at another site in the company without permission.

APPENDIX A

Security and Privacy

The Internet provides access to business and life-enhancing resources, such as distance learning, remote medical diagnostics, and the ability to work from home more effectively. Businesses, colleges and universities, and governments throughout the world depend on the Internet every day to get work done. Disruptions in the Internet can create havoc and dramatically decrease productivity.

With more and more financial transactions taking place online, *identity theft* is a growing problem, proving a person's online identity relies heavily upon their user-names and passwords. If you do online banking, there are several levels of security that you must pass through, verifying that you are who you claim to be, before gaining access to your accounts. If you divulge your usernames and passwords, someone can easily access your accounts online with devastating effects to your credit rating and to your accounts.

Phishing is a criminal activity that is used by people to fraudulently obtain your personal information, such as usernames, passwords, credit card details, and your Social Security information. Your Social Security number should never be given out online. Phishers send e-mails that look legitimate, but in fact are not. Phishing e-mails will often include fake information saying that your account needs your immediate attention because of unusual or suspected fraudulent activity. You are asked to click a link in the e-mail to access a Web site where you are then instructed to enter personal information. See **Figure A–23** and **Figure A–24**. Phishing e-mail might also come with a promise of winning some money or gifts. When you get mail from people you don't know, the rules to remember are "you never get something for nothing," and "if it looks too good to be true, it's most likely not true."

PayPal would not use a yahoo.com Domain for e-mail

No recipient

Fake URL as you can see from ScreenTip

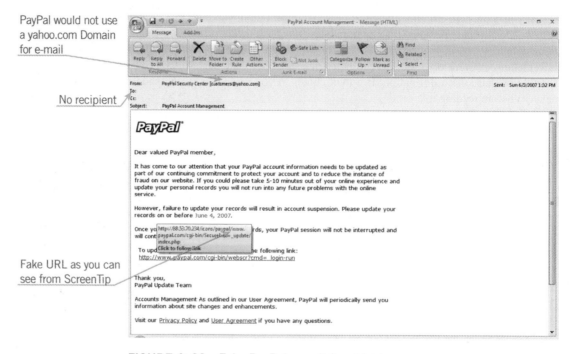

FIGURE A–23   Fake PayPal e-mail for phishing

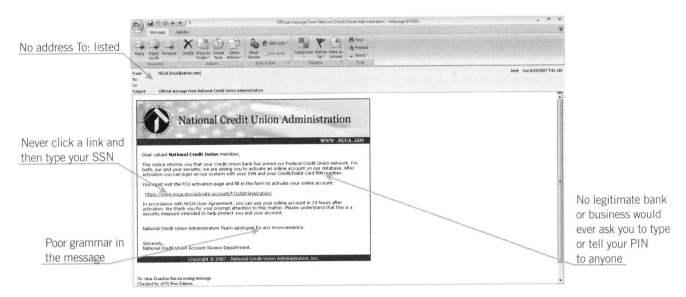

FIGURE A-24 Fake Credit Union e-mail for phishing

Whatever the ruse, when you click the link provided in the phishing e-mail, your browser will open a Web site that looks real, perhaps like your bank's site, eBay, or PayPal. But, in fact, this is a fake site set up to get you to give up your personal information. Phishing sites are growing. You should never click a link provided in an e-mail to get to sites such as your bank, eBay, or PayPal. Your bank or any other legitimate Web site will never ask you to type personal information on a page linked from an e-mail message. Always type the Web page address directly in the browser. Banks and Web sites have been trying to stop phishing sites through technology. Other attempts to reduce the growing number of reported phishing incidents include legislation and simply educating users about the practice.

Just as you would not open someone else's mail, you must respect the privacy of e-mail sent to others. When interacting with others online, you must keep confidential information confidential. Do not endanger your privacy, safety, or financial security by giving out personal information to someone you do not know.

> **EXTRA FOR EXPERTS**
>
> Ebay is an online auction Web site that provides people a way to buy and sell merchandise through the Internet. PayPal is a financial services Web site that provides a way to transfer funds between people who perform financial transactions on the Internet.

Career Opportunities

In one way or another, all careers involve the computer. Whether you are a grocery store clerk using a scanner to read the prices, a busy executive writing a report that includes charts, graphics, and detailed analysis on a laptop on an airplane, or a programmer writing new software—almost everyone uses computers in their jobs. Farmers use computers to optimize crops and order seeds and feed. Most scientific research is done using computers.

There are specific careers available if you want to work with computers in the computer industry. Schools offer degrees in computer programming, computer repair, computer engineering, and software design. The most popular jobs are systems analysts, computer operators, database managers, database specialists, and programmers. Analysts figure out ways to make computers work (or work better) for a particular business or type of business. Computer operators use the programs and devices to conduct business with computers. Programmers write the software for applications or new systems. There are degrees and jobs for people who want to create and maintain Web sites. Working for a company maintaining their Web site can be a very exciting career.

There are courses of study in using CAD (computer-aided design) and CAM (computer-aided manufacturing). There are positions available to instruct others in computer software use within companies and schools. Technical writers and editors must be available to write manuals about using computers and software. Computer-assisted instruction (CAI) is a system of teaching any given subject using the computer. Designing video games is another exciting and ever-growing field of computer work. And these are just a few of the possible career opportunities in an ever-changing work environment. See **Figure A–25**.

FIGURE A–25   Working in the computer field

What Does the Future Hold?

The possibilities for computer development and application are endless. Things that were dreams or science fiction only 10 or 20 years ago are now reality. New technologies are emerging constantly. Some new technologies are replacing old ways of doing things; others are merging with those older methods and devices. Some new technologies are creating new markets. The Internet (more specifically, the Web), cell phones, and DVD videos are just a few inventions of the past decades that did not have counterparts prior to their inventions. We are learning new ways to work and play because of the computer. It is definitely a device that has become part of our offices, our homes, and our lives.

Social networking has moved from the streets and onto the Web. People meet and greet through the Internet using sites such as MySpace, Facebook, and Twitter.

Emerging Technologies

Today the various technologies and systems are coming together to operate more efficiently. Convergence is the merging of these technologies. Telephone communication is being combined with computer e-mail and Web browsing so users can set a time to meet online and, with the addition of voice technology, actually speak to each other using one small portable device.

The Web, now an important part of commerce and education, began as a one-way vehicle where users visited to view Web pages and get information. It has evolved into sites where shopping and commerce takes place and is now evolving into a technology where users create the content. Web 2.0 and sites such as Facebook.com, flickr.com, LinkedIn.com, twitter.com, wikipedia.com, and youtube.com have content generated by the people that visit the Web sites. See **Figure A–26**.

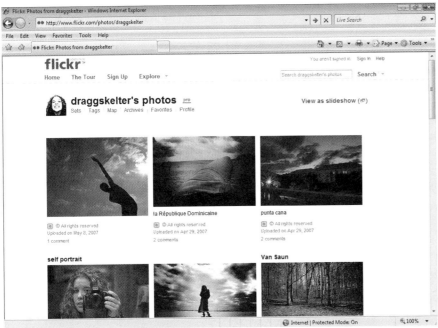

FIGURE A–26   User generated content

Computers have radically changed the way the medical profession delivers health care. Through the medical community, computers have enhanced medicine and healthcare throughout the world.

Trends

There are many trends that drive the computer industry. One trend is for larger and faster storage. From megabytes, to gigabytes, to terabytes, storage is becoming less an issue as the cost of storage is also dropping. RAM today is increasing exponentially. The trend is to sell larger blocks of RAM with every new personal computer. Newer processors also operate at speeds that are faster than the previous generation processors.

The actual size of computers is decreasing. Technology is allowing more powerful components to fit into smaller devices—laptops are lighter, monitors take up less space on the desktop, and flash drives can fit in your pocket and store gigabytes of data.

Home Offices

More and more frequently, people are working out of their homes—whether they are employees who are linked to their office in another location or individuals running their own businesses. *Telecommuting* meets the needs of many industries. Many companies allow workers to have a computer at home that is linked to their office and employees can use laptop computers to work both from home and on the road as they travel. A laptop computer, in combination with a wireless network, allows an employee to work from virtually anywhere and still keep in constant contact with her or his employer and customers.

Business communication is primarily by e-mail and telephone. It is very common for serious business transactions and communications to occur via e-mail rather than through the regular mail. Such an arrangement saves companies time and workspace and, thus, money.

Home Use

More and more households have personal computers. The statistics are constantly proving that a computer is an essential household appliance. Computers are used to access the Internet for shopping, education, and leisure. Computers are used to maintain financial records, manage household accounts, and record and manage personal information. More and more people are using electronic banking. Games and other computer applications offer another way to spend leisure dollars, and the convergence of television, the Internet, and the computer will find more households using their computers for media such as movies and music.

The future is computing. It's clear that this technology will continue to expand and provide us with new and exciting trends.

APPENDIX B

Keyboarding Touch System Improvement

Introduction

- *Your Goal—Improve your keyboarding skills using the touch system so you are able to type without looking at the keyboard.*

Why Improve Your Keyboarding Skills?

- To type faster and more accurately every time you use the computer
- To increase your enjoyment while using the computer

Instead of looking back and forth from the page to see the text you have to type and then turning back to the keyboard and pressing keys with one or two fingers, using the touch system you will type faster and more accurately.

⊣ WARNING

Using two fingers to type while looking at the keyboard is called the "hunt and peck" system and is not efficient when typing large documents.

Getting Ready to Build Skills

In order to get ready you should:

1. **Prepare your desk and computer area.**
   a. Clear your desk of all clutter, except your book, a pencil or pen, the keyboard, the mouse, and the monitor.
   b. Position your keyboard and book so that you are comfortable and able to move your hands and fingers freely on the keyboard and read the book at the same time.
   c. Keep your feet flat on the floor, sit with your back straight, and rest your arms slightly bent with your finger tips on the keyboard.
   d. Start a word-processing program, such as Microsoft Word, or any other text editor. You can also use any simple program such as the Microsoft Works word processor or WordPad that is part of the Windows operating system. Ask your teacher for assistance.

2. Take a two-minute timed typing test according to your teacher's directions.

3. Calculate your words a minute (WAM) and errors a minute (EAM) using the instructions on the timed typing progress chart. This will be the base score you will compare to future timed typing.

4. Record today's Date, WAM, and EAM on the Base Score line of the writing progress chart.

5. Repeat the timed typing test many times to see improvements in your score.

6. Record each attempt on the Introduction line of the chart.

Getting Started

Keyboarding is an essential skill in today's workplace. No matter what your job, most likely you have to learn to be an effective typist. Follow the hints below to help you achieve this goal:

- Ignore errors.
- To complete the following exercises, you will type text that is bold and is not italicized and looks **like this**.
- If you have difficulty reaching for any key, for example the y key, practice by looking at the reach your fingertips make from the j key to the y key until the reach is visualized in your mind. The reach will become natural with very little practice.
- To start on a new line, press Enter.

Skill Builder 1

Your Goal—Use the touch system to type the letters j u y h n m and to learn to press the spacebar.

Keys

What to Do

1. Place your fingertips on the home row keys as shown in **Figure B–1**.

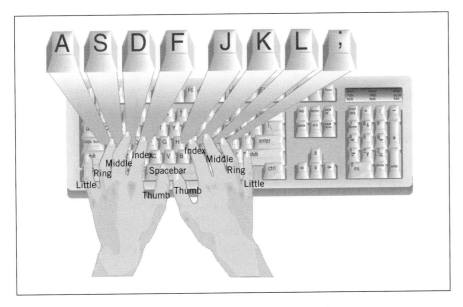

FIGURE B-1   Place your fingertips on the Home Row keys

2. Look at **Figure B–2**. In step 3, you will press the letter keys j u y h n m. To press these keys, you use your right index finger. You will press the spacebar after typing each letter three times. The spacebar is the long bar beneath the bottom row of letter keys. You will press the spacebar with your right thumb.

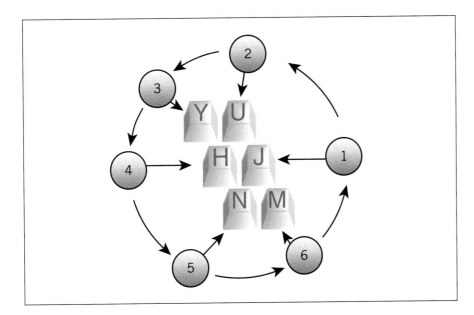

FIGURE B-2   Pressing the J U Y H N M keys

3. Look at your keyboard. Repeat the letters silently to yourself as you move your right index finger from the j key to press each key three times, and then press the spacebar. Start typing:

    jjj uuu jjj yyy jjj hhh jjj nnn jjj mmm

    jjj uuu jjj yyy jjj hhh jjj nnn jjj mmm jjj

4. Repeat the same drill as many times as it takes for you to reach your comfort level.

   jjj uuu jjj yyy jjj hhh jjj nnn jjj mmm

   jjj uuu jjj yyy jjj hhh jjj nnn jjj mmm jjj

5. Close your eyes and visualize each key under each finger as you repeat the drill in step 4.

6. Look at the following two lines and type:

   jjj jjj jjj juj juj juj jyj jyj jyj jhj jhj jhj jnj jnj jnj jmj jmj jmj

   jjj jjj jjj juj juj juj jyj jyj jyj jhj jhj jhj jnj jnj jnj jmj jmj jmj

7. Repeat step 6, this time concentrating on the rhythmic pattern of the keys.

8. Close your eyes and visualize the keys under your fingertips as you type the drill in step 4 from memory.

9. Look at the following two lines and type these groups of letters:

   j ju juj j jy jyj j jh jhj j jn jnj j jm jmj j ju juj j jy jyj j jh jhj j jn jnj j jm jmj

   jjj ju jhj jn jm ju jm jh jnj jm ju jmj jy ju jh j u ju juj jy jh jnj ju jm jmj jy

10. You may want to repeat Skill Builder 1, striving to improve typing letters that are most difficult for you.

Skill Builder 2

The left index finger is used to type the letters f r t g b v. Always return your left index finger to the f key on the home row after pressing the other keys.

Your Goal—Use the touch system to type f r t g b v .

Keys

What to Do

1. Place your fingertips on the home row keys as you did in Skill Builder 1, Figure B–1.

2. Look at **Figure B–3**. Notice how you will type the letters f r t g b v and then press the spacebar with your right thumb.

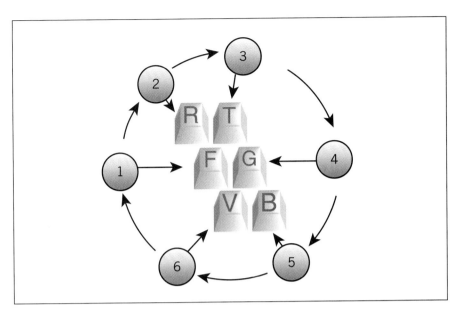

FIGURE B–3   Pressing the F R T G B V keys

3. Look at your keyboard. To press these keys, you use your left index finger. You will press the spacebar after typing each letter three times. The spacebar is the long bar beneath the bottom row of letter keys. You will press the spacebar with your right thumb.

   After pressing each letter in the circle, press the home key f three times as shown. Don't worry about errors. Ignore them.

   fff rrr fff ttt fff ggg fff bbb fff vvv

   fff rrr fff ttt fff ggg fff bbb fff vvv fff

4. Repeat the same drill two more times using a quicker, sharper stroke.

   fff rrr fff ttt fff ggg fff bbb fff vvv

   fff rrr fff ttt fff ggg fff bbb fff vvv fff

5. Close your eyes and visualize each key under each finger as you repeat the drill in step 4.

6. Look at the following two lines and key these groups of letters:

   fff fff fff frf frf frf ftf ftf ftf fgf fgf fgf fbf fbf fbf fvf fvf fvf

   fff fff fff frf frf frf ftf ftf ftf fgf fgf fgf fbf fbf fbf fvf fvf fvf

7. Repeat step 6, this time concentrating on a rhythmic pattern of the keys.

8. Close your eyes and visualize the keys under your fingertips as you type the drill in step 4 from memory.

9. Look at the following two lines and type these groups of letters:

   fr frf ft ftf fg fgf fb fbf fv fvf

   ft fgf fv frf ft fbf fv frf ft fgf

10. You are about ready to type your first words. Look at the following lines and type these groups of letters (remember to press the spacebar after each group):

jjj juj jug jug jug rrr rur rug rug rug

ttt tut tug tug tug rrr rur rub rub rub

ggg gug gum gum gum mmm mum

mug mug mug hhh huh hum hum hum

11. Complete the Keyboarding Technique Checklist.

Skill Builder 3

Your Goal—Use the touch system to type k i , d e c.

Keys ⬚K⬚ ⬚I⬚ ⬚,⬚ (comma)

What to Do

1. Place your fingertips on the home row keys. The home row key for the left middle finger is d. The home row key for the right middle finger is k. You use your left middle finger to type d, e, c. You use your right middle finger to type k, i, , as shown in **Figure B–4**.

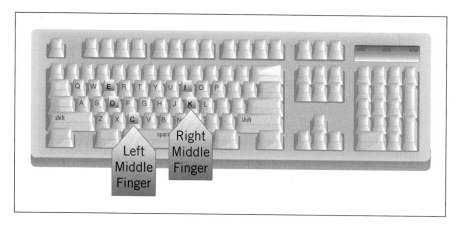

FIGURE B–4   Pressing the K I , D E C keys

2. Look at your keyboard and locate these keys: k i , (the letter k key, the letter i key, and the comma key).

3. Look at your keyboard. Repeat the letters silently to yourself as you press each key three times and put a space between each set of letters and the comma to type:

kkk iii kkk ,,, kkk iii kkk ,,, kkk iii kkk ,,, kkk iii kkk ,,, kkk iii kkk ,,, kkk

4. Look at the characters in step 3 and repeat the drill two more times using a quicker, sharper stroke.

5. Close your eyes and repeat the drill in step 3 as you visualize each key under each finger.

6. Repeat step 3, do not look at the keyboard, and concentrate on the rhythmic pattern of the keys.

Keys

What to Do

1. Place your fingertips on the home row keys.

2. Look at your keyboard and locate these keys: d e c (the letter d key, the letter e key, and the letter c key).

3. Look at your keyboard. Repeat the letters silently to yourself as you press each key three times and put a space between each set of letters to type:

   ddd eee ddd ccc ddd eee ddd ccc ddd eee ddd ccc ddd eee ddd ccc ddd

4. Look at the letters in step 3 and repeat the drill two more times using a quicker, sharper stroke.

5. Close your eyes and repeat the drill in step 3 as you visualize each key under each finger.

6. Repeat step 3, do not look at the keyboard, and concentrate on the rhythmic pattern of the keys.

7. Look at the following lines of letters and type these groups of letters and words:

   fff fuf fun fun fun ddd ded den den den

   ccc cuc cub cub cub vvv vev vet

   fff fuf fun fun fun ddd ded den den den

   ccc cuc cub cub cub vvv vev vet

8. Complete the Keyboarding Technique Checklist.

Skill Builder 4

Your Goal—Use the touch system to type l o . s w x and to press the left Shift key.

Keys    (period)

APPENDIX B

What to Do

1. Place your fingertips on the home row keys. The home row key for the left ring finger is s. The home row key for the right ring finger is l. You use your left ring finger to type s w x. You use your right ring finger to type l o . as shown in **Figure B–5**.

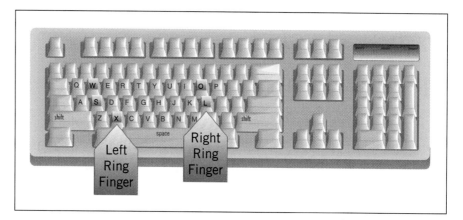

FIGURE B–5   Pressing the L O . S W X keys

2. Look at your keyboard and locate the following keys: l o . (the letter l key, the letter o key, and the period key).

3. Look at your keyboard. Repeat the letters silently to yourself as you press each key three times and put a space between each set of letters and the periods to type:

    lll ooo lll ... lll ooo lll ... lll ooo lll ... lll ooo lll ... lll ooo lll ... lll ooo lll ... lll

4. Look at the line in step 3 and repeat the drill two more times using a quicker, sharper stroke.

5. Close your eyes and repeat the drill in step 3 as you visualize each key under each finger.

6. Repeat step 3, do not look at the keyboard, and concentrate on the rhythmic pattern of the keys.

Keys

1. Place your fingertips on the home row keys.

2. Look at your keyboard and locate the following letter keys: s w x

3. Look at your keyboard. Repeat the letters silently to yourself as you press each key three times and put a space between each set of letters to type:

    sss www sss xxx sss www sss xxx sss www sss xxx sss www sss xxx sss

4. Look at the line in step 3 and repeat the same drill two more times using a quicker, sharper stroke.

5. Close your eyes and repeat the drill in step 3 as you visualize each key under each finger.

6. Repeat step 3, do not look at the keyboard, and concentrate on the rhythmic pattern of the keys.

Key Shift ⌈ SHIFT ⌉ (Left Shift Key)

You press and hold the Shift key as you press a letter key to type a capital letter. You press and hold the Shift key to type the character that appears above the numbers in the top row of the keyboard and on a few other keys that show two characters.

Press and hold down the left Shift key with the little finger on your left hand while you press each letter to type capital letters for keys that are typed with the fingertips on your right hand. See **Figure B–6**.

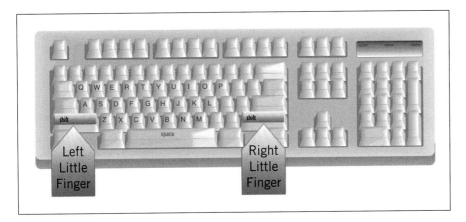

FIGURE B–6   Using the Shift keys

1. Type the following groups of letters and the sentence that follows.

   jjj JJJ jjj JJJ yyy YYY yyy YYY nnn NNN nnn NNN mmm MMM

   Just look in the book. You can see well.

2. Complete a column in the Keyboarding Technique Checklist.

Skill Builder 5

Your Goal—Use the touch system to type a q z ; p / and to press the right Shift key.

Keys ⌈ ; ⌉ (Semi-Colon) ⌈ P ⌉ ⌈ / ⌉

APPENDIX B

What to Do

1. Place your fingertips on the home row keys. The home row key for the left little finger is a. The home row key for the right little finger is ;. You use your left little finger to type a q z. You use your right little finger to type ; p / as shown in **Figure B–7**.

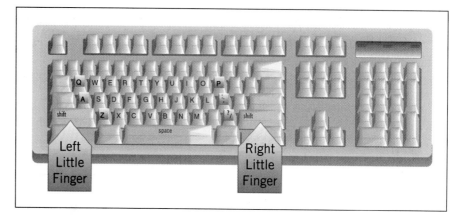

FIGURE B–7   Pressing the A Q Z ; P / and the right Shift key

2. Look at your keyboard and locate the following keys: ; p / (the semi-colon, the letter p, and the forward slash).

3. Repeat the letters silently to yourself as you press each key three times and put a space between each set of characters to type:

   ;;; ppp ;;; /// ;;; ppp ;;; /// ;;; ppp ;;; ///

   ;;; ppp ;;; /// ;;; ppp ;;; /// ;;; ppp ;;; /// ;;;

4. Look at the lines in step 3 and repeat the drill two more times using a quicker, sharper stroke.

5. Close your eyes and repeat the drill in step 3 as you visualize each key under each finger.

6. Repeat step 3, do not look at the keyboard, and concentrate on a rhythmic pattern of the keys.

Keys (A) (Q) (Z)

1. Place your fingertips on the home row keys.

2. Look at your keyboard and locate the following keys: a q z (the letter a, the letter q, and the letter z).

3. Look at your keyboard. Repeat the letters silently to yourself as you press each key three times and put a space between each set of letters and type:

   aaa qqq aaa zzz aaa qqq aaa zzz aaa qqq aaa zzz aaa qqq aaa zzz aaa

4. Look at the line in step 3 and repeat the same drill two more times using a quicker, sharper stroke.

5. Close your eyes and repeat the drill in step 3 as you visualize each key under each finger.

6. Repeat step 3, do not look at the keyboard, and concentrate on the rhythmic pattern of the keys.

Key Shift ⬚SHIFT⬚ (Right Shift Key)

Press and hold down the right Shift key with the little finger on your right hand while you press each letter to type capital letters for keys that are typed with the fingertips on your left hand.

1. Type the following lines. Press and hold down the right Shift key with the little finger of your right hand to make capitals of letters you type with the fingertips on your left hand.

   sss SSS rrr RRR

   Press each key quickly. Relax when you type.

2. Complete another column in the Keyboarding Technique Checklist.

Skill Builder 6

You will probably have to type slowly at first, but with practice you will learn to type faster and accurately.

Your Goal—Use the touch system to type all letters of the alphabet.

What to Do

1. Close your eyes. Do not look at the keyboard and type all letters of the alphabet in groups of three with a space between each set as shown:

   aaa bbb ccc ddd eee fff ggg hhh iii jjj

   kkk lll mmm nnn ooo ppp qqq rrr sss

   ttt uuu vvv www xxx yyy zzz

2. Repeat step 1, concentrating on a rhythmic pattern of the keys.

3. Repeat step 1, but faster than you did for step 2.

4. Type the following sets of letters, all letters of the alphabet in groups of two with a space between each set as shown:

   aa bb cc dd ee ff gg hh ii jj kk ll mm nn oo pp qq rr ss tt uu vv ww xx yy zz

5. Type the following letters, all letters of the alphabet with a space between each letter as shown:

   a b c d e f g h i j k l m n o p q r s t u v w x y z

6. Continue to look at this book. Do not look at the keyboard, and type all letters of the alphabet backwards in groups of three with a space between each set as shown:

zzz yyy xxx www vvv uuu ttt sss rrr

qqq ppp ooo nnn mmm lll kkk jjj iii

hhh ggg fff eee ddd ccc bbb aaa

7. Repeat step 6, but faster than the last time.

8. Type each letter of the alphabet once backwards:

z y x w v u t s r q p o n m l k j i h g f e d c b a

9. Think about the letters that took you the most amount of time to find the key on the keyboard. Go back to the Skill Builder for those letters, and repeat the drills until you are confident about their locations.

Timed Typing

Prepare to take the timed typing test, according to your teacher's directions.

1. **Prepare your desk and computer area.**
   a. Clear your desk of all clutter except your book, a pencil or pen, the keyboard, the mouse, the monitor, and the computer if it is located on the desk.
   b. Position your keyboard and book so that you are comfortable and able to move your hands and fingertips freely.
   c. Keep your feet flat on the floor, sitting with your back straight, resting your arms slightly bent with your fingertips on the keyboard.

2. Take a two-minute timed typing test according to your teacher's directions.

3. Calculate your words a minute (WAM) and errors a minute (EAM) scores using the instructions on the Timed Typing Progress Chart in this book.

4. Record the date, WAM, and EAM on the Skill Builder 6 line in the Timed Typing Progress Chart printed at the end of this appendix.

5. Repeat the timed typing test as many times as you can and record each attempt in the Timed Typing Progress Chart.

Skill Builder 7

Your Goal—Improve your typing techniques—which is the secret for improving your speed and accuracy.

What to Do

1. Rate yourself for each item on the Keyboarding Technique Checklist printed at the end of this appendix.

2. Do not time yourself as you concentrate on a single technique you marked with a "0." Type only the first paragraph of the timed typing.

3. Repeat step 2 as many times as possible for each of the items marked with an "0" that need improvement.

4. Take a two-minute timed typing test. Record your WAM and EAM on the Timed Typing Progress Chart as 1st Attempt on the Skill Builder 7 line. Compare this score with your base score.

5. Looking only at the book and using your best techniques, type the following technique sentence for one minute:

.　2　.　4　.　6　.　8　.　10　.　12　.　14　.　16

Now is the time for all good men and women to come to the aid of their country.

6. Record your WAM and EAM in the Timed Typing Progress Chart on the 7 Technique Sentence line.

7. Repeat steps 5 and 6 as many times as you can and record your scores in the Timed Typing Progress Chart.

Skill Builder 8

Your Goal—Increase your words a minute (WAM) score.

What to Do

You can now type letters in the speed line very well and with confidence. Practicing all of the other letters of the alphabet will further increase your skill and confidence in keyboarding.

1. Take a two-minute timed typing test.

2. Record your WAM and EAM scores as the 1st Attempt in the Timed Typing Progress Chart.

3. Type only the first paragraph only one time as fast as you can. Ignore errors.

4. Type only the first and second paragraphs only one time as fast as you can. Ignore errors.

5. Take a two-minute timed typing test again. Ignore errors.

6. Record only your WAM score as the 2nd Attempt in the Timed Typing Progress Chart. Compare only this WAM with your 1st Attempt WAM and your base score WAM.

Get Your Best WAM

1. To get your best WAM on easy text for 15 seconds, type the following speed line as fast as you can, as many times as you can. Ignore errors.

.　2　.　4　.　6　.　8　.　10

Now is the time, now is the time, now is the time,

2. Multiply the number of words typed by four to get your WAM (15 seconds × 4 = 1 minute). For example, if you type 12 words for 15 seconds, 12 × 4 = 48 WAM.

3. Record only your WAM in the 8 Speed Line box in the Timed Typing Progress Chart.

4. Repeat steps 1–3 as many times as you can to get your very best WAM. Ignore errors.

5. Record only your WAM for each attempt in the Timed Typing Progress Chart.

Skill Builder 9

Your Goal—Decrease errors a minute (EAM) score.

What to Do

TIP

How much you improve depends upon how much you want to improve.

1. Take a two-minute timed typing test.

2. Record your WAM and EAM as the 1st Attempt in the Timed Typing Progress Chart.

3. Type only the first paragraph only one time at a controlled rate of speed so you reduce errors. Ignore speed.

4. Type only the first and second paragraphs only one time at a controlled rate of speed so you reduce errors. Ignore speed.

5. Take a two-minute timed typing test again. Ignore speed.

6. Record only your EAM score as the 2nd Attempt in the Timed Typing Progress Chart. Compare only the EAM with your 1st Attempt EAM and your base score EAM.

Get Your Best EAM

1. To get your best EAM, type the following accuracy sentence (same as the technique sentence) for one minute. Ignore speed.

   Now is the time for all good men and women to come to the aid of their country.

2. Record only your EAM score on the Accuracy Sentence 9 line in the Timed Typing Progress Chart.

3. Repeat step 1 as many times as you can to get your best EAM. Ignore speed.

4. Record only your EAM score for each attempt in the Timed Typing Progress Chart.

Skill Builder 10

Your Goal—Use the touch system and your best techniques to type faster and more accurately than you have ever typed before.

What to Do

1. Take a one-minute timed typing test.

2. Record your WAM and EAM as the 1st Attempt on the Skill Builder 10 line in the Timed Typing Progress Chart.

3. Repeat the timed typing test for two minutes as many times as necessary to get your best ever WAM with no more than one EAM. Record your scores as 2nd, 3rd, and 4th Attempts.

> **TIP**
>
> You may want to get advice regarding which techniques you need to improve from a classmate or your instructor.

Assessing Your Improvement

1. Circle your best timed typing test for Skill Builders 6-10 in the Timed Typing Progress Chart.

2. Record your best score and your base score. Compare the two scores. Did you improve?

	WAM	EAM
Best Score	_____	_____
Base Score	_____	_____

3. Use the Keyboarding Technique Checklist to identify techniques you still need to improve. You may want to practice these techniques now to increase your WAM or decrease your EAM.

APPENDIX B

Timed Typing

Every five strokes in a timed typing test is a word, including punctuation marks and spaces. Use the scale above each line to tell you how many words you typed.

```
      .        2      .       4      .       6      .
If you learn how to key well now, it
   8      .       10     .       12     .       14     .       16
is a skill that will help you for the rest
       .       18     .       20     .       22     .       24
of your life. How you sit will help you key
   .       26     .       28     .       30     .       32     .       34
with more speed and less errors.  Sit with your
       .       36     .       38     .       40     .       42     .
feet flat on the floor and your back erect.
      44     .       46     .       48     .       50
To key fast by touch, try to keep your
   .       52     .       54     .       56     .       58     .
eyes on the copy and not on your hands or
      60     .       62     .       64     .       66     .       68
the screen.  Curve your fingers and make sharp,
   .       70     .
quick strokes.
   72     .       74     .       76     .       78     .
Work for speed first.  If you make more
      80     .       82     .       84     .       86     .       88
than two errors a minute, you are keying too
   .       90     .       92     .       94     .       96     .
fast. Slow down to get fewer errors. If you
      98     .       100    .       102    .       104    .
get fewer than two errors a minute, go for
   106    .
speed.
```

Timed Typing Progress Chart

Timed Writing Progress Chart

Last Name: _____   *First Name:* _____

Instructions

Calculate your scores as shown in the following sample. Repeat timed writings as many times as you can and record your scores for each attempt.

Base Score	Date	WAM	EAM	Time

To calculate WAM: Divide words keyed by number of minutes to get WAM. For example: 44 words keyed in 2 minutes = 22 WAM [44/2=22]

To calculate EAM: Divide errors made by minutes of typing to get EAM

For example: 7 errors made in 2 minutes of typing = 3.5 EAM [7/2=3.5]

		1st Attempt		2nd Attempt		3rd Attempt		4th Attempt	
Skill Builder	**Date**	**(a) WAM**	**(b) EAM**	**WAM**	**EAM**	**WAM**	**EAM**	**WAM**	**EAM**
Sample	9/2	22	3.5	23	2.0	25	1.0	29	2.0
Introduction									
6									
7									
8					-----				
9				-----					
10									
7 Technique Sentence									
8 Speed Line			-----		-----		-----		-----
9 Accuracy Sentence		-----		-----		-----		-----	

APPENDIX B

Keyboarding Technique Checklist

Last Name: _____   *First Name:* _____

Instructions

1. Write the Skill Builder number, the date, and the initials of the evaluator in the proper spaces.

2. Place a check mark (✓) after a technique that is performed satisfactorily.

3. Place a large zero (0) after a technique that needs improvement.

Skill Builder Number:	Sample										
Date:	9/1										
Evaluator:	SL										
Technique											
Attitude											
1. Enthusiastic about learning	✓										
2. Optimistic about improving	✓										
3. Alert but relaxed	✓										
4. Sticks to the task; not distracted	✓										
Getting Ready											
1. Desk uncluttered	✓										
2. Properly positions keyboard and book	✓										
3. Feet flat on the floor	✓										
4. Body erect, but relaxed	0										
Keyboarding											
1. Curves fingers	0										
2. Keeps eyes on the book	✓										
3. Taps the keys lightly; does not "pound" them	0										
4. Makes quick, "bouncy," strokes	0										
5. Smooth rhythm	0										
6. Minimum pauses between strokes	✓										

APPENDIX C

Differences between Windows 7, Windows Vista, and Windows XP

The Windows Experience

- Microsoft offers many new features in Windows 7 that are not available in Windows XP and Windows Vista.

- The overall Windows experience has been vastly improved from Windows XP to Windows 7. If you make the jump from XP to Windows 7, you will discover a great number of changes that are for the better. In addition, many of the new features introduced in Windows Vista were retained in this latest version of the popular operating system. Upgrading to Windows 7 is also an easier, more streamlined transition.

APPENDIX C

- With Windows 7, Microsoft has simplified everyday tasks and works more efficiently. This is all in response to issues users had with the Windows XP and Windows Vista experience. The major differences between Windows XP, Windows Vista, and Windows 7 are in the Start menu, dynamic navigation, desktop gadgets, improved security, search options, parental controls, and firewall, as well as improvements to the Windows Aero feature, see **Figure C–1**.

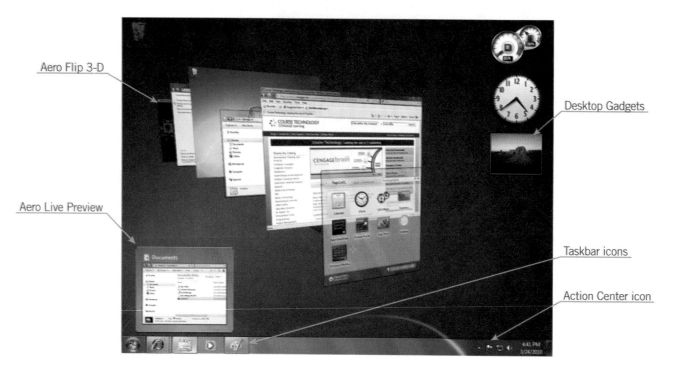

FIGURE C–1 Windows 7 Features

Windows Aero

- Windows Aero is a new graphic interface feature which gives a "transparent" quality to windows, dialog boxes, and other items in the Windows Vista and Windows 7 environment.

- Flip 3-D, or simply Flip, shows mini versions of windows and thumbnails in the Windows 7 environment when turned on.

Windows XP users had to download Windows Desktop Enhancements and PowerTools from the Microsoft Web site to change their Windows experience. Windows Vista and Windows 7 now have many different themes and options built into the operating system, making it easy to modify the Windows experience. One theme, introduced in Windows Vista is Aero.

Windows Aero is a feature which was first introduced in Windows Vista and is not available in the Windows XP operating system. Windows Aero, enabled by default in Windows 7, is a more aesthetically pleasing user interface to Windows Vista and Windows 7 systems. For example, Windows XP utilizes ScreenTips only when pointing to items on the Taskbar, Desktop, and Menus. The basic ScreenTips found in Windows XP have been enhanced to show live "sneak-previews" of windows with a simple point to the icon on the taskbar , as shown in **Figure C–2**.

Windows 7 made major improvements to the function of Aero. These new features include Aero Peek, Aero Shake, Aero Snap, Touch UI, and many other visual effects covered in this section. Compare the evolution of the Taskbar ScreenTip in Windows XP to Windows Vista and finally in Windows 7 in the figures below.

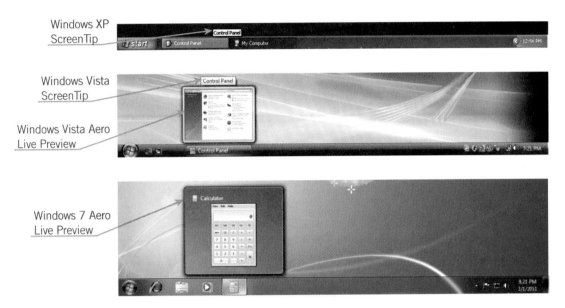

FIGURE C–2 Comparing Windows XP taskbar with Windows Vista and Windows 7

Understanding the Desktop

■ Gadgets, introduced in Windows Vista, and Jump Lists, introduced in Windows 7, are two new desktop features.

■ Windows 7 also includes multiple Aero themes to customize your desktop including the Desktop Background Slideshow.

At first glance, the Windows XP desktop only appears to differ slightly from that of Windows Vista, but the new features available with Windows 7 are substantial. The icons, shortcuts, folders, and files are generally the same; however, there are major aesthetic visual differences in this version. The most obvious addition from XP to Vista is the desktop gadget. Gadgets were not available in Windows XP. In **Figure C–4**, notice the appearance of three gadgets on the sidebar. Desktop gadgets are also available in Windows 7; however the sidebar function has been abandoned. Users simply add the gadget to the desktop.

The Taskbar in Windows XP includes the notification area, quick launch (when enabled), Start button, and icon(s) representing open programs. Beginning with Windows 7, you can now easily pin items to the Taskbar instead of using a quick launch feature. Jump lists, Aero themes and the Desktop Background Slideshow, explained in this chapter, are also new features to Windows 7.

FIGURE C–3 Windows XP Start menu and Desktop

The Start menu has been slightly enhanced from Windows XP to Windows 7. All Programs no longer appears on an additional menu, it has been merged with the Start menu. Windows Vista introduced a search function built into the Start menu, which allows users to search the computer easily for documents, applications, and help. Compare the evolution in desktops from Windows XP to Windows 7 in **Figures C–3, C–4,** and **C–5**.

FIGURE C–4   Windows Vista Start menu and Desktop

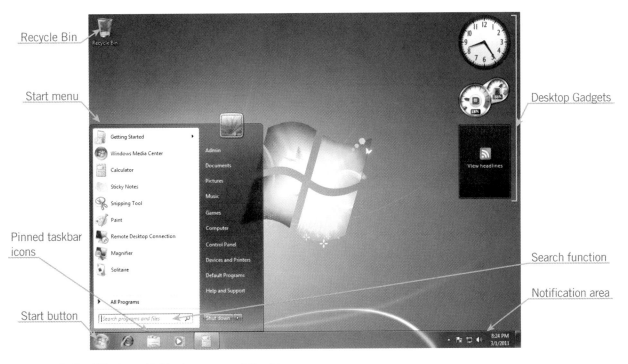

FIGURE C–5   Windows 7 Start menu and Desktop

Navigating in Windows

■ The Address bar in Windows 7 now functions differently, with more direct navigation functions.

■ Windows 7 now includes a comprehensive Navigation pane in Windows Explorer.

Windows Explorer provides the tools to navigate and locate items on your computer. The Address bar has been upgraded from Windows XP to allow for easier movement between folders. In Windows XP, the only available methods were the Back button and drop-down arrow. See **Figure C–6**. A big difference is in the function of the path. You may now click the folder in your path to move back. You may also begin a search directly from the Address bar, which is a new Windows 7 feature. Windows XP users' only option to search was to utilize the Search Companion.

The Navigation pane, which provides links to common or recently used folders, is dramatically different in Windows 7, compared to Windows XP, which only featured Favorites. "My Documents", the default user folder in Windows XP, is now a collection of folders grouped in Libraries in Windows 7. These folders, as well as Favorites, are easily found on the new Navigation pane and are easily customizable.

To switch between open programs easily, Windows XP's only option aside from clicking the icon on the Taskbar, was to tab through available programs, in a basic method with no preview of the program state. Windows Flip, introduced in Windows Vista, allows you to move to an open file, window or program by pressing the Alt+Tab keys, while showing a preview of the program's current state in Aero. The Windows Vista version of Flip was enhanced for Windows 7 users, although the function remains the same. See **Figures C–8** and **C-9** on the following pages.

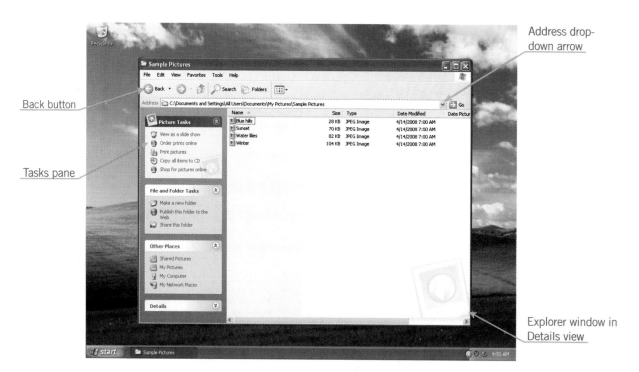

FIGURE C–6 Windows Explorer as seen in Windows XP

Dynamic Address bar

Back button

Favorite Links pane

Search text box

Explorer window in Tiles view

FIGURE C–7 Windows Explorer as seen in Windows Vista

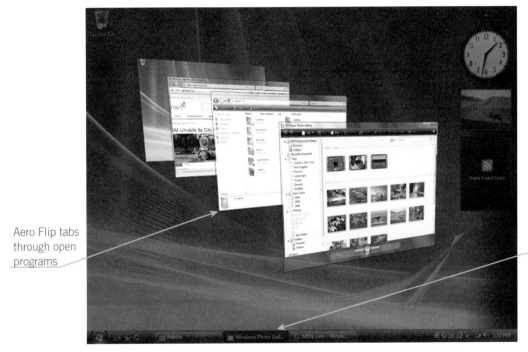

Aero Flip tabs through open programs

Taskbar buttons for open programs

FIGURE C–8 Flip in Windows Vista

Aero Flip 3-D tabs through open programs

Taskbar buttons for open programs

FIGURE C–9   Flip 3-D in Windows 7

Using Windows

- The new Aero Shake and Aero Snap allow you to easily move, resize, minimize and maximize open windows.

- The Control Panel now includes additional descriptive links, making it easy to find the item you are looking to modify.

Moving and resizing windows in Windows 7 provides the same essential functions as it did in previous Windows versions, with a few additions. In Windows XP and Vista, you had to manipulate each window individually, by clicking and dragging. You can still click and drag to resize and move windows; however this function has been upgraded and revamped in Windows 7. Aero Shake allows you to "shake" all open windows except that particular window to a minimized state. Aero Snap is a new way to easily resize open windows to expand vertically, or side-by-side.

The Control Panel, revamped in Windows Vista, has a new look in Windows 7, compared to that in Windows XP. The Search text box allows you to search for the Control Panel task you wish to perform. There are also descriptive linked items now replacing the "classic" icon format. **Figures C–10**, **C–11**, and **C–12**, which are shown on the following pages, illustrate the differences in the Control Panel from Windows XP to Windows 7. ▾

Switch to Classic View for basic icon arrangement

Control Panel

Grouped categories

FIGURE C–10 Windows XP Control Panel

Switch to Classic View for basic icon arrangement

Control Panel

Search text box

Descriptive Grouped categories with links

FIGURE C–11 Windows Vista Control Panel

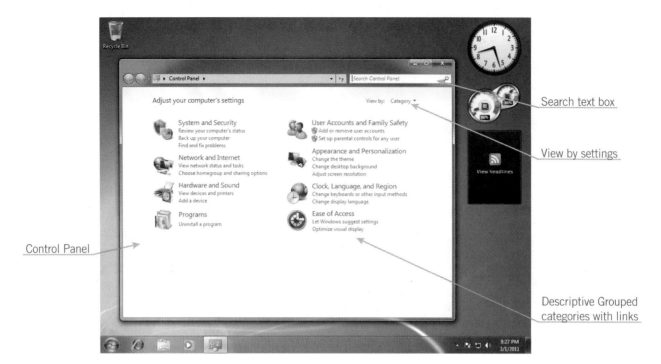

Search text box

View by settings

Control Panel

Descriptive Grouped categories with links

FIGURE C–12   Windows 7 Control Panel

Managing Your Computer

- The Action Center is a new feature in Windows 7 which consolidates message traffic from Windows maintenance and security features.

- Basic system utilities, such as Disk Cleanup and Disk Defragmenter, remain essentially the same from Windows XP to Windows 7.

Windows XP and Windows Vista's only method of receiving information on security and maintenance was the Security Center, available from the Control Panel. Windows 7 has improved this function, by creating a new Action Center, which communicates with the firewall, spyware protection, and antivirus software. Windows 7 users can now navigate to the Action Center by visiting the System and Security section of the Control Panel to view computer status and resolve issues. The Action Center is also pre-configured in Windows 7 to send important alerts to the Notification area of the taskbar.

One of the major upgrades in Windows 7 is in performance. Windows 7 was designed to run on less memory, shutting down services when not in use. In the Control Panel of Windows 7, there is a new Performance and Information Tools section. If you are a previous Windows XP user, you should familiarize yourself with this new feature. You will be able to assess your computer's performance, adjust settings, run disk cleanup, and launch advanced tools to manage your computer.

Windows Defender, introduced in Windows Vista is Microsoft's answer to spyware protection. This was not available for Windows XP users, pre Windows XP Service Pack 2. Windows XP Service Pack 2 users could download it from the Microsoft Web site and install it manually. Windows 7 also includes Windows Defender by default.

Windows Update, introduced in Windows XP has remained the same throughout the transitions through Windows Vista and Windows 7. Windows Update, which automatically downloads and installs important updates, was one of the only ways

Microsoft offered to maintain a secure PC with Windows XP. Now, in Windows 7, the Action Center, Performance Information and Tools, Windows Defender, and Windows Update work together to keep your computer secure. **Figures C–13**, **C–14**, and **C–15**, which are shown on the next few pages, compare Windows XP and Vista's Security Centers with Windows 7 Security Center and Action Center.

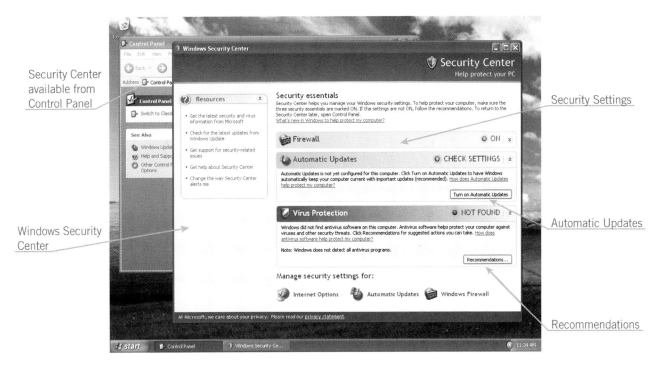

FIGURE C–13   Windows XP Security Center

FIGURE C–14   Windows Vista Security Center

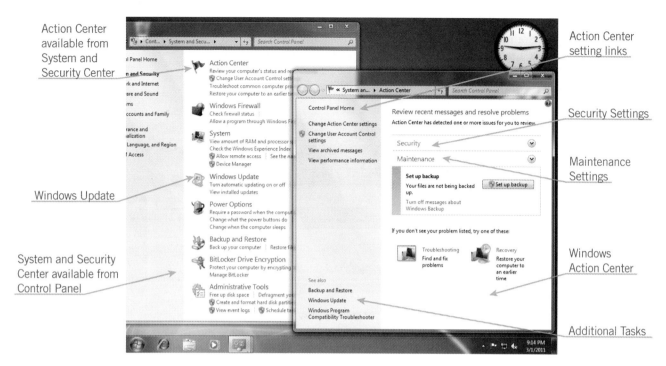

FIGURE C–15   Windows 7 Security Center and Action Center

APPENDIX D

Using SkyDrive and Office Web Apps

■ OBJECTIVES

Upon completion of this lesson, you should be able to:

- Explore cloud computing and Windows Live.
- Obtain a Windows Live ID and sign in to Windows Live.
- Upload files to SkyDrive.
- Use Office Web Apps View and Edit modes.
- Create folders on SkyDrive.
- Organize files on SkyDrive.
- Give permission for access to a folder on your SkyDrive.
- Co-author using the Excel Web App.

■ VOCABULARY

cloud computing
co-author
Office Web Apps
OneNote
SkyDrive
Windows Live

If the computer you are using has an active Internet connection, you can go to the Microsoft Windows Live Web site and use SkyDrive to store and share files. From SkyDrive, you can also use Office Web Apps to create and edit Word, PowerPoint, Excel, and OneNote files, even when you are using a computer that does not have Office 2010 installed. In this Appendix, you will learn how to obtain a Windows Live ID, how to share files with others on SkyDrive, and how to use the Word, Excel, and PowerPoint Web Apps, including co-authoring in the Excel Web App.

Understanding Cloud Computing and Windows Live

▶ **VOCABULARY**
cloud computing
Windows Live

Cloud computing refers to data, applications, and even resources that are stored on servers that you access over the Internet rather than on your own computer. With cloud computing, you access only what you need when you need it. Many individuals and companies are moving towards "the cloud" for at least some of their needs. For example, some companies provide space and computing power to developers for a fee. Individuals might subscribe to an online backup service so that data is automatically backed up on a computer at the physical location of the companies that provide that service.

Windows Live is a collection of services and Web applications that you can use to help you be more productive both personally and professionally. For example, you can use Windows Live to send and receive email, chat with friends via instant messaging, share photos, create a blog, and store and edit files. Windows Live is a free service that you sign up for. When you sign up, you receive a Windows Live ID, which you use to sign into your Windows Live account. **Table D–1** describes the services available on Windows Live.

TABLE D–1 Services available via Windows Live

SERVICE	DESCRIPTION
Email	Send and receive e-mail using a Hotmail account
Instant Messaging	Use Messenger to chat with friends, share photos, and play games
SkyDrive	Store files, work on files using Web Apps, and share files with people in your network
Photos	Upload and share photos with friends
People	Develop a network of friends and coworkers and use it to distribute information and stay in touch
Downloads	Access a variety of free programs available for download to a PC
Mobile Device	Access applications for a mobile device: text messaging, using Hotmail, networking, and sharing photos

SkyDrive is an online storage and file sharing service. With a Windows Live account, you receive access to your own SkyDrive, which is your personal storage area on the Internet. You upload files to your SkyDrive so you can share the files with other people, access the files from another computer, or use SkyDrive's additional storage. On your SkyDrive, you are given space to store up to 25 GB of data online. Each file can be a maximum size of 50 MB. You can also use your SkyDrive to share files with friends and coworkers. After you upload a file to your SkyDrive, you can choose to make the file visible to the public, to anyone you invite to share your files, or only to yourself. You can also use SkyDrive to access Office Web Apps. When you save files to SkyDrive on Windows Live, you are saving your files to an online location. SkyDrive is like having a personal hard drive "in the cloud."

Office Web Apps are versions of Microsoft Word, Excel, PowerPoint, and *OneNote*, an electronic notebook program included with Microsoft Office, that you can access online from your SkyDrive. Office Web Apps offer basic functionality, allowing you to create and edit files created in Word, PowerPoint, and Excel online in your Web browser. An Office Web App does not include all of the features and functions included with the full Office version of its associated application. However, you can use the Office Web Apps from any computer that is connected to the Internet, even if Microsoft Office 2010 is not installed on that computer.

Obtaining a Windows Live ID

To save files to SkyDrive or to use Office Web Apps, you need a Windows Live ID. You obtain a Windows Live ID by going to the Windows Live Web site and creating a new account.

Note: If you already have a Windows Live ID, you can skip Step-by-Step D.1.

> ▶ **VOCABULARY**
> **SkyDrive**
> **Office Web Apps**
> **OneNote**

Step-by-Step D.1

1. Start Internet Explorer. Click in the Address bar, type **www.windowslive.com**, and then press **Enter**. The page where you can sign into Windows Live opens.

2. Click the **Sign up** button. The Create your Windows Live ID page opens.

3. Follow the instructions on the screen to create an ID with a new, live.com email address or create an ID using an existing email address.

4. After completing the process, if you signed up with an existing email address, open your email program or go to your Web-based email home page, and open the email message automatically sent to you from the Windows Live site. Click the link to open the Sign In page again, sign in with your user name and password if necessary, and then click the **OK** button in the page that appears telling you that your email address is verified.

5. Exit Internet Explorer.

> **WARNING**
>
> If the URL doesn't bring you to the page where you can sign into Windows Live, use a search engine to search for *Windows Live*.

Uploading Files to SkyDrive

You can access your SkyDrive from the Windows Live page in your browser after you signed in with your Windows Live ID, or from Word, Excel, PowerPoint, or OneNote. Then you can upload a file to a private or public folder on your SkyDrive.

Uploading a File to SkyDrive from Backstage View

If you are working in a file in Word, Excel, or PowerPoint, you can save the file to your SkyDrive from Backstage view. To do this, you click the File tab, click Save & Send in the navigation bar, and then click Save to Web. After you do this, the right pane changes to display a Sign In button that you can use to sign in to your Windows Live account. See **Figure D–1**.

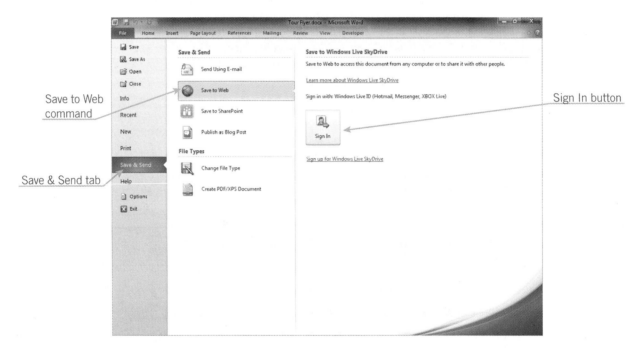

FIGURE D–1   Save & Send tab in Backstage view in Word after clicking Save to Web

Click the Sign In button to sign into Windows Live. After you enter your user name and password, the right pane in Backstage view changes to list the folders on your SkyDrive and a Save As button now appears in the right pane. See **Figure D–2**.

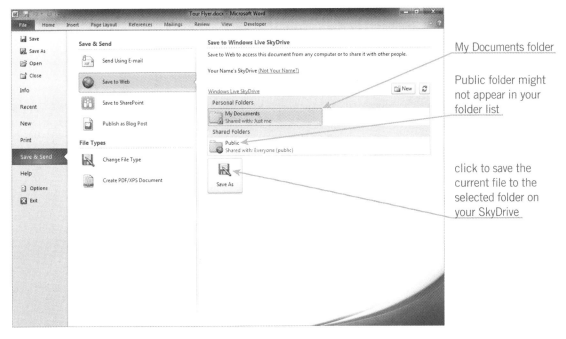

FIGURE D-2   Save & Send tab after connecting to Windows Live

To save the file, click the correct folder, and then click the Save As button.

Step-by-Step D.2

1. Start Word. Open the file named **Tour Flyer.docx** document from the drive and folder where your Data Files are stored.

2. Click the **File** tab, and then click **Save & Send** on the navigation bar. The Save & Send options appear in Backstage view as shown in Figure D–1.

3. Under Save & Send, click **Save to Web**.

4. Click the **Sign In** button. The Connecting to docs.live.net dialog box opens. See **Figure D–3**. If you are already signed into Windows Live, you will see the folders in your SkyDrive account listed instead of the Sign In button. Skip this step (Step 4) and Step 5.

FIGURE D–3
Connecting to docs.live.net dialog box

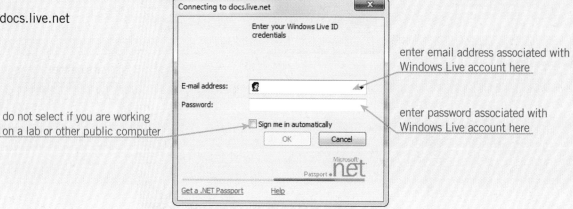

5. In the E-mail address box, type the email address associated with your Windows Live ID account. Press **Tab**, and then type the password associated with your Windows Live account in the Password box. Click the **OK** button. The dialog box closes, and another dialog box appears briefly while you connect to the Windows Live server. After you are connected, the folders on your SkyDrive appear in the right pane in Backstage view, as shown in Figure D–2.

6. In the right pane, click the **My Documents** folder, and then click the **Save As** button. Backstage view closes, and then after a few moments, the Save As dialog box opens. The path in the Address bar identifies the Public folder location on your SkyDrive.

7. Click the **Save** button. The dialog box closes and the Tour Flyer file is saved to the My Documents folder on your SkyDrive.

8. Exit Word.

Uploading a File to SkyDrive in a Browser

You can also add files to SkyDrive by starting from an Internet Explorer window. To do this, go to www.windowslive.com, and then log in to your Windows Live account. See **Figure D–4**.

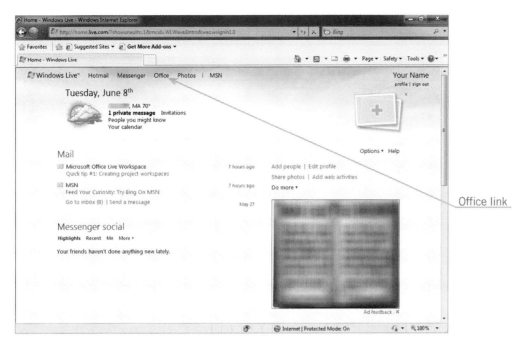

FIGURE D–4 Windows Live home page

To get to your SkyDrive, you click the Office link in the list of navigation links at the top of the window. To see all the folders on your SkyDrive, click View all in the Folders list on the left. See **Figure D–5**.

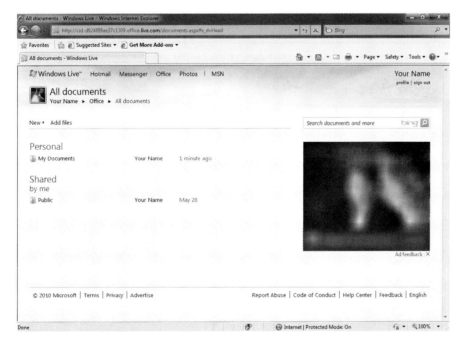

FIGURE D–5 Folders list on SkyDrive

Click the folder to which you want to add the file to open it. See **Figure D–6**.

click to add files
to this folder

contents of folder
are listed here

FIGURE D–6   My Documents folder page on SkyDrive

Click the Add files link to open the Add documents to *Folder Name* page; for example, if you click the Add files link in the My Documents folder, the Add documents to My Documents page appears. See **Figure D–7**.

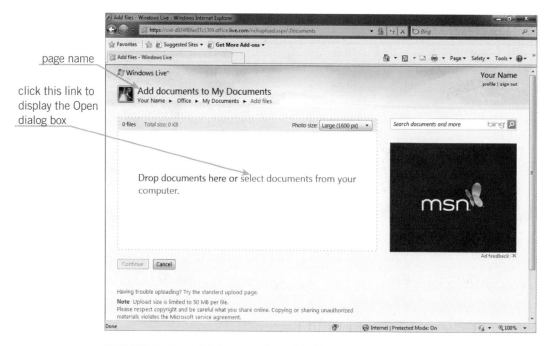

page name

click this link to
display the Open
dialog box

FIGURE D–7   Add documents to My Documents page on SkyDrive

Click the "select documents from your computer" link to display the Open dialog box. Locate the drive and folder where the file is stored, click it, and then click Open. The file uploads and is listed in the box. Click Continue to display the folder containing the files you uploaded to your SkyDrive.

Step-by-Step D.3

1. Start Internet Explorer. Click in the Address bar, type **www.windowslive.com**, and then press **Enter**.

2. If the Sign In page appears, type your Windows Live ID user name and password in the appropriate boxes, and then click **Sign in**. Your Windows Live home page appears similar to the one shown in Figure D–4.

3. In the list of command links at the top of the window, click **Office**. Your SkyDrive page appears.

4. In the list under Folders on the left, click **View all**. All the folders on your SkyDrive appear, similar to Figure D–5.

5. Click the **My Documents** folder. The My Documents page appears, similar to Figure D–6.

6. In the list of command links, click the **Add files** link. The Add documents to My Documents page appears, as shown in Figure D–7.

7. Click the **select documents from your computer** link, navigate to the drive and folder where your Data Files are stored, click **Tour Sales.pptx**, and then click the **Open** button. The file uploads and appears in the box on the Add documents to My Documents page.

8. At the bottom of the box, click the **select more documents from your computer** link. In the Open dialog box, click **Tour Data.xlsx**, and then click **Open**. The Excel file is listed in the box along with the PowerPoint file.

9. Below the box, click **Continue**. The My Documents folder page appears listing the files in that folder.

10. Keep the My Documents folder page displayed in Internet Explorer for the next Step-by-Step.

Using Office Web Apps

There are two ways to work with files using the Office Web Apps. You can view a file or you can edit it using its corresponding Office Web App. From your SkyDrive, you can also open the document directly in the full Office 2010 application if the application is installed on the computer you are using. You do not need to have Microsoft Office 2010 programs installed on the computer you use to access Office Web Apps.

Using a Web App in View Mode

To use a Web App in View mode, simply click its filename in the folder. This opens the file in View mode in the Web App. **Figure D–8** shows the Tour Flyer Word file open in the Word Web App in View mode.

File tab

commands you
can use in the
Word Web App
in View mode

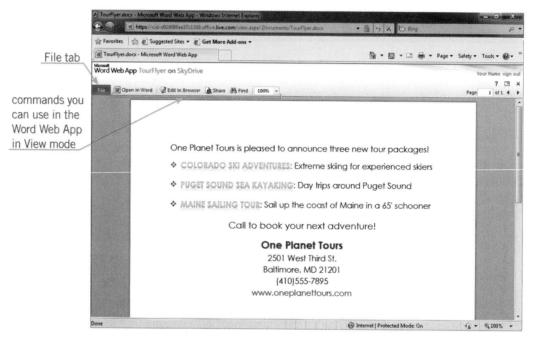

FIGURE D–8 Tour Flyer document open in View mode in Word Web App

Step-by-Step D.4

1. Click **Tour Flyer**. The Tour Flyer document opens in the Word Web App in View mode, as shown in Figure D–8.

2. Click anywhere in the document window, and then type any character. Nothing happens because you are allowed only to view the document in View mode.

3. Click the **File** tab. A list of commands opens. Note that you can print the document using the Print command on this menu.

4. Click **Close**. The document closes and the My Documents folder page appears again.

5. Leave the My Documents folder page open for the next Step-by-Step.

TIP

Position the mouse over a file icon to see the full filename and other details about the file.

Using a Web App in Edit Mode

You can also edit documents in the Office Web Apps. Although the interface for each Office Web App is similar to the interface of the full-featured program on your computer, a limited number of commands are available for editing documents using the Office Web App for each program. To edit a file in a Web App, point to the file in the folder page, and then click the Edit in browser link. You will see a Ribbon with a limited number of tabs and commands on the tabs. **Figure D–9** shows the file Tour Sales open in the PowerPoint Web App in Edit mode.

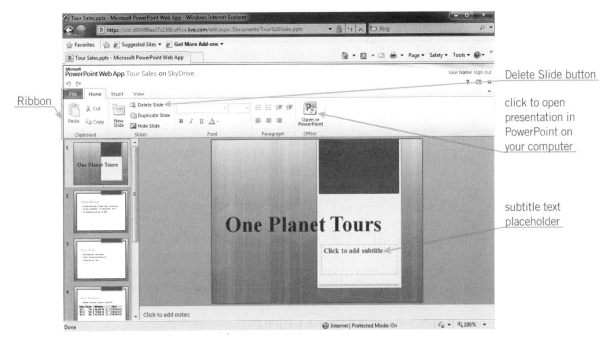

FIGURE D–9   Tour Sales presentation open in Edit mode in PowerPoint Web App

Step-by-Step D.5

1. In the list of files in the My Documents folder, point to **Tour Sales**. A list of commands for working with the file appears.

2. In the list of commands, click the **Edit in browser** link. The Tour Sales presentation appears in the PowerPoint Web App in Edit mode, as shown in Figure D–9. In Edit mode, you see a version of the familiar Ribbon.

3. In the Slide pane, click in the subtitle text placeholder, and then type your name.

4. In the Slides tab, click **Slide 3** to display it in the Slide pane. The slide title is *New Tours*.

5. On the Home tab, in the Slides group, click the **Delete Slide** button. The *New Tours* slide is deleted from the presentation and the new Slide 3 (*Tour Revenue*) appears in the Slide pane. Now you will examine the other two tabs available to you in the PowerPoint Web App.

6. Click the **Insert** tab on the Ribbon. The only objects you can insert in a slide using the PowerPoint Web App in Edit mode are pictures and SmartArt. You can also create a hyperlink.

7. Click the View tab. Note that you cannot switch to Slide Master view in the PowerPoint Web App.

8. Leave the Tour Sales file open in the PowerPoint Web App for the next Step-by-Step.

Editing a File Stored on SkyDrive in the Program on Your Computer

If you are working with a file stored on your SkyDrive and you want to use a command that is available in the full-featured program on your computer but is not available in the Web App, you need to open the file in the full-featured program on your computer. You can do this from the corresponding Office Web App by clicking the Open in *Program Name* button on the Home tab on the Web App Ribbon.

Step-by-Step D.6

1. Click the **Home** tab. In the Office group, click the **Open in PowerPoint** button. The Open Document dialog box appears warning you that some files can harm your computer. This dialog box opens when you try to open a document stored on a Web site.

2. Click the **OK** button. PowerPoint starts on your computer and the revised version of the Tour Sales presentation opens on your computer. The presentation is in Protected view because it is not stored on the local computer you are using.

3. In the yellow Protected View bar, click the **Enable Editing** button. Now you can insert a footer on the slides.

4. Click the **Insert** tab, and then click the **Header & Footer** button in the Text group.

5. Click the **Footer** check box, type **2013 Sales Projections** in the Footer box, and then click the **Apply to All** button. When you use the full-featured version of a program, you do need to save the changes you made, even when it is stored in a folder on your SkyDrive.

6. On the Quick Access Toolbar, click the **Save** button 🖫. The modified file is saved to your SkyDrive.

7. In the PowerPoint window title bar, click the **Close** button ⬛. The PowerPoint program closes and you see your browser window listing the contents of the My Documents folder.

8. Click the **Tour Sales** file. Slide 1 of the Tour Sales file appears in the PowerPoint Web app in View mode.

9. At the bottom of the window, click the **Next Slide** button 🔽 twice. Slide 3 (*Tour Revenue*) appears in the window. Remember that you deleted the original Slide 3, *New Tours*. Also note that the footer you added is on the slide.

10. Click the **File** tab, and then click **Close**. The PowerPoint Web App closes and the My Documents page appears.

11. Leave the My Documents page open for the next Step-by-Step.

WARNING

You can also open a document stored on your SkyDrive in the program stored on your computer from View mode in the corresponding Office Web App.

WARNING

If the Connecting to dialog box opens asking for your Windows Live ID credentials, type the email address associated with your Windows Live ID in the E-mail address box, type your password in the Password box, and then click the OK button.

Creating Folders on Your SkyDrive

You can keep your SkyDrive organized by using file management techniques, similar to the way you organize files on your computer's hard drive. You can create a folder in your SkyDrive in the Internet Explorer window or from Backstage view in the program on your computer.

To create a folder on your SkyDrive in Internet Explorer, click the New link in the list of commands, and then click Folder to open the Create a new folder page on your SkyDrive. See **Figure D–10**.

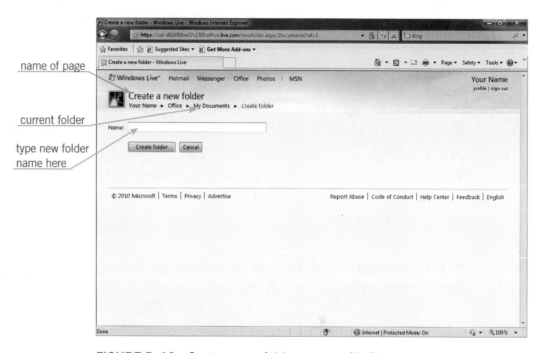

FIGURE D–10   Create a new folder page on SkyDrive

To create a new folder on your SkyDrive from the Save & Send tab in Backstage view in an application, click the New button in the upper-right. This opens the same Create a new folder page shown in Figure D–10.

Type the name for the new folder in the Name box, and then click Next. The Add files to *Folder Name* page that you saw earlier appears. If you want to upload a file to the new folder, you can do so at this point. If you don't, you can click the link for the new folder or click the SkyDrive link to return to your SkyDrive home page.

Step-by-Step D.7

1. In the list of command links, click the **New** link, and then click **Folder**. The Create a new folder page appears with the insertion point in the Name box.

2. In the Name box, type **Sales**, and then click **Create folder**. The new empty folder is displayed in the browser window. You can see that you are looking at the contents of the new folder by looking at the navigation links. See **Figure D–11**.

navigation links

command links

FIGURE D–11
Sales folder on SkyDrive

Sales folder is the current folder

3. Leave the Sales folder page open for the next Step-by-Step.

Organizing Files on Your SkyDrive

As on your hard drive, you can move and delete files on your SkyDrive. To move or delete a file, first display the commands for working with the file by pointing to its name in the file list in the folder. To move a file, click the More link, and then click Move to open the "Where would you like to move *File Name*?" page. See **Figure D–12**.

click to select this folder

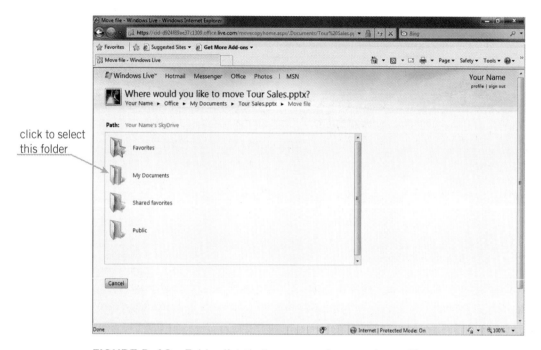

FIGURE D–12   Folder list that appears when moving a file

In the list of folders, click a folder. Then, at the top of the list, click the "Move this file into *Folder Name*" command. The folder into which you moved the file appears, along with a message telling you that the file was moved.

To delete a file, point to it to display the commands for working with the file, and then click the Delete button in the list of command links.

Step-by-Step D.8

1. In the list of navigation links, click the **My Documents** link. Point to **Tour Sales**. The commands for working with this file appear.

2. In the list of command links, click the **More** link, and then click **Move**. The "Where would you like to move Tour Sales.pptx?" page appears, and a list of folders on your SkyDrive appears.

3. In the list of folders, click the **My Documents** folder to display the list of folders located inside that folder. Click the **Sales** folder. The contents of the Sales folder appear in the list of folders. Because this folder does not contain any additional folders, you see only a command to create a New folder and the command to move the file.

4. In the list of folders, click **Move this file into Sales**. After a moment, the contents of the Sales folder appear, along with a message telling you that you have moved the Tour Sales file from the My Documents folder.

5. In the list of navigation links, click the **My Documents** link. The contents of the My Documents folder appear.

6. Point to **Tour Flyer**. In the list of command links, click the **Delete** button . A dialog box opens warning you that you are about to permanently delete the file.

7. Click **OK**. The dialog box closes, the file is deleted from the My Documents folder on your SkyDrive.

8. Leave the My Documents folder page open for the next Step-by-Step.

> **WARNING**
>
> Depending on the resolution of your computer, you might not need to click the More link to access the Move command.

Giving Permission for Access to a Folder on Your SkyDrive

If you upload a file to a private folder, you can grant permission to access the file to anyone else with a Windows Live ID. You can grant permission to folders located at the same level as the My Documents folder. You cannot grant permission to individual files or to folders located inside a locked folder. If you grant permission to someone to access a folder, that person will have access to all the files in that folder.

To grant permission to someone, click the folder to display its contents, click the Share link in the list of navigation links, and then click Edit permissions. The Edit permissions for *Folder Name* page appears. You can use the slider bar to make the contents of the new folder public by sharing it with everyone, your friends as listed on your Windows Live ID account and their friends, just your friends, or only some friends. You can also share it only with specific people that you list in the box in the Add Specific People section. When you type someone's name or email address associated with the person's Windows Live ID account in the box in the Add specific people section, and then press Enter, the person's name appears in a box below with a check box next to the name or email address. The box to the right of the person's name or email address indicates that the person can view files in the shared folder. You can then click the arrow to change this so that the person can view, edit, or delete files. See **Figure D–13**. Click Save at the bottom of the window to save the permissions you set.

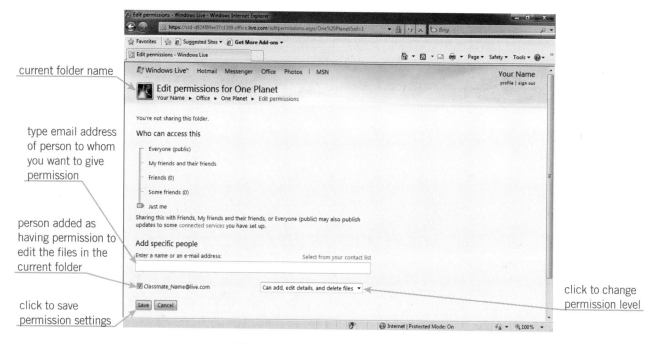

FIGURE D–13   Edit permissions for One Planet page on SkyDrive

To complete the next Step-by-Step, you need to work with a partner who also has a Windows Live ID account.

Step-by-Step D.9

1. In the list of navigation links, click the **Office** link, and then in the list of links on the left, click **View all**. The All documents page appears.

2. In the list of command links, click the **New** link, and the click **Folder**. The Create a folder page appears with a temporary folder name in the Name box. The temporary name is selected, so you can just type the new name.

3. In the Name box, type **One Planet**. Click **Next**. The One Planet folder page appears.

4. In the list of navigation links, click the **Office** link. In the list of folders on the left, click the **My Documents** link. The My Documents folder page appears.

5. In the file list, point to **Tour Data**, click the **More** link, and then click **Move**. The Where would you like to move Tour Data.xlsx? page appears.

6. In the list of folders, click **One Planet**. In the new list that appears, click the **Move this file into One Planet**. The One Planet page appears with the Tour Data file listed.

7. In the list of command links, click the **Share** link. Click **Edit permissions**. The Edit permissions for One Planet page appears.

8. Under Add specific people, click in the **Enter a name or an e-mail address** box, type the email address of your partner, and then press **Enter**. The email address you typed appears below the box. A check box next to the email address is selected, and a list box to the right identifies the level of access for this person. The default is Can add, edit details, and delete files, similar to Figure D–13. You want your partner to be able to edit the file, so you don't need to change this.

9. At the bottom of the window, click **Save**. The Send a notification for One Planet page appears. You can send a notification to each individual when you grant permission to access your files. This is a good idea so that each person will have the URL of your folder. Your partner's email address appears in the To box.

> **TIP**
>
> Because you are creating a folder at the same level as the My Documents folder, there is a Share with box below the Name box. You can set the permissions when you create the folder if you want.

> **TIP**
>
> To make the contents of the folder available to anyone, drag the slider up to the top so it is next to the Everyone (public).

10. Click in the Include your own message box, type **You can now access the contents of the One Planet folder on my SkyDrive.**, and then click **Send**. Your partner will receive an email message from you advising him or her that you have shared your One Planet folder. If your partner is completing the steps at the same time, you will receive an email message from your partner.

11. Check your email for a message from your partner advising you that your partner has shared his or her Sales folder with you. The subject of the email message will be "*Your Partner's Name* has shared documents with you."

12. If you have received the email, click the **View folder** button in the email message, and then sign in to Windows Live if you are requested to do so. You are now able to access your partner's One Planet folder on his or her SkyDrive. See **Figure D–14**.

FIGURE D–14
One Planet folder on someone else's SkyDrive

name of person who gave you permission to access the One Planet folder on his or her SkyDrive

your Windows Live name appears here

current folder

13. Leave Internet Explorer open for the next Step-by-Step.

Co-Authoring with the Excel Web App

When you work with the Excel Web App, you can use its ***co-authoring*** feature to simultaneously edit an Excel workbook at the same time as a colleague. When you co-author a workbook, a list of the people currently co-authoring the workbook appears at the bottom of the window. Co-authoring is not available in the Word or PowerPoint Web Apps. When you open a file in the Excel Web App, a notification appears at the right end of the status bar notifying you that two people are editing the document. See **Figure D–15**. You can click this to see the email addresses of the people currently editing the workbook.

▶ **VOCABULARY**

co-author

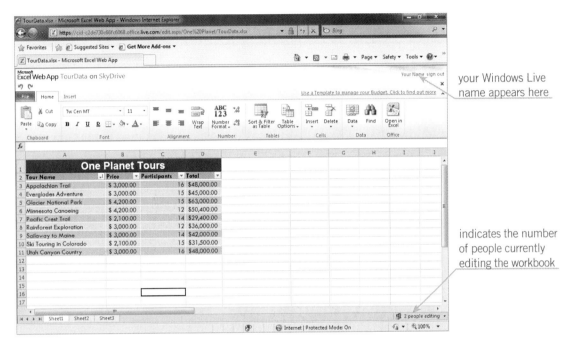

your Windows Live name appears here

indicates the number of people currently editing the workbook

FIGURE D–15   Tour Data file open in Edit mode in Excel Web App with two people editing

To complete this next Step-by-Step, you need to continue working with the partner who has permission to access the One Planet folder on your SkyDrive and who gave you permission to access his or her One Planet folder.

Step-by-Step D.10

1. Decide with your partner whether you will modify the Tour Data file stored on your SkyDrive or on his or her SkyDrive. After you decide the SkyDrive account with which you are going to work, both of you display the contents of that One Planet folder.

2. Point to **Tour Data**, and then in the list of command links, click the **Edit in browser** link.

3. In the status bar, click the **2 people editing** button. A list pops up identifying you and your partner as the two people editing the document.

   Decide with your partner which one of you will execute Step 4. The other person will then execute Step 5.

4. Either you or your partner click cell **A12**, type **Gulf Islands Sailing**, press **Tab**, type **3000**, press **Tab**, type **10**, and then press **Tab**. The formula in the other cells in column D is copied automatically to cell D12 because the data in the original Excel file was created and formatted as an Excel table. Both you and your partner see the data entered in row 12.

   If you entered the data in row 12, you partner should execute Step 5; if your partner entered the data in row 12, you should execute Step 5.

5. Either you or your partner—the person who did not execute Step 4—click cell **B12**, type **3700**, and then press **Tab**. The data entered is reformatted in the Accounting number format, and the total in cell D12 is recalculated. Again, both you and your partner see the change executed.

   Both you and your partner should execute the rest of the steps in this section.

6. Click the **File** tab, and then click **Close**. The changes you made to the Excel workbook are saved automatically on the current SkyDrive account. You are finished working with the Office Web Apps, so you can sign out of Windows Live.

7. In the upper-right of the SkyDrive window, click the **sign out** link. You are signed out of Windows Live.

8. In the title bar of your Web browser window, click the **Close** button [X] to exit your Web browser.

OneNote Web App

The other Office Web App is OneNote. As with Word, Excel, and PowerPoint files, you can share OneNote files on SkyDrive directly from OneNote. Note that you need to click the Share tab in the navigation bar in Backstage view, and then click Web and specify Windows Live as the Web location. After you upload a OneNote file to SkyDrive, you can work with it in its corresponding Web App.

GLOSSARY

3-D reference   A reference to the same cell or range in multiple worksheets that you use in a formula.

A

Absolute cell reference   A cell reference that does not change when copied or moved to a new cell.

Active cell   The cell in the worksheet in which you can type data.

Active worksheet   The worksheet that is displayed in the work area.

Adjacent range   A range where all cells touch each other and form a rectangle.

Align   To specify how the contents of a cell are lined up horizontally and vertically within the cell.

Argument   The value the function uses to perform a calculation, including a number, text, or a cell reference that acts as an operand.

Ascending sort   To arrange data with letters in alphabetical order (A to Z), data with numbers from lowest to highest, and data with dates from earliest to latest.

Audit   Check for accuracy.

AutoFit   An automatic determination of the best width for a column or the best height for a row, based on its contents.

Automatic page break   A page break Excel inserts whenever it runs out of room on a page.

Axis   A horizontal or vertical line that establishes the relationship between data in a chart.

B

Banded columns   When you create a table, the columns can appear with different formats. Typically, one column will have a lighter format and the adjacent column will have a darker format. This type of formatting is referred to as banding.

Banded rows   When you create a table, the rows can appear with different formats. Typically, one row will have a lighter format and the adjacent row will have a darker format. This type of formatting is referred to as banding.

Border   A line around the edges of a cell.

Button   Called a control because it controls the macro actions that are assigned to it.

C

Case-sensitive   Refers to uppercase and lowercase characters in a password. Passwords must be entered in the same uppercase and lowercase letters in which they were created.

Cell   The intersection of a row and a column.

Cell reference   A unique identifier for a cell that is formed by combining the cell's column letter and row number.

Cell style   A collection of formatting characteristics you apply to a cell or range of data.

Chart   A graphical representation of data.

Chart area   The entire chart and all other chart elements.

Chart floor   The foundation, or base, of a 3-D chart.

Chart layout   An arrangement that specifies which elements are included in a chart and where they are placed.

Chart sheet   A separate sheet in the workbook that stores a chart.

Chart style   Formatting applied to a chart based on the colors, fonts, and effects associated with the workbook's theme.

Chart template   A chart that you create and add unique formats and settings to, then you save the chart as a template. Chart templates are saved in the same default location as the preformatted chart templates.

Child   In a PivotTable, when there is more than one level, the main row heading is referred to as the parent and the level of detail below this level is the child.

Clear   To remove all the formatting applied to a cell or range of cells.

Code   Macro actions formatted in easy-to-read sentences, just like text in a book.

Column   Appears vertically in the worksheet; identified by letters at the top of the worksheet window.

Column chart   A chart that uses bars of varying heights to illustrate values in a worksheet.

Column heading   The column letter.

Combination chart   A chart that shows data on two y-axes for the purpose of showing different data in the same chart.

Comment   A note attached to a cell that explains or identifies information contained in the cell.

Concatenate   A function that combines the text from two or more cells into one cell.

Condition   A requirement that needs to be met.

Consolidating   Bringing data from several worksheets together into one worksheet.

Conditional formatting   Formatting that changes the look of cells that meet a specified condition.

Copy   To duplicate a cell's contents without affecting the original cell.

Criteria   The conditions you search for in a data range.

Custom AutoFilter   A feature that lets you display only cells that meet specific criteria.

Cut   To move cell contents from the original location and place in a new location.

D

Data label   Text or numbers that provide additional information about each data marker in a data series.

Data marker   A symbol (such as a bar, line, dot, or slice) that represents a single data point or value from the corresponding worksheet cell.

Data point   The actual point in the chart that corresponds with the data in the worksheet.

Data series   A group of related information in a column or row of a worksheet that is plotted on the chart.

Data source   The chart data stored in a range of cells in the worksheet.

Data table   A grid that displays the data plotted in the chart.

Data validation   A feature to ensure that the data is entered as accurately as possible.

Date and time functions   Functions that convert serial numbers to a month, a day, or a year, or that insert the current date or the current date and time.

Delimited   Data that is separated by a tab, semicolon, comma, or space.

Delimiter   A character, such as a comma, space, or a tab, used to separate data.

Dependent   The cell with a function that depends on other cells for the function results.

Descending sort   To arrange data with letters from Z to A, data with numbers from highest to lowest, and data with dates from oldest to newest.

Destination   The location where data will appear.

Destination range   The location in the worksheet where the result of a function will be placed.

Disable   To make inactive, such as tracking changes.

E

Embedded chart   A chart is inserted in the center of the worksheet.

Enable   To make active, such as tracking changes.

Encrypt   When the information in the file is scrambled into illegible data.

Exploded pie chart   A pie chart with one or more slices pulled away from the pie to distinguish them.

Export   To take Excel data from a workbook and send it to another program or to the Web.

F

Fill   The background color of a cell.

Fill handle   The black square in the lower-right corner of the active cell or range that you drag over the cells you want to fill.

Filling   Copying a cell's contents and/or formatting into an adjacent cell or range.

Filter   To display a subset of the data that meets certain criteria and temporarily hide the rows that do not meet the specified criteria.

Filter arrow   An arrow that appears in a column heading cell that opens the AutoFilter menu.

Financial functions   Functions that are used to analyze loans and investments.

Fixed width   Data that is separated at the same place in each cell, such as after 15 characters.

Font   The design of text.

Font size   The height of characters.

Font style   Emphasis added to cells, such as bold, italics, and underlining.

Footer   Text that prints in the bottom margin of each page.

Format Painter   A tool to copy formatting from one worksheet cell to another without pasting the cell's contents.

Formula   An equation that calculates a value based on values currently entered in cells.

Formula AutoComplete   A tool to help you enter a formula with a valid function name and arguments.

Formula Bar   The box to the right of the Name Box that displays a formula when the cell of a worksheet contains a calculated value (or the results of the formula).

Freeze panes   To keep selected rows and/or columns of the worksheet visible on the screen as the rest of the worksheet scrolls.

Function   A shorthand way to write an equation that performs a calculation.

Function number   A number that represents a calculation in the SUBTOTAL function.

G

Gauge chart   A chart that shows the amount of progress accomplished towards a goal. Also called a progress chart.

Grand total   The total for all the data in column(s) or row(s) in a worksheet.

H

Header   Text that prints in the top margin of each page.

Horizontal gridlines   Lines that appear within the chart itself and are horizontal.

Hyperlink   A reference that opens a Web page, a file, a specific location in the current workbook, a new document, or an e-mail address when you click it.

I

Import   To bring data from other programs, such as Access or Word, into an Excel workbook.

Indent   To shift data within a cell and insert space between the cell border and its content.

L

Landscape orientation   A page turned so that its longer side is at the top.

Legend   A list that identifies patterns, symbols, or colors used in a chart.

Line chart   A chart that uses points connected by a line to illustrate values in a worksheet.

Live Preview   The results of the formatting options displayed in the worksheet.

Logical functions   Functions that display text or values if certain conditions exist.

Lookup table   The range of data you create in either a vertical or horizontal format that Excel will use to match against criteria in a LOOKUP function.

M

Macro   Automates common, repetitive tasks you perform in Excel.

Manual calculation   Lets you determine when Excel calculates formulas in the worksheet.

Manual page break   A page break you insert to start a new page.

Margin   Blank space around the top, bottom, left, and right sides of a page.

Mathematical functions   Functions that manipulate quantitative data in a worksheet.

Merge   To combine multiple cells into one cell.

Microsoft Excel 2010 (or **Excel**)   The spreadsheet program in Microsoft Office 2010.

Mixed cell reference   A cell reference that contains both relative and absolute references.

N

Name Box   The cell reference area located below the Ribbon that displays the cell reference of the active cell.

Nonadjacent range   A range that includes two or more adjacent ranges and selected cells.

Normal view   The worksheet view best for entering and formatting data in a worksheet.

Number format   Changes the way data looks in a cell.

O

Object   Anything that appears on the screen that you can select and work with as a whole, such as a shape, picture, or chart.

Office Clipboard (or **Clipboard**)   A temporary storage area for up to 24 selections you copy or cut.

Operand   A constant (text or number) or cell reference used in a formula.

Operator   A symbol that indicates what mathematical operation to perform on the operands, such as a plus sign (+) for addition.

Order of evaluation   The sequence used to calculate the value of a formula.

Orientation   Rotates cell contents to an angle or vertically.

P

Page Break Preview   The worksheet view for adjusting page breaks in a worksheet.

Page Layout view   The worksheet view that shows how the worksheet will appear on paper.

Parent   In a PivotTable, when there is more than one level, the main row heading is referred to as the parent and the level of detail below this level is the child.

Password   A sequence of characters, known only by you, that is required for access to the file.

Paste   To place the last item from the Clipboard into the cell or range selected in the worksheet.

Picture   A digital photograph or other image file.

Pie chart   A chart that shows the relationship of a part to a whole.

PivotChart   The data in a PivotTable can be rearranged and summarized in different ways so that you can view the data from various perspectives.

Plot area   The graphical representation of all of the data series.

Point-and-click method   In a formula, to click a cell rather than type its cell reference.

Points   The measurement unit for font size.

Portrait orientation   A page turned so that its shorter side is at top.

Precedent   Cells that supply the values used in a function.

Primary axis   The y-axis on the left side of the chart.

Print area   The cells and ranges designated for printing.

Print titles   Designated rows and/or columns in a worksheet that print on each page.

R

Range   A group of selected cells.

Range reference   The unique identifier for a range, which is the cell in its upper-left corner and the cell in its lower-right corner, separated by a colon.

Relative cell reference   A cell reference that adjusts to its new location when copied or moved.

Research task pane   A task pane that provides access to information typically found in references such as dictionaries, thesauruses, and encyclopedias.

Row   Appears horizontally in the worksheet; identified by numbers on the left side of the worksheet window.

Row heading   The row number.

S

Scale   To resize a worksheet to print on a specific number of pages.

Scatter chart   A chart that shows the relationship between two categories of data; sometimes called an XY chart.

Scenario Manager   Performs a "what-if" analysis on several cells of data by changing the data in these cells.

Secondary axis   The y-axis on the right side of the chart.

Screen clipping   The area you choose to include in a screenshot.

Screenshot   A picture of all or part of something you see on your monitor, such as a Word document, an Excel workbook, a photograph, or a Web page.

Shape   Rectangles, circles, arrows, lines, flowchart symbols, or callouts that can help make a worksheet more informative.

Shared workbook   A file that can be accessed and changed by more than one person.

Sheet tab   The name of each worksheet at the bottom of the worksheet window.

Signature line   A security feature that you add to a workbook file so that someone else can sign, or verify, the information in the workbook.

SkyDrive   A program that allows you to access and share files online with friends, family members, or co-workers on the Web.

Slicer   A visual control that looks like a notepad. The slicer lets you filter your data in a PivotTable.

SmartArt graphic   A visual representation of information and ideas.

Sort   To rearrange data in a more meaningful order.

Source   The location that data is being transferred from.

Sparkline   A miniature chart that can be displayed in a single row or column of data.

Split   To divide the worksheet window into two or four panes that scroll independently.

Spreadsheet   A grid of rows and columns in which you enter text, numbers, and the results of calculations.

Statistical functions   Functions that are used to describe large quantities of data.

Style   A combination of formatting characteristics such as alignment, font, font size, font color, fill color, and borders that are applied simultaneously.

Subtotal   The total of only specific parts of the data.

Sum button   Inserts the SUM function to add long columns or rows of numbers.

T

Table Provides professional presentation features for displaying worksheet data.

Template A predesigned workbook file that you can use as the basis or model for new workbooks.

Text functions Functions that are used to format and display cell contents.

Theme A preset collection of design elements, including fonts, colors, and other effects.

Tracer arrow An arrow drawn from cells to show dependents or precedents.

Trigonometric functions Functions that manipulate quantitative data in a worksheet.

Truncate To hide text that does not fit in a cell.

V

Validation range The range of cells that you select to apply the validation rule.

Validation rule Allows you to set parameters for worksheet cells where values will be entered.

Vertical gridlines Lines that appear within the chart itself and are vertical.

Virus A computer program that is designed to reproduce by copying itself and attaching to other programs in a computer.

W

Watch Window Lets you view the data while working in another worksheet.

Workbook The file used to store worksheets; usually a collection of related worksheets.

Worksheet A computerized spreadsheet in Excel.

Worksheet range A group of adjacent worksheets.

Wrap text To move data to a new line when the cell is not wide enough to display all the contents.

X

X-axis The horizontal axis in a chart.

Y

Y-axis The vertical axis in a chart.

INDEX